A John Steinbeck Encyclopedia

A JOHN STEINBECK ENCYCLOPEDIA

Edited by Brian Railsback
and Michael J. Meyer

Greenwood Press
Westport, Connecticut • London

Library of Congress Cataloging-in-Publication Data

A John Steinbeck encyclopedia / edited by Brian Railsback and
Michael J. Meyer.
p. cm.
Includes bibliographical references and index.
ISBN 0–313–29669–3 (alk. paper)
1. Steinbeck, John, 1902–1968—Encyclopedias. 2. Authors, American—
20th century—Biography—Encyclopedias. I. Railsback, Brian E. II. Meyer, Michael J., 1943–
PS3537.T3234Z459 2006
813′.52—dc22 2006009754

British Library Cataloguing in Publication Data is available.

Library of Congress Catalog Card Number: 2006009754
ISBN: 0–313–29669–3

First published in 2006

Greenwood Press, 88 Post Road West, Westport, CT 06881
An imprint of Greenwood Publishing Group, Inc.
www.greenwood.com

Printed in the United States of America

The paper used in this book complies with the
Permanent Paper Standard issued by the National
Information Standards Organization (Z39.48–1984).

10 9 8 7 6 5 4 3 2 1

For
Charles Keith and Patricia Anne Boone Railsback
And
Christine Lisa Friberg, with the hope that from her generation a new rank of Steinbeck scholars will arise

Contents

Alphabetical List of Entries

Topical List of Entries

AWARDS

New York Drama Critics
Nobel Prize, The
Nobel Prize Acceptance Speech
Presidential Medal of Freedom
Pulitzer Prize

CHARACTERS IN STEINBECK WORKS

Abner, the Aerial Engineer
Accolon of Gaul, Sir
Advertising Man, The
Agnes
Aguirre, Fernando
Al, The Aerial Gunner
Alardine of the Outer Isles, Sir
Albertson, Judge
Albey, Kate
Alex
Alice (various works)
Allan, the Navigator
Allen, Elisa
Allen, Henry
Allen, T. B.
Alyne
Ames, Cathy
Ames, William
Ames, Mrs
Amesbury, Catherine
Anderson, Alfred
Andrews, Mabel
Anguyshaunce, King
Annie
Apolonia
Apolonio
Arbellus, Sir
Arthur, King
Arthur, King
Aryes
Athatoolagooloo
Aunt
Aunt Clara
Bacon, Abra
Bacon, Mr.
Bacon, Mrs.
Bagdemagus, Sir
Baker, Amelia
Baker, Banker
Baker, Cap'n
Baker, Red
Balan, Sir
Balin of Northumberland, Sir
Balmoure of the Marys, Sir
Balyse, Master
Ban, King of Benwick
Banks, Cleo
Banks, Raymond
Barton, John
Battle, George
Battle, John
Battle, Myrtle
Bawdewyn of Bretagne, Sir
Beavers, Butch
Becky
Bellias, Sir
Bentick, Captain
Biggers
Bill, the Bombardier
Black Hat
Blaikey, Joe
Blanco

Blanken
Bleoberis, Sir
Bolter
Bordoni, Mr.
Borre
Bors, King of Gaul
Boss, The
Boston, Milton
Bras de Fer
Brastias, Sir
Braziliano, Roche
Breed, Walter and Mrs Breed
Brethren of the Coast
Brian of the Forest
Brother Colin
Brother Death
Brother Paul
Buck, Billy
Bucke, Mrs.
Bud
Bugle, Mildred
Bulene, Pet
Bullitt, Jessie
Burgundian, The
Burgundian, The Other
Burke
Burt, William C.
Burton, Doc
Candy
Canedaria, Alicia
Captain of Rurales
Carados, King
Carlson
Carriaga, Alberto
Carriaga, Johnny
Carson, Pimples (Kit)
Casy, Jim
Cat
Cathy
Cavalier, The
Central Committee at Weedpatch Camp
Chappell, Ed
Chappell, Mrs.
Charley
Charro
Cheerleaders (Cheerladies)
Chicoy, Alice
Chicoy, Juan
Child, the
Chin Kee
Chong, Lee
Chong, Lee
Ci Gît
Claudas, King
Coachman, The
Coeur de Gris
Colleto, Tiny
Colombé, The Lady
Cook of the Bristol Girl, The
Cooper Family
Corcoran, Jesus Maria
Corell, George
Coroner
Corporal, The
Cortez, Teresina
Cotton Eye
Coyotito
Cristy, Mayor
Crooks
Culp, Miss
Curley
Curley's Wife
Dafydd
Dakin
Damas, Sir
Dan
Dane, Axel
Danny
Dark Watchers
Davis's boy, Joe
Dawes, (Captain)
Deborah, Great-Aunt
Deems, Mr.
Delphine
Dempsey Mamie Hamilton
Deuxcloches, M.; Douxpied, M.; M Rumorgue, M.; Sonnet, M.; Veauvache, M.
Doc (various works)
Doctor (various works)
Don Guiermo
Don Pedro
Dorcas, Judge
Dormody, Dr. Horace
Doubletree Mutt
Doxology
Duenna, The
Duke of the South Border
Duncan, Eric

Hamilton, Samuel
Hamilton, Tom
Hamilton, Will
Hamilton, Una Anderson
Hansen Sea Cow
Harris, the Radio Engineer
Hartnell, Alex
Hartog, Mr.
Harvey, George
Hat, Black
Hawkins, Amy
Hawkins, Emalin
Hawkins Farm
Hawley, Allen
Hawley, Cap'n
Hawley, Ellen
Hawley, Ethan Allen
Hawley, Mary
Hazel
Heiserman, Chief
Helen (various works)
Henri the Painter
Héristal, Clotilde
Héristal, Marie
Héristal, Pippin
Hervis de Revel, Sir
Hitzler
Holbert
Holman, Rabbit
Holmes, Dr.
Hopps, Martin
Horseman, The other
Horton, Ernest
Hueneker, Allen
Hugh of the Red Castle, Sir
Hughie
Humbert, Pat
Hunter, Major
Huston, Ezra
Hyacinthe, Sister (née Suzanne Lescault)
Ida, Wide
Ignacia, Tia
Igraine, The Lady
Indians
Innocénte
Jehovite Women, The Six
Jelke's cousin
Jenny
Jingleballicks, Old (Old Jay)
Joad, Al
Joad, Granma
Joad, Granpa
Joad, Ma
Joad, Noah
Joad, Pa
Joad, Ruthie
Joad, Tom
Joad, Uncle John
Joad, Winfield
Joads, The
Joan of Arc
Joe, the Italian Mechanic
Joe, the Pilot
Joey
John the Canuck
Johnson, Charlie
Johnson, Tod
Jones
Jones
Jordanus, Sir
Joseph
Joseph of Arimathea
Joy
Juan Chicoy
Juan Thomas
Juana (various works)
Juanito
Judge
Katy
Kay, Sir
Kaynes, Sir
Keef, Mr. R.
Kelly, Kiss of Death
Kemp, Corporal
King of the Lake
King of North Galys
Kino
Knowles, Floyd
Knudsen, Judge
L'Ollonais
Lady de Vawse
Lady of the Castle, The
Lady of the Lake, The
Lady of the Rock, The
Lady of the Rule, The
Laguna, Joe
Lancelot, Sir
Lanser, Colonel
Lapierre, Mr
Launceor, Sir
Lawrence, (Captain)

Norma
Norris, Miss
Nurse
Nyneve
Oaks, Camille
Old Easter
Old Juan
Old Man from Gambais
Old Tennis Shoes
Old Woman Passenger, The
Older man and the silent boy by the Colorado River, The
One-eyed Man at the Junkyard, The
Ontelake of Wenteland, Sir
Orden, Mayor
Orden, Sarah
Outlake, Sir
Overseer, The
Paulette
Pearl Buyers, The
Peele, Doc
Pelham, King
Pelleas, Sir, Lord of the Isles
Pellinore, King
Percival
Perez de Guzman, Juan (Don)
Peryne de Monte Belyarde, Sir
Perys de Foreste Savage, Sir
Phariance, Sir
Phillips, Dr.
Pierre Le Grand
Pigtails (Amy)
Pilon
Pioda, Mr.
Pirate, The
Placidas, Sir
Platt, Alex
Plutarco
Pom-pom, Johnny
Portagee, Big Joe
Portugues, Bartolomeo
Prackle, Lieutenant
Priest, The
Pritchard, Bernice
Pritchard, Elliott
Pritchard, Mildred
Pryor, Charley, and son Tom
Pulaski, Mike
Punk Kid, The
Pynnel, Sir
Ragged Man
Ralph, Tito
Ramirez, Delores (íSweets")
Randall, Emma
Randall, Peter
Rantini
Rattlesnake Club, The
Ratz, Mrs
Ratz, Timothy
Rawley, Jim
Raynald, Sir
Red
Red Saint, The
Repent
Rivers, Connie
Rivers, Rose of Sharon Joad
Roark
Robbie, The Proprietor's Son
Rocinante
Rodriguez, Mrs
Romanoff's
Romas
Romas, Willie
Romero, Mae
Root
Rosasharn
Rosasharn's baby
Royns, King of North Wales
Ruiz, Cornelia
Ruthie
Sagramor de Desyrus, Sir
Saint Katy
Sanchez, Pablo
Sandry, Mrs.
Santa Roja, La
Saul, Joe
Scot, Louis
Seer, The
Sheriff
Single, Jenny/Jennie
Slim
Small Lennie
Smasher
Smitty
Sorcerer's Farewell, The
Sorlus of the Forest
Spanish Corporal
Stutz, Jakob
Susy
Suzy
Sweetheart
Talbot, Mary

CONCEPTS

Discourse

Timshel [Timshol; Timshol-bo]

ORGANIZATIONS

Office of War Information
Work Projects Administration (WPA)

PEOPLE

Friends, Acquaintances, and Relatives

Abramson, Ben
Ainsworth, Elizabeth Steinbeck
Albee, Edward
Albee, George
Anderson, Elizabeth
Anderson, Maxwell
Anderson, Sherwood
Bailey, Margery
Bellow, Saul
Benchley, Nathaniel
Berry, Anthony
Beskow, Bo
Beswick, Kate
Blaine, Mahlon
Brace, Eleanor
Breck, John
Brigham family
Caldwell, Erskine
Calvin, Jack
Campbell, Joseph
Capa, Robert
Capp, Al
Cathcart, Robert
Chaplin, Charlie [Sir Charles Spencer]
Colleto, Vincent (Tiny)
Conrad, Barnaby
Day, A. Grove
de Kruif, Paul
Dekker, Mary Steinbeck
Enea, Sparky
Evelyn, John
Fairbanks, Douglas, Jr.
Fisher, John and Shirley
Fonda, Henry
Galbraith, John Kenneth
Gemmell, Margaret
Gragg, Hattie
Graves, Glen
Gray, Marlene
Gregory, Susan (Sue)
Hamilton, Delia
Hamilton, Dessie
Hamilton, George
Hamilton, Joe
Hamilton, Liza
Hamilton, Lizzie
Hamilton, Samuel
Hamilton, Tom
Hamilton, Will
Hamilton (Anderson), Una
Hammarskjöld, Dag
Hedgpeth, Joel
Hemingway, Ernest [Miller]
Henning, Carol
Hersey, John
Horton, Chase
Ingels, Beth
Jackson, Toni
Johnson, Lady Bird [Claudia Alta Taylor Johnson]
Johnson, Lyndon Baines
Johnson, Nunnally
Kaufman, George S.
Kazan, Elia (Gadg)
Kennedy, Jacqueline Bouvier
Kennedy, John
Kline, Herbert
Loesser, Frank and Lynn
Lorentz, Pare
Lovejoy, Ritchie and Tal (Natalie)
Ludden, Allen
McNally, Terrence
Meredith, Burgess [George Burgess]
Milestone, Lewis
Miller, Amasa "Ted"
Mirrielees, Edith Ronald
O'Hara, John
Otis, Elizabeth
Parker, Dorothy [Rothschild]
Ricketts, Edward F.
Rodgers, (Olive) Esther Steinbeck
Sandburg, Carl
Scardigli, Virginia
Shebley, Lloyd
Schulberg, Budd
Sheffield, Carlton "Dook"
Steinbeck, Carol Henning
Steinbeck, Elaine Scott
Steinbeck, Gwyndolyn Conger
Steinbeck, John Ernst
Steinbeck, John IV (Catbird)
Steinbeck, Olive Hamilton

Steinbeck, Thom
Stevenson, Adlai Ewing
Summers, Ella
Travis, Tex
Vinaver, Eugene
Wagner, Edith Gilfillan
Wagner, Jack
Wagner, Max
Whitaker, Francis
White, E(lwyn). B(rooks).

Literary, Political, and Cultural Influences

Adams, Henry
Addison, Joseph
Allee, W. C.
Allen, Fred
Anderson, Sherwood
Baker, Ray Stannard
Bellow, Saul
Benton, Thomas Hart
Bergson, Henri
Blake, William
Boodin, John Elof
Borrow, George
Boswell, James
Bourke-White, Margaret
Briffault, Robert
Bristol, Horace
Brown, Harold Chapman
Browning, Robert
Bunyan, John
Burns, Robert
Byrne, Don
Cabell, James Branch
Cage, John
Campbell, Joseph
Capote, Truman
Campbell, Joseph
Capa, Robert
Capp, Al
Carroll, Lewis
Cather, Willa
Cervantes, Miguel de
Chambers, Pat
Charles II
Chrétien de Troyes
Clemens, Samuel Langhorne [Mark Twain]
Condon, Eddie
Conrad, Barnaby
Conrad, Joseph
Cooper, James Fennimore
Crane, Stephen
Dante Alighieri
Darwin, Charles
Decker, Caroline
Dickens, Charles
Dos Passos, John
Dostoyevsky, Fyodor
Doughty, Charles Montague
Dreiser, Theodore
Eddington, Arthur
Faulkner, William
Edman, Irwin
Einstein, Albert
Eliot, George
Eliot, Thomas Stearns
Emerson, Ralph Waldo
Esquemeling, Alexandre Olivier
Fielding, Henry
Fitzgerald, F. Scott
Flaubert, Gustave
Floyd, Purty Boy
Floyd, Carlisle
Freud, Sigmund
Galbraith, John Kenneth
Geoffrey of Monmouth
Gerould, Katherine
Gibbon, Edward
Gide, Andre
Graubard, Mark
Guthrie, Woody
Hammarskjöld, Dag
Hardy, Thomas
Hargrave, John Gordon
Harte, Bret
Hedgpeth, Joel
Hemingway, Ernest [Miller]
Herodotus
Hersey, John
Howe, Julia Ward Hughes, Howard
Ibsen, Henrik
Inge, William
James, William
Jeffers, Robinson
Johnson, Lady Bird [Claudia Alta Taylor Johnson]
Johnson, Lyndon Baines
Joyce, James
Julius Caesar
Jung, Carl

Movies, Music, and Stage

Parker, Dorothy [Rothschild]
Quaid, Randy
Quinn, Anthony
Rodgers, Richard, and Oscar Hammerstein II
Schulberg, Budd
Shaw, George Bernard
Sinise, Gary
Springsteen, Bruce
Tracy, Spencer
Van Fleet, Jo
Williams, Tennessee
Williamson, Nicol
Zanuck, Darryl F.

Publishers/Agents/Critics

Astro, Richard
Ballou, Robert O.
Benson, Jackson J.
Best, Marshall
Covici-Friede
Covici, Pascal "Pat"
Cox, Martha Heasley
DeMott, Robert James
Ditsky, John
Fenton, Frank
Fontenrose, Joseph Eddy
French, Warren Graham
Friede, Donald
Gannet, Lewis
Gladstein, Mimi Reisel
Guinzburg, Harold
Guinzburg, Thomas
Hedgpeth, Joel
Jackson, Joseph Henry
Kazin, Alfred
Levant, Howard
Lisca, Peter
Martha Heasley Cox Center, The
McBride, Robert M.
McBride & Company, Robert M.
McIntosh, Mavis
McIntosh & Otis
Mizener, Arthur
Otis, Elizabeth
Owens, Louis D.
Parini, Jay (Lee)
Parker, Dorothy [Rothschild]
Simmonds, Roy
Steinbeck Societies
Thurber, James
Time Magazine
Timmerman, John H.
Viking Press
Watt, F(rank). W(illiam).
West, Anthony
Williams, Annie Laurie
Wilson, Edmund

Places, Ships, Vehicles, and Other Things (Real and Fictional)

Arvin Sanitary Camp
Bad Lands, The
Bear Flag Restaurant (Bear Flag)
Biddle Ranch, The
Bristol Girl
Café La Ida
Cannery Row
Campesino
Carmel-by-the-Sea (Carmel)
El Gabilan
Great Tide Pool
Highway 66
Hollywood (California)
Hopkins Marine Station
Hurricane Donna
Japan
Joyous Garde
La Jolla, CA
La Paz, Mexico
Lee Chong's Heavenly Flower Grocery
Katrina, The
Knight, U.S.S.
Monterey
Nantucket
Old Mexico
Old Stagecoach Road
Pacific Biological Laboratory
Pacific Grove
Palace Flophouse and Grill (Palace Flophouse)
Rebel Corners
Rocinante
Round Table,The
San Juan de la Cruz
San Ysidro
San Ysidro River
Spreckels Sugar
Stanford University

Tagus Ranch
Western Flyer, The

WORKS BY JOHN STEINBECK

Fiction

Acts of King Arthur and His Noble Knights, The
"Adventures in Arcademy: A Journey into the Ridiculous"
"Breakfast"
Burning Bright
Burning Bright (TV version)
Cannery Row (book)
Cannery Row (film)
"Case History"
"Chrysanthemums, The"
Cup of Gold
"Days of Long Marsh, The"
"Dissonant Symphony"
East of Eden (book)
East of Eden (film)
"East Third Street"
"Essay to Myself"
"Fingers of a Cloud: A Satire On College Protervity"
"First Watch, The"
"Gift, The"
"Gifts of Iban, The"
"God in the Pipes, The"
"Good Neighbors, The"
Grapes of Wrath, The (book)
Grapes of Wrath, The (film)
Grapes of Wrath, The (Steppenwolf stage and television version)
"Great Mountains, The"
"Harness, The"
"His Father"
Hooptedoodle
"How Edith McGillicuddy Met Robert Louis Stevenson"
"How Mr. Hogan Robbed a Bank"
In Dubious Battle
"Johnny Bear"
Keehan, Don
"Lady in Infra-Red, A"
"Last Joan, The"
"Leader of the People, The"
Lifeboat
"Lifeboat" (script-novelette)
Long Valley, The
Medal for Benny, A
"Miracle of Tepayac, The"
Moon Is Down, The
Moon Is Down, The (film)
Moon Is Down, The (play)
"Murder, The"
"Murder at Full Moon"
"Nail, The"
"Nothing So Monstrous"
"Nymph and Isobel, The"
Of Mice and Men (book)
Of Mice and Men (film)
"Olive Wood Cross, The"
Pastures of Heaven, The
Pearl, The (book)
Pearl, The (1947 film)
Pearl, The (2005 film)
"Piece of It Fell On My Tail, A"
"Promise, The"
"Raid, The"
Red Pony, The (book)
Red Pony, The (film and television versions)
"Saint Katy the Virgin"
Short Reign of Pippin IV, The
"Snake, The"
"Summer Before, The"
"Time the Wolves Ate the Vice-Principal, The"
To a God Unknown
Tortilla Flat (book)
Tortilla Flat (film)
Travels with Charley
Uncollected Stories of John Steinbeck
"The Vigilante"
Viva Zapata!
Wayward Bus, The
"Wizard, The"
Wizard of Maine, The
"White Sister of 14th Street, The"
"White Quail, The"
Winter of Our Discontent, The

Documentary

The Forgotten Village, The

Nonfiction

"About Ed Ricketts"
"Always Something to Do in Salinas"
America and Americans
"Americans and the Future"
"Argument of Phalanx"

WORKS (NOT BY STEINBECK)

Preface

When George Butler of Greenwood Press asked me to do *A John Steinbeck Encyclopedia*, I was delighted for the community of Steinbeck scholars. Adding Steinbeck's name to the prestigious Greenwood literary encyclopedias puts the author on the shelf next to such writers as William Faulkner and Henry James. Not long after I signed the contract, one of the foremost Steinbeck critics, Warren French, wrote me a kind letter with the caution that I had no idea what I was getting into. I had some idea—I knew that Jackson J. Benson's wonderful biography of Steinbeck had taken thirteen years to complete. Yet I was an assistant professor of English at the time, full of enthusiasm, and ready to knock out this book in two or three years. That was thirteen years ago.

Had I been as wise as French or Benson, I would have realized that John Steinbeck is a vast, complicated subject (the length of Benson's biography, over 1100 pages altogether, should have been a clue). Steinbeck himself provides fair warning to those who would attempt to set his life down in a biography or encyclopedia. "A good writer always works at the impossible," he wrote in his *Journal of a Novel*. "There is another kind who pulls in his horizons, drops his mind as one lowers rifle sights.... Whether fortunate or unfortunate, this has not happened to me." Steinbeck was above all a wanderer: he traveled the world, made numerous acquaintances and friendships along the way, read through hundreds of books in several disciplines (from art to zoology), and broke through nearly every genre: the short story, the novella, the novel, newspaper articles, creative nonfiction, screenplays, and even to a form he created for himself, the "play-novelette." He investigated life as much as possible without preconceptions, and he strove to create art without borders or horizons. To contain a writer like Steinbeck between two covers is impossible.

What you have in this encyclopedia is an attempt to capture, in a very accessible form, many elements of John Steinbeck's life: his work, from the great novels to the more obscure articles, his friends, important acquaintances, and influences; places lived, books read, and awards earned. In some 250,000 words and 1269 entries, here is the life of one of our most popular authors, a Nobel Prize winner and international figure. Years ago, when I first began my own research into Steinbeck's life, this encyclopedia would have been invaluable to me, and it would have saved me countless hours of labor. I hope this book will serve as an able companion to two other most important works about Steinbeck: Benson's narrative of the author's life, *The Adventures of John Steinbeck, Writer*, and Robert DeMott's important reference work, *Steinbeck's Reading, A Catalogue of Books Owned and Borrowed*. Perhaps, with these three works, serious readers of Steinbeck will have all they need to get started on understanding an extremely complex man.

Four years into this project, the immensity of the subject spread out in all directions. In addition, I had become founding dean of Western Carolina University's Honors College. At my request, Michael J. Meyer came on board as coeditor, and he became the project's manager as well as a major contributor of entries, including the numerous character entries for *The Grapes of Wrath*. Without his work, and the work of others mentioned in the acknowledgments, this encyclopedia would have overwhelmed me and would never have been completed.

The one great advantage of the length of time spent on this book is that we were able to invite the contributions of several generations of important Steinbeck scholars. You will find in these pages the work of such pioneering Steinbeck critics as French, Joseph Millichap, Robert Morsberger, and Roy S. Simmonds. A few representative names of the next generation—those who took Steinbeck scholarship to a broader audience—include Benson, Donald Coers, DeMott, John Ditsky, Mimi Reisel Gladstein, Kiyoshi Nakayama, and John Timmerman. The latest generation of scholars, such as Charles Etheridge and Stephen K. George (president of the New John Steinbeck Society) are here as well. Wherever possible, these contributors were asked to write entries along areas of particular expertise—no one could be better, for example, than British scholar Simmonds on *The Acts of King Arthur and His Noble Knights*, or DeMott on *East of Eden*, or Ditsky on *The Winter of Our Discontent*. Who better to write an introduction to Steinbeck, the man, than his chief biographer, Benson? While a record of Steinbeck's life and work, this book is also a record of the work and opinion of nearly every prominent scholar devoted to the author.

This encyclopedia is laid out to accommodate the high school student fascinated with John Steinbeck (that was me in 1976), the university student laboring on a paper, the teacher preparing a lesson, or the scholar who needs a quick reference to enhance a fading memory (that is me now). John Steinbeck himself is covered by Benson's introduction, which gives us the essence of the author's personality and ideas, and by the following chronology, which provides the facts. To help readers find their bearings, the book begins with a complete alphabetical list of all the entry names (or "headwords"), followed by a "Guide to Related Topics," which lists the entries by categories ("Characters," "People," "Works," and so forth.). Cross-referencing within entries either by clear direction of bolded words or by "See" references will also help the reader, as will the extensive index at the end.

The main part of the book consists of the alphabetically arranged entries, which range from brief identifications to full articles with thumbnail bibliographies ("Further Reading" sections). Some minor entries are unsigned, as are many of my own, and in some cases entries are unsigned because the author has done a group of them in one category (all the entries for one Steinbeck work, for example). After the entries, the notes on contributors provide a "who's who" of Steinbeck scholars up to 2006, and there is a substantial bibliography to help users venture off in many new directions.

Given the size of John Steinbeck as a subject and the diligence of the fifty-seven contributors, it has always been a struggle to keep this book to a manageable size. In the course of editing, I had to cut nearly 40,000 words, and still we are over a quarter of a million. Some entries had to be combined with others or, in some cases, cut entirely. And even after thirteen years, we still keep learning of more entries to add. "I guess there are never enough books," Steinbeck once wrote. In an encyclopedia on a globe-trotting man so wild in imagination, so diverse in interests, and so willing to embrace new forms in writing, there are never enough words.

Brian Railsback
The Honors College
Western Carolina University
May 9, 2006

Acknowledgments

The editors are grateful for the patience and good work of all the contributors and Steinbeck scholars who made this encyclopedia possible. At Western Carolina University, Jennifer Baumgartner and Emily Johnson worked as editorial assistants while they were MA students (they are both professionals now). Darren West, an Honors College Scholar, helped bring the book home in the last stretch. In Cullowhee, Sandra, Travis, Justin, and Cadence Railsback all helped to keep one of the co-editors sane. At Northeastern Illinois University, Gayle Orloski—a *summa cum laude* graduate—lent her superb editorial and computer skills to the project. At Greenwood, George Butler came up with the encyclopedia idea and endured a long wait for the book; Anne Thompson propelled the editors along; Susan Yates and her wonderful production staff made the finished book a handsome one.

We are grateful for the Steinbecks. Elaine Steinbeck was an amazing force for Steinbeck studies. Thom is an inspiration in conversation and as a fine writer. And without John, of course, there would be no encyclopedia.

An Introduction to John Steinbeck

Jackson J. Benson

What kind of man was John Ernst Steinbeck? He looked like a National Football League linebacker—tall, with big shoulders and barrel chest—and he talked with a gravelly voice, often so low people couldn't hear him. Out of shyness he could assume a mean look to ward off people, but he was a peaceful man who hated violence. One of his most endearing qualities was a genuine modesty, including an absolute refusal to publicize himself. When Hemingway received the Nobel Prize, he said privately that it was about time; when Steinbeck got it and was asked at a news conference whether he thought he deserved it, he replied, "Frankly, no." He was a gentle man, a man who when he wasn't writing was nearly always working with his hands making or fixing something, a man who was kind and who cared deeply about people in need or trouble. He had a wonderful sense of fun and loved jokes, parties, and any kind of celebration or holiday. Both his compassion and his sense of fun appear frequently in his work.

On the negative side, he was moody. He was not addicted to drink, but he drank a lot and that contributed to his deep depressions. He had a great sense of humor, but he could be very corny and sentimental, and he had a tendency to be over-impressed with ideas, to think something profound when it wasn't. He could be willful and demanding of friends and family. He was married three times, and although he was fond of children, he was not a good father, trying to raise his two boys according to some grand scheme or other.

Steinbeck was born in 1902, three years after Hemingway and five after Faulkner. That small difference in age meant that he missed World War I, the travel and release from home. For him there was no postwar Paris, no influence from Joyce or Pound, Stein or Eliot. Isolated on the West Coast, he was cut off from the dynamic artistic movements of his time and largely thrown back on his own resources in his development as a writer.

One positive result of this, however, was that he was able to achieve a remarkable originality of vision and technique. Steinbeck was born and raised in Salinas, a cattle and wheat town of 2,500 people at the turn of the century. It was a town that had grown up at a crossroads near the end of a narrow valley pinched longways into California's coastal mountains. His mother, Olive Hamilton Steinbeck, had been a teacher in a one room schoolhouse before she was married, and his father, John Ernst Steinbeck, was a flour mill manager and then treasurer of Monterey County of many years. The Steinbecks had a comfortable income and were highly respected in their community, and John, the only son among four children, was somewhat spoiled and in his shyness became something of a loner, more comfortable with books or wandering by himself along the seashore than being with his peers.

Out of his homelife, several aspects of the novelist would develop. The Steinbecks lived in a large Victorian frame house at the edge of town, and the father, who would rather have been a farmer, had a large garden and kept chickens, pigs, and a cow; besides supplying vegetables for the family, he was proud to be able to place flowers on the dining room table any time of the year. He taught all his children how to garden and brought them up to have a love and respect for animals—John was given Jill, the red pony, to take care of when he was six. John Ernst also taught them, out of his old-country, German heritage, respect for the land and a sense of conservation.

On the other side, Steinbeck's mother had the sense that all things about us are enchanted, that there was potential for magic everywhere and in every experience, and that, just as there were good and bad people, there were good and bad places—and special places. But readers also see this in *The Red Pony*, wherein Jody has a special place, near a spring, where he goes to be alone close to nature. In the novella the atmosphere is dominated by the two mountain ranges that run on either side of Steinbeck's long valley. On the one side are the sunny, rounded, reassuring Gabilans, while on the other are the taller, darker Santa Lucias, which, after the sun sets behind them, inspire Jody with fear.

So, out of his diverse parental influences, there developed a deep split reflected in both John Steinbeck's personality and his work. On the one hand, there developed the biological, the strong ecological perspective that he alone of major writers of his time had; on the other, there was the mystical, the philosophical, which became associated with myth and legend (particularly the Arthurian legends), with a Jungian sense of a collective unconscious and the importance of symbolism, and with materials from the bible (particularly the story of Genesis).

Where Steinbeck grew up is important as well, because much of his best work takes place in an enclosed valley, a microcosm in which fundamental human dramas work themselves out in death and life, violence and compassion. What Jody learns of birth, life, old age, and death, and the difference between romantic dream and reality, are every bit as traumatic as the lessons of Hemingway's Nick Adams, although *The Red Pony* is often thought of as a book for children. Steinbeck's perspective, a godlike re-creation of myth on one side and an acknowledgment of the inevitability of biological processes on the other, is far colder and more objective than many critics have acknowledged. His strong connection to the land and to growing things set him apart from other writers of his time, so that the phrase "Steinbeck country" has a special poignancy. One manifestation of this attachment in his life was that he was never without a garden, even in the most difficult of circumstances. During the last half of his life, while living in New York, he struggled, with compost and care, against the soot-filled air, intemperate weather, and lack of sun (his yard was surrounded by tall apartment buildings) to raise flowers and vegetables. During his last weeks, when he knew he was dying and was confined to his tower apartment, he planted seeds in pots and flower boxes, with little hope of seeing results, just to have something near him, growing.

We can only guess the full implications of what having a garden meant to him, but since the most commonly used mythic/symbolic structure in his work was the Garden of Eden, we can surmise that there was in his own gardening some sense of connection with the history of man and the processes of nature. Then, too, he probably felt a connection with his parents and a continuity with family tradition—perhaps a feeling that he was bringing a little piece of California and his heritage with him. I would guess, also, that there was connection, perhaps not so much a thought as an artistic intuition, between the magic of growing things and the magic of words, so that the fertility and vitality of the one might stimulate in him the springing forth of the other.

In Steinbeck's writing, there is always a sense that each man is but a part of a larger physical whole, a perception not uncommon among Westerners whose sense of the land, climate, and seasons can be palpable and immediate. Often in his fiction that which is outside man becomes a metaphor for that which is inside. Steinbeck asks the question of his characters, "How does your garden grow?" It is asked of his readers as well.

Unlike most of us, John, while growing up, did not rebel so much against his parents, whom he loved dearly, as he did against a narrow, provincial social environment; Salinas, and what it stood for to him emotionally, gradually became part of his geographical metaphor. Characteristics of the white middle class in Salinas and the surrounding area, as we see in many of the stories in *The Long Valley*, are tidy gardens and farms, carefully maintained, enclosed, and uniform. The emotional repression, conformity, and ultimate sterility of such gardeners as Elisa Allen in "The Chrysanthemums," Mary Teller in "The White Quail," and Peter Randall in "The Harness" contrast vividly with the *joie de vivre* of the lower class out of *Tortilla Flat*. In these surroundings, the gardens of Danny's house and his neighbors are filled with weeds, junk, and broken-down chicken coops. Disgraceful. Yet those paisanos seemed full of life and joy and often populated John's feelings. In fact, as an Anglo writer who grew up with Mexican Americans and who for periods lived in Mexico, he was unique in writing a half-dozen works of various kinds that dealt with the Mexican experience, including *The Pearl* and the classic motion picture *Viva Zapata!* Another aspect of his life that made a difference in his writings and which separates him from most other novelists was that he was engaged in hard physical labor on the land for long periods of time in his youth. One can hardly think of other writers, like Henry James, to cite an extreme example, touching bare ground with a bare hand. When Steinbeck went to Stanford, which in those day was designed to serve young people who couldn't afford the tuition at the University of California at Berkeley, he alternated one or two quarters of college with half a year of work on the farms of the Spreckels Sugar Company, which raised sugar beets and hay. *Of Mice and Men* was based on an incident that he witnessed in his early twenties, when a large, mentally retarded worker turned with a pitchfork on a straw boss who had been heckling him.

While the events of this play-novella are touching, the perspective of the author is quite objective, simply presenting in the words of the original title, "Something That Happened." Notice that Lennie kills without malice—animals and people die simply because of the biological combination of his strength with a weak mind. Lennie himself must die simply because within the society of man he is an anomaly and he is weak. The point in each case is that what happens, happens: things work themselves out according to their nature, not according to what we would like to see happen.

Such biological determinism is quite foreign to the literary sensibility, but a factor we should never forget while reading Steinbeck is that he saw life in a different way from most of us. At Stanford, although technically an English major, he took the classes in history, philosophy, and writing that interested him, without any concern for a degree. On one occasion he tried to sign up for a class in the dissection of cadavers in the Medical School. It was an odd request, so he was forced to go to the dean of the Medical School to explain. "I want to learn about human beings," Steinbeck told him. He was turned down, since cadavers are a valuable resource not to be wasted on literature students. Later in life, in the early 1950s, when many people were digging shelters during the panic over the bomb, Steinbeck observed with a shrug that sooner or later, for one reason or another, man would disappear from this earth and some other species would take over. "Species" was one of his favorite words.

His favorite virtue was "acceptance," to accept and see things as they are, rather than moralizing about them or weeping over them. For example, Doc Burton, in the strike novel *In Dubious Battle*, has sympathy for the strikers but refuses to endorse the doctrine of the union organizers. He wants—in nearly the same words used later by Jim Casy in *The Grapes of Wrath*—to be able to see the whole picture to examine it carefully as a scientist would examine an ecological pattern, so he refuses to put labels like "good" and "bad" on people or events. To do so would be to put on blinders. Doc is one of the first appearances of a character in Steinbeck's fiction based on his closest friend, the marine biologist Edward F. Ricketts, who, during the 1930s and 1940s, ran the Pacific Biological Laboratory on Cannery Row, only a few blocks away from Steinbeck's house in Pacific Grove, near Monterey. Ed, who was not only a good scientist but also a philosopher, had the acceptance and perceptiveness that Steinbeck admired, so he used Ed as the model for a series of what he called "self characters," or spokesmen for the author. In addition to Doc Burton and Jim Casy, we see him most directly in the Doc of *Cannery Row* and *Sweet Thursday*, as well as in Friend Ed in *Burning Bright*. The novelist's admiration for Ricketts raises another difficulty for the reading in addition to that of a biological perspective, and that is that Steinbeck's central characters are seldom traditional protagonists. He is concerned with characters who are central because of what they are, rather than what they do—with being rather than doing. And all such characters have their central place by a scientific role—that is, because of their ability to see, or because of their ability to learn to see.

The idea of perception—as clarity of vision, perspective, and insight—is also central to Steinbeck's work. He is concerned not only with the accurate physical vision of the scientist but also with the insight of the poet and philosopher. Notice the emphasis on eyes in *Cannery Row* and the recurring vision by various characters—underlining the two kinds of seeing, the physical and poetic—and the combination in Doc as a scientist who reads poetry aloud to his friends. The opening of the novella is poetic description of what would ordinarily be thought of as the materials of grim realism: trash, decay, and lowlife people:

> Cannery Row in Monterey in California is a poem, a stink, a grating noise, a quality of light, a tone, a habit, a nostalgia, a dream. Cannery Row is the gathered and scattered, tin and iron and splintered wood, chipped pavement and weedy lots and junk heaps, sardine canneries of corrugated iron, honky-tonks, restaurants and whore houses, and little crowded groceries, and laboratories and flophouses. Its inhabitants are, as the man once said, "whores, pimps, gamblers, and sons of bitches," by which he meant Everybody. Had the man looked through another peephole he might have said, "Saints and angels and martyrs and holy men," and he would have meant the same thing.

That peephole, or the fact that there is another peephole, is important and reverberates through the author's work—how we see is important, and our main difficulty in seeing at all is our tendency to be judgmental and our failure to try to see the whole picture. *Cannery Row* begins with a look through a peephole, and the sequel, *Sweet Thursday*, ends with a parting gift to Doc of a telescope from Mack and the boys.

To digress for a moment from Steinbeck's themes, I should mention something about his style. Several major critics have suggested that Steinbeck's and Hemingway's styles were very similar, that Steinbeck must have been a disciple of Hemingway (a suggestion that put Steinbeck's teeth on edge). Actually the two styles are quite different. Hemingway's, to oversimplify, is newspaperese that is, in response to influence of such painters as Cezanne, spatial in its conception. Steinbeck's style, which is evident in the small sample just cited, is more lyrical, and he seems to have felt prose as music—he frequently played what he felt was appropriate music while he wrote. Superficially, his style is usually romantic, that is, lyrical and emotional, but I think that it is better thought of as multidimensional, because he seems to have wanted it to work biologically, as well as intellectually and emotionally. He is concerned with nerve endings, and he has noted that he tried to write *In Dubious Battle* in such a way as to make the reader feel, in pace and sound, the things that are happening in the story.

Getting back to theme, Steinbeck's concern with perception is connected to a philosophy that the novelist worked out in connection with Ricketts called "non-teleological thinking." Teleological thinking is that which reasons according to cause and effect, that which sees a design or overall purpose, whereas non-teleological thinking focuses on what "is" and can be to some extent relative to what has been called "existentialism," although Steinbeck never used that term.

As the novelist explains in his journal of a scientific expedition to the Gulf of California, *The Log from the Sea of Cortez*, written with Ed Ricketts, too often as human beings we look for morals, for purpose, for the design of a personal God. When we suffer a disaster, we ask "Why?" or "Why me? What have I done to deserve this?" According to non-teleological thinking, these are the wrong questions; instead, we should be asking "What is this?" and "How can I deal with it?" We should not be looking to cause, but looking to understand the thing as it is. Unlike many fiction writers, Steinbeck is not primarily asking the reader to come to some moral conclusion, but to improve and enlarge his vision and to adapt and evolve in response to what he sees—which is what Steinbeck asks of his characters.

We see this kind of evolution of thinking in Tom Joad, in *The Grapes of Wrath*, which is Steinbeck's masterpiece. In response to the changes in society and in the environment, Tom is forced to change his perspective from that of rugged, Western individualism to that of a responsive member of the human community. The novel, originally thought of as merely a propaganda novel often compared to *Uncle Tom's Cabin*, or as a journalistic recounting of the Dust Bowl migration during the thirties, has been, sixty-six years after the events, elevated to a classic expression of Americana. In its background we hear the voices of Emerson and Thoreau, of Whitman and Sandburg—of the oversoul, the intimate connection of man with nature, of America singing and working, on the move, and the voice of the people questing, searching for life and liberty, for social justice. Malcolm Cowley accurately summed up the achievement of this novel when he wrote that "a whole literature is summarized in this book and much of it is carried to a new level of excellence."

At the beginning of the novel, we see the farm people of Oklahoma hit by a smothering dust storm that blankets everything—corn, fence posts, houses, and trees. Steinbeck writes,

> The people came out of their houses and smelled the hot stinging air and covered their noses from it. And the children came out of the houses, but they did not run or shout as they would have done after a rain. Men stood by their fences and looked at the ruined corn, drying fast now, only a little green showing through the film of dust. The men were silent and they did not move often. And the women came out of the houses to stand beside their men—to feel whether this time the men would break. The women studied the men's faces secretly, for the corn could go, as long as something else remained.

Of course, they must leave to try to make a life elsewhere, and they encounter brutality and prejudice and greed. But like the turtle of the early chapters of the novel, they survive, and they have brought their seed with them. This is not people standing about making witty comments in an English drawing room or four hundred pages of worrying about who is going to marry whom, but a cry out of the heart of our land and culture. This is not the American dream of a house in suburbia with two cars and a swimming pool, but the American dream of basic decency and a chance to make such decency work. Although the novel goes beyond the depiction of a historical period or its relevance to current events, we cannot help be reminded in reading it of the plight of the small family farmer, of our farm workers, of our displaced factory workers, and of our many homeless. One may be reminded of Carl Sandburg's poem "The People, Yes."

In its themes of a mass movement west, or "westering" as Steinbeck calls it in his story "The Leader of the People," and the movement from "I" to "we," the necessity for the people to share and stand together against natural and social disaster, the novel points to another basic Steinbeck concern during this period of his work: "group man." Never a Marxist or attracted to socialism, Steinbeck nevertheless was very aware during the 1930s of living in a period of mass movement, of fascism in Germany and Italy and Communism in the USSR. *In Dubious Battle* presents men gathered to become a group animal, different from its component parts, and led into violence by blood lust or hunger. In *The Grapes of Wrath* we see a more benign grouping in neighbor helping neighbor and assuming a responsibility beyond individual welfare. But even as late as the scene of the foul-mouthed mob, the cheerleaders in *Travels with Charley*, we see Steinbeck's fascination with group psychology—an important aspect of a democratic, pluralistic character.

Following the great period of *In Dubious Battle*, *Of Mice and Men*, *The Long Valley*, and *The Grapes of Wrath*, Steinbeck had several experiences that radically changed the direction of his work. First was his experience as a correspondent during World War II. Although recommended for the Silver Star for conspicuous courage while accompanying a patrol behind enemy lines, he was unable to shake the visions of wholesale slaughter, especially of young children blasted in battle, and went into a depression that lasted nearly a year. In order to shake it off, he wrote *Cannery Row* out of, as he said, "nostalgia." A scientifically flavored fairy tale, a dark comedy, and an ecological parable, it is a key work in the exposition of Steinbeck's world view as considered by Steinbeck scholars, but a book that disappointed many generalist critics who, because of their Marxist sympathies, had lauded his previous work as making a contribution to the class struggle.

Second, he found after the war, largely as a result of the hatred generated in the conservative Salinas-Monterey area by the publication of *The Grapes of Wrath* and a jealousy of his celebrity by some of his former friends, that he could not live any longer in the country that had become associated with his name. He tried to return several times but was driven away each time. It was ironic that the book which gave him his most fame and stature at the same time robbed him of the land and people that had been his inspiration. Third, in 1948 his close friend Ed Ricketts was killed when his car was hit by a train, and fourth, shortly after Ed's death, Steinbeck's second wife, Gwendolyn Conger Steinbeck, announced to her husband that she had never loved him and had been unfaithful to him for years. She even suggested that his youngest son was not his own. Overwhelmed by shock and grief, John suffered a breakdown that almost destroyed him.

Ultimately, his salvation came first from marrying another woman, Elaine Scott Steinbeck, and second from writing out his emotions in regard to what he felt was the betrayal by his wife and the loss of his children to what he now considered a thoroughly evil woman. The resulting works were the play-novelette *Burning Bright* (1950) and the epic-length novel *East of Eden* (1952), which had been in his mind for many years as a family history, "The Salinas Valley." Despite overemphasis and a certain windiness, the novel (starring his ex-wife as the vixen, Cathy Ames) has had a powerful effect on the public's imagination and has been successfully dramatized as a feature film and as a television miniseries.

Despite a generally happy marriage to Elaine, John entered a long period of frustration and uncertainty in regard to his writing. His hope was to turn from the novel to become a playwright, building on his earlier successes with *Of Mice and Men* (which had won the New York Critics Circle Award) and the wartime drama, *The Moon Is Down*. But with first the failure of *Burning Bright* (produced in 1950) and then that of the musical *Pipe Dream* (produced in 1955), he began to devote more and more time to travel and to journalism. Near the end of the decade, he moved in yet another direction to a project that had been in the back of his mind for many years, the rewriting in modern English of Malory's *Morte d'Arthur*, the book that had been his favorite as a child and which had been in part responsible for his desire to become a writer.

He was unable during these years, 1957–1960, to find a language that was adequate to convey the magic he had found in the original and left the project only partially completed. His feeling, however, that the age of Malory had its counterpart in a confused America of our own time led to the writing of two of his last three books: his last novel, *The Winter of Our Discontent* (1961), an examination of modern, middle-class values in an age of malaise, and *America and Americans* (1966), a word and picture book, which sought, again in moralistic terms, to examine the lives and values of ordinary citizens in various parts of the country. A similar quest for the pulse of America led him on his journey around the country in a camper in 1960 and resulted in *Travels with Charley* (1962).

Because of his own sense of failure and the decline of his reputation, which his recent books had done little to stem, no one was more surprised than Steinbeck himself when he was awarded the Nobel Prize for Literature in 1962. Even if one agrees with John's own assessment that he did not deserve the prize, the abuse that he suffered in the wake of the announcement, particularly at the hands of the Eastern literary establishment, seems tasteless and mean-spirited. He resolved to conduct himself with as much dignity as possible during the ceremony and throughout the controversy that followed, but the wound was so deep that, although he wrote many thousands of words before he died in 1968, he never wrote another word of fiction.

Few American writers have been the source of as much controversy as John Steinbeck. The furor over *The Grapes of Wrath* lasted for almost two years, as the author was denounced in newspaper editorials and in the Congress as a liar and a pervert. His books are still denounced by those on the political right, and more of his works are on the top-ten list of most-banned books by schools and libraries than any other writer. On the other hand, as a presumably "popular" author, he has been scorned by many academics, and the liberal-intellectual community has not yet forgiven him for what it perceived as his uncritical support for the Vietnam War. It will take a good many more years than have already passed since John Steinbeck's death for us to separate and evaluate the true merit of his work from the prejudices and misconceptions that are still attached to it.

Chronology

Brian Railsback

*Words in **bold** indicate entries in the encyclopedia.*

1902 On February 27 John Ernst Steinbeck is born in **Salinas**, California, to **Olive Hamilton Steinbeck** and **John Ernst Steinbeck**. His mother had been a schoolteacher, and at the time of Steinbeck's birth, his father managed a flour mill. He is the third child, with two older sisters: **Esther** (born 1892) and **Beth** (born 1894). Throughout his childhood, Steinbeck spends much of his summer in the family cottage at **Pacific Grove** or at his uncle **Tom Hamilton**'s ranch near King City. Otherwise, he lives at the Victorian Steinbeck home in Salinas. Thus, the middle-class life against which he would rebel is set in Salinas, his fascination with the sea and biology is set in Pacific Grove, and his regard for ranch life and the Hamiltons is set near King City.

1905 Sister **Mary Steinbeck [Dekker]** is born.

1906 Steinbeck is given a red Shetland pony to care for ("Jill"); this pet will be an inspirational source for ***The Red Pony***.

1907 Begins public school in **Salinas** and proves to be a good student. He comes to school already with a love of books, thanks to a household where books are important and his parents and older sisters read to him. This sets Steinbeck's lifelong love of reading: "I guess there are never enough books," he writes years later. As a child, he is introduced to the **Bible**, which will have a profound impact on his writing style. Other important works include ***Paradise Lost***, *Pilgrim's Progress*, the works of Romantic writers such as Walter Scott, the works of **Shakespeare**, and Thomas Malory's ***Le Morte d'Arthur***. The latter work will become an obsession in Steinbeck's last years, as he will strive unsuccessfully to complete a retelling of Arthurian Legends with ***The Acts of King Arthur and His Noble Knights***.

1910 Steinbeck's father tries his hand at owning a feed and grain store, but this soon fails. After a brief stint working for the **Spreckels Sugar** mill (where Steinbeck will work years later), he is appointed treasurer of **Monterey** County—a position he holds for the rest of his working life.

1917–1918 The United States fights in World War I.

1918 A junior at **Salinas** High School, Steinbeck suffers from pneumonia in the spring and nearly dies. His mother cares for him in the warmer and drier climate at a ranch near Jolon.

1919 Graduates from high school. Though the record suggests Steinbeck was popular—involved in athletics and elected senior class president—biographer **Jackson J. Benson** suggests Steinbeck is somewhat introverted with a few close friends (one being his sister, **Mary**). He is recognized by his teachers as a bright and promising student, and indeed Steinbeck reads voraciously and writes stories. However, Steinbeck is not a dedicated college student and in the fall starts his fitful, lackluster academic career at **Stanford University**.

1920 Steinbeck has his appendix removed. He begins work off and on at **Spreckels**.

1923 Enrolls for the summer at the **Hopkins Marine Station**, where he takes a course in general zoology and learns through professor C. V. Taylor holistic concepts of nature (specifically, **William Emerson Ritter**'s ideas regarding organismal unity). Over the years, Steinbeck will develop a holistic view of nature and the universe that will be a major theme throughout most of his writing.

1924 In the winter Steinbeck enrolls in **Harold Chapman Brown**'s history of philosophy course; Brown advocates science as a road to truth and "cosmic integration," synthesizing life and mind and physical matter; the emphasis on science and holistic thought further informs and refines Steinbeck's views. He takes two courses with **Edith Mirrielees**, a creative writing teacher he admires (he will write a brief preface for her textbook, *Story Writing*, in 1962). He publishes his first two stories, **"Fingers of Cloud: A Satire on College Protervity"** (February) and **"Adventures in Arcademy: A Journey into the Ridiculous"** (June) for *The Stanford Spectator*.

1925 Steinbeck leaves **Stanford** without a degree and embarks on a restless year in which he works at Lake Tahoe, then travels to New York via the freighter, ***Katrina***, which introduces him to Panama and Caribbean scenes that will inspire his first novel, ***Cup of Gold***. In New York he briefly finds work as a journalist and then works construction (on Madison Square Garden); his stories are rejected by **Robert M. McBride & Company**. A decade later he writes of his experience: "I guess I hate New York because I had a thin, lonely, hungry time of it there. . . . I was scared thoroughly."

1926 Steinbeck returns to California from New York. He does a number of odd jobs but finds his primary employment as a caretaker for the Bingham estate at Lake Tahoe.

1927 Intensifies his writing apprenticeship while working alone at the Bingham estate and has his first professional short story publication with **"The Gifts of Iban"** in *The Smoker's Companion*; he uses the pseudonym John Stern. Becomes acquainted with his friend **Webster "Toby" Street**'s play project, entitled "The Green Lady," which will eventually inspire Steinbeck's second novel, ***To a God Unknown***. Works on the manuscript of his first novel, ***Cup of Gold***.

1928 Meets his wife-to-be, **Carol Henning [Steinbeck]**, while working at a fish hatchery in Tahoe City.

1929 Steinbeck is able to write full time and just survive thanks to his father's financial support. ***Cup of Gold*** is published by **Robert M. McBride** in August. He regrets his first novel, a rather romantic handling of the pirate **Henry Morgan**. In a letter written at the end of the year, Steinbeck notes *Cup* "was an immature experiment written for the purpose of getting all the wise cracks (known by sophomores as epigrams) and all the autobiographical material (which hounds us until we get it said) out of my system." The book receives a small number of moderately favorable reviews, and some critics recognize the author's ambition to make it more than another historical romance; whatever chance the first novel might have in terms of sales is wiped away with the stock market crash just two months after *Cup's* publication.

1929–1933 Herbert Hoover is president of the United States. The United States and much of the world enters the Great Depression, with two major phases: 1929–1932 and 1937–1938 (though some experts consider that it lasted through World War II). Steinbeck's novel, ***The Grapes of Wrath***, published in 1939, is considered one of the great literary works to portray the effects of the Depression.

1930 Married to **Carol Henning Steinbeck** at the beginning of the year. After a couple of brief moves, the couple settles in the old Steinbeck cottage in **Pacific Grove**. Carol helps Steinbeck find a stronger, more realistic writing voice and supports him with shrewd editorial advice through his most productive period, the 1930s. He also meets **Edward F. Ricketts**, marine biologist and proprietor of **Pacific Biological Laboratory** on **Cannery Row** in **Monterey**. Ricketts quickly becomes a close friend who is an intellectual partner in Steinbeck's holistic and scientific vision; Ed leads Steinbeck to important sources such as the works of **W. C. Allee**, **Mark Briffault**, and **John Elof Boodin**. Ricketts' lab provides an intellectual and social haven for the young writer that is critical to Steinbeck's development and eventual success. ***To a God Unknown*** does not yet find a publisher, nor do two novellas, **"Murder at Full Moon"** and **"Dissonant Symphony."**

1931 Spends much of the year in poverty in **Pacific Grove**, lacking money to travel much, but puts together a short story cycle he has been working at for over a year: ***The Pastures of Heaven***. Steinbeck moves to the agency of **McIntosh & Otis**—his literary agents for the rest of his life.

1932 ***The Pastures of Heaven*** is published by Brewer, Warren, and Putnam in October (the publisher soon goes bankrupt). Reviews, including one from the *New York Times Book Review*, are favorable, but book sales are slim and do nothing to relieve the Steinbecks' poverty. Early in 1932, Carol and **Joseph Campbell** have a brief affair; Campbell tells John about it and trust in the marriage is permanently eroded. The Steinbecks move to Montrose in Los Angeles to find a better financial situation.

1933 Unable to sustain themselves in Montrose, John and Carol return to **Salinas** to care for **Olive Steinbeck**, who suffers from a stroke. While miserably caring for his mother, Steinbeck begins writing ***The Red Pony*** stories. By the late summer, Steinbeck's father also needs care as he becomes ill with stress, faltering eyesight, and heart trouble. Remaining loyal to **Robert O. Ballou**, the man who saw to the production of *Pastures* through two bankruptcies, Steinbeck does not accept an offer from Simon and Schuster to publish ***To a God Unknown***, the "apprenticeship" novel he has been working on for five years. Ballou manages to pull enough money together to publish *God* himself in September; sales are lackluster and reviewers find some power in Steinbeck's descriptions but note the book on the whole to be "strange," "obsessed," and, as the *New York Times Book Review* notes, "a novel which attempts too much; and by any standard . . . achieves too little."

1933–1945 **Franklin Delano Roosevelt** is president of the United States.

1934 **Olive Steinbeck** dies in February and John remembers her last Christmas, while his ill father tries to keep the family traditions going, as "the most terrible wrenching scene." John and Carol take care of his father in **Pacific Grove** until they arrange for family friends to care for him in the **Salinas** house. Steinbeck tries to maintain a writing pace of 1000 words a day. ***Tortilla Flat*** is rejected by Ballou and Knopf, but finds a place with **Pascal Covici** of **Covici-Friede**. Until Pascal Covici's death, he will edit Steinbeck's books (most of them for **Viking**). Steinbeck becomes acquainted with the dismal farm labor problem in California, meeting with labor organizers, and begins writing ***In Dubious Battle***.

1935 Steinbeck's father dies in May. "In my struggle to be a writer," Steinbeck writes, "it was he who supported and backed me and explained me—not my mother"; he adds that his father let responsibilities overwhelm quiet ambitions: "He was a man intensely disappointed in himself." Ironically, Steinbeck's faith in his son is finally fulfilled when ***Tortilla Flat*** is published by **Covici-Friede**—the book receives positive reviews, it sells well, and Paramount buys the movie rights for $4,000 (a large sum in the middle of the Great Depression). Steinbeck visits Mexico City and New York.

1936 **Covici-Friede** publishes Steinbeck's hard-hitting book about labor strife in California agriculture, ***In Dubious Battle***. "I guess it is a brutal book," Steinbeck writes, "more brutal because there is no author's moral point of view." The book dramatizes ideas in his unpublished 1934 essay, **"Argument of Phalanx,"** in which violent group mentality is explored. The novel is widely and favorably reviewed, and helps immensely to put Steinbeck on the map as a serious writer. He works on the manuscript for ***Of Mice and Men***; his puppy, Toby, destroys the first half of the only copy of the manuscript and Steinbeck comments that the dog may have been acting as a critic. Carol supervises construction of a new house in Los Gatos, a more secluded home where Steinbeck hopes to escape the growing publicity and attention that he despises. Steinbeck writes a series of articles for the *San Francisco News* (published together in an expanded version as *Their Blood Is Strong* in 1938). His research into the labor problem is leading him toward his first "big book": ***The Grapes of Wrath***.

1937 ***Of Mice and Men***, Steinbeck's first experiment in the "play-novelette" (a novella that might be easily adapted to a play), is a great success commercially and in the reviews. With Carol, Steinbeck makes his first trip to Europe (once again traveling the seas by freighter), visiting Denmark, Sweden, Finland, and the Soviet Union. ***The Red Pony*** is published in a special limited edition by **Covici-Friede** (*Time* attacks the price of this and other special editions of his work). ***Of Mice and Men*** is adapted by Steinbeck and **George S. Kaufman** for the stage and in November begins a successful run on Broadway. Research of the labor problem in California intensifies, with more trips to migrant camps in California.

1938 Broadway stage version of ***Tortilla Flat*** fails; John and Carol had increasing apprehension about it as they reviewed drafts, written by Jack Kirkland. With mounting pressure on Steinbeck to live the life of a famous author, which John loathes but Carol is ready to embrace, tension in an already difficult marriage increases. In February and March Steinbeck travels to camps with *Life* photographer **Horace Bristol**; he is appalled by what he witnesses, especially in some of the flooded areas, writing, "Four thousand families, drowned out of their tents are really starving to death." By the spring he takes his first run at a book on the subject in the form of a brutal satire, "L'Affaire Lettuceberg," but destroys the manuscript. After the bankruptcy of **Covici-Friede**, **Pascal Covici** moves to **Viking**, which publishes Steinbeck's second short story collection, ***The Long Valley***, in September to strong sales and good reviews. Regarding his story collection, Steinbeck writes to Covici: "Understand it will have to compete with **Hemingway's** short stories . . . in many ways he is the finest writer of our time." Steinbeck begins writing what will become ***The Grapes of Wrath*** on May 31 and finishes on October 26. The pressure he puts on himself to finish the book is immense, and by the end he is mentally and physically exhausted; worse, he is uncertain about the result: "I am sure of one thing—it isn't the great book I had hoped it would be . . . And the awful thing is that it is absolutely the best I can do." Carol works with him, typing the manuscript from his handwritten copy, offering editorial advice, and even providing the title. He dedicates the book to **Tom Collins**, a migrant camp manager who was in many ways his guide and consultant on migrant life, a man "who lived it," and to Carol, who, John writes, "willed it."

1939 Much of the first part of the year Steinbeck recuperates from leg pain and general malaise from the tremendous effort he put into writing *Grapes*. Resisting pressure from **Elizabeth Otis** and Covici, Steinbeck does minimal revision to the manuscript and refuses to alter the controversial ending (the scene in which **Rosasharn** offers her breast to a starving man). At the end of March he receives his first copies of *Grapes* and tells Covici he is "immensely pleased with them." The novel is released in April to rave reviews and becomes the number one bestseller for 1939 while screen rights sell for the large sum of $75,000; the book is also banned in places, and conservative elements in "Steinbeck country" are furious. Living now at the

Biddle Ranch, a new home on 46 acres complete with a swimming pool, Steinbeck becomes increasingly uncomfortable with all the trappings of "respectability": fame, fortune, and his marriage. He travels restlessly, often leaving Carol to handle the queries for deals and publicity back at home, and flirts with several projects (one of the more substantial is work with filmmaker **Pare Lorentz** on a documentary, *The Fight for Life*). In Hollywood he begins an on-and-off affair with the woman who will become his second wife: **Gwyndolyn Conger [Steinbeck]**. Steinbeck returns to **Ed Ricketts'** lab on **Cannery Row** (living with him for a week during one of his stormy separations from Carol), and the author is enamored with the idea of doing scientific work, of understanding the world through a greater knowledge of biology, chemistry, and physics. He sees and approves of film versions of ***The Grapes of Wrath*** (directed by **John Ford**) and ***Of Mice and Men*** (directed by **Lewis Milestone**).

1940 Throughout the winter he prepares with **Ed Ricketts** for a collecting expedition to the Gulf of California, otherwise known as the Sea of Cortez. Leaving **Monterey** on March 11, the 76-foot ***Western Flyer***, skippered by **Tony Berry**, stops at various points in the Gulf to catalogue marine specimens and returns on April 20. Carol is on board as cook, but soon that job is taken by crewmember **Sparky Enea**. The resulting book of the trip, published in 1941 with Steinbeck and Ricketts as co-authors, includes a narrative largely written by Steinbeck that articulates his and Ed's holistic view. The only person on the trip who is not included in the narrative is Carol. Later Steinbeck travels again to Mexico to work with director **Herbert Kline** on a film involving the difficulty of introducing modern medical practice in a rural village (***The Forgotten Village***); the project results in a rare dispute between John and Ricketts. Steinbeck meets twice with President **Franklin Delano Roosevelt** to discuss propaganda and the author's proposal to hurt the Axis economies with counterfeit money. He wins the **Pulitzer Prize** for *Grapes* and gives the money to his struggling writer friend, **Ritchie Lovejoy**.

1941 Steinbeck works fitfully on the ***Cortez*** manuscript and other projects; he describes himself as suffering from "restlessness." In April, in a small house he bought for himself in **Monterey**, Carol and Gwyn are left to discuss which one will have John—he and his wife permanently separate. The book version of ***The Forgotten Village*** is published (with 136 stills from the film) and Steinbeck receives enthusiastic or polite reviews; the *New Yorker* notes it is "One of the better picture books . . . ." Begins his first residence in Manhattan, living briefly at the Bedford Hotel with Gwyn. He works on his second "play-novelette": ***The Moon Is Down***. **Pascal Covici** and **Viking** are uncomfortable with the Sea of Cortez project as a work of nonfiction, a collaboration, and an expensive production with the narrative and catalogue of invertebrates (with photographs, including color plates). But the pet project of the publisher's star writer comes out in December to generally enthusiastic reviews, and the holistic, biological current of Steinbeck's work is recognized.

1941–1945 The United States enters World War II following the bombing of Pearl Harbor on December 7, 1941.

1942 ***The Moon Is Down*** published in March, with the Broadway play opening in April. This Steinbeck project generates mixed reviews—some finding it a "little masterpiece" with an inspirational, clear-headed look at an occupied country, others deciding *Moon* is a slim book, "melodramatic" and "pretentious." By June, ***Time*** notes *Moon* has "stirred up . . . the year's liveliest literary fight"; also noted is the commercial success of the book (450,000 copies sold), the play (some 56,000 tickets sold), and the payment for film rights ($300,000, an exaggeration). Though bothered by the critical reception, Steinbeck is amused as critics go after each other regarding the book; responding to criticism of the play, Steinbeck writes, "They don't really know what bothered them about the play, but I do. It was dull." Though

Steinbeck did not want to write up a picture book about the training of bomber crews, **FDR** tells him to do just that in a September 1941 meeting in the Oval Office. Working with photographer **John Swope**, Steinbeck flies with a variety of crews and aircraft and is then rushed to write up the manuscript. Clearly a propaganda piece, ***Bombs Away, The Story of a Bomber Team*** receives better reviews than *Moon*, his more serious war effort. The film version of ***Tortilla Flat*** is finally completed and released, starring **Spencer Tracy** and directed by **Victor Fleming**.

1943 In March, Steinbeck officially divorces **Carol** and marries **Gwyn**; the Steinbecks live in a Manhattan apartment. In the summer he works as a war correspondent for the *Herald Tribune*, traveling to the front in North Africa and Italy. He returns to New York in October, sick of the war, and begins the manuscript for ***Cannery Row*** in November (the book will pointedly not be about war).

1944 The film ***Lifeboat***, directed by **Alfred Hitchcock**, appears. Steinbeck worked the previous year on a screen treatment that eventually becomes this production, but he is so angered by the changes made to his story—including slurs against organized labor and the conversion of his three-dimensional black character to a stock Negro stereotype—that he demands to have his name removed from the film. (He is not successful and, ironically, receives an Academy Award nomination for his work.) His son, **Thom Steinbeck**, is born on August 2. By October, the family is back in **Monterey**.

1945 ***Cannery Row*** is published in January and receives generally negative—sometimes harsh—reviews. Steinbeck notes of the critics: "Far from being the sharpest readers, they are the dullest." The novel increases his difficulty in getting along with his old friends in California, such as **Ritchie Lovejoy** or people on **Cannery Row**, who see or do not see themselves in the book. With a completed draft of the book ***The Pearl***, he and **Gwyn** go to Cuernavaca, Mexico; John works with **Jack Wagner** on the film version. With Wagner, he receives an Academy Award nomination for his writing for ***A Medal for Benny***, directed by Irving Pichel.

1945–1953 Harry S. Truman is president of the United States.

1946 Son **John Steinbeck IV** born on June 12. With **Gwyn** and John IV both ill after the birth and with Gwyn feeling her husband has repressed her singing career, tension increases in the household. Steinbeck abandons his office at home and tries to work on the manuscript of ***The Wayward Bus*** at **Viking**. Travels again to Mexico to work on the film of ***The Pearl***. Quickly finishes the manuscript for *The Wayward Bus* in October and then travels with Gwyn to Europe. Despite the opinions of some reviewers at home, such as **James Thurber**, ***The Moon Is Down*** proved to be an inspiration in occupied Europe—Steinbeck is awarded the King Haakon Liberty Cross in Norway.

1947 Friend **Burgess Meredith** suggests the idea for a play, **"The Last Joan,"** which Steinbeck works on but never completes. ***The Wayward Bus***, Steinbeck's allegorical novel about repressed sexuality and rampant commercialism, is published in February. Identified by reviewers as his first full-length novel since ***Grapes***, some find it to be a triumph of unsentimental realism while others see it as a disappointment; Orville Prescott of the *New York Times* goes so far as to suggest that Steinbeck is a "one-book author" with an inflated reputation. Steinbeck's plans to travel to the Soviet Union with photographer **Robert Capa** are delayed when the balcony rail of his brownstone in Manhattan gives way and he falls, shattering his knee cap. In the summer he and Gwyn travel to Paris, where Steinbeck enjoys himself, and then with Capa he travels throughout the Soviet Union after Gwyn returns to New York. ***The Pearl*** is published in November to generally positive reviews, some noting that Steinbeck is at the top of his form., and many observe this modern fable has meaning beyond the simple story, as Edward Weeks of the *Atlantic* writes: "One can take this as a parable or as an active and limpid narrative whose depth . . . is far more than one would suspect."

1948 Continuing work begun the previous year, Steinbeck goes to **Monterey** in February to do background research for "The Salinas Valley," his second "big book" (after *Grapes*), which will become ***East of Eden***. He plans to go on another expedition with **Ed Ricketts**, to the Queen Charlotte Islands off British Columbia—a trip intended to lead to another joint effort, **"The Outer Shores."** The film version of ***The Pearl***, directed by Emilio Fernandez, is released. ***A Russian Journal***, with text by Steinbeck and one chapter and photographs by **Robert Capa**, is published in April; reviewers generally treat the book as a light effort and a simple, sometimes humorous look at the Soviet Union from one writer's point of view. Life for the Steinbecks in New York deteriorates: tension increases in the marriage and John recovers from an operation in April to remove varicose veins. On May 7, Ricketts is crossing train tracks in his car when he is hit by the Del Monte Express; Steinbeck rushes to see him but Ed dies on May 11. In an interview ten years later, Steinbeck notes, "He was my partner for eighteen years—he was part of my brain." Devastated by the loss of his best friend, Steinbeck returns home to Manhattan to find Gwyn wants a divorce; she tells him she has not loved him for years, and the divorce is final in October. He spends some time in Mexico with **Elia Kazan**, working on the screenplay for ***Viva Zapata!***, and goes to the **Pacific Grove** cottage where he suffers from depression. Steinbeck is elected to the American Academy of Arts and Letters.

1949 Release of film version of ***The Red Pony***, directed by **Lewis Milestone**, screenplay by Steinbeck. Recovering from depression, he has a brief affair with the actress **Paulette Goddard**. Steinbeck meets the woman who will become his third wife, **Elaine Scott [Steinbeck]**, in **Carmel** in May (at the time she is still married to the actor Zachary Scott and has one daughter by him, Waverly Scott). Continues work on ***Zapata!*** and begins work on "Everyman," which will become his third "play-novelette," ***Burning Bright***. Moves to Manhattan, and his relationship with Elaine strengthens.

1950 ***Burning Bright***, produced as a book and Broadway play in October, is reviewed as a courageous but failed experiment. After initial rage at the critics' inability to understand what he was doing with his highly abstract morality tale, he later admits that it did not work well as a play. He quickly moves on to work on ***East of Eden***. Marries Elaine in New York on December 28.

1950–1953 The United States fights in the Korean War.

1951 In February the Steinbecks move to their new home on 72nd Street in Manhattan (a four-story brownstone). Steinbeck continues work on ***East of Eden*** (working at a pace of about 800 words a day), summers in Nantucket with his sons along. The narrative portion of ***Cortez***, along with an essay, **"About Ed Ricketts,"** is published as ***The Log from the Sea of Cortez*** in September.

1952 ***Viva Zapata!*** released. Steinbeck travels to North Africa and Europe with Elaine, ostensibly paying his way by writing travel pieces for *Collier's*. ***East of Eden*** is published in September; Steinbeck dedicates what he considers his best novel to his editor, **Pascal Covici**. Some reviewers praise his ambitious novel as a return to *Grapes* form while others use the book to question Steinbeck's literary merit entirely. The novel is a number one bestseller by November.

1953 Steinbeck receives Academy Award nominations for story and screenplay for ***Zapata!*** He works on a novel called "Bear Flag," which eventually becomes ***Sweet Thursday***, with the idea it can become a musical comedy. He spends much of the year in New York.

1953–1961 Dwight D. Eisenhower is president of the United States.

1954 **Richard Rodgers and Oscar Hammerstein** work on making "Bear Flag" into a musical, ***Pipe Dream***. Steinbeck writes a satirical poem about Senator Joe McCarthy but discovers his publisher, Harold Guinzburg, does not want it to be published. Traveling from Spain to Paris, Steinbeck suffers from possibly a mild heart attack or stroke. ***East of Eden*** is published in Paris and Steinbeck is celebrated during a large reception for the book. Waiting to meet **Robert Capa** in Paris, Steinbeck discovers his friend has died from stepping on a mine in Vietnam; this death shakes him nearly as much as Ricketts'. He writes a series of articles, translated into French, for ***Le Figaro***. ***Sweet Thursday*** is published in June; most reviewers recognize it as a light work not to be taken too seriously; as a *Nation* review notes, it is "a minor pleasantry from a major novelist."

1955 Film version of ***East of Eden***, directed by **Elia Kazan** and starring **James Dean**, is a hit. Purchases a summer home in **Sag Harbor** on Long Island. Begins writing articles as "Editor at Large" for *Saturday Review.* Steinbeck enjoys watching rehearsals for ***Pipe Dream*** but recognizes trouble with the treatment of the material; his suggestions, which become increasingly urgent, are largely ignored. Though a **Rodgers and Hammerstein** production, ***Pipe Dream*** fails, and Steinbeck for the most part gives up his ambitions in theater.

1956 Publishes **"How Mr. Hogan Robbed a Bank"** in the March *Atlantic*; the story later becomes the source for his last novel, ***The Winter of Our Discontent***. Steinbeck cuts back on drinking to ease his bouts of depression. For the Louisville *Courier-Journal*, covers the Democratic and Republican national conventions; becomes friends with **Adlai Stevenson** and helps with some of the candidate's speeches. Uncharacteristically volunteers to serve on a committee of Eisenhower's People to People Program, chaired by **William Faulkner** with other members including Edna Ferber, Donald Hall, **Saul Bellow**, and William Carlos Williams. Works throughout the year on his satirical novella set in Paris, ***The Short Reign of Pippin IV***; **Covici** and **Elizabeth Otis** do not like it. Rekindles his interest in the ***Morte d'Arthur*** and begins research on a version he will write for modern times (the manuscript is never completed but is published in 1976).

1957 ***The Short Reign of Pippin IV*** is published in April; reviewers treat it as a "froth of a book"; some find the humor charming while others feel it is strained. Publicly defends Arthur Miller, who is on trial for contempt of Congress charges stemming from the investigations conducted by the House Un-American Activities Committee.

1957–1975 The duration of the Vietnam War, with the U.S. military involved primarily from 1964 to 1973.

1958 Steinbeck travels to Nassau with **Burgess Meredith** and mutual friend Kevin McClory on a disorganized and failed expedition to find sunken treasure. He worries about how his sons, who spend most of the year with Gwyn, are being raised and educated; the morality of the younger generation and the country as a whole concerns him. Prominent critic **Alfred Kazin** attacks Steinbeck's work in *The New York Times*. Working with professor **Eugene Vinaver**, Steinbeck goes to England for more research on his ***Morte d'Arthur*** project. ***Once There Was a War***, a collection of his World War II reporting, is published in September; reviews range from noting the book as a collection of humorous and moving pieces to observing that it is like yesterday's news and generally irrelevant.

1959 Beginning in February, spends the next eight months with Elaine in a cottage near Bruton, Somerset, to intensify his ***Morte d'Arthur*** work; years later, as Steinbeck lies dying, they both decide these are the best months of their time together. Returns to New York in October, depressed at the lack of progress of his *Arthur* book, and suffers from a kidney infection. He is dismayed by the TV quiz show scandals, adding to his concern about American morality. In December, possibly suffers a minor stroke and is hospitalized for two weeks.

1960 He sets aside the *Arthur* project and, between March and July, drafts out his last novel, ***The Winter of Our Discontent***, a dramatization of his concerns about the decay of the individual's morality in the United States. In September, to become reacquainted with his country and assert his physical and mental independence, he travels across the United States and back in his specially outfitted truck, ***Rocinante***, accompanied by his French poodle, Charley. During the part of his trip in **Monterey**, he is appalled at the tourism on **Cannery Row** and such things as the John Steinbeck Theatre.

1961 Works up the book of his trip across the country, ***Travels with Charley in Search of America***. His sons, **Thom** and **John IV**, decide to live with him in New York because life with **Gwyn**, an alcoholic, has become too difficult. ***The Winter of Our Discontent*** is published in June; the reviews, mixed and often unfavorable, depress Steinbeck. "Any critic knows it is no longer legal to praise John Steinbeck," one favorable *Newsweek* review begins. In September, the Steinbecks commence a ten-month stay in Europe. He suffers from another episode—possibly a minor stroke or heart attack—in Milan in November.

1961–1963 **John F. Kennedy** is president. Steinbeck attends President Kennedy's inauguration and is treated as one of the most important celebrities there.

1962 While he is in Europe, ***Travels with Charley*** is published to favorable reviews; Edward Weeks of the *Atlantic* writes, "This is a book to be read slowly for its savor, and one which, like Thoreau, will be quoted and measured by our own experience." On October 25 he hears on television that he has won the **Nobel Prize** for Literature; critical reaction to the award is negative, with questions raised as to why he should win the award when other writers are more deserving. In his **acceptance speech**, Steinbeck makes brief reference to "a pale and emasculated critical priesthood" but discusses the importance of the writer and in the new Atomic Age the need for humans to recognize that "Having taken Godlike power, we must seek in ourselves for the responsibility and the wisdom we once prayed some deity might have." The critical backlash from winning the Nobel and his waning physical strength make it impossible to finish another novel.

1963 In March, the Steinbecks move to a high-rise apartment on the same block as their brownstone. Requires surgery for a detached retina; his recovery is aided by visits from his old friend, the novelist **John O'Hara**. At the request of President **Kennedy**, Steinbeck travels on an exhausting two-month cultural exchange trip to Eastern Europe and the Soviet Union; he travels with Elaine, meets writers **Edward Albee** and **Erskine Caldwell**. He is shocked by the assassination of Kennedy in November. In December the Steinbecks are invited to a private dinner with President **Lyndon Johnson** and his wife, **Lady Bird Johnson**.

1963–1969 **Lyndon Baines Johnson** is president.

1964 **Thom** and **John IV** return to live with **Gwyn**; in March Steinbeck is sued for more child support but a large increase is denied in court the next month. In August, **Thomas H. Guinzburg**, the head of **Viking**, brings a collection of photographs taken from around the country and proposes Steinbeck write captions for a picture book; Steinbeck has one last writing streak, creating a series of essays that will become his last book published in his lifetime, ***America and Americans***. Now friends with the Johnsons, Steinbeck is asked to help with the president's acceptance speech for the Democratic Party nomination and later Johnson's inaugural speech. Steinbeck is awarded the Presidential Medal of Freedom in September. On October 14, **Pascal Covici** dies; at the small funeral service, with other Covici writers **Saul Bellow** and Arthur Miller, Steinbeck states, "He demanded of me more than I had and thereby caused me to be more than I should have been without him." Spends the first of two Christmases in Ireland with the director, **John Huston**.

1965 While in Paris he learns of his sister Mary Dekker's death, adding to a general malaise caused by his inability to write and the death of **Covici**. Back at

Sag Harbor, continues work on ***America and Americans***; suggests to **Elizabeth Otis** that his journal written alongside ***East of Eden*** be published (it will become the posthumous book, ***Journal of a Novel***). Beginning in November publishes a series of articles for *Newsday* that become known as **"Letters to Alicia,"** which run off and on until May 1967. Goes to England to conduct more research in Arthurian manuscripts.

1966 Travels to Israel and is inspired by that nation's great survival instinct, an echo of the survival theme in ***America and Americans***. At **John IV**'s request, Steinbeck helps his son (who had finished basic training in the Army) to get an assignment in Vietnam. The author and son meet with President Johnson in the White House. In the small writing studio (**Joyous Garde**) he had built on his property at Sag Harbor, Steinbeck works at a novel project, "A Piece of It Fell on My Tail," but does not get far with it. *America and Americans* is published in October, receiving generally favorable reviews. Continuing his work for *Newsday*, Steinbeck begins a six-week tour of Vietnam. He is inspired to go because his son is there and to take a first-hand look for his friend, **Lyndon Johnson**.

1967 While John tours the field in Vietnam, **Elaine** attends news briefings in Saigon and helps file dispatches. As he identifies more and more with the American soldier in battle, his **"Letters to Alicia"** pieces in *Newsday* take on a hawkish feel and his loathing of antiwar hippies gets in print, as he compares them unfavorably to the soldiers. "I suppose it is the opposite of the shiver of shame I sometimes feel at home when I see the Vietnicks, dirty clothes, dirty minds, sour smelling wastelings and their ill-favored and barren pad mates. Their shuffling, drag-ass protests . . . ." These articles irritate the leftist literary establishment, further damaging Steinbeck's reputation among critics. Leaving a village one evening with Elaine, their helicopter is fired at as it takes off; Steinbeck pushes himself to mental and physical limits during the trip. He continues a wider tour of Southeast Asia, including Laos. In Hong Kong, helping a Chinese worker, Steinbeck suffers from a slipped disk. The Steinbecks return to New York in April and in May John and Elaine visit the White House to discuss the trip with President **Johnson** and several cabinet members. By August, he understands that the war in Vietnam cannot be won. Suffering from terrible back pain, he enters a hospital in New York for surgery. **John IV** is arrested in connection with 20 pounds of marijuana found in his Washington, D.C., apartment; the Steinbecks deal with the unwelcome press coverage. After a successful back operation, Steinbeck is released from the hospital in December, and shortly afterward his son is acquitted. With Elaine, he rests in Grenada—his last trip abroad.

1968 Steinbeck suffers a small stroke in May and a heart attack in July; at New York Hospital, he has another attack. Goes to Sag Harbor in August, needing oxygen at night, and in a last unfinished letter writes, "my fingers have avoided the pencil as though it were an old and poisoned tool." Returns to the apartment in New York in November. John tells Elaine she should be prepared for his book sales to dry up after he is dead, but time proves him wrong. He dies at 5:30 P.M. on December 20. After a service at St. James Episcopal Church in Manhattan and a smaller family service at Point Lobos, John Ernst Steinbeck's ashes are buried in the Garden of Memories Cemetery in **Salinas**.

Major posthumous publications include ***Journal of a Novel, The "East of Eden" Letters*** (1969), *Steinbeck: A Life in Letters* (edited by **Elaine Steinbeck** and **Robert Wallsten**, 1975), ***The Acts of King Arthur and His Noble Knights*** (edited by **Chase Horton**, 1976), *Working Days: The Journals of "The Grapes of Wrath"* (edited by **Robert DeMott**, 1989), and ***America and Americans*** *and Selected Nonfiction* (edited by Susan Shillinglaw and **Jackson J. Benson**, 2002).

A

ABNER, THE AERIAL ENGINEER. In *Bombs Away,* the quiet and humble California garage mechanic who is capable of fixing nearly anything, but who possesses a special affection for engines; he joins the Air Force to satisfy his mechanical curiosity and to work on the B-17 Flying Fortress.

"ABOUT ED RICKETTS" (1951). This seventy-page biographical essay appeared as the preface to ***The Log from the Sea of Cortez*** in 1951, ten years after the original publication of ***Sea of Cortez***, the record of the specimen-collecting trip Steinbeck and **Edward F. Ricketts** made to the Gulf of California in 1940. Published just three years after Ricketts' death in 1948, this tribute uses the same sportive humor that characterizes Steinbeck's ***Tortilla Flat*** and ***Cannery Row.*** It is noteworthy as a well-written and fair-minded character sketch of one of Steinbeck's closest friends and perhaps the person who exerted the greatest influence on his writing.

The essay opens with an objectively narrated account of Ricketts' death—he was struck in his car by a train. Through anecdotes, Steinbeck restores the open-minded, compassionate, and roguish marine biologist who was the template for several characters in Steinbeck's fiction, most notably **Doc Burton** of ***In Dubious Battle***, **Doc** of *Cannery Row* and ***Sweet Thursday,*** and **Jim Casy** of ***The Grapes of Wrath***.

The anecdotes carefully build Ricketts' complex character. For example, recounting the fire that once destroyed Ricketts' **Pacific Biological Laboratory** on the Row in 1936, Steinbeck says that Ricketts managed to grab his typewriter and escape in his car without stopping to put pants on. When some of the habitués of the laboratory buy a three-dollar sheep to eat during the hard times of the Great Depression, none of them have the heart to slaughter the animal, except the same Ricketts who showed such kindness to the dogs, bums, and prostitutes of the Row. "With no emotion whatsoever," Steinbeck writes, "Ed cut its throat" and then explained as the rest watched how painless the process was for the sheep. Other anecdotes reveal Ricketts' lustfulness, his scientific detachment, and his nonjudgmental nature. Stories of Ricketts' relations with his Cannery Row neighbors and the wild parties in his laboratory provide further insight into their fictional counterparts in Steinbeck's *Cannery Row* and *Sweet Thursday.*

This essay also explores Ricketts' **non-teleological** outlook, which Steinbeck incorporates into much of his best work and which he expands on in *The Log from the Sea of Cortez.* In particular, Steinbeck explains Ricketts' philosophy of "breaking through," a scientifically and aesthetically transcendent phenomenon. Throughout his fiction, Steinbeck explores how this phenomenon affects people (such as **Jim Nolan** in *In Dubious Battle*) experiencing it through groups and as individuals (**Tom Joad** in *The Grapes of Wrath*, for example). Curiously, in this essay Steinbeck describes Ricketts' philosophical point of view just as many critics have described Steinbeck's—as "essentially ecological and holistic."

Further Reading: Astro, Richard. *John Stein- beck and Edward F. Ricketts: The Shaping of a Novelist*. New Berlin: University of Minnesota Press, 1973; Ricketts, Edward F. *Renaissance Man of Cannery Row: The Life and Letters of Edward F. Ricketts*. Ed. Katharine A. Rodger. Tuscaloosa: University of Alabama Press, 2002.

Scott Simkins

ABRAMSON, BEN (1898–1955). Employed by various bookstores in Chicago as a young man, Abramson established his own store, the Argus Book Shop, in 1922. To supplement his earnings after the stock market crash, Abramson added a mail order business, advertising books in a catalog, *Along the North Wall* (1930), and in a newspaper, the *Argus Decennial Tribune, the World's Greatest Book Paper* (1932). The Argus Book Shop was one of the top bookstores in Chicago for almost two decades.

Abramson read the two installments of John Steinbeck's ***The Red Pony*** in *The North American Review* in 1933 and ordered remaindered copies of Steinbeck's early works for his store. When he read **"The Murder"** in the April 1934 issue of *The North American Review,* Abramson was wholly convinced of Steinbeck's greatness and fervently promoted the author's works to his customers.

At about this time, **Pascal Covici**, a former Chicago bookstore owner himself and a friend of Abramson, dropped by the Argus Book Shop. Abramson insisted he read Steinbeck, so Covici bought ***The Pastures of Heaven*** to read on the train back to New York City, where he owned a small publishing house called **Covici-Friede**. Covici was so impressed with the book that he immediately inquired about Steinbeck's contractual obligations. After approaching Steinbeck's most recent publisher, **Robert O. Ballou**, he called **McIntosh & Otis** and discovered that Steinbeck had none. **Mavis McIntosh** explained that several publishers had already rejected ***Tortilla Flat***, and she mailed the book to Covici. Covici not only offered to publish *Tortilla Flat*, but he also promised to reissue Steinbeck's earlier works, thereafter becoming Steinbeck's lifelong editor and friend.

Deborah Covington, the Abramsons' only child, commented that if Ben (her father) liked an author's work, his generosity was limitless. In fact, she noted that her parents were such good friends with John and **Carol Henning Steinbeck** that—in the early years—the Abramsons sent stationery, stamps, and homemade foods to the couple. Abramson himself mailed letters of encouragement to Steinbeck, sometimes sending along cartons of the author's books to sign for Abramson's customers. Abramson tried to help place Steinbeck's short stories in magazines, and when Covici-Friede had financial problems, he guaranteed payment in advance for copies of *Tortilla Flat* and offered to pay printing bills.

Letters between the two men indicate that Steinbeck often told Abramson about his writing, and Steinbeck visited Abramson at least once. However, their relationship lapsed around 1941, when Harry Thornton Moore, author of *The Novels of John Steinbeck* (1939), asked Ben to help him sell his Steinbeck correspondence. Because he was aware of Steinbeck's disdain for fame, Abramson arranged to sell the correspondence privately to a buyer who would not show the letters publicly. Steinbeck was furious when Ben wrote him of it, and their relationship, for the most part, ended.

Despite contemporary claims that Abramson was Steinbeck's discoverer, Abramson himself did not feel he was so important in Steinbeck's career. He told Steinbeck, "If any one discovered you, it was Bob Ballou. That I was instrumental in getting Covici to take your manuscripts was and is of little importance. Their merit alone would have eventually brought them to the light of print."

In 1944, Abramson moved to New York City, where he was finally able to begin his publishing business. The first book to appear under the Ben Abramson, Publisher imprint was *Pilgrims through Space and Time*, by J. O. Bailey. But his business was unstable, and his final years were bleak. In 1947, Ben collapsed from pleurisy and experienced a complete breakdown, which resulted in a short stay in a sanitarium. In 1953, he returned to Chicago; two years later, on July 16, depressed and desolate, he committed suicide.

Further Reading: Benson, Jackson J. *The True Adventures of John Steinbeck, Writer*. New York: Viking, 1984; Covington, Deborah B. *The Argus Book Shop: A Memoir*. West Cornwall, CT: Tarrydiddle, 1977; Fensch, Thomas. *Steinbeck and Covici: The Story of a Friendship*. Middlebury, VT: Paul S. Eriksson, 1979.

Jennifer Baumgartner

ACCOLON OF GAUL, SIR. In ***The Acts of King Arthur***, lover of **Morgan le Fay**, who gives him **Excalibur**, the sword she has stolen from **Arthur**.

ACTS OF KING ARTHUR AND HIS NOBLE KNIGHTS, THE (1978). Published in 1978, this posthumous Steinbeck work, although uncompleted, was a book that he had arguably always been destined to write. In 1911, as a child of nine, Steinbeck was given a copy of *The Boy's King Arthur*, an edited version of the Caxton ***Morte d'Arthur*** of Sir Thomas Malory. The legend of **King Arthur** and the Knights of the Round Table became a lifelong fascination and a constant metaphor in his work. The little closed societies of **Danny** and his paisano friends in ***Tortilla Flat*** and of **Mack** and the boys in ***Cannery Row*** and ***Sweet Thursday*** possess certain analogies with the concept of the Round Table. The influence is established more importantly, however, in the Arthurian ethos, which, to one degree or another, underpins the whole of Steinbeck's fictional output and has as its starting point the image of the Holy Grail: the search for the unattainable—the never-ending quest that motivates the actions of so many Steinbeckian characters and is most memorably delineated in the story of the two bindlestiffs **George Milton** and **Lennie Small** in ***Of Mice and Men*** and in the saga of the **Joad** family's journey to the false promised land of California in ***The Grapes of Wrath***.

Steinbeck finally decided to write his own modern version of the Malory cycle of Arthurian romances in the mid-1950s. His original intention had been to modernize the text of the familiar Caxton *Morte d'Arthur*, but by the time he began to write he had decided to abandon the Caxton text and to base his work on the authentic Malorian text of the Winchester manuscript, which had been discovered in 1934, edited and interpreted by **Eugene Vinaver**, and published by the Oxford University Press in 1947 in a three-volume edition under the title *The Works of Sir Thomas Malory*. Steinbeck's change of mind immediately posed several structural problems, for whereas Caxton had effectively edited the Malory romances into a continuing narrative, the Vinaver text reverted to Malory's original eight separate romances, the first of which, *The Tale of King Arthur*, is divided into six sections.

The text of *The Acts of King Arthur and His Noble Knights*, edited by Chase Horton, contains Steinbeck's versions of these six sections of the first romance (***Merlin***, *Balin or The Knight with the Two Swords, Torre and Pellinor, The War with the Five Kings, Arthur and Accolon*, and *Gawain, Ywain, and Marhalt*) and his version of the third of the romances (*The Noble Tale of Sir Launcelot du Lake*), which together compose only approximately two-sevenths of the total Vinaver text. He visualized that his version of the whole work would run into two volumes, the first volume ending with the first part of Malory's fifth romance, *The Book of Sir Tristram de Lyones*, and the second volume containing the latter part of the fifth romance, together with the sixth, seventh, and eighth (*The Tale of the Sankgreal Briefly Drawn Out of French Which Is a Tale Chronicled for One of the Truest and One of the Holiest That Is in This World, The Book of Sir Launcelot and Queen*

Guinevere, and *The Most Piteous Tale of the Morte Arthur Saunz Guerdon*). Steinbeck did, in fact, also complete a version of the fourth of Malory's romances, *The Tale of Sir Gareth of Orkney That Was Called Bewmaynes*, but Horton has silently dropped this from the published text.

Steinbeck wrote the whole of the extant text of his Arthurian book, including the unpublished *Sir Gareth*, during the time he was staying in a tiny cottage on the outskirts of the Somerset town of Bruton, in England, from March through September 1959. He had gone there with his wife, **Elaine**, specifically to soak himself in the atmosphere of Avalon while writing his book. At first, the work went well, but after he had completed the first four sections, a growing disenchantment with what he was doing began to set in. He was by then receiving unfavorable and somewhat puzzled feedback from his New York agents, who had clearly been expecting more Steinbeck than Malory in the text. Moreover, he had from the beginning, particularly in the *Merlin* section, been plagued by a series of small but vital structural problems and these problems were further aggravated in later sections by Malory's failure to tidy up loose ends in his own narrative and by the difficulties Steinbeck experienced in necessarily putting his own construction on matters that, with the passage of time, have little meaning for the modern reader. Beginning with the sixth section of the book, *Gawain, Ewain and Marhalt,* he commenced to elaborate on Malory's text, letting his own imagination and scholarship take wing. He justified the abandonment of his earlier purist stance by observing that he was simply cutting and re-editing Malory's text in the same way that Malory himself had cut and re-edited the "Frensshe Booke" on which his romances were based. The sixth and seventh sections of *The Acts* are the most vivid and successful in the whole book and constitute some of the best prose Steinbeck ever wrote. This, unfortunately, was not a good enough solution, for the structural problems persisted and became irresolvable. Steinbeck found himself torn between carrying on with his own extended versions of the somewhat disjointed scheme of Malory's romances and either disputing the order of the remaining romances or discarding some of them, wholly or in part, as he had earlier discarded *The Tale of the Noble King Arthur.* He had still not discovered a way out his confusion when, at the end of August 1959, he broke off work on the book, and indulged in an extended round of sightseeing until mid-October, when he returned home to New York. He intended that the suspension of work on the book should be merely temporary, and comforted himself with the thought that a room in the Bruton cottage was no different in essence from a room in New York. But it would seem, as he put it, that "the flame had gone out," and, although he subsequently spoke and wrote about his *Arthur* book, the break proved to be permanent.

Steinbeck's text of the first and third of the Malory romances is supplemented in *Acts of King Arthur* by sixty-eight pages of letters, or extracts from letters, to his agents and to Chase Horton covering the period from November 1956, when he first determined he would begin concentrated research on the *Morte,* until July 1965. These letters provide a fascinating study of Steinbeck's continuing struggle to find a rationale for and a path through the overwhelming mass of material he had at his disposal.

The book was respectfully, if somewhat cautiously, received by the critics of the day. Subsequent scholarly assessment has inevitably concentrated on the Arthur-Lancelot-Guinevere aspects and has been extremely well-informed. While being viewed in certain quarters as something of an anachronism in the Steinbeck canon, the book is in fact essential reading for anyone interested in an understanding of the Steinbeckian view of life.

Further Reading: Gardner, John. "The Acts of King Arthur and His Noble Knights," *New York Times Book Review.* October 24, 1976, 31–32, 34, 36; Hodges, Laura F. "Steinbeck's

Adaptation of Malory's Launcelot: A Triumph of Realism over Supernaturalism," *Quondam et Futurus* 2 (Spring 1992) 70–81; Mitchell, Robin C. "Steinbeck and Malory: A Correspondence with Eugene Vinaver," *Steinbeck Quarterly* 10 (Summer–Fall 1977) 70–79; Simmonds, Roy S. "A Note on Steinbeck's Unpublished Arthurian Stories," in *Steinbeck and the Arthurian Theme.* Ed. Tetsumaro Hayashi. Steinbeck Monograph Series No. 5 (1975) 25–29.

Roy S. Simmonds

ADAMS, HENRY (1838–1918). American historian, philosopher of history, and cultural critic who wrote one of America's outstanding autobiographies, *The Education of Henry Adams* (1907). Steinbeck was familiar with Adams's historical theories. Adams's most impressive achievement as a historian is his *History of the United States of America During the Administrations of Thomas Jefferson and James Madison* (nine volumes, 1889–1891), in which he contended that the decisions and policies of the period from 1801 to 1817 shaped the main course of subsequent American political development.

His *Degradation of the Democratic Dogma* (1919) includes three essays on his philosophy of history. In this work Adams introduced his dynamic theory of history. Derived from the second law of thermodynamics, the theory that maintains energy is in a constant state of dissipation, Adams believed that human history is similarly devoid of purpose and consists merely of a succession of energy phases. Steinbeck knew the dynamic theory and probably read Adams's most widely read book, *The Education of Henry Adams* (for which Adams was awarded, posthumously, the **Pulitzer Prize** in 1919). The book is an autobiography written in the third person with detached skepticism and delicate irony. Its main concern was to indict the educational system of his day for its failure to prepare an intelligent man for the chaos of modern life. Adams's works reveal a profound concern with the destiny of the modern world.

Further Reading: DeMott, Robert. *Steinbeck's Reading: A Catalogue of Books Owned and Borrowed*. New York: Garland, 1984.

ADAMS, WILLIAM (1922–2005). Adapted and directed a not very successful stage version of ***The Grapes of Wrath*** that played at some colleges in 1978.

ADDISON, JOSEPH (1672–1719) AND **HENRY STEELE** (1672–1729). Addison was an English poet, essayist, and critic, and Steele an Irish-born English playwright and essayist. With the publication of their essays in the periodicals entitled *The Tatler* and ***The Spectator***, Addison and Steele helped to perfect the essay as a literary form and modeled a clear, crisp style of English. Steinbeck owned an 1883 copy of *The Spectator*, edited by Henry Morley. In ***Travels with Charley***, part II, Steinbeck noted "a love for Joseph Addison which I have never lost."

Janet L. Flood

"ADVENTURES IN ARCADEMY: A JOURNEY INTO THE RIDICULOUS" (1924). An early satire of university life by Steinbeck published in the *Stanford Spectator* in June, 1924.

ADVERTISING MAN, THE. In *The Wayward Bus*, the man with whom Camille Oaks's friend Lorraine lives. He becomes a burden when he loses his job and his mental stability after Lorraine unknowingly infects him with gonorrhea.

AGNES. One of the prostitutes at the **Bear Flag**. In ***Sweet Thursday***, she usually joins **Becky** and **Mabel** to serve as a sort of collective character, a Bear Flag chorus. Like her two companions, she is portrayed as extremely vacuous. Agnes has so little individuality that at one point Steinbeck seems to have forgotten her name (see **Alice**).

AGUIRRE, FERNANDO. In ***Viva Zapata!***, Aguirre is a fictitious character; he does not appear in the newly discovered narrative, and it is generally felt that he was invented by Steinbeck as a foil to Emiliano Zapata. While the latter can be described a warm-hearted rebel totally desirous of having his people's confiscated lands returned to them and not seeking any power or public office for himself, Fernando is a cold-hearted, calculating revolutionary. He will stop at nothing to promote his cause, and, when Emiliano leaves Mexico City to investigate the complaint brought to him by his compatriots from Morelos, Fernando warns him that he will not live long and that he is throwing his power away. He eventually betrays Emiliano as he has Madero, whose emissary he once has been; he also emphasizes Pablo Gómez's treachery, thus forcing Emiliano to execute his long-time friend.

Further Reading: Morsberger, Robert E. "Stein- beck's Zapata: Rebel versus Revolutionary." In *John Steinbeck's Zapata*. Ed. Robert E. Morsberger. New York: Penguin, 1993. 203–223.

Marcia D. Yarmus

AINSWORTH, ELIZABETH STEINBECK (1894–1992). Born in Paso Robles on May 25, 1894, Elizabeth was the oldest sister of John Steinbeck, one who understood the importance to her brother of family loyalty. In 1916 she graduated from Mills College with a degree in home economics and later attained a graduate degree in business. Known as Beth, she enjoyed success in San Francisco while working as a purchaser and manager for a department store. She eventually worked in personnel management with Shell Development, the research division of the Shell Oil Company. In 1925, Beth helped her brother John by playing host to him when he arrived in New York empty handed. Her husband was able to get John a job with the James Stewart Construction Company working on the construction of Madison Square Garden (the predecessor to the current venue), where he hauled cement to bricklayers. She lived in Berkeley before moving into the Steinbeck cottage at 147 11th Street in **Pacific Grove**, California. John Steinbeck carved her initials, "ESA," on the wooden mailbox outside the cottage.

Donating her time and original family artifacts, Beth played an important part in the Valley Guild, the nonprofit organization that maintains the Steinbeck family home in Salinas.

Further Reading: Benson, Jackson J. *The True Adventures of John Steinbeck,* Writer. New York: Viking, 1984; Parini, Jay. *John Steinbeck*. New York: Henry Holt, 1995.

John Hooper

AL, THE AERIAL GUNNER. An Army Air Force volunteer in ***Bombs Away***; he is the nervy, cocky, and tough man from the Midwest, a product of hard times and a one-time amateur boxer.

ALARDINE OF THE OUTER ISLES, SIR. Killed by Sir Gawain during the Quest of the White Stag in *Acts of King Arthur.*

ALBEE, EDWARD (1928–). American playwright and author of such plays as *Who's Afraid of Virginia Woolf?*, *Tiny Alice, A Delicate Balance,* and *Three Tall Women*, Albee is a three-time winner of the **Pulitzer Prize** for Drama. His earlier one-acts, including *The Zoo Story, The Sandbox*, and *The American Dream*, established him as an astute critic of American values and dreams, so it was no surprise that at the request of Steinbeck, the young Albee accompanied the author on a cultural exchange with the Soviet Union in 1963. Fresh from his success with *Virginia Woolf*, Albee was considered part of a new generation of younger and distinguished American writers. Despite the difference in their ages and attitudes, Steinbeck became a close friend of Albee during their stay in Russia. Albee's presence served to diffuse potential false charges of spying against Steinbeck, who was considered by the Soviets more of a government agent than an artist. Albee drew a different audience, enabling the two men to meet both students and dissidents and giving them a more balanced and clearer picture of the real nature of Soviet citizens. Albee served as one of the honorary pallbearers at Steinbeck's funeral service in New York.

Michael J. Meyer

ALBEE, GEORGE (1905–1964). Friend of and correspondent with John Steinbeck during the 1930s. Like Steinbeck, Albee was a struggling writer, and the two would often write one another about the multitudinous frustrations, concerns, and philosophies surrounding their early writing careers. Some of Steinbeck's most insightful comments about his own work as a writer are contained in his letters to George Albee. However, as Steinbeck's popularity increased, and Albee continued to flounder in mediocrity, Albee became jealous of his friend and began to ridicule Steinbeck behind his back to mutual friends. As a result, Steinbeck all but ended their relationship in an angry letter written to Albee in 1938. In it, Steinbeck expresses the pain he feels from Albee's resentment, and how he can no longer deem the two friends. Although Steinbeck resumed his correspondence with Albee almost twelve years later, the two remained somewhat distant, never again achieving the amiability of their previous relationship.

Ted Scholz

ALBEE, RICHARD (1909–1983). Younger brother of Steinbeck's good friend, **George Albee**. He considered himself a philosopher and was a particular admirer of **John Elof Boodin,** a UCLA philosophy professor of some influence on Steinbeck whose writings included *A Realistic Universe* and *Cosmic Evolution.* Steinbeck read *Cosmic Evolution* sometime in 1932–33 after discussing Albee's class notes with him and after attending a lecture by C. V. Taylor at the Hopkins Marine Station. **Jackson J. Benson** notes that Albee delivered a personal letter from Steinbeck to Boodin, complimenting him and requesting permission to use Boodin's idea in his own creative work. In taped oral histories donated to the Steinbeck Library in **Salinas**, Albee claimed to have been an influence in developing Steinbeck's "**Argument of Phalanx**," and to have been present as Steinbeck typed out his explanation of "group man." The phalanx argument was based on both men's love for ancient history, and its name was determined by the battle formation employed by Philip of Macedon and Alexander the Great. After reading the treatise, Albee commented that the Greeks often referred to the phalanx as a tortoise, a reference to the protection of a hard shell of shields as the army moved forward. Later, after reading ***The Grapes of Wrath***, Albee believed the turtle image in the initial chapters was motivated by this conversation.

Albee and his wife, Jan, were participants in conversations that clearly piqued the interest of Steinbeck and his friend, **Edward F. Ricketts**, in several complex concepts of philosophical thought that were later developed in ***The Log from the Sea of Cortez.*** Albee also claimed to have introduced the two men to the musical tenets of Gregorian chants. Although specific influences cannot be definitively confirmed, Albee clearly felt he had a significant impact on the philosophical base of Steinbeck's fictional world.

Further Reading: Benson, Jackson J. *The True Adventures of John Steinbeck, Writer.* New York: Viking, 1984; DeMott, Robert. *Steinbeck's Reading: A Catalogue of Books Owned and Borrowed*. New York: Garland, 1984.

Michael J. Meyer and Herbert Behrens

ALBERTSON, JUDGE. The judge in ***Sweet Thursday*** who discharges **the seer**, arrested for stealing candy bars, on the recommendation of the **Safeway manager**.

ALBEY, KATE. Name used by **Cathy Ames/Cathy Trask** in ***East of Eden*** when, after shooting her husband **Adam Trask**, she begins working at and eventually arranges to inherit, **Faye**'s brothel. She uses this name for the rest of her life with one exception: when she writes her will bequeathing all of her money to her son, **Aron Trask**, and signs it "Catherine Trask."

ALEX. The cook at **Faye**'s, later **Kate Albey**'s, brothel in ***East of Eden***.

ALICE. A prostitute in ***Sweet Thursday***, who along with **Mabel** and **Becky** learns of **Doc's** broken arm while having her morning orange juice. The name appears to be a slip, for there is no previous mention of an Alice in *Sweet Thursday*; rather, it is **Agnes** who is invariably in the company of the other two.

ALICE. The village prostitute in ***The Winter of Our Discontent***.

ALLAN, THE NAVIGATOR. In ***Bombs Away***, the technically-minded engineering graduate from Indiana who gets accepted into navigator training based on his mathematical aptitude.

ALLEE, W. C. (1885–1955). Highly respected professor at the University of Chicago from 1921 until 1950. Known as one of the first American ecologists, W. C. Allee is widely known for his theories involving the mutual interdependence of living organisms. In such books as *Animal Aggregations* and *Principles of Animal Ecology*, Allee demonstrated that the social behavior of animals stems from an innate fundamental harmony or automatic cooperation in nature, and not from any active conscious need within the animals themselves. Allee's theories had a profound influence on **Edward F. Ricketts**, who was a student at the University of Chicago during his tenure. Consequently, as Ricketts and Steinbeck became good friends, many of Allee's ecological theories were passed on to the author. For example, Steinbeck's phalanx theory, or the theory of the group man, can be seen as an indirect reference to Allee. Just as Allee saw animals working in harmonious social units common to all living organisms, so did Steinbeck see similarities in the social interactions between humans. He felt that, while human beings may behave differently as individuals, roused by different forces to different ends, these individual concerns are replaced by a group consciousness as groups of individuals are formed.

Further Reading: Astro, Richard. *John Stein- beck and Edward F. Ricketts: The Shaping of a Novelist*. New Berlin: University of Minnesota Press, 1973; Railsback, Brian. *Parallel Expeditions: Charles Darwin and the Art of John Steinbeck*. Moscow: University of Idaho Press, 1995.

Ted Scholz

ALLEN, ELISA. Thirty-five-year-old protagonist in **"The Chrysanthemums,"** aligned with the chrysanthemums of the story's title. A talented woman who grows huge flowers and believes that with opportunity she could succeed at traditionally male roles and tasks, she is married to **Henry Allen**, a farmer who loves her but can neither fathom nor appreciate her true nature. A chance visit by an itinerant tinker awakens Elisa's desires and longing for excitement and opportunity, but her newly formed concepts of her femininity and her abilities are dashed when she realizes that the tinker has betrayed her by discarding the chrysanthemums she has entrusted to him.

ALLEN, FRED (1894–1954). Comedian and friend of Steinbeck's, best known for "The Fred Allen Show"; Steinbeck's unpublished play, **"The Wizard of Maine,"** was to have been a vehicle for Allen.

ALLEN, HENRY. The husband of **Elisa**, the protagonist of **"The Chrysanthemums."** A well-meaning man, he is a successful rancher who cannot fathom the depths of his wife's longings and abilities. When he takes her to dinner in **Salinas** at the end of the story, he notices her mood changes, but he has no idea of the identity crisis she has suffered through the chance visit of an itinerant tinker.

ALLEN, T. B. In ***Pastures of Heaven***, the shopkeeper in Las Pasturas and member of the school board who circulates the idea that the Battle place is cursed or haunted. He also promotes the theory that the Munroe curse of never attaining or achieving success has mated with the Battle curse and produced a slew of baby curses. His major function is as a taleteller or scandalmonger.

"ALWAYS SOMETHING TO DO IN SALINAS" (1955). Appearing in the June 1955 issue of *Holiday*, this article was not entirely complimentary to Steinbeck's hometown and regenerated some of the antagonism felt by locals toward the author. It suggested that there was little inherent in the area or its cultural surroundings that influenced either Steinbeck's success or the passion that filled his fictional output.

ALYNE. The daughter of **King Pellinore**, born of his love for the **Lady of the Rule**, and affianced to **Sir Myles of the Lands** in ***The Acts of King Arthur***. While she and Sir Myles are on their way to Camelot to be wed, Sir Myles is attacked from behind and wounded by a cowardly knight, **Loraine le Sauvage**. Alyne's cries for help are ignored by King Pellinore as he rides by, intent on carrying out his quest on behalf of **King Arthur**. The two lovers are torn to pieces by wild beasts, only their heads remaining, and it is only later, on his return to Camelot with the damsel's head, that King Pellinore is told by **Merlin** who she was.

Roy S. Simmonds

AMERICA AND AMERICANS (1966). Published by **Viking Press** in October 1966, this last book published during Steinbeck's lifetime is a chronicle of the American people and their way of life, both past and present, and a testament to the future endurance of the American spirit. Often the correlation between the photos and the text is only implied, and as a result, the reader may feel, as did a few early reviewers, that the two work independently of each other. This effect is particularly evident in the paperback edition, published by Bantam in October 1968. Yet there is a consistent thread throughout—the diversity of issues and tones is always firmly rooted in Steinbeck's unwavering belief in the democratic spirit.

In August 1964, **Thomas Guinzburg**, president of Viking Press, asked Steinbeck to write an introduction and captions for a collection of photographs reflecting the American lifestyle and values; Steinbeck's own enthusiasm for the project enlarged the scope of his contribution. Apparently the photos, which represent the works of such distinguished photographers as Alfred Eisenstaedt, Ansel Adams, Henri Cartier-Bresson, Tom Hollyman and Bruce Roberts, stirred Steinbeck's imagination and provided a forum for his personal observations on American life. His collection of essays addresses the fundamental needs, goals, and idealistic values of American society: equality, freedom, democracy, world power and recognition, domestic security, civil rights, and heroism. The end result is the awareness that America is a paradox—it embodies the hope and the futility of the American Dream; it offers both assurance and despair. In the midst of financial security is moral decay; coexistent with the majestic, stunning landscape is environmental abuse. Not only is America at war globally but internally as well, and violence and chaos threaten the very fabric of American idealism.

Steinbeck's perceptions reflect the contradictions within his own personality; he is both critical and sentimental. He attacks American parenting for creating a nation of spoiled, weak, irresponsible children who grow into emotionally immature adults while he applauds these Americans for their very restlessness and dissatisfaction—qualities that keep them ever searching, ever hopeful, and therefore ever progressing. Always, no matter how unrelenting he might be in his criticism or how dark he may paint the horizon, he is forgiving and, ultimately, hopeful. Steinbeck's most probing commentary is in the final chapter, **"Americans and the Future."** Here he returns to a familiar theme: luxury and excess have weakened the moral fiber of Americans, who now refuse to accept responsibility for their actions and who resent any punishment for the consequences of those actions. He portrays Americans as greedy, selfish, and undisciplined: "I have named the destroyers of nations: comfort, plenty, and security—out of which grow a bored and slothful cynicism." He then gives the indications of a "dying people," but he refuses to condemn Americans as such. Instead, Steinbeck's optimism and sentimentality, which usually prevail over his darker vision, reaffirm his faith in the greatness and spirit of the American people. In the Afterword, he states, "We have failed sometimes, taken wrong paths, paused for renewal, filled our bellies and licked our wounds, but we have never slipped back—never."

This note of affirmation has been a consistent theme throughout Steinbeck's works. As critics have noted, Steinbeck's fascination with Malory and the Arthurian legend was a constant throughout his career and manifested itself both directly and indirectly in *America and Americans*. Malory and Steinbeck share a similar concept of heroism, and paradox is at the core of both their works. As Steinbeck says, "Americans seem to live and breathe and function by paradox." Both Malory and Steinbeck lived in worlds where the harsh realities belied the idealism, yet both chose to uphold the illusion as some distant, redeeming possibility. From ***Cup of Gold*** to *America and Americans*, Steinbeck shapes his heroes after this model. As Steinbeck illustrated in his Nobel Prize acceptance speech, he applauded mankind's "greatness of heart . . . for gallantry in defeat." This comment explains why Steinbeck can unmercifully expose American frailties and injustices and still remain optimistic about the future.

His sweeping overview of America's past illustrates various clichéd moments of history, with personal anecdotes that are usually entertaining despite their sometimes obvious biases. The particular character sketches are what Steinbeck does best—they live and breathe and seem less self-indulgent than the broad editorial strokes. For example, the tale of the Native American, Jimmy, crystallizes the white man's inability to recognize and appreciate nature as a diminishing resource that must first be respected and then maintained; the reader is as mystified and interested in Jimmy's experience as Steinbeck is. Another anecdote focuses on the "miser" Mr. Kirk, who is plagued with personal demons but is further tormented by a young Steinbeck and company, who lack compassion for and are intolerant of those who are different; the reader is as guilty as Steinbeck in being quick to judge others.

But Steinbeck as prophet takes center stage at the conclusion of *America and Americans*. A number of reasons perhaps urged Steinbeck to take a more strident moral and patriotic stand in the mid-sixties: his advancing age and ill health, his increased sense of social/moral responsibility after winning the Nobel Prize in 1962, his increased involvement in the political scene, which was no doubt a result of his friendship with **Adlai Stevenson** and **Lyndon Johnson**, and his conflicting feelings over the Vietnam War all contributed to his deepening concern for America's well-being. Whatever the reasons, Steinbeck offers no apologies for his biased assessment of America: "Of course it is opinion, conjecture, and speculation. . . . But at least it is informed by America, and inspired by curiosity, impatience, some anger and a passionate love of America and the Americans."

What is particularly unfortunate is the fact that the hardback edition of *America and Americans* is now out of print. While the paperback's written text is complete, the photos are not. All the color prints are excluded, and a good number of black and white photos are rearranged while a few are omitted. In some cases these changes affect the overall impact. For example, in the hardback edition's chapter "Pursuit of Happiness," the reader is taken aback to see a black and white photo of an army trainee determinedly taking aim at his target. This contrast with the preceding pages, which focus on varied images of America's youth in college and at play, is riveting—and it was certainly prophetic. In the paperback edition this photograph is excluded, and the emotional impact is weakened. Thus there are two very different reading experiences depending upon which edition is used. The loss is that most of today's audience will be denied access to the more unified, visually stunning work. Further, today's reader cannot adequately evaluate the overall visual impact that prompted Steinbeck's own artistic vision.

Further Reading: Benson, Jackson. *The True Adventures of John Steinbeck, Writer.* New York: Viking, 1984; Gladstein, Mimi R. *"America and Americans: The Arthurian Consummation." After 'The Grapes of Wrath': Essays on John Steinbeck.* Eds. Donald V. Coers, Paul D. Ruffin, and Robert J. DeMott. Athens, OH: Ohio University Press, 1995. 228–236; Heavilin, Barbara. "Steinbeck's *America and Americans* (1966)." *A New Study Guide to Steinbeck's Major Works, with Critical Explications.* Ed. Tetsumaro Hayashi. Metuchen: Scarecrow, 1993. 3–33; Steinbeck, John. *America and Americans.* New York: Viking, 1996; ———. *"America and Americans" and Selected Nonfiction.* Ed. Susan Shillinglaw and Jackson J. Benson. New York: Viking, 2002.

Nancy Zane

"AMERICANS AND THE FUTURE"(1966). This essay concludes the series of nine that John Steinbeck contributed to Viking Press's collection of photographs, ***America and Americans***. In it, Steinbeck essentially attributes the contemporary problems of violent crime, drug addiction, and racial unrest to a national lack of purpose or direction and an ethically enervating prosperity. While a cautionary, often solemn, tone dominates the essay, Steinbeck, whatever his own doubts, maintains an optimistic outlook about the future of the United States in this work.

AMES, CATHY. In ***East of Eden***, she is the daughter of **William** and **Mrs. Ames**, wife of **Adam Trask**, and mother of **Cal** and **Aron Trask**. In ***Journal of a Novel***, Steinbeck wrote, "Cathy Ames is a monster—don't think they do not exist. If one can be born with a twisted and deformed face or body, one can surely also come into the world with a malformed soul." Her pretty face and golden hair belie her disposition as a clever liar who wields and preys on sexuality to gain power.

When Cathy is fourteen, she engages in a sexual relationship with her Latin teacher, **James Grew**. The overwrought and probably guilt-ridden Grew goes to the Ames house late at night to speak to Mr. Ames, but he is turned away and subsequently kills himself in front of the church altar. In the absence of a suicide note, Cathy's lie about some problems Grew had in Boston become the accepted explanation for his death. Grew's is the first death Cathy causes.

Cathy Ames thus becomes **Catherine Amesbury**, a prostitute in Boston. As she did with James Grew, she bewitches the whoremaster, **Mr. Edwards**, who is so smitten by her that he buys her a house, supports her, and is blind to her real motive: using sex to exploit him for money. He remains her dupe until he insists that they drink champagne together; alcohol has a powerful effect on Cathy and strips her of her facade. She spits bitter words of loathing at Mr. Edwards and cuts his face with her broken champagne glass. He beats her fiercely and leaves her for dead. When Cathy is sixteen, she refuses to return to school and runs away to Boston. Her father brings her back and whips her, and thereafter she becomes a model daughter, though she is methodically preparing to kill her parents, steal money from her father's tannery, and fake her own death. Her plan succeeds, and her parents die in a fire that she sets. This incident establishes murder as Cathy's method of eliminating people who impede her ability to get what she wants. Moreover, it establishes how she abandons one identity and assumes another to erase and disassociate herself from the scene.

Cathy crawls onto the Trask front porch, where she is taken in and cared for by the solicitous Adam and his reluctant brother, **Charles Trask**, who sees through her facade. She is badly frightened and feigns amnesia—Catherine Amesbury no longer exists, and she is now only "Cathy." She is wary of Charles Trask because "he had something in his face that she recognized, that made her uneasy. She saw that he touched the scar on his forehead very often, rubbed it, and drew its outline with his fingers." When Charles tells her that "You're going to have one like it, maybe a better one," he is confirming the kinship between them that their scars, intended as Cain-signs, establish.

Even though Charles sees through Cathy and taunts her, Cathy exploits and encourages Adam's sympathies and care, for he is completely taken in by her. Despite Charles's warnings, Adam proposes to Cathy. On their wedding night, she drugs the unsuspecting Adam with laudanum and climbs into bed with Charles. She wants to be able to use her encounter with Charles should she later require a weapon to wound or destroy Adam. Perhaps she also wants to gain power over Charles. Or, as she tells Adam later, perhaps it is because she "could have loved Charles. He was like me in a way."

Still enchanted, Adam sells his share of the farm in Connecticut to Charles and moves with an unwilling Cathy to the Salinas Valley in California. Pregnant, Cathy does what she has done before—attempts to murder what stands in her way: She tries to induce an abortion but almost dies in the process. She gives birth to twins, but later shoots Adam, leaves him for dead, and abandons her squalling babies.

The pattern of murder and self-obliteration is repeated, for **Cathy Trask** disappears and **Kate Albey**, a prostitute at **Faye's** brothel in **Salinas**, materializes. She ingratiates herself with Faye and manipulates and preys upon Faye's sincere desire for a daughter by repeatedly calling her "mother." Eventually Faye is duped by Kate's feigned affection and arranges to make Kate the beneficiary of her estate, worth over $60,000. Doing so precipitates Faye's death for, like Cathy's parents, husband, and children, Faye is an obstacle that must be removed by murder. Kate slowly and systematically poisons Faye, takes over the brothel, and turns it into a place that caters to perversions and unnatural sex. Inheriting the brothel solidifies the connection between sex and money for Kate and ensures that she can use sex to gain and maintain power and control, which she does by blackmailing many of the men who frequent her house. She uses the name Kate Albey for the rest of her life with one exception, when she signs her will as Catherine Trask.

As a child, Cathy's favorite book was ***Alice in Wonderland***. In Carroll's story, Alice eats or drinks substances that cause her to grow unnaturally big or unnaturally small. This growing and shrinking seem a metaphor of Cathy/Kate's growth into a powerful, monstrous figure who leaves human wreckage in her wake—examined in parts 1 and 2—and of her decline, deterioration, and tentative humanization—examined in parts 3 and 4.

The first evidence of Kate's "shrinkage" occurs when Adam visits her for the first time since the shooting. After being informed of Adam's desire to see her, Kate becomes wary and frightened. She is self-conscious about her appearance because, while her hair is again blonde and she is still pretty, she seems swollen. Her hands have aged prematurely, the result of painful arthritis. Kate's appearance, her unease, and her need to protect herself from Adam by secreting a loaded revolver on her desk indicate a decline in her power and metaphorical size. After Adam enters her room, Kate drinks rum, well aware of what the alcohol will do to her, because she feels threatened and wants to hurt him. She attempts to show him her clear understanding of human nature—that it is composed of hypocrisy, filth, and perversion—and when Adam calls her inhuman, she replies, "Do you think I want to be human? . . . I'm smarter than humans. Nobody can hurt me." Hoping to destroy the foundations of his world, she tells him that Charles may be the father of their sons. When Adam remains unshaken, she resorts to seduction, but her old strategies don't work; Adam "twisted her hands from his arm as though they were wire." Realizing her power is no longer sufficiently strong, Kate screams to bring the house pimp, **Ralph**. Whereas earlier she had always acted alone, she now relies on another for help. Though Ralph knocks Adam down, this isn't enough to appease Kate's hate and anger. Kate knows that she's lost Adam and that she has shrunk in power and threat.

When Adam next sees Kate, by now an aged madam, for the first time her power and stature have severely declined. She is suspicious of Adam and thinks that he is trying to trick her. She is afraid of him, taunts his manhood, and calls him "Mr. Mouse" to try to make him feel small and helpless. When he tells her that "there's a part of you missing . . . you are only part of a human," Kate stands with fists clenched, angry and terrified. Adam leaves and her vision is "distorted by tears and . . . her body shook with something that felt like rage and also felt like sorrow." Tears and sorrow are new to Kate and are part of the process that is weakening her. Fear controls Kate and ultimately dissipates her powers. She develops an increasing reluctance to go out; she has a gray, stark lean-to built in her room; and she wears a chain around her neck from which suspends a tube containing enough morphine to kill her.

Two incidents contribute to the ever-present "crouching fear" that Kate experiences. The first is a visit from her son, Cal, who discovers his mother is alive. He follows her for eight weeks before she confronts him outside her brothel, learns who he is, and invites him into her lean-to sanctuary. Cal reminds her of Charles, and lost in a reverie about how well she fooled and manipulated others, she even addresses Cal by his uncle's name. When Cal realizes that he doesn't have her in him, which is to say, a genetic predisposition to evil, he tells her, "I'm glad you're afraid." Besides manifesting Kate's increased fear, this episode is important for thematic reasons also: it establishes for Cal that he is not fated by blood to succumb to his bad impulses; rather, he "mayest [rule over sin]" (***timshel***).

Cal's visit unnerves Kate and feeds her fear, but an earlier visit from **Ethel**, a whore who had worked at Faye's, has already shaken her control. Ethel claims that in a dream she had seen Kate bury the medicine bottles and eyedropper, evidence that Faye had been murdered, and had dug up and kept the shattered glass in an envelope. Ethel tries blackmailing Kate, but Kate arranges to have her framed for robbery and run out of Salinas. Although Kate doesn't think much about Ethel's visit at the time, she becomes more and more frightened by it. Kate realizes she has made mistakes, first by not disposing of the bottles and eyedropper more cleverly and second by not dealing more surely and permanently with Ethel. Kate seems no longer to be the towering, intimidating monster who successfully murdered, duped, and tyrannized. Her lean-to is really a retreat for a wounded, frightened animal—"a cave to hide in" and her painful, disfiguring arthritis a form of retribution for her deeds.

Nevertheless, the maelstrom of her deterioration spirals more tightly. When, to punish Aron, Cal takes his brother to meet their mother for the first time, Kate sees "the face of the blond and beautiful boy, his eyes mad with shock." Afterward Kate gains stark insight into her own nature: "She was cold and desolate, alone and desolate. Whatever she had done, she had been driven to do. She was different—she had something more than other people." She seems more human as she sits at her desk with tears running down her face and realizes the truth of what Adam had told her before, that people "had something she lacked, and she didn't know what it was. Once she knew this, she was ready" to commit suicide.

Kate writes her will, leaving everything to Aron. Her bequest to Aron relates back to **Cyrus Trask**'s bequest to his sons, Charles and Adam, for both she and Cyrus had made their money by cheating, extorting, or stealing from others. She then retreats into her lean-to, thinking of the imaginary Alice who "was her friend, always waiting to welcome her to tinyness." To join Alice, Kate swallows the morphine capsule and waits to die, thinking of Cal and his taunting words before "she grew smaller and smaller and then disappeared and she had never been."

The process of Kate's humanization, or more sympathetic handling, culminates in death. In fact, the beginning of Chapter 17 had proposed a softening of the reader's attitude toward her: "It is easy to say she was bad, but there is little meaning unless we know why."

Cathy/Kate is perhaps another species of human, solitary and isolated and incapable of communicating with other humans. In this light, Cathy/Kate becomes a tragic figure, a freak of nature, and a permanent outsider whose actions can be understood, though her motivations—if there even are any—remain unknown. Like Adam, Cathy/Kate is prey to her own nature because she seems to have no choice or awareness of choice. But in the end, unlike Adam, she gains a painful self-awareness. The consequence must be, as it is for her son Aron, self-annihilation. Much critical speculation suggests that Ames is based on Steinbeck's second wife, **Gwyndolyn Conger Steinbeck**, with whom he suffered a bitter divorce.

Margaret Seligman

AMES, MRS. The mother of **Cathy Ames** and wife of **William Ames** in *East of Eden*. Portrayed as a woman who is naïve and afraid of her daughter, she is repeatedly fooled by Cathy's feigned innocence. She is killed along with her husband in a fire Cathy sets.

AMES, WILLIAM. The father of **Cathy Ames** and husband of **Mrs. Ames** in *East of Eden*. Mr. Ames has nagging suspicions that something isn't right with his daughter, but he either ignores or forgets them. However, when Cathy runs away to Boston, he brings her back and whips her at the insistence of his wife. Thereafter, Cathy becomes a model daughter, though she is secretly planning to murder her parents. A year later, Mr. Ames and his wife are killed in a fire set by Cathy, who robs her father's tannery, fakes her own death, and runs away to Boston.

Margaret Seligman

AMESBURY, CATHERINE. Name used by **Cathy Ames** in *East of Eden* during the time that she lives and works as a prostitute in Boston and is kept by **Mr. Edwards**.

ANDERSON, ALFRED. In ***In Dubious Battle***, lunch wagon operator in the city of Torgas who sympathizes with the Party organizers and feeds them. He asks to join the Party when growers beat him up and burn his lunch wagon. He also persuades his reluctant father to let the migrant strikers camp on his farm in return for picking his apples, but the father is alienated when the growers burn the barn containing his crop.

ANDERSON, ELIZABETH. *See* **Breck, John**.

ANDERSON, MAXWELL (1888–1959). American playwright and author of *Candle in the Wind* (1941). When Steinbeck and his second wife **Gwyndolyn Conger Steinbeck** decided to move to Sneden's Landing in New York, Anderson was a neighbor. During the summer that the Steinbecks resided near this playwright, John and **Burgess Meredith** conceived the idea for the play **"The Last Joan."**

ANDERSON, SHERWOOD (1876–1941). An American novelist and short story writer who strongly influenced American writing throughout the early twentieth century. Known for his use of everyday speech and his renegotiation of the formal constraints of the novel, his influence on **Ernest Hemingway** is markedly clear, and **William Faulkner** described him as "the father of all [his] literary generation." Anderson's 1919 composite novel *Winesburg, Ohio*—one of Steinbeck's favorite books—established his reputation as a formidable writer.

While at **Stanford University,** Steinbeck heard Anderson speak, but it would be nearly twenty years before Steinbeck actually met him in the fall of 1939. After their meeting, Anderson, in his personal diary, spoke warmly of Steinbeck. Although there is no explicit record of Steinbeck's personal feelings toward Anderson, it can be inferred from his public comments about the man and his work that the feelings were mutual. On several occasions, Steinbeck lauded Anderson's innovation and celebrated his impact on the American literary landscape. In a 1951 letter to his publisher **Pascal Covici**, Steinbeck stated that "Sherwood Anderson made the modern novel and it has not gone much beyond him." Later, in ***America and Americans***, he noted America's indebtedness to Anderson's work: "But in considering the American past, how poor we would be in information without . . . *Winesburg, Ohio*." Anderson's influence on Steinbeck's writing can be best seen in ***The Pastures of Heaven***, where Steinbeck experiments with formal conventions (a short story cycle) in a manner reminiscent of Anderson's masterwork, *Winesburg, Ohio*.

Further Reading: White, Ray Lewis. "Sherwood Anderson Meets John Steinbeck: 1939." *Steinbeck Quarterly* 11.1 (Winter 1978): 20–22; DeMott, Robert. *Steinbeck's Reading; A Catalogue of Books Owned and Borrowed*. New York: Garland Publishing, 1984.

Gregory Hill, Jr.

ANDREWS, MABEL. In ***Sweet Thursday***, a resident of **Monterey** who occasionally calls the police to report a burglary because of a rat in her dining room, an actual burglar, or mere wishful thinking. She is mentioned briefly to illustrate how well a constable such as **Joe Blaikey** understands the members of his community.

ANGUYSHAUNCE, KING. King of Ireland, father of Launceor in ***The Acts of King Arthur***. He is one of the eleven rebel kings of the North who take arms against **Arthur** and are defeated in the battle at Bedgrayne and one of the five kings to invade Arthur's England after the death of **Merlin**. He is killed, together with the other four kings, by Arthur, **Sir Gawain**, **Sir Gryffet**, and **Sir Kay**.

ANNIE. In ***The Moon Is Down***, the straw-haired kitchen maid who works in the household of **Mayor Orden**. Temperamental and strong-willed, she is also known by her fellow townspeople to have a bad disposition. After a foreign army invades her village, she vents her anger by pouring scalding water on some enemy soldiers. Later, she also gathers crucial intelligence for the resistance. Through such actions, Annie successfully translates simple ire into patriotic emotion and thereby becomes transformed from a simple servant to Steinbeck's figure of the local heroine.

APOLONIA. **Juan Thomas**'s wife in ***The Pearl***, whose behavior represents that of an ordinary native Mexican housewife. When **Kino's** house is being burnt down, she raises "an official lament for the dead of the family" because she is the nearest female relative. However, Kino and the family are actually hiding themselves in her house.

APOLONIO. In ***Viva Zapata!***, Apolonio is described as a grizzled old man who, upon turning in his rifle with the other **Zapatistas**, is praised by **Emiliano** to Madero.

ARBELLUS, SIR. In ***The Acts of King Arthur***, a murderer and a false knight killed by **Sir Torre** on the Quest of the White Brachet.

"ARGUMENT OF PHALANX." Unpublished essay Steinbeck wrote in 1935 in which he discussed the "phalanx" idea, essentially a theory of human behavior that notes the personality of the individual can be subsumed by the personality of a group. Steinbeck dramatized this concept in his handling of mob scenes, most notably in the novels ***In Dubious Battle*** and ***The Grapes of Wrath***.

ARTHUR, KING. In *The Acts of King Arthur*, son of King **Uther Pendragon** and **Igraine**. Reared by **Sir Ector de Marys**, he claims his rightful place as Uther Pendragon's successor when he draws the sword from the stone. In due course, he becomes king and, with the help of the magician **Merlin** and the French kings **Ban** and **Bors**, routs the eleven rebel lords of the North at the battle of Bedgrayne. He is father of **Mordred** as a result of his unknowing incestuous relationship with his half-sister **Margawse**. The sword **Excalibur** is given to him by the **Lady of the Lake**. He marries **Guinevere**, daughter of **King Lodegrance of Camylarde**, despite Merlin's warning that she will be unfaithful to him with his dearest and most trusted friend. He establishes his court at Camelot and creates the Fellowship of the **Round Table**. He defeats all his enemies and peace prevails over the land. Peace, however, brings its own problems, for his knights become soft, lazy, and uninterested, quarreling among themselves. On Guinevere's suggestion, he sends **Sir Lancelot** out on a quest accompanied by **Sir Lyonel**, as his pupil, to search out and correct injustice wherever he finds it, punish evil, and overcome traitors to the King's Peace.

Roy S. Simmonds

ARTHUR, KING. In *Cup of Gold*, the Arthurian legend is an allusion and a backdrop. Old **Robert**, **Henry Morgan**'s father, fondly speaks of Arthurian legend while the local curate finds such tales to be heathen.

ARVIN SANITARY CAMP. Also known as Weedpatch by those who lived there, the Arvin Sanitary Camp was one of the most successful migration camps set up by the **Roosevelt** administration to deal with the influx of homeless farmers flooding into California during the Great Depression. Headed by **Tom Collins**, the Arvin Sanitary Camp was successful because those who lived there were allowed the authority to govern themselves. Steinbeck spent a week in 1936 at Weedpatch while on assignment by the *San Francisco News* to write a series of articles on the state of the migrant worker. He interviewed its residents and observed its daily operations. Steinbeck left the camp with a briefcase full of notes and reports given to him by Collins, which would soon be the primary resources for a significant portion of ***The Grapes of Wrath***. When *Grapes of Wrath* was finally made into a film in 1940, the Weedpatch camp became the location for much of its shooting, and Tom Collins served as a consultant.

Ted Scholz

ARYES. In ***The Acts of King Arthur***, a cowherd who raises **Sir Torre,** believing him to be his own son.

ASTRO, RICHARD. One of the most informed writers and critics about Steinbeck's philosophical beliefs, including **non-teleological thinking** and the phalanx theory, Astro wrote a biographical study of the friendship between Steinbeck and **Edward F. Ricketts**: *John Steinbeck and Edward F. Ricketts: The Shaping of a Novelist* (1973). The biography is invaluable in that it elucidates Steinbeck's worldview and philosophy of life by considering his relationship to Ricketts. In addition, Astro's biography provides a careful study of the life, work, and ideas of Ricketts, who was Steinbeck's closest personal and intellectual companion for almost twenty years. It also lays the groundwork regarding the influence Ricketts exerted over his friend's life. Astro also wrote the introduction for Twentieth Century Classics' edition of ***The Log from the Sea of Cortez***. Astro is also credited with discovering and enabling the first publication of a joint memorandum written by Ricketts and Steinbeck and addressed to **Pascal Covici** and the other **Viking Press**

editors. The memorandum described the collaborative procedure used in the composition of the narrative.

Further Reading: Astro, Richard. *John Steinbeck and Edward F. Ricketts: The Shaping of a Novelist*. New Berlin: University of Minnesota Press, 1973; ———. "Introduction." *The Log from the Sea of Cortez*. John Steinbeck. New York: Penguin, 1995.

Harry Karahalios

ATHATOOLAGOOLOO. In *Sweet Thursday*, a native con man outfoxed by **Fauna** when she served as a missionary and shrunken-head dealer in South America. In one of the most extravagantly improbable episodes in *Sweet Thursday*, Fauna tells the story of this swindler, who sold shrunken monkey heads as the genuine human article. She says that she bought his overpriced supply of counterfeit heads to keep him from contaminating the market and destroying customer confidence. However, in her desk drawer, she retains proof of her ultimate triumph over him in the form of his own head, black as ebony and shrunken to the size of a lemon. Steinbeck takes an old tradition of Southwest humor to a new extreme in this tale of the trickster tricked.

Bruce Ouderkirk

"ATQUE VALE" (1960). A meditative essay on the black man's burden in America and a celebration of his courage and dignity in the face of trials and tribulation, "Atque Vale" was published by *The Saturday Review* in May of 1960. It depicted the white behavior at Little Rock as "faces drooling hatred, spitting their venom at children" while praising the restraint black families practiced in the midst of such cruel harassment and hatred. Noting that parts of the article had been altered and cut before its publication in the magazine, Steinbeck later refused any further contributions solicited by its editor, assuming that the changes were motivated by a desire not to offend its predominantly white readership.

Michael J. Meyer

AUNT. Described in ***Viva Zapata!*** as "middle aged," she accompanies **Josefa Espejo** to the church where **Emiliano Zapata** and his brother **Eufemio** come upon them. Eufemio pins the Aunt's arms back and covers her mouth while Emiliano inquires of Josefa when he may call on her father to ask his permission for her hand in marriage. When the brothers leave the church, the Aunt shocks and surprises Josefa with her comment that she likes Emiliano even though "he's a terrible man . . . a fugitive—a criminal," to which Josefa responds in kind, saying that she likes him, too. The Aunt appears twice more but does not speak. When Emiliano goes to Señor Espejo's place of business to speak with him regarding his desire to marry Josefa, she, Josefa, and her mother are embroidering and overhear their confrontation while pretending not to listen.

Marcia D. Yarmus

AUNT CLARA. **Lennie Small**'s dead aunt in ***Of Mice and Men***. She was a little obese old woman who gave Lennie a rubber mouse so he would not kill any live pets, but Lennie did not like it. Before she died, **George** promised her that he would look after Lennie. At the end of the novel, when Lennie hides himself in the bushes, the ghost spirit of Aunt Clara appears in front of Lennie. She wears thick bull's-eye glasses and a huge gingham apron with pockets. She stands in front of Lennie and frowns disapprovingly at him because he has broken his promise not to bring any trouble for George. Lennie tells Aunt Clara, in fact thinking to himself, "I'll fin' a cave an' I'll live there so I won't be no more trouble to George."

Luchen Li

"AUTOBIOGRAPHY: MAKING OF A NEW YORKER." *See* **"Making of a New Yorker."**

B

BACON, ABRA. The daughter of **Mr.** and **Mrs. Bacon** in *East of Eden*. Abra meets **Cal** and **Aron Trask**—she is ten and they are eleven—when she and her parents take shelter during a rainstorm at Adam Trask's ranch. Even in their earliest interactions, the dynamics of Abra's mothering love toward Aron, Aron's response to that love, and Cal's jealousy are established. Abra's relationship with Aron continues, and in their hideaway beneath the willow tree, she provides the mothering that he wants so badly. Abra tells Aron that she heard her parents say that his mother isn't dead, but Aron is unable to accept this information because the news disorders his conception of the world.

After Aron goes to college, Abra spends a great deal of time at the Trask house, where she and **Lee** develop a strong and touching father-daughter relationship. During one of her visits, Abra confides to Lee that she feels different about Aron, that it's as if Aron has "made someone up, and it's like he put my skin on her. I'm not like that—not like the made-up one." Because Abra wants to be herself and because she understands that she comprises both good and bad impulses, she realizes that she cannot fulfill Aron's dream of purity. She outgrows her relationship with him and falls in love with his brother, Cal.

When Aron is killed in battle and Adam has a second stoke, Cal runs to Abra and attempts to shock her by telling her that he caused these occurrences. He goes on to tell her that his mother, **Kate Albey**, is a prostitute and he's "got her blood," a genetic predisposition to evil. Abra's rhetorical responses to Cal reflect the intent of ***timshel*** [thou mayest], the thematic emphasis of the book, because they express that the choices he makes are up to him, not a result of heredity.

Steinbeck characterizes Abra as balanced and integrated, in contrast with **Mrs. Trask**, **Alice Trask**, and **Cathy Ames**, who represent extreme polarities. Moreover, Abra, like Cal, is related to the theme of *timshel* because she recognizes and understands the responsibility of choice.

Margaret Seligman

BACON, MR. The father of **Abra Bacon** and a county supervisor in ***East of Eden***. Desirous of a son, he considers Abra a disappointment and disapproves of her relationship with **Aron Trask**. When under suspicion for embezzlement, Mr. Bacon retreats into feigned illness.

BACON, MRS. The conservative, controlling, and overly protective mother of **Abra Bacon** in *East of Eden*.

BAGDEMAGUS, SIR. In ***The Acts of King Arthur***, a knight who is hurt when **Arthur** chooses **Sir Torre** in preference to him for one of the vacant seats at the **Round Table** after the war with the five kings. He vows never to return to Arthur's court until men speak of him with honor and say he is worthy to be a Knight of the Round Table.

BAILEY, MARGERY (1891–1963). Yale PhD who was one of Steinbeck's professors of English while he was at **Stanford University**. She was reputed to have had little tolerance for slothful students, she gave low grades, she was passionate about her subject, and she is often referred to as a "dragon" of a woman in Steinbeck biographies. She and Steinbeck shared a mutual friend in **John Breck**, and they often visited in Bailey's house as they smoked, drank, and discussed the literary merits of such contemporary writers as **Sinclair Lewis**, **Willa Cather**, and **F. Scott Fitzgerald**. Bailey and Steinbeck shared a grudging, mutual respect for each another.

Further Reading: Benson, Jackson J. *The True Adventures of John Steinbeck, Writer*. New York: Viking, 1984.

Tracy Michaels

BAKER, AMELIA. The wife of **Banker Baker** in ***The Winter of Our Discontent***, she is something of a cipher at the tea ceremony that brings together the Bakers and the **Hawleys**.

BAKER, BANKER. A character in *The Winter of Our Discontent* who owes his inherited wealth to an insurance payoff for the burning of the *Belle-Adair*, a ship **Ethan Allen Hawley's** grandfather had co-owned with Baker's own forefather. Baker urges Ethan to invest his wife's inherited money to recoup the family losses, particularly in a land scheme for a new local airport. One of the persons whose money-based values tempt Ethan the most, Baker is also a male chauvinist. As one of the town fathers, he manipulates the local government in order to further his own financial gain. Hawley also imagines robbing Baker's bank.

John Ditsky

BAKER, CAP'N. Former business partner of **Ethan Allen Hawley**'s grandfather in ***The Winter of Our Discontent***, Cap'n Baker is remembered as the one who held on to the insurance profits from the burning of the men's ship.

BAKER, RAY STANNARD (1870–1946). Journalist, author, and biographer of Woodrow Wilson, Baker was one of the leading journalists of his generation. In 1897, he joined the staff of *McClure's Magazine*, a leader in the "New Journalism" that was transforming the national press. During the 1890s he dreamed of writing the "Great American Novel" and published numerous stories for young people in the *Youth's Companion*, a magazine he himself enjoyed as a boy. Along with fellow journalists **Lincoln Steffens** and Ida Tarbell, Baker soon gained a national reputation as one of the leading "muckrakers"—a term Theodore Roosevelt applied to crusading journalists in 1906. That same year Baker published the first of a series of "adventures in contentment" under the pen name David Grayson. Totaling nine volumes in all, the David Grayson adventures attracted millions of readers worldwide, probably including Steinbeck, since he mentions the pseudonym and *Adventures in Contentment* in the **Junius Maltby** episode of ***Pastures of Heaven***. In later years, Baker abandoned the hard-hitting journalism of the *McClure's* years, but continued to chronicle the social and political life of the nation, becoming the first prominent journalist to focus on America's racial divide in a 1908 book titled *Following the Color Line*. He was also highly involved in government, serving as Woodrow Wilson's press secretary at Versailles, and eventually becoming his biographer, with an eight-volume study titled *Woodrow Wilson: Life and Letters* (1927–39).

BAKER, RED. In ***The Winter of Our Discontent***, Red is the town banker's dog that **Ethan Allen Hawley** sees each morning. Ethan addresses the dog with respect and confidence, probably another trait shared with Steinbeck himself, a notable lover of dogs. Ethan's conversation with the dog, "I met you in pissing," was part of the questionable humor that critics berated in the novel.

BALAN, SIR. Brother of **Sir Balin of Northumberland**, the Knight of the Two Swords in ***The Acts of King Arthur***. He is tricked into a joust against his brother, neither knowing the other's identity, and they are both mortally wounded.

BALIN OF NORTHUMBERLAND, SIR. Known as "The Knight of the Two Swords" in ***The Acts of King Arthur***, he gains the magic sword of the **Lady Lyle of Avalon**, but refuses to return it. It is prophesied that he will use it to kill his best friend and the man he loves best in the world; this prophecy is fulfilled when he unwittingly kills his own brother, **Balan**.

BALLOU, ROBERT O. (1892–1977). Former literary editor of the *Chicago Daily News*, Robert Ballou joined the publishing company of Cape and Smith Inc., whose client list included many established writers published by the parent company of Jonathan Cape in England. In 1932, the company became Jonathan Cape and Robert Ballou, Inc.; at about the same time, contracts for Steinbeck's ***The Pastures of Heaven*** and two subsequent novels were signed. *The Pastures of Heaven* was published in September 1932, and 1,499 copies of ***To a God Unknown*** were then published in 1933, both by Robert O. Ballou.

John Hooper

BALMOURE OF THE MARYS, SIR. Beaten in a fight with **Sir Gawain** during the Quest of the White Stag in ***The Acts of King Arthur***. As Sir Gawain is about to deliver the mortal blow, Balmoure's lady accidentally falls on his body and is killed by Gawain's sword.

BALYSE, MASTER. In ***The Acts of King Arthur***, he lives in Northumberland and keeps a chronicle of **Arthur**'s deeds from the stories told to him by **Merlin**.

BAN, KING OF BENWICK. One of the two French kings who help **Arthur** in his war against the eleven rebel kings of the North in ***The Acts of King Arthur***. He is the father of **Sir Lancelot**.

BANKS, CLEO. In ***Pastures of Heaven***, **Raymond Banks**'s wife; her cheerful, jolly manner is most appreciated by her neighbors.

BANKS, RAYMOND. In ***Pastures of Heaven***, a chicken farmer in Las Pasturas who has the most admired house and farm. Described as a strong and dedicated worker, Banks is painstakingly portrayed by Steinbeck as having two sides to his physical appearance as well as to his personality. For example, his jovial mouth is compared with his "villainously beaked nose" Similarly, though he is the local Santa Claus at Christmas, he also enjoys the efficient killing of his chickens and his biannual trips to San Quentin prison to witness the execution of prisoners. During the latter events, Banks revels in the pleasure he experiences, even though he is unaware of the real reasons that the morbid events appeal to him. When he is manipulated into extending an invitation to **Bert Munroe** to attend an execution with him, Banks forfeits his former pleasure forever as Munroe relates his fears that watching a hanging might be somewhat like the killing of a chicken he once saw, a process that was mishandled and cruel rather than precise and efficient.

Michael J. Meyer

BARTON, JOHN. *See* **Breck, John**.

BATTLE, GEORGE. In ***Pastures of Heaven***, the original owner of the best piece of land in Las Pasturas, a farm that is now thought by the townspeople to be cursed. His garden is described as meticulously cared for, and his hands have formed in the shape of farm instruments as a result of his hard work. His property becomes his poem, his art, a thing of beauty as he ignores his responsibility to his family in order to give more of himself to the land.

BATTLE, JOHN. In ***Pastures of Heaven***, the only son of the Battles, he inherits his mother's "mad knowledge of God." He dies of a rattlesnake bite after trying to scourge out the devil from his land. His neglect of the prime property he inherits defines his nature as the opposite of his father, who treated it with great care and devotion. John's strange actions establish the reputation of the farm as haunted or cursed.

BATTLE, MYRTLE. In ***Pastures of Heaven***, **George Battle**'s wife. A victim of epilepsy and mental stress, she is eventually committed to a sanitarium for the insane after bearing Battle an infant son. She is known as a religious fanatic.

BAWDEWYN OF BRETAGNE, SIR. One of the four knights who protect **Arthur** from his enemies before he becomes king in ***The Acts of King Arthur***. He is made Constable by **Arthur** to keep law and peace in the realm.

BEAR FLAG RESTAURANT (BEAR FLAG). In ***Sweet Thursday***, a brothel on **Cannery Row** that is separated by a vacant lot from **Lee Chong**'s grocery store and is across the street, catercornered, from **Western Biological Laboratories**. In the book ***Cannery Row***, the Bear Flag was run as "a sturdy, virtuous club" by the generous **Dora Flood**, and now, run by her equally magnanimous sister, **Fauna**, it has become "a kind of finishing school for girls." In this oddly wholesome house of prostitution, a special room is set aside for the women to relax and study. Fauna gives the young women scheduled lessons on etiquette and inspires them to dream of matrimony. At night, after the last trick is turned, she requires the women to assemble for a rest break at which refreshments are served and the women sometimes join in song.

Steinbeck clearly considered the brothel to be of central importance in *Sweet Thursday* given that he originally titled the novel "Bear Flag." However, in the chapters dealing with the house, his satire tends to be overdone. Although he takes his usual delight in defying the conventional moral judgments about such an institution, his portrait of the house is sentimentalized.

Bruce Ouderkirk

BEAVERS, BUTCH. Acquaintance of **Joe Valery** in ***East of Eden***.

BECKY. One of the three prostitutes at the **Bear Flag** who usually appear in unison, like a chorus in ***Sweet Thursday***. She and her two companions, **Agnes** and **Mabel**, are more comfortable working in the brothel than is **Suzy**. Shortly after Suzy is hired, Becky tells the others that she doesn't think Suzy will stay long because she goes out on walks and has "a nuts look in her eye." Becky shows few signs of intelligence; although she works in a brothel, she is unfamiliar with the word *harlot*.

Becky also figures in one politically incorrect incident that may seem offensive to readers today. She is seen perusing a letter from a pen pal in **Japan**, and Steinbeck quotes the pidgin English at length: "Your interest missive receipt. How gondola the Goldy State. Japan girl do hair-kink likewise, but not using blitch." Although Steinbeck generally shows respect for Asian people in his fiction, he delighted in writing mimicking parodies of their struggles with the English language, as he enjoyed wordplay in general. When he went to Tokyo to attend the P.E.N. conference in 1957, for instance, he wrote home to his wife that he was receiving bundles of correspondence that said, "I are Japan girl higher student which like you bookings."

Further Reading: Steinbeck, John. *Steinbeck: A Life in Letters*. Ed. Elaine Steinbeck and Robert Wallsten. New York: Viking, 1975.

Bruce Ouderkirk

BELLIAS, SIR. In *The Acts of King Arthur*, **Lancelot** recommends that **Bellias** be made a Knight of the **Round Table** in exchange for Bellias's not revealing to the court the rather ludicrous circumstances in which they have met.

BELLOW, SAUL (1915–2005). American novelist and 1976 **Nobel Prize** laureate in Literature, Bellow is the author of such works as *Henderson the Rain King* (1959), *Herzog* (1964), *Mr. Sammler's Planet* (1970), and *Humboldt's Gift* (1975); he also won three National Book Awards and a **Pulitzer Prize** for fiction. Bellow came to know Steinbeck early in his career, when the older author wrote to magazines regarding a younger writer whose works he held in esteem and whom he deemed to have been criticized unjustly. Later in life, Bellow returned the favor when he defended Steinbeck's talent on the dust jacket of ***The Winter of Our Discontent***, stating, "In this book John Steinbeck returns to his high standards of ***The Grapes of Wrath*** and to the social themes that made his early work so impressive and so powerful. Critics who said of him that he had seen his best days had better tie on their napkins and prepare to eat crow."

Additionally, Bellow crossed paths with Steinbeck in November of 1956 as a fellow member of the Eisenhower administration's People to People group (along with William Carlos Williams and **William Faulkner**), through which several well-known authors traveled behind the Iron Curtain at the government's expense in order to promote cultural understanding between nations. Bellow was also a fellow eulogist with Steinbeck at the funeral of **Pat Covici**, Steinbeck's editor at **Covici-Friede** and later at **Viking**.

Further Reading: Parini, Jay. *John Steinbeck*. New York: Henry Holt, 1995.

Tracy Michaels

BENCHLEY, NATHANIEL (1915–1981). Steinbeck's friend from April 1946, when the Benchleys rented the second of two houses that the Steinbecks had purchased and remodeled on East Seventy-eighth Street in New York. The two families struck an immediate rapport.

For Steinbeck, Nat Benchley represented a return to the kind of vigor and frenetic mayhem he knew and missed from his friends during his younger days in California. Steinbeck and Benchley enjoyed the quality of each other's company and a particularly close friendship for the next three years. In Benchley, Steinbeck found someone who was willing to engage in his constant scheming and revelry. As such, Benchley quickly became a Steinbeck confidant.

During this period, the Steinbeck marriage was disintegrating at an increasing pace with Steinbeck's frequent absences. **Gwyndolyn Conger Steinbeck** (Gwyn) was consistently ill and depressed, and Steinbeck felt the need to surround himself with unhelpful diversions. The two began to partake in a kind of antagonism that ensured the failure of their marriage.

True to the spirit of the times, neither was the friendship without troubles. As confidants, the Benchleys were asked to shoulder a great deal of the tension and were an easy source for misplaced emotions. Although impossible to substantiate unequivocally, Nat and Gwyn may have had an affair at some point near the end of the marriage. By 1949 Steinbeck felt somewhat bitter toward Benchley for publishing a series of stories in *The New Yorker* and other magazines that apparently involved the Steinbeck family.

Further Reading: Benson, Jackson J. *The True Adventures of John Steinbeck, Writer*. New York: Viking, 1984.

Brian Niro

BENSON, JACKSON J. (1931–). Born and raised in San Francisco, Jackson J. Benson graduated from **Stanford University** (Honors Humanities) and received his MA from the University of Southern California. From 1966 to 1997, he served as professor of

English and comparative literature at San Diego State University, where he taught twentieth-century American literature.

Twice a fellow of the National Endowment of the Humanities, he has published eleven books on modern American literature. Among them is the authorized biography *The True Adventures of John Steinbeck, Writer* (1984), which won the PEN-WEST USA award for nonfiction. One of his latest works is the authorized biography *Wallace Stegner: His Life and Work* (1996), which won the David Wolley and Beatrice Cannon Evans Biography Award. Over a thousand pages long, Benson's biography of Steinbeck's life is so complete that, as John Kenneth Galbraith wrote, "There will not be another book like it nor will we need one."

Further Reading: Benson, Jackson J. *Looking for Steinbeck's Ghost*. Norman: University of Oklahoma Press, 1988.

BENTICK, CAPTAIN. In ***The Moon Is Down***, one of five members of **Colonel Lanser**'s staff, each of whom manifest "herd men" characteristics that make them ill-suited for the profession of arms. In Bentick's case, he is too old to be a captain and fails to get promoted because he is a dilettante who lacks ambition. He has misguided dreams of success predicated on outmoded Victorian culture. Bentick is hardly the model of the battle-hardened warrior. His death at the hands of alderman **Alexander Morden**, an angry citizen who kills him with a pickax, symbolically figures the ineffectuality of nineteenth-century values in the face of such modern barbarisms as fascism.

Rodney P. Rice

BENTON, THOMAS HART (1889–1975). Born in Neosho, Missouri, Benton was a painter of the American scene. He achieved national prominence in the 1930s for such larger-than-life murals as *America Today* for the New School of Social Research, *The Arts of Life in America* for the Whitney Museum, and *A Social History of Missouri* in the rotunda of the Missouri State Capitol. In 1934 Benton's self-portrait was featured on the cover of ***Time***. The cover story linked him with two other Midwestern painters: Grant Wood and John Stuart Curry. All three were soon to be known as American "regionalists."

Benton's family background undoubtedly sparked his interest in painting American subjects. Benton's parents had named him, the eldest of four children, after the hero of the clan, his granduncle, Thomas Hart Benton, Missouri's first senator. Senator Benton, an avid defender of Western interests, held office for five terms. The artist's father, Maecenas Benton, was a lawyer and prominent Democrat in the populist mold of William Jennings Bryan.

Although John Steinbeck and Benton never met, their work converged upon several occasions during the Depression era. In 1939, Twentieth-Century Fox Film Corporation, in conjunction with its advertising campaign promoting the film ***The Grapes of Wrath***, commissioned Benton to create a series of lithographs depicting Steinbeck's main characters: **Ma** and **Pa Joad**, **Tom Joad**, **Rosasharn**, and the Reverend **Jim Casy**. Although Benton wrote that the original drawings were made when he was on a sketching trip through Oklahoma and Arkansas, he apparently altered the originals so that they would more closely conform to studio stills of the main players in the film. Thus the portrait of Ma resembles the actress **Jane Darwell**, the portrait of Tom Joad resembles **Henry Fonda**, and so on.

A sixth lithograph, *The Departure of the Joads*, was reproduced billboard size and was eventually made into a painting. The lithograph includes two separate scenes. One depicts the Joads in the final stage of loading their possessions into the old jalopy that will take them from Oklahoma to California, and the other depicts the home that they are leaving. Situated in the front yard, a table with a lantern on it testifies to the Joads' imminent departure. A forlorn-looking figure suggestive of **Muley Graves**, the Joads' neighbor who elected to stay behind without his family, is seated directly in front of the house. This lithograph also appeared in a 1940 issue of *Life* magazine in "Movie of the Week," which featured a half dozen movie stills from *The Grapes of Wrath*.

Benton continued to produce notable artworks with American themes, both narrative paintings and landscapes, until his death in 1975. His most ambitious late work, *Independence and the Opening of the West*, was completed in 1962 for the Truman Library in Independence, Missouri. George Macy, the New York publisher of Limited Editions Club, happened to see Benton's movie series at the studio of the artist's New York City printer, George Miller. Macy immediately wrote to Benton proposing that the artist illustrate an edition of *The Grapes of Wrath* for The Limited Editions Club. The resulting two-volume book, published in 1940, contains sixty-one lithographic illustrations: thirty horizontal vignettes for chapter headings, twenty-seven full-page illustrations, and four double-page end paper designs, one end paper design being a reproduction of *The Departure of the Joads*.

Further Reading: Adams, Henry. *Thomas Hart Benton: An American Original*. New York: Alfred Knopf, 1989; Benton, Thomas Hart. *An Artist in America*. New York: McBride, 1937; "Movie of the Week," *Life* 8. January 22, 1940, 10–11; Steinbeck, John. *The Grapes of Wrath*. 2 vols. Illustrated by Thomas Hart Benton. With prefaces by Joseph Henry Jackson and Thomas Craven. New York: Limited Editions Club, 1940.

Nina Allen

BERGSON, HENRI (1859–1941). A French philosopher. He became a professor at the Collège de France in 1900, devoted some time to politics, and, after World War I, took an interest in international affairs. He is well known for his brilliant and imaginative philosophical works, which won him the 1927 Nobel Prize in Literature. Among his works that have been translated into English are *Time and Free Will* (1889), *Matter and Memory* (1896), *Laughter* (1901), *Introduction to Metaphysics* (1903), *Creative Evolution* (1907), *The Two Sources of Morality and Religion* (1932), and *The Creative Mind* (1934). Bergson's philosophy is dualistic: the world contains two opposing tendencies—the life force (*élan vital*) and the resistance of the material world against that force. **Edward F. Ricketts** owned a copy of *Creative Evolution*, which Steinbeck may have read.

Further Reading: Railsback, Brian. *Parallel Expeditions: Charles Darwin and the Art of John Steinbeck*. Moscow: University of Idaho Press, 1995.

Michael J. Meyer

BERRY, ANTHONY (TONY) (1906–1995). Usually referred to as "Tony Berry," he captained the ***Western Flyer***. He was described by Steinbeck as a "quiet" and "serious" young man whose virtues also included being "intelligent" and "tolerant" and who had "one great passion; he loves rightness and hates wrongness." Steinbeck, according to **Jackson J. Benson**, impressed Berry because the author knew how to steer a boat as well as the principles of navigation. In later years, Berry would recall that Steinbeck was the driving force behind the voyage, saying, "If not for him . . . [w]e wouldn't have collected anything."

Further Reading: Benson, Jackson J. *The True Adventures of John Steinbeck, Writer*. New York: Viking, 1984.

BESKOW, BO (1906–1989). Swedish artist and writer who was a friend of John Steinbeck for over thirty years, Beskow was born in Djursholm, Sweden, and studied at the Royal Academy of Fine Arts in Stockholm (1923–26). Among Beskow's notable paintings are a fresco mural in the United Nations Headquarters in New York and portraits of Swedish statesmen and of his friends Dag Hammarskjöld, Secretary-General of the United Nations from 1953 to 1961, and John Steinbeck. He also created stained glass windows for cathedrals in Skara and Växsjö. Beskow and Steinbeck met for the first time in a publisher's office in New York during the spring of 1937. That June, on his way to Russia, Steinbeck and his first wife, **Carol Henning Steinbeck**, visited Beskow and his wife Zita in Stockholm, where Beskow painted his first portrait of Steinbeck.

Following this visit, Steinbeck and Beskow began a correspondence that would continue almost to Steinbeck's death. In 1946, the two met again in Scandinavia. In Copenhagen, where he and Beskow toured refugee camps, Steinbeck was acclaimed as a hero because of the extraordinary success of his novel, ***The Moon Is Down***, which was hailed as anti-Nazi propaganda during the occupation of Denmark. Beskow then accompanied his friend to Oslo, where the king of Norway personally honored Steinbeck by awarding him the Haakon VII Cross for his contribution through his novelistic effort to the patriotic resistance in occupied Norway. When they returned to Stockholm, Beskow painted his second portrait of Steinbeck.

The following year, Steinbeck and the photographer **Robert Capa** stopped over in Sweden on their trip to Russia. Finally, in 1952 Beskow joined Steinbeck and Steinbeck's new wife, **Elaine Scott Steinbeck**, in Madrid, where Steinbeck shared his optimism about his new book, ***East of Eden***, and his recent marriage.

Over the next few years, Beskow sensed a cooling in his relationship with Steinbeck caused by, or at least exacerbated by, growing political distance between the two. Beginning in 1948, Beskow had supported the World Federation Movement mobilized by former American GI Garry Davis, who, declaring himself no longer subject to national laws, had begun issuing passports for "World Citizens." When Beskow asked Steinbeck how Davis's efforts were viewed in the United States, Steinbeck, apparently unaware of Beskow's strong commitment to the movement, belittled Davis and his followers as quixotic. During the McCarthy hearings of the early 1950s, Beskow, obviously unfamiliar with Steinbeck's spirited defense of playwright Arthur Miller, believed his friend had been intimidated by the Wisconsin senator. According to Beskow, Steinbeck also felt compelled to defend America when other intellectuals were attacking it. In Beskow's view, Steinbeck's sense of vulnerability to the attacks of conservatives such as McCarthy and his need to speak positively for America explained Steinbeck's support later of America's role in Vietnam, a political stance with which Beskow disagreed.

Despite their political differences, Beskow and Steinbeck continued to correspond and to see each other. Steinbeck and Elaine visited Beskow and his second wife, Greta, at Rytterskulle in the summer of 1957. During this time, Beskow painted his third and final portrait of Steinbeck. That August, Beskow and Greta came to New York, where Beskow spent the remainder of the summer and that fall painting the modernistic fresco mural on the wall of the Meditation Room at the United Nations Building. His friend Dag Hammarskjöld had commissioned him for that task.

While they were in New York, the Beskows visited the Steinbecks in both Manhattan and Sag Harbor. Five years later, when Steinbeck traveled to Stockholm to receive the **Nobel Prize** for Literature, Beskow met him at the airport and accompanied him and Elaine to their official ceremonial activities. According to Beskow, their time together in Stockholm was "the last blaze of a smoldering friendship," although Beskow did defend his old friend when several Swedish writers and critics attacked the Swedish Academy for selecting Steinbeck. In an article appearing in Stockholm's *Radio TV Magazine*, Beskow blasted one critic in particular, the Swedish Marxist writer Artur Lundkvist, for suggesting that awarding the Nobel Prize to Steinbeck was the Swedish Academy's "biggest mistake."

In some ways the rift between Steinbeck and Beskow seems to have resulted from Beskow's view that Steinbeck changed during the course of his career from a social idealist into an American apologist, a perception Beskow shared with those American critics who were never able to forgive Steinbeck for what they regarded as political betrayal—his supposed abandoning of socialist doctrine after he achieved fame and financial security.

Further Reading: Benson, Jackson J. *The True Adventures of John Steinbeck, Writer.* New York: Viking, 1984; Beskow, Bo. *Krokodilens middag.* Stockholm: Bonnier, 1969; Steinbeck, John. *Steinbeck: A Life in Letters.* Ed. Elaine Steinbeck and Robert Wallsten. New York: Viking, 1975.

Donald Coers

BEST, MARSHALL. One of Steinbeck's senior editors at **Viking Press** when ***The Grapes of Wrath*** was published, Best, along with editors **Pat Covici** and **Harold Guinzburg**, objected to the manuscript's language, which he considered "rough" in places. His main concern was that bookstores would refuse to carry a book filled with "obscene" dialogue and that the book might also be banned. Consequently, he put pressure on Steinbeck's agents **McIntosh and Otis** to persuade their client to modify the language of the manuscript.

The overall conflict between Best and Steinbeck, after the success of *The Grapes of Wrath*, was due to Beck's preoccupation with sales and his willingness to appease the public's appetite for more books like *Grapes* when Steinbeck's desire, on the contrary, was to escape from the best-seller category and concentrate on more experimental work. This conflict continued for several years. By 1950, when Steinbeck submitted to Viking a draft of his profile of **Edward F. Ricketts**, an impressionistic memoir rather than biographical profile, Best had developed an unusual yet subtle shift in attitude toward Steinbeck's work by becoming more critical toward the writer's productions. In 1997 the Viking Critical Editions restored all the language contained in the original manuscript of *The Grapes of Wrath*, including rougher language and sexual explicitness.

Harry Karahalios

BESWICK, KATE (d. 1975). Beswick was a member **Stanford University**'s English Club with Steinbeck during his last year of school. Although many biographers have assumed she was a girlfriend of Steinbeck's, this has never been confirmed. The author's correspondence with Beswick between 1928 and 1931 reveals the attitudes Steinbeck struggled with regarding his writing while he lived in New York and in Tahoe. For example, on April 10, 1928, he wrote, "I know that ***Cup of Gold*** is a bad book, but on its shoulders I shall climb to a good book." Beswick is known to have voluntarily typed Steinbeck's manuscript of *Cup of Gold* without pay and to have provided honest critiques of the same work to Steinbeck.

Tracy Michaels

BETWEEN PACIFIC TIDES (1939). Published in 1939 by **Stanford University** Press, this title was written by Steinbeck's close friend **Edward F. Ricketts** and was coauthored by **Jack Calvin**. Although only 1000 copies of the first edition were printed, and despite the fact that the book was out of print within three years, the volume remains a definitive source book for studying marine life on the Pacific Coast and is still used at oceanographic research centers in the area. The text discusses marine invertebrates of the California shores and tidepools inductively instead of by phylogenetic classification. In the book, animals are observed according to their manner of living and are discussed as a living and integral part of a whole ecology rather than as separate entities. Steinbeck's high interest in Ricketts' discoveries later led to his accompanying his close friend on the boat the ***Western Flyer*** in a collecting voyage that later resulted in the publication of ***Sea of Cortez*** and its corresponding ***Log from the Sea of Cortez***, a commentary on the trip authored by Steinbeck. In 1947 Ricketts and Steinbeck hoped to but never took one final voyage together. The resulting third book was to be ***The Outer Shores***, with a narrative provided by Steinbeck. The three books were to be a trilogy that recorded observations of marine life on the Western coastline of America, moving from the tip of Baja to the very edge of Alaska.

Michael J. Meyer

BIBLE, THE. Like other notable American writers, Steinbeck relied upon, wrestled with, and rewrote biblical stories, finding the legacy of biblical Protestantism at once confining and compelling. His narrative voice is sometimes that of a prophet, sometimes of a psalmist, sometimes of a chronicler of sacred stories. Most of his major novels feature characters based on biblical prototypes: Jesus, Cain and Abel, Eve, Mary, Moses, John the Baptist, Paul, and the prodigal son, among others. Biblical settings (the desert, the mountaintop, the heavens, green pastures, Edenic valleys) and situations (a people exiled and wandering, a son returning to his father, a prophet indicting pharisaism, rowdy low-class disciples with a beloved leader) abound. Sometimes these parallels are deliberately ironic, as in ***The Pastures of Heaven***. In other works, most notably in ***The Grapes of Wrath*** and ***East of Eden***, the underlying biblical material provides, through the transforming medium of fiction, a way of understanding in radically biblical, loosely Christian terms not only human history (in which there seems to be a recurrent compulsion to reenact the dramas of Genesis, Exodus, and the gospels) but also, more specifically, American history and culture. The **Joads**, like the wandering Jews, for instance, leave a place where they suffered political exploitation and ecological disasters. They wander in the desert, accompanied by a prophet figure (**Casy**) who sees their journey in cosmic dimensions, and arrive at a promised land (California) only to find it the site of a new struggle. Permeating Steinbeck's thematic material are biblical, or Christian, ideas such as the fall and exile from paradise, necessary evil (*felix culpa*), curse and blessing, repentance, conversion, baptism, love of neighbor, universal brotherhood, discipleship, law, prophecy, wisdom, gospel, apocalypse, division of brother against brother and son against father, and women as agents of temptation. His stories have often been called allegories or parables, and some (such as ***The Pearl*** and ***The Wayward Bus***) are clearly designed as such. Even where they are least explicit, the biblical stories emerge as inescapable structural archetypes. The oft-drunken rabble who populate several of Steinbeck's novels (***Tortilla Flat*** and ***Cannery Row***, for instance) not only provide both comedy and pathos, but also recall the "publicans and sinners" with whom Jesus deigned to consort and among whom he found disciples. These men, the fallen women with whom they associate, and the communities that tolerate them with grace are "saved" by the rough socialism of their makeshift community and by their loyalty to and dependence on "Christ-figures" such as **Doc**, who have compassion on them.

The dominant ethic articulated in and drawn from the biblical foundations of Steinbeck's work is one of compassion, generosity, recognition of a debt owed to mankind, and willingness to take responsibility for that debt even to the point of self-sacrifice. ***Of Mice and Men***, for instance, emphasizes the importance of voluntary acceptance of dreadful responsibility for the good of the community. *Cannery Row*, taking another route to a similar point, challenges a system that justifies preying upon others and that, with pharisaic alliance, makes a virtue of success at the expense of the downtrodden. Among those downtrodden, both in this novel and in *Tortilla Flat*, sharing of resources is a rule of life. The two earliest novels, ***Cup of Gold*** and ***To a God Unknown***, clearly function as parables, the first warning about the consequences of conquest and the second combining the story of Joseph and elements of Christ's life to comment on patterns (and ironies) of settlement and conquest. Both dramatize a kind of universalism that becomes much more explicit in the later novels. In *Tortilla*

Flat, for instance, **Pilon**'s epiphany emerges in the invocation "Our Father who art in Nature." In this later novel, too, we see a merging of Arthurian legend with Christian tradition that recurs throughout the writing. Indeed, the biblical/Christian legacy in Steinbeck's writing is frequently filtered through allusion to later sources in Christian writing: medieval morality plays and legends, Chaucer, **John Milton**, and **Dante**. The Dantean schema is probably most explicit in *The Wayward Bus,* in which, as **Peter Lisca** has pointed out, characters are divided into "the damned, those in purgatory, and the saved or elect," and the journey moves from hell to purgatory to heaven. Repentance is a recurrent motif, and conversion manifested in self-knowledge comes through relationship with community.

Though Steinbeck's broad humanism can hardly in itself be called Christian or even specifically biblical (his philosophical roots can be traced also to **Lao Tze** and even to Hindu writings), the biblical structures and archetypes that recur consistently throughout his work may be seen as an abiding habit of mind, a prototype for the moral universe of his fiction, and the story from which his stories emerge and to which they point in their ultimate implications: that we are born into a struggle between good and evil with apocalyptic potential and that we must love one another, attend to the poor, share resources, exercise choice responsibly, respect wisdom, and recognize in nature itself the intelligent design in which we have a place.

Further Reading: DeMott, Robert. *Steinbeck's Reading; A Catalogue of Books Owned and Borrowed*. New York: Garland, 1984.

Marilyn Chandler McEntyre

BIDDLE RANCH, THE. Property of about forty-seven acres near Los Gatos, California, that was purchased by John and **Carol Henning Steinbeck** on August 25, 1938. Steinbeck described the ranch as one of the most beautiful places he had ever seen, though the purchase of the land and construction of a new house on the property occurred while he was under great self-imposed pressure to finish ***The Grapes of Wrath***. As a gift to Carol, Steinbeck had a swimming pool built on the property. The Steinbecks entertained such famous guests as **Charlie Chaplin**, Broderick Crawford, and Spencer Tracy at the Biddle property. But as the author suffered from exhaustion due to the completion of his great novel and his subsequent fame, the property became the unhappy setting of his failing marriage to Carol.

BIGGERS. A traveling salesman of grocery commodities in ***The Winter of Our Discontent***, he attempts to bribe **Ethan Allen Hawley** by offering him money and a 5 percent share of new orders, an offer made without owner **Marullo**'s knowledge, and he also makes recreational use of **Margie Young-Hunt**'s services when he is in town.

BILL, THE BOMBARDIER. In *Bombs Away,* the good-humored and taciturn young bombardier from Idaho. While in college waiting for the Depression to pass, he is inducted into the Army Air Force and becomes the guardian of the bomber crew's secret bombsight.

BLACK HAT. In ***The Grapes of Wrath***, one of the men **Pa** chats with in the **Weedpatch** (**Arvin Sanitary**) camp. He enlightens Pa about how the Okies are discriminated against by the local educational system and how after twelve hours of work each day, a family can still be hungry. Later, Black Hat reveals that the dilemma of owners manipulating labor exists nationwide as he discusses worker strife in Ohio.

"BLACK MAN'S IRONIC BURDEN" (1960). Article first published in the *Saturday Review* in 1960 and reprinted in the *Negro History Bulletin* (24, April 1961) in which Steinbeck asserts whites hold blacks to impossibly high standards possibly because the whites themselves feel inferior and therefore hostile toward the other race.

BLAIKEY, JOE. A constable in **Monterey** who is liked and trusted by everyone in town in ***Sweet Thursday***. He developed his social skills and learned how to deal with violence from being the youngest of fifteen children. Joe has the instinctive ability to size up a newcomer to town at first sight. Thus, on **Suzy**'s arrival at Monterey, he surmises that she is a transient who may start working the streets. He informs her that the town authorities will not allow street walking and that it is difficult to find other work with the canneries closed. Knowing she is broke, he offers to loan her money if she wants to leave town. Although Suzy declines his offer and begins working at the **Bear Flag**, she is grateful for his assistance later when she decides to leave the brothel. He helps talk **Ella** into hiring her as a waitress at the Golden Poppy Restaurant, and he loans her $25 so that she can buy the supplies needed to convert an abandoned boiler into her home.

Steinbeck admired small-town law-enforcement officers such as Joe Blaikey who knew and respected the other members of their community. Blaikey participates in all the connected aspects of the life of the town. For instance, when the **Cannery Row** community is selling raffle tickets to buy **Doc** a new microscope, Joe Blaikey carries some with him and cancels $2 parking tickets if the offender will spend the money on the raffle instead. Blaikey has his counterpart in such other small-town law enforcers as Jake Lake in ***Tortilla Flat*** and **Horace Quinn** in ***East of Eden***. As opposed to these understanding law enforcers, Steinbeck detested deputized thugs, such as those who help break up the strikes in ***The Grapes of Wrath*** and ***In Dubious Battle***.

Bruce Ouderkirk

BLAINE, MAHLON (1894–1970). Illustrator with one glass eye and a penchant for playing jokes with it whom Steinbeck met on board the freighter *Katrina* during his first trip to New York in 1925. Once in New York, Steinbeck eventually settled into a tiny, vermin-infested, walk-up apartment six floors above Blaine's more spacious place. Despite Prohibition laws, Steinbeck joined other friends at Blaine's for regular parties with wine. Blaine suggested that Steinbeck put together a collection of stories and try to get them published, leading to Steinbeck's first contact with **Robert M. McBride & Company**. Blaine also illustrated the cover, which Steinbeck didn't like, for ***Cup of Gold***.

Further Reading: Benson, Jackson J. *The True Adventures of John Steinbeck, Writer*. New York: Viking, 1984.

Kevin Hearle

BLAKE, ROBERT (1933–). Film actor who produced, and played **George** in, the 1981 television version of ***Of Mice and Men***. Blake gave a performance that some critics found superior to the sometimes-ingratiating mannerisms of **Burgess Meredith** in the 1939 film; Blake's George is a no-nonsense working man who smiles only when expressing his affection for **Lennie Small** (played by **Randy Quaid**).

BLAKE, WILLIAM (1757–1827). An early nineteenth-century English poet and artist who instilled his poetry with mysticism and symbolism. One of Steinbeck's least successful plays, ***Burning Bright***, originally titled *In the Forest of the Night*, derives its title from Blake's poem titled "The Tiger." Though the play-novelette suggests that mankind has the ability to withstand prejudice and that all men are fathers to all children in the world, critics dismissed its positive message that light would overcome darkness as in the Blake poem.

BLANCO. In the film ***Viva Zapata!*** he is Emiliano's beloved white stallion (his name means "white" in Spanish). When Emiliano is introduced to a little boy, who along with his brother had lassoed and dislodged a machine gun out of a gunner's hands, Emiliano offers the young boy a reward upon hearing of the brother's death. Nothing less than Emiliano's horse will satisfy the boy. The boy is later killed, and the horse is not seen again until the end of the film, when Blanco is used as an enticement for Emiliano to enter the courtyard of the Hacienda Chinameca. When Emiliano asks Guajardo where the horse was found, Guajardo informs him that a federal officer had him. Emiliano speaks to the horse as though it were human, lamenting that it has aged. He is so distracted that he does not notice Guajardo backing away, signaling to the men in the parapets. Emiliano is showered with a fusillade of bullets, and Blanco rears and bolts. In the final image in the film, Blanco is grazing riderless in the mountains, prompting all the peasants to say that Emiliano will one day be back if ever he is needed again.

Marcia D. Yarmus

BLANKENS. In ***The Wayward Bus***, a family of Southern sympathizers during the Civil War. The Blankens were transplanted Kentuckians who seceded 160 acres and a blacksmith shop from the Union, causing their land to become known as Rebel Corners, California. The Blankens brought their prejudices with them to California and were admired for their courage by their neighbors, who showered them with gifts of food. Eventually the Blankens degenerated through laziness and an argumentative nature and lost their land and business.

BLEOBERIS, SIR. Standard-bearer and godson of **King Bors** in ***The Acts of King Arthur***.

BOLTER. Mr. Bolter is the new President of the Torgas Valley Fruit Growers' Association in ***In Dubious Battle***. He tries to induce the strikers to return to work, but when they reject the terms he offers, he threatens to call in government troops to drive them out of the valley.

BOMBS AWAY: THE STORY OF A BOMBER TEAM (1942). When the United States entered World War II in 1941, John Steinbeck recognized his patriotic duty to his country and voluntarily served in a number of governmental agencies. In addition to working as an unpaid consultant for the Office of the Coordinator of Information (COI), a precursor to the Central Intelligence Agency (CIA), he was also a foreign news editor for the Office of War Information, and he worked for the Writer's War Board. However, the genesis of *Bombs Away* occurred in 1942, when he was appointed special consultant to the Secretary of War and assigned to Army Air Force Headquarters.

In May of 1942, Steinbeck was summoned to Washington for an interview with General Henry A. "Hap" Arnold, who outlined an ambitious plan to have him write a book detailing the training of a bomber crew. Arnold also suggested that if the first book were successful, there would be an opportunity for a sequel that followed the newly trained crew into combat. At first, Steinbeck was wary of the project, mainly because he did not want to be held responsible for someone going to war and getting killed. Nonetheless, he was ultimately persuaded to do the job, partly through the combined ministrations of General Arnold and Steinbeck's close friend, actor **Burgess Meredith**, but primarily as a result of a mandatory meeting with **Franklin Delano Roosevelt**, during which the president affably, yet assuredly, commanded Steinbeck to take on the task.

Subsequent to his meeting with Roosevelt, Steinbeck was briefed on the project, wined and dined by several generals, and introduced to **John Swope**, who would accompany him as a photographer for the text. He also learned he would be flying in a variety of Army aircraft, from trainers to bombers, and would be traveling all over the United States in an exhausting journey that would take him all the way from Texas to New Orleans and on to places such as Albuquerque, Phoenix, Las Vegas, Los Angeles, San Diego, Sacramento, Illinois,

Florida, and finally to New York. Steinbeck traveled roughly 20,000 miles for about a month in the early summer of 1942. He immersed himself in the military flying culture by training with the crews, getting up at 0500 hours, accompanying crews on flights, attending classes, taking tests, and socializing with crew members in roadhouses and bars.

Steinbeck worked slavishly through the summer, although he missed the original August 1 deadline he was given because the Army Air Force did not furnish him with the materials he needed to complete the task. Notwithstanding such frustrations, the writer's output was prodigious: to meet the pressing requirements, Steinbeck for the first time resorted to using an ediphone to dictate some 4,000 words a day. By the end of August, he had produced a final manuscript. After *Bombs Away* went to press, Steinbeck began work on a movie version in September, and he moved to Los Angeles to get it produced. But even though Hollywood paid roughly $250,000 for the rights to the book, they made little commitment to the project, and it languished. Steinbeck generously gave all his royalties from *Bombs Away* to the Army Air Forces Aid Society Trust Fund.

On November 27, 1942, *Bombs Away* was finally published to mostly favorable reviews. Clifton Fadiman, a writer for *The New Yorker* who had negatively viewed Steinbeck's earlier work, ***The Moon Is Down***, called *Bombs Away* an "extraordinary fine job of recruiting propaganda." However, *The New Republic* scorned *Bombs Away* as a work of dangerously debased ideas that bear "about the same relationship to literature that a recruiting poster does to art."

Later, several literary scholars would echo some of the same sentiments voiced by *The New Republic*. Lester Jay Marks, for instance, alleges a "pathetic" quality in *Bombs Away* because Steinbeck intruded upon his ethical and esthetic standards in writing it. Likewise, **Richard Astro** finds that the central flaw in the work is that in capitulating to political expediency, Steinbeck abandoned the "whole picture" view that had characterized great works such as ***In Dubious Battle*** and ***The Grapes of Wrath***. In perhaps the most damning statement of all, **John Ditsky** variously refers to it as Steinbeck's "weakest book" and as a "hurriedly written hack work with a patently propagandistic purpose." On a more positive note, however, Robert Morsberger argues that though *Bombs Away* is Steinbeck's most neglected work, it also contains his most elaborate treatment of his so-called phalanx theory and what happens when people work together as a group.

Though not generally regarded as one of Steinbeck's finest artistic efforts, *Bombs Away* can be appreciated on its own terms as a significant piece of war propaganda that fulfilled its avowed purpose to reassure Americans that victory was coming and that American men, aircraft, and material were the best in the world. It is the theme of teamwork that *Bombs Away* most effectively chimes, through its repeated emphasis on the importance of group endeavor and cooperation as a way of transforming individuals into cohesive fighting units.

Structurally, *Bombs Away* does not contain a plot in the conventional sense, but it is arranged to produce a concentrated communication of theme through the emphasis of particular functions performed by each member of the bomber team. In doing so, counting the preface, the book is organized into eleven chapters, with each chapter providing both an individual and a collective emphasis that coalesce into a central image of a particular entity: the bomber team. The chapters also form three larger groups that outline the contours of the discussion. The first group includes the "Preface" and "Introduction," which establish the purpose of the work and highlight the overarching teamwork motif. The middle sections describe the key members of the team, including the bomber, bombardier, gunner, navigator, pilot, aerial engineer, and radio engineer. Significant to this discussion is the order in which each position is treated. Normally, one might expect the most commonly recognized member of the team, the pilot, to be the first person discussed. However, Steinbeck deliberately delays his treatment of this vital crewmember in order to underscore his conception of an aircrew as a democratic organization. Steinbeck uses his concluding chapter, "The Mission," not only to dramatize the principles demonstrated in each of the preceding chapters, but also to highlight the central concept of the entire work, ultimately depicted as a cross section of men from all over the country who "had become one thing—bomber crew."

Unfortunately, in the process of condensing his focus and simplifying his theme, Steinbeck also flattened his characters. As a result, the figures peopling *Bombs Away* actually look more like allegorical types than rounded human beings. Although the characters are wooden, they do effectively serve the propagandist's aims by suggesting an easily apprehensible range of human temperaments aptly suited to Steinbeck's purposes. Of special significance, too, is the fact that virtually all of these crewmembers come from either Midwestern or Western rural and small-town stock, which connects them closely to mythic American ideals of agrarian frontier expansion and mass democracy. **Bill**, for example, the bombardier from Idaho, is an average Joe whose vitality, hard work, and faith are the product of what Steinbeck refers to as the "alert" democracy of the West. **Al, the aerial gunner**, is a former soda jerk from the Midwest who is transformed through training into the modern descendant of the Kentucky rifleman, the western Indian fighter, and the frontiersman.

Naturally, themes such as specialized mission, intelligence, and teamwork also figure prominently in the sixty photographs included in the book. Consequently, the relationship of photographs and words in *Bombs Away* helps unify groups of information while underscoring key concepts elucidated in the text. For example, the central symbol for the fighting group, the bomber, is featured in five of the first seven photographs. However, two of these photos, which depict respective ground and air profiles of the B-17 Flying Fortress and the B-24 Liberator, are placed on the same pages as Steinbeck's preliminary description of the bombers' primary role. The same practice also is used elsewhere to unify and outline other crucial concepts. In each case, the photographs are located in close proximity to the ideas they illustrate.

The characters, the photographs, and the structuring of events in *Bombs Away* ultimately combine to project the bomber crew as yet another illustration of Steinbeck's group man, or "phalanx" theory, an idea dramatized in such novels as *The Grapes of Wrath* and *In Dubious Battle* and explained in ***The Log from the Sea of Cortez***. The bomber crew functions in a way similar to the Joad family in that it becomes a coalition of individuals forming a small group that subsequently joins with other small groups to become part of a larger entity. The bomber crew is part of a flight, the flight is part of a squadron, the squadron part of a wing, the wing part of the Air Force, and the Air Force an extension of a supra-phalanx, the Allied powers that form a united front against Axis tyranny and oppression.

This concept is consistent with Steinbeck's belief that thoughtful group action functioning within the framework of a democratic society can ultimately triumph over spiritless machinations of corporate groupthink or fascist political dogma. As *Bombs Away* illustrates, the outbreak of worldwide war placed unique demands on the writer's talent in that it aroused patriotic instincts and propelled Steinbeck into a new situation that demanded a particular rhetorical response designed to counter an ominous threat—fascism. The propaganda that obtrudes in *Bombs Away*, though unsophisticated, can thereby be justified as a reasonable response to an unreasonable threat.

Further Reading: Astro, Richard. *John Steinbeck and Edward F. Ricketts: The Shaping of a Novelist*. Minneapolis: University of Minnesota Press, 1973; Benson, Jackson J. *The True Adventures of John Steinbeck, Writer*. New York: Penguin, 1984; Ditsky, John. "Steinbeck's

Bombs Away: The Group-man in the Wild Blue Yonder." *Steinbeck Quarterly* 12 (Winter/ Spring 1979): 5–14; Lewis, Cliff. "Art for Politics: John Steinbeck and FDR." In *After "The Grapes of Wrath": Essays on John Steinbeck*. Ed. Donald Coers, Paul D. Ruffin, and Robert J. DeMott. Athens: Ohio University Press, 1995. 23–38; Marks, Lester Jay. *Thematic Design in the Novels of John Steinbeck*. The Hague, the Netherlands: Mouton, 1969; McElrath, Joseph, Jr., Jesse S. Crisler, and Susan Shillinglaw, eds. *John Steinbeck: The Contemporary Reviews*. Cambridge, England: Cambridge University Press, 1996. 259–67; Morsberger, Robert E. "Steinbeck's War." *The Steinbeck Question: New Essays in Criticism*. Ed. Donald R. Noble. Troy, NY: Whitson Publishing, 1993. 183–212.

Rodney P. Rice

BOODIN, JOHN ELOF (1869–1950). This UCLA professor of philosophy's "cosmic idealism" theory appealed to Steinbeck. Steinbeck is known to have read Boodin's *A Realistic Universe and Cosmic Evolution* sometime between 1932 and1933. He was especially interested in the idea of the intersection of individual minds being combined to create a great whole with properties of its own (i.e., a new collective form). In this theory, an impersonal god or form controls matter that responds to the god or form.

Steinbeck was first introduced to Boodin's work when he attended a summer session at Hopkins Marine Station (a **Stanford University** extension) held by Professor **C. V. Taylor.** Later in life, Steinbeck's friend **Richard Albee**, a student of Boodin's, further enlightened Steinbeck to the professor's theories via discussion and review of his class notes.

It is generally thought that speculation about Boodin's theories inspired Steinbeck to script his unpublished essay, "**Argument of Phalanx**." In addition, his philosophical ideas played a great role in influencing the beliefs and dialogue of **Casy** in ***The Grapes of Wrath***.

Further Reading: Railsback, Brian. *Parallel Expeditions: Charles Darwin and the Art of John Steinbeck*. Moscow: University of Idaho Press, 1995.

Tracy Michaels

BORDONI, MR. Swiss immigrant in ***East of Eden*** who owns what is left of the old Sanchez grant—about nine hundred acres—in the Salinas Valley. Shortly after he arrives in California, **Adam Trask** buys Bordoni's ranch.

BORRE. Bastard son of **Arthur** by **Lyonors** in ***The Acts of King Arthur***, he eventually becomes a Knight of the **Round Table**.

BORROW, GEORGE (1803–1881). An English writer and traveler, he led a nomadic life in England and on the Continent, where he was a translator and agent for the British and Foreign Bible Society. Although his most famous book is *The Bible in Spain* (1843), his best is probably the autobiographical *Lavengro* (1851), with its sequel, *Romany Rye* (1857). All Borrow's works are based on his wanderings. Steinbeck read Borrow's *Wild Wales: Its People, Language and Scenery* for background information for his first published novel, ***Cup of Gold***.

BORS, KING OF GAUL. One of the two French kings in ***The Acts of King Arthur*** who help **Arthur** in his war against the eleven rebel kings of the North.

BOSS, THE. Owner of a ranch near Soledad in ***Of Mice and Men***, he is a little stocky man who walks with his thumbs stuck in his belt. He wears blue jeans, a flannel shirt, a black, unbuttoned vest, and a black coat. He also wears a soiled brown Stetson hat and high-heeled boots with spurs to distinguish himself from the laborers. When **George Milton** and **Lennie Small** first arrive on the farm by noon, he meets with them and warns them not to make any trouble. Because George does much of the talking for Lennie when the Boss asks him questions, the Boss is suspicious that George is "selling" Lennie—he believes that George is taking Lennie's pay.

Luchen Li

BOSTON, MILTON. In ***The Wayward Bus***, owner of the drugstore where **Van Brunt** bought cyanide as insurance against his feared disabling by stroke. Boston and Van Brunt were longtime friends, fellow members of the Blue Lodge.

BOSWELL, JAMES (1740–1795). Journal writer and close friend of the English lexicographer and essayist Samuel Johnson. Best remembered for his magnificent biography on Samuel Johnson, *The Life of Samuel Johnson LL.D*, Boswell also published *The Journal of a Tour to the Hebrides*, a record of their 1773 travel through Scotland, a work that contains similarities to Steinbeck's musings on his trip with **Edward F. Ricketts** titled ***The Log from The Sea of Cortez***. Boswell's biography of Johnson was one of Steinbeck's favorites during the late 1920s, and Steinbeck possessed a copy of it bound in a blue denim cover so that it would withstand the toils of overuse. Steinbeck's interest in Samuel Johnson was inspired by **Margery Bailey**, a professor and mentor to Steinbeck during his years at **Stanford University**.

Ted Scholz

BOURKE-WHITE, MARGARET (1904–1971). Famed American photojournalist whose work for the magazines *Fortune* and *Life* brought notice not only to herself, but also to the field of photojournalism. She is best remembered today for her collaboration with the author **Erskine Caldwell** on *You Have Seen Their Faces* (1937), a frank and evocative look at rural poverty in the United States. In particular, the photographs she and others, including **Dorothea Lange**, took during the Great Depression brought the suffering of Dust Bowl refugees to the forefront of public consciousness, indirectly developing an audience for books like ***The Grapes of Wrath*** and undoubtedly contributing to Steinbeck's dissatisfaction with the migrants' conditions.

Further Reading: Bourke-White, Margaret. *Portrait of Myself*. New York: Simon & Schuster, 1963; Goldberg, Vickie. *Margaret Bourke-White: A Biography*. New York: Harper & Row, 1986.

Scott Simkins

BRACE, ELEANOR. During the first leg of his trip in ***Travels with Charley***, Steinbeck stops in Deer Isle, Maine, where he has been invited to stay with Miss Eleanor Brace, a friend of **Elizabeth Otis**, Steinbeck's longtime friend and agent.

BRANDO, MARLON (1924–2004). Often considered the greatest movie actor of all time, Brando appeared in a string of Academy-nominated performances—including Steinbeck's ***Viva Zapata!***, directed by **Elia Kazan**. In this film, Brando portrayed the Mexican title hero, **Emiliano Zapata**, a role for which he received an Oscar nomination for Best Actor in a Leading Role. Brando's most famous roles after *Zapata!* were his portrayal of Terry Malloy in *On the Waterfront* (1954) and his appearance as Don Vito Corleone in *The Godfather* (1971), with both performances garnering Oscars. Most critics consider his last great performance to be the role of Colonel Kurtz in Francis Ford Coppola's *Apocalypse Now* (1979).

BRAS DE FER. Actual pirate captain as well as a character in ***Cup of Gold***. His name is French for "Arms of Iron." In Steinbeck's book, he is reputedly the father of **Henry Morgan**'s favorite lieutenant, **Coeur de Gris**.

BRASTIAS, SIR. Trusted knight of the Duke of Cornwall in ***The Acts of King Arthur***, who becomes knight of **Uther Pendragon** after the Duke's death. One of the four knights who protect **Arthur** from his enemies before he becomes king. He is made warden of the northern boundaries by Arthur and acts as messenger between Arthur and the French kings, **Ban** and **Bors**.

BRAZILIANO, ROCHE. Pirate captain with an extreme hatred of Spaniards in ***Cup of Gold***.

"BREAKFAST" (1936). First published in ***Pacific Weekly*** in 1936, a first-person narrated sketch that, although brief, forms a vividly depicted and useful transition in ***The Long Valley*** between the depictions of the male-female relationships in the earlier stories and some of the plights and concerns of the migrant workers appearing in **"The Raid."** In "Breakfast" the unidentified narrator thinks back to a scene that has stayed in his memory for years, and he tries to recapture it as it had seemed to him at the time: Traveling through the Long Valley at daybreak, shivering with cold and sensing more "pure night" than light, the narrator comes across a tent, a stove, and a young woman. He notices that as she prepares breakfast, the young woman nurses her baby, holding it in the crook of one arm and keeping its head inside her blouse for warmth. This maternal image suffuses the entire story, for the woman represents warmth and food and nourishment to the narrator and to her husband and father-in-law who appear moments later while the narrator warms his hands at the stove. In the present day, the narrator vividly recalls the smell of frying bacon and freshly baked bread. In the memory, the woman's husband and father-in-law (presumably: they never introduce themselves) invite the narrator to sit down and join them at their meal. The two men are wearing new clothes, and their faces still shine with water from their morning washing. The woman, her husband, and father-in-law all seem proud to have found jobs picking cotton and to have worked twelve days; they are proud to have food that they can share with a stranger, but the unaccustomed abundance is suggested by the way that all of them, including the narrator, devour their food. All the while, the light is growing swiftly, and although there may be an element of sexual attraction in the narrator's attention to the woman, there is a spiritual quality to it as well. An unemphatic but discernible religious element permeates the story, not only in the way the young man and his father intone "Keerist!" and "God Almighty" in praise of the aroma and taste of the food, but also in subtler ways: the father, the son, the mother, and the child suggest the Christian Holy Family, and their generous concern and goodness infuses the narrator's memory with a kind of beauty that transcends the physical sensations he has enjoyed.

"Breakfast" has typically been seen as a warm-up for ***The Grapes of Wrath***. **Jackson J. Benson**, however, asserts that "Breakfast," written three years before Steinbeck's earliest drafts of *Grapes*, actually constituted part of Steinbeck's preparatory work for ***In Dubious Battle***. An examination of the characters in "Breakfast" shows clearly their similarity to Lisa, **Joey Morphy**, their baby, and **Mr. London** in *In Dubious Battle*, and the narrator of "Breakfast" relates to this family in a way very similar to the way **Jim Nolan** relates to the London family. Nonetheless, most readers cannot help seeing in the nameless young woman of "Breakfast" an early version of **Rose of Sharon** in *The Grapes of Wrath*.

Further Reading: Benson, Jackson J. *The True Adventures of John Steinbeck, Writer*. New York: Viking, 1984; Benton, Robert M. "'Breakfast' I and II." In *A Study Guide to Steinbeck's "The Long Valley."* Ed. Tetsumaro Hayashi and Reloy Garcia. Ann Arbor, MI: Pierian, 1976. 33–39; Hamby, James A. "Steinbeck's Biblical Vision: 'Breakfast' and the Nobel Acceptance Speech." *Western Review: A Journal of the Humanities* 10.1 (1973): 57–59; Hughes, Robert S. Jr., *John Steinbeck: A Study of the Short Fiction*. New York: Twayne, 1989; Schmidt, Gary D. "Steinbeck's 'Breakfast': A Reconsideration." *Western American Literature* 26.4 (Winter 1992): 303–11.

Abby H. P. Werlock

BRECK, JOHN. Masculine pseudonym used by Elizabeth Smith, a wealthy student in her thirties who was Steinbeck's classmate while he attended **Stanford University**. Breck was a member of the informal English Club at the university, a discussion group devoted to the extension of reading and analysis beyond the classroom. An ardent feminist, Breck had assumed a masculine name in order to gain recognition as a writer (at that time typically a male field). No doubt Steinbeck was first impressed by the fact that she had actually succeeded in placing several of her stories in national magazines, and he often sought her advice about his work. Breck's house became a gathering place for the artistically minded, especially the writers of **Stanford University** in the late 1920s. Using a writing studio Breck had constructed behind her house, Steinbeck was often a guest of the family, and no doubt it was this residence that established a pattern of constructing lean-tos or add-ons to his future homes as he became accustomed to an isolated space where he could compose without disruption.

Breck's influence extended further and impacted Steinbeck's choice of subject material. For instance, Breck's primary interest as a writer lay in man's relation to his environment and the drama of mankind as he encountered the wilderness, a theme often repeated in Steinbeck. Since Breck was also a dedicated proponent of ecology, perhaps some of her ideas influenced Steinbeck's later interest in environmental issues and his attempt to foster conservation and to protect animal life and land. What is more certain, however, is that under Breck's roof and with her sponsorship, Steinbeck was able to experiment safely and was given some positive feedback. Moreover, the author's depiction of masculine women such as **Elisa Allen** in **"The Chrysanthemums"** and **Mary Teller** in **"The White Quail"** were possibly based on Breck's strong personality.

Perhaps the most important contribution of Breck to Steinbeck's career, however, was that she introduced him to **Mavis McIntosh** and **Elizabeth Otis** in 1930. Impressed by their firm's business acumen (they had placed her novel within a short time), Breck recommended the young Steinbeck as a new client for the agency, thus beginning his lifelong association with McIntosh and Otis.

Michael J. Meyer

BREED, WALTER, AND MRS. BREED. In ***The Wayward Bus***, owners of a general store and service station on the road between Rebel Corners and San Juan. The Breeds and **Juan Chicoy** are good friends. Walter Breed's frightened appraisal of the flooding river adds suspense to the novel as the bus approaches the store.

BRETHREN OF THE COAST. Historic name for a loose alliance of buccaneers in the Caribbean in the seventeenth century, and in ***Cup of Gold*** an alternate name for what Steinbeck usually calls the **Free Brotherhood of the Coast**.

Further Reading: Eddy, Darlene. "To Go A-Buccaneering and Take a Spanish Town: Some Seventeenth-Century Aspects of *Cup of Gold*." *Steinbeck Quarterly* 8 (Winter 1975): 3–12.

BRIAN OF THE FOREST. In ***The Acts of King Arthur***, Brother of **Sorlus of the Forest**, both of whom are encountered by **Gawain** on his Quest of the White Stag.

BRIFFAULT, ROBERT (1876–1948). The writings of Briffault, author of *The Mothers: A Study of Origins of Sentiments and Institutions* (1927), formed a partial background for Steinbeck's mystical and mythical composition titled ***To a God Unknown***. This novel considers nature as an organic whole larger than human attempts to control or understand it. In order to present a wide spectrum of relationship between man and nature in his novel, Steinbeck drew on his reading of Briffault, as well as from James Frazer's *The Golden Bough* (1890), Jessie Weston's *From Ritual to Romance* (1920), and the biblical Old Testament. Ultimately, Steinbeck makes the point that man will experience delusion and suffering whenever he selects and gives precedence to any closed system of beliefs and ignores wider possibilities.

Michael J. Meyer

BRIGHAM FAMILY. Mrs. Alice Brigham, a widow of a prominent San Francisco surgeon, hired Steinbeck in the fall of 1926 through 1928 to be the caretaker of the family summer home estate on the south shore of Lake Tahoe. Here, during the cold winter months when the extended Brigham family was not in residence, Steinbeck had access to the ample library of the home and time to write. Among his duties were serving as driver and also tutoring the grandchildren. After overcoming initial lethargy, Steinbeck wrote his first novel, ***Cup of Gold***, while employed by the Brighams.

Paul M. Blobaum

BRISTOL GIRL. Ship on which **Henry Morgan** first sails to the Caribbean in ***Cup of Gold***.

BRISTOL, HORACE (1908–1997). American photographer who worked with Steinbeck in 1938. After studying at **Stanford University** and in Europe during the 1920s, Bristol enrolled in the newly founded photography department at the Los Angeles Art Center School of Design in 1931. He joined *Life* in 1937 and *Fortune* in 1939 as a photojournalist, traveling the country to capture a wide variety of images and stories. During World War II, Bristol was one of five photographers selected to work under Edward Steichen in the Pacific for the Department of the Navy. In 1947, Bristol began his own company, East West Photo Agency, which he ran until his retirement in 1965. A native Californian, Bristol's world travels eventually brought him to Ojai, California, where he resided from 1976 until his death in 1997.

Bristol occasionally worked side by side with **Dorothea Lange** during the Depression, capturing images of migrant workers. Inspired by **Margaret Bourke-White**'s and **Erskine Caldwell**'s photographic book *You Have Seen Their Faces* and Steinbeck's own ***In Dubious Battle***, Bristol asked Steinbeck if he was interested in working with him on a photographic book documenting the migration. Steinbeck agreed, but on the condition that they work only on weekends.

According to Bristol, the two would drive to camps in the California valley with cheap food, trading it for stories and the permission to photograph the workers. Often encountering antagonistic people both within and outside the camps, Bristol tried to calm a nervous Steinbeck: "He thought that the farmers wanted to kill him. I would say to Steinbeck, 'Nobody's going to hurt you.' I never felt any danger at all." After seven weekends of work, Bristol felt he had enough material for their book, but Steinbeck chose to write a novel, ***The Grapes of Wrath***, instead.

After Bristol's wife, Virginia, committed suicide, the despondent photographer destroyed nearly all of his photographs in 1956. The surviving photographs from his time with Steinbeck resonate with what became the **Joads**' story. "Rose of Sharon," with its strong contrasts of light and dark and the intensity of **Rose of Sharon**'s distant gaze as she nurses her baby, exemplifies the drama of the situation in which the migrants found themselves. "Pea Pickers," a more traditionally reportorial image, shows a diversity of people engaged in arduous menial labor under the glare of a California sun. Although clearly aesthetically founded in their careful compositions and use of light, both images represent Bristol's fundamental interest in reportage over the more artistic endeavors of friends Edward Weston and Imogen Cunningham. "My idea was to get a picture to illustrate a point or a story. I really didn't care if it was f4.5 or f64 as long as the picture was successful in illustrating a story." Like Steinbeck, Bristol was keenly interested in expressing the terrible conditions of the migrant workers in a way that would affect the public audience for his work.

Bristol's influence on the creation of *The Grapes of Wrath* extended beyond the text to the film: "Twentieth Century Fox asked if they could see my pictures to assist them in casting. Some of the characters look exactly like people I photographed." Together, Steinbeck and Bristol used their visual and textual images to alter the American public's consciousness of the migrant laborers' plight.

Further Reading: Bristol, Horace. *Stories From Life: The Photography of Horace Bristol.* Athens: Georgia Museum of Art/University of Georgia Press, 1995; Harris, Mark Edward. *Master Photographers and Their Work.* New York: Abbeville Press, 1998; Railsback, Brian. "Style and Image: John Steinbeck and Photography." In *John Steinbeck: A Centennial Tribute.* Ed. Syed Mashkoor Ali. Jaipur, India: Surabhi, 2004; *Watkins to Weston: 101 Years of California Photography 1849–1950,* Exhibition Catalogue. Santa Barbara, CA: Santa Barbara Museum of Art in Cooperation with Roberts Rinehart Publishers, 1992.

Kirstin Ringelberg

BROTHER COLIN. One of the brothers of the "Monastery of M—" in **"Saint Katy the Virgin,"** who, while tithing with **Brother Paul** in the "County of P—," thinks that they have the best of the bargain when the evil **Roark** gives them Katy, his enormous pig. Brother Colin, a rotund man more worldly than his companion, thinks of the fine ham and bacon Katy will produce—until she takes a bite out of his calf and sends both brothers scurrying up a tree.

BROTHER DEATH. **Henry Morgan**'s dying vision of death approaching in ***Cup of Gold***.

BROTHER PAUL. Companion to **Brother Colin** in **"Saint Katy the Virgin,"** together with whom he accepts the offer of Katy the pig from **Roark**, her first owner. After Katy bites Brother Colin and sends both men up a tree, Brother Paul, a thin, pious man, fails at his attempt to exorcise the devil from Katy, but finally converts her to Christianity. At the monastery, however, **Father Benedict** does not give Paul the praise he had expected, but instead calls him a fool for converting Katy. Annoyed, Father Benedict tells him that one cannot slaughter and eat a Christian pig, and thus Brother Paul has unwittingly set Katy on her road to sainthood.

Abby H. P. Werlock

BROWN, HAROLD CHAPMAN (1879–1943). Prior to Steinbeck's reading of **John Elof Boodin**, Brown was one of the essential pillars in constructing Steinbeck's philosophies of humanity. Brown taught a course in the history of philosophy while Steinbeck attended **Stanford University**, and Steinbeck often spoke of this independent-minded professor in glowing terms. He made a point of attending all of Brown's offered lectures, even when not enrolled in a course, and he also discussed issues presented in class with Brown at his home. Brown emphasized openness to all experience, and he suggested that modern philosophy and scientific law could work together simultaneously as integrated wholes. Utilizing this concept, Steinbeck's holistic style of writing often presents characters who fail because of their inability to incorporate philosophy and science and thus are defeated by their limited vision (e.g., **Joy** in ***In Dubious Battle***, **Lennie Small** in ***Of Mice and Men***, and **Noah Joad** in ***The Grapes of Wrath***).

Tracy Michaels

BROWNING, KIRK. Directed the Steppenwolf Theatre production of ***The Grapes of Wrath*** for its television version on PBS's *American Playhouse* in March 1991.

BROWNING, ROBERT (1812–1891). Victorian poet whose influence perhaps is evident in the structure of some Steinbeck works. In Steinbeck's early experimental, unpublished work **"Dissonant Symphony,"** he emulated the style Browning used in his famous poem "The Ring and the Book," wherein the central character was never directly seen except through the eyes of characters around him. Each character then provides a new layer or dimension to the main character. This is particularly true of Steinbeck's technique in ***The Pastures of Heaven***, a short-story cycle.

BUCK, BILLY. In all four of the stories that make up *The Red Pony,* Billy Buck, a ranch hand, serves as a mentor and surrogate father to **Jody Tiflin**. Acknowledged by all the people in the area as being an expert horseman, Billy Buck is key throughout **"The Gift"** in educating Jody about the care and training of **Gabilan**. He proves fallible when he assures Jody that it will not rain and it does. Then he fails to save the ailing colt that falls ill from exposure to the weather. Billy attempts to make amends in **"The Promise."** After the pony dies, Jody's father (**Carl Tiflin**) promises that if Jody will work all summer to pay for breeding of the mare, **Nellie**, and will take care of her during the long months following, Jody will have earned the colt. When the time for delivery arrives, Billy is obliged to kill the mare in order to save the colt. Despite the loss, Jody's new colt is saved. In **"The Great Mountains,"** Buck is the voice of compassion for the old paisano who visits the ranch. The contrast between Billy and Tiflin is brought out most clearly in **"The Leader of the People."** When Mr. Tiflin becomes impatient with his wife's father's frequently retold tale of leading the settlers across the continent, Billy patiently puts up with the disgruntled leader who no longer has followers. In return, **Grandfather**, even though he considers this middle-aged man a boy, acknowledges the quality of his character and welcomes his respectful behavior toward an older man. Jody learns, too, to be compassionate toward his grandfather.

Mimi Reisel Gladstein

BUCKE, MRS. In *Sweet Thursday,* a first-grade teacher in **Pacific Grove** who stands accused by a student of giving him the dust cover of the Kinsey Report. Under questioning, she reveals that in 1918 her father signed a petition for the release of the socialist leader Eugene Debs. Through this incident and some others in *Sweet Thursday,* Steinbeck lampoons the McCarthyism rampant at the time. Steinbeck thoroughly detested Senator McCarthy, whom he referred to as "Josephine" in his private correspondence. He published a mocking essay called **"How to Tell Good Guys from Bad Guys"** in *The Reporter* in 1950.

Bruce Ouderkirk

BUD. In *The Wayward Bus,* the man to whom **Alice Chicoy** lost her virginity when she was young. The memory surfaces when she starts drinking following the bus's departure for San Juan de la Cruz. For Alice this is a bitter memory, for what had begun as a bucolic picnic ended with Bud's callousness following intercourse. In Alice's view, Bud's attitude foreshadows the general attitude of the men she will encounter in her life.

BUGLE, MILDRED. In *Sweet Thursday,* a precocious thirteen-year-old, discriminating in botany, who discovers plants of *Cannabis americana* growing in the Los Angeles Plaza where **Joseph and Mary Rivas** have cultivated them.

BULENE, PET. Taxi driver in Salinas in ***East of Eden***.

BULLITT, JESSIE. *See* **Women's Committee at the Weedpatch camp**.

BUNYAN, JOHN (1628–1688). An English writer of allegorical fiction, Bunyan was the son of a tinker who had little schooling. During the English Civil War, while he served in the Parliamentary Army, he underwent a period of acute spiritual anxiety and finally became a lay preacher while earning his living as a tinker. His first substantial work was an autobiography, *Grace Abounding to the Chief of Sinners*. This was followed by other works, of which the most read and most loved by far is his *The Pilgrim's Progress from This World to That Which Is to Come*, usually called *Pilgrim's Progress;* this work, which Steinbeck read, was likely an early influence. Steinbeck himself, particularly in later works, delved into allegory (***The Pearl***, for example, or ***Burning Bright***).

Michael J. Meyer

Further Reading: DeMott, Robert. *Steinbeck's Reading; A Catalogue of Books Owned and Borrowed*. New York: Garland, 1984.

BURGUNDIAN, THE. Pirate captain under **Henry Morgan**'s command in the campaign against Panama in ***Cup of Gold***. His first name is Emil, and he and The Other Burgundian, whose name is Antoine, are inseparable. The closeness of the two brothers is captured in Steinbeck's portrayal of The Other Burgundian's always having his one good arm placed protectively around the shoulders of his brother. As young men, they and two friends had all been in competition for the love of the same young woman, named **Delphine**. The Burgundian won her love by giving her a single rose-colored pearl, and they were happily married even though she was the mistress to the three other friends. Eventually, when public opinion required a duel, Emil killed two friends and cut Antoine in defense of his wife's honor. Antoine's cut became infected, and the left arm had to be amputated at the elbow. When Emil and Antoine were brought before Lieutenant Governor Henry Morgan to be tried for piracy, Henry reminisced with them about Panama, found them guilty, and sentenced them to be hanged. The Burgundian gave Henry Morgan the rose pearl to give to Henry's wife.

Kevin Hearle.

BURGUNDIAN, THE OTHER. *See* **"Burgundian, The."**

BURKE. A strike leader in charge of camp security in ***In Dubious Battle***, who supports **Dakin**. During a confrontation in the struggle for power, he accuses **London** of selling out, and the short-tempered and powerful London breaks Burke's jaw.

BURNING BRIGHT (1950). John Steinbeck's third and last experiment with his "play-novelette" form, it was performed as a play and produced as a book in October 1950. Both forms were panned by the critics, and Steinbeck himself admitted later that *Burning Bright* did not work as a play. Unlike other slight works in Steinbeck's canon, such as ***Bombs Away*** or ***The Short Reign of Pippin IV***, *Burning Bright* is an admirable attempt by the author to strive for something important, and this slim work could be viewed as a spectacular failure.

Most readers would agree that *Burning Bright* has been neglected for good reason. Steinbeck's attempt to make a play and book out of a philosophical treatise utterly fails to entertain. Set in three acts—"The Circus," "The Farm," and "The Sea"—*Burning Bright* concerns **Joe Saul**, a man nearing fifty who suffers from sterility. Following the death of his first wife, **Cathy**, he has married a healthy young woman named **Mordeen**. She surmises that an early bout with rheumatic fever has made Saul sterile, but he does not know about his condition. **Friend Ed**, a protective companion, consoles Saul and consults with Mordeen. Tension mounts as **Victor**, a strong young man, senses Saul's weakness and wants to have Mordeen for himself. Because Saul desperately wants children to continue his bloodline, Mordeen decides she will do anything to please him. Out of love for her husband, Mordeen lets Victor impregnate her, using him like a stud animal. Victor cannot stand to be used, however, and threatens to tell Saul how Mordeen became pregnant. She decides to kill Victor and, in a climactic scene, takes a knife to do the hapless man in. However, Friend Ed intervenes, crushing Victor's skull and disposing of the body (this is softened in the play, in which Friend Ed arranges for Victor to be shanghaied). Meanwhile, Saul discovers he is sterile after a visit with **Dr. Zorn**. Saul confronts Mordeen but, with some mediation from Friend Ed, accepts her gift of great love. In the last scene, the **Child** is born and love conquers all. This odd tale suffers from strange dialogue, odd setting, and abstract characterization.

The dialogue is strained and highly artificial because Steinbeck created "a kind of universal language" for his everyman characters. In a response to his critics, Steinbeck noted that *Burning Bright* was an attempt to "lift the story to the parable expression of the morality plays." This artistic aim results in lines like this one, when Ed is trying to help Saul: "Three years it is since Cathy died. You were strong in your wife-loss. You were not nervy then." This universalized language annoyed critics, as evident by L. A. G. Strong's parody of the work: "Have I, I wonder, the admirer-right to tell Mr. Steinbeck that this trick has set me screaming silently in my reader-loss?" Most literary critics, from **Peter Lisca** to Jay Parini, have echoed the laments of the contemporary reviewers. Steinbeck's odd shifting of scene, as characters walk through circus, farm, and sea settings, also was an attempt to universalize the experience. Critics have generally dismissed this device as a highly artificial gimmick that confused readers and viewers alike. Literary critic Howard Levant asserts that Steinbeck had been struggling with form, and the odd structure of the play-novelettes, *Burning Bright* in particular, demonstrates Steinbeck's tendency "to substitute mechanics and manipulation for organic form."

Characterization also suffers from Steinbeck's attempt to make *Burning Bright* a lofty, universal experience. Joe Saul, Friend Ed, and Mordeen are walking abstractions; ironically, Victor is the most dynamic character in the work, and he shows some flashes of real humanity. Lisca wrote that with *Burning Bright*, Steinbeck was reverting to his earlier mode in ***To a God Unknown***, in which characters were overloaded with symbolism. **John Ditsky** summed up the combination of problems for this play-novelette, noting that "unreal dialogue is spoken by unreal characters in unreal settings."

Burning Bright was published during a turbulent time in Steinbeck's personal life and artistic career. In 1948 he suffered an ugly separation from his second wife, **Gwyndolyn Conger Steinbeck**, and the untimely death of his great friend and literary muse **Edward F. Ricketts**. At the end of 1949, he married his third wife, **Elaine Scott Steinbeck**, who had been a successful Broadway stage manager and who assured that his residence would remain in New York rather than his native California. Steinbeck's third play-novelette was inspired by meeting Elaine's theater friends and being immersed in the Broadway scene; he wanted to create a vehicle for the theater. Given his recent personal traumas, moral issues came to the forefront of his writing as he moved away (but never completely) from the sweeping **non-teleological** ideas that he had worked out with Ricketts. This change of direction culminated in ***East of Eden***, but *Burning Bright* (as a modern morality play) represents a major artistic turning point for Steinbeck. It is difficult to believe that the allegorical play-novelette was written by the same man who wrote the cold, scientific ***In Dubious Battle***. The difficulty for *Burning Bright* is the collision of Steinbeck's objective, scientific direction (the realities of human animal/sexual nature) with higher notions of morality (the human ability to love deeply and forgive). Although Mordeen and Friend Ed conspire compassionately to give Saul his child, they have little trouble doing away with Victor when he gets in the way. Critic John S. Kennedy explained the problem thus: the "thoughtful reader is appalled by the complete severance of man from morality which the book's argument represents."

The biblical allegory is heavy-handed in *Burning Bright*, but Steinbeck used the most important stories of the western world to give his little play gravity. There are elements of several Bible stories, and Joe Saul's name and the action of the story suggest the rivalry of King Saul and David (Victor) or Saul on the road to Damascus (as Old Saul drifts in darkness until he literally is enlightened). However, as Lisca has observed, many elements in the play-novelette indicate the Christ story: Joe Saul's first name (for Joseph), Mordeen's blue gown (traditional for Mary), that Joe is not the father of the Child, and that the Child is born at Christmas. The scene changes are meaningful as Joe and Mordeen wander from place to place, in a sense searching for the inn (which becomes a rather austere hospital room). But once again, the allegory is undercut by unsavory realities: Victor is the father, Mordeen suggests an earlier career as a prostitute, and Joe Saul is a raging, impotent man.

Burning Bright, with its eccentricities of language, setting, characters such as Mordeen or Friend Ed who oscillate unpredictably between good and evil, and odd biblical allusions, is ultimately a reflection of chaos. Steinbeck has created a dark little universe, and the central character—with one foot in hell and the other in heaven—is the human being: here is the "fearful symmetry" referred to in William Blake's poem "The Tiger," from which Steinbeck's title is derived. In a world of shifting scenes and moral conundrums, one cannot rely on old teleologies from a manufactured god; as Steinbeck noted in his **Nobel Prize acceptance speech**, "We must seek in ourselves for the responsibility and the wisdom we once prayed some diety might have."

The moral message of Steinbeck's allegorical play-novelette is that humans are both animal and god; if humans would recognize this chaotic existence, they might survive themselves. That Joe Saul and his family survive the convoluted mess that leads to the Child (a product of the best and worst of humanity) is the positive theme of *Burning Bright*. Norman Cousins praised the message of the Steinbeck's book: "He has written his most mature book, a book which, if carefully and slowly read, can be as rewarding a literary experience as any of us is likely to have for a long time." The form and execution of *Burning Bright*, however, has made it difficult for readers to heed Cousins's advice.

Further Reading: Cousins, Norman. "Hemingway and Steinbeck," *Saturday Review of Literature*. October 28, 1950, 26–27; Kennedy, John S. "John Steinbeck: Life Affirmed and Dissolved." In *Steinbeck and His Critics: A Record of Twenty-Five Years*. Ed. E. W. Tedlock and C. V. Wicker. Albuquerque: University of New Mexico Press, 1957; Lisca, Peter. *John Steinbeck: Nature and Myth*. New York: Crowell, 1978; Railsback, Brian. "The *Bright* Failure: What Are We to Make of Chaos?" In *The Betrayal of Brotherhood in the Work of John Steinbeck*. Ed. Michael J. Meyer. Lewiston, NY: Mellen Press, 2000; Steinbeck, John. "Mr. Steinbeck's Foreword to 'Burning Bright,'" *New York Times*. October 15, 1950, 1; ———. "Critics, Critics, Burning Bright," *Saturday Review of Literature*. November 11, 1950, 20–21; Strong, L. A. G. Rev. of *Burning Bright*, by John Steinbeck, *Spectator*. August 10, 1951, 196.

Brian Railsback

BURNING BRIGHT (TV ADAPTATION) (1959). Produced in 1959 and directed by Curt Conway, this production starred Colleen Dewhurst as **Mordeen** and Myron McCormick and Victor Madden as **Joe Saul** and **Victor**, respectively. **Friend Ed** was played by Dana Elcar. A Broadway Theater Archive play, it was released on DVD in 2003. Details on the DVD are available at http://movies2.nytimes.com/gst/movies/dvd.html?v_id=290006.

BURNS, ROBERT (1759–1796). Eighteenth-century Scottish poet whose work "To a Mouse" provided the title for Steinbeck's ***Of Mice and Men***. Tradition holds that Burns was plowing a field and turned up a mouse's nest, which prompted the lines "But Mousie, thou art no thy-lane, / In proving foresight may be vain: / The best laid schemes o' Mice an' Men / Gang aft agley, / An' lea'e us nought but grief an' pain, / For promis'd joy!" Critics often draw parallels between the situation of Burns's mouse, who has carefully planned a home only to have it suddenly taken away, and the situation of **George Milton** and **Lennie Small** in the novel, whose carefully crafted plans of owning a home of their own are dashed as well.

BURT, WILLIAM C. Member of the Salinas Home Guard in ***East of Eden***, a group of men over fifty who want to join the war effort. He dies while doing push-ups on the armory floor.

BURTON, DOC. In ***In Dubious Battle,*** one of the first characters based on Steinbeck's friend, the marine biologist **Edward F. Ricketts**, especially in the way that Doc Burton expresses Ricketts' **non-teleological** philosophy and rejection of commitments that put "blinders" on people. He takes care of the medical and sanitary needs of the strikers, but he refuses to join the party. His arguments with **Mac** about the differences between the thoughts and actions of individuals and "groupmen" and the possibility of establishing a lasting commune have been the focus of much of the critical discussion of the book, although Steinbeck had said that the novel offered no moral point of view. Burton disappears mysteriously; most interpreters have theorized that he met with foul play, although, having served his purpose, he may simply have gone his way.

Warren French

BYRNE, DON (1889–1928). Popular American author of historical romances who was born in New York but educated in Ireland. Much of Byrne's work relies on romanticized Celtic history. Steinbeck cited Byrne as an early and bad influence on his apprentice writing and claimed to have conquered that influence by writing ***Cup of Gold***.

Further Reading: Benson, Jackson J. *The True Adventures of John Steinbeck, Writer*. New York: Viking, 1984; Steinbeck, John. *Steinbeck: A Life in Letters*. Ed. Elaine Steinbeck and Robert Wallsten. New York: Viking, 1975.

Kevin Hearle

C

"CAB DRIVER DOESN'T GIVE A HOOT, THE" (1956). Article in the *Daily Mail* (4, August 14, 1956) in which Steinbeck addresses public perceptions at the height of the 1956 political convention season. While he notes that most Americans are ambivalent about the candidates until it is time to vote, he tells the story of his cab driver who, when pressed by Steinbeck, concludes that all politicians are crooks.

Eric Skipper

CABELL, JAMES BRANCH (1879–1958). Popular American author of historical romances. His most famous works were set in an idealized medieval world of sophisticated manners. Steinbeck cited Cabell as an early and bad influence on his apprentice writing, and claimed to have conquered that influence by writing ***Cup of Gold***.

Further Reading: Benson, Jackson J. *The True Adventures of John Steinbeck, Writer.* New York: Viking Press, 1984; Steinbeck, John. *Steinbeck: A Life in Letters.* Elaine Steinbeck and Robert Wallsten, eds. New York: Viking Press, 1975.

Kevin Hearle

CAFÉ LA IDA. A bar on **Cannery Row** run by **Wide Ida** in ***Sweet Thursday.***

CAGE, JOHN (1912–1992). During his six-decade career in music, Cage's restless intellect led him down many paths as he experimented with unusual percussion instruments, weird notation, and even silence. Cage was an occasional visitor at the **Pacific Biological Laboratory** in **Monterey**, the business owned by **Edward F. Ricketts**. During the 1940s, possibly through discussions with other artistic individuals at the lab (including Steinbeck, **Joseph Campbell**, Elwood Graham, the **Lovejoys,** and Ricketts himself), Cage became interested in Eastern philosophy, especially Zen, from which he gained a respect for non-intention (see **non-teleological thinking**). He worked to remove creative choice from his compositions, preferring at times to simply employ coin or dice tosses to determine events and intervals. His belief that art was basically something that happened made him a musical parallel to Steinbeck. Cage probably added to Steinbeck's keen interest in and knowledge of musical techniques and how to employ them in the written word.

CALDWELL, ERSKINE (1903–1987). Author contemporary of Steinbeck who was famous for his novels and short stories that revealed the absurd and pitiful poverty of white and black sharecroppers in rural Georgia. He is best known for *Tobacco Road* (1932), *God's Little Acre* (1933), and *You Have Seen Their Faces* (1937). The two met on a trans-Atlantic trip as Steinbeck prepared to research material for his book on **King Arthur**, and they became good friends. Caldwell traveled with Steinbeck to the

Soviet Union during the Cold War as part of a cultural exchange program between the United States and the U.S.S.R. Caldwell had another connection with Steinbeck, since *Tobacco Road* was adapted and rewritten as an extremely successful Broadway production by Jack Kirkland, who also adapted Steinbeck's ***Tortilla Flat*** for the stage.

Further Reading: Benson, Jackson J. *The True Adventures of John Steinbeck, Writer.* New York: Viking, 1984; Parini, Jay. *John Steinbeck: A Biography.* New York: Henry Holt, 1995.

Tracy Michaels

CALVIN, JACK (1901–1985). A writer of children's stories and pulp fiction, as well as a photographer and illustrator, Calvin, like Steinbeck, had attended **Stanford University**. Calvin was a close friend of **Edward F. Ricketts** and may have introduced Ricketts to Steinbeck in 1930. He also introduced Steinbeck to his young protégé, **Ritchie Lovejoy**, an aspiring writer whose work Steinbeck tried to foster. Despite his close relationship to Ricketts (he coauthored ***Between Pacific Tides*** with him in 1939), Calvin was not particularly fond of Steinbeck, perhaps because he envied the success of the younger author. In fact, his reaction to Steinbeck's work was condescending, and he leveled accusations that it was often flimsy and derivative. Despite the negative feedback, Steinbeck and Calvin often met informally to discuss books and writing, and occasionally Calvin was part of the group that gathered at Ricketts' lab. Some critics attribute Calvin's initial hostility to Steinbeck to his belief that the author's ideas for ***The Pastures of Heaven*** actually belonged to Calvin's friend, **Beth Ingels**. Steinbeck grouped Calvin with artists who he claimed didn't take writing seriously, who wrote merely for money, and who saw no dignity in craftsmanship.

Michael J. Meyer

CAMPBELL, JOSEPH (1904–1987). Authority on world and comparative mythology and author of *The Hero With 1000 Faces* (1949) and the multivolume *The Masks of God* (first volume, 1959), Campbell was a member of the group of friends who gathered with Steinbeck and **Edward F. Ricketts** in the latter's **Monterey** lab for drinking, songs, philosophical conversations, experimental discourses, and costume parties. Steinbeck acquired a good deal of useful material from Campbell and often used him as a critical listener or judge of his work, especially for ***To a God Unknown***, which had a significant mythological base. Steinbeck read Fraser's ***The Golden Bough*** (1922) under Campbell's careful tutelage. Erudite discussions between Ricketts, Steinbeck, and Campbell also occurred over other texts, including works by Johann Peter Eckermann, Johann Wolfgang von Goethe, **Edward Gibbon, Carl Jung,** and **Oswald Spengler**. The latter's two volume *Decline of the West* (first volume, 1918) especially drew Campbell's attention with its vision of history as an ever-evolving myth. Campbell's discussions about **Sigmund Freud** and Jung influenced the archetypal characters Steinbeck drew in *To a God Unknown*, especially the Fisher King depiction of **Joseph Wayne**. They may also have affected **"The Snake"** and **"Flight,"** two stories from Steinbeck's ***The Long Valley***.

In 1932, Campbell began an affair with Steinbeck's first wife, **Carol Henning Steinbeck**, creating an emotionally painful time for John as his fragile marriage relationship was tested. According to **Jay Parini**, the affair was broken off abruptly after Campbell realized his mistake and discussed it with his friend, but Steinbeck was devastated by the betrayal. An incurable romantic, Steinbeck ultimately saw the event as destructive of his trust in Carol and a prefigurement of his divorce.

Further Reading: Parini, Jay. *John Steinbeck: A Biography.* New York: Henry Holt, 1995.

Michael J. Meyer

"CAMPING IS FOR THE BIRDS" (1967). Article published in *Popular Science* (190.5, May 1967) in which Steinbeck expresses his dislike for camping via the misadventures of a fictional family.

Eric Skipper

CANDY. In ***Of Mice and Men,*** an old crippled ranch hand, or "swamper," who cleans up around the ranch. He had been working on the ranch before **George Milton** and **Lennie Small** arrive but has been relegated to the bunkhouse after injuring his hand. He has an old dog, which **Carlson** insists on killing. He has saved some money and expresses interest in joining George and Lennie's effort to buy a place of their own. An important scene in the novel is the shooting of Candy's old dog. When Carlson persuades him to kill his dog, Candy feels that one day he himself might be killed when he becomes useless. The shooting of his dog makes him more pessimistic about life and also foreshadows George's execution of Lennie at the end of the story.

Luchen Li

CANEDARIA, ALICIA. In ***Viva Zapata!,*** a maid in the Espejo household who is asked by **Señora Espejo** to bring chocolate after **Emiliano**'s proposal of marriage to **Josefa Espejo** has been accepted.

CANNERY ROW. During the 1930s and 1940s, a rundown district in **Monterey,** California, that served as the setting for two of Steinbeck's novels: ***Cannery Row*** and ***Sweet Thursday.*** Steinbeck draws highly sympathetic portraits of the loafers, hookers, pimps, and assorted social outcasts of this area. In fact, he frequently shows them to surpass in natural goodness the staid members of Monterey's middle class, whose pretensions of moral superiority fail to conceal their underlying greed and hypocrisy.

CANNERY ROW **(NOVEL)** (1945). Steinbeck's sixth novel, published in 1945, is a fictional application of the author's ecological views of human behavior and frequently cited by scholars as among his very best works. Set on the street in **Monterey** that gives the book its name, the novel examines the old fish-processing neighborhood. The novel's opening declares Steinbeck's intent, invoking his experience collecting marine animals. **Jackson J. Benson** goes so far as to say that *Cannery Row* is "a fictionalized version" of ***Sea of Cortez***. Alternating biblical language, the language of heroic myth, and **non-teleological** observation applied often for comic effect, the novel alternates a plot that has an overall comic nature with moments of great pathos and tragedy.

The plot's central thread begins when a lovable bum named **Mack** decides that he and his "boys," who live in a shack that has been grandiosely christened **The Palace Flophouse and Grill,** decide they want to have a party for **Doc** (another of Steinbeck's fictionalized versions of **Edward F. Ricketts**). Like **Danny** in ***Tortilla Flat,*** Mack has often been likened to **King Arthur**, whereas his "boys" have been compared to mock-knights and the Palace Flophouse to Camelot. The Arthur/Mack connection is strengthened in ***Sweet Thursday,*** the sequel to *Cannery Row.*

In *Cannery Row,* Mack and his knights errant have no money to stage the planned festivities for Doc. After considering getting work (a suggestion that is roundly dismissed by the group), they approach Doc, who eventually agrees to pay the men five cents each for frogs, which Doc will then embalm and sell as specimens. The men borrow a truck from the local grocer **Lee Chong,** who is also their landlord, on the condition that they get the truck in working order. They embark on a frog hunting expedition that is comic both in tone and incident—filching chickens, getting progressively drunker, and then having one of the most successful frog-catching expeditions in "frog history." The men make a triumphant return to **Cannery Row** and want to celebrate their victory over frogdom, but find they lack the funds for a fiesta. Mack approaches Lee Chong, and the two create a barter system that makes the frogs into currency.

The story line is punctuated by separate chapters that give brief life stories of people on the Row; usually these tales are sad, tragic, or bittersweet. These stories include the tale of Horace Abbeville, whose mounting debts led him to deed a building to Lee Chong (which eventually becomes the Palace Flophouse and Grill) and who eventually commits suicide; of a mentally handicapped child named **Frankie** who hangs around Doc's lab and whose kindhearted attempts to be helpful result in his own demise; of **Henri the painter**, whose name was not Henri, who was not French, and who was not really a painter—a man whose life's work seemed to be building a boat, though he feared the water; of **Mary Talbot**, who was poor but nevertheless managed to throw elaborate teas for the cats in her neighborhood; of a boy named **Joey,** whose father committed suicide by taking rat poison and who must endure the taunts of other boys his age as a result. These stories, as described in the preface to the novel, are observed, collected, and reported in much the same way as biological specimens were examined in *Sea of Cortez*.

While Mack and the boys have been questing across the countryside in a pickup truck, relentlessly pursuing their frog quarry, Doc heads south on a collecting expedition. The expedition is successful, but during it he discovers the dead body of a beautiful girl. In Doc's absence, Mack and the boys have prepared for the party, which is attended by all of the denizens of the Row. Long before the guest of honor arrives, the revelers have gotten out of hand and a fight has ensued. Doc arrives to find his place badly damaged. Mack and the boys are disgraced, a "black gloom" settles over them and the Palace, and matters remain thus until the puppy, Darling, takes ill and Mack and the boys are forced to go visit Doc for help.

Meanwhile, some sort of "benignant influence" begins to affect all of the inhabitants, from the humans to the sea lions. Wanting to make amends, Mack plans a second party, hoping to surprise Doc for his birthday. The growth of the second party is traced in terms of biology: Mack and the boys' planning is "the stone dropped in the pool" and "the impulse" sends out "ripples to all of Cannery Row." Before long, all of the inhabitants learn of the party and plan on various presents. Doc gets wind of the party and makes his own preparations, which include removing the breakables and providing food, because he is confident that the guests will remember to bring alcohol but will not think about things to eat.

This second, organic party is a great success, although Doc spends as much time cooking and caring for his guests as he does enjoying it. At **Dora Flood**'s request for nice music, Doc plays recordings of Monteverdi. Feeling the specialness of the moment, Doc takes out a translation of the Sanskrit poem "Black Marigolds" and recites from it. The guests are moved to "sweet sadness," until a group of tuna boat fishermen enters and a glorious fight breaks out, even the police who come to break up the fight wind up joining the party.

The next morning a tired Doc awakens, still hearing music in his head, and puts a record on, cleaning up as he listens. He picks up the copy of "Black Marigolds" and reads from it again. Not only is the novel Steinbeck's most poetic, the thematic and plot resolution actually resides within a poem. **Warren French** calls the novel "a defense of poetry."

The initial reviews of *Cannery Row* were almost uniformly negative. A reviewer for the *New York Times* wrote, "This little tribute to a waterfront block in Monterey and its indecorous inhabitants has some of the Steinbeck mannerisms, much of the Steinbeck charm and simple felicity of expression, but it is as transparent as a cobweb." A reviewer for the *Nation* dismissed the book as "cheap, fancy, and false." The *New York Times Book Review* declared it "inconsequential and . . . pretentious." The *Boston Globe*'s reviewer pronounced the work "a terrible disappointment." The negative reviews are typical of the post–World War II criticism that characterized reaction to Steinbeck's work, a pattern of commentary about Steinbeck's work that **John Ditsky** once lamented as "cookie cutter criticism" that took Steinbeck's "decline" as an *a priori* assumption.

The novel's reputation has benefited enormously from serious critical study, and in marked contrast to the reviews, *Cannery Row*'s present critical reputation is very positive. Less than five years after the novel's initial publication, Frederick Bracher, writing in *The Pacific Spectator*, was content to analyze the work on its own terms. He was one of the first to draw comparisons between the world view espoused in *Sea of Cortez* and the novelistic method of *Cannery Row*, praising Doc for his "non-teleological virtue," which is defined as "the ability to see what 'is' . . . with 'the love and understanding of instant acceptance.'" Warren French notes that "the novel is about the man who has learned with the assistance of art to triumph over his immediate sensations and surroundings, to move from Monterey to 'the cosmic Monterey.'"

Howard Levant says the book shows "the creative depth and force of Steinbeck's fictive powers at their best." **John H. Timmerman** treats the three *Cannery Row* novels as a unified body of work (he includes *Tortilla Flat* and *Sweet Thursday*), meditates on the nature of comedy, and concludes that the "comedy of the novel is charged with human-animal energy and spirit but ultimately acquires a grim aspect. Civilization, a term Steinbeck uses freely for both a technological-materialistic society and for the darker side of man lurking along the ocean bottom of his spirit, always encroaches on human affairs." Emphasizing the connection between *Cannery Row* and Steinbeck's most important work of nonfiction, Jackson J. Benson notes that the narrative portion of *Sea of Cortez* is "the foundation for the novel" and that *Cannery Row* "may be the only thoroughly non-teleological novel ever written." Despite its initial reception, Steinbeck critics now tend to see the novel as among his best works.

Further Reading: Benson, Jackson J. *The True Adventures of John Steinbeck, Writer.* New York: Viking, 1983; French, Warren. *John Steinbeck.* Rev. ed. Boston: Twayne/G.K. Hall, 1975; Levant, Howard. *The Novels of John Steinbeck: A Critical Study.* Introduction by Warren French. Columbia: University of Missouri Press, 1974; Crisler, Jesse S., Joseph R. McElrath, Jr., and Susan Shillingslaw, eds. *John Steinbeck: The Contemporary Reviews.* New York: Cambridge University Press, 1996; Railsback, Brian. "Dreams of an Elegant Universe on Cannery Row." *Beyond Boundaries: Rereading John Steinbeck.* Ed. Susan Shillinglaw and Kevin Hearle. Tuscaloosa: University of Alabama Press, 2002; Timmerman, John H. *John Steinbeck's Fiction: The Aesthetics of the Road Taken.* Norman: University of Oklahoma Press, 1986.

Charles Etheridge, Jr.

CANNERY ROW* (FILM)** (1982). A film version of ***Cannery Row, directed by David Ward and narrated by Steinbeck's friend **John Huston**, was released by MGM in February 1982. Despite its title, the film draws primarily on the events of ***Sweet Thursday***, the romantic plotline of the sequel providing a more suitable vehicle for a big-studio release.

In spite of solid performances by Nick Nolte as **Doc** and Debra Winger as **Suzy** (from *Sweet Thursday*), the film is not fully successful as an adaptation. In writing the script, Ward made some startling departures from the sources, and they damage the film's credibility. The most confusing aspect of the script is the characterization of Doc. In an apparent attempt to make Doc a more popular figure in an era of athletic hero worship, Ward converts Doc into a former big-league pitcher whose emotional malaise derives from his guilt at having accidentally beaned an opposing batter, who turns out to be **the Seer.** Yet this washed-up pitcher, like Steinbeck's Doc, has improbably become a scientist with a PhD in marine biology. Although the acting, production design, and cinematography are impressive, Ward's unfaithfulness to his sources blurs the thematic focus and harms the credibility of the film.

Despite the drawing power of its stars, *Cannery Row* received mixed reviews and was a commercial failure, falling far short of earning back its $11.3 million cost.

Further Reading: Morsberger, Robert E. "*Cannery Row* Revisited." *Steinbeck Quarterly* 16 (Summer–Fall 1983): 89–95.

Joseph Millichap

CAPA, ROBERT (1913–1954). War photojournalist. Born in Budapest, Hungary as Andre Erno Friedman, Capa spent most of his life traveling from war to war, documenting scenes of terror, destruction, and hope among the bombed-out ruins of Spain, China, and Israel. The handsome and celebrated photographer rubbed elbows with famous politicians, writers (including **Ernest Hemingway**), and film stars, and had a brief affair with Ingrid Bergman. Despite this cosmopolitan lifestyle, the majority of Capa's images focus on the bleak landscapes he witnessed during the turmoil of the 1930s, 40s, and 50s.

Capa met Steinbeck during World War II, when they shared a room in an Algiers hotel with a dozen other war correspondents awaiting the Allied invasion of Italy. This meeting was brief, however, and their friendship did not begin until later, in March 1947, when they met again at the bar of a New York hotel. Both men were at an unhappy stage of their lives (Steinbeck's marriage to his second wife **Gwyndolyn Conger Steinbeck** was floundering, and his work was not going well; Capa had just broken up with Bergman and was gambling large amounts of money away), but Steinbeck found Capa's sense of humor refreshing. Steinbeck was thinking about visiting the Soviet Union, and when Capa suggested a joint trip and possible collaboration on a book, Steinbeck immediately agreed.

The two arrived in Moscow on July 31, 1947. Although their trip was carefully monitored and limited, Steinbeck's popularity in the USSR—coupled with Soviet hopes for positive propaganda—garnered Capa and Steinbeck far greater access to people and sites than was available to other Western writers and photographers. The trip resulted in the publication of ***A Russian Journal***, both as a book and a syndicated newspaper serial. Unfortunately, the *Journal* pleased neither the Soviet bureaucracy (criticized by Steinbeck) nor the increasingly anti-Soviet U.S. government.

Steinbeck and Capa remained good friends until Capa's death, although they had occasional disagreements over disparities in pay for work from the Soviet trip—Capa was paid more by *The Ladies' Home Journal* for his photos than Steinbeck was paid for his accompanying text, although Steinbeck was paid more for the newspaper syndication rights. The two joined radio director Henry S. White in founding World Video, a television production company. That move deepened their personal animosities, because Steinbeck and White placed unrealistic expectations on Capa to direct and produce a fashion series of eight programs in six weeks. Eventually, Steinbeck and Capa sold their stock and resigned, becoming fast friends once more.

Capa had changed his name in 1936 to fit an invented persona he used to sell his photographs of the Spanish Civil War. He became an American citizen in 1946, and in 1947 he co-founded Magnum, a photography cooperative that included Henri Cartier-Bresson. On assignment from *Life* magazine to cover the French Indochina War, Capa stepped on a land mine while traveling with a French convoy and was killed. Steinbeck, then waiting to meet Capa in Paris, took the news very hard, for by then the photographer had become a very close friend.

Further Reading: Steinbeck, John. *A Russian Journal* (1948). New York: Penguin Books, 1999; Steinbeck, John. "Robert Capa: An Appreciation," *Photography.* September, 1954, 48–53; Stojko, Wolodymyr and Wolodymyr Serhiychuk. "John Steinbeck in Ukraine: What the Secret Soviet Archives Reveal." *The Ukrainian Quarterly* 51 (1995): 62–76; Whelan, Richard. *Robert Capa: A Biography.* New York: Alfred A. Knopf, 1985.

Kirstin Ringelberg

CAPOTE, TRUMAN (1924–1984). American author known for various works of fiction such as *Other Voices, Other Rooms*

(1948), *The Grass Harp* (1951), and *Breakfast at Tiffany's* (1958). In 1966, Capote entered the world of nonfiction with the publication of the controversial *In Cold Blood*. Steinbeck read two of Capote's works: *The Grass Harp* and *Other Voices, Other Rooms*. Steinbeck disliked Capote's writing, which he labeled as decadent. According to **Warren French**, Steinbeck's character **Joe Elegant,** of ***Sweet Thursday,*** was based on a publicity photo of Capote taken for *Other Voices, Other Rooms*.

CAPP, AL (1909–1979). Celebrated creator of the *Li'l Abner* comic strip, which ran in daily newspapers from 1934 to 1977. Considered one of the most important comics of its time, *L'il Abner* featured "hillbilly" characters who ridiculed the upper echelons of society. The strip featured a subtle sophistication that was consistently downplayed by Capp's ironic use of southern dialect. Steinbeck wrote a generous introduction to Capp's compilation titled *The World of Li'l Abner* (1953). In the introduction, Steinbeck argued against critical highbrow conceptualizations of art, insisting instead that literature is first and foremost what people read, and that the role of literature and art was to instruct changes and otherwise perform a criticism of society.

Brian Niro

CAPTAIN OF RURALES. In ***Viva Zapata!***, he is the one who orders his men to capture Emiliano Zapata. The captain indicates that he is under orders to bring Zapata in.

CARADOS, KING. One of the eleven rebel kings of the North defeated by **Arthur** at Bedgrayne in ***The Acts of King Arthur***; later killed by **Sir Lancelot**.

CARLSON. A powerful and big-stomached ranch hand in ***Of Mice and Men***. He is described as a blunt and unfeeling man who insists on shooting **Candy's** aged sheep dog. He encourages **Slim** to give one of his pups to Candy in an attempt to convince the old swamper to kill his aged and ailing pet. Having outlived its usefulness, the dog has become an annoyance to the men who occupy the bunkhouse. Carlson tells Candy, "If you want me to, I'll put the old devil out of his misery right now and get it over with. Ain't nothing left for him. Can't eat, can't see, can't even walk without hurtin." This episode anticipates George's mercy killing of Lennie at the conclusion of the novel. It is Carlson's Luger that George uses to kill Lennie at the end. *See also* **Milton, George**; **Small, Lennie**.

Luchen Li

CARMEL-BY-THE-SEA (CARMEL). Small seaside village in California near the most important places in Steinbeck's early years: **Monterey**, **Pacific Grove**, and **Salinas**. In the 1920s and 30s, Carmel—much as it is to this day—was a place for liberal intellectuals, writers, and artists. Steinbeck saw author **Jack Calvin** there, as well as actor **Charlie Chaplin**, political activist **Francis Whitaker**, poet **Robinson Jeffers**, and famous muckraker and author **Lincoln Steffens**. In addition, he first encountered his third wife, **Elaine Anderson Scott**, while she stayed at Carmel's Pine Inn.

CARRADINE, JOHN (1906–1988). Gaunt character actor who played **Jim Casy** in **John Ford's** 1940 movie of ***The Grapes of Wrath*** and again on stage in a touring version adapted and directed by **William Adams**. Carradine had some distinguished roles in the 1930s and 40s but later often appeared in B-grade horror films. He did some of his best work in eight films directed by John Ford, including *The Hurricane* (1937), *Stagecoach* (1939), *Drums Along the Mohawk* (1939), and *The Man Who Shot Liberty Valance* (1962).

CARRIAGA, ALBERTO. Father of little **Johnny Carriaga** in ***Sweet Thursday***. He allows **Mack** and the boys to use his first-born son at their masquerade for a fee of sixty-two cents, enough to buy himself a gallon of wine.

CARRIAGA, JOHNNY. A streetwise youth hired by **Mack** and the boys in ***Sweet Thursday*** to play Cupid at their masquerade party. However, Johnny gets out of control and shoots his rubber-tipped arrows with abandon, including one that strikes a lantern, causing it to crash in flames and set fire to the costumes of three partiers. Although Steinbeck has often been accused of sentimentality, he rarely creates romanticized portraits of the children in his fiction. The wild, mouthy Johnny Carriaga is one of many troublemaking youths in Steinbeck's work.

CARROLL, LEWIS (1832–1898). A pseudonym for Victorian author Charles Dodgson, whose major works included *Alice's Adventures in Wonderland* (1865) and *Through the Looking Glass* (1871). Steinbeck employed frequent literary allusions to these works in ***East of Eden,*** where the character **Cathy Ames** associates herself with Alice. Especially relevant is Cathy's desire to disappear at the end of the novel, to become smaller and smaller and eventually vanish from sight. When combined with her earlier fascination with Lewis' text, this event offers a clear parallel to Alice's use of mushrooms and liquids in order to grow and shrink and thus follow the White Rabbit (perhaps associated with Cathy's addiction to drugs and sex in *East of Eden*).

Michael J. Meyer

CARSON, PIMPLES (ALSO KNOWN AS "KIT," OR ED). In ***The Wayward Bus***, a seventeen-year-old apprentice mechanic who works at **Juan Chicoy's** business (a combination of garage/lunchroom/bus station) in **Rebel Corners**, California. Pimples epitomizes the acne-ravaged, concupiscent adolescent. Steinbeck makes it clear that Pimples views Juan Chicoy as a role model and desires his approval.

On the morning of the bus trip, two events loom large to him. The first is Juan's tacit agreement to call him "Kit" Carson, thus recognizing that he possesses a potential for heroic rather than inconsequential stature. The second is the appearance of **Camille Oaks**, a woman of pinup beauty and proportions, who emits a powerful sexual magnetism that excites the attentions of virtually every male she encounters. Recognizing Pimples' response to Camille, Juan invites him to join her and the other passengers on the bus trip to **San Juan de la Cruz**. Later, on a desolate detour necessitated by a flooding river, Juan mires the bus and elevates Pimples' stature by leaving him in charge. However, his rise in station and growing confidence are short-lived. Recognizing that Camille is far beyond his sexual reach, Pimples instead tries to force his attentions on **Norma**, a waitress in the Chicoys' lunchroom who quit earlier in the day. When he is violently rejected, his heroic dream bursts.

Pimples is an important figure in the novel because he embodies the diminution of modern American character. Unlike the Carson of frontier fame, Pimples struggles simply to awake in the morning, and he spends the remainder of the day in menial attempts to discover ways to worm another piece of pie out of **Alice Chicoy**. Pimples is in fact a character marred by excess—gustatory as well as sexual—and his fumbling, yet violent pawing of Norma near the novel's end leaves little doubt that the frontier hero won't be found on this bus.

Christopher S. Busch

"CASE HISTORY" (1934). Early 1934 version of the short story, **"The Vigilante."** John Ramsey returns from the war, and despite his hatred of the events he finds he misses the huge design the war provided for his life. He hungers to belong to a group, to join a phalanx. He finds solace in a mob and eventually participates in a lynching. The original draft discusses Steinbeck's concept of a phalanx. After three failed attempts, Steinbeck decided to change the emphasis from a man looking for a phalanx to a man deprived of a phalanx. In the revision, a story included in ***The Long Valley,*** the lynching becomes the central focus. Steinbeck's attempts to portray a lynching were probably inspired by the vigilante hanging of two kidnap/murder suspects outside the San Jose jail in November 1933.

Michael J. Meyer

CASY, JIM. A former Burning Bush preacher, Jim Casy meets **Tom Joad** in ***The Grapes of Wrath***, shortly after Tom is released from prison. To this congregation of one, Casy relates his struggle to regain the original "sperit" that motivated him in the past. Casy has had a hard time separating the sensual pleasures of life (sex) from the intensity of the rewards of the spirit (faith in a higher power). Attempting to sort out his paradoxical sexual sinning after each religious revival meeting, Casy—like Christ—isolates himself in the wilderness, hoping to discover the true nature of his faith. He has a Thoreauvian/Emersonian revelation that the Holy Spirit is just love—love for people.

After meeting **Muley Graves**, Casy discovers that he is not the only one who has discovered universal brotherhood during a struggle in the wilderness. Later he acknowledges that perhaps he can preach again, and that maybe there's a place for preachers because the need of the growing migrant population is so great.

Casy then follows Tom Joad home and is accepted as part of the tight group traveling from the wasteland of Oklahoma to the Eden of California. Willing to perform even so-called women's work, and thereby denying the correctness of gender labeling of tasks, he is readily seen as practicing the equality he preaches. On the road, Casy is very sensitive to the migrant society he confronts, comparing its movement to his own acquisition of knowledge. Eventually he becomes the Joads' spiritual advisor, saying the Lord's Prayer over **Granpa Joad** and officiating when the old man dies from a stroke. Both times Casy suggests a lack of belief in sin, first by leaving out the "forgive us our trespasses" section of the famous prayer and then by using his eulogy to assert once again that "all that lives is holy."

As the journey continues, Casy worries about his physical lust as evidence of his own selfishness and his inability to live up to his new creed, but he also continues to learn from those around him, including **Sairy Wilson** and **Uncle John**. By the time the Joads reach California, Casy's insight and his knowledge have solidified. His speech about the difference between the rich and the poor reveals his understanding that true riches lie not in having money and possessions but in the self, and in the willingness of the self to give to others out of its own richness.

At the Hooverville, Casy demonstrates just such an ability by taking the blame for Tom's tripping of the deputy and for the flight of **Floyd Knowles**. Though Casy does enter the fight by kicking the deputy into unconsciousness, he convinces the others to let him take full blame, thus keeping Tom's parole violation from being discovered. Casy's calm reaction and acceptance of his arrest allow him to protest the laws of the Establishment in a way first advocated by **Thoreau** in "Civil Disobedience." As he is led off to jail, Casy also displays a curious look of conquest, indicating his superior position despite his confinement.

Upon his release, Casy becomes a union organizer, and he rejoins the Joads during the Hooper Ranch uprising over inadequate wages. He is beaten to death by a vigilante, a strikebreaker hired by the growers. If his initials and his role as the herald of a new consciousness had not been sufficient to suggest the Christlike imagery being employed by Steinbeck, this final section of chapter 26—where Casy is shown to possess a shining appearance and to repeat the Savior's last words on the cross ("You don' know what you're doin'.")—strongly suggests the desired analogue.

As a vision-pierced prophet, Casy serves as a wedge to open up the Joads, baptizing Tom in the manner of John the Baptist and recalling to Tom's consciousness his earlier label as "Jesus Meek," a recognition that will establish him as the one who will continue to spread Casy's "gospel." Casy also helps several of the family members to break down their beliefs in traditional social customs and mores and to establish new insights about being human.

Casy's paradoxical embracing of Christian commitment with a sensual celebration of the life force will evidently continue after his death in the actions of **Ma Joad**, Tom, and **Rosasharn**. Moving from judgmental Calvinistic tenets to the broader transcendental concepts espoused by Thoreau and **Emerson**, Casy is Steinbeck's call for a shift away from wrath and anger to the more positive goals of self-sacrifice and sharing as solutions to the people's greatest problems.

Michael J. Meyer

CAT. In ***East of Eden***, the bartender in Niagara Falls, where **Adam Trask** travels after his discharge in 1885. Cat explains to Adam that he got his nickname from the shape of a strawberry mark on his forehead, and Adam comments that his brother, **Charles Trask**, also has a scar on his forehead. This mark is another instance of the "Cain sign" that is present on the forehead of **Cathy Ames** and is a vital part of the biblical myth that Steinbeck uses as a controlling element of his plot.

CATHCART, ROBERT. Along with **Webster Street** and **"Dook" Sheffield**, Cathcart was one of Steinbeck's friends while he attended **Stanford University**. Cathcart was a member of the English Club and often looked to the older Steinbeck for critical response to his own writing. The two often exchanged letters, in which Steinbeck offered speculation and reflection about his own stylistic experimentation. Steinbeck's most famous letter to Cathcart was written in 1929. In it he praises the young writer's potential and notes his fascination with paradox, a fascination Steinbeck seems to share.

CATHER, WILLA (1876–1947). American author who wrote *My Antonia* (1918), one in a series of books that dealt with the life of immigrants in the Midwest. Steinbeck owned copies of her novels, *Death Comes for the Archbishop* (1927), *My Antonia*, *O Pioneers* (1913), and *The Professor's House* (1925). In the 1975 edition of *John Steinbeck*, **Warren French** points to remarkable similarities in the careers of the two writers.

In the winter and spring of 1925, Steinbeck returned to **Stanford University**, where he continued to meet with members of the English Club. **Margery Bailey**, **John Breck** (Elizabeth Anderson), and Steinbeck would meet at Breck's house to smoke, drink, and discuss authors of the day, including Willa Cather, whose *The Professor's House* was published that year.

Janet L. Flood

CATHY. **Joe Saul's** deceased wife in ***Burning Bright***.

CAVALIER, THE. **Henry Morgan's** escort for his triumphal entry into Port Royal, in ***Cup of Gold***.

CENTRAL COMMITTEE AT WEEDPATCH CAMP. In ***The Grapes of Wrath***, depicted as godlike figures who run Weedpatch Camp (**Arvin Sanitary Camp**) without the taint of corruption that infects the outside world, these men (**Jim Rawley**, **Ezra Huston**, and **Willie Eaton**) are admired by the entire **Joad** clan. The committee keeps the camp an ideal place to live, and their anticipation of outside trouble also prevents a major clash at the square dance, an arranged fight that could have given local California authorities the opportunity to invade the camp and suggest its breakup for not being able to maintain order.

CERVANTES, MIGUEL DE (1547–1616). Miguel de Cervantes, the Spanish novelist and author of *Don Quixote*, influenced John Steinbeck in much the same way as Sir Thomas Malory and ***Morte D'Arthur*** did. Both provided a code of chivalry and sense of moral purpose that profoundly affected the themes of Steinbeck's later works. His focus on integrity and individual moral responsibility in ***Viva Zapata!***, ***East of Eden***, ***The***

Winter of Our Discontent, and ***Travels with Charley*** has much of its genesis in Cervantes's errant knight attacking windmills and saving damsels in distress.

Steinbeck loved the writing of Cervantes, especially *Don Quixote*, so much that near the end of his life he was reading the text in the original Old Spanish. When his friend and editor **Pascal Covici** gave him a new edition as a gift, John responded to his wife **Elaine Scott Steinbeck**, "[This] book is not an attack on knight errantry but a celebration of the human spirit." Steinbeck later tried to write a modern version of *Don Quixote* set in the American West—his novel ***Don Keehan***—but after several drafts he abandoned the effort as unsatisfactory. Still, as with "L'Affaire Lettuceberg," an aborted forerunner to ***The Grapes of Wrath***, his struggles with *Don Keehan* served as a preliminary warm-up for his last novel, ***The Winter of Our Discontent***, and its stricken knight, **Ethan Hawley**.

Ultimately the appeal of Cervantes and the knight's code of chivalry was personal. John Steinbeck saw Don Quixote as a symbol of himself, and the novel's morally arid time as a mirror of mid-twentieth-century America. Thus, Steinbeck described ***The Wayward Bus*** as something like the "*Don Quixote* of Mexico," traveled to Spain and La Mancha in 1954 out of a special affinity for the place, and began his journey to rediscover the soul of America in a camper he affectionately christened **Rocinante.** The fruits of this journey (Operation Windmill, as he called it) eventually found expression in ***Travels with Charley.*** To the very end, the romantic ideals expressed in the work of Miguel de Cervantes stoked the moral and artistic imagination of John Steinbeck.

Stephen K. George

CHAMBERS, PAT. A strike organizer who in 1933 became involved in the civil rights complaint of some migrant workers at the **Tagus Ranch** in California. According to Chambers, the migrant workers at the ranch had worked for three or four seasons harvesting the peach crops, upon which the ranch was financially dependent, without pay. Chambers was made aware of this problem via a friend who had contact with the ranch. Chambers managed to sneak his way into the camp to make contact with the workers. He encouraged the workers to form a union, and then chose leaders within the camp to devise an organized strike. Chambers warned the workers that once the strike commenced, the ranch would probably cut their food rations, so they began to store up food in advance to enable them to hold out for a longer period of time. Time was what the ranch did not have, because peach crops spoil easily; consequently, an agreement was reached and the workers won their wages as well as higher pay.

In an effort to recover from the strike, the Tagus Ranch removed its peach crops and planted cotton. As a result, a cotton strike began to brew. The Cannery and Agricultural Workers' Industrial Union (CAWIU) dispatched **Caroline Decker** to join Pat Chambers and help organize the workers' cause. Days of violence ensued. Strikers were beaten, shot at, and killed. Finally, government intervention between the growers and the strikers brought an end to the ordeal. Chambers and Decker were arrested for criminal syndicalism under California's antiunion law.

Steinbeck first came into contact with the situation in 1934 when he met Cicil McKiddy, who had been involved in the cotton strike with Chambers and Decker. Steinbeck obtained much of the information about the strike from McKiddy's testimony, and it became a major source of inspiration behind the writing of ***In Dubious Battle.*** Steinbeck altered the Tagus Ranch story into a fictitious account of a strike to suit the theme of the novel, but the character of **Mac** in the novel was based on the profile of Chambers that Steinbeck had gathered from McKiddy. Although it is not clear that Steinbeck ever met Chambers, Chambers did read *In Dubious Battle*. Chambers disliked Steinbeck's profile of him, claiming that Steinbeck based Mac's organization on manipulation rather than on the spirit of a united brotherhood.

Further Reading: Benson, Jackson J. *The True Adventures of John Steinbeck*. New York: Viking, 1984.

CHANEY, LON JR. (1906–1973). Film actor whose finest performance was as **Lennie Small** in the 1939 version of ***Of Mice and Men***. Thereafter he was type-cast as monsters (the Wolf Man, the Mummy, and Frankenstein's monster) in B-grade horror films, though he also played small character roles in innumerable films, including *High Noon* (1952) and *The Defiant Ones* (1958). Critics unanimously applauded his performance as Lennie, which *Newsweek* called "compelling."

CHAPLIN, CHARLIE [SIR CHARLES SPENCER] (1889–1977). A famous comedian and early film star, Chaplin admired Steinbeck's writing and met him at Los Gatos in August of 1938, while Steinbeck was writing ***The Grapes of Wrath***. Chaplin rented a home in nearby Pebble Beach, and the two became friends—they shared many political views. Chaplin was also romantically linked with Geraldine Spreckels, of the **Spreckels Sugar Company** family, who had employed Steinbeck in his youth. After his divorce from his first wife, **Carol Henning Steinbeck,** Steinbeck was linked romantically with **Paulette Goddard**, who lived with Chaplin and was married to another Hollywood friend, **Burgess Meredith**.

Paul M. Blobaum

CHAPPELL, ED. A significant minor character and friend of **Peter Randall** in **"The Harness"** to whom Peter reveals his secrets and his psychological condition. Although he drinks with Peter on the night of **Emma Randall**'s funeral and becomes the confidant that Peter so clearly needs, Ed sees habit and stability as a cure for whatever ails Peter.

CHAPPELL, MRS. In **"The Harness,"** she is the wife of **Ed Chappell**, the sounding board and voice of reason who exists in striking contrast to the tormented **Peter Randall** and even to his long-suffering wife, **Emma**. Mrs. Chappell reflects the attitude of the community that views hard work as not only a panacea for sorrow, but as a goal in and of itself.

CHARLEY. Steinbeck's faithful traveling companion in ***Travels with Charley***. *Charles le Chien* (Charley the Dog) was a giant "blue" poodle. One of Steinbeck's favorite authors was **Robert Louis Stevenson**, whose travelogue, *Travels with a Donkey in the Cevennes* (1879), served as Steinbeck's model for his own book. Charley is to Steinbeck as Sancho Panza was to Don Quixote.

CHARRO. In the narrative Steinbeck wrote to accompany ***Viva Zapata!***, the term is defined as "cowboy." The charros were "slightly above" the peasant and "usually of Mestizo blood." The charro in *Zapata* appears in the midst of the delegation that has arrived to meet with **Emiliano Zapata** to complain about **Eufemio**, Emiliano's brother and fellow revolutionary.

"CHEERLEADERS" (CHEERLADIES). In Part Four of ***Travels with Charley***, Steinbeck encounters a group of white mothers who are protesting the integration of the public schools in New Orleans. The vulgar, hateful language the mothers direct at the black school children makes Steinbeck "sick with nausea" and hastens his return home to Sag Harbor; it is one of the most distressing scenes described in the book.

CHICOY, ALICE. In ***The Wayward Bus***, the wife of **Juan Chicoy** and co-operator of their garage/lunchroom/bus station located in **Rebel Corners**, California. Alice is responsible for running the lunchroom. She views the world from a totally self-centered perspective, and is concerned with others only to the extent that they "augment or take away from her immediate life." Juan figures largest in her life, and she is fearful that her aging body and waning sexual attractiveness will not be enough to hold him. She much prefers Juan's infrequent anger—and even violence—which she takes as an indication of his love for and interest in her, to his overt demonstrations of kindness, which she feels are a sign of his losing interest in her.

Alice is the only significant character in the novel who does not participate in the bus journey from Rebel Corners to **San Juan de la Cruz**. Instead, she uses the opportunity to be alone at the lunchroom to indulge in a daylong bender, in part prompted by Juan's reaction to one of the passengers, the beautiful **Camille Oaks**. Alice wages an ongoing war against houseflies entering the lunchroom. On the day of the bus trip, her drunken efforts to kill a solitary fly—both comic and grotesque—end with the destruction of the interior of the lunchroom and her lapse into defeated unconsciousness.

Christopher S. Busch and Bradd Burningham

CHICOY, JUAN. In *The Wayward Bus*, the owner of a franchise to provide bus service from **Rebel Corners** to **San Juan de la Cruz** and proprietor of the garage/lunchroom/bus station located at Rebel Corners, California. Married to **Alice Chicoy**, Juan is described as a handsome, steady man—Mexican and Irish—who is about fifty years old. He is a first-rate mechanic. Juan's central importance in this highly allegorical novel is underlined not only by his initials (J[esus] C[hrist]), but by this early description: "he was a man and there aren't very many of them, as Alice Chicoy had found out. There aren't very many of them in the world, as everybody finds out sooner or later." Juan's religiosity is more pagan and personal than Christian and formal, however. He has renamed his bus "Sweetheart" from its original *el Gran Poder de Jesus* (the great power of Christ).

Chicoy represents much of what Steinbeck admires in a man: he is virile, mechanically adept, and independent, both of his wife's demands and of his fiduciary duties as holder of the bus franchise. Yet, as **Jackson J. Benson** notes in his biography of Steinbeck, Chicoy—like Steinbeck's first protagonist **Henry Morgan** (*Cup of Gold*)—suffers from a "distant and . . . unsympathetic presentation" by Steinbeck. Through much of the novel, Juan's inner thoughts become Steinbeck's subject. Finding himself increasingly disgusted by Alice's alcohol-induced moods and the passenger's inane demands, Juan dreams of his youth and contemplates leaving his wife, Alice, in particular, but also the business, and perhaps the whole of contemporary America as it is portrayed and understood by Steinbeck.

On a perilous detour around a flooded area during the eventful bus journey, Juan makes a bargain with himself: should the bus mire, he will simply walk away from it and continue on to Mexico. Juan intentionally disables the bus in axle-deep mud and walks away, ostensibly for help but actually to recapture his freedom. He falls asleep in the Hawkins barn, where young **Mildred Pritchard**, another freedom-seeker, discovers him, and they have intercourse. Despite Mildred's encouragement of his quest for freedom, he returns to the bus. Although his eventual sacrifice and demonstration of personal integrity are hardly Christlike, he does finally decide to return—to the bus, to the passengers, and presumably to his life with Alice. In the modern day America that Steinbeck increasingly portrayed (especially in his later novels) as having shrunken, diminished, and corrupted the human soul and spirit, such acts and characters are presented not so much as heroic, but simply as good as America is capable of getting.

Brad Burningham and Christopher S. Busch

CHILD, THE. In *Burning Bright*, the Child is **Mordeen's** infant son fathered by **Victor**, though she is married to the impotent **Joe Saul**. Mordeen uses Victor because she wants a child for Saul and knows that he cannot father one. "the Child" is the title of the second scene of the play-novelette's third act, in which the infant appears. Mordeen is distraught by what she has done to conceive the Child, and she fears she has lost Saul's love (he has learned who the father is). But in the final scene, Saul's love for the Child overcomes his anger and her grief. The Child represents the continuance not only of Saul's line, but of the human race. Saul realizes that the species must continue, and this realization makes him literally shine with a knowledge that is much greater than his own personal needs.

Brian Railsback

CHIN KEE. In ***Tortilla Flat***, the proprietor of a **Monterey** squid yard whose employment serves as the last resort for paisanos in need of money. Whenever **Danny's** friends are especially desperate, they make the ultimate sacrifice by doing a day's work at the messy, smelly job of cleaning squid. Employment at Chin Kee's represents the value of industry and a hard day's work for a hard day's pay—and nothing could be more antithetical to the paisanos of *Tortilla Flat*. It is significant that one of the rumors that comes from the squid yard when all the paisanos are at work is that Chin Kee has kicked **the Pirate's** dogs, which are symbols of the ideal of communal brotherhood Danny and his friends are supposed to embody, however imperfectly. Chin Kee himself never appears in *Tortilla Flat*; he represents the values of an outside world that are only gradually making headway into the life of the Flat.

Bryan Vescio

CHONG, LEE. Proprietor of **Lee Chong's Heavenly Flower Grocery** in ***Cannery Row***. Lee is an eminent person along the Row, the owner of an abandoned storage area that has been inhabited by **Mack** and the boys and christened **"The Palace Flophouse and Grill."** Although Lee never receives any money in rent, we are told that although "he made business errors," they are "turned to advantage in good will if in no other way."

Charles Etheridge, Jr.

CHONG, LEE. In ***Sweet Thursday***, the former owner of the business on **Cannery Row** still called **Lee Chong's Heavenly Flower Grocery**, though it is now owned by **Joseph** and **Mary Rivas**. After his many years as a central figure in the community, Lee's absence leaves a large vacancy on the Row. Having sold his store, he bought a schooner, loaded his stock in its hold, and sailed off for the South Seas to trade with the Polynesians. Before leaving, Lee secretly deeded the **Palace Flophouse** to **Mack** and the boys and left the money for ten years' taxes so that they would continue to have a home.

Bruce Ouderkirk

CHRÉTIEN DE TROYES. A twelfth-century French author of courtly romances. His *Yvain, Lancelot,* and the unfinished *Perceval* were some of the books consulted by Thomas Malory, during the composition of ***Le Morte D'Arthur,*** and by Steinbeck during the preparation of ***The Acts of King Arthur and His Noble Knights***.

"CHRYSANTHEMUMS, THE" (1937). According to most critics, "The Chrysanthemums"—first published in *Harper's Magazine* in October 1937—is the greatest story Steinbeck ever wrote, and a significant number consider it one of the best American stories of the twentieth century. It has been examined from several critical perspectives: from biblical, **Freud**ian, **Jung**ian, and modernist, to sociological and feminist. That an astonishing number of these readings are persuasive helps to underscore Steinbeck's own comment on the story. Speaking to his friend **George Albee** in 1933, he said that he designed the story "to strike without the reader's knowledge," and that after reading it, the reader will realize "that something profound has happened to him, although he does not know what nor how."

Steinbeck is admired for his meticulously conceived and implemented uses of setting, and "The Chrysanthemums" showcases this talent. The setting of the story establishes the season and the locale, and also becomes an apparent metaphor for **Elisa Allen**, one of Steinbeck's most sympathetically drawn protagonists. The story opens in winter, yet from the beginning it exudes a sense of optimism as the slumbering earth readies itself to receive the fertilizing rain. With this sense of possibility established, the third-person narrator introduces Elisa Allen, who lives with her husband **Henry** on a well-tended ranch. Working in her garden, Elisa is immediately contrasted with Henry and the visiting men, all of whom are associated with the metallic, mechanistic imagery of tractors and automobiles. Unlike the men, Elisa is overtly aligned with the earth, with planting and life-giving—and, later, with sexual desire—in contrast to Henry, who, although he is a farmer, is overtly aligned with cars, farm machinery, boxing matches, and business deals.

Elisa is not contrastively feminine in the traditional sense, however. In fact, her character suggests a slumbering yet powerful potential that, like the winter earth, awaits arousal. Like the chrysanthemums, which are fall-blooming rather than spring-blooming flowers, the 35-year-old Elisa is a late bloomer. Handsome rather than beautiful, she wears a man's hat, gloves, and heavy-duty shoes, her androgynous appearance suggesting the strength, power, and energy that lie just beneath her frustration with her female role. She is enclosed in her tidy and flower-filled yard, whose fence protects it from intruders, animal or human. Although he compliments her success in growing her enormous, healthy chrysanthemums, Henry—though not consciously—implies that Elisa's talents and achievements are not as significant as his. Part of the power of the characterization derives from Steinbeck's portrait of Henry as a man who is not evil, but merely ignorant of his wife's unarticulated frustrations and desires.

In keeping with the male mechanistic imagery, the tinker appears with a squeak of wheels and advertisements for his skill at fixing metal articles. Like the earth of the valley with which she is associated, Elisa is ready for renewal, but this man is self-centered, neither comprehending nor caring about her. Elisa is innocently attracted by his free and itinerant life. The sexual tension appears in the quite obvious phallic imagery of sharpening scissors and the feminine imagery of mending pots. The tinker, like that other intruder in the Old Testament garden, discovers her weakness. He sees that she loves flowers and compliments her chrysanthemums. In the ensuing conversation the tinker, again like Henry, leans farther and farther over the fence. When he asks for chrysanthemums, she gives the tinker careful instructions, growing passionate and eloquent in a scene of unmistakable sexual innuendo and desire. His ploy has worked: now that she believes he cares about the flowers, she hands him the sprouts, invites him into her yard, and gives him two pots to mend. Like the biblical serpent, the tinker leads the woman into his trap. Of her own free will, she invites him into her enclosed paradise.

Elisa comments on the life he lives, yearningly wishing that women could live freely as he does. He responds that such a life would be too lonely and frightening for a woman, but he has enticed her out of her garden, and she will never be able to return to her former state of innocent ignorance. With his departure, Elisa believes that the tinker values the chrysanthemums she has entrusted to him.

In a scene of ritualistic cleansing and heightened self-awareness, she prepares to have dinner with her husband at a **Salinas** restaurant. After bathing and dressing herself to look beautiful, however, she stiffens as Henry noisily bangs and crashes into her room. As they head down the road toward Salinas for dinner, she sees the dark spot on the road and immediately knows that the tinker has dumped her chrysanthemums and kept the pot. Elisa now determinedly asks Henry for wine at dinner and briefly contemplates attending the prizefight, but in the end she opts for only the wine.

The final sentence, which describes her "crying weakly—like an old woman," continues to invite debate over the question of Elisa's future. Roughly half the critics argue persuasively that she has been defeated, whereas the other half contends, with equal vigor, that Elisa, like the chrysanthemum shoots she so carefully prepares for winter, will reappear in the spring to bloom again. Some even view the chrysanthemums as metaphors for pregnancy and children. Because most critics believe **Carol Henning Steinbeck** was the model for Elisa—as she does, herself—it is tempting to view the story from biographical perspectives as well and to speculate about Steinbeck's artistic intention. The interpretive possibilities offered by "The Chrysanthemums" continue to attract new generations of readers and promise to keep the story in the forefront of the best of its genre.

Further Reading: Benson, Jackson J. *The True Adventures of John Steinbeck, Writer.* New York: Viking, 1984. Ditsky, John. "A Kind of Play: Dramatic Elements in John Steinbeck's 'The Chrysanthemums.'" *Wascana Review of Contemporary Poetry and Short Fiction* 21.1 (Spring, 1986): 62–72. Hadella, Charlotte. "Steinbeck's Cloistered Women." In *The Steinbeck Question: New Essays in Criticism.* Ed. Donald R. Noble. Troy, NY: Whitston, 1993. Osborne, William R. "The Texts of Steinbeck's 'The Chrysanthemums.'" *Interpretations: Studies in Language and Literature* 9 (1977): 34–39. Owens, Louis. "'The Chrysanthemums': Waiting for Rain." In *John Steinbeck's Re-Vision of America.* Athens: University of Georgia Press, 1985. 108–13.

Abby H. P. Werlock

CI GÎT. A character in ***Travels with Charley.*** Just outside of New Orleans, having just fled from the incident with the **"Cheerleaders,"** which left him unnerved, Steinbeck finds a pleasant spot near the Mississippi River where he stops to eat and restore his spirit. He is soon joined by a neatly dressed older man; the two share coffee and conversation, focusing primarily on the "Cheerleaders" and race relations. When Steinbeck asks the philosophical visitor his name, he replies "Ci Gît . . . Monsieur Ci Gît—a big family, a common name."

"CIRCUS" (1954). Appeared in *Ringling Bros and Barnum & Bailey Circus Magazine* (1954: 6–7) as the lead article, preceded by a giant photo of Steinbeck by Philippe Halsman. In this reminiscence, Steinbeck recalls his fascination with the traveling Big Top and how it affected him as a young boy. He reminds his readers that the circus was the future, and that it got into people's blood because it brought a change of pace and offered an escape from boredom. Steinbeck felt that: "every man and woman and child comes from the circus refreshed and renewed and ready to survive."

Further Reading: John Steinbeck. "Circus." In *America and Americans and Selected Nonfiction*. Ed. Susan Shillinglaw and Jackson J. Benson. New York: Viking, 2002. 136–38.

Herbert Behrens and Michael J. Meyer

CLAUDAS, KING. The enemy of **King Ban** and **King Bors** in ***The Acts of King Arthur and His Noble Knights***.

CLEMENS, SAMUEL LANGHORNE [MARK TWAIN] (1835–1910). American novelist and humorist, Twain's major works included *The Adventures of Tom Sawyer* (1876), *The Adventures of Huckleberry Finn* (1884), and *A Connecticut Yankee in King Arthur's Court* (1889), as well as the autobiographical *Life on the Mississippi* (1883). Like Twain, Steinbeck wrote about what interested him rather than following others' critical suggestions.

Other similarities shared by the two writers include their extensive use of allegory and their reliance on caustic humor, which often satirized American mores and attitudes. Both authors also received criticism for what some evaluators called lapses of good taste and for their failure to exhibit a firm control of their material. Their appeal to the masses was primarily based on their down-to-earth storytelling and the "moral caveats" these tales presented. Twain's interest in the Middle Ages and Arthurian legend was also appreciated by Steinbeck, who struggled for many years to complete ***The Adventures of King Arthur and His Noble Knights.*** Steinbeck was perhaps influenced by *Huckleberry*

Finn when he wrote the manuscript that later evolved into the script for Alfred Hitchcock's ***Lifeboat***.

Further Reading: DeMott, Robert J. *Steinbeck's Reading; A Catalogue of Books Owned and Borrowed.* New York: Garland Publishing, 1984.

Michael J. Meyer and Paul M. Blobaum

COACHMAN, THE. The coachman of **Henry** and **Elizabeth Morgan** in ***Cup of Gold***. He tends to be drunk on the job

COEUR DE GRIS. Member of **Henry Morgan's** pirate crew in ***Cup of Gold***. His name is French for "Heart of Gray." After making him his sole friend among the pirates, Henry promotes Coeur de Gris to second in command. Henry Morgan shoots him during the sacking of Panama, because the drunken Coeur de Gris has the bad timing to ask if Henry has had sex with **La Santa Roja**—shortly after Henry's dismal failure with her. Half-mad with grief, Henry vacillates for a while as to what should be done with the corpse of his friend.

COLLETO, VINCENT (TINY) (1909–1945). One of the seamen who crewed the ***Western Flyer*** for Steinbeck's 1940 expedition to the **Sea of Cortez**. He and **Sparky Enea** are a matched pair who often provide comic relief. Both are described by Steinbeck as a "counterbalance" to **Tony Berry's** truthfulness, although both prove to be hardworking seamen and effective collectors of marine life. The two are almost always mentioned in tandem with one another, competing for women or embarking on some adventure that involves alcohol. In a merger of fiction and nonfiction, Sparky and Tiny appear in ***Cannery Row*** and get into a bar fight with **Gay**, one of the inhabitants of the **Palace Flophouse and Grill**.

Charles Etheridge, Jr.

COLLINS, TOM. Head of the **Arvin Sanitary Camp** (or Weedpatch, as its residents called it), one of many migration camps set up by the **Roosevelt** Administration for the migrant farmers flooding into California during the Great Depression. Collins's sanitary camp was successful because he tried to build a sense of community among its denizens. Steinbeck first met Collins while on assignment for the *San Francisco News* to write a series of pieces about the situation of the migrant farmer. While at Weedpatch, Steinbeck followed Collins around the camp, observing the daily operations and listening to stories. Steinbeck left the camp with a briefcase full of notes and reports given to him by Collins, which would soon be the primary resources for a large portion of ***The Grapes of Wrath***. Collins also provided Steinbeck with a record of migrant dialects and camp songs, which would prove invaluable for the young writer. When *The Grapes of Wrath* was finally made into a movie, Collins was hired as a technical advisor for $15,000. Steinbeck dedicated *The Grapes of Wrath* partially "To Tom—who lived it."

Ted Scholz

"COLLOQUY OF BUGS, A." Patterned after **Cervantes'** "A Colloquy of Dogs," Steinbeck's idea for a play with this title came after he read a 1962 *New York Times* article claiming that nuclear radiation sufficient enough to wipe out humanity would have little effect on cockroaches. Satirical in nature, the play was to feature a conversation between two cockroaches discussing how humankind had succeeded in destroying itself. Referring to the absurdist playwright Samuel Beckett, Steinbeck told his agent **Elizabeth Otis** he didn't see why two cockroaches talking couldn't hold the stage as well as two people in garbage cans or a woman buried in sand, a reference to Beckett's plays.

Michael J. Meyer

COLOMBÉ, THE LADY. Lover of **Sir Launceor** in ***The Acts of King Arthur and His Noble Knights***.

CONDON, EDWARD (EDDIE) (1905–1973). Steinbeck met this jazz guitarist in the 1940s in Greenwich Village, while living with **Gwyndolyn Conger Steinbeck** at the Bedford Hotel in Manhattan. Condon and Steinbeck often discussed American jazz, and the musician later composed a blues piece entitled "Tortilla B Flat" exclusively with Steinbeck in mind.

CONGER, GWYNDOLYN (GWYN). *See* **Steinbeck, Gwnydolyn Conger**.

CONRAD, BARNABY (1922–). American novelist. In 1952 *The New York Times Book Review* polled various celebrities and asked them to catalog the books they most liked from the past year. Steinbeck listed Conrad's *Matador* (1952). In a letter addressed to Conrad on December 12, 1952, Steinbeck wrote that he liked *Matador* because he believed it. In the winter of 1953 John and **Elaine Scott Steinbeck** vacationed with Conrad in the Virgin Islands.

CONRAD, JOSEPH (1857–1924). English novelist and short-story writer. In a letter to **Ted Miller**, Steinbeck acknowledges Conrad's philosophy that only two types of writing can be sold: "the very best and the very worst." Conrad's lush descriptions appear to have influenced Steinbeck as he composed ***Cup of Gold***, because the vivid imagery and lyrical prose employed (especially the description of **Morgan's** entrance into Panama) appear to imitate Conrad's style.

"CONVERSATION AT SAG HARBOR" (1961). Written for *Holiday* in 1961, this piece features a 1958 visit by Steinbeck and his sons, **Thom** and **John IV**, to this area of New York's Long Island where Steinbeck owned a home. Echoing some of his ideas in ***East of Eden***, Steinbeck as father discusses the problems of adolescence and offers his sons freedom by agreeing to "get off their backs." Paraphrasing **Lee's** advice to **Cal Trask** in the novel, he tells his sons that if they succeed it is their success, and if they fail it is their failure. He indicates that true freedom implies personal responsibility, and that only by willingly accepting this challenge can children become adults.

Michael J. Meyer

COOK OF THE BRISTOL GIRL, THE. In ***Cup of Gold***, he befriends **Henry Morgan** on Henry's first voyage.

COOPER FAMILY. Prior to his encounter with the racist New Orleans **"Cheerleaders"** in ***Travels with Charley***, Steinbeck recalls an African American family in **Salinas**, the Coopers. As a child, Steinbeck writes, his "Negro experience" was limited to his experiences with the Cooper family, an honest, hardworking, dignified family of five. Steinbeck carefully positions this discussion of race matters at the end of this section of Part Four—just before his departure from Texas and prior to his entry into New Orleans, where he will witness the infamous "Cheerleaders." Steinbeck is quick to show his hatred of the racism he encounters in New Orleans and, later on, in a brief encounter with a white racist in Mississippi.

Thom Tammaro

COOPER, JAMES FENNIMORE (1789–1851). American novelist who is best known for the character of Natty Bumppo, introduced in *The Pioneers* (1823). In the chapter "Americans and the World" from ***America and Americans***, Steinbeck criticized Cooper, saying "Cooper made up a fund of misinformation about American Indians." However, **Robert J. DeMott** attributes this uncomplimentary assessment to **Mark Twain**'s "Fennimore Cooper's Literary Offenses" (1895), which Steinbeck enjoyed reading out loud.

Further Reading: DeMott, Robert J. *Steinbeck's Reading; A Catalogue of Books Owned and Borrowed*. New York: Garland Publishing, 1984.

Janet L. Flood

COPLAND, AARON (1900–1990). A prominent twentieth-century composer, Copland began serious musical study as a teenager and developed a folksy American style that won him a wide audience. Most famous for his ballet scores *Billy The Kid* (1938), *Rodeo* (1942), and *Appalachian Spring* (1944), all of which featured American folk music, Copland also composed the film scores for two movies based on Steinbeck novels. ***Of Mice and Men*** was nominated for an Academy Award for best score. After rereading *Of Mice and Men* to ensure that it would suit his musical aesthetic, Copland said, "Here was an American Theme, by a great American writer, demanding appropriate music." After viewing the unscored film, he stated, "I was genuinely moved by *Of Mice and Men* and by the inspired performances, and I found that the scenes induced the music if I turned to them while composing."

Avoiding the full-blown orchestration of most film scores at the time, Copland composed minimally scored themes reminiscent of film songs, with, in his own words, "more naturally sounding instrumentation—solo flute, flutes together, and a guitar for a campfire scene." In 1942, Copland reworked the themes "Barley Wagons" and "Threshing Machines" from his *Of Mice and Men* score as two of the five movements in his suite *Music for Movies*. In 1949, **Lewis Milestone**, who had directed *Of Mice and Men*, asked Copland to score the film version of Steinbeck's ***The Red Pony***. Unlike some studio composers who scored hundreds of films, Copland was very selective about the films he scored. Of *The Red Pony*, he said, "I admired Steinbeck, and after reading the book, I knew this was a film for me." Before the film was released, he adapted his score into a suite. Steinbeck himself said that the music was far better than the rest of the film.

Steinbeck's little known and unpublished "Narration" for "The Red Pony Suite" was written in response to Copland's request for an introduction to this suite, which consisted of music drawn from the musical score he had written for the film. Copland wished to perform it before performances of the suite at children's concerts. Steinbeck responded enthusiastically with the "Narration," which was about 300 words long. He was indicating through his portrayal of a day in the life of Everybody that he conceived of this "self character" as a universal figure symbolic of the aspirations and experiences that every child should enjoy. Although Copland felt that it was not suitable for children, who probably would not understand this symbolic interpretation of the work, Steinbeck did not wish to revise it.

Further Reading: Copland, Aaron. "Copland: Music for Films." (Compact disc).

Warren French and Michael J. Meyer

CORCORAN, JESUS MARIA. In ***Tortilla Flat***, the fourth member of **Danny's** ersatz round table of paisanos, after Danny, **Pilon**, and **Pablo Sanchez**. Pilon and Pablo stumble across the drunken, red-headed Jesus Maria passed out in a ditch with a half-full gallon bottle of wine. Jesus Maria is rich for a paisano, having sold a rowboat he found for seven dollars. Discovering that he still has three dollars left, his friends take him to the house they are renting from Danny on the pretense that he is sick, and they rent space in their house to him.

Jesus Maria quickly becomes something of a fall guy for the rest of the group. In the debate over what to do with the money Jesus Maria has contributed, Pilon and Pablo wait silently for Jesus Maria to make the suggestion they had resolved to act on all along: to use the money to buy wine rather than to give it to Danny as rent. But the two double-cross Jesus Maria, sending him into Monterey for food while they head to **Mr. Torrelli's** for the wine that they will inevitably drink without him.

The defining feature of Jesus Maria, according to Steinbeck, is gentleness and humanity. At the beginning of chapter 10, Steinbeck provides a long list of Jesus Maria's humanitarian deeds. The rest of the chapter recounts another one, describing Jesus Maria's attempts to help a young corporal with a baby. It is also Jesus Maria who, in a drunken moment of contrition over the burning of Danny's house, declares that the friends will take the responsibility for providing food for Danny from that point forward, a declaration that the otherss—and even Jesus Maria himselff—hope Danny will forget.

Steinbeck always takes care to temper the gentleness and humanity of Jesus Maria. It is Jesus Maria who suggests that **the Pirate** come to live with the paisanos, but his motives, like Pilon's, are to discover the whereabouts of the Pirate's treasure. At other times, Steinbeck's use of "humanitarian" seems only to be a euphemism for "womanizer." Jesus Maria's dalliance with **Arabella Gross**, which is supported by gift-giving, is prominent in the first half of the novel, and in the second half Steinbeck strongly intimates that his charity toward **Teresina Cortez** and her starving children is inspired by ulterior motives (he may be responsible for a new addition to the brood). Like all the paisanos, Jesus Maria is a mixed character, proving Pilon's wisdom that there is evil in every good.

Charles Etheridge, Jr.

CORELL, GEORGE. In *The Moon Is Down*, Corell is a popular storekeeper who is also a traitor to his country. Corell is Steinbeck's symbol for the maligned social outcast, a quisling figure who prepares the town for invasion by diverting the local militia from the invading forces, making lists of every firearm in the village, and providing valuable information on topography and resources to the enemy. Self-serving and ambitious, he seeks to overthrow local authority and ultimately climb the political ladder. His plans backfire when he goes over the head of **Colonel Lanser**, the commander of the invading forces, in seeking the execution of **Mayor Orden**. Eventually, Corell outlives his usefulness and becomes a Cain-like exile, not only from the community of his own people, but also from the world of the invaders.

Rodney P. Rice

CORONER. He investigates **Jim Moore's** murder of **Jelke Moore's** lover in **"The Murder,"** assures Jim that he and **Will**, the deputy sheriff, can dismiss the technical murder charge, and advises Jim not to punish his wife too harshly. His attitude epitomizes that of the region: no serious criminal charges need accrue to a crime of passion—particularly, the text implies, if the murderer is a peer of the coroner and the victim is the son of immigrants.

CORPORAL, THE. In *Tortilla Flat*, a sixteen-year-old soldier with a baby in tow. **Jesus Maria Corcoran** finds him being harassed by a policeman and brings him to **Danny's** house. The corporal explains to the paisanos that he had been a soldier in Chihuahua, married to a beautiful girl and father of a new baby boy, when a captain claimed the corporal's wife as a privilege of his rank. When he says that he is going back to the army to try to improve his own rank, the paisanos wholly approve, believing they have learned a lesson in parental ethics from the corporal. In fact, their reaction to the corporal's story shows that they, like the corporal, are being swayed from the true values of family and friendship toward a false ethic of success, represented by military hierarchy.

Bryan Vescio

CORTEZ, TERESINA. In *Tortilla Flat*, an abandoned mother of eight who is helped to feed her children by the paisanos, in one of their more or less philanthropic acts. Teresina lives with her children and her mother on the edge of the gulch south of Tortilla Flat; they are impoverished and hungry. **Jesus Maria Corcoran**, one of the paisanos, visits Teresina and convinces his friends to help her, mostly by cheating and stealing. But when they present her with their ill-gotten food and she explains that her children can only eat beans, they steal 400 pounds of beans for her directly from a warehouse. Teresina's story demonstrates the fragility of life on Tortilla Flat, and also the way life depends on fallible natural rhythms rather than the well-designed supernatural order Teresina, in her shaky piety, assigns to all events. The story is also another example of the way even the paisanos' questionable ulterior motives can result in genuinely good deeds.

Bryan Vescio

COTTON EYE. Blind piano player at **Faye's** whorehouse, then at **Kate Albey's**, in ***East of Eden***.

COVICI, PASCAL "PAT" (1885–1964). John Steinbeck's editor and publisher for 30 years, from prior to the publication of ***Tortilla Flat*** in 1935 until Covici's death in 1964. After Covici's death, Steinbeck wrote, "Pat Covici was much more than my friend. He was my editor. Only a writer can understand how a great editor is a father, mother, teacher, personal devil and personal god. For 30 years Pat was my collaborator and my conscience. He demanded more than I had and thereby caused me to be more than I should have been without him." Although Covici was most closely tied to Steinbeck, Steinbeck was not the only major literary figure Covici published. **Arthur Miller** and **Saul Bellow**, and many others, published successfully under Pascal Covici's aegis.

As Steinbeck was completing *Tortilla Flat*, a chance meeting between two old friends helped change Steinbeck's career. The meeting was between a Chicago bookstore owner, **Ben Abramson,** and Covici, who had previously owned a Chicago bookstore and later his own publishing company.

Covici had been urged by Abramson to read Steinbeck's first three books; Covici did so and contacted Steinbeck through Steinbeck's literary agency, **McIntosh and Otis**. Covici contracted to publish *Tortilla Flat*, which appeared in 1935. The relationship between Steinbeck as author and Covici as editor and publisher remained stable and grew stronger through the years, to be broken only by Covici's death in 1964. In 1936, Covici-Friede published ***In Dubious Battle***, and in 1937, ***Of Mice and Men*** (as a play and as a novel) and ***The Red Pony***. The Covici-Friede firm was liquidated in 1938.

Steinbeck was then free to publish with any other major publishing house, but he chose to follow Covici, who had taken a position with **The Viking Press**. Steinbeck's first book published under the Viking imprint was ***The Long Valley*** in 1938, but as Covici joined The Viking Press, Steinbeck already had a partially completed manuscript that would make them both famous: ***The Grapes of Wrath***, published in 1939.

Covici knew instinctively how Steinbeck should prepare himself to begin a novel. In the mid-1940s, when Steinbeck was contemplating his short novel ***The Pearl***, Covici wrote, "I hope you will take a few days off and relax completely before you start working on Pearl. Quietly soak in some ocean breezes and let your mind dwell in the depths measureless to man, then cover yourself with the hills, and the dreams will come. *The Pearl* should be pure fantasy, grounded on reality."

After ***Cannery Row*** had been published and the publication date excitement had abated, Covici reread the book. He then wrote Steinbeck, "I read *Cannery Row* over again. It's a good book, John. You poured a great deal of poetry into it. You give a good many reasons for living and for dying. And I am glad you were born and happy you are alive. Certainly life is an accident. Man is no more important to the Universe than an ant on the Sahara Desert. But we are important to each other—we are born in each other's image."

Covici always stood ready to aid Steinbeck in more mundane ways. For many years, Covici supplied Steinbeck with pencils and yellow legal pads (Steinbeck wrote in longhand when working on a book manuscript). Covici sent the pencils, dozens and dozens, without ever questioning why Steinbeck couldn't keep himself in the tools of his own trade.

Covici also acted as surrogate father to Steinbeck's sons, **Thom** and **John IV.** As Steinbeck traveled, Covici remembered dates and occasions that Steinbeck forgot. With two boys in summer camp, Steinbeck forgot a birthday for Thom. Covici responded with presents for both boys and their camp friends. It is logical to assume that Covici happily ran errands for Steinbeck because "walking in Steinbeck's shoes" kept Covici closer to understanding the day-to-day problems of Steinbeck's life. There is no indication that Covici ever passed these minor errands to a secretary or office worker at The Viking Press. He did everything for Steinbeck himself.

There were, however, episodes of disagreement between the two. Covici never liked Steinbeck's ***Burning Bright***. By 1964, Covici's well-intentioned notes of encouragement to Steinbeck to write and be more productive, and Covici's lack of interest in Steinbeck's **King Arthur** project, were a source of frustration for the author. In the summer of 1964 the two had some irritable exchanges; on October 14, Covici died.

After Covici's death, Arthur Miller, the playwright, said that Covici "stood rather alone, superbly himself, eager to be moved by something true. . . . He was the slave of an appetite for excellence, and, while he could set forth all the right reasons for his judgments, his real calculus was the human heart. He loved best whatever lifted up the human possibility; what really made him slap the table and roar out his laugh was the outbreak of light over passionate dark." **Thomas Guinzburg**, who succeeded his father, **Harold Guinzburg**, as president of The Viking Press, said of Covici, "He was an extraordinary guy—he was some part psychiatrist, some part lawyer, some part priest. . . . Covici didn't work on books, he worked on people. He fought for his people, inside and outside the publishing house."

Covici was able to explain Steinbeck's problems, conflicts, and psyche in ways Steinbeck appreciated. Steinbeck was better able to write when Covici charted the course of the author's personality. A letter to Steinbeck from Covici in late 1948 is indicative of this: "You are best when you do the things you know best. You often stray in alien places. You can't always help that because of your restless and creative spirit. When done with one thing you must immediately tangle up with something else, whether it's writing or other things. I only know that when you paint your house or weed a garden . . . and you talk of many things, something passes through you, something deep and human is communicated to your soul and becomes part of your book and it is great." Covici's letter is a litany of Steinbeck's personal characteristics.

Although Covici's methodology was often mysterious to Steinbeck during their relationship, Steinbeck ultimately recognized Covici's worth. When ***East of Eden*** was published (and Steinbeck considered it his best work), Steinbeck presented the manuscript to Covici in a hand-crafted box. *East of Eden* was dedicated to Pascal "Pat" Covici.

Further Reading: Benson, Jackson J. *The True Adventures of John Steinbeck, Writer.* New York: Viking, 1984; Fensch, Thomas. *Conversations with John Steinbeck.* Jackson: The University Press of Mississippi, 1988; *Steinbeck and Covici: The story of a Friendship.* Middlebury, VT: Paul S. Eriksson, Publisher, 1979; Friede, Donald. *The Mechanical Angel.* New York: Alfred Knopf, 1948; Parini, Jay. *John Steinbeck: A Biography.* New York: Henry Holt, 1995.

Thomas Fensch

COVICI-FRIEDE. Variously typeset as Covici-Friede or Covici•Friede, the publishing firm established by **Pascal Covici** and **Donald Friede** existed for almost ten years, 1928–1938 (Donald Friede left the firm in 1935). Notable publishing successes were: *The Front Page* (1931) by Ben Hecht and Charles MacArthur; Theodore Drieser's *An American Tragedy* (1925); Radclyffe Hall's early fictional work about lesbianism, *The Well of Loneliness* (1928); books by e. e. cummings; and a modern version of *The Canterbury Tales,* with illustrations by Rockwell Kent. The firm published genteel erotica and, even before Steinbeck's ***In Dubious Battle,*** had published *Revolt Among the Sharecroppers, Revolt on the Campus, The Decline of American Capitalism,* and *America Faces the Barricades*. Covici-Friede also published Steinbeck's ***Tortilla Flat, Of Mice and Men*** (as a novel and a play), and ***The Red Pony.*** The printing firm J. J. Little & Ives called notes due which could not be paid, and Covici-Friede was dissolved in 1938. Pascal Covici moved to **The Viking Press** and took John Steinbeck with him.

Further Reading: Fensch, Thomas. *Steinbeck and Covici: The Story of a Friendship*. Middlebury, VT: Paul S. Eriksson, 1979; Friede, Donald. *The Technical Angel*. New York: Alfred Knopf, 1948.

COX, MARTHA HEASLEY. Emerita professor at San Jose State University, Cox founded the Steinbeck Research Center at that university in 1974. She is also the author of numerous textbooks on writing and American literature, including *Image and Value: An Invitation to Literature* (1966) and *A Reading Approach to College Writing* (1970). In 1997 Cox received the university's highest honor, the Tower Award, and was further recognized when the Center was officially rechristened the **Martha Heasley Cox Center for Steinbeck Studies** the same year. Cox was an integral figure in securing donations that allowed the center to become a central location for continuing Steinbeck research. In 1998 she initiated the Steinbeck Fellows Program at San Jose, a program that provides research grants to young Steinbeck scholars.

COYOTITO. Infant son and only child of **Kino** and **Juana** in ***The Pearl***, who is stung by a scorpion at the beginning of the story. The incident causes his parents to make a tireless journey in search of a cure. This cure is supposedly attained when Kino discovers a pearl of great price, a gem that will not only pay for medical help but will also ensure that the child receives a competent education and an upbringing among a higher social class. However, jealousy over the pearl causes the doctor who treats Coyotito to exploit the baby's illness for his own gain, and eventually the family's possession of the jewel causes them to lose their house and their livelihood. As most parents do, Kino and Juana see Coyotito as their future. However, these dreams of education and success vanish when Coyotito is accidentally shot to death by a tracker, because the baby's cries in a cave sounded like a coyote. Without his death, Kino would not have learned that the son is much more valuable than the pearl—a symbol of earthly wealth.

Stephen K. George

CRANE, STEPHEN (1871–1900). American novelist, short-story writer, and poet, known for his naturalistic works *The Red Badge of Courage* (1895) and "The Open Boat" (1898). Steinbeck read Crane's work in his twenties, and although he admired his fiction, Steinbeck's perspective on man's place in the universe differed from Crane's. Crane's characters were primarily trying to reconcile themselves to an indifferent universe, which often led to anger and disillusionment, whereas Steinbeck's **non-teleological** vision allows at least some of his characters to find reconciliation with their ancillary place within a larger whole.

CRISTY, MAYOR. In ***Sweet Thursday***, the mayor of **Pacific Grove** who is under attack when the butterflies fail to arrive in time for the community's annual festival. Later, he has to leave town when it becomes known that he had a tryst with a blonde in a hotel room. Typically, Steinbeck uses such incidents to attack "respectable society" for scapegoating and for moral hypocrisy.

"CRITICS, CRITICS BURNING BRIGHT" (1950). Steinbeck's response to critical attacks of his play-novelette, *Burning Bright*, was published in *The Saturday Review* (33.45, 11 Nov. 1950). He defends his right to boldly experiment and laments the critics' inability to truly appreciate artistic innovation. The article is reprinted in *Steinbeck and His Critics* (1957).

"CRITICS—FROM A WRITER'S VIEWPOINT" (1955). In this article, published in *The Saturday Review* (27 Aug.: 20, 28),

Steinbeck attempts to understand the erratic and often hostile nature of literary criticism. He attributes such ill treatment to the fact that critics are writers themselves, and are "subject to all of the virtues and vices of other writers in other fields." More often than not they bring jealousy, self-interest, personal prejudices, or a desire to be original to the writing table.

Further Reading: *America and Americans and Selected Nonfiction*. Ed. Susan Shillinglaw and Jackson J. Benson. New York: Viking, 2002.

CROOKS. In ***Of Mice and Men***, a black "stable buck" who has a crooked back from being kicked by a horse. He is ostracized except on Christmas, when the boss brings in a gallon of whiskey for the entire crew. Crooks keeps his distance from the white people, a choice that results in his loneliness. During the daytime, he can work together with the white folks, but at night he has to go to his own place, the harness room, to sleep. Crooks tells **Lennie Small** that the white ranch hands do not allow him to play cards with them because he is black, and he tells **George Milton,** Lennie, and **Candy** that they will never attain their dreams. His skepticism is based on the fact that he has known many workers who wanted land of their own, but he has never heard of anyone who has actually realized this ambition.

Luchen Li

CULP, MISS. **Cal** and **Aron Trask's** elementary school teacher in ***East of Eden***.

CUP OF GOLD (1929). Steinbeck's first novel, published in September 1929. The arrangements for its publication by Robert M. McBride & Company of New York were made by Steinbeck's old **Stanford University** classmate, **Amasa "Ted" Miller**. Steinbeck had spent much of the years 1924 through 1928 converting **"A Lady in Infra-Red,"** a short story he had written while still a student at Stanford University, into what would become his first novel, but his letters of 1928 and 1929 make it clear that he was dissatisfied with almost every aspect of the published book. He complained that the cover design, by his friend **Mahlon Blaine**, made the book appear to be a swashbuckling tale for adolescents, and that the publisher had done a poor job of marketing the book.

Steinbeck reserved his harshest criticism for the contents of the book, however. In one letter, he concluded that it was, "as a whole, utterly worthless," and in another he called it "the Morgan atrocity." Steinbeck approved of the "lyric" qualities of various passages, but later seemed to feel that his most important accomplishment in *Cup of Gold* was overcoming the influence of **Don Byrne** and **James Branch Cabell** on his writing. Although most critics have agreed that Steinbeck's reading of Byrne and Cabell was a hindrance to his development as a writer, there has been occasional disagreement as to how thoroughly he banished their influence. In general, critics have been only slightly kinder in their evaluations of *Cup of Gold* than Steinbeck was. But "Ted" Miller thought it was Steinbeck's most characteristic and best work, and **Jackson J. Benson** claims it is Steinbeck's most ambitiously literary work.

Steinbeck appears to have loosely based this *Bildungsroman* on a portion of **Alexandre Olivier** Exquemelin's (spelled **Esquemeling** in the first English edition of 1684 or 1685) *The Buccaneers of America*. Although his claim to have been among the pirates **Henry Morgan** led in the sacking of Panama is generally accepted, many of the "facts" in Esquemeling's narrative were denied by Henry Morgan and continue to be questioned by historians. Steinbeck's narrative of the life of Henry Morgan parallels the outlines of Esquemeling's biographical sketch of Morgan.

Esquemeling begins Morgan's story with the tale of an adolescent boy, heading off to sea, who is tricked by a seeming friend and sold into slavery. Steinbeck adds a number of characters: **Robert Morgan**, Henry's father, who is drenched in Welsh lore; **Gwenliana Morgan**, Henry's paternal grandmother, who is a seer and necromancer of dubious distinction; **"Mother" Morgan**, Henry's mother and a superstitious Christian peasant, who is essentially a stock character; and a young girl named **Elizabeth,** with whom the young Henry fancies himself in love. A visit to the Morgan family home by **Daffyd**, a former farmhand who had gone off to sea, sets off in Henry a desire for adventure. Hoping to dissuade his son from leaving, Henry's father asks him to confer with **Merlin** before he leaves. Merlin reminds Henry of the importance of Arthurian lore and Welsh history, but when Henry tells Merlin that he feels half of him is missing and that he will return when he is "whole again," Merlin predicts that Henry will be "a great man" as long as he remains "a little child." Henry then goes to say his farewells to Elizabeth, but when he gets there, he sees her silhouetted in the doorway and runs away before she can see him. Henry then heads to Cardiff, where he is tricked into passage as an indentured slave.

Once landed, Henry quickly advances from slave to overseer. He takes advantage of his owner's library to study military history, and he embezzles sufficient funds from the man, **James Flower**, to buy his first captaincy once his period of indenture is ended. After a number of early battles are successes because Morgan uses unconventional tactics and weaponry, he becomes the vice admiral in **Edward Mansveldt's** attack on St. Catherine. When Mansveldt disappears near Cuba, Morgan becomes the preeminent pirate in the Caribbean.

Meanwhile, as in Esquemeling's history, a legend is spreading across the Americas about a woman of unique beauty living in the legendary *Cup of Gold*, the fabulously wealthy city of Panama. Henry develops a fascination for the woman Steinbeck calls variously **The Red Saint** or **La Santa Roja** and decides to take the supposedly unconquerable city of Panama. Steinbeck's descriptions of Morgan collecting an army, crossing the isthmus, and sacking the city appear to draw on Esquemeling's account once again.

Esquemeling also tells the story of Henry's failed attempt to romance the lovely lady, and of receiving ransom for her safe return. But Steinbeck makes this tale the climactic episode of the plot, and he ties it closely both to Henry's earlier failure to even attempt to win the love of the Welsh girl, Elizabeth, and to the ultimate emptiness of his materialistic ambitions. La Santa Roja's laughter at his inept romancing so unnerves Henry that out of misplaced rage he kills both an inoffensive Cockney sailor named **Jones** and his favorite lieutenant and only friend, **Coeur de Gris**. Steinbeck again follows Esquemeling, in that Henry's great final deed as a pirate is to sail off in the middle of the drunken celebration and keep all of the plunder for himself. The remainder of the book quickly describes Henry's worldly successes—marriage to his too-proper cousin, a knighthood, and the lieutenant governorship of Jamaica—and his growing sense of alienation from what he has become. Ironic to the end, Morgan's dying thought is of the Welsh heritage he left behind: "Where is Merlin? If I could only find him."

Most critics, if they bother to discuss *Cup of Gold* at all, comment briefly on the allegorical aspects of Henry Morgan's self-creation and of his ironic grail quest. Some note its paradoxical message; in a complex combination typical of Steinbeck, the image of a cup of gold serves many purposes. It functions as title, symbol, place, and artifact. As a title, it is a reminiscent, but skewed, allusion to **King Arthur** and the Grail Legend. As a symbol, it is the ever-receding fulfillment of Henry Morgan's desires—as soon as he achieves one desire, another takes its place, ad infinitum. As a place, it is Panama, a seemingly unattainable pearl of great price—offering not only vast wealth, but also the allure of a woman reputed to be the most beautiful, the most fascinating in the world. As an object, it is the golden cup that Henry Morgan lifted from the heap of loot after the fall of Panama to his buccaneers.

As the novel continues, readers find that Henry Morgan functions more and more like an automaton, disappointingly lacking in the human and humane qualities of compassion and love—a lack that is reminiscent of Albert Camus' *The Stranger.* In fact, *Cup of Gold* is more an examination of how such a vacuous human being functions than an account of events that may be historically documented, although there are some of these as well. There seem to be several underlying questions that Steinbeck explores: What motivates a human being whose mind and heart are set on ravage and rapine? What effects do such motivations have on the human psyche? How does such a mind function? In the character of Henry Morgan, *Cup of Gold* draws the portrait and sets forth "heroic" actions that illustrate, and to an extent answer these questions. *Cup of Gold*, then, is more a fable than it is a historical novel or a biography. As a fable, its moral is similar to that of the ancient Sisyphus myth: when a self-absorbed person pursues desires, satisfaction and contentment will be impossible.

Yet this fable is hardly a glorification of violence, as some critics suggest. As is true of his later works, *Cup of Gold* indicates that Steinbeck has read and studied deeply, dissecting and examining the various facets of human behavior, including what Wordsworth calls "man's inhumanity to man." In his portrait of the single-minded, self-absorbed Henry Morgan, Steinbeck has provided a portrait of a criminal mind—one moving from atrocity to atrocity, with little evidence of any regret or compassion. *Cup of Gold*, therefore, is a study of good and evil, in which evil is not in the least appealing and does not bring gratification, and in which its emptiness and vacuity are made clear. This story of Henry Morgan is one of Steinbeck's versions of "the only story we have," which is the story of good and evil. No doubt is left in the reader's mind about which side of good and evil Steinbeck would choose to take his stand.

One final indication of *Cup of Gold*'s complexity is the fact that, through the years, critics such as **Joseph Eddy Fontenrose** have claimed such varied literary sources for the book as **Shakespeare**'s *Henry V*, Sabatini's *Captain Blood*, Goethe's *Faust*, the romances of Nathaniel Hawthorne, Greek and Celtic myth, and Jacobean drama. More important, however, is biographer **Jackson J. Benson**'s assertion that Steinbeck thought of Morgan's story as "autobiographical." In short, Benson believes that psychologically, for Steinbeck, both Morgan's loneliness and his heroic efforts to create himself were reflections on Steinbeck's own difficult years as an apprentice writer. More recent critics, including Dennis Prindle, have focused on the tension between the allegorical and mythic aspects of the novel and Steinbeck's penchant for biology and literary naturalism. Despite the varied responses, however, most critics suggest that there is more beneath the surface of Steinbeck's first novel than is initially evident to a cursory reader.

Further Reading: Benson, Jackson J. *The True Adventures of John Steinbeck, Writer.* New York: Viking, 1984; Eddy, Darlene. "To Go A-Buccaneering and Take a Spanish Town: Some Seventeenth-Century Aspects of *Cup of Gold.*" *Steinbeck Quarterly* 8 (Winter 1975): 3–12; Fontenrose, Joseph. *John Steinbeck: An Introduction and Interpretation.* New York: Holt, Rinehart and Winston, 1963; Prindle, Dennis. "The Pretexts of Romance: Steinbeck's Allegorical Naturalism from *Cup of Gold* to Tortilla Flat." In *The Steinbeck Question: New Essays in Criticism*. Ed. Donald R. Noble. Troy, NY: Whitston Publishing, 1993; Steinbeck, John. *Steinbeck: A Life in Letters.* Ed. Elaine Steinbeck and Robert Wallsten. New York: Viking, 1975.

Kevin Hearle and Barbara A. Heavilin

CURLEY. **The Boss**'s son in ***Of Mice and Men***. He is a thin young man with a brown face, brown eyes, and tightly curled hair. Like the Boss, he wears high-heeled boots. Rumor also has it that Curley wears a glove full of Vaseline on his left hand. The implication is that this practice is intended to keep his hand soft for his wife. Curley loves to pick fights and develops an instant dislike for **Lennie Small** because of his massive size. Lennie crushes Curley's hand after Curley picks a fight with him. At the end of the novel, Curley organizes a posse to find Lennie and get revenge for Lennie's senseless murder of Curley's wife.

Luchen Li

CURLEY'S WIFE. In ***Of Mice and Men***, a flirt who likes to give men "the eye." She is heavily made up, with full rouged lips and taunting eyes. **George Milton** refers to Curley's wife as a tramp and a trap. Afraid that her beauty and her femininity itself may "trap" **Lennie Small**, who once touched a little girl's dress just to feel it, George warns Lennie to stay away from her. Lennie is attracted to her because she is soft like the rabbit he dreams of owning, or the mouse he accidentally killed on the way to their new job. To the ranch hands, she is known as a "tart" because she often comes to the bunkhouse to flirt with the laborers.

Since her husband **Curley** does not give her much attention, Curley's wife makes every effort to find someone to talk to. She eventually approaches Lennie and tells him her life story: She used to live in **Salinas**, and at the age of fifteen she met an actor who promised to take her to Hollywood, where she dreamed of having an exciting life. She also tells Lennie of her dreams to be a movie star, and she discloses that she never liked Curley, although she married him. One day Curley's wife flirts with Lennie and invites him to stroke her hair. Lennie's strength scares her, and in the struggle to quiet her screams he breaks her neck.

Curley's wife may come on to the men as playful and seductive, but she is acutely aware of the hostile reception she receives from the ranch hands. She realizes that they will tolerate her presence around the bunkhouse only if she uses her usual excuse, "I'm lookin' for Curley." Her more honest explanation, "I'm jus' lookin' for somebody to talk to. Don't you never jus' want to talk to somebody?" meets with coldness and resentment from the men. Like George and others in the novel, she is trapped in a lonely life in a pitiless world.

Luchen Li

D

"'D' FOR DANGEROUS"(1957) Published in *McCall's* (85.1 Oct. 1957: 57,82), Steinbeck's essay sets forth a humorous plan for careless drivers whereby they would be sentenced to display a large red "D" (for dangerous) on their license plates for at least three years, after which the "D" could be removed by a record of good driving.

Eric Skipper

DAFYDD. In *Cup of Gold,* Dafydd worked on the Morgan farm as a boy and then went away to sea. He returns from the Indies, visits the Morgans, and seems quite broken up by the brutality in which he has been engaged. Yet he also leaves **Henry Morgan** with a desire to go to sea to seek his own destiny and fortune in the Indies. Dafydd must return to the Indies as well, to seek out again the heat that he loathes but which he needs to live.

DAKIN. The first leader of the striking migrants in ***In Dubious Battle***, a capable organizer and thrifty man, who is inordinately proud of the new truck he has been able to buy. When it is destroyed by the growers' hirelings, he goes berserk and is jailed.

DAMAS, SIR. A mean and recreant knight in ***The Acts of King Arthur,*** who refuses to share inherited lands with his brother, **Sir Outlake,** and in whose dungeon Arthur is imprisoned. Arthur acts as his champion against **Sir Accolon of Gaul,** the champion of Sir Outlake, but subsequently dispossesses him of all his lands in favor of his brother.

DAN. An old migrant in ***In Dubious Battle*** who has been through many strikes and scoffs at the efforts of the young organizers. When he falls through a defective ladder and breaks a hip, he becomes a rallying focus for the strikers' demonstrations.

DANE, AXEL. San Jose recruiting sergeant in ***East of Eden,*** who allows the shocked and disillusioned seventeen-year-old **Aron Trask** to enlist in the army the morning after Aron meets his mother, **Kate Albey.**

DANNY. In ***Tortilla Flat,*** the main character and the central figure in the title community. He is a paisano, a mixture of Spanish, Indian, and assorted Caucasian bloods. His last name is never given, and the only physical description calls him small, dark, intent, and bowlegged from working on ranches. Danny chooses to live the life of most of his fellow paisanos, eking out a meager living, spending most of his earnings on wine, and sleeping wherever he can. All of these make Danny not just a paisano, but the epitome of a paisano, the very embodiment of Tortilla Flat.

When Danny returns home at the end of World War I, he finds that his grandfather has died, leaving him two houses in Tortilla Flat. Danny considers his inheritance a burden rather than a windfall, and he goes on a drinking binge that lands him in jail. His discomfort with the responsibility of ownership becomes a recurring theme in the novel, and after he escapes from jail, his friend **Pilon** plays upon that discomfort, first to get Danny to let him share one of the two houses and then to get Danny to rent the other house to him.

Soon there are more friends taking advantage of Danny's generosity, such as **Pablo Sanchez** and **Jesus Maria Corcoran,** who move into the second house as a result of Pilon's machinations. One night, these characters accidentally burn down the house they inhabit. However, Danny is actually happy to be rid of at least part of his property. He even invites all of them to stay in his remaining house. From this point on, the friends share everything, inviting more acquaintances, including the **Pirate** and **Big Joe Portagee,** to join the household. Danny's generosity and disdain of property, then, become not only his personal characteristics but also the principles that bind a community together.

In the closing chapters, Danny grows strangely morose, for he longs for freedom from "the weight of property." At first, this longing is manifested in an angry "amok," in which Danny spends weeks drinking, stealing, fighting, and trading all of his possessions (including his house) for more wine. The friends give him a reprieve when they destroy the bill of sale for the house, but Danny's return only postpones the inevitable. He enters a deep depression at the beginning of the penultimate chapter and experiences intimations of death. His friends earn a day's pay to throw him a party, but the party proves to be his last. After behaving like his old self one last time, Danny ends the party by plunging to his death in the gulch south of Tortilla Flat. All Tortilla Flat gathers for his funeral, as they had gathered for his party, but Danny's death signals the end of the community of paisanos he had built: the novel ends when the remaining friends let Danny's house burn and go their separate ways.

Steinbeck tells us in the preface that Danny's house is like Camelot, and his friends are like the Knights of the **Round Table.** This makes Danny the **King Arthur** figure. His rise from humble origins to relative wealth makes him like Arthur, an apparently ordinary boy who becomes king of the Britons when he pulls the sword from the stone. Danny's generosity may be Steinbeck's equivalent of Arthur's moral superiority, although this has been a contentious issue among critics. But certainly Steinbeck intended Danny's crises about the burdens of property to echo Arthur's crises about the responsibility of leadership. Like Arthur, Danny holds his community together, and his death, like Arthur's, leads to the dissolution of a quasi-mystical brotherhood.

Danny also serves as an embodiment of Steinbeck's populist ideal. Danny's relationship with his friends creates a tension between the kind of communal generosity that Steinbeck most admired and the encroaching capitalist values of selfishness and greed.

Bryan Vescio

DANTE ALIGHIERI (1265–1321). Italian poet, generally considered one of the supreme figures of world literature. Dante was admired for the depth of his spiritual vision and for the range of his intellectual accomplishment. His epic masterpiece, *The Divine Comedy,* was begun about 1307 and was completed shortly before his death. The work is an allegorical narrative, in verse of great precision and dramatic force, of the poet's imaginary journey through hell, purgatory, and heaven. **Robert DeMott,** in his extensive study of Steinbeck's reading, notes that Steinbeck had "read the entire *Divine Comedy,* probably at a fairly early age."

Michael J. Meyer

DARK WATCHERS. **Mama Torres,** in "Flight," warns her son **Pepé** about these mysterious figures who appear unpredictably and sporadically along the trail that Pepé rides through the Santa Lucia Mountains. He ignores them, knowing that the best course is to pretend one does not see them. Although Steinbeck declared that he knew neither who they were nor what they symbolized, most readers have no trouble identifying them as metaphors for death, the fate that awaits Pepé.

Steinbeck's ***The Pearl*** is filled with images and figures of darkness: the "dark thing" and "watchful evil" that wait outside **Kino** and **Juana**'s hut after the pearl's discovery; the bleeding "dark figures" lying in Juana's path after she has been beaten by Kino; the "dark enemy" and "watcher[s]" who are tracking them down like animals at the novella's end. Darkness is always accompanied by violence and evil in *The Pearl.* Yet one must also wonder how much of the evil is exterior, and how much comes from within Kino himself, for he is also one of the work's "dark figures," both in his wife's path and at the end when he kills his three pursuers. In this sense, the "dark watchers" may represent the moral and psychic potential within us all.

Stephen K. George

DARWELL, JANE (1880–1967). A character actress (born Patti Woodward) noted for strong, motherly roles, who won the Academy Award as best supporting actress for her performance as **Ma Joad** in **John Ford**'s film version of ***The Grapes of Wrath.***

DARWIN, CHARLES (1809–1882). Famous British naturalist, whose theory of evolution created a revolution in biology, philosophy, and sociology. Serving as a naturalist on H.M.S. *Beagle* while the ship was on a surveying expedition (1831–36), Darwin made observations of animal and plant life that would form much of the evidence for his famous theory. He published *On the Origin of Species by Means of Natural Selection* in 1859, with five revisions through 1872. Darwin's theory defied the reigning creationist theology when it was published.

Steinbeck embraced Darwin's methods and theories, dramatizing them in many novels and short stories. The author formally encountered evolutionary theory in zoology class at **Stanford University**'s Hopkins Marine Station in 1923, but most of his contact with Darwinian ideas came in his reading from 1930 to 1940. Many of the books he read were in friend **Edward F. Ricketts**' small library at his lab in **Monterey**, California. Steinbeck read several volumes concerning evolutionary concepts, including works by **John Elof Boodin**, **Jan Christian Smuts**, and **Henri Bergson**. He probably read Darwin's *Origin* and did read the published journal of the *Beagle*. Steinbeck read the latter volume in preparation for his own expedition, when, in 1940, he and Ricketts spent six weeks in the Gulf of California (**Sea of Cortez**). In his most important nonfiction work, ***The Log from the Sea of Cortez***, he lauds the holistic, inductive methodology of the naturalist, and at one point, Steinbeck compares his collecting expedition to Darwin's.

Critical to Steinbeck's artistic vision is the Darwinian placement of the human species within the whole, defying theological and philosophical preconceptions that would set the human apart (or above) the rest of nature. This viewpoint, largely originated by Darwin, permeates Steinbeck's work in style and in content. From a narrative stance that levels humans and nature through personification, anthropomorphism, theriomorphosis (rendering human characters as beasts), and pervasive motifs (such as a preoccupation with primitive settings), Steinbeck demonstrates that civilization simply veneers what Darwin calls the human's "lowly origin." The biological substructure of the novelist's art undercuts political and social overtones. Novels like ***In Dubious Battle*** and ***The Grapes of Wrath*** are violent pictures of the struggle for survival—competition for land and food. ***The Wayward Bus*** is a brutal consideration of sex, with a view similar to Darwin's theory of sexual selection, in which strength and physical attractiveness decide who wins the privilege of procreation. With the notable exception of ***East of Eden***, Steinbeck rarely strays far from his biological view of humanity. In the last book that he wrote and published in his lifetime, ***America and Americans***, he asks people to look at themselves as a species. He fears above all that Americans have lost their survival drive, their competitive edge. Through much of Steinbeck's work, Darwin's ideas parallel the novelist's biological view of humanity.

Further Reading: Darwin, Charles. *Voyage of the Beagle* (1839). London: Penguin, 1989; ———. *The Origin of Species* (1859). New York: Norton, 1979; Railsback, Brian. *Parallel Expeditions: Charles Darwin and the Art of John Steinbeck.* Moscow, ID: University of Idaho Press, 1995; Steinbeck, John. *The Log from the Sea of Cortez* (1941; 1951). New York: Penguin, 1995; ———. *America and Americans.* New York: Viking, 1966.

Brian Railsback

DAVIS'S BOY, JOE. In *The Grapes of Wrath*, Joe works for the banks that are forcing the Okies from their land. Joe Davis's boy, in intercalary chapter 5, is more concerned about self-survival, earning $3 a day to tractor the tenants from their land. Besides this betrayal of his own, he is also important because his speeches to the victims reveal the impossibility of ever finding who is ultimately responsible for the evictions. Corporations and banks are abstract entities that are insensitive to personal needs and will not respond to an individual's concerns the way they will to the Almighty dollar.

In chapter 6, **Willie Feeley** is mentioned by **Muley Graves** as a similar betrayer, a friend who has been hired to tractor out the Joads, and whom the Joads are reluctant to attack because he appears to be one of their own. When confronted by Muley, Willie, too, identifies his family's needs as taking precedence over those of the landholders. The survival of his wife and children demand his attention, and he is forced to become an enemy of his former friends, enduring violence (Muley hits him over the head with a fence post to avoid capture) in order to complete his task.

Michael J. Meyer

DAWES, (CAPTAIN). Pirate captain in ***Cup of Gold.***

DAY, A. GROVE (1904–1994). Educator, prolific author, and Hawaiian historian, who wrote or edited more than fifty books, including *Mark Twain's Letters from Hawaii. Mad about Islands: Of a Vanished Pacific* is a collection of biographical essays on **Herman Melville**, **Robert Louis Stevenson,** Mark Twain, and other famous writers who spent time in the islands. Born in Philadelphia, Day earned his bachelor's and graduate degrees at **Stanford University**, where he began a lifelong friendship with Steinbeck. Their relationship is documented in Steinbeck's letters. (*See also* **Clemens, Samuel Langhorne**.)

"DAYS OF LONG MARSH, THE" (circa 1924). This unpublished short story, probably written while Steinbeck was at **Stanford University**, concerns a lone, unnamed narrator, who walks alone and slips in the muck of Long Marsh one moonlit night. He is taken in by a mysterious hermit, who lives alone in a hut on the marsh. Here, the narrator listens to the tale of how the hermit sets up a trap for his wife's lover (if indeed she has a lover) by cutting the supports from one of the bridges that lead over the muck to his shack. When the suspected lover falls into the quicksand, the hermit's wife, Nellie, falls in herself and perishes trying to save the man. The hermit is left to consider his deeds, and, in the ensuing years, drifts into various states of reality. The hermit's story and presence are so powerful that the narrator feels he is losing a grip on permanent reality as well. The story demonstrates Steinbeck's early interest in Edgar Allan Poe (like the unpublished "**Murder at Full Moon**" and the more sophisticated short story "**Johnny Bear**," with its eerie, gothic descriptions and its Poesque, first-person narration). Also, this early tale emphasizes Steinbeck's interest in varying perceptions, or the warp of the individual, against the external reality. The unsigned manuscript of this story is at Harvard's Houghton Library.

Brian Railsback

DE KRUIF, PAUL (1890–1971). American bacteriologist and author whose work included writing a film documentary, titled *The Fight for Life*, directed by **Pare Lorentz**. De Kruif became a close friend of Steinbeck. His script for the documentary was written in an attempt to reduce the rate of infant mortality, caused primarily by poverty and ignorance, at the Chicago Maternity Center. Later Steinbeck himself was involved in scripting a similar film titled ***The Forgotten Village***, a documentary that depicted attempts to bring modern medicine to an isolated village in Mexico. Both films combined factual events with a social message, and both men seemed to realize that although they embraced the progress brought about by new technology, they still needed to express reservations about the mixed blessings provided by the social reforms brought about through **Franklin Delano Roosevelt**'s New Deal policies. Paul de Kruif was also famous for his books *Arrowsmith* (1925), which he anonymously co-wrote with Sinclair Lewis, and *The Microbe Hunters* (1926).

Michael J. Meyer

DEAN, JAMES (1931–1955). Although a Hollywood legend, he had major roles in only three movies, one of which was the **Elia Kazan** production of John Steinbeck's ***East of Eden***. Dean played **Cal Trask**. Since the motion picture only covered the last half of the novel, the role was significantly enhanced, and Dean won rave reviews. Like **Marlon Brando**, after whom he modeled himself, Dean seemed destined to play lonely outsiders, who refused to conform to the demands of society.

"DEATH OF A RACKET, THE" (1955). In a response to the Red Scare testimony of Harvey Matusow in Congress during the infamous McCarthy hearings, Steinbeck wrote this article questioning the use of informants by the FBI. In his testimony, Matusow said being such an informer was a good racket and his testimony had "ruined the racket." Indeed, the FBI informant was an important cog in sabotaging the misguided crusade history remembers as McCarthyism. In his appearance before Congress, Matusow admitted telling a string of outrageous lies that McCarthy and others never questioned. This damaged the senator's credibility, and years later, the Ford Foundation declared Matusow's hoax to be the major catalyst for defusing the Red Scare. Later, in his book *False Witness*, Matusow's further revelations made fools of some of the most powerful politicians of the day. Steinbeck's reaction here centers on his hope that Matusow's testimony will push the pendulum of common sense back, as more citizens realize that over "165,000,000 people have been shuddering in terror at a problematical 50,000 communists."

Further Reading: *Saturday Review.* April 12, 1955, 26.

Herbert Behrens and Michael J. Meyer

DEBORAH, GREAT-AUNT. In ***The Winter of Our Discontent***, **Ethan Allen Hawley**'s precursor had emphasized the reality of the Crucifixion and Resurrection for him, and she is vivid in his memory as someone in tune with the occult.

DECKER, CAROLINE (1912–1992). District secretary for the Cannery and Industrial Workers Union, she was an active strike organizer/leader in the cotton strike in the San Joaquin Valley of 1933 that lasted twenty-four days. She was arrested under the California anti-union syndicalism law in 1934, and was found to be carrying a list of sympathizers with her at the time of arrest. Convicted, she spent three years (1934–37) in prison for her activism. She is considered by many critics as a role model for **Jim Nolan** in the novel ***In Dubious Battle***.

Tracy Michaels

DEEMS, MR. A philanthropist in ***Sweet Thursday*** who donates two courts for playing roque, a form of croquet, to the community of **Pacific Grove**. He is a kind man, who kept up his good health by smoking opium occasionally, when it was legal. When he sees the feuding between rival roque teams that results from his benign gift, he sends a bulldozer to demolish the roque courts on the eve of the annual tournament. The people of Pacific Grove, far from being grateful for the removal of this source of dissension, drive Mr. Deems out of town. Thereafter, on tournament day, the entire community holds a celebration at which they burn Mr. Deems in effigy.

Bruce Ouderkirk

DEKKER, MARY STEINBECK (1905–1965). The youngest sister of John Steinbeck, Mary seems to have been his favorite sibling. An early family photograph shows John and sister Mary on their pony, Jill, the "red pony." Sharing an interest in Sir Thomas Malory's book ***Le Morte d'Arthur***, John and Mary borrowed Malory's words to create their own secret language. As a remembrance of this, Steinbeck dedicated ***The Acts of King Arthur*** to his sister, writing the words in calligraphy and referring to her as an unappreciated squire. Steinbeck further suggests that, by these words, he raises Mary to the deserving status of knighthood, investing her with the title Syr Mayrie Stynebec.

John and Mary also shared a summer class at **Stanford University**'s Hopkins Marine Station in **Pacific Grove** in 1923. The next fall, Mary enrolled at Stanford University and was affiliated with the Alpha Phi sorority. It was at Stanford University where she met her future husband, William N. Dekker. They were married when Mary finished college. While serving in the air force during World War II, William Dekker died in the line of duty in 1943. Mary died on January 28, 1965, in **Carmel**, California, and was buried at the Garden of Memories cemetery in **Salinas**.

John Hooper

DELPHINE. The wife of Emil, **the Burgundian**, in ***Cup of Gold***. She was the object of a competition among four friends, but Emil won her love by giving her a single, rose-colored pearl. Although they were happily married, despite her also being the mistress to the three other friends, eventually public opinion required a duel. In that duel, her husband killed two of his friends and cut the arm of his friend Antoine, the other Burgundian. Antoine's cut became infected, and his left arm had to be amputated at the elbow. Emil was forced into exile for having killed his two friends, and Antoine joined him in exile.

Kevin Hearle

DEMOTT, ROBERT JAMES (1943–). Influential Steinbeck critic and author, born in New Canaan, Connecticut, of Italian-American working-class parents, and educated at public schools there and in Norwalk, Connecticut. DeMott received a BA in English from Assumption College (Worcester, MA) in 1965, with a senior thesis on John Steinbeck. His MA in English was awarded by John Carroll University (Cleveland, OH) in 1967, with a thesis on **T. S. Eliot** and W. H. Auden, and his PhD in American literature was earned from Kent State University (Kent, OH) in 1969, with specialization in American Renaissance and philosopher **Henry David Thoreau**. Except for two years at San Jose State University, California, as visiting professor and director of the Steinbeck Research Center, DeMott has taught at Ohio University (Athens) since 1969. In 1998 he was named Edwin and Ruth Kennedy Distinguished Professor at Ohio University.

DeMott served as a member of the editorial boards of the *Steinbeck Quarterly*, the *Steinbeck Newsletter*, and *Steinbeck Studies*. He has published widely in American literature and in creative writing (including poetry collections, *News of Loss* and *The Weather in Athens*); his essays, articles, and reviews on Steinbeck specifically have appeared in numerous journals. And he has contributed chapters to numerous books. He has also written lengthy introductions to Penguin's Twentieth-Century Classics Series reprints of ***To a God Unknown*** and ***The***

Grapes of Wrath. DeMott's books include a loosely linked trilogy on creative aspects of Steinbeck's life and work: *Steinbeck's Reading: A Catalogue of Books Owned and Borrowed* (Garland, 1984); an annotated edition of Steinbeck's composition book, *Working Days: The Journals of "The Grapes of Wrath," 1938–1941* (Viking, 1989; paperback, Penguin, 1990), chosen as a *New York Times* notable book of 1989; and *Steinbeck's Typewriter: Essays on His Art* (Whitston, 1996), which received the Nancy Dasher Book Award from the College English Association of Ohio in 1998. He also published a limited edition chapbook with preface and notes, "Your Only Weapon Is Your Work: A Letter by John Steinbeck to Denis Murphy" (Steinbeck Research Center, 1985), a festschrift, *After "The Grapes of Wrath": Essays on John Steinbeck in Honor of Tetsumaro Hayashi*, edited with Donald V. Coers and Paul R. Ruffin (Ohio University Press, 1995), and is editor (with Elaine Steinbeck as special consultant) of these Library of America volumes for which he planned the contents and also wrote the notes: *John Steinbeck: Novels and Stories 1932–1937* (1994) and *John Steinbeck: "The Grapes of Wrath" and Other Writings 1936–1941* (1996). A third Library of America volume, *Steinbeck: Novels, 1942–1952*, including ***The Moon Is Down***, ***Cannery Row***, ***The Pearl***, and ***East of Eden***, was published in 2001.

DEMPSEY (HAMILTON), MAMIE. Wife of George Hamilton in ***East of Eden***, and Steinbeck's aunt by marriage.

DEUXCLOCHES, M.; DOUXPIED, M.; RUMORGUE, M.; SONNET, M.; VEAUVACHE, M. In ***The Short Reign of Pippin IV***, these are petty bureaucrats and party leaders in the French government, which elects to reinstitute the monarchy and establish the reluctant and retiring **Pippin Héristal** as the new king because of his royal ancestry.

"DICHOS: THE WAY OF WISDOM." (1957). A *Saturday Review* (40.45, 9 Nov. 1957: 13) article in which Steinbeck gives a brief overview of the Spanish *dichos*, which are one-line pithy sayings that might concern a situation, question, or idea.

Eric Skipper

DICK. *See* **Root**.

DISCOURSE. In his post–***Grapes of Wrath*** writing, Steinbeck often turned toward the problem of language. There is evidence of his concern with the ability of language to shape perception. Steinbeck's almost obsessive interest in ***Sea of Cortez*** with the limitations of taxonomic systems is one reflection of this, as are his discussions of ***Cannery Row*** as a "poem" or as "nonfiction" being shaped by the mind of the author (or authors) in the opening paragraphs of *Sea of Cortez*.

As Steinbeck began to examine the world as shaped by discourse, he reaffirmed that truth was at best relative; it could be continually approached from a variety of different directions, but it could never be completely known through concepts provided by language. He also discovered that discourse, and therefore language itself, was to some extent a hindrance to any unmediated experience of reality. The process-oriented **non-teleological thinking**, as outlined in *Sea of Cortez*, was Steinbeck's and **Edward F. Ricketts**' answer to their need to be unhindered by the restrictions of any one discourse; however, in much of Steinbeck's post–World War II fiction and nonfiction, he is less than sanguine about the opportunities afforded by the sort of relativism that non-teleological thinking presupposes. In many of these works, he both dissects the hypocrisies of various discourses and decries the lack of a single discourse that could serve to unify a nation he saw as becoming increasingly decadent.

Further Reading: Bakhtin, Mikhail M. *The Dialogic Imagination: Four Essays*. Caryl Emerson and Michael Holquist, trans. Austin: University of Texas Press, 1981; Hearle, Kevin. "The Boat-Shaped Mind: Steinbeck's Sense of Language as Discourse in *Cannery Row* and

Sea of Cortez." In *After "The Grapes of Wrath": Essays on John Steinbeck in Honor of Tetsumaro Hayashi*. Ed. Donald V. Coers, Paul Ruffin, and Robert J. DeMott. Athens: Ohio University Press, 1995. 101–112.

Kevin Hearle

"DISCOVERING THE PEOPLE OF PARIS." This brief piece first appeared in *Holiday* 20:2 (August 1956, 36–37), which also included articles by Paul Bowles, August Derleth, Bernard De Voto, and others. In it, Steinbeck speaks of the acceptance he felt while living in Paris, stating, "In Paris, my district has become my city, the gendarme on the corner is my gendarme, the neighborhood people have become my neighbors. I am no longer a stranger."

Herbert Behrens and Michael J. Meyer

"DISSONANT SYMPHONY." In 1930, while working on ***To a God Unknown*** and ***The Pastures of Heaven***, John Steinbeck experimented with a collection of linked stories he titled "Dissonant Symphony." According to **Jay Parini**, the work focused on several northern California families—specifically on how their lives were influenced by environment or other circumstances—and thus moved "in the philosophical and aesthetic direction that would [eventually] culminate in ***The Grapes of Wrath***." The title suggests Steinbeck's lifelong interest in music. Later musical references would find their way into Steinbeck's literature, including ***Cannery Row*** (**Doc**'s playing of Monteverdi and Gregorian chants) and ***The Pearl*** (**Kino**'s "Song of the Family" and "Song of the Enemy").

"Dissonant Symphony" went through two major revisions and eventually reached a length of some thirty thousand words. The author even considered combining it with the stories in *Pastures*, which it surely influenced. But this idea was abandoned when he found the episodes wouldn't hold together logically; as Steinbeck bluntly admitted, "Everything I try [with 'Dissonant Symphony'] seems so damned forced." Ultimately, the novel was aborted, as were many of the author's creative endeavors that he considered inferior or inadequate.

Further Reading: Parini, Jay. *John Steinbeck, A Biography*. New York: Holt, 1995.

Stephen K. George

DITSKY, JOHN (1938–2006). University of Windsor professor of English (PhD, MA from the University of Detroit), he earned his doctorate (1967) from New York University, with a dissertation partially devoted to John Steinbeck. Since then, he has written well over a hundred articles and chapters on dozens of American and Canadian poets and fiction writers, as well as a number on American and European modern dramatists; a collection of drama criticism, *The Onstage Christ*, appeared in 1980. Ditsky also published three collections of poetry, a monograph—*Essays on "**East of Eden**"* (1977)—a student manual, *John Steinbeck: Life, Work, and Criticism* (1985), and an edition of largely new work, titled *Critical Essays on John Steinbeck's "**The Grapes of Wrath**"* (1989). Much of his work has been devoted to Steinbeck's previously under-discussed or disparaged later writing. For a quarter-century, he has been variously active in the affairs of the *Steinbeck Quarterly* and the Steinbeck Society. His most recent publication is *John Steinbeck and the Critics* (Rochester, NY: Camden House, 2000), which assesses the literary criticism written about the author over the decades.

DOC. Steinbeck's unique conception of the hero figure is most fully shown through the various "Doc" characters. Whether Doc appears as **Dr. Phillips** of **"The Snake,"** **Doc Burton** of ***In Dubious Battle***, or just plain **Doc** of ***Cannery Row*** and ***Sweet Thursday***, Steinbeck handles him with respect and admiration, as he bases the Doc figures, roughly, on his friend **Edward F. Ricketts**, a resident of **Cannery Row**, biologist, and collector of marine specimens with whom Steinbeck had a close relationship for eighteen years. When readers look at the first three works in which Doc appears, they see a character combining all the best traits of Steinbeck's humanitarian: Doc is humble, compassionate, and strong, an inductive seeker of truth and knowledge—a man in touch with the whole. He sees the wide picture and, therefore, cooperates with others and is quick to forgive. Above all, Doc is a patient teacher—his life as a gatherer of specimens for high schools and universities underscores his desire to observe and pass on to others his knowledge of the natural world. He suffers one important lack, however, and *Sweet Thursday* is a novel bent on solving Doc's loneliness by finding him a good woman.

Doc first appears in "The Snake" (written in 1934 but published later). A mysterious woman visits him at the lab and pays to see a rattlesnake consume a rat; when he senses her perverse interest in the scene, Doc's rational, scientific mind is repulsed. The Doc of *In Dubious Battle* shows he is a man of compassion and action by risking his profession, and possibly his life, as he directs sanitation efforts at the strikers' camp. But he is after a much larger view than the politics of the strike; he equates social injustice among men with physiological injustice among microbes. "I want to see the whole picture," he notes. His life as a lonely, set-apart man is introduced in this novel. In *Cannery Row*, a much fuller presentation of Doc shows him as a nearly whole man, one who knows science and compassion, and who knows the truth about things—from life on the Row to the **Great Tide Pool**. In *Sweet Thursday*, his character continues as a great sympathizer, thinker, and teacher. Yet his loneliness nearly overwhelms him, for he cannot just observe his species—ultimately, the need for close human companionship breaks through. Through an absurd romance often kept alive by the denizens of the Row, Doc finds his true love in **Suzy**. Doc leaves his life on the page a fully realized hero—a man embodying the entire range of human potential. In one of Steinbeck's most poignant scenes, Doc drives off with Suzy on a voyage into life and discovery, rather than accidentally turning his car into a train as Ed Ricketts did on May 7, 1948. *Sweet Thursday* is Steinbeck's wish book for his lost friend, his real-life hero.

Further Reading: Astro, Richard. *John Steinbeck and Edward F. Ricketts: The Shaping of a Novelist*. Minneapolis: University of Minnesota Press, 1973; Lisca, Peter. *The Wide World of John Steinbeck*. New Brunswick, NJ: Rutgers University Press, 1958; Railsback, Brian. *Parallel Expeditions: Charles Darwin and the Art of John Steinbeck*. Moscow, ID: University of Idaho Press, 1995.

Brian Railsback

DOCTOR. Connecticut doctor who treats **Cathy Ames/Catherine Amesbury** at **Adam** and **Charles Trask**'s farm in ***East of Eden*** after she is beaten by **Mr. Edwards**.

DOCTOR, THE. The physician who attends the dying **Henry Morgan** in ***Cup of Gold***. At the end, he bleeds Henry.

DOCTOR, THE. In ***The Pearl***, a greedy Spaniard, whose attitude toward native Mexicans represents the conquistadors' position in the history of Mexico. He embodies the source of evil for the native Indians: exploitation. When **Kino** and **Juana** ask him to see their son, he refuses because they have no money. When he hears of the pearl of great size, however, he visits Kino's house twice to give the baby questionable treatment.

DOCUMENTARIES. John Steinbeck came of age as a writer during the 1930s, which might be called the decade of the documentary as much as of the Depression. The historical convergence of new documentary technologies (in particular the sound motion picture) and new cultural imperatives (in particular economic restructuring) created a new emphasis on realistic documentation. Often these documentary efforts were sponsored by government agencies, as the New Deal documented both the conditions that necessitated change and the improvements that resulted from its new programs. Notable examples included the photographic evidence collected by the Farm Security Administration (FSA) and the illustrated guidebooks published by the Works Progress Administration (WPA). The arts were influenced by these realistic and documentary impulses, and an important new development was the documentary book, which combined photographic illustration with its prose text. Some of the most famous include **Erskine Caldwell** and **Margaret Bourke-White**'s *You Have Seen Their Faces* (1937), **Dorothea Lange** and Paul Taylor's *An American Exodus* (1939), and James Agee and Walker Evans's *Let Us Now Praise Famous Men* (1941).

The significant changes in Steinbeck's work between the beginning and the end of the 1930s can be explained partially by the general influence of this movement toward realism and documentary. For example, his classic novel ***The Grapes of Wrath*** evolved from an initial impulse to create a documentary book on the harsh conditions of the migrant workers' camps in California's great valley. Early in 1937, Steinbeck, accompanied by *Life* photographer **Horace Bristol**, began work on a long photo-essay documenting conditions in the migrant camps. Although the Steinbeck/Bristol project never came to fruition, the author did publish a series of articles in the *San Francisco News*, which were later expanded and republished with photos by Dorothea Lange as *Their Blood Is Strong* (1938). Reworking this material after additional personal observation and research in the files of government agencies, Steinbeck discovered the design of his great novel. Although the narrative would follow the **Joad** family on their desperate journey from the Dust Bowl to California, it would be intercut with documentary chapters much in the manner of the film documentarians such as **Pare Lorentz**, later a friend of the author. The same documentary films also influenced **John Ford**'s classic movie adaptation of Steinbeck's literary masterpiece in 1940.

The documentary direction of Steinbeck's evolution as a writer during the 1930s is confirmed by the projects that followed the success of *The Grapes of Wrath*, both as novel and as film. In 1941, he coauthored a nonfiction account of a voyage in the Gulf of California, *The* ***Sea of Cortez****: A Leisurely Journal of Travel and Research*, with his friend, marine biologist **Edward F. Ricketts**. He later collaborated on another Mexican project with a new friend, documentary film director **Herbert Kline**. Steinbeck wrote the screenplay for Kline's documentary film, ***The Forgotten Village***, concerning the introduction of modern medicine into rural Mexico during this period; the author also arranged for its publication as a photobook, illustrated by frames from the film. After considerable complications, both versions appeared late in 1941, to some critical praise, only to be forgotten because of Pearl Harbor and America's immediate preoccupation with the war effort.

Steinbeck's war work to a great extent consisted of various documentary projects. The first was ***Bombs Away: The Story of a Bomber Team***, another photo-book also intended as the basis for a documentary film. Photographer **John Swope** accompanied Steinbeck as they traveled across the country to the training fields set up for newly formed bomber crews. Their collaborative efforts were structured by the process of training that turned a half-dozen raw recruits into a precision bombing team, ready by the final frame to fly off into air combat and bring the war home to the Axis enemies. This handsome volume was well received, but the film project languished and finally perished. Another of Steinbeck's wartime film works was finished, although to the writer's frustration. ***Lifeboat***, directed by Alfred Hitchcock, was conceived as a docudrama in the mode of *Bombs Away!* but this time dramatizing the accomplishments of the merchant marine in the battle of the Atlantic. Steinbeck's unpublished "novelette" strikes a neat balance between documentary realism and allegorical symbolism that was lost in several subsequent Hollywood treatments.

When Hitchcock's film opened, Steinbeck asked that his name be removed from what he saw as a muddled melodrama. Later in the war, the author turned to straightforward news writing for the New York *Herald-Tribune*, dispatches collected as ***Once There Was a War*** in 1958.

In the postwar period, Steinbeck's documentary works for the most part concerned the Cold War. In 1947, he traveled in the Soviet Union, just as the Iron Curtain was falling across Europe. On this trip, he was accompanied by the famous photographer **Robert Capa**, and the result of their collaboration was the photo-book ***A Russian Journal***, published in 1948 to very positive reviews. Like Capa's photographs, Steinbeck's writing was objective yet sympathetic, in a period when the Cold War was beginning to freeze American/Soviet relations. Steinbeck's strong screenplay for director **Elia Kazan**'s ***Viva Zapata!***, essentially a dramatized biography, also rejected McCarthy-era hysteria about leftist politics. The film uses the congenial subject matter of Mexican history to project Steinbeck's own recognition of the need for concerted, even militant, social action to protect the rights of all the people from ideologues of the right or the left.

Steinbeck's last two documentary texts, ***Travels with Charley*** and ***America and Americans*** (made into a documentary film for television), address social problems he saw dividing the nation in the civil rights and Vietnam eras. Both books unfortunately tend toward personal rather than social observation. However, given the importance of the documentary mode to Steinbeck's lifelong concern for the permutations of the American Dream, it is appropriate that the last of his works published in his lifetime was *America and Americans*, a photo-book celebrating the persistence of this topic.

Further Reading: Millichap, Joseph R. *Steinbeck and Film*. New York: Ungar, 1983.

Joseph Millichap

DON GUIERMO. A representative citizen of Panama in ***Cup of Gold***.

"DON KEEHAN." During John Steinbeck's modern language translation work on ***Morte d'Arthur***, he began a project he hoped would provide a fresh start to Malory's work. This project was the unpublished "Don Keehan," a modern-day version of **Miguel de Cervantes**'s *Don Quixote* set in the rough and tumble American West. As **Jackson J. Benson** notes, Steinbeck considered it a "novelette-movie combination," much in the same way he pictured ***Sweet Thursday*** as a novel-musical drama. He even tried to interest his friends **Elia Kazan** and **Henry Fonda** in the screen version, with Fonda in the leading role. This endeavor, however, was short lived, and after several false starts and periods of intense revision, Steinbeck discarded the manuscript. As he explained to **Pat Covici** in a letter dated December 1958, "It isn't a bad book. It just isn't good enough. . . . It is a nice idea—even a clever idea but that isn't sufficient reason for writing it. . . . Frankly, this is a hack book, and I'm not ready for that yet." Clearly, a combination of guilt over abandoning his beloved translation and a lingering sensitivity from **Alfred Kazin**'s stinging attack in the *New York Times Book Review* in May 1958 (in which Kazin claimed that nothing after ***The Grapes of Wrath*** here was worth reading) prompted the author to abandon the work. Nevertheless, "Don Keehan" did play a role in John Steinbeck's creative life by serving as a dry run for his last novel, ***The Winter of Our Discontent***, which also depicts a quest for moral integrity.

Stephen K. George

DON PEDRO. A representative citizen of Panama in ***Cup of Gold***.

DON QUIXOTE. *See* **Cervantes, Miguel de**.

DORCAS, JUDGE. He is used as an example of routine corruption, fixing traffic tickets in ***The Winter of Our Discontent***; a Dorcas Hoar was reputedly the first to confess to witchcraft in the Salem witch trials.

DORMODY, DR. HORACE. A **Monterey** physician in ***Sweet Thursday***, with whom **Doc** schedules an examination to see if there is any biological cause for his discontent. Later, Doc calls Dormody in the middle of the night to treat his broken arm, which Doc thinks he injured by turning over in his sleep. Dormody suspects, rightly, that Doc's arm was broken by a hard blow. Professional ethics prevent Dormody from discussing the case with anyone, but he can't help chuckling about it to himself at odd moments.

DOS PASSOS, JOHN (1896–1970). As an experimental author, Dos Passos subscribed to the practice of emphasizing the form of a work itself and the effect it could have upon the reading audience. He used materials from various documents (e.g., diaries, newspapers) to enlarge the perspective of a character and the themes of his novels. Steinbeck emulated this practice when he composed his destroyed work **"Dissonant Symphony,"** in which he attempted to give weight to the contrast between the public and private, or inside and outside, dimensions of his main character. The structure of ***The Grapes of Wrath*** and ***East of Eden*** was probably inspired by Dos Passos, with different narrators and different scenes separating the main stream of the narratives. **Robert DeMott** notes Steinbeck read Dos Passos's *USA*, which certainly influenced the structure of *The Grapes of Wrath*. When Steinbeck flew to Tokyo to attend the P.E.N. meeting, Dos Passos and **John Hersey** were also on the flight, and both became Steinbeck's friends.

Tracy Michaels

DOSTOYEVSKY, FYODOR (1821–1881). Dostoyevsky was a Russian novelist and short-story writer, whose psychological penetration into the darkest recesses of the human heart, together with his unsurpassed moments of illumination, had an immense influence on twentieth-century fiction. Dostoyevsky's major works include *Crime and Punishment* and *The Brothers Karamazov*.

Steinbeck's reaction to reading Dostoyevsky was one of admiration. Early on, he commented that certain books were more real than experience, citing the Russian author's work along with **Gustave Flaubert**'s *Madame Bovary*, the novels of **George Eliot**, and **Thomas Hardy**'s *Return of the Native* as examples of such creative genius. **Jackson J. Benson**, in delineating Steinbeck's high school reading, notes that the novels mentioned above were seen by the author not as books but as something that happened to him.

DOUBLETREE MUTT. This dog, who first appears in **"The Gift,"** is one of two ranch dogs. He is described as having a thick tail and as having once gotten his leg caught in a coyote trap. In **"The Great Mountains,"** he is the object of **Jody Tiflin**'s cruel pranks.

DOXOLOGY. A hymn or praise to God and the name of **Samuel Hamilton**'s horse in ***East of Eden***. Although the horse is old and stubborn, Samuel keeps him because he is faithful.

DRAYSON, DAVID. *See* **Baker, Ray Stannard**.

DREISER, THEODORE (1871–1945). One of the great literary figures of American Naturalism. His novels *Sister Carrie* (1900) and *An American Tragedy* (1925) are among his most critically acclaimed works, as well as archetypes for Dreiser's vision of the individual struggling with social and economic forces beyond his or her control. Dreiser often depicted characters from ordinary backgrounds, who possessed little if any education. Creating these types of characters allowed him to effectively portray the failure of an individual's will within problematic scenes of moral importance. Steinbeck owned copies of *Sister Carrie* and *An American Tragedy*, which he read and admired. However, where Dreiser was destroyed by his realization of man's place within the universe, Steinbeck relished it, always believing that there is a profound freedom in that discovery.

T. Adrian Lewis

"DUBIOUS BATTLE IN CALIFORNIA" (1936). First appearing in the *Nation* (September 12, 1936, 302–304), this essay outlines the struggles of the modern California migratory worker and the ever-increasing efforts of large farm owners to suppress them, often with brutality and threats. Steinbeck exposes a corrupt system in which workers are paid trifling wages, subjected to unsanitary living conditions, and labeled communists when they try to organize.

Further Reading: Reprinted in *America and Americans and Selected Nonfiction*. Ed. Susan Shillinglaw and Jackson J. Benson. New York: Viking, 2002. 71–77.

"DUEL WITHOUT PISTOLS" (1952). Written in 1952, while Steinbeck and his wife **Elaine Scott Steinbeck** were traveling abroad, this essay is a reply by Steinbeck to a communist newspaper in Italy that had printed a vicious open letter to him, attacking the United States and Steinbeck's writing in particular. Although Steinbeck acknowledges that he had never answered criticism in his life, feeling that responding was always a losing game, he did send a response to the newspaper, which was communistically cut by the editors. Steinbeck then sent his original piece to *Il Tempo*, a Rome newspaper. When the communist paper replied, it claimed that Steinbeck's books "were no damn good," and in "Duel without Pistols" the author comments regretfully that he wishes he could "learn to keep his 'big' mouth shut."

Further Reading: "Duel without Pistols," *Collier's* 130:8. August 23, 1952, 13–15. Reprinted in *America and Americans and Selected Nonfiction*. Ed. Susan Shillinglaw and Jackson J. Benson. New York: Viking, 2002. 91–100.

Herbert Behrens and Michael J. Meyer

DUENNA, THE. An old woman in the service of **Ysobel Espinoza, La Santa Roja**, in ***Cup of Gold***. When Ysobel at one point lapses into rapid Spanish in the presence of **Henry Morgan**, the Duenna translates for her. The Duenna urges Henry to kill Ysobel because, as a good Catholic woman, Ysobel will surely go directly to heaven, and might even be canonized if killed in defense of her married virtue by the Protestant Henry Morgan.

Kevin Hearle

DUKE OF THE SOUTH BORDER. In ***The Acts of King Arthur***, the enemy of **King Arthur** who challenges **Sir Marhalt**, during the Triple Quest, to fight him and his six sons. Marhalt does so and defeats them, sparing them with the understanding that they will go to the court of Arthur and beg the king's forgiveness.

DUNCAN, ERIC. According to **Robert DeMott**, Steinbeck consulted Duncan's *From Shetland to Vancouver Island* and *The Rich Fisherman and Other Sketches* for background information on Norwegian ancestry and the Lofoden Islands while writing ***The Moon Is Down***.

DUNCAN, RED. One of **Tom Hamilton**'s neighbors in ***East of Eden***. When **Dessie Hamilton** becomes severely ill, Tom rides in a panic to Red's house so he can use his telephone to call **Dr. Tilson** in King City.

E

"THE EASIEST WAY TO DIE" (1958). This article appeared in the *Saturday Review* (41.34, August 23, 1958: 12, 37), subtitled "Reflections of a Man about to Run for His Life." In it Steinbeck ponders the psychological effect life insurance has on those who have it. He theorizes that people live indefinitely as long as they continue to work and lead a productive life, while those who retire die quickly. Where life insurance is concerned, the danger is even greater. He asserts, "I believe that by far the greatest number of heavily insured men simply die because it is expected of them."

Eric Skipper

EAST OF EDEN **(NOVEL)** (1952). Although ***The Grapes of Wrath*** is generally acknowledged as John Steinbeck's masterpiece, he later considered *East of Eden* as his "big" book, for which he felt all the others were merely practice. First known by its working title, "The **Salinas** Valley," then given its present title, *East of Eden*, on June 11, 1951, this epic saga of California, which relates the contrapuntal tales of the **Trask** and the **Hamilton** families, was considered by Steinbeck to be the capstone of his career as a novelist: "I think perhaps it is the only book I have ever written. I think there is only one book to a man," he wrote in the journal that documents the daily vicissitudes of his "attempt to find symbols for the wordlessness" (published as ***Journal of a Novel***, 1969).

The 602-page *East of Eden* was published in September 1952 in a limited, signed edition of 1,500 copies in a brown paperboard slipcase, and a trade edition of 112,621 copies with a colored pictorial dust jacket. Because *East of Eden* was written in a subjective style unlike his earlier fiction, Steinbeck predicted critics would "bitterly resent" its eccentricities, and readers would be unsettled by its graphic content. However, in fact, the novel sold vigorously and was reviewed widely and seriously (although by no means evenly or with consensus). A few years later, it became the basis for a popular movie starring **James Dean** as **Cal Trask** and **Jo Van Fleet** as **Cathy Ames/Kate Albey**, indicating the ease with which visual mediums can appropriate Steinbeck's work. (In 1981, ABC transformed Steinbeck's book into an eight-hour-long "Novel for Television" mini-series starring Jane Seymour as Cathy Ampes/Kate Albey, Timothy Bottoms as **Adam Trask**, and Lloyd Bridges as **Samuel Hamilton**; recently playwright Alan Cook adapted a faithful dramatic version.) Steinbeck produced a text centered around the dynamic issues of individual (and often aberrant) identity, responsibility, and belief; the failure of rigid adherence to institutionally constructed norms of morality; the melding of history, (auto)biography, and fiction (which provides a critique of both genre and objectivity); and the redefinition of the family along psychological/emotional lines of difference rather than along lines of monolithic propriety. Perhaps, for these reasons and for its unflinching presentation of evil in American life, *East of Eden* has continued to fascinate readers ever since and, as a consequence, has never been out of print.

For years, Steinbeck had dreamed of writing a major book on his home area, the Salinas Valley, but it wasn't until early 1948 that he actually began taking steps to realize that ambition. He visited the area to reacquaint himself with its flora, fauna, geography, and landscape; he talked to family members, friends, and a few trusted old timers; and he arranged to carry out research in the back files of the daily *Salinas Californian*. He steeped himself in the social and domestic atmosphere of nineteenth- and early twentieth-century Salinas.

A couple of traumatic events, however, delayed his actual writing of the novel. First, in May 1948, his closest friend, collaborator, and soul mate, **Edward F. Ricketts**, was killed in a car-train accident in **Monterey**. Then, a few months later, Steinbeck's world was shattered even more by his second wife **Gwyndolyn Conger Steinbeck**'s demand for a divorce. Steinbeck retreated to his family's cottage on 11th Street in **Pacific Grove** (Gwyn and their two sons, **Thom** and **John IV**, stayed in Manhattan) and was again close to his old Salinas Valley haunts during 1948 and 1949. But, given Steinbeck's mental and emotional distress, his misogyny and feelings of victimization, and his increasingly complicated involvement in writing a film script of the life of Mexican revolutionary Emiliano Zapata for **Elia Kazan** (***Viva Zapata!***) and later—in 1950—writing his controversial play-novelette ***Burning Bright***, he managed to accomplish very little on the novel during that three-year period, except to brood deeply over its potential direction and shape. Normally with Steinbeck, such brooding, percolating, and gestating were always integral to his creative process, and he accepted the extensive period of interior rehearsal that generally preceded the actual writing of his fiction. Regarding this project, however, perhaps because Steinbeck felt so much was riding on the success of his personal vision, he seemed to have been particularly anxious and guilt-ridden about failing to compose any hard copy at all for several years. In fact, however, the themes of trust and betrayal, and the issues of brotherhood and paternity, that came to figure prominently in *East of Eden* were being worked out by Steinbeck in *Zapata* and *Burning Bright* (script published in 1975).

By late January 1951, however, Steinbeck's life had taken a momentous turn for the better. Recently married to **Elaine** Anderson **Scott Steinbeck** (his third wife), and living again in New York City not far from his two children, Steinbeck, feeling at last settled and supported, was ready to begin writing his coveted work. While his intense personal turmoil and anger had considerably subsided, the aftermath of his divorce from Gwyn would give emotional coloration to the book and help quicken the portraits of several characters, notably that of Cathy Ames herself and of Cathy's disastrous, nightmarish conjugal relationship with Adam and **Charles Trask**. In the meantime, certain aspects of his sons Tom and John's temperaments, habits, and physiques went into his creation of Cal and **Aron Trask**, the sons of Adam and Cathy. In addition, Steinbeck's ongoing anxieties over his role as absentee father to his young sons figured prominently in the creation of the neglectful relationship between Adam Trask and his twin sons. Steinbeck's acute awareness of being emotionally reborn through his marriage to Elaine (whose daughter, Waverly, lived with them) also contributed to the salutary emphasis of some of the discursive chapters and to the redemptive climax in which Steinbeck reconfigures the makeup of the American family.

Another sea change also informed the novel in progress. Galvanized by positive changes in his own psyche and also responding to his 1947 trip to Russia and to the larger shift in the climate of post-1945 Cold War America, Steinbeck made a dramatic break with his own aesthetic. He turned his back on the phalanx concept that had informed and made possible his brand of social realism and communitarian vision in his earlier fiction, and he embraced instead the sanctity of individual creativity. "The only creative thing our species has is the individual, lonely mind," he reported to novelist **John O'Hara** on June 8, 1949, because "the group ungoverned by individual thinking is a horrible destructive principle." His anti-totalitarian thinking, his hatred of official communist and fascist systems, codified in a 1951 broadcast for Voice of America, helped shape the subjective aesthetic matrix of his new novel, and may have contributed to the text's pronounced dualism, its sense of American exceptionalism (although not offered without irony), and its aggressive pronouncement in chapter 13 on "the freedom of the mind to take any direction it wishes," which produces moments of "glory." In any event, Steinbeck's literary expressivism affected everything from the book's themes of individual redemption and creative choice, to its use of literary symbolism, to its binary technique of interspersing the realistic, omnisciently narrated sections of plot with the fictive interventions of first-person commentary by the author/narrator. As an example of how Steinbeck sought to unsettle the boundaries between history and fiction, in chapter 31 of this experiment in narration, fictional character Adam Trask visits the real-life Steinbeck house on Central Avenue in Salinas, where young sister and brother, Mary (*see* **Dekker, Mary Steinbeck**) and John Steinbeck, peeked out at Adam from behind the skirts of their mother, **Olive Hamilton Steinbeck**.

In carrying out his radical textual project, Steinbeck was breaking with the tradition of seamless realism produced by a completely omniscient or removed narrator, and was instead drawing on examples of what for him were innovative, self-aware fictions, such as Joseph Fielding's digressive *Tom Jones*, **Herman Melville**'s highly symbolic *Moby-Dick*, and **Andre Gide**'s journal/novel hybrid *The Counterfeiters*. Indeed, self-consciously literary, *East of Eden* also shows the impact of many other writers from Steinbeck's life as a reader—**Plutarch**, **Herodotus**, Marcus Aurelius, Dr. John Gunn, **William James**, **Erich Fromm** (*Steinbeck's Reading*, passim). In 1953, Steinbeck told Charles Mercer "that the author has become so absent from the modern novel, that it's actually become a stereotype. I felt I could tell *East of Eden* better by being in it myself." By being "in" his fiction, Steinbeck granted himself artistic permission to use autobiographical reminiscences and memories (and both family stories and secrets) of the kind that open the novel in chapters 1 and 2, for instance, and to present unabashedly personal opinions on a wide variety of topics, such as direct speeches to his audience in chapters 13, 19, and 34. Reviewers and critics who were his contemporaries often took this mixture of modes and genres as a signal of artistic failure; current literary theory is more tolerant regarding Steinbeck's hybridization of discourses and his shifting roles of narrative agency, although it is still difficult to know exactly what to call *East of Eden*—it has elements of novel, autobiography, confession, memoir, history, and essay—and manages to resist taxonomy. Moreover, given Steinbeck's contention that all worthy literature has something "preposterous" about it, it is possible to consider *East of Eden* as a fiction of unfolding narrative consciousness, or even as a fictive memoir, rather than as a traditionally well-made, "straight-line narrative" (*Journal of a Novel*).

On Monday, January 29, 1951, Steinbeck sat down to begin the long-awaited process of composition by writing a preliminary journal entry. He had before him a blue-lined, oversized (10 3/4" x 14") ledger book given to him by **Pascal Covici**, his editor at the **Viking Press**, and his plan was to repeat a practice he had started with *The Grapes of Wrath* and ***The Wayward Bus***; that is, to keep a complete running record of his day's writing progress. But where the two previous daily diaries had been private—almost arcane—in purpose, this journalizing effort would have a self-justifying air to it, because it was consciously addressed to Pat Covici. (Steinbeck not only dedicated the novel to his cherished editor and friend, but also presented him with the completed manuscript in a special mahogany box he had carved himself.) After taking two weeks off while his writing room/library on the top floor of the house at East 72nd was being finished, he began again on Monday, February 12, and at the start of each day's work, Steinbeck made a letter-like entry of varying length to Covici on the left-hand page of the "double-entry" record book; then, when that was finished, he launched his day's novel stint—usually between 1000 and 2000 words—on the right-hand page of the ledger. Steinbeck dawdled with isolated entries for a few days before penciling the first lines of his fiction on Thursday, February 15, but once he started in earnest, he hardly missed a beat for the next nine months, the longest period of sustained novel writing in his career.

On a weekly basis, Steinbeck sent or gave Covici manuscript pages of the novel, carefully removed from the ledger; Covici had the manuscript typed and just as regularly returned both manuscript and typed pages to Steinbeck. Occasionally, Steinbeck also read aloud sections of the novel to his wife, his editor, and his agent, **Elizabeth Otis**, in order to ensure a properly sustained rhythm, but he discouraged the voicing of direct criticism, a point Elaine Steinbeck learned firsthand. Steinbeck debated the feasibility of printing the novel and its work letters together as an integrated text; had that been the case, the result would have been a truly intertextual, double-voiced product. However, Viking Press published them separately, with *Journal of a Novel: The "East of Eden" Letters* not appearing until 1969, a year after Steinbeck's death and five years after Covici's. It has generally been thought that *Journal of a Novel* was the only diary Steinbeck kept during the writing of *East of Eden*, but Steinbeck, addicted to self notation, also made fairly regular and lengthy private commentary—"secret writing," he called it on February 12—in two other as-yet unpublished 1951 leather-bound record books (housed at the Pierpont Morgan Library, New York City). These three journals provide a synchronistic view into the cluttered personal, historical, and social context in which Steinbeck wrote, and considered together, they serve to demystify his compositional process at the same time they indicate how central, how definitive, how salvational all modes of inscription were in his life, and the degree to which Steinbeck required the presence of an audience to address as he wrote.

When the Steinbecks, children in tow, moved to a rented house next to Sankaty Light on Siasconset Bluff on the island of Nantucket for the summer, the writer kept up his daily regimen, despite a very busy domestic routine; back in Manhattan in September, Steinbeck completed the first draft of his book on Thursday, November 1, 1951. During the next four months, he trimmed the huge typescript (over 900 pages long, and approximately 265,000 words) by carefully revising, rewriting, and eventually cutting out over 90,000 words, according to his own estimate. It is important to understand the ramifications of Steinbeck's revisions. Originally, the novel was addressed directly to Steinbeck's sons, then six and four years old. The opening page of "The Salinas Valley" autograph manuscript reads, "Dear Tom and John: You are little boys now when I am writing this . . . I think I will tell you a book about that Valley so that you will come in time to know what your father was like and how he lived." Although later excised in the revision process, these numerous and sometimes lengthy first-person addresses to Tom and John help explain the instructional tone (sometimes tendentiously so) of the published book, and situate Steinbeck's paternal desire to tell them its highly symbolic, almost allegorical tale, the "greatest story of all—the story of good and evil" (*Journal of a Novel*), at the same time instructing them in the grittiest aspects of human conduct, mores, and sexuality. On one level, then, the novel was intended as a kind of young person's guide book, or manner book, with which to negotiate the intricacies of social intrigue, sexual politics and power, and familial history.

The elevated theme of the universal war of good and evil, the eternal battle of virtue and vice, is given a secular cast and underscores the casually unfolding and intertwined plot of *East of Eden*. Steinbeck clearly felt that Americans had lost a sense of evil, and that this absence limited the full range of felt life. And, yet, the novel's morality, insofar as it can be said to promote such terms, arises from the actions of its characters and from the narrator's shared ground of inquiry, not from the imposition of a predetermined order of behavior or any machinery of theological transcendence.

Steinbeck's fascination with the biblical story of Genesis (4:1–16) had been explicitly on his mind at least since 1946, according to his unpublished "*Wayward Bus* Journal," especially the tragic tale of brothers Cain and Abel, a story that was to provide the thematic backbone for the novel. Many of Steinbeck's previous characters also had names beginning with C or A, and his C characters (**Juan Chicoy** in *The Wayward Bus* and Cathy Ames and Charles Trask in *East of Eden*, for example) are additionally physically marked with a Cain sign. *East of Eden* narrates three generations of the tyrannical **Cyrus Trask**'s family, in time from the Civil War to World War I, in place from Connecticut to California. Through it all, no Trask brother ever quite escapes being visited by the sins of his parents, or ever quite fully resolves the burden of neglect, inarticulateness, abandonment, or misplaced love. The Trask plot of Steinbeck's novel attempts to confront head-on the unspeakable horror of childhood rejection, dysfunctional parenting, and wayward, irrational affection.

The main thread in this multilayered history concerns Cyrus's favored son, Adam Trask, a Civil War veteran and former chain gang convict, who nevertheless remains a type of the unsuspecting American innocent. Steinbeck relates Adam's impulsive marriage to Cathy Ames in Connecticut (in earlier chapters, she has killed a teacher/lover as well as her parents, has run away, and has served as a prostitute and been almost bludgeoned to death by her whoremaster). On their wedding night, this heartless incarnation of evil drugs Adam and has intercourse with his brother, Charles. In an attempt to escape the traumatic memories of his past, Adam then moves to the King City area of California's Salinas Valley, where, clueless about Cathy's real nature, Adam intends to build a family dynasty in the Edenic countryside. However, Cathy, desperate to be free, tries to abort her dual pregnancy and shoots Adam in the shoulder with his own Colt pistol, ultimately abandoning their twin sons, Aron and Cal, shortly after their birth. Adam wallows in self-pity and inertia for ten years. He then begins a gradual restoration, first, by standing up to Cathy (now named Kate), who has become the sadistic madam of a notorious Salinas brothel, and then, on his deathbed, by forgiving the transgressions of his own son, Cal.

While most other characters can be considered at least nominally good, in creating the murderous Cathy/Kate, Steinbeck created a character of conscienceless evil and, like Melville's Captain Ahab, of unmitigated pride. Cathy/Kate is so sensational that she cannot be contained by the definition of "monster," which Steinbeck attributed to her in chapter 8; rather, everything about her is unsettling or disorienting, including her fascination with Alice in Wonderland and her own unpredictable suicide, so that her textual presence is constantly subject to revision by the narrator. Nevertheless, her influence on the book and its various characters is deep and pivotal and cannot be erased, for she is the image of depravity that all people have in themselves. In that sense, her demonic power defies gender boundaries.

This dynastic, Gothic-like tale of betrayal, corruption, and suffering among the Trasks, however, is juxtaposed with the more socially normative, quasi-pastoral tale of the Hamilton family's existence in the Salinas Valley. Steinbeck presents a fictionalized portrait of his maternal family, with special emphasis on Samuel Hamilton, his Irish grandfather, colorful patriarch of the clan and avid reader of **William James**'s 1890 *Principles of Psychology*. Steinbeck's evocation of the natural environment and physical attributes of the Salinas Valley provides a resonant backdrop for his depiction of the nimble-minded Samuel and his wife, **Liza**, and their children, including four boys—**George**, **Will**, **Tom**, and **Joe**—and five girls—**Una**, **Lizzie**, **Dessie**, **Olive**, and **Mollie**—all of whom Steinbeck sketches in varying detail and weaves throughout the book. A man of many parts—blacksmith, inventor, midwife, farmer—Samuel Hamilton is painted in a near-mythic way as a representative of compassion, clear thinking, integrity, honor, and—given the paucity of their farm—skillful economic survival.

It is Samuel, along with **Lee** (Adam's trustworthy, intellectual Chinese servant), who, in a symbolic way, grant an identity to the abandoned twins by naming them **Caleb** and Aron. Part Three of the novel (chapters 23–33) contains a philosophical turn: Samuel, Lee, and Adam discuss the Cain and Abel story and debate the meaning of various translations; in the Hebrew word ***timshel*** (actually *timshol*), which Lee translates as "thou mayest," is found the central ideogramic, textual key of the novel. Rather than ordering man to triumph over sin—or promising man that would happen—God gave man a choice. "It might be the most important word in the world," Lee says. "That says the way is open. That throws it right back on man. For if 'Thou mayest'—it is also true that 'Thou mayest not.'" Although existential freedom is the hallmark of Samuel's character, Steinbeck's emphasis on intelligent, pragmatic choice as a creative action radiates throughout the novel, so that when Samuel dies, his legacy as a fixer, a nurturer, is not completely lost. In particular, Lee, Steinbeck's androgynous male, carries on the tradition of domestic spiritual economy by single-handedly holding the Trask family together.

In the fourth and final section of the novel, chapters 34–55 (the basis for Elia Kazan's 1955 film version), the focus shifts to Cal, whom Steinbeck thought of as a kind of **Everyman** figure in this "symbol story of the human soul." With Cal, however, the drama is given a realistic rather than mythic dimension. The animosity between the brothers Adam and Charles over their father's love is here repeated in Aron and Cal's oppositional feelings toward Adam's inconsistent shows of affection and his differing expectations for each boy. Fair-haired, high-minded Aron, who resembles Adam, turns out to be defeated by what life deals him—he is too rigid to roll with the punches. His brother, moody, dark Cal, who resembles Charles, struggles to resolve the issues of his mother's inherited blood; for him, the path to self-identity is painful and troubled, because it continually forces Cal to redefine himself with candor and honesty. **Abra Bacon**'s disenchantment with Aron and her eventual love for Cal is enhanced by the latter's capacity for self-doubt, his uneasiness with his own "badness." Cal's mistaken need to prove his love for Adam by giving him money earned from a crop sales scheme engineered by Will Hamilton (Adam rejects the $15,000 gift, which Cal later burns) and his vengeful desire to wound Aron by unmasking their mother Kate as a whore have significant repercussions. When Aron is shown who his mother really is, he quits **Stanford University**, enlists in the army, and shortly afterward is killed. Upon learning the news of Aron's death, Adam has a stroke. Cal, believing he has, in effect, murdered his brother and hastened the incapacity of his father, is beside himself with guilt until Lee intercedes and implores Adam to bless his son, which he does: "His whispered word seemed to hang in the air: 'Timshel!' His eyes closed and he slept," Steinbeck concludes. Just as Steinbeck had done at the end of *The Grapes of Wrath* when **Rose of Sharon (Rosasharn)** gave her breast to the dying man, this final tableau scene draws a picture of a new kind of household—here Cal, Lee, and Abra, all social, racial, or gendered outsiders—coming together in mutual love and concern over Adam's deathbed and symbolically subverting the legacy of masculine inheritance that has propelled the novel since the days of Cyrus Trask and Samuel Hamilton. Recognition of this subtle transformation in the power structure of the American family may have been the greatest lesson Steinbeck wished to impart to his own children, a legacy at least partly demonstrated by the late John Steinbeck IV in a 1990 talk in Salinas called "Adam's Wound."

Scholarly criticism of *East of Eden* has relentlessly detailed its structural flaws, character inconsistencies, stylistic gaffes, and plot failures, as the influential critics **Peter Lisca**, R. W. B. Lewis, and **Warren French** demonstrate. Many other critics, such as **Howard Levant** and **Roy S. Simmonds**, consider it a kind of magnificent failure or qualified success, especially in comparison to *The Grapes of Wrath*. **John Ditsky** and Mark Govoni have performed important foundational work on the novel; **Martha Heasley Cox** has established the relatedness of real-life and fictional Hamiltons.

Some recent discussions of the novel by **Robert DeMott**, Steven Mulder, **Louis Owens**, **John H. Timmerman**, and David Wyatt are less influenced by hegemonic New Critical principles that held sway through the 1970s and, as a result, treat the novel on its own terms, either by accepting Eden's self-reflexive constructedness or by viewing its experimental techniques and tendencies as prophetic postmodernist strategy. But despite four decades of steady critical conversation, no thorough consensus regarding its rank in Steinbeck's canon has been reached, and, in fact, a great deal remains to be investigated in this work. Matters of critical taste aside, Steinbeck's immersion in a matrix of internal and external forces gives *East of Eden* a contextual richness and helps explain why he considered it "the book" with "all the things I have wanted to write all my life."

Further Reading: Cox, Martha Heasley. "Steinbeck's Family Portraits: The Hamiltons." In *Mapping "East of Eden."* Ed. Robert DeMott. Special issue of *Steinbeck Quarterly* 14 (Winter–Spring 1981): 23–32; DeMott, Robert. "'Working at the Impossible': The Presence of *Moby-Dick* in *East of Eden*." In *Steinbeck's Typewriter: Essays on His Art*. Troy, NY: Whitston, 1996. 75–106, 206–232; Ditsky, John. *Essays on "East of Eden."* Steinbeck Monograph Series, No. 7. Muncie, IN: John Steinbeck Society of America/Ball State University, 1977; ———. "'We Are Cain's Children': Towards a Newer Testament." *South Dakota Review* 35 (Summer 1997): 47–59; Fontenrose, Joseph. *John Steinbeck: An Introduction and Interpretation*. New York: Barnes and Noble, 1963; French, Warren. *John Steinbeck's Fiction Revisited*. New York: Twayne, 1994; Gladstein, Mimi Reisel. "The Strong Female Principle of Good—or Evil: The Women of *East of Eden*." *Steinbeck Quarterly* 24 (Winter–Spring 1991): 30–40; Hayashi, Tetsumaro. "'The Chinese Servant' in *East of Eden*." *San Jose Studies* 18 (Winter 1992): 52–60; Levant, Howard. *The Novels of John Steinbeck: A Critical Study*. Columbia: University of Missouri Press, 1974; Lewis, R. W. B. "John Steinbeck: The Fitful Daemon." In *Steinbeck: A Collection of Critical Essays*. Ed. Robert Murray Davis. Englewood Cliffs, NJ: Prentice Hall, 1972. 163–175; Lisca, Peter. *The Wide World of John Steinbeck*. New Brunswick, NJ: Rutgers University Press, 1958; McElrath, Joseph R., Jesse S. Crisler, and Susan Shillinglaw, eds. *John Steinbeck: The Contemporary Reviews*. New York: Cambridge University Press, 1996; Mulder, Steven. "The Reader's Story: East of Eden as Postmodernist Metafiction." *Steinbeck Quarterly* 25 (Summer–Fall 1992): 109–118; Owens, Louis. "Steinbeck's *East of Eden* (1952)." In *A New Guide to Steinbeck's Major Works with Critical Explications*. Ed. Tetsumaro Hayashi. Metuchen, NJ: Scarecrow Press, 1993. 66–89; Simmonds, Roy S. "'And Still the Box Is Not Full': Steinbeck's *East of Eden*." *San Jose Studies* 18 (Fall 1992): 56–71; Timmerman, John H. *John Steinbeck's Fiction: The Aesthetics of the Road Taken*. Norman: University of Oklahoma Press, 1986; Wyatt, David. Introduction to *East of Eden* by John Steinbeck. New York: Penguin Books, 1992.

Robert DeMott

EAST OF EDEN* (FILM)** (1955). In September 1952, John Steinbeck published his major postwar fictional effort, *East of Eden*, to mixed critical response but best-seller popularity that ensured film adaptation. **Elia Kazan**, Steinbeck's collaborator on ***Viva Zapata!, directed a screen version of

East of Eden, which was released in March 1955 and won more critical praise than Steinbeck's novel. The persistence of *East of Eden*'s popularity was demonstrated by a major television presentation broadcast by ABC over three evenings' prime-time viewing in February 1981. Both adaptations remain most interesting as indirect commentaries on the work Steinbeck thought his most important, but which most critics find less interesting than his fiction of the Depression decade.

After the long and difficult gestation period of his "big California book," the author was happy to leave the task of screen adaptation for *East of Eden* to Kazan, who enlisted the aid of Paul Osborn, a successful playwright and film writer. They tightened the focus of the sprawling narrative to the dramatic and symbolic conflict of twin brothers **Cal** and **Aron Trask** for the love of their father, **Adam Trask**, the central figure in Steinbeck's family saga. Their film makes Cal the pivotal character, even as it excises roughly the first two-thirds of the original narrative to emphasize the confrontations of the brothers with each other, as well as with their patriarchal single parent. This strategy tightens Steinbeck's somewhat diffuse plot lines, but it places great importance on the casting.

In fact, the 1955 film is best remembered precisely for its casting. Because Kazan saw the romantic, inarticulate, and frustrated Cal as the dramatic center of the work, he wanted to cast **Marlon Brando**, who had starred in his Kazan's memorable adaptation of Tennessee Williams's *A Streetcar Named Desire* (1951). Because Brando was already committed to other projects, Osborn suggested a young actor who struck him as a budding Brando type, and Kazan quickly signed **James Dean** for the role, establishing the screen persona that grew to cult proportions after the new star's untimely death. Dean's screen presence also creates much of the difficulty with the film version, notably an exaggerated reliance on the emotions of "Method Acting" to achieve melodramatic catharsis. Despite competent performances by the rest of the cast—notably Raymond Massey as Adam Trask, **Jo Van Fleet** as **Cathy Trask**, and Julie Harris as **Abra**—Dean's histrionic excesses make the movie something of a period piece. Kazan's attempts at an experimental filmic style that would match the overwrought emotions of the characters also contribute to the inauthentic quality of this adaptation, although his direction did win praise for effective use of the new, wider screen.

Quirky casting also created major problems for the 1981 eight-hour television miniseries based on Steinbeck's California saga. In particular, the presence of the comely British actress Jane Seymour as Cathy Trask, as well as that of the boyish brothers Timothy and Sam Bottoms as father and son Adam and Cal Trask, evoked a sense of prime-time soap opera, a form then dominating the television ratings in series such as *Dallas*, *Dynasty*, and *Falcon's Crest*. Although the longer format was more capable of realizing Steinbeck's epic sweep by including the first two-thirds of the plot excised in the earlier film, it also abandoned the writer's attempts at archetypal and intellectual symbolism to emphasize the more prurient aspects of the novel. The lavish, location-shot production reinforced director Harvey Hart's simplistic reading of Steinbeck's text with a "television epic" style. Again, this version of Steinbeck's novel seems most interesting as a period piece or as an oblique commentary on its original. Although John Steinbeck cannot be held accountable for the vagaries of either production, both suggest difficulties may be inherent in his own vision of *East of Eden*—especially in terms of one-dimensional characters, melodramatic plot lines, and overwrought emotions and themes.

Further Reading: Millichap, Joseph R. *Steinbeck and Film*. New York: Ungar, 1983; Morsberger, Robert E. "*East of Eden* on Film." *Steinbeck Quarterly* 25:1–2 (Winter–Spring 1992): 28–42; Steinbeck, John. *East of Eden*. New York: Viking, 1952.

Joseph Millichap

"EAST THIRD STREET." *See* **"Days of Long Marsh, The."**

EATON, WILLIE. *See* **Central Committee at Weedpatch Camp**.

ECTOR DE MARYS, SIR. Father of **Sir Kay** and elder brother of **Sir Lyonel** in *The Acts of King Arthur*. Chosen by **Merlin** to rear **Arthur** from a newborn baby. He is one of the knights captured and imprisoned by **Sir Tarquin**. When released by **Sir Lancelot,** he decides, together with his son and his brother, to ride after Lancelot and join him on his quest.

EDDIE. One of **Mack**'s "boys" in ***Cannery Row*** and ***Sweet Thursday,*** he lives at the **Palace Flophouse Bar and Grill**. Eddie is a "desirable inhabitant" of the flophouse because of his duties as the understudy bartender at the **Café La Ida**. When a customer leaves an unfinished drink, Eddie pours the remains into a jug, which he takes home with him; this habit gives Mack and the boys a steady, although chaotic, supply of alcohol.

EDDIE. In ***The Wayward Bus***, one-time fiancé of **Camille Oaks**'s friend, Lorraine.

EDDINGTON, ARTHUR (1882–1944). British physicist and astronomer. Eddington's *The Nature of the Physical World* (1929) was a work of influence for Steinbeck, and it is referred to in ***Sea of Cortez***. In 1932, when mythologist **Joseph Campbell** lived near **Edward F. Ricketts**, Eddington was a topic of conversation for John and Joseph at Ed's lab. Eddington's wide-open discussions from the quantum to the cosmic were probably appealing to John and Ed as they developed their holistic viewpoint.

EDGAR. In ***The Wayward Bus***, the ticket clerk at the **San Ysidro** bus station. Edgar admires Louie, the Greyhound bus driver. He emulates Louie's sexually degrading references toward **Camille Oaks** in their conversation prior to the bus's departure, and sports the beginnings of a long nail on his left little finger, copying Louie's fully grown one. Edgar displays his provincial prejudice in dealing with a pair of Hindu passengers, thinking of them as "rag heads," who ought to learn English.

EDMAN, IRWIN (1896–1954). New York writer and professor of philosophy at Columbia University. He published in a variety of genres, beginning with *Poems* (1925). From there, he completed the novel *Richard Kane Looks at Life* (1925), and an introduction to the nonfiction work *The World, the Arts, and the Artist* (1928). Steinbeck read two 1939 publications by Edman, *Candle in the Dark* and *Philosopher's Holiday,* and noted that he had enjoyed them.

EDUARDO. In ***Viva Zapata!*** he is the guerilla fighter who tells Emiliano of the bravery of a little boy (who he brings with him) and his brother. Eduardo describes how the two boys had pulled a machine gun out of the gunner's hands.

EDWARD OF THE RED CASTLE, SIR. One of the two brothers who have taken the Red Castle and lands from the **Lady of the Rock** in ***The Acts of King Arthur***. He is killed by Sir Ewain during the Triple Quest.

EDWARDS, CHARLEY. An officer under whom **Ethan Allen Hawley** (in ***The Winter of Our Discontent***) had served. Ethan remembers him as a figure of military efficiency, whose objectivity he had once admired.

EDWARDS, DR. VICTOR. A physician who treats **Adam Trask** in ***East of Eden***. Adam has a stroke at the post office, when he discovers that his son **Aron Trask** has run away and enlisted in the army. Edwards is also in attendance after Adam's second stroke, a result of receiving the telegram that brings the news of Aron's death.

EDWARDS, MR. Married, wealthy Boston whoremaster in ***East of Eden***, who hires, then falls in love with, **Cathy Ames**, now **Catherine Amesbury**. Edwards buys a house for her, gives her money, and buys her presents. He is so smitten with her that he easily becomes her dupe. Only when she drinks champagne at his insistence, insults him, taunts him, and cuts his face does he come to his senses. After learning about the money that she stole from him and about her past, he exacts revenge. He forces her to accompany him to Connecticut, where he intends to whip her and put her to work at an inn, but, overcome with passion, he beats her first with his fists and then with a stone, leaving her for dead. He runs from the scene, leaving behind the suitcase, whip, and box of money, all found later by **Alex Platt**. The scar on Cathy/Catherine's forehead—intended as a Cain sign—results from this beating.

EDWARDS, MRS. Wife of **Mr. Edwards**, the wealthy Boston whoremaster who falls in love with **Catherine Amesbury** in ***East of Eden***. Mrs. Edwards is involved with church and children, and she believes her husband is in the importing business. She feels helpless when she finds her husband weeping over Catherine and concludes that he is sick beyond any remedy.

EGGLAME, SIR. One of **King Arthur**'s knights in ***The Acts of King Arthur***, who has a fight with **King Pellinore** and finally flees to save his life.

EGLAN, SIR. A young and untried knight beaten in combat by **Sir Ewain** in ***The Acts of King Arthur***.

EINSTEIN, ALBERT (1879–1955). Arguably one of the most famous names in mathematics and physics, Einstein won the major awards in his field, including the Nobel Prize in 1921. His work was as revolutionary in physics as **Darwin**'s was in natural science. Ever interested in the science of his day, Steinbeck investigated physics, noting as early as 1929 in a letter that he was enjoying his study of quantum theory. Steinbeck likely read a 1920 translation of Einstein's *Relativity* and **Arthur Eddington**'s sweeping discussion of physics, *The Nature of the Physical World*. Steinbeck and **Edward F. Ricketts**' **non-teleological** concept of "is" thinking (focusing on *what* rather than *why*) would naturally involve Einstein's theory of relativity, that measurement of space and time are relative to one's position—there are no absolutes. Steinbeck was very interested in the hint of chaos in things suggested in physics, where concepts that explain the subatomic universe do not work for the cosmic universe, and where there exists the quest to reconcile the subatomic and cosmic universes. Steinbeck's fiction often highlights what he calls the "warp" of perception that he discusses in ***The Log from the Sea of Cortez***. ***The Grapes of Wrath*** oscillates between the micro view of the **Joad** family and the macro view of the intercalary chapters that present the big picture. ***Cannery Row***'s realities depend on one's relative position on the Row or, as the famous prologue suggests, which "peephole" one peers through. As he did with Darwin, Steinbeck admired the inductive leap Einstein made in creating theory that challenged popular preconceptions, and he put Einstein on his lists of great thinkers in both *Sea of Cortez* and later in his sequel to *Cannery Row*, ***Sweet Thursday***.

Further Reading: DeMott, Robert. *Steinbeck's Reading: A Catalogue of Books Owned and Borrowed*. New York: Garland, 1984; Railsback, Brian. "An Elegant Universe on Cannery Row." In *Beyond Boundaries, Rereading John Steinbeck*. Ed. Susan Shillinglaw and Kevin Hearle. Tuscaloosa: University of Alabama Press, 2002; Steinbeck, John. *Cannery Row* (1945). New York: Penguin, 1994; ———. *The Log from the Sea of Cortez* (1941; 1951). New York: Penguin, 1995.

Brian Railsback

EL GABILAN. The Salinas High School yearbook; Steinbeck served as associate editor. In his senior year (1918–1919), he contributed a number of signed and unsigned articles to *El Gabilan*, most of which indicate the wit and literary skill of a budding author.

ELAINE. Second daughter of **Lady Igraine** in ***The Acts of King Arthur***. She is the wife of King Nentres of Garlot.

ELAINE, QUEEN. Wife of **King Ban of Benwick** and mother of **Sir Lancelot** in *The Acts of King Arthur*.

ELEGANT, JOE. In ***Sweet Thursday***, an aspiring writer of a mythic, symbol-laden novel, *The Pi Root of Oedipus*, who supports himself by working as a cook at the **Bear Flag Restaurant**. Vain, effeminate, posturing, Elegant is the object of Steinbeck's harshest satire in the novel. When free of his cooking duties, this pale young writer keeps to himself in a lean-to behind the Bear Flag. He works late at night, typing his ponderous novel in green type on green paper. *The Pi Root of Oedipus* is apparently a novel of elaborate psychological symbolism with Gothic settings. While writing the book, he also imagines the picture of himself that will grace the dust cover, considers how the novel will be reviewed, and dreams of setting off to Rome after its publication.

For those who would argue that *Sweet Thursday* is escapist fantasy, Steinbeck has prepared his rebuttal in advance, demonstrating through the portrayal of Joe Elegant that much highbrow fiction praised by the critics does not mirror reality either. Despite Elegant's claim that he is reaching for deep truths, Steinbeck depicts him as completely out of touch with his physical and human environment. Feeling superior to those around him, Elegant keeps people at a psychological distance and interacts with them only to augment his own vanity. As **John H. Timmerman** has explained, Joe Elegant's book "serves as an antithesis to the kind of novel Steinbeck is writing in *Sweet Thursday*." Steinbeck's novel is frankly for the masses, as well as for specialists, and its light tone contributes to its celebration of life and love.

Steinbeck's portrayal of Joe Elegant seems less "spiteful"—the term **Warren French** uses to describe it (John Steinbeck, 155)—when one realizes that the character is based to some extent on the younger John Steinbeck. As **Louis Owens** has observed, Steinbeck began his career by writing mythic novels that are almost oppressive in their reliance on symbol, and he himself later worked on a manuscript called "Pi Root." Some, however, have suggested that the character may also have been based on writer **Truman Capote**.

Further Reading: Benson, Jackson, J. *The True Adventures of John Steinbeck, Writer*. New York: Viking, 1984; French, Warren. *John Steinbeck*. Second edition. Boston: Twayne, 1975; Owens, Louis. *John Steinbeck's Re-Vision of America*. Athens: University of Georgia Press, 1985; Timmerman, John H. *John Steinbeck's Fiction: The Aesthetics of the Road Taken*. Norman: University of Oklahoma Press, 1986.

Bruce Ouderkirk

ELEVEN REBEL LORDS OF THE NORTH, THE. King Anguystaunce of Ireland, King Brandegoris, **King Carados**, King Clarivaus, King Cradilment, the Duke of Cambenet, King Idris, King of a Hundred Knights, **King Lot of Lothian and Orkney**, King Morganoure, and King Nentres, who take arms against **Arthur** and are defeated by him and the two French kings **Ban** and **Bors** at the battle of Bedgrayne in ***The Acts of King Arthur***.

ELGAR, MISS. In ***The Winter of Our Discontent***, she is an acquaintance of **Ethan Allen Hawley**'s, whose sense of real time has long since elapsed.

ELIOT, GEORGE (1819–1880). Pen name of Victorian English novelist Mary Ann Evans, who wrote *Silas Marner* (1861). She is also known for writing about the social and moral problems of her time. Steinbeck read *Silas Marner* and *Adam Bede* (1859). In a 1936 letter to **Ben Abramson**, Steinbeck counted her books among those that are "realer than experience."

ELIOT, THOMAS STEARNS (1888–1965). Modernist poet, whose work was considered influential on novelists such as **F. Scott Fitzgerald** and **Ernest Hemingway**. Essentially, Eliot influenced the writings of Steinbeck in two ways. First, Steinbeck subscribed to Eliot's theory of literary impersonality, wherein, during the process of invention of a text, the author loses himself in a continual surrender to a new creation or a new character. This continual self-sacrifice was a practice of Steinbeck's as he penned ***The Pastures of Heaven*** in 1931, and he noted in a letter to his friend **George Albee** that he had no emotions of his own. Second, **Robert DeMott** notes that in the late 1950s Steinbeck had read Eliot's *The Waste Land* (1922), a text that became a strong influence on Steinbeck's last novel, ***The Winter of Our Discontent***. *Winter* emphasizes the moral decay and emptiness that still exist in America, traits Eliot also descried. Donna Gerstenberger points out additional parallels, including a questor knight and similarities to Eliot's Madame Sosostris and Mr. Eugenides from the original poems. She also calls attention to Steinbeck's time structure (from Easter to the Fourth of July) and suggests that it mirrors Eliot's in its concern with images of death and life, imprisonment and freedom.

The novel contains other Eliot parallels: secular rituals have replaced religious beliefs, meaningful speech and conversations are difficult to find, and hollow friendships are the rule rather than the exception. Only when non-action is converted into actual seeking is hope restored for **Ethan Allen Hawley**, the novel's protagonist. Although Ethan's spiritual dryness is emphasized throughout the book, his return to the watery cave, his place near the sea's edge, indicates a potential, if not assured, renewal. Such an ambiguous ending mirrors Eliot's poem in suggesting that the questor has gained some self-knowledge but remains enmeshed in the corruption and hypocrisy of the American wasteland, unsure of what to do next.

Further Reading: DeMott, Robert. *Steinbeck's Reading: A Catalogue of Books Owned and Borrowed*. New York: Garland, 1984; Gerstenberger, Donna. "Steinbeck's American Waste Land," *Modern Fiction Studies* 11 (1965): 59–65.

Tracy Michaels and Michael J. Meyer

ELIZABETH. The girl whom the young **Henry Morgan** believes he loves in ***Cup of Gold***. When he sees her silhouetted in the doorway of her family's home on the last night before he leaves his hometown forever, he runs away without speaking to her. He names his first ship after her. In the stories Henry tells other men, he and Elizabeth were in love, and he left Wales because her family wouldn't accept him. In those stories, she is at first a squire's daughter, then the daughter of an earl. Finally, when he tells the story to Charles II, Henry says she is a French princess, but then admits she was a peasant girl. On his deathbed, Henry has a vision of her.

ELLA. The waitress-manager of the Golden Poppy restaurant in ***Sweet Thursday***. Before **Suzy**'s arrival, she is used to working eighteen-hour days and refuses to acknowledge to herself her weariness and pain. She has a tough exterior, but she takes a personal interest in her customers and is willing to give the untested Suzy a chance to prove herself. Ella seems much like an older version of **Mae**, the tough but kind-hearted waitress in ***The Grapes of Wrath***. Steinbeck admired people who worked hard for a living, whether as farmers, shopkeepers, or waitresses. Steinbeck's own strong work ethic is reflected in his sympathetic portrayal of this exhausted waitress.

Bruce Ouderkirk

ELLEN. In ***The Wayward Bus***, friend of **Bernice Pritchard**, and the audience for the letters Bernice composes in her mind on the bus trip.

ELOISE. Prostitute at **Kate Albey**'s brothel in ***East of Eden***.

EMERSON, RALPH WALDO (1803–1882). American essayist and poet, a leader of the philosophical movement of transcendentalism. Influenced by such schools of thought as English romanticism, Neoplatonism, and Hindu philosophy, Emerson is noted for his skill in presenting his ideas eloquently and in poetic language. Steinbeck's work is replete with Emersonian echoes. Key among these are his repeated emphasis on resistance to institutions or systems that exploit, co-opt, or dull individual genius; his emphasis on nature as a source of wisdom and renewal; the recurrent theme of self-reliance, complemented by a vision of organic community in which individuals act in freedom; and the transposition and secularization of biblical and Christian ideas and values.

Robert DeMott notes that Steinbeck read Emerson's "Self-Reliance," "The Oversoul," "The American Scholar," and "Experience" prior to 1935, although, in a 1954 letter, Steinbeck pointedly wrote that Emerson was not a "direct influence." Rather, their ideas were parallel. Like Emerson, Steinbeck is often at his most lyrical when he is articulating this essentially romantic credo, pausing in the midst of narrative movement to make space for a soliloquy, a moment of philosophical musing, or, as in ***The Grapes of Wrath***, an intercalary chapter that takes us "inward" rather than "onward." His reliance upon a Christian tradition toward which he, like Emerson, felt great personal ambivalence, is evident in the many iterations of biblical archetypes (especially "Christ-figures") and biblical stories (original temptation and fall; Cain and Abel; wandering in the wilderness; struggles over patrimony; elevation of the poor and marginalized; and portrayals of the wise man, teacher, and prophet who is marginalized and rejected).

Both writers appear to have retrieved from traditions they found binding and moribund an image of Jesus as a man of original genius, a prophet luminous with self-knowledge, and a model of ultimate compassion toward humankind and nature, unsubmissive to even the most sacred institutions of his time. These characteristics, which Emerson describes in his portrayal of Poet, Prophet, and Seer, emerge in Steinbeck's novels in characters such as **Doc** (and even the Chinaman) in ***Cannery Row***; **Jim Casy** in *The Grapes of Wrath*; **Slim** in ***Of Mice and Men***, **Jim Nolan** in ***In Dubious Battle***, **Father Angelo** in ***To a God Unknown***, and **Joseph** in *To a God Unknown*. What is rejected in all his invocations of Christianity is the pharisaism, hypocrisy, and stultifying suppression of original thought presumed to be an inevitable function of institutionalization, tradition, and social respectability. This anti-institutionalism is a legacy of Emerson, whose skepticism about both church and government has fueled much subsequent political rhetoric on individual freedom. Similarly, Steinbeck's representation of the macrocosm in the microcosm, which suggests a cosmology of "circles," or correspondences between the immediate and the transcendent is Emersonian. The famous image of the turtle crossing the road in *The Grapes of Wrath* is one clear instance of such a habit of mind, where an ordinary image assumes metaphorical and finally iconographic significance.

Further Reading: DeMott, Robert. *Steinbeck's Reading: A Catalogue of Books Owned and Borrowed*. New York: Garland, 1984.

Marilyn Chandler McEntyre

EMILE DE, LIEUTENANT. In ***The Short Reign of Pippin IV***, a guard at Versailles where **Pippin Héristal** is being protected, although to him it seems like captivity. When Pippin learns the lieutenant wants to see the rioting in Paris that has resulted from Pippin's egalitarian speech, Pippin releases him from his responsibility, thus freeing himself from intrusive supervision.

ENEA, SPARKY (1910–1994). One of the seamen who crewed the ***Western Flyer*** during Steinbeck's expedition to the Sea of Cortez in 1941; he became the ship's cook after Steinbeck's wife, **Carol Henning Steinbeck**, gave it up. He and **Tiny Colleto** are a matched pair, often providing comic relief; both are described by Steinbeck as a "counterbalance" to **Anthony Berry**'s truthfulness, although both prove to be hardworking men and effective collectors of marine life. The two are almost always mentioned in tandem with one another, competing for women or embarking on some adventure that involves alcohol. Steinbeck's narration rarely distinguishes between **Sparky** and Tiny; the reader is told the two men "grew up together in **Monterey**" and that "it is said lightly that the police department had a special detail to supervise the growth and development of Tiny and Sparky." In a merger of fiction and nonfiction, Sparky and Tiny appear in ***Cannery Row*** and get into a bar fight with ***Gay***, one of the inhabitants of the **Palace Flophouse and Grill**.

Further Reading: Enea, Sparky, and Audrey Lynch. With *Steinbeck in the Sea of Cortez*. Los Osos, CA: Sand River Press, 1991.

Charles Etheridge, Jr.

ESPALDAS MOJADAS. A dance band consisting of a group of illegal aliens from Mexico in ***Sweet Thursday***. They perform at the **Palace Flophouse** on the night of the riotous Snow White masquerade.

ESPÉJO, JOSEFA. In ***Viva Zapata!***, when **Emiliano Zapata** meets her in church to ask when he can meet with her father to request her hand in marriage, Josefa adamantly admits that he needn't bother, for what she is looking for is a rich husband. It is clear that she is romantically smitten. She does marry Emiliano after a traditional sayings (*dichos*) proposal, and it is clearly a love match from the start. Subsequently, she has a premonition of Emiliano's death. In *Viva Zapata!* (the movie), it was the curandera who foresaw Emiliano's birth and death; in *Viva Zapata!* (the screenplay), this is transferred very movingly and more meaningfully to his wife Josefa.

Marcia D. Yarmus

ESPÉJO, SEÑOR. In ***Viva Zapata!*** he is the wealthy and aristocratic man of business, the father of **Josefa** and the father-in-law of Emiliano Zapata. At first, he opposes his daughter's marriage to Emiliano because he considers him to be a man without substance; he fears that his daughter will end up squatting on the bare earth, patting tortillas like a common Indian. He changes his mind, however, when Emiliano is declared "General of the Armies of the Fourth," and, at that moment, introduces Emiliano to several officers. He then invites Emiliano to come to the house and honor them with his presence. The historical father of Josefa had died the year before Emiliano and Josefa married, but had left money for her dowry.

Marcia D. Yarmus

ESPÉJO, SEÑORA. In ***Viva Zapata!***, she is **Josefa**'s mother and **Señor Espejo**'s wife.

ESPINOZA, (DON). Husband of the woman commonly known as the **Red Saint** or **La Santa Roja**, **Dona Ysobel Espinoza, Valdez y Gabilanes**, in ***Cup of Gold***. He pays **Henry Morgan** a ransom of twenty thousand pieces of eight for her release, because she is the sole heir to ten silver mines in Peru. Don is his title; his first name is not given.

ESPINOZA, VALDEZ Y GABILANES, YSOBEL (DONA). Full name of **La Santa Roja**, the **Red Saint**, in ***Cup of Gold***. Dona is her title. Ysobel is her Christian name. Espinoza is her husband's family name. Valdez y Gabilanes refers to her maiden name and her mother's maiden name, and Gabilanes appears to also be a sly reference on Steinbeck's part to the Gabilan Mountains, which form the eastern border of his native **Salinas** Valley.

ESQUEMELING, ALEXANDRE OLIVIER (JOHN). Steinbeck appears to have loosely based his ***Cup of Gold*** on a portion of Exquemelin's (spelled Esquemeling in the first English edition of 1684 or 1685) *The Buccaneers of America*. Although his claim to have been among the pirates **Henry Morgan** led in the sacking of Panama is generally accepted, many of the "facts" in Esquemeling's narrative were denied by Morgan and continue to be questioned by historians. Steinbeck's narrative of the life of Henry Morgan parallels the outlines of Esquemeling's biographical sketch of Morgan.

"ESSAY TO MYSELF" (1954). Title given by **Jackson J. Benson** in *True Adventures* to an untitled and unsigned one-page typescript that Steinbeck enclosed in a September 17, 1954, letter to **Elizabeth Otis**. In this brief essay, Steinbeck expresses dissatisfaction with his writing technique. He wonders if technique, once it is firmly established after years of writing, "not only dictates how a story is to be written but also what story is to be written." He goes on to say that a writer's facility with his or her technique may be extremely limiting in another way: "Suppose I want to change my themes and my approach. Will not my technique, which has become almost [unconscious], warp and drag me around to the old attitudes and subtly force the new work to be the old [?]"

Steinbeck continued to talk about these ideas in various interviews and letters throughout 1955. In an interview included in *Conversations with John Steinbeck*, Steinbeck echoes "Essay to Myself": "I'm tired of my own technique . . . Once [a writer] develops the technique, the technique starts choosing his subject matter." He apparently began an experimental novel about a man building his own spaceship. And the technique he began experimenting with in this work is touched on in *Letters to Elizabeth*: "I want to work this with an absolute minimum of description and exposition—perhaps none—except in so far as the protagonists themselves are able to describe and expose." Steinbeck later abandoned this experimental novel.

Edited versions of "Essay to Myself" have been included in *Steinbeck: A Life in Letters* (497) and Benson's *True Adventures* (766). The original typescript is part of the John Steinbeck Collection at Stanford University, where it is also known as "A Little Private Essay Written to Myself."

Further Reading: Benson, Jackson J. *The True Adventures of John Steinbeck, Writer: A Biography*. New York: Viking, 1984; Buchwald, Art. "John Steinbeck Turns His Hand to Tale of Space Ship, Flying Saucers," *International Herald Tribune*. March 19, 1955. Rpt. in *Conversations with John Steinbeck*. Ed. Thomas Fensch. Jackson: University Press of Mississippi, 1988.

Michael Cody

ETHEL. Prostitute who works at **Faye**'s and then at **Kate Albey**'s brothel in ***East of Eden*** until Kate fires her. Ethel observes Kate bury the glass from the smashed bottles of cascara sagrada, nux vomica, and croton oil, and the eyedropper Kate used to administer the compounds to Faye during the time that Kate was slowly murdering her. Suspecting that what she'd seen and found is significant, and after a run of hard luck, Ethel returns to **Salinas** many years later to use this evidence to blackmail Kate who, after agreeing to pay her a hundred dollars a month and offering her a job, has Ethel framed for robbery and run out of Salinas. Later, perhaps as part of the "humanizing" process that Kate goes through, she acknowledges her mistakes in letting Ethel go and disposing of the bottles as she did. Kate asks **Joe Valery**, her bouncer, to find Ethel, threatening to expose his past if he does not. Joe, perceiving that Kate is afraid of Ethel and realizing this fear could give him power and possibly a way to blackmail Kate, traces Ethel to Santa Cruz. From **Hal V. Mahler**, Joe discovers that Ethel has died an ignominious death, having been pushed off a sardine boat after serving the pleasure of its drug-crazed sailors. Joe returns to Salinas and, hoping to extort money, does not tell Kate that Ethel is dead.

The convoluted circle of blackmail initiated by Ethel results in death for her and Joe, and suicide for Kate. Through the whole episode with Ethel, Kate's increasing fear, acknowledgment of her mistakes, loss of control and power, and ultimate suicide suggest that Ethel is part of the mechanism that works to "humanize" Kate.

Margaret Seligman

ETTARDE, THE LADY. In ***The Acts of King Arthur***, holds a three-day tournament at which **Sir Pelleas**, an unwanted suitor, overturns five hundred knights. She is tricked by **Sir Gawain** into giving him her love when Gawain falsely tells her he has killed Pelleas. When she realizes how Gawain has tricked her, she rejects him, warning all ladies against his love and all knights against his friendship.

EUSKADI, JULIUS. Well-to-do rancher in the **Salinas** Valley in ***East of Eden*** who tells **Horace Quinn** about **Faye**'s brothel while they are on their way to **Adam Trask**'s ranch to investigate the shooting that, to protect his wife, **Cathy Trask**, Adam says was an accident. Skeptical of Adam's account and thinking that Adam may have killed Cathy, Horace deputizes Julius, who remains at the Trask ranch while Horace pursues his investigation.

EVA. Prostitute at **Kate Albey**'s brothel in ***East of Eden***, who takes **Adam Trask** into Kate's room after he attends **Samuel Hamilton**'s funeral. It is the first time Adam and Kate have seen each other since she shot him and left him for dead eleven years before.

EVELYN, JOHN. Courtier at the court of **King Charles II** of England in ***Cup of Gold***. He is there for **Henry Morgan**'s otherwise private audience with King Charles.

EVERYMAN. One of the best surviving examples of a medieval morality play, *Everyman* is a nine-hundred-line poem that illustrates the life of an "Everyman" nearing its end, and his road to redemption. Along with ***Le Morte D'Arthur*** and ***Paradise Lost***, Everyman was one of the classic texts Steinbeck chose to "rewrite" or "reshape" in his fiction. Using a technique similar to that in his Preface to ***Tortilla Flat***, Steinbeck drew attention to his intent to mirror *Everyman* in his novel ***The Wayward Bus*** by beginning the volume with an epigram that clearly suggested the connection between the two. The intent was to create a new morality play with modern characters filling similar roles to those in the original. *Everyman* was also an early working title for ***Burning Bright***, Steinbeck's three-act play that depicted the human condition through intensely allegorical characters and symbolic settings. As in the medieval text, both protagonists are involved in a struggle of how to be selfless and self-fulfilling simultaneously, and both suggest Steinbeck's belief that by working to realize one's individual potential, one serves mankind as well as one's self.

Michael J. Meyer

EWAIN, SIR. Nephew of **King Arthur**, son of **Morgan le Fay** and **Sir Uryens, King of Gore**, and cousin of **Sir Gawain** in ***The Acts of King Arthur***. He foils his mother's attempt to kill his father, but he is later banished from the court of King Arthur as proof of his father's loyalty to Arthur following Morgan le Fay's treachery. Voluntarily joined by his cousin Gawain in banishment, he and Gawain encounter Sir Malhalt, and, after knightly combat, the three of them become companions and embark on the Triple Quest. Ewain takes with him on his quest the **Lady Lyne**, under whose guidance he frees the **Lady of the Rock** from the tyranny of the two brothers, **Sir Edward** and **Sir Hugh of the Red Castle**.

Roy S. Simmonds

EXCALIBUR. Sword given to **King Arthur** by the **Lady of the Lake** in ***The Acts***

of King Arthur in exchange for an unspecified gift in return. The scabbard of the sword is the most precious part of the gift, for while he is wearing it Arthur cannot lose any blood, no matter how grievously wounded he might be. This protection is, of course, lost to him when the scabbard is stolen by **Morgan le Fay** and thrown into a lake.

Roy S. Simmonds

EXTERMINATOR, THE. Pirate captain in *Cup of Gold*.

EZYZINSKI, MRS. She only negotiates the purchases of a quarter of a pound of butter in ***The Winter of Our Discontent***, but she also stands for all the people **Ethan Allen Hawley** has to deal with in his reduced status as store clerk and indicates most individuals believe they can negotiate deals to better their personal lives.

F

FACTORIES IN THE FIELD. Published in 1939, **Carey McWilliams**'s nonfiction tract was based on his research in California agricultural areas and on conversations with actual workers. It is often considered the factual companion to ***The Grapes of Wrath***. McWilliams's book revealed the impetus that led to the California farm labor strikes in the 1930s, observing the conditions of low wages and starvation that greeted many aspiring immigrant and nonimmigrant farm laborers. The corporate agriculture industry was greatly offended by this book due to its revelation of sordid labor conditions for migrant workers. Steinbeck endorsed the work and offered to write a blurb for it to help the book's promotion.

Tracy Michaels

FAIRBANKS, DOUGLAS, JR. (1909–2000). Actor who appeared in approximately seventy-nine films, including *The Prisoner of Zenda* (1937) and *Gunga Din* (1939), but was overshadowed by his more famous father, Douglas (the swashbuckling hero of the 1920s). Steinbeck and Fairbanks Jr. enjoyed a cordial friendship. In light of his father's swashbuckling past, it seems appropriate that Fairbanks led a daring naval unit during World War II. Lieutenant Fairbanks led this special unit on a variety of heroic diversionary missions designed to misdirect Axis resources in and along the Mediterranean, a feat that earned him the Silver Star. While working as a correspondent for the Office of Strategic Services, Steinbeck signed up with Fairbanks's team and participated in a number of these raids during 1943 (Steinbeck was also recommended for the Silver Star, but as a war correspondent he was not eligible). In one particular raid to take the Italian island of Ventotene, Steinbeck removed his foreign correspondent badge (without the badge, he would have been executed if captured) and became involved in the operation, earning the respect of Fairbanks's team.

Much later, Steinbeck called upon his friendship with Fairbanks for assistance with his incomplete project on **King Arthur**. In 1965, Steinbeck used Fairbanks's connection with the British upper class to gain access to a series of expansive, but private, libraries belonging to noble estates. Along with **Eugene Vinaver**, Steinbeck hoped to find lost manuscripts pertaining to Arthurian legend.

Further Reading: Benson, Jackson J. *The True Adventures of John Steinbeck, Writer*. New York: Viking, 1984.

Brian Niro

FARNOL, JEFFREY (1878–1952). Author of *The Broad Highway*, published in 1910. Steinbeck read the book in 1924 and was intrigued by its rustic dialogue.

FAT CARL. In the short story, "**Johnny Bear**" he is the owner and bartender of the Buffalo Bar in Loma, the setting of the story. Sullen and unfriendly, Fat Carl serves only one kind of whiskey, and he does not tolerate fools gladly. His saloon provides the only available entertainment to the men of the village, and it is here that Johnny often performs.

Abby H. P. Werlock

FAT MAN, THE/THE GAS STATION ATTENDANT. A parallel in ***The Grapes of Wrath*** to the unnamed attendant in intercalary chapter 12, the fat man is also a worrier, trying to determine "what the country's comin' to," a phrase he repeats frequently. His pessimism about the fate of the nation is countered by his generosity to the **Joads**. He allows them to use the station's washroom facilities and permits them to procure water for their car's radiator. Intuitively recognized by **Tom Joad** as being in a similar predicament to the Okies in regard to his business prospects, the fat man is depicted as fated to also become homeless.

Michael J. Meyer

FATHER ANGELO. Roman Catholic priest in ***To a God Unknown*** who represents one of the traditional religious views. After praying for **Joseph Wayne**'s soul, he also prays for rain and believes that his God is responsible for the end of the drought. He is depicted as an unshakable Catholic, and yet he practices tolerance—trying his best to counsel Joseph Wayne. Toward the end of the novel, he understands Wayne's power and plight. When rain finally comes, Angelo has the last scene of the book as he thinks of forgiving the people for their wild orgy in the storm and, ironically, thinks that Wayne must be pleased that the drought has finally ended. He does not know that Joseph Wayne is dead.

FATHER BENEDICT. In "**Saint Katy the Virgin**," the Abbot of the Monastery of M____. Disappointed in **Brother Paul** for converting **Katy** (a pig) to Christianity, Father Benedict calls him a fool and reminds him that Christians abound, but pigs are scarce. Ironically, Father Benedict's ruling saves Katy's life and paves the way for her salvation and ultimate sainthood.

Abby H. P. Werlock

FAULKNER, WILLIAM (1897–1962). Though few parallels were noted initially between Steinbeck and the famous Southern writer and fellow Nobel laureate, Faulkner himself once remarked that he and Steinbeck were actually working at the same thing. Later commentators have noted important thematic parallels in the two writers, such as a pronounced native regionalism, an obvious admiration for the working poor, and a strong interest in generational influences. Five years Steinbeck's senior, Faulkner is more noticeably influenced by great early modernists such as **Joyce** and **Eliot**, but Steinbeck's work is similarly marked by the quintessential modernist tendency toward formal experimentation and, as was the case with Faulkner, a **non-teleological** approach.

Other notable literary influences shared by both writers include **Sherwood Anderson**, **James Branch Cabell**, and philosopher **Henri Bergson**. The prime similarity between the two writers appears to be an overriding concern with what Steinbeck scholarship refers to as the individual's struggle with "group man," as discussed in his "**Argument of Phalanx**," which in Faulkner studies translates to an individual struggle with the community. This struggle is likewise a function of the historical modernist dialectic that connects the two writers, and the preponderance of their early work clearly favors the wild, tragic-tending individual versus the more secure group or community.

Following World War II, however, both writers would tend to speak more often in what Faulkner has described as "the national voice." This initially awkward shift in orientation can be evidenced in the remarkable hybrid works ***Burning Bright*** and *Requiem for a Nun* (1951). Both are plays/novellas, and both are concerned with preserving a harsh order at the cost of literal human sacrifice. Echoing Faulkner's "national voice" sentiments upon his acceptance of the **Nobel Prize** in 1950, Steinbeck's own Nobel Prize acceptance speech twelve years later holds a similar view: "the writer is delegated to declare and to celebrate man's proven capacity for greatness of heart and spirit—for gallantry in defeat, for courage, compassion and love. . . . I hold that a writer who does not passionately believe in the perfectibility of man has no dedication nor any membership in literature."

Although he admired Faulkner's work, Steinbeck was at odds with the writer's dwelling on abnormality and decay and would on occasion privately refer to Faulkner's work as part of the trend of neurotic Southern literature. In addition, he felt that Faulkner had lost some of his integrity as a writer by becoming a "public figure." Steinbeck was always primarily interested in the quality of a person as an individual and less interested in the status and impact the person had in the public eye. Consequently, the connection between the two men was strained by Steinbeck's abhorrence of what he perceived as Faulkner's (and other writers') preoccupation with literary immortality. After meeting aboard the *Andrea Doria* in December 1954, Steinbeck and Faulkner began a difficult but cordial relationship (not off to a good start when Faulkner showed up very drunk at a party at the Steinbeck home in New York City in January 1955). The relationship warmed up through later meetings associated with Eisenhower's People-to-People Program (the two authors served on a committee together), and in Steinbeck's Nobel Prize speech and in ***America and Americans*** he refers to Faulkner's greatness (in the latter citing *As I Lay Dying*, in particular).

Further Reading: Benson, Jackson J. *The True Adventures of John Steinbeck, Writer*. New York: Viking, 1984.

Gene Norton

FAUNA. As proprietor of the **Bear Flag Restaurant**, a brothel on **Cannery Row**, she has a major role in the plot of ***Sweet Thursday***. Next to **Doc**, Fauna is the person on the Row whom the residents are most likely to consult for advice. It is Fauna who first suggests a marriage as the remedy for Doc's discontent, and who gives **Suzy** hope for this match by casting a horoscope that finds her compatible with Doc. Fauna plans a romantic date for the couple and teaches Suzy how to act with social grace. Her creative scheme to secure their engagement at a masquerade party fails because of Suzy's deliberate subversion. Although **Hazel**'s assistance is required to bring the plot to a close, it is chiefly because of Fauna's machinations that, at the end of the novel, the couple has all but tied the matrimonial knot.

In *Sweet Thursday*, as in many of his other novels, Steinbeck depicts the house of prostitution as an important social institution. In fact, it is not accidental that Fauna had once worked as a missionary and then became a madam, for Steinbeck held in ***East of Eden*** that the church and the whorehouse not only "arrived in the Far West simultaneously," but were designed "to accomplish the same thing" by serving to "take a man out of his bleakness for a time." As Robert Morsberger has pointed out, Steinbeck frequently used prostitution as a focus for satirizing middle-class prudery and respectability.

Further Reading: Morsberger, Robert. "Steinbeck's Happy Hookers." *Steinbeck Quarterly* 9 (Summer–Fall 1976): 101–15.

Bruce Ouderkirk

FAURE, RAOUL. Author of *Lady Godiva and Master Tom* (1948). **Robert DeMott** has asserted that Steinbeck borrowed details from Faure's characterization of Lady Godiva in the creation of **Cathy Ames** in ***East of Eden***.

Further Reading: DeMott, Robert. "Lady Godiva and Cathy Ames: A Contribution to *East of Eden's* Background." *Steinbeck Quarterly* 14 (1981): 72–83.

FAYE. Owner/operator of a **Salinas** house of prostitution in ***East of Eden*** which, in contrast to **Jenny**'s or **The Nigger**'s, offered comfort, reassurance, and a homey atmosphere. Although Faye is a shrewd businesswoman and cautious, she is not particularly bright, so she is easily duped by **Cathy Ames/Kate Albey**. Kate wheedles her way into Faye's affections by establishing and then taking advantage of an imaginary mother-daughter relationship between them. When Faye writes a will making her "daughter" the sole beneficiary, Kate embarks on her plan to murder Faye. Over a period of four months, Kate appears to nurse Faye devotedly, when in fact she is weakening her gradually by administering doses of croton oil, a cathartic, and nux vomica, an emetic, which were stolen from **Dr. Wilde**'s dispensary. Finally, when Dr. Wilde tells Kate that Faye is very near death, Kate finishes her off by administering both substances simultaneously. When Faye dies, Kate seems overcome with grief, although this emotion, like her devotion to Faye, is nothing more than an appearance intended to deceive. Faye's murder, like that of **William** and **Mrs. Ames**, demonstrates Kate's ability to plan a murder and to proceed patiently and without remorse, qualities consonant with Steinbeck's characterization of her as a monster.

Margaret Seligman

FDR. *See* **Roosevelt, Franklin Delano**.

FAYRE ELEYNE. Steinbeck's twenty-two-foot cabin boat, named after his third wife, **Elaine Scott Steinbeck**. In the opening scenes of ***Travels with Charley***, Steinbeck battles with **Hurricane Donna** and successfully saves the boat from damage.

FEELEY, WILLIE/JOE DAVIS'S BOY. In ***The Grapes of Wrath***, these two characters are similar in their betrayal of their friends and relatives by working for the banks that are forcing the Okies from their land. Joe Davis's boy, in intercalary chapter 5, is more concerned about self-survival ($3 a day to tractor the tenants from their land) than about a common cause of brotherhood. Besides his ironic betrayal by taking the tractoring job, he is also important because his speeches to the victims reveal the impossibility of ever finding who is ultimately responsible for the evictions. Corporations and banks are seen as abstract entities that are insensitive to personal needs. In chapter 6, Willie Feeley is mentioned by **Muley Graves** as a similar betrayer, a friend who has been hired to tractor the **Joads** out. The Joads are reluctant to attack Willie because he appears to be one of their own. When confronted by Muley, Willie also identifies his family's needs as holding precedence over those of the landholders. The survival of his wife and children demands his attention, and he is forced to become an enemy to his former friends, enduring violence (Muley hits him over the head with a fence post to avoid capture) in order to complete his task.

Michael J. Meyer

FENCHEL, MR. In ***East of Eden***, a German tailor in **Salinas** who is ostracized and victimized during World War I because of his nationality. About thirty Salinas men tear down his picket fence and burn out the front of his house. In ***Journal of a Novel***, Steinbeck reveals that he and his sister **Mary Steinbeck** did in fact taunt **Mr. Fenchel** as they do in the novel, something Steinbeck remembered with guilt for years.

Margaret Seligman

FENTON, FRANK. Editor of the ***Stanford*** *Spectator* during his college years, Fenton published Steinbeck's first short stories, including **"Fingers of a Cloud"** and **"Adventures in Arcademy."** He later served as the president of San Francisco State University.

FERGUS, EARL. In ***The Acts of King Arthur***, he engages the services of **Sir** Marhalt while he is on the Triple Quest for the purpose of killing the giant **Taulurd**.

FIELDING, HENRY (1707–1754). English essayist, dramatist, and novelist, primarily known for his novels *The History of the Adventures of Joseph Andrews and of his Friend Mr. Abraham Adams* (1742) and *Tom Jones, a Foundling* (1749). Fielding was undoubtedly one of the fathers of the modern novel, achieving structural innovations through his break from the epistolary form. Steinbeck compared his works to Fielding's. Referring to his composition of ***East of Eden***, he wrote in ***Journal of a Novel***: "[I]n pace it is much more like Fielding than like **Hemingway**." Likewise, Steinbeck enjoyed Fielding's use of humor, especially his slapstick. He owned a copy of *Tom Jones*, which he read more than once.

Further Reading: DeMott, Robert. *Steinbeck's Reading; A Catalog of Books Owned and Borrowed*. New York: Garland, 1984.

T. Adrian Lewis

FILM. John Steinbeck's relations with film are many and complex. Steinbeck is one of the most frequently adapted major American literary authors of the twentieth century. He also wrote screen treatments and screenplays, several of which were finally developed into movie productions. Steinbeck's fiction maintained an intertextual affinity with film, so that it became an important influence on his writing. His films also provide a rough index of his popular and critical success.

Although Steinbeck grew up with the American film, his early efforts seem less aware of the new medium than his mature work. It may be that the young author was simply more interested in literary models during an era when film was most often considered only popular entertainment. As Steinbeck matured, film itself rapidly changed with the development of sound technology, which created artistic achievements more analogous to the literary than to the graphic arts. In the 1930s, American film exhibited a realistic and documentary thrust that parallels the best of Steinbeck's fiction. When his books became bestsellers, they were candidates for screen adaptation; Steinbeck was drawn into the world of Hollywood, becoming a screenwriter himself.

The first screen productions of Steinbeck's fiction appeared at the high point of both American cinematic realism and the Hollywood studio system in the years directly before World War II. The author's writing had become more realistic—at least somewhat under the influence of documentary photography and film—so that such novels as ***Of Mice and Men*** and ***The Grapes of Wrath*** transferred easily to the screen. Director **Lewis Milestone**'s ***Of Mice and Men*** (1939) remains the most faithful filmic adaptation of Steinbeck's work, with excellent performances by **Burgess Meredith** and **Lon Chaney, Jr.** as **George Milton** and **Lennie Small**, but the movie failed at the box office because it was not easily pigeonholed within a single Hollywood genre. Thus, **John Ford**'s version of ***The Grapes of Wrath*** (1940) must be considered the most popular and important of the Steinbeck films. A brilliant cast, led by **Henry Fonda** as **Tom Joad**, combined with excellent production values to create a screen classic.

Although the documentary film ***The Forgotten Village*** appeared right before Pearl Harbor, it can be more readily classified with the grab-bag of film projects that filled Steinbeck's war years. The newly successful writer scripted this study of cultural transitions in a Mexican village, which was then directed by **Herbert Kline**. Director **Victor Fleming**'s sanitized version of Steinbeck's first bestseller, ***Tortilla Flat***, was released in 1942, confirming the consensus critical view of the novel as lightweight entertainment. Another weak adaptation, this one of Steinbeck's novel concerning the Nazi occupation of Norway (***The Moon Is Down***), was directed by Irving Pichel in 1943.

Perhaps the oddest of the Steinbeck films is Alfred Hitchcock's ***Lifeboat*** (1944), which began as an unpublished Steinbeck novelette about the Merchant Marine and became a melodramatic allegory of wartime allies adrift with an evil Nazi supervillain. When Steinbeck saw what Hitchcock had done with his script (for example, the more rounded African American character had been turned into a disparaging, stock stereotype), he tried to have his name pulled from the credits. Another unpublished story, this time about the paisanos of ***Tortilla Flat*** aiding the war effort, forms the basis of the very forgettable ***A Medal For Benny*** (1945), also directed by Irving Pichel.

Steinbeck's connections with film proved more productive in the postwar period. The author returned to Mexico to supervise the screenplay of his classic short novel, ***The Pearl***, for the interesting, though unsuccessful, Mexican/American co-production directed by Emilio Fernandez and released in 1948. In the same period Steinbeck completed a screenplay based on his short story sequence, ***The Red Pony.*** It was for his earlier collaborator, Lewis Milestone, and again their 1949 production was weakened by the need to fulfill Hollywood expectations about genre. However, Steinbeck's original screenplay for director **Elia Kazan**, ***Viva Zapata!*** (1952), avoided the clichés of movie biography in the story of Mexican revolutionary **Emiliano Zapata**, who was brilliantly portrayed by a mercurial **Marlon Brando**. Elia Kazan also directed the 1955 movie version of Steinbeck's ***East of Eden*** and, when Marlon Brando was occupied elsewhere, cast an unknown **James Dean** in the role of the **Cal Trask**. Kazan and screenwriter Paul Osborn tightened Steinbeck's diffuse epic, narrowing its scope to the generational conflict between **Adam Trask** (played by Raymond Massey) and his rebellious son, in roughly the final third of the novel. Although the movie became a box office success, it received a mixed critical reception—much like the original novel. Viewed today it seems more a period piece of method acting, overwrought symbolism, and wide-screen technicolor style. Director Victor Vicas's 1957 version of Steinbeck's ***The Wayward Bus*** proved unsuccessful in every regard, including its miscasting of Hollywood sex symbol Jayne Mansfield.

Steinbeck's artistic affinity for film and his enduring popularity as the most accessible of our major writers are demonstrated by posthumous productions, particularly television movies. Television remakes of *The Red Pony* (1973), *East of Eden* (1981), and *Of Mice and Men* (1968, 1981, and a theatrical release in 1992) owed as much to the earlier film versions as to Steinbeck's original work. The 1973 reprise of Steinbeck's classic initiation story was notable for the casting of Henry Fonda and Maureen O'Hara as the protagonist's parents, but the television production by Robert Totten retained the "boy and his horse" elements of the Steinbeck/Milestone film version. **Robert Blake**'s 1981 retelling of George and Lennie's tale—something of an homage to Lewis Milestone, who was Blake's mentor in Hollywood—proves almost as fine as the original. The 1981 television miniseries based on Steinbeck's *East of Eden* dramatizes the entire novel, though it seems to be influenced by Elia Kazan's earlier vision of the novel's dramatic final third. Also worth noting is a 1983 network production of Steinbeck's ***The Winter of Our Discontent***, which rewrote the ending of Steinbeck's last novel.

Many other filmic and televised productions of Steinbeck's shorter works have become standards in high school classrooms as well. Later feature films include a 1982 big-screen adaptation (generally panned by critics) of Steinbeck's ***Cannery Row,*** and yet another version of *Of Mice and Men* in 1992. Robert Ward's ***Cannery Row,*** which is really based more on the novel's weaker sequel, ***Sweet Thursday,*** proves to be a forgettable effort that miscasts Nick Nolte as **Doc** and Debra Winger as the stereotypical **Suzy**. Although the latest incarnations of George and Lennie, **Gary Sinise** and **John Malkovich**, are much better at their parts, Sinise's new production was criticized for its disjunction of the setting—more glamorous than the bleak surroundings shown in the 1939 and 1981 versions. Finally, although a new screen production of *The Grapes of Wrath* has been discussed, only a televised production of the prize-winning stage version appeared, in 1990.

Further Reading: Millichap, Joseph R. *Steinbeck and Film*. New York: Ungar, 1983.

Joseph Millichap

"FINGERS OF CLOUD: A SATIRE ON COLLEGE PROTERVITY" (1923). Early Steinbeck short story, published in the February 1923 issue of the *Stanford Spectator,* that concerns Gertie, a retarded albino woman in her late teens. Leaving home, she wanders into the bunkhouse of a Filipino work gang, meets Pedro, the boss, and marries him. Finally, bothered by Pedro's superstitions and occasional beatings, she leaves him to wander as aimlessly as she did at the beginning of the story. **Jackson J. Benson** notes that the story shows some flashes of promise but is hampered by the overblown, romantic language characteristic of Steinbeck's early efforts.

Further Reading: Benson, Jackson J. *The True Adventures of John Steinbeck, Writer.* New York: Viking, 1984.

"FIRST WATCH, THE." Six pages in length, the text is a letter by Steinbeck to *Esquire* editor Arnold Gingrich dated January 5, 1938. Printed in 1947 by the Ward Ritchie Press, this first and only separate edition was published in a total run of sixty numbered copies; ten were for the author and fifty for presentation to friends of Marguerite and Louis Henry Cohn. In addition to purchasing several of Steinbeck's stories that *Esquire* magazine had previously rejected, Gingrich also sent Steinbeck a watch as a gift, the consideration of which is the subject of the letter.

John Hooper

FISHER, SHIRLEY (1925–1981). One of the principal agents for **McIntosh & Otis**, Fisher was not directly responsible for the Steinbeck account. She and her husband John, however, became friends with Steinbeck and his third wife, **Elaine Scott Steinbeck**, while they resided in New York City and at Sag Harbor. John Fisher did interior decorating for both Steinbeck homes. A petite but somewhat masculine Scotswoman, Shirley grew closer to Steinbeck as time passed, often joining him as a fishing companion on his boat. According to **Jackson J. Benson**, Steinbeck considered her friendship to be comparable to his association with **Edward F. Ricketts,** and he gave her the pet name "Elfinheimer." When Steinbeck decided to take the cross-country journey that resulted in ***Travels with Charley***, Fisher painted ***Rocinante*** on his truck/camper in reference to his Don Quixote-like quest. She was so keen on this symbolism that she repainted the letters in early seventeenth-century script when the original lettering was destroyed by **Hurricane Donna**. As one of Steinbeck's confidantes in his later years, Fisher was one of only a few friends who were invited to visit him and say goodbye when it became apparent that his death was imminent.

Further Reading: Benson, Jackson J. *The True Adventures of John Steinbeck, Writer.* New York: Viking, 1984.

Michael J. Meyer

"FISHING IN PARIS" (1954). Appearing in the August 25, 1954, issue of *Punch*, this is an essay in which Steinbeck takes a humorous look at fishing practices in America, Britain, and France. He suggests that the particular characteristics of the people in each country are revealed in their attitudes toward, and methods of, fishing. In America, Steinbeck writes, fishing pits the individual against nature. The American fisherman loads himself with heaps of equipment, buys a boat, learns a fishy lexicon, and travels thousands of miles to challenge and conquer the fish he considers the most intelligent and powerful. Fishing in America also has a political aspect, as it seems to be a requirement that any candidate for office must first catch a fish and be photographed with it.

In Britain, historical passions for private property make fishing altogether different from its American manifestations. The British fisherman goes out in the evening to his privately owned stream, after the same adversary that has eluded him for years. If the old trout is finally caught, he is boiled, eaten with Brussels sprouts, and mourned at the local pub for years. In France, particularly on the River Oise in Paris, fishing is a contemplative and leisurely sport in which nothing is expected nor desired to happen. Each fisherman has his quiet place on the bank of the river, and both fish and other fishermen are to leave him alone. Going fishing on the Oise is a time for rest without seeming idle, not for sentiment, contest, and glory. Steinbeck concludes by placing his stamp of approval on the French method of fishing.

A condensed version of the essay, renamed "How to Fish in French," was reprinted in the December 1954 issue of *Reader's Digest*. The essay was then translated into French as "Sur les Bords de l'Oise" and appeared as the eighth essay in ***Un Américain à New York et à Paris***. Critics have seen "Fishing in Paris" as "corny" (Benson) and as "third-rate popular" journalism (Lisca). However, Steinbeck enjoyed writing it. In a letter to **Carlton Sheffield** dated September 23, 1955, Steinbeck says, "I'm having fun doing some little pieces for *Punch*—real crazy ones but the English seem to like them and I like doing them" (*Life in Letters*).

Further Reading: Benson, Jackson J. *The True Adventures of John Steinbeck, Writer*. New York: Viking, 1984; Lisca, Peter. *The Wide World of John Steinbeck*. New Brunswick: Rutgers University Press, 1958; Steinbeck, John. "Fishing in Paris," *Punch*. 227# August 25, 1954, 248–49; ———. *Steinbeck: A Life in Letters*. New York: Viking, 1975; ———. "Sur les Bords de l'Oise." *Un Américain à New York et à Paris*. Paris: Julliard, 1956.

Michael Cody

FITZGERALD, F. SCOTT (FRANCIS SCOTT KEY FITZGERALD) (1896–1940). Self-appointed chronicler of the "Jazz Age" (1919–1929, a period he named), Fitzgerald was a highly popular and successful short story writer in the 1920s and 1930s. Among his novels is the masterpiece, *The Great Gatsby* (1925). Steinbeck read Fitzgerald later in life, and noted in a 1949 letter that he was not among the many young writers Fitzgerald influenced. In ***America and Americans***, Steinbeck counted *The Great Gatsby* among the great works of American literature. Fitzgerald, like **Hemingway**, privately disliked Steinbeck and his work. In letters of the late 1930s and 1940, Fitzgerald accused Steinbeck of imitating D. H. Lawrence and of lifting a scene for ***Of Mice and Men*** from Frank Norris's *Mc Teague* (1899). "I'd like to put you on to something about Steinbeck," Fitzgerald wrote in a 1940 letter to his friend, the famous critic **Edmund Wilson**, "he is a rather cagey cribber." Fitzgerald's comments appear to be tainted with some professional jealousy, as they come at a time when his career was at a low and Steinbeck's was at its height.

Further Reading: DeMott, Robert. *Steinbeck's Reading; A Catalogue of Books Owned and Borrowed*. New York: Garland, 1984; Fitzgerald, F. Scott. *F. Scott Fitzgerald, A Life in Letters*. Ed. Matthew J. Bruccoli. New York: Scribner, 1994.

FIVE KINGS, THE. In ***The Acts of King Arthur***, **King Anguyshaunce** of Ireland, the King of Denmark, the King of Longtaynse, The King of Sorleyse, and the King of the Vale, all of whom invade **Arthur**'s kingdom after the death of **Merlin**. They are unsuccessful in killing Arthur when they ambush his camp at night, and later, while riding together unescorted, they are themselves ambushed and killed by Arthur, **Sir Kay**, **Sir Gawain**, and **Sir Gryffet**, and are killed.

FLAUBERT, GUSTAVE (1821–1880). French novelist, primarily known for his realist novel *Madame Bovary* (1857). Steinbeck read *Madame Bovary* and, according to **Peter Lisca** in *The Wide World of John Steinbeck*, he included that work in a list of books he described as "realer than experience." Steinbeck's friend and fellow researcher **Eugene Vinaver**, an authority on Arthurian literature, urged Steinbeck to also read Flaubert's *Legend of St. Julien the Hospitaller* (1877). Steinbeck later wrote Vinaver that it was brilliant.

Further Reading: DeMott, Robert. *Steinbeck's Reading; A Catalogue of Books Owned and Borrowed*. New York: Garland, 1984; Lisca, Peter. *The Wide World of John Steinbeck*. New Brunswick, NJ: Rutgers University Press, 1958.

Janet L. Flood

FLEMING, VICTOR (1883–1949). Film director who made ***Tortilla Flat*** (1942) and who is best remembered for *Captains Courageous* (1937), *The Wizard of Oz* (1939), and *Gone with the Wind* (1939).

"FLIGHT" (1938). The third short story in Steinbeck's ***The Long Valley*** and one of his most widely anthologized. Because the main characters in "Flight" are Mexican Americans living in greatly impoverished circumstances compared to those of the Anglos of "**The Chrysanthemums**" and "**The White Quail**," the story may, at first glance, seem to depart from the initial concerns of the first two stories. Despite these surface differences, however, the **Salinas Valley** setting and the author's persistent attention to gender differences and issues remain thematically significant. In "Flight," Steinbeck uses both his setting and his nineteen-year-old protagonist **Pepé Torres** to demonstrate the ironies involved in defining manhood. Originally entitled "Manhunt," it also differs from the other stories in *The Long Valley* in that it was unpublished until its appearance in this collection.

The story opens with a focus on **Mama Torres**, a strong and wise woman who runs a small farm and has raised three children since her husband's fall death from a rattlesnake bite ten years earlier. Considering Steinbeck's fascination with Eden myth, this intrusion by the snake indicates that the Eden of California had already lost much of its promise for the Torres family. Nor has the process ceased, as we watch Pepé follow in the footsteps of his father. He literally inherits the father's clothing, saddle, knife, and gun—not to mention the partially gender- and culture-based propensity to defend one's honor with violence. Mama seeks out Pepé to ask him to ride into **Monterey** for medicine, but she finds his younger brother **Emilio** and sister **Rosy** concentrating on Pepé's deadly aim with the knife. The conjunction of this skill with his first ride alone into Monterey and his belief that he is now a man produces predictably tragic results. Before dawn, he returns home to tell his mother that he drank wine in Monterey and killed a man who insulted him, so he must now flee to the mountains.

As numerous critics have noted, Steinbeck does not examine the morality of Pepé's actions. Instead, the author's psychological concern here appears as an ironic Steinbeckian version of the **Hemingway** code (the importance of facing certain death with courage and dignity) and an implicit questioning of the value of such a masculine code. Pepé's impulsive, male *Bildungsroman* is implicitly juxtaposed with his mother's long-suffering knowledge, understanding, and wisdom. On the eve of his departure for Monterey she still views Pepé as a boy, calling him "little one" and "foolish chicken" and telling him she would not send him alone if they did not need the medicine. She is powerless to change her son's behavior, however. As Pepé returns from Monterey to embark on his odyssey toward certain death, Mama Torres can do nothing but advise him how to stay safe as long as possible. After their formal farewell, she mourns her son with the traditional death wail and then turns back to their house. She has lost the second adult male in her life.

As Pepé rides the trail away from his family and toward his coming death, the landscape becomes more and more sterile, increasingly dotted with fragments of rock and with less water and vegetation. As he moves farther and farther into the barren, hostile mountains, he discards or loses his few accoutrements of civilization—his father's horse, his father's hat, his father's rifle—and is depicted in increasingly animalistic terms. Like the snake, the wildcat, and the mountain lion that he passes, he slithers and climbs across the rocks, sleeping and hiding whenever he has the opportunity. Indeed, with his physical condition weakened by the infected gunshot wound inflicted by his pursuers, he increasingly resembles a snake, his father's nemesis. Pepé's tongue turns black on the tip, and when he tries to speak only a hiss emerges from his lips.

Ironically, Pepé never understands that his view of manhood has actually hastened his youthful death, but the young man does face death bravely, managing to rise to his feet in a perhaps unconscious attempt to soar like the eagle above him. The final lines, however, make him seem more reptilian than birdlike as he slowly rises, sways, and stands before his pursuers gun him down. Pepé rolls over, starts a little avalanche, and ends up against a bush, his head buried under the debris and the rocks. His flight from the results of the male code has helped him not to soar, but to reenact the Fall of Man from the bright promise of the biblical garden.

Further Reading: Ditsky, John M. "Steinbeck's 'Flight': The Ambiguity of Manhood." In *A Study Guide to Steinbeck's "The Long Valley."* Ed. Tetsumaro Hayashi and Reloy Garcia. Ann Arbor: Pierian, 1976; Hughes, Robert S., Jr. *John Steinbeck: A Study of The Short Fiction.* New York: Twayne, 1989; Owens, Louis. "'Flight': Into the Jaw of Death." In *John Steinbeck's Re-Vision of America.* Athens: University of Georgia Press, 1985; Ware, Elaine. "Struggle for Survival: Parallel Themes and Techniques in Steinbeck's 'Flight' and Norris's *McTeague.*" *Steinbeck Quarterly* 21. 3–4 (Summer–Fall 1988): 96–103.

Abby H. P. Werlock

FLOOD, DORA. The madam and proprietor of the innocuously named **Bear Flag Restaurant**, which is ***Cannery Row***'s house of prostitution. Known as someone who is kind and fair to her employees, she is also philanthropic and is, in an ironic way, a pillar of her community. Once, when an influenza epidemic afflicted Cannery Row, Dora had her employees deliver soup to the sick. Dora is one of many characters in Steinbeck's work whose existence offends middle class sensibilities, but whose actions speak admirably for her. In ***Sweet Thursday***, **Mack** tells **Doc** that during the war Dora died peacefully in her sleep and that the broken-hearted prostitutes sang drunken hymns in mourning. With Dora's death, the ownership of the Bear Flag passed on to her sister, **Fauna**.

Bruce Ouderkirk

FLORENCE. Prostitute at **Kate Albey**'s brothel in ***East of Eden***.

"FLORENCE: THE EXPLOSION OF THE CHARIOT" (1957). This article, one of twenty-three travel pieces by Steinbeck in the *Louisville Courier-Journal* between April 17 and July 17, 1957, resulted from the author's stay in Florence during Easter week. He describes the Scopio del Carro (the explosion of the chariot), which is the high point of the week and foremost among the city's many celebratory displays.

Further Reading: Steinbeck, John. "Florence: The Explosion of the Chariot." *"America and Americans" and Selected Nonfiction.* Ed. Susan Shillinglaw and Jackson J. Benson. New York: Viking, 2002.

Eric Skipper

FLOWER, JAMES. **Henry Morgan**'s master on the plantation in Barbados, in ***Cup of Gold***. He is a failed English intellectual who was exiled for getting drunk and hitting a soldier. He becomes very fond of Henry and teaches him to read Greek, Latin, and Hebrew. Henry becomes Flower's overseer and manages the plantation with great efficiency, but he skims off money and uses the excellent library on the plantation to prepare for his future life as a pirate. When, after four years, Flower gives Henry his canceled indenture papers as a Christmas present, Henry thanks him and departs.

Kevin Hearle

FLOYD, CARLISLE (1926–). Composer of several modern operas, Floyd has often based his plots on novels, including *Wuthering Heights* (1958) and *Willie Stark* (1982). His style has been described as generally conservative, melodic, and lyrical, although more recent compositions have become increasingly complicated and eclectic. Floyd adapted Steinbeck's ***Of Mice and Men*** for operatic performances and debuted his composition at The Seattle Opera Company in 1970. In recent years, it has been revived to higher acclaim than it received originally. Perhaps best known for his opera *Susannah*, a folk story about religious bigotry, Floyd is considered one of the foremost composers of opera in America today. His most recent adaptation is *Cold Sassy Tree* (2000), based on the novel by Olive Ann Burns. In 2004, Floyd was awarded the National Medal of the Arts by President George W. Bush.

Further Reading and Listening: Brunelle, Phillip, ed. *American Arias / Baritone Bass (Male).* Book and CD. London: Boosey and

Hawkes, 2004. (includes George's aria, "You Bet It's Going to Be Different"); Floyd, Carlisle. *Of Mice and Men: An Opera in Three Acts*. An Albany CD. Released April 2004. Featuring the Houston Grand Opera Company under the direction of Patrick Summers.

FLOYD, PURTY BOY ("PRETTY BOY FLOYD"/CHARLES ARTHUR FLOYD) (1904–1934). Actual historical figure and folk hero, Floyd is used by **Ma Joad** in ***The Grapes of Wrath*** as an example of how one can become "mean-mad" when pursued and hassled by the law. His time in prison does not reform him, and the bitterness Floyd acquires there is later taken out on the victims of his aggressive robberies and random murders. In this way, his supposed innate goodness is transformed into evil. Ma is afraid that Tom has been inculcated with a bitterness such as Floyd's and that, like Floyd, he will react in animal-like fashion, being inclined to hurt others rather than to help them. Symbolically, Floyd's rising bitterness is also being compared to the upcoming harvest of the migrant community's own grapes of wrath.

Michael J. Meyer

FONDA, HENRY (1905–1982) Distinguished actor of stage and screen. Having read and admired Steinbeck's work, Fonda was eager to play **Tom Joad** in ***The Grapes of Wrath***. **Darryl F. Zanuck**, the head of 20th Century-Fox, wanted the studio's favorite, Tyrone Power, for the role. But director **John Ford**, who had just starred Fonda in *Young Mr. Lincoln* and *Drums along the Mohawk* (both 1939), insisted on Fonda, who gave one of his most memorable performances as Tom. Henry Fonda was nominated for the Academy Award as best actor in 1940, but he lost to James Stewart in *The Philadelphia Story*. Steinbeck was riveted by Fonda's performance as Tom Joad, and the two became lifelong friends.

Steinbeck stated that he wrote ***Sweet Thursday*** (from which **Richard Rodgers** and Oscar Hammerstein II derived their musical ***Pipe Dream***) with Fonda in mind for the role of **Doc**, but Fonda, though interested, could not sing. In 1972, Fonda starred in a television remake of ***The Red Pony***, playing the father, whose role is fused with that of **Billy Buck**. He also did the narration for television documentaries based on ***Travels with Charley*** and ***America and Americans***. During **Adlai Stevenson**'s campaigns for the presidency, Fonda delivered some speeches on Stevenson's behalf that were written by Steinbeck. He was one of the speakers at Steinbeck's funeral. Henry Fonda finally won the Oscar for *On Golden Pond* (1981), his last picture.

Further Reading: Fonda, Henry. *Fonda, My Life, as told to Howard Teichmann*. New York: The New American Library, 1981.

FONTENROSE, JOSEPH EDDY (1903–1986). Author of *John Steinbeck: An Introduction and Interpretation* (1963) for the American Authors and Critics Series. Fontenrose taught at the University of California at Berkeley and published scholarly articles and reviews, as well as longer studies including *Python: A Study of Delphic Myth and Its Origins* (1959) and *The Ritual Theory of Myth* (1966). One of a generation of scholars writing myth criticism in the 1960s, Fontenrose found Steinbeck's work amenable to mythic interpretation, and so his work is a mythic and thematic study of Steinbeck's oeuvre. "Steinbeck," Fontenrose writes, "translates myth and legend into twentieth-century realism." Among observations about Steinbeck's recurrent themes and his use of plant and animal metaphors, Fontenrose also comments on his use of Arthurian myth in ***Tortilla Flat***; **Milton**'s ***Paradise Lost*** in ***In Dubious Battle***; Edenic myth in ***The Long Valley***; biblical parallels in ***The Grapes of Wrath***; the concept of Logos in ***Cannery Row***; and, of course, the tale of Cain and Abel in ***East of Eden***. His privately published text, entitled *Steinbeck's Unhappy Valley: A Study on "The Pastures of Heaven,"* is generally considered the most authoritative analysis of Steinbeck's short story cycle.

Scott Simkins

FORD, JOHN (SEAN O'FEARNA) (1895–1973). Distinguished film director who won the Academy Award as best director for the film, ***The Grapes of Wrath*** (1940). Ford had previously won an Oscar for *The Informer* (1935), and he subsequently won for *How Green Was My Valley* (1941) and *The Quiet Man* (1952). Among Ford's many notable films are *Arrowsmith* (1931), *The Hurricane* (1937), *Stagecoach* (1939), *The Long Voyage Home* (1940), *My Darling Clementine* (1946), *The Searchers* (1956), and *The Man Who Shot Liberty Valance* (1962). Before World War II, Ford made powerful dramas about humans in crisis, often focusing on the unity of families, as in *How Green Was My Valley.* After the war, he made mostly Westerns starring John Wayne.

FORGOTTEN VILLAGE, THE (1941). Set in Mexico, this semidocumentary grew out of Steinbeck's concern for the health of the natives he met there. The script that Steinbeck wrote was intended to be made into a movie, with filming to take place in Mexico during the early months of 1940. It grew out of an invitation to participate in a project with the documentary film maker, **Herbert Kline**. Steinbeck welcomed the chance to apply his scientific theories to the practical example of a forgotten Mexican village facing a social crisis. In his Preface to the documentary book, Steinbeck insists that the movie-makers filmed what they found, employing an inductive logic but arranging the materials "to form a coherent story."

The plot centers around a young boy named Juan Diego, who has left the village for a stint at the new government school named for the idealistic leader of the Mexican revolution, Francisco Madero. When his little brother Paco sickens and eventually dies from cholera, Juan rejects the traditional explanations of Trini, the folk healer, and insists that the village purify its water supply. Both his own family and his fellow villagers doubt him until another child is stricken. This time, Juan asserts himself by giving his little sister a healing injection despite the folk healer's objections, while government workers also purify the water supply. The boy's goal is to return as a doctor and to fight the native ignorance with scientific knowledge, transforming the village from primitive to progressive in its values.

The tenet of the film is unusual in that Steinbeck advocates the importance of science and progress, whereas he usually displays mixed feeling about technology and industrialization. This uncharacteristic advocacy caused a temporary rift between Steinbeck and his friend **Edward F. Ricketts**, who advocated that noble primitives be left alone, even when confronted with disease. Ricketts felt that the knowledge attained by factual scientific observation was not always in the best interest of native cultures, and he even composed an antiscript to protest the film project. The fact that Steinbeck's script reveals a paradox of thoughts regarding right and wrong emphasizes the author's interest in the moral ambiguity of life itself. Often one can find intrinsic value both in what society deems positive and in what it considers negative.

Both book and film faced many production and distribution problems before they were released to a sympathetic critical reaction late in November of 1941. The music director, Mexican composer Silvestre Revueltas, died while the film was being shot, and the score was finished by Hanns Eisler. The original choice for the narrator, **Spencer Tracy**, was removed from the project by the MGM studio, but the narration was well read by **Burgess Meredith**, who played **George Milton** in the 1939 film version of ***Of Mice and Men***. The production faced even more problems in distribution; the film was held captive by the New York State Board of Censors and labeled indecent. First lady Eleanor Roosevelt had to intervene with the New York Board of Review to let the film open with a childbirth scene intact. It was further attacked by the America First Committee as advocating socialism. Although Steinbeck considered such criticism an overt effort to suppress the information given in the film and to thwart the social reforms it advocated, eventually *The Forgotten Village* was plagued by inadequate distribution and by a lack of interest because of the United States' entry into World War II. Ultimately, it failed to gain critical acclaim because of these problems and because of the critical limbo. It became just another competent film that sat dormant on a studio shelf, gaining little recognition for the causes it espoused.

Further Reading: Kline, Herbert. "On John Steinbeck." *Steinbeck Quarterly* 4 (Summer 1971): 80–88; Millichap, Joseph R. *Steinbeck and Film*. New York: Ungar, 1983; Steinbeck, John. *The Forgotten Village*. New York: Viking, 1941.

Joseph Millichap and Michael J. Meyer

FOUR QUEENS, THE. In ***The Acts of King Arthur***, the Queen of Eastland, the Queen of North Galys, the Queen of the Outer Isles, and their leader, the Queen of the Land of Gore (**Morgan le Fay**). They discover **Sir Lancelot** sleeping under an apple tree, drug him, and carry him off to Maiden's Castle, where they incarcerate him in the dungeon until he chooses one to have possession of him. But Lancelot escapes from their clutches, with the help of **Sir Bagdemagus**'s daughter.

FRANKIE. In ***Cannery Row***, a mentally handicapped boy who admires **Doc** greatly and who tries to help around **Western Biological** when he can. Frankie cannot learn, and his parents are not interested in paying to keep the boy in an institution. Twice in the novel Frankie tries to please Doc, and twice Frankie's efforts end disastrously. The first time, Frankie drops a serving tray of beer and is humiliated; the second time, he breaks into a store and attempts to steal a clock because he wants to give Doc a gift at his birthday party. After the attempted theft, and given the fact that Frankie is entering puberty, the local authorities decide that the boy must be institutionalized, much to Doc's despair. Frankie is yet another of Steinbeck's characters who suffers just enough deficiency to be unable to survive in a community.

Charles Etheridge, Jr.

FRANKLIN, MINNIE. Owner of a beauty parlor in **Salinas** frequented by **Kate Albey,** in ***East of Eden***.

FRAZER, SIR JAMES. *See* ***The Golden Bough.***

FREE BROTHERHOOD OF THE COAST. The loose alliance of Caribbean pirates in ***Cup of Gold***.

FRENCH, WARREN GRAHAM (1922–). A prominent Steinbeck critic and the author of many books, Warren French is a direct descendant of America's "Tenth Muse"—Anne Bradstreet—and one of the founding families of the Massachusetts Bay Colony. He was born in Philadelphia and graduated from the University of Pennsylvania (B.A., English and Journalism). He served in the U.S. Army (1943–46), training in Texas and California. After the war, he returned to the University of Texas at Austin, where he received his M.A. (English) and Ph.D. (American Literature and History). Much of French's research concerned John Steinbeck's canon, including works that he had become enthusiastic about after reading ***Cannery Row***.

French taught at several universities, and in 1958 Sylvia Bowman asked him to write the first book especially designed to establish the format for Twayne's United States Authors Series. That first volume was *John Steinbeck* (1961). He followed it up quickly with series books on **Frank Norris** and J. D. Salinger, and *A Companion to The Grapes of Wrath* (1963) that was commissioned by Steinbeck's editor, **Pascal Covici**. In 1970, just as he began work as chairman of the department of English at the newly created Indiana University/ Purdue University at Indianapolis, he was asked by Tetsumaro Hayashi to serve as president of the newly organized John Steinbeck Society of America, with its headquarters at Ball State University in Muncie, Indiana.

In 1975 French published an update to his book on Steinbeck for the Twayne series and became an editor for Twayne. During that period he became president of the newly organized International John Steinbeck Society, while continuing to produce a number of journal essays and chapters of books on Steinbeck. In 1985 French was awarded a Doctor of Humane Letters degree from Ohio University, and the following year he decided to retire early and spend the second six months of each year at the University of Wales-Swansea, where he was appointed an

Honorary Professor of American Studies. In 1996 he established a permanent residence in Tallahassee, Florida.

Warren French

FREUD, SIGMUND (1856–1939). Known as the father of psychoanalysis, Freud devoted most of the rest of his life to formulating and extending his theories of mental health. As the originator of psychoanalysis, Freud distinguished himself as an intellectual giant and pioneered new techniques for understanding human behavior. Steinbeck tended to reject Freud's psychoanalytical focus on the individual unconscious; instead, he preferred **Karl Jung**'s distinction between the collective unconscious and the personal unconscious, a theory that was more nearly parallel to the theories of **John Elof Boodin** and **Edward F. Ricketts**. Steinbeck and **Joseph Campbell** were known to have discussed the differences between these psychologists around the time Steinbeck attempted to incorporate archetypal imagery in ***To a God Unknown***.

Tracy Michaels

FRIEDE, DONALD (1901–1965). Born in New York City and widely traveled internationally in his youth, Friede returned to New York in 1915. In 1925 he became a partner in the publishing firm of Boni & Liveright. He cofounded the firm **Covici-Friede** in 1935 and moved to Hollywood to become a literary and film agent. Friede's life in the 1920s and his literary career with Boni & Liveright and Covici-Friede are described in his autobiography *The Mechanical Angel* (Alfred Knopf, 1948), now long out of print. Through **Pascal Covici**, the new firm brought out *Tortilla Flat* in 1935 and enabled Steinbeck to at last become a financially successful author.

FRIEND ED. One of the most curious of Steinbeck's fictionalized avatars of **Edward F. Ricketts**, Friend Ed acts in the role of a **Doc** character in ***Burning Bright***. Like the other characters in this, the last of Steinbeck's play-novelettes, Friend Ed is a type, an abstraction. In the course of three acts, Friend Ed is a clown, then a farmer, and then a seaman (in "captain's uniform"). Ed offers advice to **Joe Saul** and is a protective companion—the one man who has Saul's respect. He listens to Ed. Until the third act, Ed is a soothing, rational mediator for Saul, helping the older man to work through feelings of inadequacy, suspicion, fear, and rage. Friend Ed, with the "warm cool" mind of the Doc characters, is both rational and capable of passion—his love for Saul has no bounds. In the entangled story of *Burning Bright*, in which **Mordeen** uses **Victor** as a kind of stud animal so she can finally present Saul with a baby, Victor fears Ed—and for good reason. When Victor threatens to reveal his role in the conception of Saul's child, Friend Ed crushes the young man's skull and tosses him into the sea (in the stage version, he merely arranges to have Victor shanghaied).

As Steinbeck was working on *Burning Bright* in 1950, he also had Ricketts on his mind; he was composing the long essay regarding his friend, **"About Ed Ricketts."** At this time Steinbeck was moving from realism to allegory, from the objective to the subjective, from showing to telling. In general, he was shifting away from the biological viewpoint to a moralistic one. Yet, as Friend Ed shows, Ricketts was still an influence. Friend Ed, a character caught at the crossroads of Steinbeck's artistic direction, is therefore an odd fellow: a calm mediator and, when necessary, a murderer. Oscillating wildly, he is the most extreme of the Ricketts characterizations. The one constant is his devotion to Saul, however misguided the end result.

Further Reading: Railsback, Brian. "The *Bright* Failure: What Shall We Make of Chaos?" In *The Betrayal of Brotherhood in the Works of John Steinbeck*. Ed. Michael Meyer. Lewiston, NY: Mellon Press, 2000: 327–56.

FROMM, ERICH (1900–1980). An influential and popular psychoanalyst in America, his books include *Escape from Freedom*

(1941) and *Man for Himself* (1947). He is perhaps best known for his interesting treatise on love in the modern world, *The Art of Loving* (1956). Fromm's psychoanalytic theories are a rather unique blend of **Sigmund Freud** and Karl Marx. Whereas Freud postulated that our characters are determined by biology, Marx, on the other hand, saw people as determined by their society, and most especially by their economic systems. Fromm added to this mix of two deterministic systems something quite foreign to them: the idea of freedom. He allows people to transcend the determinisms that Freud and Marx attribute to them. In fact, Fromm makes freedom the central characteristic of human nature, a concept Steinbeck explores in ***East of Eden***'s ***timshel***. **Robert DeMott** notes that Steinbeck read and greatly admired Fromm's *Psychoanalysis and Religion* (1950) and that "Fromm's insistence on the ethical role of individual conscience and his discussion of 'inner strength and integrity' bore directly on JS's characterization of **Samuel Hamilton**" in *East of Eden* (148).

Further Reading: DeMott, Robert. *Steinbeck's Reading; A Catalogue of Books Owned and Borrowed*. New York: Garland, 1984.

Michael J. Meyer

FROST, RICHARD. A nervous but intelligent man, Frost appears twice in ***Cannery Row***. Consumed by the question of how a flagpole skater relieves himself without descending, Frost leaves home in the middle of the night to find out. The skater solves the mystery by revealing that he uses a can. Later, Frost serves as a sounding board for **Doc**'s philosophic explorations into how **Mac** and the boys eschew societal expectations. Doc bets Frost that Mac and the boys will take no notice of an approaching parade. Frost, convinced that no person could fail to turn to watch a parade, takes the bet and loses.

Charles Etheridge, Jr.

FUENTES, GENERAL. In ***Viva Zapata!***, he is the second neighbor *hacendado* and is described by Steinbeck as wearing "full-dress uniform of a Mexican general with decorations that include the Iron Cross." He will not relinquish his land, but he feels it is absurd to let politics ruin a dinner party with **Don Nacio de la Torre y Mier** (excised from the film, but still in the screenplay). **Emiliano Zapata** meets with Don Nacio and learns he is to receive no help from him other than his attempt to persuade them to give up the lands and return them to the natives who really own them. Fuentes draws a pistol and aims it at Emiliano's back as he leaves. Nacio grabs his wrist and succeeds in preventing harm from being done, but Fuentes ominously remarks that "by saving him you may have killed a thousand men. You may have killed yourself."

FUENTES'S WIFE. In ***Viva Zapata!***, she also appears at **Don Nacio**'s dinner party with her husband, **General Fuentes**.

G

GABILAN. In **"The Gift"** (first short story in *The Red Pony*), Gabilan is the name that **Jody Tiflin** gives to the red pony his father buys from a carnival that was shut down. Jody names the pony after his favorite mountains, choosing an appellation that means *hawk*.

GABLE, CLARK (1901–1960). In *The Wayward Bus,* the well-known Hollywood movie star who is the object of **Norma**'s obsession.

GAHERIS, SIR. In *The Acts of King Arthur,* the nephew of **King Arthur**, son of **Margawse** and **King Lot of Lothian and Orkney**, and brother of **Sir Gawain**. He is the last of the long series of knights to be captured and imprisoned by **Sir Tarquin**. He is rescued by **Sir Lancelot** and instructed to go to Tarquin's castle, release all the other prisoners, and tell them to return to Camelot, where Lancelot will greet them all at court at Pentecost.

GALAGARS, SIR. In *The Acts of King Arthur,* he is made a knight of the **Round Table** on **King Pellinore**'s recommendation following the war with the **Five Kings**.

GALAHAD. In *The Acts of King Arthur,* the original name of the son of **King Ban of Benwick** and **Queen Elaine**, changed to **Sir Lancelot** at his christening. **Merlin** prophesies that he will become the greatest knight in all the world.

GALATI, FRANK. Associate director of the Goodman Theatre, who adapted and directed a stage version of *The Grapes of Wrath* for Chicago's Steppenwolf Theatre Company that won the Tony Award as the best play of 1990. Galati himself won the Tony for best director.

GALATINE, SIR. In *The Acts of King Arthur,* one of the four knights beaten in a tournament by **Sir Lancelot** and the four white knights, who were acting as champions for **Sir Bagdemagus**.

GALBRAITH, JOHN KENNETH (1908–2006). Noted Harvard economist who served as **Franklin Delano Roosevelt**'s war price czar in 1938. He attained worldwide fame after the publication of *The Affluent Society* in 1958, a book that motivated the War on Poverty undertaken during the presidencies of **John F. Kennedy** and **Lyndon Baines Johnson**. He also wrote *The New Industrial State* (1967) and served as ambassador to India under Kennedy. Galbraith and his wife, Kitty, met **Elaine Scott Steinbeck** and John Steinbeck in 1954, when both couples were vacationing in the Caribbean. They became friends, spending many afternoons in intellectual conversation and political speculation. The friendship deepened when both men supported the candidacy of

Adlai E. Stevenson and helped write speeches and political press releases for him. Galbraith agreed with Steinbeck in deploring corporate greed. However, the two differed over the Vietnam War. Galbraith condemned American policy in Asia, the war, and the inordinate cost of America's military machine and its effect on other public affairs. Steinbeck's **"Letters to Alicia"** and his friendship with Johnson resulted in the author's public support of the troops in Vietnam. Years after Steinbeck's death, Galbraith remembered him with fondness, commenting in particular on the author's great sense of humor.

Further Reading: Galbraith, John Kenneth. "John Steinbeck: Footnote for a Memoir." In *John Steinbeck: A Centennial Tribute*. Ed. Stephen K. George. Westport, CT: Praeger, 2002.

"A GAME OF HOSPITALITY" (1957). This article, published in *The Saturday Review* (April 20), chastises a U.S. government that prohibits foreign writers from entering the country, mostly because of the perceived threat posed by their leftist politics. Steinbeck lists fifty great people in history who would have been kept out of the country under current law—Socrates, Pericles, and **Joan of Arc** among them—and lists the various reasons, often trivial, why they would have been kept out. He concludes that "a great majority of the desirable and creative men of all ages would not be welcome, or permitted, in our country."

GANNET, LEWIS (1891–1966). Critic for the *New York Herald Tribune*'s "Books" section and husband of Ruth Gannet, who did the illustrations for the first edition of ***Tortilla Flat***. In 1936, Gannet wrote the preface for the second issue of ***Cup of Gold***. He wrote one of the earliest books about Steinbeck, *John Steinbeck Personal and Bibliographical Notes* (1939). It was at a dinner party at the Gannets' when Lewis suggested to Steinbeck that he should go overseas as a war correspondent for his newspaper, the *Herald Tribune*.

John Hooper

GANYMEDE, THE. **Henry Morgan**'s first pirate ship in ***Cup of Gold***. Upon first seeing her, Henry decides she is fast and discovers, through inquiries, that she is well armed. He buys a half stake in the ship and the captaincy from **Black Grippo** for five hundred pounds, promising that if he should have one failure as captain, then Grippo will keep the five hundred pounds and once more become captain and sole owner of the ship. Henry doesn't fail.

Kevin Hearle

GARCIA, ALICE. **Juanito**'s wife in ***To a God Unknown***, daughter of Jesus Garcia. She is seduced by **Benjamin Wayne** and probably bears his child, who will be raised as Juanito's and her son. Her infidelity later results in Benjamin's murder.

GARCÍA, DON. In ***Viva Zapata!***, he is a neighbor ***hacendado*** of **Don Nacio** who invites Don Nacio and his wife, as well as **General Fuentes** and his wife, to a dinner party in the hope that he will give the land back to the people. Even though Don García paid for the land, Don Nacio's theory is that if something is not done, all the land will be lost in revolution. García is obtusely adamant about the fact that, if need be, he will fight for the property.

GARCIA, JOHNNY. In ***Travels with Charley***, Steinbeck visits Johnny Garcia's bar in **Monterey**. Johnny, Steinbeck, and other bar patrons drink and reminisce. Johnny begs Steinbeck to return home to Monterey to live. However, Steinbeck knows one cannot go home again.

Thom Tammarro

GARCÍA'S WIFE. In ***Viva Zapata!***, she appears at **Don Nacio**'s dinner party given for two of his neighbor ***hacendados***, one of whom is her husband, **Don García**. When Don García gets worked up about the fighting that will have to come in defense of the *hacendados*' lands, his wife calms him with a pill. This scene and her role are excised from the film.

GARFIELD, JOHN (JULIUS GARFINKLE) (1913–1952). Actor who usually played a New York tough guy, which he was, but whose appearance as **Danny** in ***Tortilla Flat*** (1942) was considered by critics to be miscasting. Among Garfield's most notable films were *Four Daughters* (1938), *The Sea Wolf* (1941), *The Postman Always Rings Twice* (1946), *Gentleman's Agreement* (1947), *Body and Soul* (1947), and *Force of Evil* (1949).

GARLON, SIR. In ***The Acts of King Arthur***, evil knight and brother of **King Pelham**. Bested in jousting by a gentleman, Garlon makes himself invisible and wounds the gentleman's son. He kills Sir Harleus de Berbeus and **Sir Peryne de Monte Belyarde**, and is himself killed by **Sir Balin of Northumberland**.

GARNISH OF THE MOUNTAIN, SIR. In ***The Acts of King Arthur***, the knight of Duke Harmel, who loves the duke's daughter. He kills his love and her lover when he finds them sleeping together in the garden, and then kills himself, after blaming **Sir Balin of Northumberland** for destroying his illusions about the duke's daughter.

GARRISIERE, JOE. Owner of a liquor store in **Salinas** where, in ***East of Eden***, **Cal Trask** takes his brother, **Aron Trask,** to buy three bottles of champagne for their father, **Adam Trask**. Cal wants to pay for the gift, although he wants it to seem as if it were from Aron. This incident is reminiscent of the one with a rabbit six years earlier, when Cal had shot the rabbit but was eager to give Aron credit for doing so. These gifts and attribution to the giver are connected to the Cain/Abel story that informs many aspects of Steinbeck's novel. In the previous generation, a similar event had occurred when **Charles** and Adam tried to please their father, **Cyrus**.

Margaret Seligman

GASTON, MRS. A **Monterey** resident who has a kidney stone removed that is as large as a hand and shaped like a beagle's head. Early in ***Sweet Thursday***, this peculiar circumstance is cited in retrospect as an unnoticed portent of the momentous changes coming to the area.

GAWAIN, SIR. In ***The Acts of King Arthur***, **King Arthur**'s nephew, son of Arthur's half sister, **Margawse**, and **King Lot of Lothian and Orkney**, brother of **Sir Gaheris**, cousin of **Sir Ewain**, and the second knight to be made after the creation of the Fellowship of the **Round Table**. He is sent by King Arthur on the Quest of the White Stag, accompanied by his brother, Gaheris, who is also his squire. Gawain is merciless in his quest, and although he brings back the white stag's head as proof of his success, he incurs the displeasure of Arthur, for his ruthlessness has caused the accidental death of a lady. **Guinevere** sets an eternal quest on him that he should ever after defend all ladies and fight in their cause, be courteous always, and grant mercy when it is asked. Gawain is made a Knight of the Round Table on **King Pellinore**'s recommendation after the war with **the five kings**. He leaves with Ewain when his cousin is banished from Arthur's court and, after joining up with **Sir Marhalt**, embarks with them on the Triple Quest, accompanied on his chosen path by the youngest and fairest of the ladies of the Triple Quest, who soon leaves him for a dwarf knight.

GAWTER, SIR. In *The Acts of King Arthur*, challenges **Sir Lancelot**, who is wearing the armor and bearing the device of **Sir Kay**. Gawter is beaten by Lancelot and sent to the court to submit to **Guinevere** as one of Sir Kay's prizes.

GAY. In *Cannery Row*, as the most recent addition to **Mack**'s group in the **Palace Flophouse**, Gay is a talented mechanic known for violent fights with his wife. He is able to get **Lee Chong**'s old Ford running, which makes the *Cannery Row*'s frog collecting trip possible. However, when the truck breaks down and Gay goes to find a needle valve for a carburetor, he goes into Jimmy

Bruccis', where he gets into a bar fight with **Sparky Enea** and **Tiny Colleto**, the real-life engineers from the ***Western Flyer***, the sardine boat chartered by Steinbeck for his expedition to the **Sea of Cortez**. As a result of this misadventure, Gay receives 180 days in jail, although later in the novel he is able to secure a two-day pass from jail and borrow bus-fare money from his jailer in order to attend the second party in **Doc**'s honor.

GAY. In ***Sweet Thursday***, a former resident of the **Palace Flophouse** who was killed by antiaircraft fallback during World War II. When they learn of his death, **Mack** and the boys throw a memorial party at which it is rumored that three more people have died. They leave his bed just as it was before he departed for war, with the patchwork quilt turned down, and they keep a fresh nosegay on the shelf over his bed, knowing how much he liked to eat flowers. They maintain the hope that he may return someday, even though his wife has already used his army insurance to remarry. Since in ***Cannery Row*** Gay is known mostly for having violent fights with his wife, Steinbeck may have eliminated him from *Sweet Thursday* to prevent his marriage from appearing as a possible parallel to **Doc** and **Suzy**'s union in the future. However, the absence of Gay softens the novel by removing a crude example of matrimony gone wrong.

Bruce Ouderkirk

GELTHAIN, MR. A customer at the Golden Poppy restaurant in ***Sweet Thursday***, who would have left his umbrella without **Suzy**'s timely reminder. Suzy's determination to succeed in establishing a new life for herself is evident in her interactions with Mr. Gelthain and the other diners. The spelling of Mr. Gelthain's name may have been an error, since it is very close to that of **Mr. Geltham**.

GELTHAM, MR. A resident of **Monterey** in ***Sweet Thursday***, who is having an extramarital affair with a school teacher. He is mentioned briefly to illustrate how much a good constable like **Joe Blaikey** knows about his community.

GELTHAM, MRS. In ***Sweet Thursday***, a resident of **Monterey**, whose parties are mentioned briefly to demonstrate how much **Joe Blaikey** knows about the community.

GEMMELL, MARGARET (1904–1988). An early romantic interest of Steinbeck's when he attended **Stanford University**, Gemmell shared a class with the author (Edward Martin Hulme's course, "The History of European Thought") and both were members of the English Club. Although the two dated in 1925, when Steinbeck left Stanford University for New York, he became enamored with Mary Ardath, a showgirl at the Greenwich Village Follies, and the affair with Gemmell began to fade. Nevertheless, he maintained an elevated and idealized correspondence with Gemmell, based on his earlier sentimental attachment. It is also thought by some critics that his portrait of **Henry Morgan** in ***Cup of Gold*** is a fictional depiction of himself at this confusing juncture of his life: a solitary, lonely individual who decides to pursue his dream at great costs, including the loss of love.

GENOESE SLAVE DEALERS. In ***Cup of Gold***, the Genoese slave dealers in Panama build a large warehouse for their merchandise. In it are tiers of cages where the black men sit until they are brought. The slave dealers are part of the backdrop of general inhumanity against which the specific psychological portrait of **Henry Morgan** is drawn.

GEOFFREY OF MONMOUTH (1100–1155). A twelfth-century Benedictine monk who chronicled the kings of the British Isles. His *History of the Kings of Britain*, drawn from a variety of accounts both historical and literary, is widely credited with popularizing Arthurian legend. Geoffrey's work was known to Steinbeck and was one of the sources he consulted during the composition of ***The Acts of King Arthur and His Noble Knights***.

GEORGE. The chief of the volunteer firemen in **Cathy Ames**'s Massachusetts hometown in ***East of Eden***. He searches the rubble of the Ameses' house, the result of the fire set by Cathy to kill her parents, **William** and **Mrs. Ames**. George discovers that Cathy's parents were apparently locked inside the house when the fire was set, and that the keys are missing.

Margaret Seligman

GEORGE. **Jim Moore**'s neighbor in **"The Murder,"** who unwittingly precipitates Jim's murder of his wife's lover. Chancing upon Jim on his way into town on a Saturday night, George tells him that he has discovered evidence of cattle thieves on Jim's ranch. Jim returns and, although he finds no thieves, discovers that his wife, **Jelke**, is sleeping with her cousin.

Abby H. P. Werlock

GEORGE. *See* **Milton, George.**

GEORGE. In ***The Wayward Bus***, the black swamper responsible for cleaning the Greyhound buses between runs. In preparation for a run to **Rebel Corners**, George finds a wallet with two $50 bills and a certified check for $500. Seeking to elude the glance of the window washer and pocket the cash in order to go on a drinking binge, George fails in this attempt when **Louie**, the driver, asks about the wallet at the passenger's request. George is finally the victim of Louie's brutality and greed when he receives only a token of the reward given to Louie by the passenger. Race clearly plays a role in George's vulnerable position.

GEORGIA. Prostitute at **Faye**'s (later **Kate Albey**'s) brothel in ***East of Eden***; Georgia takes piano lessons from **Cotton Eye**.

GEROULD, KATHERINE (1879–1944). Mentioned by Steinbeck in a 1924 letter to **Edith Wagner** as being on an eclectic list of writers he had begun to read; he admired Gerould's short stories and, as noted by **Robert DeMott**, probably read her collection, *The Great Tradition and Other Stories* (1915).

"GHOST OF ANTHONY DALY, THE" (1965–1966). This epistolary, one in a series of **"Letters to Alicia,"** published in *Newsday* (20 Nov. 1965–28 May 1966), is a compilation of several different accounts of the hanging death of an Irishman, Daly, who was falsely accused of murder. According to local legend, Daly's ghost still roams St. Cleran, the Georgian house in which Steinbeck stayed during his visit to Ireland. To Steinbeck, the fact the story is still argued over is proof that "Ireland is still Ireland, and you don't have to dig down for it, either."

Further Reading: Steinbeck, John. "The Ghost of Anthony Daly." In *America and Americans and Selected Nonfiction.* Ed. Susan Shillinglaw and Jackson J. Benson. New York: Viking, 2002.

Eric Skipper

GIBBON, EDWARD (1737–1794). British historian known for his massive multivolume work, *The Decline and Fall of the Roman Empire.* As **Robert DeMott** notes, Steinbeck read *Decline*, and Steinbeck cites Gibbon among the great historians in ***America and Americans.***

GIDE, ANDRE (1869–1951). French writer and intellectual who won the **Nobel Prize** for Literature in 1947. Steinbeck read at least a few of Gide's books and greatly admired Gide's novel *The Counterfeiters* (Steinbeck read a 1928 translation). In turn, Gide admired Steinbeck's works, ***In Dubious Battle*** in particular.

Further Reading: DeMott, Robert. *Steinbeck's Reading: A Catalogue of Books Owned and Borrowed.* New York: Garland, 1984.

"GIFT, THE" (1933). The first short story in ***The Red Pony***, originally published in the *North American Review* of November 1933. The young son of a **Salinas** Valley rancher,

Jody Tiflin, is given a trick show pony his father has bought from a bankrupt circus. Excited that his father trusts him at such a young age to care for an animal, Jody delightedly accepts the pony and names him **Gabilan**, meaning *hawk* and recalling the mountains of the same name that border the Tiflin ranch. As time progresses and the horse matures, Jody learns how to train and care for his animal by listening to the advice of **Billy Buck**, a stable hand; specifically, Jody finds out how to use a halter, how to rein in the pony, and how to groom and saddle it. In this way, Jody becomes more and more responsible and mature. Unfortunately, when the rainy season comes to central California, so does disaster. Realizing the danger if Gabilan is exposed to the cold rain, Jody is loath to let him out in the corral while he attends school, fearing the pony will get wet and develop an illness. However, Billy Buck encourages Jody to let Gabilan stay out, predicting fair weather and promising to take Gabilan in should it begin to rain. Surprisingly, Billy fails to keep his commitment, and Gabilan does catch a chill that becomes life threatening. Throughout Gabilan's illness, Billy reassures Jody that all will be well and that Gabilan will survive, despite the fact that the horse's health appears worse as the days pass.

As a dependable owner would, Jody helps nurse the pony and does all in his power to save it. However, one morning he awakes from his vigil in the barn to discover that Gabilan is missing. Following the sick pony's tracks, he discovers to his dismay that Gabilan is dying and is surrounded by buzzards waiting to prey on his carcass. By the time Jody arrives at the pony's dead body, the buzzards are at work, and all Jody can do is manage to strangle one who is feasting on Gabilan's eye. This violent reaction, however, does not assuage his sorrow at the death of his pony and his disappointment in Billy Buck, whom he trusted to keep his promise and to be truthful about the pony's real condition.

Michael J. Meyer

"GIFTS OF IBAN, THE" (1927). Likely written in 1926, the first short story John Steinbeck published in a professional venue (the March 1927 issue of the *Smoker's Companion*). **Jackson J. Benson** considers it "one of the best-written of Steinbeck's early stories." Iban, a fairy living in an enchanted forest, suffers when his great love, Cantha, eventually turns from him when she realizes his gifts are poetic and ephemeral, while Glump, the king of the gnomes, can offer her material goods. Benson notes that the themes of this story, such as the destructive power of pride and materialism or the hopeless quest for idealized feminine beauty, are precursors to themes more fully explored in Steinbeck's first novel, ***Cup of Gold***.

Further Reading: Benson, Jackson J. *The True Adventures of John Steinbeck, Writer.* New York: Viking, 1984.

GILMERE, SIR. In ***The Acts of King Arthur***, he challenges **Sir Lancelot**, who is wearing the armor and bearing the device of **Sir Kay**, and is beaten by him. Gilmere is sent to the court to submit to **Guinevere** as one of Sir Kay's prizes.

GIRL WITH DOC. A young woman who accompanies **Doc** on his first collecting trip to **La Jolla** in *Sweet Thursday*. She becomes disappointed, then angry, when Doc ignores her to lavish his attention on the baby octopi he has found in the intertidal zone. Doc's lack of interest in this willing romantic companion is a symptom of the unsettling change that has come over him. Ironically, while this first trip to La Jolla disrupts his romantic life, the later trip will promote the consummation of his relationship with **Suzy**.

GITANO. An old paisano; in **"The Great Mountains,"** the second story in ***The Red Pony***, he returns to the **Tiflin** ranch to die, because the old adobe in which he and his father were born had been on that land. Mr. Tiflin makes cruel jibes at him about being old and useless. Gitano is last seen returning to the mountains from whence he came.

GLADSTEIN, MIMI REISEL (1936–). Critic who has been a pioneer in feminist approaches to the study of women in Steinbeck's works. Gladstein has examined his women characters and noted the lack of women—an ironic absence, given the number of women who played crucial roles in Steinbeck's life. Two of her articles, "Deletions in the Battle; Gaps in the *Grapes*" and "Missing Women: The Inexplicable Disparity between Women in Steinbeck's Life and Those in His Fiction," brought attention to the issue. Gladstein has also published articles on Steinbeck's prophetic environmentalism, coauthored with her son, Clifford, and a study of the immigrant paradigm that undergirds the universality of ***The Grapes of Wrath***. Her Jewish heritage has also proved fruitful in her discussion of the maturation process of **Jody** in ***The Red Pony***. Most recent of her varied essays on Steinbeck is her intertextual reading of ***East of Eden***, ***Journal of a Novel***, and **John Steinbeck IV**'s "Adam's Wound" in *Cain Sign: The Betrayal of Brotherhood in the Works of John Steinbeck*. Gladstein is the author of four books, among them *The Indestructible Woman in the Works of Faulkner, Hemingway, and Steinbeck*. She has chaired the English department at the University of Texas at El Paso, directed the Women's Studies Program, and has served as associate dean of liberal arts.

Further Reading: Gladstein, Mimi Reisel and A. Walton Litz, eds. *The Indestructible Woman in the Works of Faulkner, Hemingway, and Steinbeck*. Ann Arbor, MI: UMI Research Press, 1986.

"GOD IN THE PIPES." An incomplete manuscript, in form along the lines of ***Of Mice and Men***, which was the object of Steinbeck's sporadic attention. The initial impetus for the text seems to have come from material related to his experience in Mexico while he was working on ***The Forgotten Village*** during 1940. **Pat Covici** urged Steinbeck to return to the piece while he was completing ***Sea of Cortez*** in 1941. After *Cortez*, Steinbeck once again abandoned "God in the Pipes" when the long-awaited contract for ***The Red Pony*** script came through. Although intending to return to the project later that year, Steinbeck once again left it in favor of material that would eventually become ***The Moon Is Down***.

Brian Niro

GODDARD, PAULETTE (PAULINE MARION LEVY) (1910–1990). Glamorous Hollywood movie star of the 1930s and 1940s, who appeared in such movies as *The Great Dictator* (1940) with **Charlie Chaplin**, Cecil B. DeMille's *Reap the Wild Wind* (1942), and *The Diary of a Chambermaid* (1946) with **Burgess Meredith**. For a time she lived with Chaplin, Steinbeck's friend, and then she married Meredith, another good Steinbeck friend, so it was inevitable that he knew her. In 1949, Goddard and Steinbeck were both unattached, and they had a brief affair that ended when Steinbeck met the woman who would be his third wife, **Elaine Scott Steinbeck**.

Further Reading: Benson, Jackson J. *The True Adventures of John Steinbeck, Writer*. New York: Viking, 1984.

GOLDEN BOUGH, THE. *The Golden Bough: A Study in Magic and Religion*, by Sir James George Frazer, may have been recommended to Steinbeck by **Joseph Campbell**, another writer famous for his work on myths, during their intellectual conversations at the lab of **Edward F. Ricketts** in the early 1930s. As **Robert DeMott** notes, this reference book—a monumental survey of primitive worship, sex practices, rituals, and festivals—had a widespread influence on much of Steinbeck's work. Most notably, however, *The Golden Bough* plays a prominent role in Steinbeck's rewriting of ***To a God Unknown***. An entire spectrum of relationships between man and nature is presented in the novel, from the narrowly conventional to the bizarre and absurd—a variety of responses to nature constructed out of Steinbeck's readings of the Old Testament,

The Golden Bough, Jessie Weston's *From Ritual to Romance* (1920), and Robert Briffault's *The Mothers: A Study of the Origins of Sentiments and Institutions* (1927). Moreover, considering that Christ is a representation of such dying and reviving vegetation gods, Steinbeck employed extensive imagery in the novel that was designed to make the reader identify **Joseph Wayne** as a resurrected god and **Rama Wayne** as a primitive earth mother. According to **Jackson J. Benson**, the point of the novel is that none of the mythology ultimately means anything, "although there is much conflict, prejudice, and suffering generated by man's delusions and the competition between closed systems of belief."

Further Reading: DeMott, Robert. *Steinbeck's Reading; A Catalogue of Books Owned and Borrowed.* New York: Garland, 1984; Benson, Jackson J. *The True Adventures of John Steinbeck, Writer.* New York: Viking, 1984.

Harry Karahalios

"THE GOLDEN HANDCUFF" (1958). First appearing in the *San Francisco Examiner* (November 23, 1958), this essay is a reminiscence of the cherished San Francisco of Steinbeck's youth, where he spent time as a struggling writer. The author reflects fondly on the cheap dwellings, love, music, food, and drink of a city that is so personal that "once you know her, you can never again sort out which is San Francisco and which is you." "The Golden Handcuff" is the city itself, in its magical, magnetic appeal.

Further Reading: Shillinglaw, Susan, and Jackson J. Benson, eds. *America and Americans and Selected Nonfiction.* New York: Viking, 2002.

GOMEZ, FRANKLIN. Kindly rancher who takes in the mysterious, deformed "Frog Boy," **Tuleracito**, in the fourth story of ***The Pastures of Heaven***. When Tuleracito is hauled in for assault, Gomez tries to keep him, but a **Salinas** judge orders the boy sent away to an asylum for the criminally insane.

"GOOD NEIGHBORS, THE." Unfinished manuscript that Steinbeck hoped would accompany ***The Pearl*** and another (never completed) novelette. "Neighbors" was begun in the summer of 1944, based on **Pascal Covici**'s thoughts of a trilogy of works with a Mexican setting. Although this piece of fiction was begun while Steinbeck was still living in New York and had been abandoned earlier, there was a brief attempt to resurrect it in a fictional mode. Finally, however, Steinbeck considered it to be beyond rescue and turned instead to another tale of Mexico that he had been developing, later titling it *El Camion Vacilidor* or ***The Wayward Bus*** (although the published *Bus* was set in the United States.).

Michael J. Meyer

GRACE. Prostitute at **Faye**'s (later **Kate Albey**'s) brothel in ***East of Eden***.

"GRADUATES: THESE ARE YOUR LIVES!" A faux commencement address that Steinbeck never gave; he wrote it in May 1956 for James S. Pope, executive editor of the Louisville, Kentucky, *Courier-Journal* (who was to give an address at Emory University in Georgia). In the address, Steinbeck attacks what he conceived as the contemporary mindset—preoccupation with fear, hatred, and war—as opposed to real thought and some recognition of the world's wonders. Subtitled "An Unspeakable Commencement Address," it was published in *Esquire* (84, September, 1975: 69, 142–143).

Eric Skipper

GRAGG, HARRIET ("HATTIE"). *See* **Gregory, Susan.**

GRANDFATHER. In *The Red Pony*'s fourth story (**"The Leader of the People"**), **Mrs. Tiflin**'s father is an old man, remembering how he led a wagon train of settlers across the plains to the coast of California. It was the big event of his life, and he has not been able to replicate it. Grandfather is held in reverence by **Billy Buck**, but **Carl Tiflin** finds the constant repetition of the stories of the crossing boring and irksome. **Jody** loves to hear the stories. After Grandfather has been humiliated by his son-in-law, Grandfather muses about the significance of his great adventure. Grandfather concludes that the westering impulse has died out of the people, and that Jody cannot be a leader of the people because there is no place to go. The westering movement has reached the ocean.

Mimi Reisel Gladstein

GRAPES OF WRATH, THE **(NOVEL)** (1939). Published by the **Viking Press** on April 14, 1939, *The Grapes of Wrath* was Steinbeck's sixth novel and is widely considered to be his masterpiece (although Steinbeck probably felt that ***East of Eden*** was his best novel). Generally included in most lists of the best novels of the twentieth century (the Modern Library ranked it as tenth), it was also heralded by the Book of the Month Club as one of sixty books that "defined the American character." By 1940, the novel was a huge national bestseller, with wide acclaim from reviewers that culminated in the **Pulitzer Prize** and a highly praised film version that year. However, the negative portrayal of his fellow Californians cost Steinbeck dearly in terms of the support of his local community—the author was burned in effigy and his novel denounced as scandalous and as a distortion of the truth. Moreover, the graphic detail, the sexual innuendoes, and the scatological references that Steinbeck had included in the novel offended conservative readers; indeed, Viking had pressured the author to eliminate certain words or to modify his vocabulary in order to avoid censorship. Although he complied with some of the requests for change, it was not until Viking reissued the text in 1997 that the references that were offensive to 1930s middle-class sensibility were restored in the text. Despite the controversy *The Grapes of Wrath* caused—it has often been banned from schools or library shelves—the book remains one of the few in regular consideration as the Great American Novel.

For over five years, Steinbeck gathered information and ideas that would lead to the novel (**Jackson J. Benson**'s biography provides the most extensive account of this period). Steinbeck entered the world of migrant labor in California when he interviewed two starving, fugitive strike organizers in Seaside in early 1934. He learned as much as he could about the labor strikes in the Imperial Valley (1934) and the **Salinas** lettuce strike (1936). Steinbeck and his first wife, **Carol Henning Steinbeck**, understood more about labor strife from organizers who visited them in their **Pacific Grove** home, and from visits with the famous social reformer Lincoln Steffens in **Carmel**. As early as 1934, Steinbeck explored migrant labor camps, and by 1936 he had published an objective, almost scientific portrait of labor strife in California with ***In Dubious Battle***. More intensive research into the subject of *Grapes* began with Steinbeck's assignment for the *San Francisco News* to write a series of articles about migrant farm labor in California (see ***The Harvest Gypsies***). He saw firsthand the destitution of migrant families in government camps and spontaneous Hoovervilles. A tremendous influence and source of information was **Tom Collins**, the manager of "Weedpatch," the government sanitary camp at **Arvin**. Collins made meticulous reports and gathered statistics about migrant life, which Steinbeck used. In 1937, Steinbeck toured camps with Collins, and in February and March of 1938, with *Life* photographer **Horace Bristol**, he toured camps hopelessly bogged down in the cold rainy season. Venturing into the flooded areas of Visalia, Steinbeck was appalled by the conditions of families, and he feared many would starve to death. As **Robert DeMott** writes, "What he witnessed there became the backdrop for the final scenes of *The Grapes of Wrath*."

Writing *Grapes* exhausted Steinbeck, wearing him down physically and emotionally. The best account of the composition of the novel is found in the journal Steinbeck wrote as he worked, edited by DeMott and published as *Working Days, The Journals of "The Grapes of Wrath,"* Steinbeck had burned his first complete run at his subject, a bitterly satirical novel called "L'Affaire Lettuceberg."

From May 31 to October 26, 1938, in a cramped little room in his Los Gatos home, Steinbeck handwrote the 200,000-word manuscript in his most sustained, even relentless, writing experience. During this period, too many friends visited, the business of a successful writer (with potential movie deals and huge sales) had to be conducted, his marriage to Carol endured a fatal level of strain, and by the end, Steinbeck complained of stomach problems, flu, and sciatica. After it was over, he sank into a deep depression. Although the journal exudes his excitement as the novel progresses, there is a building self-doubt just as he finishes his masterpiece. "I am sure of one thing—it isn't the great book I had hoped it would be," Steinbeck wrote, a week before finishing. "It's just a run-of-the-mill book. And the awful thing is that it is absolutely the best I can do." But his editor, **Pascal Covici**, and Viking had great confidence in the work, ordering a large press run and enjoying the fact that some one million copies had sold by 1941.

In the spirit of the **non-teleological** philosophy he worked out with **Edward F. Ricketts**, Steinbeck portrayed the plight of migrant laborers from two distinct perspectives in an attempt to capture the crisis holistically. One was the dramatic, narrower view of a single extended family, the **Joads**, on their journey from the Oklahoma Dust Bowl to the potentially Edenic state of California. The other was from the wider perspective of the larger labor migration through intercalary chapters—almost essay like—narrated with far-seeing omniscience. Dispossessed by banks and corporations, the Joads and their neighbors are helpless against the power of a faceless bureaucracy and lose the heritage of the land that has sustained them for generations. Steeling themselves to this loss, they set out on an exodus they believe will terminate at a promised land of milk and honey (similar to the first exodus led by Moses). However, they soon discover that this Canaan (California), like the Egypt (Oklahoma) they are leaving, is in reality rife with enemies. After a strenuous journey across the deserts of Arizona and New Mexico, the Joads, like the Israelites who wandered in a wilderness for forty years, are weary and discouraged by the prospect of ever attaining a promised land. In yet another biblical parallel to the Jews, the Joads lose several of their number as they undertake the demanding journey. First of all, members of the older generation, **Granma** and **Granpa Joad**, are casualties of the harsh demands created by forsaking their family home. Similarly, the oldest son of the Joads, **Noah**, a misfit both physically and socially, leaves the family when they reach the Colorado River. Steinbeck shows there is no place for a life-saving ark in this narrative, even though the new Noah is drawn by the promise of water's renewal. Instead of helping to save others, this Noah sets out on his own, abandoning his family. The biblical allusions reinforce Steinbeck's point that a chosen people must often suffer and undergo hardships in order to learn and profit in the future from the mistakes they make in the present.

At the novel's beginning, **Tom** arrives home from prison just in time to accompany his family—his parents, **Ma and Pa**, his brothers, **Winfield** and **Al**, and his sisters, Rose of Sharon (**Rosasharn**) and **Ruthie**—on a trek that the family neither anticipates nor desires. Along with his grandparents, Noah, **Uncle John,** and Rosasharn's husband, **Connie Rivers**, the group comprises the symbolic number twelve. They are disciples of a new faith, who will be instructed by a former preacher named **Jim Casy**, whom Tom encountered when he returned to search for his parents after discovering their deserted homestead. Unlike their neighbor, **Muley Graves**, whose stubbornness causes him to stay on the land his father bled for, the Joads have given up the struggle against progress and machines, desperately believing that their fate will improve in the richness of California. Steinbeck's portrayal of machines as unfeeling and destructive elements rather than as indicators of human progress is a central emphasis of the early chapters. Even though there is little to reassure them, they invite Casy to join them in the journey, unaware that en route they will discover that a new way of living will be required of them. The family begins to rely on Casy, whose symbolic initials are J. C., to formulate a way to cope. Casy relates that he has weathered a temptation in the wilderness, similar to his namesake, Jesus, and has discovered a new philosophy that supersedes his previous religious convictions. Casy's belief in the brotherhood of all humans causes the family to make drastic adjustments in their actions in order to survive the hostile environment that encompasses them. One indication of this is their eventual acceptance of the **Wilsons**, **Ivy** and **Sairy**, a couple they meet along Route 66. Motivated by the couple's willingness to share their tent and mattress to accommodate Granpa Joad when he suffers a stroke, the Joads ignore their differences. Later they decide to travel together and to share Al's and Tom's mechanical expertise when the Wilsons' car breaks down.

From the beginning of the text, it becomes evident that Steinbeck is in no hurry to move along the primary narrative; instead, he deliberately employs the intercalary, or general, chapters to set the fictional Joads within the larger social context. Using techniques similar to those used by **John Dos Passos** in his earlier trilogy, *U.S.A.* (1919–1923), Steinbeck broadens the scope of the novel and gives it the characteristic of social realism on a larger scale. As a result, some early critics labeled the work as a socialistic or communistic tract, considering it more propaganda than artistic accomplishment. Citing the fact that *The Grapes of Wrath* included scathing criticisms of banks, agricultural monopolies, the political practices of former president Herbert Hoover, and the federal prison system, such critics saw Steinbeck as an advocate of radical reform and even as a supporter of the revolutionary overthrow of democracy. The novel was politicized even further by its literary allusions to Homer's *The Odyssey*, wherein the title character's many stops are met with a lack of hospitality and brotherhood. Rather than offer aid and sustenance, most of Homer's characters seem bent instead on the destruction of the hero, Odysseus. However, unlike the pattern used in the epic poem, Steinbeck chooses to allow the Joads to confront a variety of human intentions along their journey. Not all are inhospitable. For example, the Wilsons, the gas station attendant, the man at the junk yard, the "bull simple" mayor of the Hooverville, **Floyd Knowles**, and the **Wainwright** family all offer positive examples of individuals working together for a common cause. On the other hand, the policemen, the strike busters, and some members of the Joad family themselves (e.g., Uncle John, Ruthie, and Rosasharn) demonstrate the dilemma caused by selfishness, greed, and a lack of hospitality.

Like Odysseus, the Joads discover the consequences of greed and violence as well as the value of sharing. Since the true scope of the human family includes all things living, Steinbeck illustrates his advocacy of caring for others in the novel by such episodes as Ma Joad sharing the meager stew with the children in the Hooverville, Casy's willingness to be imprisoned for Tom's act of violence, the shared breakfast Tom experiences outside the Weedpatch camp, and the cooperation of the Wainwrights and the Joads in the flood that concludes the novel. In episodes such as these, the Joads, Ma, and Tom in particular, realize that it is only through a sense of unity with all living things that humanity can advance.

Another element of the novel that stresses the wide sense of community Steinbeck wished to support was the author's use of animal imagery throughout *Grapes*. Employing land turtles, bees, cats, dogs, gila monsters, snakes, and chickens as symbols representing human traits and actions, Steinbeck suggests that all individuals need to realize that a universal connection between all species of life is necessary before an ecological balance can occur, resulting in a world, specifically an America, where equality and peace can flourish. As the Joads discover the importance of a larger family, one that springs from more than a nuclear or genetic root, Steinbeck advocates a moral imperative that emphasizes *we* rather than *I*, that conserves natural resources, and that promotes brotherhood rather than the destruction of the land through selfishness and greed.

Ultimately, the Joads' trek expands their horizons in several ways. The discoveries made by Ma, Tom, and Rosasharn in particular offer evidence of growth and understanding of a larger social picture and a recognition of the importance of a unified sense of responsibility for all things. As Ma expresses her faith in the people who go on, as Rosasharn offers her breast to the dying man in the bar, and as Tom recognizes that his life's purpose is to assume Casy's mantle as an advocate for the poor and disadvantaged, the novel draws to a close. Although its ending is deliberately inconclusive, reflecting Steinbeck's unwillingness to tie up loose ends neatly or to solve the insoluble, both **Elizabeth Otis** and Steinbeck's editors at Viking urged the writer to redraft his depiction of the mystic scene that closes the novel. Not only were they disturbed by the erotic image of Rosasharn breast-feeding a total stranger, but they were also concerned that other central figures in the novel, including Jim Casy (who disappears for almost one hundred pages in the center of the book) and Tom, were no longer in focus when the novel ended. Yet Steinbeck resisted these calls for change, opting for a cyclical return to water (this time in overabundance as a flood) in direct contrast to the opening depiction of drought and dust. Just as the death of Rosasharn's stillborn baby is used by Uncle John to awaken Californians to the desperate plight of the migrants (he sends the shriveled body that had suffered from malnutrition in the womb down the swollen river as a tragic new Moses), so Steinbeck leaves his readers of *Grapes* with no easy solutions and a family whose fate is in doubt, despite their apparent strength and desire to conquer the odds. Since some of the Joads (particularly Al, Uncle John, and Ruthie) still seem to hold self-indulgence and a predisposition to greed in high regard, the reader cannot assume that the harsh lessons of the exodus have been learned, or that right will defeat might. Instead, like life itself, the book closes with an indefinite and uneasy vignette, and the reader, unsettled and unsure of its meaning, must contemplate the author's intent and realize its ambiguous nature.

Recent works of criticism have presented a thorough overview of the varied initial reactions to the novel and the controversy over it (see *Steinbeck: The Contemporary Reviews*. Ed. Crisler, Shillinglaw, and McElrath. Cambridge: University of Cambridge Press, 1995; *The Critical Response to John Steinbeck's "The Grapes of Wrath."* Ed. Barbara Heavilin. Westport, CT: Greenwood Press, 2000; and *The Viking Critical Edition of "The Grapes of Wrath."* Ed. Peter Lisca and Kevin Hearle. New York: Viking, 1997). Assertive and often confrontational in their insistence on their viewpoints, reviewers such as Charles Poore of the *New York Times* offered positive comments like this statement on the characters: "You can't help believing in these people, in their courage and their integrity" (*Contemporary Reviews*, 154). Clifton Fadiman of the *New Yorker* found the book so effective he believed it could impact the country's future: "What sticks with me is that here is a book, nonpolitical, non-dogmatic, which dramatizes so that you can't forget it the terrible facts of a wholesale injustice committed by society" (*Contemporary Reviews*, 154). Early negative reviewers, however, based their responses primarily on Steinbeck's unusual organization or on their sense that the novel was ill-disguised propaganda. Arthur D. Spearman, writing in the *San Francisco Examiner*, notes this of the novel's point of view: "The arguments are selected from the customary communistic sources and strategy; a highlighted appeal for the behaviouristic philosophy of sex-indulgence; an animated cartoon of the useless, discouraging influence of religion upon human welfare, a tincture saturating the whole book. . . . Consistency is not, and any informed thinker knows that it can not be, a quality either of Communistic mind or of Communistic propaganda" (*Contemporary Reviews*, 171). The expansion of textual analysis in philosophical, psychological, and political arenas, however, led to recognition of the novel's complexity and to many claims that asserted its high status in the literary scene. These studies seemed to make it clear that *Grapes* was far more than a story of emotional bathos designed to promote a specific political or social agenda. Instead critics discovered what some called an intentional balance, since Steinbeck employed equal parts of characters, structure, and language in order to transcend the potential flaws the story line included.

Although Steinbeck's reputation as a writer slipped among the reviewers of his time, *The Grapes of Wrath* has been continually reassessed. Despite passionate defenses from a number of Steinbeck advocates, leaders in the literary establishment, led by Harold Bloom, continued the negative attacks of the book in more recent assessments; one notable example occurred when Leslie Fiedler appeared before a gathering of Steinbeck scholars celebrating the fiftieth anniversary of the novel's publication, arguing that the book and author were hopelessly sentimental, exhibiting befuddled philosophy and ambiguous politics.

Arguing that such lack of respect was unwarranted, later defenders of the work's artistic greatness refused to be silent. John H. Timmerman, for example, argued that the novel "is a treasure trove, ceaselessly yielding up new treasures under the probing hands of historians, theologians, and critics of every caste, method and meaning" and **Louis Owens** commented that it is "a superbly crafted work of fiction, a novel that takes impressive risks and succeeds." The status of *The Grapes of Wrath* has been heightened by the variety of approaches critics have employed in discussing the novel's place in the literary canon. Whether speculating about the author's naturalism or romanticism, employing cultural or religious mythology to plumb its meaning, using feminist or Marxist approaches to the text, or contemplating the scientific concepts Steinbeck dramatized in the book, the end result seems to be a furthering of *Grapes'* meaning and significance. The breadth of the literary allusions and parallels alone (Homer, **Shakespeare**, **Milton**, Hawthorne, **Melville**, **Thoreau**, **Emerson**, **D. H. Lawrence**, and **T. S. Eliot** to name a few) suggest that *The Grapes of Wrath* needs to be considered a classic American novel. As criticism continues to grow, new analyses will no doubt address postmodernist concerns with discourse analysis and the rhetorical strategies employed by the author, as well as pursue psychoanalytical studies of the novel's characters. In such an environment of discovery, claims of the novel's flaws will hardly stand up to scrutiny. (*See also* **Joads, The; *Grapes of Wrath, The* (film); *Grapes of Wrath, The* (Steppenwolf stage and television version).**)

Further Reading: Ditsky, John. *Critical Essays on "The Grapes of Wrath."* Boston: G. K. Hall, 1989; Donohue, Agnes McNeill. *A Casebook on "The Grapes of Wrath."* New York: Crowell, 1968; Fontenrose, Joseph. *John Steinbeck: An Introduction and Interpretation.* New York: Barnes and Noble, 1963; French, Warren. *John Steinbeck.* New York: Twayne, 1961; French, Warren. *"The Grapes of Wrath."* In *A Study Guide to Steinbeck: A Handbook to His Major Works.* Ed. Tetsumaro Hayashi. Metuchen, NJ: Scarecrow Press, 1974; Gladstein, Mimi Reisel. *"The Grapes of Wrath:* Steinbeck and The Eternal Immigrant." In *John Steinbeck: The Years of Greatness. 1936–1939.* Ed. Tetsumaro Hayashi. Tuscaloosa: University of Alabama Press, 1994, 132–144; Heavilin, Barbara, ed. *The Critical Response to John Steinbeck's "The Grapes of Wrath."* Westport, CT: Greenwood Press, 2000; Levant, Howard. *The Novels of John Steinbeck: A Critical Study.* Columbia: University of Missouri Press, 1974; Lisca, Peter. *The Wide World of John Steinbeck.* New Brunswick, NJ: Rutgers University Press, 1958; Lisca, Peter, with Kevin Hearle. *The Viking Critical Edition of "The Grapes of Wrath."* New York: Viking, 1997; Moore, Harry Thornton. *The Novels of John Steinbeck: A First Study.* Chicago: Normandie House, 1939; Owens, Louis. *"The Grapes of Wrath:* Eden Exposed." In *John Steinbeck's Re-Vision of America.* Athens: University of Georgia Press, 1985, 128–139; ———. *"The Grapes of Wrath": Trouble in the Promised Land.* New York: Twayne, 1989. ———. "Steinbeck's *The*

Grapes of Wrath (1939)." In *A New Study Guide to Steinbeck's Major Works, with Critical Explications.* Ed. Tetsumaro Hayashi. Metuchen, NJ: Scarecrow Press, 1993; Railsback, Brian. *Parallel Expeditions: Charles Darwin and the Art of John Steinbeck.* Moscow: University of Idaho Press, 1995; Timmerman, John H. *John Steinbeck's Fiction: The Aesthetics of the Road Taken.* Norman: University of Oklahoma Press, 1986.

Michael J. Meyer and Brian Railsback

GRAPES OF WRATH, THE* (FILM)** (1940). In 1940, a year after ***The Grapes of Wrath was published and in the year it won the **Pulitzer Prize, Darryl F. Zanuck** produced a movie version for Twentieth Century Fox that has been honored as a classic, often ranked among the ten best American films. Considering the controversy over the book, which militant conservatives denounced as obscene and subversive and which was burned in several communities, it is impressive that the film was made at all, let alone with reasonable fidelity to the novel. Enemies on the right denounced the project as un-American and threatened to boycott it, while liberals feared that Zanuck would either shelve it or sentimentalize it. But Zanuck wanted Steinbeck to be involved and told the suspicious novelist that the production would stay true to the novel, except for the scene where **Rosasharn** suckles the starving old man (this scene would never pass the Hays Office—the film regulation body responsible for the production code put into effect in the early 1930s by the Motion Pictures Producers and Distributors Association of America).

Screenwriter **Nunnally Johnson** used much of Steinbeck's own language but somewhat softened the novel's rage against the inhumane treatment of migrant farm workers. Johnson moved the concentration camp episode of the Hooper ranch and the murder of **Casy** so that they take place before the government camp, where the film ends, thus giving the film a more upbeat conclusion, as the **Joads** and other families leave the camp with renewed confidence in their ability to find jobs. Missing are the floods, the starvation, and the wretchedness with which the book ends. Instead, Zanuck himself took two lines from the end of chapter 20 and elaborated on them so that **Ma Joad** proclaims, in the film's last speech, "We're the people that live. Can't nobody wipe us out. Can't nobody lick us. We'll go on forever, **Pa**. We're the people." Thus, the film implies that the migrants will triumph without any action against their oppressors, who are generalized, leaving only irregular hired guards, unidentified vigilantes, and the Hooper ranch management as the enemy.

Nevertheless, the film retains much of Steinbeck's wrath against cruelty, greed, and exploitation, so much so that Zanuck maintained unprecedented security, refusing to let reporters see the script and using the counterfeit title *Highway 66* to hide the production. Despite attacks by zealous conservatives, who denounced what was perceived as Steinbeck's exaggeration and propaganda, much of the critical response was superlative, praising the film's integrity and stark realism. Under **John Ford**'s direction, photographer Gregg Toland captured the gritty look of the Depression in photographs by **Dorothea Lange**, Walker Evans, **Horace Bristol**, and others. The superlative cast looked like a genuine family suffering hard times. Only **Henry Fonda**, who played **Tom Joad**, was a star, but he was then noted for subtly underplaying proletariat characters, and he immersed himself in the interaction of the ensemble players. John Ford won the Academy Award for best director, and **Jane Darwell** won the award for best supporting actress. Fonda was nominated for best actor but was beaten by James Stewart's far less memorable performance in the sophisticated comedy *The Philadelphia Story*, while the film itself lost as best picture to Alfred Hitchcock's romantic thriller, *Rebecca*. (*See also* **Joads, The; *Grapes of Wrath, The* (novel); *Grapes of Wrath, The* (Steppenwolf stage and television version).**)

Further Reading: Bluestone, George. *Novels into Film.* Baltimore: Johns Hopkins Press, 1957; French, Warren. *Filmguide to "The Grapes* *of Wrath."* Bloomington: Indiana University Press, 1973; Gassner, John, and Dudley Nichols, eds. *Twenty Best Film Plays.* New York: Crown, 1943 (contains the screenplay of *The Grapes of Wrath*); Morsberger, Robert. "Steinbeck on Screen." In *A Study Guide to Steinbeck: A Handbook to His Major Works.* Ed. Tetsumaro Hayashi. Metuchen, NJ: Scarecrow Press, 1974.

Robert E. Morsberger

***GRAPES OF WRATH, THE* (STEPPENWOLF STAGE AND TELEVISION VERSION).** With its epic scope and episodic structure, *The Grapes of Wrath* would not at first seem suitable for adaptation to the stage. And indeed, a sprawling stage version by **William Adams**, who also directed it in a production by Paul Gregory, played at only a few colleges in 1978, and then went nowhere. It was notable mainly for having **John Carradine** repeat his film role as **Jim Casy**.

A far more successful stage adaptation appeared when **Frank Galati** wrote and directed his version for Chicago's Steppenwolf Theatre Company. This version opened in September 1988 at the Royal George Theatre in Chicago, was restaged the following May at the **La Jolla** Playhouse, and opened in June for an extended run in London. On March 22, 1990, it started a highly acclaimed run at the Cort Theater in New York, where it won the Tony Award as best play of 1990. Galati also won the Tony as best director, and several cast members (**Gary Sinise** as **Tom Joad**, Lois Smith as **Ma**, and Terry Kinney as Casy) were nominated. Galati condensed the 619 pages and thirty chapters of the novel into ten scenes and ninety pages of acting script, published in 1991 by the Dramatists Play Service. In doing so, he used Steinbeck's dialogue almost entirely verbatim, stating that only five or six lines in the play are not from the novel. Unlike Adams, who lifted large blocks of language unedited, Galati skillfully cut not only episodes but lines of dialogue within scenes, reducing each scene to its essence, tightening and speeding the narrative. For Steinbeck's interchapters, which Adams had chanted in clumsy choral reading, Galati provided musical transitions by Michael Smith, who played the Man with a Guitar; other transitions were accompanied by musical saw, jaw harp, fiddle, banjo, harmonica, accordion, and bass. Although **Nunnally Johnson**'s screenplay also retained much of Steinbeck's language, the Steppenwolf production is far more faithful to Steinbeck's narrative, especially at the end, which retains the flood, starvation, and the conclusion of Rosasharn's offering her breast to feed a starving old man, who in this case is black.

Galati's production was also far more realistic than that of Adams, which used a bare stage with several platforms that functioned as a truck and various buildings. The Steppenwolf staging included an actual truck that could move ahead, back up, and turn; three fire boxes for campfires; a tank of water that functioned variously as the Colorado River and the final flood, and a downpour of rain on an immense barn gate. Galati said that he had to retain the story's vital elements of earth, air, fire, and water.

The Steppenwolf production was reprised for television on PBS's *American Playhouse* in March 1991. It was introduced by **Elaine Scott Steinbeck**, on the stage of the Cort Theater, who explained why her husband would have loved it. Because of the filming, this time it was directed by **Kirk Browning**, who took full advantage of camera angles, medium shots, and close-ups to minimize the sense that it was a filmed stage production and to create a greater sense of realism. Unlike the 1940 movie, with its newsreel-looking black and white photography, this version was in color, so Browning had to recapture the look of the Depression through the performances, and he succeeded to a remarkable degree. Presented during a severe recession, with hordes of homeless and hungry people in the United States, the Steppenwolf production showed that Steinbeck's drama is by no means dated; its rage is as alive as ever, as many reviews at the time indicated. (*See also* **Joads, The; *Grapes of Wrath, The* (book); *Grapes of Wrath, The* [film]**.)

Further Reading: Morsberger, Robert. "Steinbeck and Steppenwolf: The Enduring Rage for Justice." *Steinbeck Newsletter* 7 (Winter 1994): 6–11.

Robert E. Morsberger

GRASTIAN, SIR. In ***The Acts of King Arthur***, the knight who guards and protects the kingdoms of **Ban** and **Bors** while they are in England helping **King Arthur** in his war against the eleven rebel lords of the North.

GRAUBARD, MARK (1904–). Steinbeck may have read Graubard's *Man the Slave and Master: A Biological Approach to the Potentialities of Modern Society* (1938) around the time he was writing ***The Grapes of Wrath***; **Robert DeMott** notes that a copy of the book bears his and **Carol Henning Steinbeck**'s stamp. Graubard's aim with this book, as he states, is "to present a picture of man's place in the biologic world from the viewpoint of the species as a whole," and thus squares with Steinbeck's philosophical and artistic goals in *Grapes*. The book culminates in "A Call for Scientific Humanism," reflecting Graubard's (and largely Steinbeck's) desire to see the true place of the human species by breaking through anthropocentric preconceptions and by adopting a scientifically objective perspective. Like Steinbeck, Graubard understood **Darwin**'s prominence in this holistic understanding.

Further Reading: Railsback, Brian. *Parallel Expeditions: Charles Darwin and the Art of John Steinbeck*. Moscow: University of Idaho Press, 1995.

GRAVES, GLEN (1902–1983). One of Steinbeck's earliest neighborhood friends. Steinbeck spent most of his youth in **Salinas** with Graves and his other close friend, **Max Wagner**. When Steinbeck left Salinas to attend **Stanford University**, Graves and Steinbeck stayed in contact, with Steinbeck often coming home during school hiatuses to play cards and hike with his childhood friend.

Ted Scholz

GRAVES, MISS. A resident of **Pacific Grove** who sings the lead in the annual Butterfly Pageant in ***Sweet Thursday***. She is a young, fourth-grade teacher, described as nice, rather pretty, and rather tired. Apparently a woman of some imagination, she sees a leprechaun in back of the reservoir on Sweet Thursday. However, two days before the Great Butterfly Festival is scheduled to begin, she loses her voice. Sprays and injections prove ineffectual in restoring her voice, reduced to a dry squawk and a croak. On the second Sweet Thursday, her voice finally comes back all by itself, as do the tardy millions of monarch butterflies.

Bruce Ouderkirk

GRAVES, MULEY. A neighbor of the **Joads** in ***The Grapes of Wrath***, Muley meets **Tom Joad** and **Jim Casy** at the former **Joad** residence and relates the tale of how families are being tractored out and why the homestead is deserted. As his name suggests, Muley is stubborn, especially about being evicted from his land. He describes himself as a ghost, haunting the drought-stricken land, in hopes of finding renewal or at least of preventing his property from falling into the hands of strangers. Like **Granpa**, Muley cannot imagine being separated from the land, which he identifies with such important events as birth and death in his personal history. Muley tells Casy and Tom of his determination to stay despite the nightly threats he receives from the landowners. When he offers Tom and Casy a meal of cooked jackrabbit, Muley not only provides the first witness to the necessity of sharing, but he also gives Tom an opportunity to relate the full details of the crime that caused him to be confined in prison. Determined to retain his heritage and refusing the opportunity of a new life, Muley retreats to his cave hideaway after the Joads' departure, preferring to hold out for as long as possible rather than transfer his life elsewhere.

Michael J. Meyer

GRAY, MARLENE. Gray was a young college graduate whom John and **Elaine Scott**

Steinbeck met in 1952 and who served as a personal secretary to the author during his stay in Paris in 1954. As typist for the articles Steinbeck was commissioned to write for *Le Figaro*, Gray was responsible not only for transcription of the dictated text but also was charged with its translation into French, a task that was not so easily accomplished. When a faulty translation was withdrawn by Gray as an inadequate representation of Steinbeck's thoughts, an editor for *Le Figaro* complained to the author about missed deadlines. Initially Steinbeck was exasperated by Gray's actions, which he felt damaged his reputation, but later he and Gray became close friends. Gray also helped critique Steinbeck's speech given over Radio Free Europe in the summer of 1954, assisting in his desire to deliver the address in the languages of the Soviet satellite countries: Hungarian, Rumanian, Polish, and Czech.

Further Reading: Benson, Jackson J. *The True Adventures of John Steinbeck, Writer.* New York: Viking, 1984.

Michael J. Meyer

"GREAT MOUNTAINS, THE" (1933). The second short story in ***The Red Pony*** cycle was first published in the *North American Review* in December 1933. **Gitano**, an old Hispanic man, returns to the ranch where his family formerly lived so that he might die where his father did. **Jody Tiflin**'s father, **Carl**, says that the old man may stay overnight but cannot remain on the ranch. During the night, after Gitano shows Jody the rapier that is his one remaining treasure, Gitano takes a once fine horse named Easter (an old animal Carl says must be shot) and wanders off with him into the **Gabilan** mountains.

GREAT TIDE POOL. In ***Cannery Row*** and ***Sweet Thursday***, an area on the tip of the peninsula of **Monterey** where **Doc** collects various marine species. The Great Tide Pool, rich in diversity, is a microcosm of nature, a place of life and death, of procreation and murder. Ordinarily, Doc takes great pleasure in witnessing the drama of this marine theater, just as he enjoys observing the teeming life around him on **Cannery Row**. Early in *Sweet Thursday*, when Doc begins to turn over a large rock in the tide pool and then, preoccupied, drops it back into place, it is a clear sign that something is seriously wrong with him, and at that point, he also wonders why a strange discontent has settled over him.

Bruce Ouderkirk

GREEN LADY, THE. Play authored by Steinbeck's friend **Webster "Toby" Street**. Steinbeck's later involvement with the material resulted in the novel ***To a God Unknown***, his third book to be published but begun before his second, ***The Pastures of Heaven***. The original play, like the Steinbeck novel, has a protagonist who experiences a very close connection with nature. Additionally, the material appealed to Steinbeck's impulses toward the grotesque and the mystical he observed in the natural world. According to **Jackson J. Benson**, the key factor in Steinbeck's adaptation of the material was the fact that he was able to create settings and characters with which he was familiar, often imbuing the latter with traits belonging to relatives and close friends. In addition, the play provided him with a chance to refine his prose and to restrain his somewhat lyrical poetical excesses of expression. Steinbeck tried to reshape Street's ideas until the summer of 1929, but he finally abandoned the rewrite and began his own version of the material. Taking his title from one of the Vedic hymns, he gradually eliminated the plot line of the original source and moved toward a psychological study that was entirely his own and that incorporated several of the fertility myths he had been discussing with **Joseph Campbell**.

Michael J. Meyer

GREGORY, SUSAN ("SUE"). A Spanish teacher at the high school in **Monterey**, she was a friend of Steinbeck's in 1933 while he was composing ***Tortilla Flat***. She knew the local paisanos who lived on the outskirts of town and provided Steinbeck numerous stories and information, therefore helping as an important resource as he put the book together. Steinbeck also saw Harriet Gragg, an older woman who also spoke Spanish. "Both Hattie and Sue were good storytellers, excellent sources for Steinbeck," **Jackson J. Benson** notes. Though both women helped Steinbeck, they were not his only sources about paisano life as he composed *Tortilla Flat*.

Further Reading: Benson, Jackson J. *The True Adventures of John Steinbeck, Writer.* New York: Viking, 1984.

GREW, JAMES. **Cathy Ames**'s high school Latin teacher in ***East of Eden***, who had failed divinity school. He and the fourteen-year-old Cathy become involved romantically and probably sexually as well. One night, James goes to the Ameses' house late, demanding to talk to **William Ames**, Cathy's father, who denies James entrance and forestalls the conversation. Later that night, probably out of guilt and desperation, James shoots himself in the head with a shotgun in front of the church altar. Afterward, and in the absence of any suicide note, Cathy tells her parents that James had been in trouble in Boston, a lie that spreads and is unquestioningly accepted as truth.

Margaret Seligman

GRIFFIN, MR. Owner of Griffin's Saloon in ***East of Eden***, where **Alf Nichelson** tells **Joe Valery** that **Faye**'s death might be suspicious and that **Kate Albey** is **Adam Trask**'s wife.

GRIPPO, BLACK. In ***Cup of Gold***, Black Grippo and **Henry Morgan** sail together on the ***Ganymede***. Henry had believed that taking a Spanish ship in battle would bring happiness. He is disappointed, however, because these victories do not bring even contentment.

GROSS, ARABELLA. In ***Tortilla Flat***, the fickle woman **Jesus Maria Corcoran** tries unsuccessfully to woo with lingerie. When we first meet Jesus Maria sleeping in a ditch, he explains how he found a rowboat the previous day and sold it to buy Arabella a bottle of whiskey and a pair of silk drawers, only to have her taken away from him by a group of soldiers. Jesus Maria vows this night to use his remaining money to buy Arabella a brassiere to match her drawers, but when he tries to give it to her, the soldiers return and beat him, with Arabella's help. He never gives up on the elusive Arabella, as evidenced by his opposition to his friends' plan to give the brassiere to **Danny** instead as a gift for **Mrs. Morales**. The failed courtship of Arabella may be read as one of the novel's many instances in which false values such as materialism disrupt the natural course of relationships.

GROSS, MR. A customer at the Golden Poppy restaurant in ***Sweet Thursday***. After **Suzy** learns about **Doc**'s broken arm, she is so distraught that she calls Mr. Gross "you" and nauseates him by serving his eggs straight up.

GRYFFET, SIR. In ***The Acts of King Arthur***, the young squire, later made a knight by **King Arthur**, who rides to challenge **King Pellinore** after the death of **Sir Miles**. He is wounded in the ensuing joust but made a Knight of the **Round Table** on King Pellinore's recommendation after the war with the **Five Kings**.

GUAJARDO, JESÚS COLONEL. In ***Viva Zapata!***, he is the direct cause of **Emiliano Zapata**'s death. He is not the mastermind of the plan to assassinate Emiliano—that was **Fernando Aguirre**'s idea—but he is the one who carries out the plan. In a courtyard, Guajardo presents Emiliano with his beloved horse, Blanco. Guajardo steps backward, steadily and silently pulling out his sword, which signals his men to send a fusillade of bullets into Emiliano's body. Jesús is the ironic name of Zapata's murderer.

GUINEVERE. In *The Acts of King Arthur,* the daughter of **King Lodegrance of Camylarde,** who gives her hand in marriage to **King Arthur**. Arthur has loved her from the time he first set eyes on her when he visited King Lodegrance's court some years before, and is determined to marry her despite **Merlin**'s warnings that she will be unfaithful to him with his dearest and most trusted friend. She becomes the lover of **Sir Lancelot**, thus fulfilling Merlin's prophecy.

GUINZBURG, HAROLD (1899–1961). President of the **Viking Press** during the principal part of Steinbeck's career. Key executives at Viking besides Guinzburg were **Pascal Covici,** Ben W. Huebsch (who had owned his own firm previously, as had Covici), and **Marshall Best**.

GUINZBURG, THOMAS (1926–). Succeeded his father, **Harold Guinzburg,** as president of the **Viking Press** and was president when Viking merged with the British firm Penguin Books in 1977. Thomas Guinzburg was instrumental in starting Steinbeck on the last book published in the author's lifetime, ***America and Americans***. In 1964, he gave Steinbeck a collection of photographs featuring life across America, with the idea that John would write captions and perhaps an introduction. Instead, Steinbeck wrote a collection of essays to go along with the photos.

GUNN'S NEW FAMILY PHYSICIAN; OR HOME BOOK OF HEALTH. Steinbeck's grandfather, **Samuel Hamilton**, had owned an 1865 edition of the book, and it was greatly admired by young John as he pored over it during his childhood in **Salinas**. **Robert DeMott** has established that the book had an early and lasting impact on Steinbeck. While writing ***East of Eden,*** Steinbeck "drew heavily on Gunn's book for various medical details, moral and ethical attitudes, and thematic configurations."

Further Reading: DeMott, Robert. *Steinbeck's Reading; A Catalogue of Books Owned and Borrowed.* New York: Garland, 1984; ———. "'A Great Black Book': *East of Eden* and Dr. Gunn's *Family Medicine." American Studies* 22 (1981): 41–57.

GUTHRIE, WOODY (1912–1967). A famous American folk singer and guitarist, Woody Guthrie was born in Okemah, Oklahoma, and became a popular representative of the folk music character emerging in the migrant communities throughout Oklahoma and California. In 1940, Guthrie recorded his *Dust Bowl Ballads,* which are in many ways a narrative of the Okie migration. Guthrie's recordings include an entire cast of characters, each of whom represents a facet of the traveling life. In particular, the album features the two-part "Ballad of **Tom Joad**." Although Joad represents only one in the list of characters contained in the recording, his inclusion in the folk wisdom and mythology of the album signifies his place in the substance of the migrant culture.

Brian Niro

GUZMAN, DON JUAN PEREZ. In ***Cup of Gold,*** he is the governor of Panama, one who devotes his life to being a gentleman and nothing else. Noted for his oratory and his wardrobe, he is no match for the invading pirate, **Henry Morgan**.

GWENLIANA. In *Cup of Gold,* Gwenliana is **Henry Morgan**'s grandmother on his father's side. She practices and takes pride in her gift of "second sight," but her family considers her prophecies to be mere guesses, although they listen to her with some respect.

H

HACENDADO. In *Viva Zapata!* the Spanish term means landowner. It is the *hacendado* who has taken away the lands on which the peasants have worked and which their village has owned. However, the peasants cannot verify their boundaries and are constantly forced off land that they have planted.

HALL, BECK, MACDOWELL, RANDOLPH, LUCE, WANTONER, STRAIT. These form a cross section of the populace of New Baytown encountered and considered by **Ethan Allen Hawley** in a crucial passage in ***The Winter of Our Discontent***. They all are undeveloped as characters, which may account for Steinbeck's naming one of them Luce, the surname of the unfriendly owner of ***Time magazine***.

HALLAM, MR. A Connecticut innkeeper in ***East of Eden*** who rents rooms to **Mr. Edwards**'s prostitutes. About every two weeks, **Charles Trask** goes to the inn to visit one of them and to get slightly drunk.

HALSING, DICK. In ***In Dubious Battle***, an attractive young radical who is used by Mac's party to win needed support and supplies from wealthy women susceptible to his charms.

HAMILTON, DELIA. Wife of **Will Hamilton** in ***East of Eden***. Steinbeck's aunt through marriage.

HAMILTON, DESSIE. Bubbly daughter of **Samuel** and **Liza Hamilton** in ***East of Eden*** and owner of a dressmaking shop in **Salinas** where women go to talk and relax. After a love affair ends tragically and her father dies, a despondent Dessie decides to sell her business and move back to the farm with her brother **Tom Hamilton**. When Dessie returns to the farm, the chronic and undiagnosed pains in her side increase in frequency and intensity. One night, Dessie finally confesses to Tom that she is ill, and he administers salts, thinking a cathartic will help. However, the salts aggravate her condition, and she dies. A week after Dessie's funeral, feeling responsible for her death and filled with despair, Tom shoots himself, completing the tragedy.

Margaret Seligman

HAMILTON, GEORGE. Eldest son of **Samuel** and **Liza Hamilton** in *East of Eden* and husband of **Mamie (Dempsey) Hamilton.** George is in the insurance business. He is gentle and sweet and deeply moved by the death of his sister, **Una Hamilton (Anderson)**, even many years later when he talks about it to his nephew, John Steinbeck.

HAMILTON, JOE. In *East of Eden*, youngest son of **Liza** and **Samuel Hamilton.** Joe is a daydreamer who feigns helplessness to avoid farm work. The family, believing he is unfit for anything else, sends him to college. He makes a fortune in advertising in the East.

HAMILTON, LIZA. Wife of **Samuel Hamilton** in *East of Eden*. She and Samuel migrate to the **Salinas** Valley from Northern Ireland around 1870. Liza is a tiny, strict woman who raises nine children. A devout Presbyterian, she dislikes all forms of tomfoolery, especially drinking alcohol, although later in life she becomes a teetotaler.

Liza is a strong woman who rarely shows her feelings. She is grounded in practical, factual reality and is a perfect foil for her husband. This is particularly apparent when, after the birth of **Cathy Trask**'s twins, Samuel sends **Lee** to get **Liza**, whose no-nonsense approach will ground Samuel's flights of fancy regarding the impending darkness about to descend on the Trask house. Once there, Liza takes charge, and though she is unable to see anything wrong with Cathy, she later confesses to Samuel that she doesn't like her very much.

On Thanksgiving of 1911, the Hamilton children decide that it is time for Samuel and Liza to leave the ranch and stay with their children. When the letter of invitation from **Olive Hamilton** (**Steinbeck**) arrives, Samuel convinces Liza to go. After Samuel dies, Liza continues to live with Olive and her family. At Liza's suggestion, **Adam Trask** buys **Dessie Hamilton**'s house in Salinas, where he intends to move so that his sons, **Cal** and **Aron Trask**, can attend school in town.

Margaret Seligman

HAMILTON, LIZZIE. One of the eldest daughters of **Samuel** and **Liza Hamilton** in *East of Eden*. She marries young and moves away. Unlike any of her family, she is bitter and full of hatred.

HAMILTON, MOLLIE. The beautiful, youngest daughter of **Samuel** and **Liza Hamilton** and wife of William J. Martin in *East of Eden*. After her marriage, Mollie lives a life of elegance and affluence in San Francisco.

HAMILTON (STEINBECK), OLIVE (IN EAST OF EDEN). Daughter of **Samuel** and **Liza Hamilton**, wife of **John Ernst Steinbeck**, and mother of John Steinbeck and **Mary Steinbeck Dekker** in *East of Eden*. Olive is a teacher at the Peach Tree School and successfully avoids myriad marriage proposals until she meets Ernst Steinbeck, to whom she becomes secretly engaged. They are married and eventually settle in **Salinas**. John describes his mother as loving, firm, intuitive, frugal, and courageous.

When, during World War I, their young neighbor, **Martin Hopps**, is killed, Olive essentially declares war on the Germans and sells so many Liberty bonds that she wins a ride in an army plane. John recounts with great fondness this anecdote that further characterizes his mother: After making a will, burning her personal papers, buying all new underwear, treating her children more gently, and giving Mary her engagement ring, Olive boards a plane and is strapped into the cockpit. The pilot performs fancy dives and loops, and Olive, thinking the plane is crashing, tries to encourage the pilot who mistakes her gestures and performs more aerial tricks. Once they land and Olive is finally wedged out of the cockpit, it takes her two days in bed to recover.

When they leave their ranch, Samuel and Liza live with Olive and her family, and after Samuel dies, Liza continues to reside with the Steinbecks until her death. (*See also* **Steinbeck, Olive Hamilton**.)

Margaret Seligman

HAMILTON, SAMUEL. In *East of Eden*, husband of **Liza Hamilton**, father of **George**, **Will**, **Tom**, **Joe**, **Una**, **Lizzie**, **Dessie**, **Olive**, and **Mollie Hamilton**, and grandfather of John Steinbeck and **Mary Steinbeck Dekker**. Steinbeck's fondness for his grandfather is revealed in his characterization of Samuel, whose warmth, wisdom, stature, and patriarchal bearing make him seem larger than life.

As outlined in *East of Eden*, Samuel and Liza migrate to the **Salinas** Valley from Northern Ireland around 1870 and settle on a particularly arid patch of land. Samuel is known and respected in the valley as a blacksmith, water witch, midwife, and comical genius. He and Liza are well regarded for being fine parents and raising fine children. Samuel and Liza create an effective balance. Whereas Samuel is a creative, probing thinker and dreamer, Liza is down to earth, practical, and pragmatic.

Samuel meets **Adam Trask** when Louis Lippo brings him to the Hamilton ranch to discuss the feasibility of finding water on the Bordoni place, which Adam is thinking of buying. Later, after he indeed buys Bordoni's ranch, Adam sends **Lee** to get Samuel so that they can discuss the specifics of digging wells. As they drive back, Samuel surprises Lee by seeing through his guise of speaking Pidgin and wearing a queue. In acknowledgment, Lee tells Samuel, "You are one of the rare people who can separate your observation from your preconception" (a major characteristic of Steinbeck's heroes).

Samuel's ability to see *what is* also allows him to understand that the beautiful and apparently sweet and contented **Cathy Trask** is not what she seems. The next autumn, as Samuel is drilling on Adam's land, Lee rides into his camp yelling in Pidgin English that Cathy has gone into labor and that Samuel must attend the birth. In Cathy's darkened bedroom, during her intense but unnaturally brief labor, Cathy seems more animal than human. When Samuel inquires how she got the scar on her forehead, she savagely bites his hand. Samuel then delivers one baby and, to his astonishment, a second. As a result of the vicious bite, Samuel is feverish and delirious for three days, as if Cathy had injected poison into his system.

Fifteen months later, Samuel runs into Lee in King City and learns that Adam is still in the trance-like state he's been in since Cathy shot him and left him and the twins. More distressingly, Samuel learns that the twins are yet unnamed. When he tells this to Liza, she shares his outrage and warns him that unless he does something about it, she will not let him back in the house. Samuel rides to the Trask ranch where he insults Adam, tries to strangle him, and finally knocks him down twice, shocking him out of his trance.

Lee brings a table and chairs, some whisky, and the boys. The men discuss the Bible as part of their concern about the effect of names on the boys' personalities. Adam, remembering his own brother's hatred, is concerned about not repeating the pattern of the past. The boys are then named, and Samuel rides home.

Change and sadness enter Samuel's life when his beloved daughter Una dies. Though her death is considered an accident, Samuel believes otherwise. He blames himself, and the sadness and loss age him. At Thanksgiving, the Hamilton children decide that he and Liza need to leave the ranch and stay with the children. Feeling resigned but content, Samuel agrees to the plan.

Before leaving, however, Samuel rides to the Trask ranch to say goodbye. Ten years have passed, and the twins are eleven. After dinner that night, Lee describes how he and four Chinese scholars studied the story of Cain and Abel. He speaks excitedly about the word ***timshel***, which means "thou mayest [rule over sin]." Lee explains, "That gives a choice. It might be the most important word in the world." Samuel, too, is excited by Lee's discovery.

In fact, as Samuel is leaving, he chooses to tell Adam the truth about Cathy, that she is now **Kate Albey** and runs a brothel in Monterey. Telling Adam is not only a choice that Samuel makes, but it also represents a gift of choice to Adam, for now Adam can choose to see his wife or to forget her. Rather than allow his delusional image of her purity to dominate his life and cause him depression, Adam can free himself and move on to a more positive future. Samuel and Lee say goodbye, and Samuel rides home.

While staying in Salinas with Olive and her family, Samuel dies. Adam attends his funeral and then decides to see Cathy/Kate. Surprisingly, he discovers that he is impervious to her attempts to manipulate, seduce, and humiliate him, and when he returns to his ranch, he is a different man—one who is alive to the present and to his children. Samuel's gift of choice to Adam is, therefore, a gift of freedom. It is comparable to Adam's blessing to Cal at the end of the novel, suggesting that *timshel* is the legacy of spiritual and real fathers to their sons, a reflection of God's gift of choice to Cain.

Margaret Seligman

HAMILTON, TOM. Third eldest son of **Samuel** and **Liza Hamilton** in *East of Eden*. Tom is more like his father than any of the other children. A man of passion and extremes, he is bold, inventive, concupiscent, shy, and violent. John Steinbeck and **Mary Steinbeck Dekker** regard him as their favorite uncle. After his parents move away, Tom remains on the ranch.

When Tom's sister **Dessie Hamilton** is disappointed in love, Tom rides to **Salinas** in a rage. Alerted by a telegram from Samuel, the sheriff waits for Tom, disarms him, and keeps him in a cell until Samuel arrives to take him home. After Samuel's death, Dessie returns to the ranch to live with Tom. One night, attempting to treat Dessie's stomach pains (heretofore kept secret), Tom administers Epsom salts, an old family remedy. Unfortunately, the salts exacerbate Dessie's condition, and she dies. Tom, bereft by the death of his father and in despair and feeling responsible for Dessie's death, shoots himself after writing one letter to his mother and another to his brother **Will Hamilton**, requesting that Will keep his suicide a secret.

Margaret Seligman

HAMILTON, WILL. Second eldest son of **Samuel** and **Liza Hamilton** and husband of **Delia Hamilton** in *East of Eden*. Will is conservative and hard-working and essentially a conformist. In contrast to his father, Will has luck financially; an entrepreneur, Will makes a small fortune in the automobile industry. He is well regarded in **Salinas**, where he lives with his wife.

When **Adam Trask** develops an interest in refrigeration, he invites Will over to discuss his plan to buy an ice plant and ship lettuce to the East in refrigerated railcars. Will attempts to discourage Adam, citing the serious risk, and urges him to plant beans instead. Disregarding Will's advice, Adam goes ahead with his plans, with disastrous financial results.

Shortly thereafter, **Cal Trask** visits Will in his office to ask him how to make a lot of money. When Will asks why, Cal tells him that he wants to recompense his father for the money lost in the lettuce venture and confesses that, as Will suggests, he is trying to buy his father's love. Will and Cal then drive to the Trask ranch, where Will asks Cal to be his partner; Will's intention is to have Rantini, the Trask tenant, plant beans that can then be sold to the British and American armies.

Though Will is always generous with money when his family needs it and loves his family dearly, he feels that they are ashamed of him and perhaps regard him as inadequate. These feelings allow Will to feel a kinship with Cal, for he can identify with Cal's passion to gain his father's love and approval, even if they must be bought. Again, the desire of the child to please and receive love from the father is a direct link to the Cain and Abel story that informs Steinbeck's novel.

Margaret Seligman

HAMILTON (ANDERSON), UNA. One of the eldest daughters of **Samuel** and **Liza Hamilton** in *East of Eden*. Una is a thoughtful, studious girl who shares with her father a love of learning and reading. She marries Anderson, a photographer, with whom she lives in squalor on the Oregon border while he attempts to discover color film. She dies, and Anderson ships her body back to her family.

Una's death devastates her family and particularly Samuel, who regards it not as an accident but as a suicide and feels responsible for it. He ages rapidly thereafter. Una's brother, **Joe Hamilton**, is still quite affected by her death, evident when he tells his nephew, John Steinbeck, about it some years later.

Margaret Seligman

HAMMARSKJÖLD, DAG (1905–1961). Swedish statesman and United Nations official. Initially, Hammarskjöld worked in the Swedish government on the economic advisory board and later as a member of the Organization for European Economic Cooperation. Hammarskjöld served as the United Nations secretary general for over eight years (1953–61). While traveling in Africa, Hammarskjöld was tragically killed in a plane crash. He was posthumously awarded the Nobel Peace Prize in 1961. Also, a book of Hammarskjöld's meditations on his religious and ethical philosophy was posthumously published in 1964.

During his time as the secretary general, Hammarskjöld greatly extended the influence of the United Nations. Likewise, Hammarskjöld's intimate approach to his duties increased the prestige of the position. By all accounts, Hammarskjöld was a personable statesman and directly led a tremendous variety of missions to lessen tension or arrange peace settlements. Under his surveillance, a UN emergency force was established. Indeed, Hammarskjöld was on a mission to the Congo when his plane went down over Rhodesia (now Zambia).

Steinbeck was often a tangential part of political machinations. His friendships with **Franklin Delano Roosevelt** and **Adlai Stevenson** placed him in close proximity to a number of significant politicians and statesmen. Steinbeck appears to have held a deep affection for Hammarskjöld, whom he met through his work with the United Nations. Steinbeck took a number of opportunities to meet and converse with the statesman, and he was greatly upset by news of his friend's death and sank into a brief malaise. In a letter to **Bo Beskow**, Steinbeck listed a visit to Hammarskjöld's grave (with a small gesture of lavender) as one of the most significant points of his visit to Stockholm. For Steinbeck, Hammarskjöld embodied the spirit of patient and diligent resilience working toward a global aim of cooperation and peace.

Brian Niro

HAMMERSTEIN II, OSCAR. *See* **Richard Rodgers.**

HANSEN SEA COW. During John Steinbeck's 1940 trip to the Sea of Cortez, the Sea Cow was the undependable outboard motor attached to the small craft used by the crew of the ***Western Flyer*** to reach shore or to collect specimens in shallow water. In the narrative, the motor is more than a machine; it is a malevolent force. Steinbeck makes a scientific experiment of observing the Sea Cow and its reactions to work, to weather, and to the ministrations of **Tex Travis**, the engineer aboard the *Western Flyer* whom the Sea Cow "hated." The Sea Cow is mentioned so often in the narrative that **Jackson J. Benson** notes that it almost becomes "the leading character" of the work.

Charles Etheridge, Jr.

HARDWICKE, SIR CEDRIC (1893–1964). Cerebral British actor whose performance as Colonel Lanser in the film version of ***The Moon Is Down*** was widely praised.

HARDY, THOMAS (1840–1928). Victorian English novelist, poet, and dramatist. His novels, which primarily depict man's struggle with an indifferent universe, include *Far From the Madding Crowd* (1874), *The Return of the Native* (1878), *The Mayor of Casterbridge* (1886), *Tess of the D'Urbervilles* (1891), and *Jude the Obscure* (1896). Steinbeck read and admired Hardy, even though he felt Hardy's fiction frequently drew upon "divine coincidences" that were often "absurd." Nevertheless, he lauded Hardy for his humility when it came to his artistic prowess, particularly admiring the fact that his "greatness bored him." Steinbeck's library contained copies of *Jude the Obscure*, *The Return of the Native*, and *Tess of the D'Urbervilles*.

T. Adrian Lewis

HARGRAVE, JOHN GORDON (1894–1982). British artist, illustrator, cartoonist, copywriter, Boy Scout Commissioner, lexicographer, inventor, author, and psychic healer best remembered as "White Fox," the dynamic leader of the Kibbo Kift, a movement every bit as extraordinary as its founder: a non-political "camping handicraft and world peace movement" that was launched in 1920. Steinbeck greatly admired Hargrave's 1935 novel, *Summer Time Ends* (he noted that he had read the book three times), and wrote Hargrave to tell him so. Some of Steinbeck's comments were published on the cover of a later issue of Hargrave's book.

"HARNESS, THE" (1938). Placed between **"The Raid"** and **"The Vigilante"** in the collection, ***The Long Valley,*** "The Harness" is a curious story that Steinbeck originally titled "The Fool" before publishing it in *The Atlantic Monthly* in 1938. The title of the published story focuses attention on the concept of restraint as well as on **Peter** and **Emma Randall**, the protagonist and his wife. Peter, a sober and successful farmer and Mason, has earned respect as the proverbial pillar of **Monterey** County. The community views his bearing, his authority, and even his posture (ironically, as it turns out) as attributes for others to emulate. Emma, on the other hand, the daughter of a prominent Mason, is a sickly woman who looks far older than her forty-five years. Not until her death do we learn that, according to Peter, she has been responsible for his standing in the community, and her will—along with the harness that she made him wear—kept Peter's slovenly tendencies in check.

During their twenty-one–year marriage, Peter behaves in exemplary fashion but takes one weeklong business trip each year. On his return, Emma invariably falls ill for a month or two, and Peter, clad in an apron, does the housework until she recovers. Their property boasts rich soil and an immaculate farmhouse with a neat fenced yard and garden. On the surface, at least, their lives sound Edenic, a perfect illustration of the American Dream. Suggesting one of the Fates who spun the thread of life, Emma knits constantly. Not until after her death, however, do we learn the extent to which she wove together the fabric of their life and Peter's standing in the community. When Emma dies, Peter appears half-mad from grief, sobbing hysterically. Because the doctor fears for his safety, he enlists Ed Chappell, a neighbor, to spend the night with him after the funeral. When Peter awakens from the morphine the doctor had given him, he strips off a web harness and a wide elastic belt that he says Emma had insisted that he wear. Pouring whiskey for himself and Ed, he tells his version of the story, explaining that Emma made him a good man for fifty-one weeks each year and allowed him to go away for one week a year so that he could keep from going berserk. During these furloughs, he would go to San Francisco, get drunk, and visit a "fancy house" each night. On his return he would do penance, repairing household items and doing housework for Emma during her invariable illnesses. Now, however, Peter says he intends to keep brandy on the shelf, to refuse to wind the clock, and to allow his shoulders to sag and his stomach to protrude. The rest of the story reads almost like a fable or fairy tale. Peter successfully grows forty acres of sweetly scented and colorful sweet peas, engendering both envy and awe in his less imaginative peers and even attracting the attention of children in school buses. Yet when Ed, unexpectedly in San Francisco, sees Peter returning from an evening of drunken revelry, Peter has clearly reverted to his annual binging, and Peter confesses to the kindly if unimaginative Ed that Emma still lives in him. Like a sort of super-ego, she never lets him enjoy his success, he says, instead making him worry about all the ways he has opened himself to risk and failure. And so Peter continues to live his life as if Emma were still alive, carousing for one week of the year, but afterward, as he confides to Ed at the end of the story, he plans to install lights in the farmhouse because Emma always wanted them.

Although most critics see Emma as a metaphor for restraint and responsibility, without which Peter's drunkenness and lust would run wild, it is worthy of note that the metaphor of the harness is itself a metaphor for a woman and a wife, one who impedes creativity, happiness, and self-fulfillment. The restraint and respectability that Emma represents has been viewed, on the one hand, as a victory for the community and the female, or, on the other, as an unfortunate shackle that impedes the natural happiness of the male and the artist. Commenting on the large "number of husbands and wives in *The Long Valley* who live at each other's throats," **Jay Parini**, along with **Jackson J. Benson**, sees a similarity to Steinbeck and his wife Carol (who had legendary fights before they divorced).

The fact that the story was first titled "The Fool" suggests Steinbeck's bleak state of mind vis-á-vis male-female relationships at that time. Notably in this story, published a year after "The Chrysanthemums," the male rather than the female is the gardener, a likely metaphor for the artist, and even though Steinbeck kills off the wife who reigns in the artistic protagonist, Peter Randall cannot escape the restrictive effect of her feminine influence. Ironically, regardless of Steinbeck's anxieties about the restraining natures of civilizing forces such as spouses or society, he wrote many of *The Long Valley* stories during his mother's illness, shortly before her death. Despite his commitment to such sickroom responsibilities as changing sheets and emptying bedpans, the period in which Steinbeck wrote "The Harness," among other Long Valley stories, has been recognized as one of his most richly productive.

Further Reading: Fontenrose, Joseph. "'The Harness.'" In *A Study Guide to Steinbeck's* The Long Valley. Ed. Tetsumaro Hayashi and Reloy Garcia. Ann Arbor, MI: Pierian, 1976. 47–52; Hughes, Jr., Robert S. *John Steinbeck: A Study of The Short Fiction.* New York: Twayne, 1989; Owens, Louis. "'Bottom and Upland': The Balanced Man in Steinbeck's 'The Harness.'" In *Steinbeck's Short Stories in* The Long Valley: *Essays in Criticism.* Ed. Tetsumaro Hayashi. Muncie, IN: Steinbeck Research Institute, Ball State University, 1991. 44–48; Steinbeck, John. "The Harness." *The Long Valley.* New York: Viking, 1939. 111–129.

Abby H. P. Werlock

HARRIS, THE RADIO ENGINEER. In ***Bombs Away***, a high school graduate and short-wave radio hobbyist interested in physics and chemistry. Unsatisfied with working in a large chain grocery, Harris joins the Air Force to get into military radio.

HARTE, BRET (1836–1902). Born in Albany, New York, Harte moved to California in 1854 and became a successful editor and famous writer. His gritty and romantic stories concerned the closing of the last frontier and the rough life in California mining camps. Steinbeck likely read Harte's *The Luck of Roaring Camp* (1906) and *On the Frontier* (1893). Critics Paul McCarthy and **Peter Lisca** have noted some echoes of Harte in Steinbeck's writing, and **Robert DeMott** suggests the two authors share an oscillation between the realistic and the romantic as well as some similarities in their treatment of women characters.

Further Reading: DeMott, Robert. *Steinbeck's Reading; A Catalogue of Books Owned and Borrowed*. New York: Garland, 1984.

HARTNELL, ALEX. Resident of Loma who forms a friendship with the narrator in **"Johnny Bear."** Alex provides the narrator (and the reader) with essential information about the town history and the backgrounds of many of its inhabitants. He also personifies the conscience of the town and its shame when, after Johnny Bear reveals their most painful secrets, the aristocratic Hawkins sisters tumble from their pedestal.

HARTOG, MR. A hearty dinner companion of the Hawleys (***The Winter of Our Discontent***) and **Margie Young-Hunt**, his presence is used largely as a foil for Margie's interest in Ethan.

"HARVEST GYPSIES, THE" (1938). This is the title of a series of seven articles Steinbeck wrote in 1938 for the *San Francisco News* on the plight of Dust Bowl migrants arriving in the region. Researching these articles brought the migrants' struggle to exist and the injustices they suffered to Steinbeck's attention not long before he wrote ***The Grapes of Wrath***. The articles were first published as a collection in the 1938 pamphlet *Their Blood Is Strong* with Steinbeck's newly written epilogue "Starvation Under the Orange Trees" and with select photographs by **Dorothea Lange**. They were last published, under the series' original title *The Harvest Gypsies* and without the epilogue, in 1988 by Heyday Books, a publisher specializing in California history and literature. Charles Wollenberg provides an introduction to this edition that places the articles in the context of Steinbeck's career and the history of that era.

The first article describes the need for migrant labor in California and outlines the history of the different non-European, and often foreign, peoples who fulfilled that need. In contrast, Steinbeck describes the latest migrants as Americans of European stock, unaccustomed to being ostracized and herded and more familiar with democracy.

The second article describes the conditions inside the migrant camps. The specific detail of this chapter often goes beyond Steinbeck's descriptions of squalor in *The Grapes of Wrath*. For example, Steinbeck records how the typical new migrants live: "The tent is full of flies clinging to the apple box that is the dinner table, buzzing about the foul clothes of the children, particularly the baby, who has not been bathed or cleaned for several days. . . There is no toilet here, but there is a clump of willows nearby where human feces lie exposed to the flies—the same flies that are in the tent." Steinbeck also describes the high mortality rate for infants and children in these camps, the routine interrogations by social workers, and the vigilantes who appear when there is labor trouble. The third article details the fearful and suspicious reaction of the large landowners to this new migration. The facilities in which the large farms house migrant labor—one-room buildings, ten by twelve feet—are patrolled by deputized company employees. Steinbeck's references to centralized authority and company guns would no doubt have tapped into his contemporary audience's fear of that decade's rising fascism.

As an alternative means of providing for these new migrants, Steinbeck explores the federal government's creation of sanitary camps in the fourth article. Much like the fictional Weedpatch camp in *The Grapes of Wrath*, the government camps at **Arvin** and Marysville are more sanitary than their "Hooverville" counterparts. Moreover, Steinbeck writes that the federal government's insistence that the workers help maintain these sanitary conditions and contribute to the general upkeep, combined with a system of self-government established among the migrants, restores the dignity and decency of the migrant laborers. However, Steinbeck reports, the local authorities resist these government camps, which, by design, will ultimately provide the migrants with a permanent home. These authorities argue that if the migrants settle there permanently, the local government will need more money for police and for schools, property values will decrease, and strikes will grow more likely. Despite the experimental government camps, Steinbeck details in the fifth article the still insufficient bureaucratic response to the migrants' plight. For example, because the migrants are only seasonally employed, the nature of their work and lifestyle prevents their fulfilling the residency requirements for relief, nor has the government yet made the procedures for relief application better known.

Steinbeck returns to the history of migrant farm labor in California in the sixth article, this time emphasizing the racism and injustice the migrants have faced. "The history of California's importation and treatment of foreign labor is a disgraceful picture of greed and cruelty," he writes. He relates the importation of Chinese labor to the railroads (who want to avoid paying higher wages to white laborers), and then he writes of the supplanting of Chinese by Japanese imported labor and the subsequent rise of literature about the "yellow peril." The third wave of immigrants from Mexico, he says, led local authorities to support racial quotas on immigration. And, with the arrival of Filipinos, California lawmakers once again had to amend the laws prohibiting interracial marriage to include these arrivals. Now, however, with the recent arrival of Dust Bowl refugees, Steinbeck suggests that California agriculture must readjust itself because "white American labor" will "refuse to accept the role of field peon, with its attendant terrorism, squalor and starvation."

Steinbeck proposes specific remedies for the migrants' difficulties in the seventh article. Federal land should be leased for subsistence farming, only employable men should migrate rather than whole families, more self-government should be encouraged, a migratory labor board should be established to publish just how much labor is needed and where, agricultural labor should be allowed to organize, and the state attorney general should investigate all vigilante crime.

Scott Simkins

HARVEY, GEORGE. In ***East of Eden*** a Connecticut lawyer who notifies **Adam Trask** that his brother, **Charles Trask**, has died and willed his money, a sum in excess of $100,000, to be divided equally between Adam and his wife, **Cathy Trask**, now **Kate Albey**.

When Horace Quinn tells Adam about Cathy/Kate's death and that she willed all her money to their son, **Aron Trask**, Adam addresses Quinn as "George," revealing his confusion and also that the moral dilemma regarding the money is the same to him as the one he experienced after Charles's death. At that time, Adam was reluctant to give Cathy/Kate her share of the inheritance because he knew that what she'd do with the money would be terrible. Now, Adam is faced with a similar but more complex problem. Adam does not know that Aron has seen his mother. Thus, Adam thinks that for Aron to receive the inheritance, he must be told that his mother had been alive and where the money came from, thereby sullying Aron's construction of a virtuous dream world and revealing Adam as a liar. As Lee observes ironically, Adam, an honest man, has been living on stolen money, and Aron, the seeker of purity, would be living on the money made in a brothel. These issues seem to follow the novel's attention to the consequences of inherited money, particularly when it is ill gotten.

Margaret Seligman

HAWKINS, AMY. Representing the town's moral as well as social aristocracy in **"Johnny Bear,"** Amy, along with her sister **Emalin Hawkins**, has inherited the mantle of standard-bearer for the entire village of Loma. Between forty and forty-five years of age, Amy is similar to **Peter Randall** in **"The Harness,"** in that she also suffers from a sexuality repressed by moral standards, public reputation, and a family member (in Amy's case, her sister). By entering into a clandestine affair with a Chinese worker, Amy risks tarnishing the respectability of the family name. Later, fueled by Emalin's shocked reaction (presumably to both the affair and the mixed race pregnancy that results), Amy commits suicide. She epitomizes the tragedy of single women who are seen more as symbols of the town's morality than as human beings.

Abby H. P. Werlock

HAWKINS, EMALIN. The elder of the two Hawkins sisters in **"Johnny Bear,"** Emalin is between fifty and fifty-five years of age and is the complete opposite of her warm and vibrant sister, **Amy Hawkins**. Cold and morally rigid, she upbraids Amy for her sensuality and tells her that she might be better off dead than alive and sinful. Emalin thus not only suggests suicide to her pregnant, conflicted, and guilt-ridden sister, but, as **Dr. Holmes** suggests, also does not try very hard to save Amy's life when she discovers that her sister has hanged herself.

Abby H. P. Werlock

HAWKINS FARM. In ***The Wayward Bus,*** a deserted old farm foreclosed by the Bank of America and left to decay. The farm initially seems to symbolize a lost America, a time when family and the farming way of life were central to the American identity. Now considered worthless and simply a stopping place for bums and foraging schoolboys, the farm provides the first (and, as it turns out, the only) stop for **Juan Chicoy** on his intended flight to Mexico. **Mildred Pritchard** follows him and, finding him in the barn, eventually has intercourse with him in a scene that seems to have a vitality and authenticity in marked distinction to events transpiring simultaneously at the mired bus.

Christopher S. Busch

HAWLEY, ALLEN. Unscrupulous son of **Ethan Allen Hawley** in ***The Winter of Our Discontent*** and rival to his sister **Ellen Hawley.** Allen is a baby-boomer and slave to the "everybody does it" mentality of the times. Allen's "I Love America" essay is plagiarized from books in the Hawley family library that celebrate America's idealistic past. Ironically, it wins a prize in a national contest complete with a monetary award. This episode alludes to the Charles Van Doren quiz-show scandal of the era, an event that involved fixed answers for large amounts of money. Allen admires himself in the faded Knight Templar hat and the symbolic sword of the order that he has borrowed from his father, thus visually bridging the worlds of piracy and business. He calls his sister a sneak for disapproving of his actions and for revealing his cheating to the contest director. But it is Ethan, their father, who diagnoses Allen's discontent—and the nation's—as a pervasive moral degeneracy.

John Ditsky

HAWLEY, CAP'N. In ***The Winter of Our Discontent***, the last mariner in the Hawley family and the one whose ship, the *Belle-Adair,* is suspiciously burned to the waterline, sending the Hawley family on a downward plummet toward relative poverty. Ethan remembers the Cap'n as a highly disciplined sailor of a school now long-vanished.

HAWLEY, ELLEN. The thirteen-year-old daughter of **Ethan Allen Hawley** in ***The Winter of Our Discontent***. Intelligent and intuitive, she is watched by Ethan as she caresses a family talisman while sleepwalking. Early on, she asks her father about plagiarism, and she later turns her brother **Allen Hawley** in to the directors of the "I Love America" essay contest. She senses that Ethan will not be coming back when he takes his last walk. Yet it appears to be her "light" that saves him from suicide and brings him home again as he remembers her belief in righteous and upright actions. He vows to go back to return the talisman (a type of grail) to its rightful owner, "Else another light might go out."

John Ditsky

HAWLEY, ETHAN ALLEN. Protagonist of Steinbeck's final completed novel, ***The Winter of Our Discontent***, Ethan is nearly forty but otherwise similar to Steinbeck in several aspects of temperament. His "discontent" (he even sings **Shakespeare**'s lines at one point) is less a matter of what we have learned to call a mid-life crisis but more a growing awareness that a New England family—pirates, pilgrims, and whaling captains—has come down to himself, a clerk in a grocery store who talks to the canned goods. Ethan is very much aware of the implications of Eastertide when the novel opens and is being simultaneously pressured by his fellow citizens and his restless family—wife, son, and daughter—to improve his and also their financial circumstances by whatever means are necessary.

Ethan can quote his **Bible**, and apparently sees himself as a kind of Christ figure as Lent of 1960 enters its final catastrophe. Ironically, though money is apparently the answer to all problems, Ethan is staunchly against investing his wife **Mary Hawley**'s inheritance from her brother. Yet he is strangely motivated to theft when the teller at the nearby bank (whose director urges investment) gives him the idea of staging a quick holdup to improve his monetary status. Retreating from playing his games of "silly" with his wife, Ethan walks the night streets of New Baytown until he comes to his "Place," a gap in the old Hawley dock where he can be alone with his thoughts. He contemplates his heretofore-relaxed existence in a time and place devoted to achievement, success, and the material rewards of ambition. Earlier he also receives encouragement in the form of the tarot readings carried out in his behalf by **Margie Young-Hunt**, the local seductress with a penchant for Wicca and a yen for the newly empowered Ethan. Margie sees fortune in Ethan's future, as if she were at once the three witches who make their promises to Macbeth.

Setting aside Ethan's initial perception of himself as a Christ-figure, a martyr to his own goodness, and also any further Shakespearean referents, a reader can see the opening section as a parody of the death of Jesus. In the Place, Ethan enters the domain of death, as he becomes increasingly the victim of his nascent ambitions. This event occurs on Good Friday; on Holy Saturday, Ethan clearly enters a private hell, and his personality begins to change in the direction of moral corruption, almost as though he were possessed by a demon.

On Easter Sunday, Ethan dreams of his friend **Danny Taylor**, who owns a piece of inherited property. Ethan comes to know the town's moneyed types want it for an airport—something Ethan discusses with Banker Baker over tea, where investment is again urged. The irony of this Easter is confirmed when, the next day, Ethan acts on his new impulses. He loans Danny the money for treatment for his chronic alcoholism, knowing that Danny will use the money to, in effect, commit suicide by drinking himself to death—after signing the property over to Ethan. In four days, Ethan the Christ has become Ethan the Judas.

The novel's first part largely ends the religious associations only to replace them with civic ones. That is, the making of money replaces ethics. Though Ethan impresses his employer **Alfio Marullo** by refusing to take a bribe from the traveling grocery supplier **Biggers**, and though he thinks of his gift to Danny as "poisoned," the gift is reciprocated. "In business and in politics," Ethan concludes, "a man must carve and maul his way through men to get to be King of the Mountain. Once there, he can be great and kind-but he must get there first." One wonders if, when Ethan sings Richard III's famous lines once his schemes are set in motion, he is actually joyous or already bitterly aware of himself as no longer a Christ but rather a Judas figure or a tragic villain.

Steinbeck's clever construction in *The Winter of Our Discontent* means a shifting from the religious or moral to the secular and amoral; he bridges the gap between the two with the occult. Margie's tarot reading is a means of showing Ethan to be a changed character—a snake shedding its skin, as she puts it. Yet Ethan is too savvy to be fooled by promises about Birnam Wood coming to Dunsinane or enemies not of woman born. The transition between the novel's two parts is handled by an emphasis on the past, as if there had been a time when civic and moral ideals were one and the same. Ethan violates the past when he unwittingly shows his son Allen the historical materials in the Hawley attic that Allen will use to concoct his fraudulent "I Love America" essay. But Ethan worships that past when he watches his daughter Ellen, while sleepwalking, lovingly stroke the family talisman—a mound of carved stone with a pattern of seemingly endless carving upon it. In fact, he sees the talisman as a protective guard for all the Hawley family, and Ellen as its mistress, the keeper of light and goodness. In fact Ethan's own eventual salvation—something Margie avers is possible in her tarot reading—comes as a result of faith in the redemptive power of womanhood, as adumbrated in ***East of Eden***'s **Abra Bacon**.

By July 4, Ethan has sunk low enough to be a model of American success. He has called the INS to report Marullo's illegal-alien status, and it is only the ironically timely—or untimely—arrival of an INS agent that keeps him from going through with a bank robbery he has already rehearsed. Ethan has been given the store by Marullo, lest "another" light go out, as Ethan finally understands his bequest. Steinbeck's venture into the conscience of an individual, perhaps for the first time at full length, leaves the reader to wrestle with the question of the degree to which Ethan internalizes what he has done. There are of course explicit clues, as when Ethan dreams of giving Danny a Judas kiss. Ethan convicts us all: "Everybody does it." But when he sits in his Place at the end, with razor blades for his wrists in his pocket and contemplates the lights and the tides, and then discovers the talisman in his pocket and recognizes his duty to the past and to the future, he finally celebrates the Fourth of July with an oddly-timed new burst of freedom in that societal transitional year of 1960; that is, he seems to have achieved his "salvation" after all.

As Steinbeck's last major character and also his most internalized one, Ethan Allen Hawley is something of an anomaly in Steinbeck's fiction. He represents an extension of the "Steinbeck" voice in *East of Eden*, yet he also comes to a point of self-discovery resembling **Cal Trask**'s in the latter novel. Curiously, the book starts out with the usual exterior presentation of Ethan, but soon the reader is allowed to listen to the workings of his mind, learning in the process how clever and disingenuous Ethan can be—a man never given full credit for shrewdness by his New Baytown neighbors. Because his self-seduction begins roughly when his internalization does, the reader is tempted along with Ethan to enter a state of denial. Yet the novel ends with renewed hope, for Ethan emerges having possibly achieved full moral awareness. This occurs in place of Macbeth's despair at having been tricked—for Danny has been the Banquo's ghost at Ethan's banquet.

Further Reading: Burningham, Bradd. "Relation, Vision, and Tracking the Welsh Rats in *East of Eden* and *The Winter of Our Discontent*." *Steinbeck Quarterly* 15 (Summer/Fall 1982): 77–90; Ditsky, John. "*The Winter of Our Discontent*: Steinbeck's Testament on Naturalism." *Research Studies* 44 (March 1976): 42–51; French, Warren. "Steinbeck's *Winter Tale*." *Modern Fiction Studies* 11 (Spring 1965): 66–74; Gerstenberger, Donna. "Steinbeck's American Waste Land." *Modern Fiction Studies* (Spring 1965): 59–65; Steinbeck, John. *The Winter of Our Discontent*. New York: Viking, 1960; Stone, Donal. "Steinbeck, Jung and *The Winter of Our Discontent*." In *Steinbeck's Literary Dimension. Series II*. Ed. Tetsumaro Hayashi. Metuchen, NJ: Scarecrow Press, 1991. 91–101; Verdier, Douglas L. "Ethan Allen Hawley and the Hanged Man: Free Will and Fate in *The Winter of Our Discontent*." *Steinbeck Quarterly* 15 (Winter/Spring 1982): 44–50.

John Ditsky

HAWLEY, MARY. **Ethan Allen Hawley**'s wife in ***The Winter of Our Discontent***, she is a naïve but loving spouse whom Ethan addresses with pet names. She is drawn in stark contrast to the other female character in the novel, **Margie Young-Hunt**. Ethan marvels at her capacity for placid sleep and regards her as a naïve innocent and something of a "mystery" to him as a protecting saint who helps him avoid worldly temptations. Though she does not nag Ethan as such, her constant reminders of what the Hawleys no longer have constitute one of the familial pressures on Ethan to acquire more in the name of his dependents. The money she has inherited from her brother is used by Ethan to supply **Danny Taylor** with a potential cure for alcoholism, though he realizes Danny will use it to drink himself to death and Ethan will become the beneficiary of Danny's property.

John Ditsky

HAYASHI, TETSUMARO (1929–). *See* **Steinbeck Societies**.

HAZEL (*CANNERY ROW*). One of **Mack**'s "boys" in ***Cannery Row***, Hazel got his name because his mother became confused about his sex when he was born. He is twenty-six, large, and mild in disposition, and he spent four years in grammar school and another four in reform school. His affability makes him an ideal companion for **Doc**, whom Hazel often accompanies on collecting trips.

HAZEL (*SWEET THURSDAY*). A man of limited mental ability who lives in the **Palace Flophouse** in ***Sweet Thursday***. Hazel is famous for his habit of asking questions just to hear the sound of speech, not to listen to the answers. In *Sweet Thursday*, he finally commits the treachery of actually attending to the responses to his questions in order to achieve the communal goal of uniting **Doc** and **Suzy**.

During the war, Hazel served in the Army long enough to qualify for the GI bill, and he later enrolled at the University of California, majoring in astrophysics for his three-month stay. Back on the Row now, he loves living at the Palace Flophouse, telling **Mack** and the boys that it is the only place where he was ever happy. Once **Fauna** casts his horoscope, however, he feels set apart from his peers by the oppressive burden of his future responsibility, for she predicts that he will one day become President of the United States. Because of his incipient sense of honor, he feels that it is not properly dignified for him to attend the community masquerade party as a mere dwarf. Instead, he seeks **Joe Elegant**'s assistance in developing a Prince Charming costume, and Joe cruelly designs him a ridiculous outfit with a missing drop-seat that reveals a target drawn on his posterior. Hazel's sense of responsibility also drives him to assume a leadership role in rousing Doc from his lethargy. After consulting all the major citizens of Cannery Row, he reluctantly decides that his best course is to break Doc's arm in the hopes that Suzy will rush to Doc's aid. The plan is successful, but to ensure that Hazel gets no more ideas, Mack talks Fauna into recanting her prediction of the presidency so that he can return to living in a blissful haze.

It is in keeping with the mock-romance flavor of *Sweet Thursday* that it is Hazel who enacts the collective will of the Row to bring the plot to its storybook resolution. Knowing that he is inadequate to the task of devising a plan alone, he visits one member of the Row after another for advice. As Brian Railsback has observed, Hazel uses an inductive method in gathering information from Joe Elegant, **Becky**, Fauna, the Patron, Suzy, Doc, and the **seer**. He then synthesizes the views of the community to arrive at his final plan of breaking Doc's arm, a physical crippling that he hopes will eventuate in Doc's spiritual healing. By using Hazel as the vehicle of the final resolution, Steinbeck casts derision on the happily-ever-after ending required of the romance genre—for with Hazel's intercession, the alliance of Doc and Suzy seems more like a match made in Bedlam than in heaven.

Hazel is one of a long list of mentally deficient characters in Steinbeck, a group that includes **Tuleracito**, the **Pirate**, **Johnny Bear**, and **Lennie Small**. Like the children in his fiction, these less socialized adults are revealing of Steinbeck's conception of human nature. Hazel differs from many of the other mentally limited characters in that he is not portrayed as having a potentially dangerous, uncontrollable sexual drive. He is similar to most of the others, however, in acting on violent impulses. While essentially good-spirited, he tends to choose the most direct method of dealing with a threat, which may involve the use of physical force. Steinbeck clearly had little confidence in the ability of people to control their violent impulses without the socialization of ethics, morals, and codes of conduct. The mentally deficient characters, on whom much of this socialization is lost, are usually unable to remain in society and are either destroyed or institutionalized. Hazel is an exception only because of the protection and guidance he is provided by Doc, Mack, and other members of the Cannery Row community.

Further Reading: Railsback, Brian. *Parallel Expeditions: Charles Darwin and the Art of John Steinbeck.* Moscow: University of Idaho Press, 1995.

Bruce Ouderkirk

HEDGPETH, JOEL (1912–). Naturalist and prolific writer who, out of a mutual interest in Pacific marine species, struck up an acquaintance with **Edward F. Ricketts** and subsequently John Steinbeck in late 1939. Hedgpeth writes about some of his visits to Ed's lab, noting Ricketts' fascination with music (particularly choral forms and Bach's works) and Ed's prediction, after reading advance galleys of ***The Grapes of Wrath***, that the novel would win the **Pulitzer Prize**. Hedgpeth lent his considerable expertise to revising later editions of ***Between Pacific Tides*** (originally authored by Ricketts and **Jack Calvin** and published by the Stanford University Press in 1939). Still later, Hedgpeth became a good friend and colleague of Ed, and he edited Ricketts' naturalist and philosophical writings in two volumes titled *The Outer Shores* (1978).

Further Reading: Hedgpeth, Joel W. "Philosophy on Cannery Row." In *Steinbeck: The Man and His Work.* Ed. Richard Astro and Tetsumaro Hayashi. Corvallis: Oregon State University Press, 1971; Ricketts, Edward F. *The Outer Shores*. 2 vols. Ed. Joel W. Hedgpeth. Eureka, CA: Mad River Press, 1978.

HEISERMAN, CHIEF. Constable in ***East of Eden*** who observes and checks up on **Cal Trask** as Cal walks the **Salinas** streets at night.

HELEN (*EAST OF EDEN*). Prostitute at **Kate Albey**'s brothel in ***East of Eden***.

HELEN (*SWEET THURSDAY*). In ***Sweet Thursday***, a prostitute at the **Bear Flag** who is unable to help entertain the members of the Rattlesnake Club of **Salinas** because she is serving sixty days in jail for fighting with another prostitute.

HEMINGWAY, ERNEST [MILLER] (1899–1961). American short-story writer and novelist whose spare dialogue, understated prose style, and objective realism have become synonymous with literary modernism. His apprenticeship to expatriate authors Gertrude Stein and **Ezra Pound** in 1920s Paris helped shape his achievement. Hemingway's short stories, collected in *In Our Time* (1925), *Men Without Women* (1927), *Winner Take Nothing* (1933), and *The Fifth Column and the First Forty-nine Stories* (1938), are considered among the finest in our language. Four of the seven novels he published during his lifetime are major contributions to American literature: *The Sun Also Rises* (1926), *A Farewell to Arms* (1929), *For Whom the Bell Tolls* (1940), and *The Old Man and the Sea* (1952). His less successful efforts in the genre include *The Torrents of Spring* (1926), *To Have and Have Not* (1937), and *Across the River and Into the Trees* (1950). Hemingway also produced two distinguished works of book-length nonfiction: *Death in the Afternoon* (1932), a treatise on bullfighting, and *Green Hills of Africa* (1935), about big-game hunting. In 1954, Hemingway won the **Nobel Prize** for Literature, and in 1961 he committed suicide. At his death, Hemingway left a considerable legacy of unpublished work. Among materials subsequently published by the Hemingway estate, his memoir of the Paris years, *A Moveable Feast* (1964), and three unfinished novels, *Islands in the Stream* (1970), *The Garden of Eden* (1986), and *True at First Light: A Fictional Memoir* (1999), have received considerable critical attention.

Because his fiction is intensely autobiographical and because he crafted a mythic persona for himself in his nonfiction, Hemingway is as well known for his Byronic life as he is for his literary attainment. He married four times, sired three sons, and came under fire in the two World Wars and the Spanish Civil War. Hemingway lived in Italy, France, Key West, Cuba, and Idaho and traveled widely in Spain and East Africa. A world-roving journalist and war correspondent, known to millions as "Papa Hemingway," he followed bullfighting with avidity, hunted big game in Africa, and fished the Gulf Stream for giant marlin. This adventurous, hypermasculine public activity camouflaged a sensitive, troubled man who suffered from alcoholism and an inherited mood disorder (Hemingway's father and two of his five siblings also committed suicide). When he put a shotgun to his forehead and pulled the trigger just days before his sixty-first birthday, the world was stunned. Ill health (Hemingway suffered from hypertension, diabetes, and cirrhosis of the liver), profound depression, the conviction that electro-shock treatments had destroyed his ability to write, and the loss of his Cuban home following Castro's rise to power all helped precipitate his death.

John Steinbeck claimed that he had met Ernest Hemingway only twice and that he couldn't remember what they had talked about because at both meetings the two men had a lot to drink. On one occasion, when Steinbeck and Hemingway gathered with other writers in a New York bar, Hemingway bet novelist **John O'Hara** fifty dollars that he could break O'Hara's antique Irish blackthorn cane, a gift from Steinbeck, over his own head. Hemingway made good on his bet, O'Hara lost his money and his cane, and Steinbeck was reportedly disgusted. Yet Steinbeck and Hemingway were far more important to each other than this anecdote suggests.

Three years younger than Hemingway, Steinbeck just missed the literary revolution that took place in 1920s Paris. While Hemingway sat at the feet of Stein and Pound, Steinbeck took creative writing classes at **Stanford University**. However, from such Hemingway short stories as "The Killers," Steinbeck absorbed the principal lesson of modernism: "throw out the words that do not say anything." Like all writers in the grip of a powerful influence, Steinbeck sometimes insisted that he "never never read Hemingway." Steinbeck once startled friends by suddenly exclaiming, "Hemingway . . . that shit!" although no one had mentioned the other author, and one evening, he entertained dinner guests by mocking dialogue from *The Sun Also Rises*. Yet in 1939 Steinbeck wrote to tell Hemingway that his "The Butterfly and the Tank" was one of the finest short stories of all time, and in 1962, the year after Hemingway's death, Steinbeck publicly acknowledged that Hemingway's short stories were, with Faulkner's novels, one of the two most significant influences on his career.

When Steinbeck's short-story collection, ***The Long Valley,*** was published the same year as Hemingway's *The First Forty-nine*, Steinbeck worried about comparisons: "Competing with Hemingway isn't my idea of good business." He did not realize that Hemingway was worried too. Concerned that the public would not understand that his book contained new stories in addition to reprints, Hemingway wrote defensively to his publisher: "There is enough new stuff in the book to make a book a good deal longer than ***Of Mice and Men*** say. Mention that." Hemingway's attention here to the commercial and literary success of Steinbeck's 1937 novella is telling. Either *Of Mice and Men* or ***The Pearl*** may have influenced Hemingway to experiment with the novella in *The Old Man and the Sea* (1952).

On Hemingway's side, the anxiety of influence led to disparaging remarks that unfortunately got back to the younger writer. Hemingway proclaimed that he could not read Steinbeck any more after the scene in ***The Grapes of Wrath*** where Rose of Sharon gives her breast to a starving man, and he reportedly said that "aside from anything else, that's hardly the solution to our economic problem." Steinbeck saw the humor in this jab but still felt hurt by this criticism. He never saw the letter Hemingway wrote to Charles Scribner when Hemingway was pondering the fate of his own sweeping novel of political and social turmoil *For Whom the Bell Tolls* (1940) published just one year after *The Grapes of Wrath*. Hemingway ranked *Grapes* with **Richard Wright**'s *Native Son*, **Dostoyevsky**'s *The Brothers Karamazov,* and **Flaubert**'s *Madame Bovary* and decided, perhaps insincerely, that his own new book was "not in that class." Steinbeck's masterpiece had to have been much on Hemingway's mind as he completed *Bell*.

Certainly, Hemingway was much on Steinbeck's mind during the early 1950s. Concerned about his own failing critical fortunes, Steinbeck was wounded by the "obscene joy" with which critics "trampled" on Hemingway's *Across the River and Into the Trees*. He fretted that "the lovers of Hemingway" would not love his own ***East of Eden,*** and he contemplated attacking Hemingway on his own ground by attempting a short story about the bullfighter Litri. Always ambivalent about the older writer, Steinbeck next rejoiced over the public adulation accorded *The Old Man and the Sea* (1952) and Hemingway's 1954 receipt of the Nobel Prize.

In 1959, the deterioration of Hemingway's physical and mental health accelerated, and Steinbeck's productivity haunted Hemingway as he became increasingly unable to write. When publisher Charles Scribner, Jr. nagged him for material, Hemingway lashed out: "I could give [Scribner] a book every year like Steinbeck composed of my toenail parings. . . . little fantasies about King Poo Poo [Steinbeck's ***The Short Reign of Pippin IV***] or other author toe jam. But that is all shit and just the byproducts of egotism or avarice or both." Steinbeck, meanwhile, more charitably refused to be baited into criticizing the alter ego down on his luck.

Because Hemingway's great theme had been courage in the face of adversity, his 1961 suicide shocked and disturbed Steinbeck. In an insightful letter to **Pascal Covici**, Steinbeck contemplated how Hemingway's fiction might have predicted his suicide. Despite his distaste for Hemingway's vanity and competitiveness, he acknowledged the profundity of Hemingway's effect on contemporary writing and his certain literary immortality. Steinbeck paid homage to the influential writer "called Papa" when for a tribute he chose Prince Hamlet's lines on the dead king, his father: "He was a man, take him all in all, / We shall not look upon his like again."

The strong parallels between their careers returned to haunt Steinbeck when he received the Nobel Prize the year after Hemingway's suicide. "I've always been afraid of it because of what it does to people," Steinbeck wrote. "For one thing I don't remember anyone doing any work after getting it save maybe **Shaw**. . . . Hemingway went into a kind of hysterical haze. . . . It has in effect amounted to an epitaph." Sadly, Steinbeck's words were prophetic as he would complete little significant work between receiving the prize in 1962 and his death in 1968. Although Steinbeck died of emphysema and coronary artery disease, he did contemplate and prepare for suicide during his protracted and painful final illness, citing *Ecclesiastes*, perhaps not coincidentally Hemingway's favorite book of the **Bible**, to his doctor. They met only twice, but the extent to which these two great writers of the American twentieth century influenced one another, competed with one another, and finally found their literary destinies woven together, cannot be understated.

Further Reading: Baker, Carlos. *Ernest Hemingway: A Life Story.* New York: Charles Scribner's Sons, 1969; Benson, Jackson J. *The True Adventures of John Steinbeck, Writer.* New York: Viking, 1984; Hemingway, Ernest. *Ernest Hemingway: Selected Letters, 1917–1961.* Ed. Carlos Baker. New York: Charles Scribner's Sons, 1981; Steinbeck, John. *Steinbeck: A Life in Letters.* Ed. Elaine Steinbeck and Robert Wallsten. New York: Viking, 1975.

Susan F. Beegel

HENNING, CAROL. *See* **Steinbeck, Carol Henning**.

HENRI THE PAINTER. In ***Sweet Thursday***, a former resident of **Cannery Row** who, though afraid of water, lived in a boat he had built in the woods. As a practical joke, **Mack** and the boys glued barnacles to the bottom of the boat at night. After the second time this occurred, Henri sold the boat and left town, afraid that the vessel was going to the ocean while he slept. This practical joke seems uncharacteristically cruel of Mack and the boys, who are generally tolerant of the eccentricities of their neighbors on the Row, and in fact they are ashamed about the outcome.

Bruce Ouderkirk

HERE'S WHERE I BELONG. Like ***Pipe Dream***, the Rodgers and Hammerstein musical adaptation of ***Sweet Thursday***, this title was also an adaptation of a Steinbeck novel, ***East of Eden***. It opened in New York City on March 3, 1968, with a book by **Terrence McNally**, lyrics by Alfred Uhry, and music by Robert Waldman. Though McNally and Uhry later became famous as playwrights (McNally with such controversial works as *Love, Valor and Compassion!*,

Corpus Christi, and *Master Class* and Uhry with *Driving Miss Daisy* and *The Last Night at Ballyhoo*), this ill-starred conception closed after one performance. The failure was perhaps due to the fact that the artists tried to yoke the serious social issue of turn-of-the-century progress and change with a romance, played out in a ménage à trois between **Cal** and **Aron Trask** and **Abra Bacon**. In addition to these central plot concerns, the musical also contained a subplot and a song about Kaiser Wilhelm and World War I and a maudlin tune entitled "Soft As the Sparrow," which dealt with Adam Trask's idealization of his monster wife, Cathy. This jumble of emphases and moods in the musical's book became even more conflicted when a ballet of lettuce pickers was inserted in Act 1, Scene 6. Produced by Mitch Miller and directed by Michael Kahn, only a few copies of the original script are extant, and most Steinbeck critics are unaware of its existence.

Michael J. Meyer

HÉRISTAL, CLOTILDE. In ***The Short Reign of Pippin IV***, star-struck daughter to **Pippin Héristal**, the newly crowned king of France. Clotilde is obsessed with film, particularly American film. She spends many afternoons at the movies and manages to get parts in a couple of movies whose reviews are so negative that she retreats conveniently from those ambitions when she finds herself suddenly in the role of princess royal. In that capacity she meets **Tod Johnson** while waiting with fellow members of the Tab Hunter fan club for that star to put in an appearance at Les Ambassadeurs. She also considers herself a novelist, having written a best-seller at fifteen titled *Adieu, ma vie*, and is given to public political gestures that identify her as a communist rebel until her father's ascension to the throne and her involvement with Tod, an arch-capitalist, change her politics.

Marilyn Chandler McEntyre

HÉRISTAL, MARIE. In ***The Short Reign of Pippin IV***, wife of **Pippin Héristal**. She is elevated suddenly from bourgeois housewife to Queen of France when her husband is made the new king. A practical bourgeois wife, Marie provides a comic foil to her studious, somewhat abstracted husband whose expenditures and daily habits she supervises with the eye of a sympathetic but tough manager. She acclimates to their surprising change of fortunes by remaining essentially unchanged; the habits of cleanliness, order, frugality, and common sense that have served her in her flat on the Rue de Marigny enable her to function as queen with little disruption of her essential fidelities to family, friendship, and household order. She serves as a satirical comment on what virtues are to be sought among those in public life; she is not an idealist and is not as reflective as Pippin, and she consents to observe the forms, but manages to maintain a practical and therefore sometimes jaundiced view of politics.

Marilyn Chandler McEntyre

HÉRISTAL, PIPPIN. In ***The Short Reign of Pippin IV***, a mild-mannered amateur astronomer who lives quietly in Paris. Two facts of Pippin's identity link him to the history and fate of his country: his ancestry can be traced to Charlemagne's royal blood, and his home is the historical headquarters of the Knights of St. John, a medieval order devoted to chivalrous and charitable work. When representatives of many disputing political parties meet to try to work out a viable compromise government, they decide to reinstate the ancient monarchy and, after a search, identify the surprised and reluctant Pippin as hereditary monarch. Bewildered at first, Pippin seeks to avoid both notoriety and ceremonial royal duties, but over time, as he begins to reflect on the political environment from which he has studiously maintained his distance, he recognizes the opportunity to use his position to advocate for protection for the laboring classes, for better distribution of wealth and use of resources, and for protection for the poor. Pippin's reflections are developed in conversation with an odd assortment of other characters whose practical and philosophical wisdom help him articulate the philosophy he finally brings to court. His uncle, **Charles Martel**, a small entrepreneur, warns him against offending those with the power of the guillotine; an old friend, now a nun, encourages him to speak truth; an old forest-dwelling hermit reminds him of and represents the significance of ordinary people, and, oddly, the son of an American chicken farmer from Petaluma exposes the actual workings of American capitalism. Having presented his political philosophy to the assembly of party leaders, Pippin quietly leaves by the back door, sheds his royal robes, and returns to his home to play his harmonica and polish his telescope, convinced that the rioting factions will forget him and expend their energies on each other. Though the character is not deeply developed, he does offer a genuinely endearing portrait of a man of sense and sensibility, capable of minding his own business, caring for others' welfare, and motivated by love of knowledge rather than greed.

Marilyn Chandler McEntyre

HERODOTUS (480–425 BCE). Greek historian who has been termed the "Father of History." He is perhaps best known for his history of the Persian invasion of Greece. In 1930, the newly married Steinbeck wrote to Amasa **'Ted' Miller** from his home at Eagle Rock, California, that he was rereading Herodotus, along with Plutarch and Xenophon, in an effort to streamline his writing style. During this time, he was working on revising ***To a God Unknown***. By reading and rereading the classics, Steinbeck engaged in a reeducation process. This was the beginning of a transition that would "culminate" with ***The Grapes of Wrath***.

Janet L. Flood

HERSEY, JOHN (1914–1993). American novelist and journalist noted for his documentary fiction about catastrophic events during World War II. Hersey's early novel, *A Bell for Adano,* won the 1945 Pulitzer prize for fiction, but his most famous books are *Hiroshima* (1946), an objective account of the atomic bomb explosion as experienced by survivors of the blast, and *The Wall* (1950), which recounts the Warsaw ghetto uprisings in Poland during the war. Steinbeck met Hersey in 1944, and they became casual friends, visiting each other occasionally at home. Perhaps Steinbeck's affinity for Hersey is related to their similar penchant for relaying facts charged with imaginative fictionalization. Hersey, like Steinbeck, was a journalist at one point in his career, serving as a foreign correspondent in East Asia, Italy, and the Soviet Union for *Time* and *Life* magazines from 1937 to 1946.

Michael J. Meyer

HERVIS DE REVEL, SIR. In ***The Acts of King Arthur***, a knight of the line of Sir Thomas Malory who distinguishes himself in the service of **King Arthur** during the battle with **Nero**, the brother of **King Royns**; he is made a Knight of the **Round Table** on **King Pellinore**'s recommendation after the war with the **Five Kings**.

"HIGH DRAMA OF BOLD THRUST THROUGH OCEAN FLOOR" (1961). A publication in *Life* magazine (50.15, April 14, 1961), this is Steinbeck's account of his trip with a *Life* photographer on a voyage that was the beginning of a long-term plan for an exploration of the unknown two-thirds of the planet that lies under the sea. Considered an amateur oceanographer by the crew, Steinbeck records his pleasure at being part of the first journey and records the tight smiles of deepest satisfaction of the men who planned the voyage. He also expresses his hope to be invited back when a new ship sails toward new wonders in about two years.

Herbert Behrens and Michael J. Meyer

HIGHWAY 66. Often called the Mother Road, this highway prefigured the modern-day expressway. Running from Chicago to Los Angeles, it was the main road used by the Okies as they migrated westward looking for work. Constructed in 1926, the road was intended to link rural and urban communities and to make it easier for small farmers to market their products using larger trucks. Though Steinbeck's ***The Grapes of Wrath*** was one of the first to popularize the road and inscribe it into the imaginations of Americans in the late 1930s, later media, including songs and television, also appropriated the highway as a symbol for travel and for seeking the unknown.

"HIS FATHER" (1949). A short story written by Steinbeck in 1949 after visiting his children in New York. Of the three stories Steinbeck wrote then, two of them were destroyed; the third, "His Father," was sent to his agent, **Elizabeth Otis**, with the comment, "I don't know whether you will like or approve of the enclosed. It is what happened anyway. Maybe it isn't good to even think of printing it. But it occurs to me that if **Nat Benchley** can write the things that didn't happen in my family, perhaps I can write some that did." Published in *Reader's Digest* in September 1949, in a Turkish publication of an American short-story anthology in 1951, and in the *Uncollected Stories of John Steinbeck* in 1986, "His Father" deals with a young child's secret concerning his father's absence. Nearly seven years old, the boy lives in the city (probably New York) and is tortured by other children who demand to know where his father has gone. The boy lamely says his father is working indoors or on long trips, but the children—a boy named Alvin in the lead—keep taunting him until an older boy in the street reveals the father is gone because of divorce. The boy flies into a rage and beats his tormentors, though they silently taunt him thereafter. One day, while the boy is sitting on the steps of his brownstone coping, his father appears, and the boy screams it out to the neighborhood. Written not long after Steinbeck's own divorce from his second wife, **Gwyndolyn Conger Steinbeck**, the story seems haunted by the author's anxiety about being separated from his two young sons, **John IV** and **Thom Steinbeck**. There is also the suggestion that even before the divorce, the father was often away on business—working—as Steinbeck often was during his marriage to Gwyn.

Further Reading: Steinbeck, John. "His Father." *Uncollected Stories of John Steinbeck*. Ed. Kiyoshi Nakayama. Tokyo: Nan'un-do, 1986.

John Hooper

HITZLER. In ***Sweet Thursday***, a man who reports to **Doc** that **Old Jingleballicks** was seen kneeling on a lawn in Berkeley, trying to pull a worm from the ground with his teeth. Old Jay insists that he was simply conducting an experiment to determine how much pull a robin has to exert to overcome the worm's resistance.

HOLBERT. Pirate captain under **Henry Morgan**'s command in the campaign against Panama in ***Cup of Gold***.

HOLLYWOOD. In ***The Wayward Bus***, this motion picture capital of the world elicits Steinbeck's particular disdain, beginning in the first chapter. It is the place where "eventually, all the adolescents in the world will be congregated," a kind of intellectually empty yet compelling attraction for the mousy **Norma** and perhaps millions of other adolescents who fill their empty lives with movies and thoughts of movie stars.

HOLMAN, RABBIT. Worker at **Adam Trask**'s ranch in ***East of Eden***. One night, when Rabbit goes to **Salinas**, he encounters **Cal Trask** and gets so drunk that he forgets who Cal is. Rabbit tells him that **Kate Albey** is **Cathy Trask**, that she shot and deserted Cal's father, and that her brothel is excitingly depraved. Cal then accompanies Rabbit to Kate's. This chance encounter with Rabbit and what results from it provide a pivotal point in the plot and in the development of Cal's character.

HOLMES, DR. A minor character in **"Johnny Bear"** who is called in twice to tend to **Amy Hawkins** (for the first attempted suicide and for the second ensuing attempt that succeeds), he differs from the rigidly respectable **Emalin Hawkins**, whom he cautions to behave kindly toward Amy. The last time he is called in, he sees the mark made by the rope Amy used to hang herself, correctly diagnoses her pregnancy and her suicide, and suggests that Emalin left Amy hanging longer than she should have. He retreats almost immediately, however, and, as the trusted family doctor, assures Emalin of his cooperation and discretion.

Abby H. P. Werlock

HOOPTEDOODLE. A literary term introduced by **Mack** in the prologue of ***Sweet Thursday***. Although Mack's definition is rather vague, the term apparently refers to a passage of lyricism, interpolated narration, or impressionistic description that does not move forward the main plotline of a novel. Mack's preference is that passages of hooptedoodle be kept distinct from the material depicting the central events. Oddly enough, however, Steinbeck seems to use a different definition of hooptedoodle than Mack does. Steinbeck assigns chapter 3 the title of "Hooptedoodle (1)," although actually only its first four paragraphs fit Mack's definition. The rest of that chapter focuses on matters that are central both to the novel's plot and to its thematic development.

If one keeps to Mack's, rather than Steinbeck's apparent use of the term, the only chapters *completely* composed of hooptedoodle are "The Great Roque War" and "Hooptedoodle (2), or The Pacific Grove Butterfly Festival." Although **Peter Lisca** claims that hooptedoodle is "ubiquitous" in the novel, Steinbeck does follow Mack's advice to the extent that most of it is confined to the opening paragraphs of a few chapters. Thus, the chapters "Lousy Wednesday," "Sweet Thursday (1)," and "Waiting Friday" all begin with hooptedoodle to describe these sorts of days in general before moving into the specific events that advance the plot. With other chapters, such as "Sweet Thursday Revisited," Steinbeck sometimes indulges in additional hooptedoodle when he begins a new segment. In *Sweet Thursday,* and perhaps in ***Cannery Row*** as well, the hooptedoodle passages are often more interesting than the account of the central events. A reader who skips the incidents about the Pacific Grove roque war or butterfly festival is missing out on some of the best satire in *Sweet Thursday.*

Bruce Ouderkirk

HOPKINS MARINE STATION. Located near **Pacific Grove**, this station was an extended campus for **Stanford University** where Steinbeck studied zoology and humanities during the summer of 1923. The zoology course was taught by C. V. Taylor and exposed Steinbeck to the philosophical doctrines of **William Emerson Ritter** concerning the organismal nature of all life. Critics have often speculated that the author's interest in nature in general and in the ocean's ecosystem specifically began about this time and eventually led to his exploratory expedition of the **Sea of Cortez** with his friend **Edward F. Ricketts** in 1940.

HOPPS, MARTIN. A **Salinas** boy killed in World War I in ***East of Eden***. His death angers **Olive Hamilton** (**Steinbeck**) and spurs her to join the war effort, which she does by aggressively selling Liberty bonds. Her success in doing so earns her a ride in a plane, the story of which her son, John Steinbeck, narrates with warmth and humor.

HORSEMAN, THE OTHER. In ***Viva Zapata!*** at the beginning of the screenplay, he accompanies the man on the white horse who is later identified as **Emiliano Zapata**. When the man on the white horse stops to speak to the peasants at a train whistle-stop, he turns the reins of his horse over to his brother, the other horseman, who has been telling him that he is wasting his time. This scene was excised entirely from the film. We later learn that the other horseman is Emiliano's older brother, **Eufemio Zapata**.

HORTON, CHASE (1897–1985). Owner of the Washington Square Bookshop, Horton was a close friend and frequent companion of **Elizabeth Otis**, Steinbeck's agent. An avid fan of Arthurian legend, he recognized that no update of Malory's ***Le Morte D'Arthur*** had been written since the 1890s, and he tried to interest prominent authors in creating such a revision/translation. After discovering through Otis that Steinbeck's personal passion for Malory mirrored his own, Horton convinced the author to begin a modern version of the legend, a task Steinbeck had often envisioned for himself. Horton pledged to assist Steinbeck by doing the legwork and obtaining the materials necessary for research.

However, Steinbeck tired of the collaboration, often becoming annoyed at the slow methodical planning of Horton and yet feeling an obligation to the bookseller. The emotional strain heightened when Steinbeck asked Otis and Horton for a critique of one of his drafts and was told that his efforts had produced a dull text. Furious, Steinbeck broke off contact with Horton and only wrote Otis intermittently. Later, he reluctantly returned to the matter of Arthur, feeling that he had discovered the correct voice for a modern version; unfortunately, Otis's continued negative reactions and Horton's silence (he preferred not to offend Steinbeck twice) left Steinbeck unsure of his ability to revise Malory's classic text. The book, ***The Acts of King Arthur***, remained incomplete at Steinbeck's death and was published posthumously in a fragmented version edited by Horton in 1975.

HORTON, ERNEST. In ***Wayward Bus***, a traveling salesman and decorated war veteran. Discharged from service just five months earlier, Horton is more pitiable than unlikable, the embodiment of the contemporary American caught up in an economy and a consumerist culture in which everything is for sale. Though he claims to long for a home, wife, and children, Horton prefers to spend his life on the road. Indeed, he had been married, but walked out on his wife the second day of their marriage. Horton's character reminds the reader of a young Willy Loman, pursuing the dream of wealth through personality and cleverness yet destined to discover the emptiness of American materialism. In many ways, like Loman, Horton is the stereotypical traveling salesman, an extroverted seller of novelties and gadgets of questionable taste and utility, including a line of "gag" gifts and novelties in his sample case. Horton sweetens his wares' appeal by claiming that each item is a sample, not for sale, yet by trip's end, he has managed to unload a respectable amount of merchandise. Though always on the lookout for the main chance, be it in business or with women, Horton, like **Juan Chicoy,** the driver of the bus during its eventful journey, has a personal set of ethics and an integrity that he will not violate. When **Norma**, a star-struck waitress at Juan Chicoy's lunchroom, suggests she is related to **Clark Gable** and asks Horton to deliver a letter to him in **Hollywood**, Horton plays along with her thin deceit rather than humiliating her as he easily could do. Like virtually every other man who encounters her, he responds to the sexual allure of **Camille Oaks**; however, unlike most other men, including several on the bus journey; his response is honest, straightforward, and not manipulative. Horton is not unlike several later Steinbeck characters—for instance, **Ethan Hawley** in ***Winter of Our Discontent***—who retain a residue of the spirit and integrity that Steinbeck felt existed in the early days of America, but who have been diminished and brought to humiliating levels by life in contemporary, capitalistic America.

Christopher S. Busch

"HOW EDITH MCGILLICUDDY MET ROBERT LOUIS STEVENSON" (1943). A story based on an incident that actually happened to **Max Wagner**'s mother, **Edith Gilfillan Wagner**, this story tells of her encounter with the famous author as a child after she had wandered away from a funeral ceremony. Mrs. Wagner had written her own version of the story in 1933 and submitted it to *Reader's Digest*, so Steinbeck was later forced to apologize for his appropriation of the details for his own account. Later, Steinbeck sold the story to *Harper's* magazine in 1941 when it was obvious that Mrs. Wagner's version would not be published. At the time of the publication, Mrs. Wagner was ill and in need of money, and Steinbeck hoped that the story would cheer her in her old age and that the money acquired from the sale of the manuscript would alleviate the family's financial crisis.

Michael J. Meyer

"HOW MR. HOGAN ROBBED A BANK" (1956). Steinbeck's most irreverently whimsical fable since the 1936 short story, **"Saint Katy the Virgin,"** it surprised readers of the *Atlantic Monthly* (March 1956) because it was his first short story since 1949. While still under the influence of his summer in Paris during a period when he was publishing mostly articles, Steinbeck was preparing a satirical novel about France, ***The Short Reign of Pippin IV.*** The story is told with the same kind of deadpan humor. Mr. Hogan has worked out a plan for robbing a local bank while his son and daughter are busy writing essays for William Randolph Hearst's "I Love America" contest. The robbery is successful, and the son wins honorable mention in the contest. After hiding the $500 he has taken in the box with his Knight Templar's regalia, Hogan gives the son $5 for winning and the daughter $5 for being a good loser. Steinbeck reworked the basic situation with renamed characters in his final novel, ***The Winter of Our Discontent,*** but in this latter, more somber tale, **Ethan Allen Hawley** realizes in time that his clever scheme will not work and that subtle thievery pays better than outright stealing. In addition, the hero's son in *Winter* is exposed as plagiarizing his essay from great American patriotic writers.

Little has been written about this clever fantasy, which Steinbeck told his agents he had not intended to write, but **Pascal Covici, Jr.** included it in the revised edition of *The Portable Steinbeck* (New York: Viking, 1971), and in his "Introduction" to the collection, Covici discusses in detail the similarities and differences between the treatment of the material in the short story and the novel.

"HOW TO RECOGNIZE A CANDIDATE" (1955). In this article, which appeared in *Punch* (229, August 10, 1955: 146–148), Steinbeck notes the superficial changes (being nice to dogs, taking up fishing, etc.) men undergo when they run for office in the United States.

"HOW TO TELL GOOD GUYS FROM BAD GUYS" (1954). Unlike the fantastic "The Affair at 7 Rue de M—" (see entry for ***Le Figaro***), this work is a comic narrative involving Steinbeck and his son "Catbird" (**John IV**), and it draws upon conventional symbolism from stereotyped American Western movies. Steinbeck wrote this piece quickly in London, shortly after leaving Paris in early September 1954. It was published in *Punch* on September 22, with the title "Good Guy—Bad Guy." It was not picked up in the United States until March 1955, when it appeared in *The Reporter* with its final title. It soon became enormously popular as a putdown of the witch-hunting Senator Joseph McCarthy and was reprinted a number of times, though it is not included in any collection of Steinbeck's work published in the United States. Steinbeck had been out of the country when the Senate hearings that led to McCarthy's downfall were being televised, but his son had watched the hearings with great interest and had identified McCarthy as a "bad guy" because he wore a black hat like the villains of the old "B" Western movies, whereas the good guys wore white. Steinbeck writes that he explained Catbird's criticism to a musical comedy producer (probably Ernest Martin), who told him, "It's not kid stuff at all. There's a whole generation in this country which makes its judgment pretty much on that basis." Despite its popularity, little has been written about the piece. **Jackson J. Benson** describes it as a "marvelously innocent little bit of mockery"; **Peter Lisca** mentions it without comment as an article of a political nature, and recent critics, including biographer **Jay Parini**, seem content to ignore it completely.

HOWE, JULIA WARD (1819–1910). Composer of "The Battle Hymn of the Republic" during the Civil War. Steinbeck later chose a portion of the text of this anthem as the title for his masterpiece, ***The Grapes of Wrath***. **John H. Timmerman** has suggested that although Steinbeck credited his wife **Carol Henning Steinbeck** with the suggestion for the title, he was also aware of several **biblical** connections to the plight of the Okies in *Grapes*, as offered by the Civil War tune. Noting that Steinbeck insisted on the publication of Howe's words in the frontispiece of the novel, **Timmerman** also quotes Steinbeck's letters to **Elizabeth Otis** as evidence of such awareness. Steinbeck writes, "As you read the book, you will realize that the words have a special meaning." References to Howe's "trampling out the vintage where the grapes of wrath are stored" are then traced to the avenging angel of God in Revelation 14:19–20 and to earlier Old Testament references to bitter grapes in Deuteronomy 32:32 and Jeremiah 31:29, where God prefigures divine retribution for the oppression of his people. The grapes of plenty, the dream of a verdant California winery to replace the arid farmland of Oklahoma, also find a biblical parallel in the account of the Israelites' exodus from Egypt and their discovery of the Promised Land in Canaan, an event recorded in Numbers 13:23–27. Finally, the huge bunch of grapes that signify the "land of milk and honey" and the prophecy of Deuteronomy 23:24 that the people of God would eat their fill of grapes, are reversed by Steinbeck as his chosen people, the **Joads** (whom some critics equate with the chosen tribe of Judah), find only misery and starvation in the lush soil of the California valleys.

The fact that Howe's song was associated with the Civil War also appealed to Steinbeck's plan for his novel given that he envisioned a new battle being waged for American soil—this time between the migrants and the large landowners.

Michael J. Meyer

HUENEKER, ALLEN. In ***The Pastures of Heaven***, Allen Hueneker, described as the ugliest, shyest man in the valley, is also set apart by his ape-like actions. Embarrassed by his looks, Allen's wife tells stories of his sexual prowess to account for their marriage, so it is no wonder that when he is seen on his way to **Monterey** with one of the Lopez sisters (known for their free sexual favors), the rumors begin. Started by **Bert Munroe**, these rumors eventually cause **Rosa** and **Maria Lopez**'s place of business to be shut down and shape their decision to leave the sheltered valley and become real prostitutes in San Francisco.

Michael J. Meyer

HUGH OF THE RED CASTLE, SIR. In ***The Acts of King Arthur*** one of two brothers who have taken the lands and Red Castle from the **Lady of the Rock**. He was defeated in combat by **Sir Gawain** during the Triple Quest.

HUGHES, HOWARD (1905–1976). Famous, eccentric Texas billionaire who took the tool-company fortune he inherited into ventures in film and aviation, among other things. As detailed in **Jackson J. Benson**'s biography, Steinbeck spent a long evening with Hughes at Chasen's Beverly Hills restaurant in 1940. Hughes, who had been producing Hollywood movies since 1924 and who eventually purchased RKO in 1947, wanted to involve Steinbeck in a movie project. Steinbeck had arranged for plans to get out of the dinner early, but these plans went awry when **Gwyndolyn Conger Steinbeck** and friend **Max Wagner**—vexed because Steinbeck had called for their help much later than planned—showed up with Gwyn's teeth blackened out and a great artificial globule hanging from Max's nose. Outside of the restaurant and away from Hughes, Steinbeck thought the gag was hilarious. Never really interested, Steinbeck did not go into a film venture with Hughes.

Further Reading: Benson, Jackson J. *The True Adventures of John Steinbeck, Writer.* New York: Viking, 1984.

HUGHIE. One of **Mack**'s "boys" in ***Cannery Row.***

HUMBERT, PAT. In ***The Pastures of Heaven***, an eligible bachelor in Las Pasturas, Pat Humbert is the only son of older parents, who are intolerant of his youthful ideas and who create a depressing atmosphere for his childhood. After his parents' death, Humbert is initially unable to suppress, either through work or through the companionship of his neighbors, the guilt or loneliness they have instilled in him. It is as if they are still alive, dominating his life. Plagued by the loneliness of his place, Humbert seeks companionship and participation in the community to help him erase the dismal past. When **Mae Munroe** provides the possibility of a love interest, he tries to restore the inside of the house and make it as beautiful as the Vermont farmhouse that Mae seems to covet. Soon, motivated by the cascading white rose bush that adorns the outside of the Humbert family place, Pat Humbert destroys the furniture and uncomfortable memories by burning them up. Then, using catalogs and pictures, he attempts to create an idyllic home suitable for a young wife, but he fails to tell Mae that his future wedding plans involve her. Thus, his effort to destroy the past and reconstruct a future fails when Mae announces her engagement to **Bill Whiteside.** The restored and redecorated home becomes a hollow shell without love, and Humbert retreats to the barn in despair at his failed plans.

Michael J. Meyer

HUNTER, MAJOR. In ***The Moon Is Down***, the senior-ranking member of the five who make up **Colonel Lanser**'s staff, all of whom manifest "herd men" characteristics that make them ill-suited as professional soldiers. Hunter is Steinbeck's character type for the cold, calculated view of war as nothing more than a technological puzzle. Aptly symbolized by the T-square and triangle he often wields, Hunter is an engineer and a technocrat who simplistically views men as mere numbers to be added and subtracted with mathematical precision. Like other members of the staff such as **Captain Bentick** and **Captain Loft**, he also is crippled by misguided dreams. However, unlike the others, Hunter's vision seems to be clouded not by lofty visions of military success or the good country life, but by his unswerving belief in the power of scientific logic and mathematical proficiency to solve the thorny problems of life. Unfortunately, such a perspective, though orderly and precise, also dehumanizes and limits. His several marriages fail, and he is unable to perceive the "humor, the music, or the mysticism" that a more qualitative perspective could provide.

Rodney P. Rice

HURRICANE DONNA. In the third section of part 1 of ***Travels with Charley***, Steinbeck battles to save his twenty-foot cabin boat, ***Fayre Eleyne*** (named after his wife, **Elaine Scott Steinbeck**), from Hurricane Donna. Although the hurricane causes substantial damage to the **Sag Harbor** (Long Island) area, Steinbeck manages to save the boat. The truck with which he plans to cross the country, **Rocinante**, is spared as well.

HUSTON, EZRA. *See* **Central Committee at Weedpatch Camp.**

HUSTON, JOHN (1906–1987). Famous, Oscar- nominated and -winning writer, director, and screenwriter—a true Hollywood Renaissance man whose career spanned six decades. During Steinbeck's marriage to **Elaine Scott Steinbeck**, the couple developed a good friendship with Huston, often visiting the director when they were overseas in Europe. Steinbeck and Huston discussed possible projects they might work on together, but these ideas were floated too late in Steinbeck's career (in the mid-1960s) and nothing came of their schemes.

Further Reading: Benson, Jackson J. *The True Adventures of John Steinbeck, Writer.* New York: Viking, 1984.

HYACINTHE, SISTER (NÉE SUZANNE LESCAULT). In ***The Short Reign of Pippin IV***, a nun and former dancer in the Follies

Bergère and a friend of **Pippin Héristal**'s wife, **Marie Héristal**. She serves as confidante and advisor to the new queen and her bewildered king. Sister Hyacinthe combines compassion and a long sense of history with a practical and skeptical assessment of human nature as well as a lively irreverence. When Pippin refuses her ruse to help him escape, facing instead possible persecution for confronting the parties who put him into office, she lauds his courage, recognizing more than others the nobility of his readiness for self-sacrifice.

Marilyn Chandler McEntyre

I

"I AM A REVOLUTIONARY" (1954). In this essay, first published in *Le Figaro* in 1954, Steinbeck disputes a published claim that he is not a revolutionary. He observes that Communist groups don't like him or his books precisely because he is revolutionary in his thinking and that the so-called revolutionaries (Communists) perpetually stamp out all strains of individuality and creativity because they threaten the status quo. Steinbeck expresses his resolve to "fight for the right of the individual to function as an individual without pressure from any direction."

Further Reading: Steinbeck, John. "I Am a Revolutionary." *America and Americans and Selected Nonfiction*. Ed. Susan Shillinglaw and Jackson J. Benson. New York: Viking, 2002. 89–90.

"I EVEN SAW MANOLETE . . ." (1970). A condensed version of **"Then My Arm Glassed Up"** (*Sports Illustrated*, December 20, 1965: 94–96, 99–102), published in *A Thousand Afternoons: An Anthology of Bull Fighting* (1970). Steinbeck critiques bull fighting, noting the bulls are laden with impediments and the matadors are avaricious cowards outside the ring. The bull fighter's dubious courage, Steinbeck asserts, is "not the kind the audience and the world needed or needs." He adds that he did see the matador, Manolete, even more times than **Hemingway** did.

Further Reading: Steinbeck, John. "I Even Saw Manolete . . ." *A Thousand Afternoons: An Anthology of Bull Fighting*. Ed. Peter Haining. New York: Cowles Book Co., 1970.

"I GO BACK TO IRELAND" (1953). Published in *Collier's* (January 31, 1953: 48–50), this reminiscence followed the completion of ***East of Eden*** and, according to **Jackson J. Benson**, reflects Steinbeck's urge to dwell on his own past and to compose based on nostalgia and personal memory. Other nostalgic pieces of the same era include **"The Making of a New Yorker"** and **"A Model T Named It."**

Further Reading: Steinbeck, John. "I Go Back to Ireland." *America and Americans and Selected Nonfiction*. Ed. Susan Shillinglaw and Jackson J. Benson. New York: Viking, 2002. 262–269.

IBSEN, HENRIK (1828–1906). Famous Norwegian dramatist considered the father of modern drama. Steinbeck praised Ibsen's great character construction and development of relationships. Like Steinbeck's novels, Ibsen's plays realistically deal with psychological and social problems. Later in life, during his stay in Paris in the fall of 1952, Steinbeck worked on a script based on an early Ibsen play called *The Vikings of Helgoland* (1858). Steinbeck had asked Ingrid Bergman whether she was interested in the lead role of the mythical woman Hjordis.

Bergman replied, "Thou art minded I play a woman mighty as Hjordis? Set thy hand at work." Though he ultimately produced a crude screenplay, the project was never realized, despite Bergmann's interest and support.

Steinbeck's earliest association with Ibsen, however, can be traced back to his college years at **Stanford University**, where he had developed an incongruous air around his persona as the introvert who knew a lot of people. What set him apart from his peers, though, can be attributed to his singular motivation rather than his solitary lifestyle. In a letter to **Carl Wilhelmson** in July of 1924, he writes, "I think rebellion man's highest state. . . . In the *Enemy of the People*, the Doctor says in his last speech that the strongest man in the world is he who is most alone. That line has come to mean more and more to me." Steinbeck's identification with Dr. Stockman of the Ibsen play suggests that he saw himself as the lonely idealist, a man cast out from and opposed by the respectable majority—a man ahead of his time, radical in his adherence to principle and in his vision.

Harry Karahalios

IDA, WIDE. In *Sweet Thursday*, owner of the **Café La Ida**, a bar on **Cannery Row** where **Eddie** works as a bartender. A strong woman, she is renowned for her ability to throw drunks out of her bar, though with one particularly vigorous launch she sprains her shoulder. **Mack**'s worries about the ownership of the **Palace Flophouse** begin when Wide Ida tells him that she has received her tax notice in the mail. She participates in the meeting at which Mack explains his plan to use a raffle to transfer ownership of the Palace to **Doc**. She also attends the masquerade party, where she is seen arm wrestling with **Whitey No. 2**.

Bruce Ouderkirk

"IF THIS BE TREASON" (1953). An unpublished article written in the fall of 1953 expressing Steinbeck's response to Senator Joseph McCarthy and the congressional committee that was investigating the influence of Communism in the arts and film community as well as in the government. While in Spain the following spring, Steinbeck wrote a strongly anti-McCarthy poem that, to his shock, upset his **Viking** publisher, **Harold Guinzburg**. Guinzburg did not want the poem published, and it suffered the same fate of "If This Be Treason."

IGNACIA, TIA. In *Tortilla Flat*, a successful forty-five-year-old widow who is able to seduce **Big Joe Portagee** in spite of himself. Tia is something of an outcast even in Tortilla Flat because of her "indecent" amount of Indian blood, and she is known for her harsh demeanor. But she has wine, and when Big Joe seeks refuge in her house on a rainy night, she attempts to use this commodity to satisfy the needs he awakens in her. When Joe falls asleep during her wooing, she chases him out of the house, and it is only when he embraces her to prevent her from beating him that Joe comes to share her feelings. The episode seems designed to demonstrate the brutality of Joe's character, which can only be stirred to love through violence.

Bryan Vescio

IGRAINE, THE LADY. In *The Acts of King Arthur*/ by **Merlin**'s magic contrivance, accepts **Uther Pendragon** to her bed, believing him to be her husband, the Duke of Cornwall, who had, unknown to her, been killed in battle three hours earlier. **Arthur** is conceived by their act of love. Shortly after her husband's death, she marries Uther Pendragon and Arthur is accordingly born in wedlock.

"IN AWE OF WORDS" (1954). Steinbeck's piece about writing that appeared in the seventy-sixth anniversary issue of the *Exonian* (March 3, 1954), the publication of Exeter Prep School. It was requested by the son of Steinbeck's close friend, **Nathaniel Benchley**, and was later reprinted posthumously as part of a Steinbeck interview that appeared in *The Paris Review* in Fall of 1969.

Considered by Steinbeck collector Preston Beyer to be a significant comment by the author on his craft, the piece echoes some of the ideas of Steinbeck's **Nobel Prize** acceptance speech, stating that "a man who writes a story is forced to put into the best of his knowledge and the best of his feeling. . . . a writer lives in awe of words for they can be cruel or kind, and they can change their meaning right in front of you."

Further Reading: Rice, Barbara A., Marilyn S. Shuffler, and Lynne B. Sagalyn. *John Steinbeck: The Collection of Preston Beyer.* Princeton, NJ: Princeton University Press, 1998. xv.

Michael J. Meyer

IN DUBIOUS BATTLE (1936). Steinbeck's fifth published novel narrates the last few days of the life of **Jim Nolan**, a young man who has lost his job in a department store after the police picked him up for watching a radical speaker; he was unjustly sentenced for vagrancy. The reader first meets him on the evening that he decides to leave his shabby rooming house and make a trip across the dark city (that resembles San Jose, California) to join an otherwise unidentified radical party. He is assigned to join the organizers of an applepickers' strike in the fictitious Torgas Valley. Steinbeck keeps his authorial spotlight focused always on Jim until he is killed during the strike by an explosion that blows off his face. This is a chronicle of a wasted life.

Because the novel appeared at the height of the production and condemnation of "proletarian" novels in the United States, it has frequently been consigned to that category and viewed as a political-philosophical tract, but such an assessment is an oversimplified and mistaken interpretation of Steinbeck's intentions.

Though influential theorist-critic Harold Bloom, in his series of collections of "Modern Critical Views," lists *In Dubious Battle* as one of Steinbeck's three best novels (with ***Of Mice and Men*** and ***The Grapes of Wrath***), he does not include an essay devoted to that novel perhaps because such critiques are infrequent and repetitious. Famed as a mapper of literary misreading, Bloom notes that *In Dubious Battle* "is now quite certainly a period piece, and is of more interest to social historians than to literary critics." Although it was praised even by radical reviewers and by such later critics as James Woodress as possibly the best strike novel that this country had produced, it is rather a fictional fantasy (like much of Steinbeck's work) that provides little information for social historians. However, as the **Milton**ic title suggests, the novel is a timely yet timeless recounting of the unending struggle between inimical forces seeking to control human destiny.

Although Steinbeck rarely chose to explain his writings publicly and often boasted gleefully about cocksure critics missing his point, he often worked out and defended his ideas in letters to his friends that were published only after his death. Not surprisingly, these provide more trenchant explanations of *In Dubious Battle* than his critics have. Maintaining that he was writing novels, not tracts, he explained to another aspiring novelist, **George Albee**, in January 1935, "I'm not interested in strikes as a means of raising men's wages, and I'm not interested in ranting about justice and oppression, mere outcroppings which indicate the condition, but man hates something in himself. He has been able to defeat every natural obstacle but himself, he cannot win unless he kills every individual."

Although these letters appeared only posthumously, the comments of Harry T. Moore, the distinguished author of the first monograph about Steinbeck, resemble closely the writer's own explanations. Moore may have talked to the author or his close associates in confidence. A **D. H. Lawrence** scholar, Moore admired the brutality that Steinbeck acknowledged in the novel and the hard-hitting style of narration. (Later he lost interest in what he considered the increasing sentimentalism in Steinbeck's later work.) He denied that *In Dubious Battle* was a "party line story," explaining that Steinbeck was trying not to take sides and quoting a letter to Steinbeck's agents in which the author avers that this novel has "no moral point of view." Steinbeck also denied that any character was autobiographical.

No more detailed review of *In Dubious Battle* was published for two decades, until **Peter Lisca**'s *The Wide World of John Steinbeck* (1958) appeared. Lisca established the long-continuing trend to emphasize the debates between the strike organizer **Mac** and **Doc Burton**, theorizing about the differences between group men and individual men, arguing that the mob and the strike through which it exists are the real protagonists of the book. But this counters Steinbeck's assertion that the strike is a mere "outcropping." The mob is not introduced until chapter 4, and it is never physically the central focus of the narrative. Readers never know, although the outcome seems in little doubt, what becomes of the strike or the mob. They rarely even view the action through the eyes of the strikers but rather view it through the speculations of the theorists. Nevertheless, Lisca's ideas—supported by **Richard Astro**'s important analysis of Steinbeck's use of his friend **Edward F. Ricketts**' ideas—have generally prevailed in subsequent criticism of the novel.

Since Steinbeck borrowed his title from John Milton, a small substream of influence hunters has attempted to find characters in the novel paralleling Christ, Satan, and other rebellious angels, as others have sought Arthurian parallels in ***Tortilla Flat***; but they have found it difficult to establish any consistent pattern of **biblical** or Miltonic influences in this novel that the author denied had any moral point of view. The tenor of Steinbeck's remarks to George Albee is that all human battles are "dubious," not in their outcome but in the nature of their sources. **Louis Owens** revitalized the discussion in *John Steinbeck's Revision of America* (1985). Though he still sees the strike as the surface story and Mac and Doc's debate as providing the novel "with much of its dynamic force," he examines principally Doc's position to argue that "the only conclusion that stands out clear and certain in this complex and ambiguous novel is that commitment is a necessity for man . . . even to the point of selfsacrifice and even for a cause of questionable merit." Although it is difficult to agree with Clifford Lewis's opinion that "Doc Burton's psychological and philosophical theories nearly destroy the novel," they certainly have served to obscure the focus of the novel. Owens undermines his summary argument by pointing out earlier that Jim's tragedy is indeed over-commitment—too much or too little, the outcome is the same. Owens has not taken seriously enough Steinbeck's injunction in his letter to George Albee: "I wanted to be merely a recording consciousness, judging nothing, simply putting down the thing." Owens is certainly justified in finding that *Tortilla Flat* and *In Dubious Battle* are Steinbeck's two most pessimistic novels, but he may also find that the endings of *Of Mice and Men* and *The Grapes of Wrath*, which followed, are now viewed more hopefully than may be warranted. In all four novels the "consciousness" that Steinbeck wished to be recorded was not a failure to make commitments, but was a matter of characters' making commitments that they were not capable of carrying out. (In *The Grapes of Wrath*, this failure applies mainly to **Casy**, not **Tom Joad**; however, one must recall that even in that novel, the characters in the end are still locked "in dubious battle.")

If one looks at *In Dubious Battle* from the viewpoint of "simply putting down the thing," as Steinbeck sought to do, it is hard to argue that the novel is about either a strike that has not been settled or an unresolved philosophical dispute—if there were any interest in such unfinished business; the novel is not fictionalized journalism about such "outcroppings," but a speculation about underlying conditions—both external and internal—that destroy individuals' opportunities for self-fulfillment.

In reading Steinbeck's novels of this early period, one must also take into consideration that much biographical information is available now about Steinbeck's own situation at that time. On April 26, 1957,

Steinbeck sent his editor **Elizabeth Otis** and his advisor **Chase Horton** copies of a letter about his continuing work on Malory. This correspondence contains an important paragraph for considering his concept of a "recording consciousness." "A novel may be said to be the man who writes it," he begins.

> Now it is nearly always true that a novelist, perhaps unconsciously identifies himself with one chief or central character in his novel. . . . We can call this spokesman the selfcharacter. You will find one in every one of my books. . . . I suppose my own symbol character has my dream wish of wisdom and *acceptance*.

Because many of Steinbeck's novels present characters with no parallels in his experience, his explaining that his "self-character" shares his dream is important. At the time that Steinbeck was writing *In Dubious Battle*, he was engaged in a dubious battle of his own. His first three novels, which had received little attention, were out of print, their publishers bankrupt; *Tortilla Flat*, his first successful work, had been turned down by so many publishers that he was about to give up on it. It was not until the success of *Of Mice and Men* as a novel and play that he had a sense of winning any of the "acceptance" of which he dreamed. In rapid succession, he produced three novels whose central characters are doomed by the frustration of their dreams, resulting in part from unwise actions. **Danny** in *Tortilla Flat* destroys himself and his dream of an ideal community for his friends because he cannot adjust to the demands that civilized society imposes upon a property owner; Jim Nolan is destroyed because others seek to exploit talents that he has not had adequate opportunity to develop; and **George Milton** in *Of Mice and Men* ends up with a blasted dream because **Lennie Small** is destroyed by natural defects that are beyond George's ability to control. All three reflect aspects of Steinbeck's despair over his apparent failure as a writer, the lack of acceptance of his work.

The self-character in *In Dubious Battle* is neither of the debaters, but the figure who is at the center of the action from the first words of the novel to the last. Through his eyes the reader perceives the action, from the curt, defeatist opening sentence, "At last it was evening," to the lantern light rhetoric of Mac's funeral oration, "'This guy didn't want nothing for himself'" (of course, he did want something—the very wisdom and acceptance that Steinbeck did). This is the tragedy of a wasted life, a promising young person whose talents and energies are not properly recognized or directed. Although Jim's actual experiences in no way mirror the author's, the fantasy is, as Steinbeck called it, "honest," because he draws upon his own feelings and frustrations in a world in which he is struggling desperately for his own survival, fearful that he may be predicting his own doom. After the unexpected success of these three doomsday novels, the writer's own life and work were to change greatly, somewhat ironically, on the success of what can be accurately called a trilogy of the underdogs.

Further Reading: Benson, Jackson J. *The True Adventures of John Steinbeck, Writer.* New York: Viking, 1984; Bloom, Harold, ed. *Modern Critical Views: John Steinbeck.* New York: Chelsea House, 1987; French, Warren. "Introduction," *In Dubious Battle.* New York: Penguin, 1992; Owens, Louis. *John Steinbeck's Re-vision of America.* Athens: University of Georgia Press, 1985; Steinbeck, Elaine, and Robert Wallsten, eds. *Steinbeck: A Life in Letters.* New York: Viking, 1975.

Warren French

IN TOUCH (1971). The Vietnam memoir by **John Steinbeck IV** (John Steinbeck's son) was published by Knopf in 1971. John IV writes about his experiences with the Vietnamese, the GIs, and his romantic interlude with that culture. He describes the tense and surrealistic atmosphere of demonstrations in the streets, knifings in bars, and bombs exploding everywhere. "In a duality that was getting harder for me to accept, Saigon Warriors. . . . could watch the war every night, sipping gin or smoking marijuana on the rooftop bars of all the hotels in Saigon. How insane that people should be fighting and dying and at the same time provide a cordite-flavored stage show for a military cocktail crowd while Filipino rock-and-roll singers at the bar produced the musical background. The drums and cymbals would sometimes sizzle with the concussion of a nearby explosion." In his depiction of the use of drugs during the war, John IV writes, "When the realization finally strikes home. . . . that each day may be his last the average soldier sees that for all intents and purposes the entire country is stoned. For a kid who has spent the last few years of his life going through much shoe leather and money in trying to locate marijuana, Vietnam is that huge garden he has always dreamed about. And to think the Army sent him there!"

John IV had gone to Vietnam as a hawk, but he returned to Washington as a dove. He writes about his drug bust, the trial, and the acquittal. His testimony to the Senate about the use of marijuana by American soldiers in Vietnam is included in his book as an appendix. In the final chapter, he tells the reader about a drive across the United States as he talks with friends about issues that were urgent to his generation-freedom, responsibility, education, the direction of their lives, meditation, and drugs.

Nancy Steinbeck

INDIANS. In *Viva Zapata!* many Mexican Indians appear, but those who are chatting and laughing in the stables where both **Don Nacio** and **Emiliano Zapata** are viewing some Arabian horses speak what Don Nacio calls "the Aztec language," which is actually Náhuatl, and because Emiliano, a Mexican Indian himself, is fluent in the language, he overhears that instead of a shipment of five Arabian horses, there were really ten. This fact enables Emiliano to be more of service to his boss, Don Nacio, and raises the latter's appreciation of Emiliano even more because he enviously admires Emiliano's ability to "understand the Indians."

INDIVIDUAL RIGHTS. The right of individuals to be treated justly is the heart of Steinbeck's political vision. The Joad family in ***The Grapes of Wrath*** embodies the revolutionary spirit that brought America's independence and its sense of individual worth. The novel expresses the feeling that economic and political oppression underlie the discontent of peoples everywhere. Steinbeck's strong belief in individual rights led to a December 15, 1941, letter to President **Franklin Delano Roosevelt** requesting that he respect the civil rights of Japanese American citizens during the war. In 1944, when Steinbeck listed programs that Roosevelt should pursue for America after the war, several dealt with individual welfare, including a call for the United States to protect human rights and to oppose tyranny abroad and a proposal "to protect our racial, religious and political minorities."

Mexico's revolutionary leader **Emiliano Zapata** was Steinbeck's ideal of the democratic man who fought to bring justice and asked for nothing in return. (In fact Steinbeck himself frequently reminded political leaders he advised that he wanted no rewards). Steinbeck researched Zapata and planned a movie that would celebrate the capability of the common man to defeat his oppressors. Steinbeck's script, however, prepared in the early 1950s, ran afoul of the House Un-American Activities Committee that saw a Communist conspiracy lurking everywhere. Consequently, Steinbeck's Hollywood bosses revised the ***Viva Zapata!*** script and turned a movie about an extraordinary man of justice into a feeble piece of anti-Communist propaganda.

This bitter experience with censorship led Steinbeck to identify with the presidential candidate **Adlai Stevenson**, who reminded Americans that freedom to think and to express one's ideas were essential to maintain our democracy. Steinbeck admired him for emphasizing that our nation should place integrity over profit. In their correspondence, each of the men condemned President Eisenhower's failure to offer the nation a moral vision. National decadence was Steinbeck's subject in ***The Winter of Our Discontent***, in which he argued that individuals knowingly elect evil deeds. Crooked quiz shows and crooked national leaders in business and politics (the first Nixon scandal) represent the declining state of public morality. But in the unconscious dreams that lead **Ellen Hawley** to pursue a moral course in life, Steinbeck reminds us that he has not lost faith in humanity's moral heritage or in the power of the moral individual.

Clifford Lewis

INGE, WILLIAM (1913–1973). American playwright, winner of the 1953 **Pulitzer Prize** for his play *Picnic*. Although it seems that Inge and Steinbeck never met, Steinbeck was familiar with his work, enough so that following Steinbeck's attendance of **Elia Kazan**'s Boston production of Inge's *The Dark at the Top of the Stairs*, Kazan asked him to make suggestions for improvements before the production opened in New York.

INGELS, BETH (1906–1975). Family friend of **Carol Henning Steinbeck** and John, Ingels was said to have supplied the author's initial idea for ***The Pastures of Heaven***. There is no doubt she knew the Steinbecks well, having opened an advertising agency with Carol in **Monterey** in 1931. Raised in the Corral de Tierra, Ingels had collected several real life experiences that she thought would make good material for a short-story sequence in the fashion of **Sherwood Anderson**'s *Winesburg, Ohio* (1919). Her idea for a unifying device was to depict a family that interacts with other valley residents and whose motives are ambiguous and questionable. As Steinbeck became more interested in the idea, he came to see the small valley as a microcosm for the world and determined to give his work the ironic title of *The Pastures of Heaven*. The powerful integration of individuals' dreams with societal expectations and the problematic use of scapegoats to escape personal flaws and problems both find a place in this story cycle. Ingels later became a part of the group of close friends who met at **Edward F. Ricketts**' lab.

Michael J. Meyer

INNOCÉNTE. In ***Viva Zapata!*** he is an old Mexican Indian farmer taken prisoner by five *rurales* for planting corn in what he still considered his field, but which no longer belongs to him or his fellow compatriots. It is now fenced in and heavily guarded, but he persists in going in and planting and defying the guards. When **Emiliano Zapata** finds a man in the custody of two rurales with a noose around his neck, he realizes that the Mexican Indian in custody is Innocénte. **Eufemio Zapata** offers him a drink and Emiliano begs one of the rurales to release him, but instead the rural jerks on the rope, and Innocénte falls to the ground and dies.

"IS" THINKING. *See* **Non-teleological Thinking**.

J

JACKSON, JOSEPH HENRY (1894–1955). Employed by the *San Francisico Chronicle* as a book critic, Jackson was one of the first to acknowledge Steinbeck's talent in the early thirties before the success of ***Tortilla Flat***. Later he and his wife, Charlotte, became close friends with Steinbeck and his first wife, Carol, often inviting them to parties in their Berkeley home and even vacationing with them in Mexico.

JACKSON, TONI (1911–). Born Eleanor Susan Solomons, she married Ben O. Jackson (1894–1963) and divorced him at a later unknown date. They had a daughter, Kate. Solomons was known as Toni Jackson when **Edward F. Ricketts** met her. Associated with the group of discussants who met at Ricketts' lab, Jackson lived with Ed Ricketts for seven years as his common-law wife and even took his name for a time. A journalist and political liberal, she also served as secretary to Steinbeck in 1941, answering letters from his admirers and doing much of the typing of the manuscript of *The **Sea of Cortez***.

After her daughter died in 1947, she left Ed and eventually married Ben. E. Volcani (1915–99). They had one child, son Yanon, born 1949. In 1948, Jackson became Steinbeck's office manager during his participation in a venture called World Video and warned the author about the risks involved in the company's attempt to package film shows for sale to TV networks.

Michael J. Meyer

JAMES, WILLIAM (1842–1910). American psychologist, philosopher, and writer of inspirational literature, James was also a radical empiricist, a pluralist, and a pragmatic teacher. James had a rather unique upbringing, thanks to his father, studying both science and art before receiving a degree in medicine from Harvard University in 1869. His *The Varieties of Religious Experience* (1902) combines philosophy and psychology and embraces nondogmatic religions, which need be neither isolated nor universal to be valid. As briefly discussed by **Robert DeMott**, Steinbeck at least reviewed several of James's books, including *Varieties* and *Pragmatism* (1907; read while a student at **Stanford University**). Steinbeck makes direct reference to *Psychology, A Briefer Course* (1892) and to the two-volume *Principles of Psychology* (1928) in ***East of Eden***.

Further Reading: DeMott, Robert. *Steinbeck's Reading; A Catalogue of Books Owned and Borrowed*. New York: Garland, 1984.

JAPAN. After the United States, arguably the country most involved with Steinbeck studies. The first Steinbeck works printed in Japanese, ***Of Mice and Men*** and ***The Grapes of Wrath*** (chapters 1–17), were published in 1939, one year before the first two scholarly articles appeared in 1940. Today, most of Steinbeck's works have been translated into Japanese. In 2000, the Osaka Kyoiku Tosho Publishing Company completed a 20-volume

Japanese translation: *The Complete Works of John Steinbeck*. In addition, Steinbeck works such at *The Grapes of Wrath* and *Of Mice and Men* have been performed in Japanese theaters. Although scholars lagged behind general readers in Steinbeck reception initially, the situation has improved. In Japan, Steinbeck now competes favorably with his American contemporaries in terms of the number of scholarly works written about him. Moreover, Steinbeck studies in Japan have an international aspect. The John Steinbeck Society of Japan has cosponsored four international congresses with the International John Steinbeck Society and another with the **Martha Heasley Cox Steinbeck Research Center** of San Jose State University. Moreover, its annual conferences have attracted major Steinbeck scholars from abroad. Studies have indicated Steinbeck's interest in Eastern thought—Taoism, Buddhism, and Confucianism—which may account for an American author having such a vibrant following in the Pacific Rim.

Further Reading: *Kenkyusha Yearbook of English*. Tokyo: Kenkyusha, annual; Nakayama, Kiyoshi, ed. *Steinbeck in Japan: A Bibliography* (1939–1992). Suita-shi, Osaka: Kansai University Press, 1992; Nakayama, Kiyoshi, Scott Pugh, and Shigeharu Yano, eds. *John Steinbeck: Asian Perspectives*. Osaka: Osaka Kyoiku Tosho, 1992.

Yasuo Hashiguchi

JEFFERS, ROBINSON (1887–1962). American poet who was born in Pittsburgh, Pennsylvania, and moved to California with his family when still a teenager; Steinbeck read several of his books. Jeffers graduated from Occidental College when only seventeen and later studied at the University of Southern California and the University of Washington. In 1913 he married the recently divorced Una Call Kuster, and the following year, he moved to **Carmel**. Jeffers spent his life there, writing verse that brought to readers the rugged beauty of the central California coast, often through the use of symbols suggested by the natural world, most notably the red-tailed hawk whose characteristics of fierce courage and disinterestedness Jeffers admired. Jeffers set an example for the young John Steinbeck, who respected the work of the older writer and, like Jeffers, responded to his surrounding landscape with great sensitivity and imagination, though Steinbeck found inspiration in rural valley settings more often than Jeffers did.

In 1925 Jeffers published his breakthrough book, *Roan Stallion, Tamar and Other Poems*. "Tamar" voiced Jeffers's feeling for how archetypal patterns are embedded in human behavior and his developing sense of the place of human beings as only a small part of the majestic natural world (represented in the poem through Jeffers's vivid descriptions of the Point Lobos setting). Jeffers later coined the term *inhumanism* to describe this perspective. After *Tamar*, most of Jeffers's books appeared in volumes containing a substantial narrative poem—usually set along the California coast between Big Sur and Carmel—and a gathering of shorter ones. Among these volumes are *The Women at Point Sur* (1927), *Cawdor and Other Poems* (1928), and *Give Your Heart to the Hawks and Other Poems* (1933). In 1932 Jeffers published one of his best collections, *Thurso's Landing and Other Poems*, and his photograph appeared on the cover of *Time*.

Meanwhile, Steinbeck was just discovering the poetry of his **Monterey** County neighbor, with "Roan Stallion" making a particular impression. Steinbeck's aim at the time was translating "my people and my country" into his third book, ***To a God Unknown***. In fact, Steinbeck's novel seems influenced by Jeffers's "The Women at Point Sur," given that the main characters in both works—**Joseph Wayne** in Steinbeck's novel and Reverend Barclay in Jeffers's poem—sacrifice themselves, believing that their deaths are necessary to bring renewal to the land. Jeffers's reputation declined after he became the subject of harsh treatment by New Critics, who often felt that Jeffers's long narratives were too loosely constructed and didactic. (Critics sometimes assailed Steinbeck's work for the same faults.) Still, Jeffers continued to write memorable works, including his free adaptation of Euripides' *Medea* (1946)—written for Judith Anderson—and *Hungerfield and Other Poems* (1954), the title poem written to express grief over Una's death from cancer in 1950.

Further Reading: Beers, Terry. *". . . a thousand graceful subtleties": Rhetoric in the Poetry of Robinson Jeffers*. New York: Lang, 1995; Brophy, Robert. *Robinson Jeffers: Myth, Ritual and Symbol in His Narrative Poems*. Cleveland, OH: Case Western Reserve University Press, 1973; Karman, James. *Robinson Jeffers: Poet of California*, rev. ed. Brownsville, OR: Story Line Press, 1995. The standard text for Jeffers's work is *The Collected Poetry of Robinson Jeffers*. Ed. Tim Hunt. 5 vols. Stanford: Stanford University Press, 1988.

Terry Beers

JEHOVITE WOMEN, THE SIX. These women offer to say prayers over **Granma** in ***The Grapes of Wrath*** when the Joads are about to cross over into California. Implying that a revivalist meeting of shouting and wailing will be more beneficial to Granma than the careful concern of **Ma Joad** and **Rosasharn**, these women provide still another instance of Steinbeck's dislike for formal religions. Lacking sensitivity, the Jehovites howl and jump like beasts or hyenas, sobbing and grunting as if they were less than human; in short they bring more disturbance than comfort and consolation to a dying soul.

JELKA'S COUSIN. The nameless cousin and lover of **Jelka Moore** in **"The Murder."** Although **Jim Moore** has rid his farm of "pigs" in favor of stallions, a metaphorical one returns in the form of the Slavic man whose attention Jelka prefers to Jim's. Jim murders the cousin—whom he pointedly refers to as a pig—and, aided by other law-enforcement officials, avoids paying any penalty for his crime.

JENNY. In ***East of Eden***, also known as "Fartin' Jenny," the owner of one of the whorehouses in **Salinas**. In contrast to **The Nigger**'s or **Faye**'s, Jenny's was merry and light-hearted.

JINGLEBALLICKS, OLD (OLD JAY). A wealthy scientist who visits **Doc** at Western Biological and later offers him a research position. In a novel that features a panoply of unusual characters, the Dickensian Old Jingleballicks stands out as the most eccentric figure of ***Sweet Thursday***. The suggestive name is one that **Edward F. Ricketts** had used to refer to a professor he disliked. Steinbeck brings Old Jay into the novel after Doc and **Suzy**'s first date to provide some comic relief during the period leading up to the masquerade party. The presence of Old Jay during this stage reduces the sentimentality of the love story. Through his discussions with Doc, Old Jay also serves to raise some serious ideas that provide a thematic counterweight to the banal concerns of the romance's plotline. At the same time, Old Jay helps to advance this plot to its obligatory happy conclusion.

He is described as a stubby man with yellow hair and with eyes "bright as a bird's." His friendship with Doc is probably based on his intellectual curiosity, a trait demonstrated when he is seen kneeling on his hands and knees, with a scale between his teeth, pulling a worm from the ground to discover how much resistance it would exert. If Old Jay seems too bizarre to be believed, Steinbeck frankly concedes as much, introducing this character with the admission, "It is madness to write about Old Jingleballicks." Similarly, Doc tells Old Jay, "you're just not possible! You're a ridiculous idea." Through such reflexive touches, Steinbeck ensures that his plot is openly viewed as a fiction, and this is one way that *Sweet Thursday* escapes the banality of the conventional romance.

Old Jingleballicks is also used to introduce into the novel ideas that confute those derived from its romance formula. First, when he engages in a debate with Doc about whether the human race is likely to endure long, Old Jay takes the position that humanity will reproduce itself into oblivion—an idea that clearly undercuts the romantic theme that love conquers all.

Further Reading: Fontenrose, Joseph. *John Steinbeck: An Introduction and Interpretation*. New York: Barnes and Noble, 1963.

Bruce Ouderkirk

JOAD, AL. The sixteen-year-old son of the Joads in ***The Grapes of Wrath***, Al reaches maturity abruptly and acquires credibility in the family council when his knowledge of car and machines becomes essential to the group. Generally cocksure of himself at the book's start, Al does admire his brother **Tom Joad** for his violent temperament and his refusal to let others push him around. In fact, it is a trait Al tries to emulate. Yet he also resents Tom's return to the family just as Al has acquired respect as an adult, for it undermines his newly acquired confidence. Al's recently found sexuality is also a factor throughout the book, and early on he is depicted as a "tom-cat," concerned for the most part with his own sexual satisfaction rather than a lengthy commitment to another. Perhaps this emphasis on his sexual prowess is designed to reflect an earlier version of his brother, Tom, or of the preacher **Casy**. Al also mirrors the pride and stubbornness of his younger sister **Ruthie Joad** in his desire to receive attention, praise, and recognition rather than give credit and acknowledgment to others, and like his brother-in law, **Connie Rivers**, he fantasizes about having a lot of "jack" and living a "Hollywood" life as portrayed in the motion pictures. Although his sense of commitment seems to develop toward the end of the book with his engagement to **Aggie Wainwright**, for the majority of the novel he is a character whose selfish nature overcomes his more noble tendencies toward brotherhood and whose short temper often leads to arguments.

Michael J. Meyer

JOAD, GRANMA. In ***The Grapes of Wrath*** Granma is described by Steinbeck as very religious, and therefore she is attracted to the preacher **Casy**, often replying to his words with "Amen!" and "Hallelujah!" Though she lacks true understanding of his new philosophy, there is a sense of security in a reliance on a higher being. She seems to enjoy a domineering role over her failing husband, who in his senility is becoming uncontrollable and forgetful. Rather than fostering charity, she points out his flaws, berating his inability to control himself. Immediately after his death, Granma seems to crumble physically, reacting with stunned surprise to **Granpa Joad**'s quick stroke and slowly deteriorating as she realizes the loneliness that any move will now bring. By the time the Joads reach the California border, Granma is hallucinating and talking to her dead husband. Although **Ma Joad** rejects the Jehovite women's offer to pray over her, the old woman momentarily seems better and sleeps peacefully for a short time. However, by the time the family crosses the desert, she has become the second of the Joads (again from the first generation) who is unable to survive the wilderness journey and who succumbs before she can be transplanted successfully into the longed-for promised land.

Michael J. Meyer

JOAD, GRANPA. In ***The Grapes of Wrath***, Granpa is portrayed as a randy old man who is gradually falling into senility. His brash nature often causes conflicts with his wife, and though his mind is failing, he is initially very vocal about his desire to experience the "promised land" of California. But as the departure time looms, Granpa becomes more reluctant and reticent, refusing to board the truck and asserting his right to remain on the land of Oklahoma even though it has lost its fertility. Nevertheless, the family decides he must accompany them, and he is drugged with a "soothin' syrup" that puts him to sleep and allows him to be loaded for the journey. His trip is short, however, because he falls ill quickly, speaking incoherently and expressing regret at his forced departure from his home. Before they pass the Oklahoma border, the Joads are forced to stop because of his illness, and Granpa dies of a quick stroke in the tent of **Ivy** and **Sairy Wilson**, two other migrants. Despite the fact that it is illegal, Granpa's body is buried in an unmarked grave with the help of the Wilsons. His grandson, **Tom Joad**, provides a Bible passage that suggests forgiveness of his sins, and in his eulogy, **Casy** suggests his death resulted from separation from the land. Granpa's death is the first indication that the older generation will not survive the wilderness journey and will not enjoy the land of milk and honey that has been promised in the handbills.

Michael J. Meyer

JOAD, MA. Initially described by Steinbeck in ***The Grapes of Wrath*** as "the citadel of the family, the strong place that can not be taken," Ma demonstrates a high sense of dignity and calm in this time of trouble. She is consistently the protector of the family, but she is especially concerned for **Tom Joad** because of his former imprisonment at McAlester. Although she begins the journey with a limited idea of brotherhood, concentrating rather on her individual family, she demonstrates her willingness to share with others, even as she is first introduced, by inviting **Jim Casy** to join them at breakfast and to accompany them on their journey.

Early on, she demonstrates her flexibility, a key factor in surviving the odyssey she faces, through her acceptance of Casy's doing "women's work" and in her sorting through the remnants of the Joads' life and determining what is of ultimate value and what will be discarded. Her comment, "I never heard tell of no Joads, or no Hazletts neither, ever refusin' food and shelter or a lift on the road to any body that asked" sets the stage for her openness to the new philosophy of self that is advocated by Casy, a philosophy in which sharing is a dominant feature of faith. As the journey continues, many episodes evidence Ma's learning process in this new way of living. For example, she embraces the Wilson's cooperation and help after **Granpa Joad**'s death, and she successfully conceals **Granma Joad**'s death from the border inspectors as the family enters California.

Ma initially seems to shift back and forth between a limited perspective of family and Casy's far wider definition, and her determination to keep the group together without losses is fierce. As the size of the entourage begins to dwindle, however, Ma is one of the earliest to realize the truth of Casy's discovery of the oneness of all mankind. Although she is dismayed by the negative treatment the family receives from the Californians and the demeaning and derogatory use of the term "Okie," Ma learns to stop feeling mean and ashamed and to feel like "people" again.

Often labeled an Earth Mother by critics, Ma is readily associated with nourishment, food, and shelter, demonstrating her generosity by sharing meals with Casy and the Wilsons, offering the leftovers of a stew to the children in the Hooverville and coffee and pone to the **Women's Committee at the Weedpatch camp**, and always scrimping and saving to provide special meals for the family when possible. In addition, she shows marked concern for Tom's safety and shelter when he kills the vigilante, and she shares the railway car with the Wainwrights in acknowledgment that their need is as great as the Joads.

Nonetheless, Ma's power and strength are given equal space by the author as shown in the jack-handle incident, in the threatening of the deputy with the skillet, and in her determined decision-making and assertiveness, accepting the role of leader almost instinctively. Though it takes Ma a while to comprehend the fact that her initial dreams of a house and steady work in the new Eden will not be forthcoming, she tries to convince Tom about the importance of staying together: "Goin' away ain't goin' to ease us. It's gonna bear us down. . . . There ain't no fambly anymore." This speech, when combined with her comment to Mrs. Wainwright—"Use t'be fambly was fust. It ain't so now. It's any body. Worse off we get, the more we got to do" indicates how far Ma has progressed in her thinking. All men and women are now her responsibility.

As Ma plans Tom's escape and helps him hide from the vigilantes, her self-sacrificial attitude grows. As a woman she is like a river "all one flow, like a stream, little eddies, little waterfalls, but goin' right on." Her knowledge that the people will survive even if individuals are lost, as expressed to Tom—"Why we're the people—we go on"—is now brought to fruition as she endures the death of **Rosasharn**'s baby in the boxcar and is then rewarded by her daughter's totally unselfish act of offering her breast to an old man whom they find dying of starvation in a deserted barn. With her eldest daughter's sacrificial act, Ma sees clearly how committed to others one must be; like Tom and Rosasharn, she is willing to turn disasters into the divine for the sake of brotherhood.

Michael J. Meyer

JOAD, NOAH. The oldest Joad brother in *The Grapes of Wrath* is described by Steinbeck as strange, having been misshapen at birth by **Pa Joad** when the midwife arrived late. Isolated from others, "yet not lonely," Noah is characterized by listlessness and a lack of caring about life in general. Silent and calm, he seems to follow his family blindly and without reason until he arrives at the Colorado River, which proves a soothing and relaxing source of life for him. Unwilling to leave this place, Noah announces to **Tom Joad** his intention to stay by the reviving water, living simply from his immediate surroundings. His leaving and his decision to conceal himself in a cave of willows foreshadow Tom's later departure. His removal lessens the nuclear family once again, but it also symbolically predicts the future of the Joads. Despite the impending floods in California, there is no place for a Noah figure there. There are no new beginnings, no second chances, no opportunities for starting over. Though the water images found at the river are positive signals for the Joads after the wasteland drought of Oklahoma, the myth of man's rebirth and God's promise for renewal is shown to be increasingly unattainable in California. Biblical savior figures such as Noah, Moses, and even the historical Christ himself are ineffectual when men refuse to help each other and have such a limited concept of brotherhood.

JOAD, PA. After **Granpa Joad**'s death, Pa is the titular male head of the family in *The Grapes of Wrath*, though his wife makes most of the decisions. Pa is cowed by the major changes that have taken place in his world, including the loss of his land, the aggressiveness of his wife, the newly found mechanical talents of his son **Al Joad**, and the unexpected return of **Tom**. He feels guilty about the condition of his oldest son, **Noah Joad,** and is constantly upbraiding himself for his offspring's isolated condition, blaming his own panic at the child's birth for Noah's misshapen body and his inability to fit in with others.

Pa attempts, mostly unsuccessfully, to cope with these changes and to help **Uncle John Joad** cope with his guilt as well. But as **Ma Joad** notes, men live in jerks and starts, and Pa often finds himself puzzled and dismayed by a world that seems confused and unreal. Often his reaction expresses his own personal frustration at his condition. Only toward the end of the novel, when he organizes the working crew to build the dike that will hold back the water from the boxcars, does he begin to understand the lessons of **Casy** regarding the brotherhood of all humankind; he states, "If we was all to get our shovels an' throw up a bank, I bet we could keep her out!" Before that, he is merely stunned by the large requirements of brotherhood and the shift brought about in his family, especially in Ma, by Casy's new philosophy.

Michael J. Meyer

JOAD, ROSE OF SHARON (ROSASHARN). *See* **Rivers, Rose of Sharon Joad ("Rosasharn").**

JOAD, RUTHIE. In *The Grapes of Wrath,* known for her selfishness, Ruthie is the second-youngest Joad. Part little girl and part developing woman, Ruthie is at the awkward age of twelve, recognizing her impending maturity but still drawn to immature actions. She prides herself on her knowledge and ability and enjoys bullying others with her supposed expertise even when her intelligence is obviously lacking.

Episodes throughout the book indicate Ruthie's unchanging negative attitude about others. For example, she is unwilling to share when playing ball at the **Weedpatch** camp, and later in the novel, she refuses to share her Cracker Jack with other children, resulting in a fight. Finally, near the novel's conclusion, she is reluctant to share the petals from the red geranium with her brother **Winfield Joad**, seemingly never learning the lessons of brotherhood so evident in the experiences that surround the family. Often depicted as cruel and mean, Ruthie is evidence that the lessons of charity and generosity do not reach everybody. Her insensitivity is also shown by her consistent tattling about her brother Winfield's mistakes and by her revelation in a childish quarrel that her brother **Tom Joad** is a killer and is hiding out nearby, thereby threatening his safety and the general good of all the Joads.

Michael J. Meyer

JOAD, TOM. Considered by many the protagonist in ***The Grapes of Wrath***, despite his early departure before the book's end, Tom—like **Ma Joad** and **Rosasharn**—is deeply affected by **Jim Casy** and his new doctrine of brotherhood. As the book begins, Tom is on his way home to Sallisaw, having just been released from McAlester Prison, where he had been serving time for the killing of Herb Turnbull in a barroom brawl. Clearly not known for his belief in brotherhood at this point, Tom demonstrates his mistrust in humanity first in his surly attitude toward the truck driver whom he accuses of being too nosy and later when he relates his lack of remorse for his crime as he talks to Jim Casy. In addition, his decision to pick up the land turtle and interrupt its journey also demonstrates his insensitivity to nature and his desire to impose his will on others rather than offer help or assistance.

But Tom discovers that much has changed in Oklahoma since his imprisonment. His family has been tractored off their land and is preparing to head off for California. It is only by chance that he arrives in time to join them on this journey, which often bears resemblances to the stories of biblical Exodus or the classical *Odyssey*. When Tom reacquaints himself with the preacher, Jim Casy, his spiritual and physical journeys begin, and the changes that result are the most important ones in the novel. As Tom listens to Casy recount his self-evaluation in the wilderness and tell of the changes in his belief system, Tom is initially cynical, but he begins to relate to some elements of the new faith. His first step in adapting Casy's doctrine of brotherhood to his own life is his invitation to the preacher to accompany the family on their journey. Despite the fact that this will mean less for the Joads and will add another individual to an already crowded truck, the family agrees, citing the history of sharing in their Joad and Hazlett ancestors.

Tom's return is given another biblical analogy in Casy's reference to the parable of the prodigal son, in which the selfish and reckless younger son is welcomed back after squandering his inheritance and is even given a feast to celebrate his safe return. When Tom relates his nickname, "Jesus Meek," readers also are able to predict his eventual role as the leader of the tribe that is headed toward a new Eden, a heavenly Jerusalem in the West. Like Moses in the wilderness, Tom and Casy will lead the Joads through the desert and the dustbowl toward a promised land. Although Casy is the one with the striking initials of J. C., his new doctrine is destined to be spread by his converts, and Tom begins his education for such a task along the road.

Though Tom at first has a tendency to be clannish and isolated, he finds new approaches to brotherhood as he watches Casy in action. Here the analogue to the Good Samaritan is evident as Casy attempts to bind up the wounds of the travelers, and Tom follows in his footsteps. For example, upon **Granpa Joad**'s death, Tom applies Casy's doctrine of "There ain't no sin" in his choice of Bible verses to be interred with the old man. He rejects "God have mercy on his soul" as too judgmental and chooses instead a passage that stresses forgiveness and sin being covered. He also recognizes that a travel partnership with the **Wilsons** will be beneficial to both families, acknowledging that one car can be used for transporting goods, thus lightening the human load and making hills more manageable and traveling more comfortable.

At other times, however, Tom is quick-tempered and stubbornly proud, and his initial reactions to others he meets along Route 66 indicate that he has not totally understood Casy's newfound faith and that the education of his heart is incomplete. For example, he upbraids both the fat man at the service station and the one-eyed man at the junkyard, at times cruelly mocking them and chastening them for their lack of action and for their whining and complaining about the conditions they are forced to endure. In another situation, Tom blames his brother **Al Joad** when a bearing on the truck burns out, accusing him of not accepting responsibility for his actions. Such hot-headed acts of anger and spite indicate that Tom is still leery of trust and commitment to his neighbors as well as to his own immediate family and that perhaps Ma's fear that he has become "mean-mad" like **Purty Boy Floyd** as a result of his imprisonment is justified.

Tom also functions as the realist in the Joad family, realizing early on the deception of the handbills about available work and pragmatically trying to cope with the potential disasters that may face the family in California after they cross the desert. Discussing his doubts with Ma, he receives reassurance of the strength of "the people" whom Ma sees as enduring even as the immediate family begins to crumble around her.

After reaching the Hooverville in California, Tom learns firsthand about the lack of brotherhood practiced by the growers and producers, and he performs his first deliberate act of brotherhood by tripping the deputy who is turning to shoot the escaping **Floyd Knowles**. His own selfless act for a stranger, however, is soon superseded by Casy, who agrees to take the blame for Tom's defiance and thus prevents a potential discovery of Tom's past criminal record and the fact that he has broken parole.

Tom's continued education in brotherhood and sharing is then fostered at the Weedpatch Camp where Timothy and Wilkie **Wallace** not only invite him for breakfast but also help him get work by sharing their jobs with him. Of course, Tom is also influenced in Casy's absence by the role-modeling of Ma Joad, who continues to demonstrate generosity in her interactions with the poor and helpless who surround the family. He also is affected by the deterioration and disintegration of his nuclear family, which by this point in the novel, has lost Granpa Joad, **Granma Joad**, **Noah Joad**, and **Connie Rivers**. All of the lost fall victim to two potential roadblocks to success, succumbing either to exhaustion and inability to cope with despair or to a more selfish lifestyle that places the individual before the group.

As the novel draws to a close, Tom's reencounter with Casy at the Hooper Ranch offers the final lesson in his spiritual education and completes his journey toward a new faith. Casy, like Christ, is not only willing to suffer imprisonment to bring about a sense of brotherhood; he is also ready to die for it. His example of fearless sacrifice inspires Tom's total commitment to his cause. Like the biblical Saul turned Paul, he is converted, and like the biblical Peter, his first reaction is to try to save his master through violence, striking down those who attack him.

As his personal story repeats itself with a second murder, Tom's face is marked, Cain-like, and like his biblical predecessor, Tom is forced to go into exile or hiding to avoid retribution for his crime. Though he must live in hiding like the nomadic wanderer of old, Tom vows to pick up Casy's mantle and to continue his fight. He will cope with his dual heritage as Cain and "Jesus Meek," trying to emphasize the light over the dark, letting good triumph over evil.

Quoting Ecclesiastes, Tom stresses the importance of brotherhood and then reiterates Casy's earlier contention that "a feller ain't got a soul of his own, but only a piece of a big one." His emotional speech to Ma, before disappearing from sight, reiterates the transition he has made from his early stages to a more confident savior figure. Like Christ, he even enters a cave and then reappears, suggesting a type of resurrection. Echoing Jesus's promise to his disciples before his ascension ("Lo I am with you always, even to the end of an age," Matthew 28:20), Tom says, "I'll be aroun' in the dark. I'll be ever'where—wherever you look. Wherever they's a fight so hungry people can eat, I'll be there. Wherever they's a cop beatin' up a guy, I'll be there. . . . Why, I'll be in the way guys yell when they're mad an—I'll be in the way kids laugh when they're hungry and they know supper's ready. And when *our folks* [italics added] eat the stuff they raise an' live in the houses they build—why I'll be there."

Michael J. Meyer

JOAD, UNCLE JOHN. **Pa Joad**'s brother, John is depicted in ***The Grapes of Wrath*** as an isolated and sorrowful man. Cut off from society because of his guilt over the accidental death of his young wife from appendicitis, John is described as "crazy" and "mean." Later, **Tom Joad** relates that because he ignored and minimized another's pain out of his own ignorance, Uncle John needed two years of a trance-like state before he began his self-punishment.

Becoming more and more depressed as the journey continues, John yearns for death, hoping to find release in a spiritual rather than physical Eden. Using money that he has selfishly withheld from the group, he gets drunk to dull his pained senses. He refuses to acknowledge that his sins are no greater than anyone else's, and his glum disposition allows him to bring down the emotional highs of others. At times family members have to physically assault him to break his depression. At the end of the novel, John is given the task of burying **Rosasharn**'s stillborn baby. Instead, he places the body in a discarded apple box (symbolic of man's fallen state) and sets it on the flood, urging the corpse to go down to the town and tell of the dilemma of the poor. For most of the book, however, he is inactive, trying to recede from brotherhood, eliciting sympathy and pity for his own personal state. Through Uncle John, Steinbeck seems to suggest that at critical times a strict rule-bound religion, insistent on punishment and revenge, is an unconscionable luxury and must be rejected before the guilt-engendered person brings about destruction.

Michael J. Meyer

JOAD, WINFIELD. Innocent, naïve, and the youngest of the Joads in ***The Grapes of Wrath***, Winfield, age ten, is described as grime-faced and wild. He is often awed by the newness of what he sees as he journeys from Oklahoma to California. Surprisingly, although he begins as a snot-nosed kid, he changes to a confused preteen, and his usual childish reactions are occasionally replaced by thoughtful reflection. For the most part, Winfield serves as a foil for **Ruthie Joad**'s pride, and his rivalry with his sibling is his essential role, revealing the lack of brotherhood even in a nuclear family. Eventually, Winfield's illness, a result of lack of nutrition, causes the Joads to become even more desperate for money so that they can buy nourishing food for their youngest.

Michael J. Meyer

JOADS, THE. Steinbeck's representative "Okies" in ***The Grapes of Wrath*** consist of eleven extended family members, including three generations: the elderly grandparents; **Ma** and **Pa Joad** and **Uncle John Joad**, Pa's brother; and Ma and Pa's six children, **Noah, Tom, Rose of Sharon, Al, Ruthie**, and **Winfield Joad**. When joined by Rose of Sharon's husband, **Connie Rivers**, the twelve family members become disciples of the newly reborn preacher **Jim Casy**, who has discovered a new religion based on the concept that all men need to recognize themselves as a part of a larger whole. Though the Joads have previously been a nuclear family merely concerned with their own welfare, and though they have failed in their responsibility to their land and to their fellow man in the past, they are found worthy. Some critics, such as **Peter Lisca**, have even likened their last name to that of the chosen people: the tribe of Judah, the Jewish nation. As they begin their journey from the wasteland of Oklahoma to the paradise of California, each member of the family is given the opportunity to examine whether he or she will adapt to this new philosophy, a philosophy that advocates the family of man rather than a selective and specific nuclear family. Some Joads die, some leave the group, and some reject the proffered opportunity, preferring to remain self-centered. However, some receive Casy's message and choose to become newly orientated to all humankind instead of to a select few.

Michael J. Meyer

"JOAN IN ALL OF US, THE" (1954). Appearing in 1954 in *Le Figaro* and *John O' London's Weekly*, and then in 1956 in *The Saturday Review* (January 14), Steinbeck's article comments on the appeal of the Joan of Arc story as a constant theme for writers. He believes the miraculous details of the story with the documented facts of it mean it "could not possibly have happened—and did," which to Steinbeck is the true miracle. Steinbeck himself explored the story in an unpublished work, "**The Last Joan**."

Further Reading: Steinbeck, John. "The Joan in All of Us." In *America and Americans and Selected Nonfiction*. Ed. Susan Shillinglaw and Jackson J. Benson. New York: Viking, 2002.

Eric Skipper

JOAN OF ARC. *See* "***Last Joan, The***."

JOE, THE ITALIAN MECHANIC. In his discussion about mobile homes and mobile home parks near the end of part 2 of ***Travels with Charley***, Steinbeck recalls a dinner he shared with a family who lived in a mobile home. In their conversation, the father—the son of Italian immigrants—and Steinbeck discuss the meaning of family roots and permanency. Joe, a good auto mechanic, has a dream of buying a used mobile home and gutting it out so that he can use it as a repair shop. He then wants to travel from park to park, rent a temporary spot, and repair the cars of mobile-home owners. When business would drop off, he would then move on to another park. Near Toledo, Ohio, the memory leads Steinbeck to one of his "conversations" with **Charley** about American immigration, rootedness, restlessness, and mobility.

Thom Tammaro

JOE, THE PILOT. In ***Bombs Away***, the farm boy from South Carolina who graduates from agricultural school and applies for entrance into the Air Force. After completing a variety of tests, he gets accepted for flight training on the basis of his intelligence, poise, and alertness.

Rodney P. Rice

JOE SAUL. *See* **Saul, Joe**.

JOEY. A boy in ***Cannery Row*** whose father killed himself because he could not get a job. Joey starts a rumor among the other boys on the Row that **Doc** keeps human fetuses in jars in his lab.

JOHN THE CANUCK. Near a lake in Aroostock County, Maine, where he camps for the evening in ***Travels with Charley***, Steinbeck meets a French Canadian migrant family from Quebec, headed by John, who have come to work the potato fields of Maine. Steinbeck invites the family of eight for after-dinner conversation and coffee and cognac for the adults and soda pop for the children.

"JOHNNY BEAR" (1937). In ***The Long Valley*** and originally published in *Esquire* in 1937 as "The Ears of Johnny Bear," this short story has attracted attention from Steinbeck scholars who see it as unquestionably compelling, despite their complaints about a plot divided between the two settings of the swamp and the town. However, this so-called plot weakness may also be viewed as part of Steinbeck's carefully planned attention to setting. So viewed, "Johnny Bear," appearing between **"The Vigilante"** and **"The Murder,"** examines aspects of the sexual and racial issues introduced in "The Vigilante" and further explores the sex and gender differences (already introduced in such earlier stories as **"The Snake"**) that culminate dramatically in "The Murder." "Johnny Bear" once again depicts the lost Eden of California and continues the theme of loneliness that threads its way throughout the *Long Valley* stories. The swamp and the town, Loma, are linked through the almost daily moving back and forth of the nameless narrator who is employed as a swamp dredger. Because Loma appears as an extension of the swamp, Steinbeck implies that the evil nature of the swamp has enveloped the surrounding world, and thus the two settings become metaphorically one and the same. Not surprisingly, then, as the constant dredging of the swamp occurs in the background, the narrator, **Alex Hartnell**, and the source of the title, Johnny Bear, engage in their own sort of dredging, digging into the private lives of townsfolk.

In addition to the chasm between men and women, a theme common to numerous *Long Valley* stories, Steinbeck achieves a rich artistic complexity through his use of multiple narrators: the nameless narrator, an outsider who divides his time between his job in the swamp and the Buffalo Bar in Loma; Johnny Bear, a grossly described bear-like idiot savant who can mimic with precision any voice he hears; Alex Hartnell, a native of Loma and one of its elite, who befriends the nameless narrator and provides information on the backgrounds of various characters; and Steinbeck himself, of course, who was known as "Johnny Boy" when, like the fictional narrator, he worked on a swamp dredger near Castroville, California.

One of the issues Steinbeck raises in this story is the role of the writer: Does he just replay the voices of the characters in return for some sort of payment each time he tells a story? Is his purpose strictly to entertain? When does entertainment become an invasion of privacy? Should the writer interpret the story he tells, as the narrator and Alex do to varying degrees? Or, like Johnny Bear, should he simply replicate the voices of "real life"? To what degree is the writer—as Johnny Bear, the narrator, Alex, and even, presumably, Steinbeck himself—simply a voyeur?

The fictional narrators play active roles as characters, too—but critics have difficulty agreeing on a single protagonist. The unnamed narrator is befriended by Alex, who introduces him to the history and background of Loma and its inhabitants and takes him to the Buffalo Bar. The prime actor is Johnny Bear, rewarded by the men in the bar for his stories only if he gives them juicy gossip or some secret in the private lives of individuals. The only individuals on whom he focuses in this story are two women, **Amy** and **Emalin Hawkins**. The distance between these women and the Buffalo Bar is enormous; in one sense at least, the men in the saloon are merely less obvious copies of Johnny Bear himself. Encouraging and even colluding with Johnny Bear's voyeurism, they echo his Neanderthal image.

The narrator agrees with Alex that "a place like Loma, with its fogs, with its great swamp like a hideous sin, needed, really needed, the Hawkins women." The story raises other issues besides those of the artist. It was originally titled "The Sisters," in recognition of the most frequent subjects of Johnny Bear's nocturnal voyeurism. The sisters were likely based on two prominent **Salinas** women, one of whom had an affair with an Asian (according to **Jackson J. Benson**), and Robert Hughes, Jr. points out that Steinbeck's high school mathematics teacher was named Emma Hawkins. The daughters of the late Loma Congressman Hawkins, the characters Amy and Emalin are the town's aristocrats. Yet they have had no say in the storytelling process; indeed, they never speak directly, but are disembodied voices heard only through the mouth of Johnny Bear. According to Alex, this male community has invested in Amy and Emalin the virtues that the men lack: the sisters embody goodness and morality. Steinbeck portrays two female stereotypes in these sisters. Emalin is the one who obeys the male codes that she has inherited, protecting the family name and espousing both chastity and respectability. Amy has a passionate, clandestine affair with a Chinese sharecropper who lives nearby. The unmarried Amy becomes pregnant and commits suicide. Because she falls from her pedestal, Amy joins a long line of fictional women in literature—from Leo Tolstoy's Anna Karenina to Nathaniel Hawthorne's Hester Prynne to **Ernest Hemingway**'s Catherine Barkley—who fulfill Edgar Allan Poe's dictum that the most poetic subject for fiction is the "death of a beautiful woman"; because Amy and these others have crossed forbidden sexual lines, they must die.

Steinbeck also includes a third female stereotype in this story in the character of **Mae Romero**, who is the first woman whom Johnny Bear overhears as she has a date with the narrator. Not an aristocrat, however, Mae is condescendingly presented as a promiscuous woman who, unlike Amy and Emalin, has no reputation to protect. She, like them, is voiceless, connected to them through her gender but distanced because of her class and ethnicity. Indeed, Johnny Bear's depiction of her evening with the narrator prepares us not only for the mesmerizing appeal of stories of furtive sex in the dark, but also for the racial issues, particularly the issue of miscegenation. Significantly, though Johnny Bear tells the story of the narrator's evening with the Mexican woman, the narrator's role is quickly forgotten. When the roles are reversed, however, and an upper-class woman has a romance with a lower-class Chinese immigrant, Steinbeck stunningly demonstrates the hypocrisy about class, race, and gender that leads to the death of a woman and her unborn baby.

Further Reading: Byrd, Charlotte. "The First-Person Narrator in 'Johnny Bear'": A Writer's Mind and Conscience." *Steinbeck Quarterly* 21.1–2 (Winter–Spring 1988): 6–13; French, Warren. "'Johnny Bear': Steinbeck's 'Yellow Peril' Story." In *A Study Guide to Steinbeck's 'The Long Valley': Essays in Criticism.* Ed. Tetsumaro Hayashi. Ann Arbor, MI: Pierian, 1976. 57–64; Hughes, Robert S., Jr. *John Steinbeck: A Study of the Short Fiction*. Boston: Twayne, 1989; Mandia, Patricia M. "Chaos, Evil, and the Dredger Subplot in Steinbeck's 'Johnny Bear.'" In *Steinbeck's Short Stories in "The Long Valley": Essays in Criticism*. Ed. Tetsumaro Hayashi. Muncie, IN: Steinbeck Research Institute, Ball State University, 1991. 54–62; Owens, Louis. *John Steinbeck's Re-Vision of America.* Athens: University of Georgia Press, 1985; Steinbeck, John. "Johnny Bear." In *The Long Valley.* New York: Viking, 1939. 145–168.

Abby H. P. Werlock

JOHNSON, CHARLIE. In *The Wayward Bus*, a successful businessman whom **Elliott Pritchard** admires.

JOHNSON, LADY BIRD [CLAUDIA ALTA TAYLOR JOHNSON] (1912–). Former First Lady of the United States, wife of President **Lyndon B. Johnson**. Steinbeck's third wife, **Elaine Scott Steinbeck**, knew Lady Bird at the University of Texas, and the Steinbecks and Johnsons were close friends. While visiting the White House, the Steinbecks stayed on the second floor where the president's family lived.

JOHNSON, LYNDON BAINES (1908–1973). As a senator from Texas (1948–1960) and as President of the United States (1963–1968), Lyndon Johnson earned a reputation as one of America's greatest legislators. Vice President Johnson assumed the Presidency upon the assassination of John F. Kennedy, and a year later won election by an overwhelming margin. Although Johnson was vilified by the public for continuing the Vietnam War, his major accomplishment during his term of office was to enact civil rights legislation. In passing social legislation, Johnson attempted to give women and the poor their share of the American Dream, and this was, of course, an issue that Steinbeck cared about deeply. Johnson extended government aid to early education, housing, and medical care for the poor and the elderly. But many argue that his social programs were hastily conceived and too expensive.

Others remember his presidency as a period of civil unrest: some Americans marched and were beaten or jailed for protesting racism, a few rebelled against poverty by burning their neighborhoods, and others applied civil disobedience to protest the Vietnam War. Because Johnson held office during this tumultuous era, he often received blame for the unrest, but historians also cite his Great Society speech at Michigan, in which he set goals to end racism and poverty, called for environmental awareness, and challenged the materialistic attitudes of most Americans. Most Americans never trusted Johnson, who used questionable means to achieve his ends. Although he was a president with a social conscience, he remained a controversial personality who conducted an unpopular war and whose presidency was associated with tragedy.

John Steinbeck publicly supported Lyndon Johnson's military and social programs. The acquaintanceship of **Lady Bird Johnson** and **Elaine Scott Steinbeck** originated in their college days and was renewed in the White House, where the Steinbecks were guests for dinner and overnight visits. In time, Steinbeck developed a close relationship with President Johnson, often scripting or offering ideas for speeches he delivered. Johnson even had the 1964 Democratic platform sent to Steinbeck for improvement. But Steinbeck feared that his involvement in the editing and revising of the Great Society platform would never be known to the public. Steinbeck mailed his revisions August 12, 1964, to White House aide Jack Valenti with the comment, "I have changed and rewritten the beginning and the ending because these are the two places where emotion can be added." Steinbeck's stylistic changes appear throughout the draft; however, Johnson, still unsatisfied, flew Steinbeck to the White House for a weekend of solitary labor on the document. Steinbeck had reason to be pleased that his last important writing improved a document that stressed liberty and argued that the individual and the nation would be enriched by an attack on poverty and illiteracy; liberty and the fight against these social problems were causes to which he was surely committed. Steinbeck also drafted Johnson's acceptance speech for the Democratic Convention; unfortunately, his draft of Johnson's inaugural speech went to speechwriter Richard Goodwin, who retained but one sentence.

With his friend **Adlai Stevenson** at the United Nations and urged on by the president, Steinbeck became an international ambassador of goodwill. He spoke to student audiences and to government officials in the Soviet Union and in the third world. A Steinbeck report that the White House files dated June 1965—perhaps sent to Dean Rusk, Secretary of State—offered advice on Central Europe and Cuba. In considering his tour of Russia, Czechoslovakia, Hungary, and Poland, Steinbeck prophetically wrote, "the block is beginning to fragment. . . . Russia will hesitate to use the Red Army again." He added that Castro's Communist government had failed, but the United States should not expect the former dictatorship by the wealthy to replace Castro.

As his life drew to a close, support for the Vietnam War occupied much of Steinbeck's discussions and correspondence with the White House and became the subject of his column for the Long Island paper, *Newsday*. His support pleased the president but alienated his readers. Although he spent six weeks in Vietnam as a correspondent examining the conflict, his firsthand assessments were largely dismissed by the reading public. Nonetheless, there is evidence he persisted in offering his conclusions. In fact, a report he sent summarizes a conversation with the president about bombing North Vietnam and about proposed treatment of war prisoners and dropping medicine to win converts. Steinbeck and Johnson both thought that they were carrying out a foreign policy that evolved from the aftermath of World War II. By 1967, Steinbeck did have doubts about the war, but he was not in a position to publicly contradict his friend, the sitting president.

Further Reading: Benson, Jackson, J. *The True Adventures of John Steinbeck, Writer*. New York: Viking, 1984; Dallek, Robert. *Lone Star Rising: Lyndon Johnson and His Times 1908–1960*. New York: 1991; Kearns, Doris. *Lyndon B. Johnson and the American Dream*. New York: 1971; Miller, Merle. *Lyndon: An Oral Biography*. New York: 1980. *See also* the Steinbeck Files at the Johnson Presidential Library in Austin Texas.

Cliff Lewis

JOHNSON, NUNNALLY (1897–1977). Screenwriter, producer, and film director, who wrote the screenplays for ***The Grapes of Wrath*** (1940) and ***The Moon Is Down*** (1943), which he also produced. Steinbeck became friends with Johnson and had several lengthy conversations with the screenwriter concerning the film version of *Grapes*. Steinbeck feared it would be watered down, with hard-hitting scenes ending up on the cutting room floor. When Steinbeck saw a screening of the film in December 1939, he was very pleased and in fact thought the movie "a harsher thing than the book." His faith in Johnson was such that when the screenwriter asked Steinbeck for suggestions about adapting *The Moon Is Down*, the novelist replied, "Tamper with it." Johnson's wife, Dorris Bowdon (1915–), played **Rosasharn** in *The Grapes of Wrath* and **Molly Morden** in *The Moon Is Down*. Johnson's work is extremely varied, including comedies (*How to Marry a Millionaire* [1953]), mysteries (*Bulldog Drummond Strikes Back* [1934], *The Dark Mirror* [1946]), historical dramas (*Cardinal Richelieu* [1935]), Westerns (*Jesse James* [1939], *The Gunfighter* [1950]), and psychological dramas (*The Three Faces of Eve* [1957]). Citing *The Grapes of Wrath*, Leslie Hallowell praises Johnson "for being involved in so many of Hollywood's most intelligent pictures." Thomas Burton wrote in *The Saturday Review of Literature* that Johnson's handling of the script for *The Grapes of Wrath* was "superb." Gene Bluestone and Warren French praise Johnson for using much of Steinbeck's dialogue verbatim but criticize him for evading mention of the most specific targets of Steinbeck's wrath and for rearranging some sequences to give the film an upbeat ending.

Joseph Millichap

JOHNSON, TOD. In ***The Short Reign of Pippin IV***, son of the "Chicken King" of Petaluma (an American millionaire chicken rancher) who befriends both **Pippin Héristal** and Pippin's daughter, **Clotilde Héristal**. Having graduated from Princeton, Johnson is enjoying leisure in France before entering the world of American commerce via his father's immense chicken farm. He proposes that Pippin sell aristocratic titles in Texas to alleviate French debt, and as his intimacy with the royal family grows apace, he offers other suggestions about government drawn from the model of American advertising and corporate enterprise. When Pippin delivers the speech that generates rioting among the aristocracy, Tod offers to drive him and Clotilde to safety, but Pippin sends him off with his daughter and his blessing.

Marilyn Chandler McEntyre

JONES (*CANNERY ROW*). One of **Mack**'s "boys" in ***Cannery Row***.

JONES (*CUP OF GOLD*). Also known as The Cockney. He is an epileptic pirate under **Henry Morgan**'s command in ***Cup of Gold***. His life's ambition is to be a minister, but he is married to a Catholic former prostitute whom he was given in the division of spoils after a previous victory. During the trek to Panama, **Coeur de Gris** upsets Henry Morgan when he tells Henry that Jones has the same depth of feeling and the same desires as Henry. During the collection of booty in Panama, Henry Morgan discovers that Jones is concealing a jeweled crucifix for his wife. Henry, who has just failed to win over **La Santa Roja**, shoots Jones dead and blames his actions on Coeur de Gris's words.

Kevin Hearle

JORDANUS, SIR. In ***The Acts of King Arthur,*** one of the trusted knights of the Duke of Cornwall.

JOSEPH. In ***The Moon Is Down***, a butler who works in the household of Mayor **Orden**. Elderly, lean, and serious, he rarely expresses an opinion about anything and seems content to follow the wishes of Mayor Orden. However, after the arrival of the invaders, like his fellow servant **Annie**, he learns to transform passive acceptance into active resistance and finds a role as one of the mayor's secret mouthpieces for relaying information to the people.

JOSEPH OF ARIMATHEA. In ***The Acts of King Arthur***, the merchant who gives his sepulcher to receive Christ's body after it is taken down from the cross. He brings to Britain the sacred cup of the Last Supper (the Holy Grail) and the spear with which Longinus the Roman wounded Christ on the cross. His dead body lies in a room in **King Pelham**'s castle, where the unarmed **Sir Balin**, fleeing from the vengeful wrath of the king, finds it and uses the spear to wound his adversary.

JOURNAL OF A NOVEL (1969). Steinbeck's journal written while he wrote ***East of Eden***, it was published in 1969, a year after the author's death. From January 29 through November 1, 1951, Steinbeck kept a running commentary and record of events while writing the first draft of *East of Eden*. Handwritten in pencil, the journal was composed in a 10¾ by 14 inch notebook that was given to him by his editor, **Pat Covici**. The first few pages contain prefatory comments to Covici; then Steinbeck wrote dated letters to his editor on the left-hand pages and the text of the draft on the right-hand pages. Steinbeck used these "letters" (which were never mailed) to prepare himself for the day's writing by commenting on plans for the novel's strategies, character development, themes and writing techniques. He also recorded many personal thoughts about his family, some daily happenings, and his hobbies. Rambling and repetitious at times, this journal, much like his previous commentaries on earlier works such as ***To a God Unknown*** and ***The Grapes of Wrath***, illuminates the mind, moods, and creative methods of the writer as his novel progresses. The initial reception of *Journal of a Novel* was generally positive but somewhat querulous. The *Christian Science Monitor* called it "worth reading" but used a sports analogy to say, "You still don't know what's going on in [Steinbeck's] head when he's playing the game." Other reviewers noted severe editorial oversights but praised the wealth of information that had been made available. *The Saturday Review*, for instance, noted that Steinbeck's comments "will be indispensable to future studies of his work," but the *New Republic*, after noting the book's "precious insights," concluded that Steinbeck's "comments on pace, construction, and so on, are professionally worthless." Many subsequent critics, however, have found *Journal of a Novel* an invaluable repository of many of the intricate keys to an understanding of *East of Eden*.

Most significant for readers are Steinbeck's specific comments made as he composed his most ambitious novel, in which he portrays the existence of good and evil by using and alluding to as many viewpoints as possible of the known world: ethnic, religious, intellectual, scientific, historical, political, and literary. In his remarks about how he plans to write his book, Steinbeck explains here for the only time his now refined technique of syncretic allegory, by which he uses precise literary and other recorded references in a distinctly untraditional way. Briefly stated, syncretic allegory abandons the traditional one-to-one relationship of traditional allegory (for instance, as seen in "The Fox and the Grapes" and Aesop's other fables). Instead, Steinbeck often combines many symbolic referents into one or inverts them completely in an attempt to reconcile their differences while at the same time acknowledging their significance. For example, in *East of Eden*, the character of **Cathy Trask** evidences characteristics and demonstrable echoes of Catherine the Great, Cain, Satan, and Alice in Wonderland—each of whose myth, Steinbeck believed, had always been considered individually instead of being seen as part of the whole truth about human existence. Accordingly, Steinbeck fused and inverted allegorical references in a manner, as he predicted over and over again in *Journal of a Novel*, that most traditional literary critics would not recognize. Only by understanding this often subversive and always contradictory allegorical technique can a reader understand what Steinbeck's major works, especially *East of Eden*, really mean.

In *Journal of a Novel*, some of the most relevant entries provide the following clues to what Steinbeck was trying to do as he drafted his novel. January 29: He states that the overall "philosophy" of the novel will be "old and yet new born." February 12: He thinks of naming the family "Canable" (Cain-Able) but does not want the obvious "double or rather . . . triple meaning." February 22: He tells Covici to find out for himself the nature of the characters and "their symbol meanings," noting that a "key" exists and that "there are many leads." He refuses, however, to identify what these secrets are, adding that they should be "found by accident." February 23: He notes how complicated the book has become.

Continuing in to the next month, on March 7, he wonders if readers will understand how the Cain–Abel echoes actually work in the novel. March 12: Steinbeck changes the name of Carl **Trask** to Charles because "he has changed his symbolic nature to a certain extent" and then notes that he has tried to "throw in history and make it sound like conversation." He also defines a symbol as "usually a kind of part of an equation . . . The symbol is never the whole . . . But in this book . . . I want to clothe my symbol people in the trappings of experience." March 13: He states that critics are never able to pick out the subtleties of his technique. March 26: He writes about "a tremendously powerful force in the book. And her name is Catherine or Cathy—Does that give you any clue to her?" March 29 (a key entry): "Since this book is about everything, it should use every form, every method, every technique. I do not think this will make it obvious because even though I bring most everything to the surface, there will still be the great covered thing." April 16 (another significant entry): Listing the names that start with A and C, he indicates his intention to echo characteristics of Adam, Able, and Cain in female as well as male characters.

On May 9, he asks if his intention to write a story with "immediacy" but also as "a record of a past truth" makes sense to Covici. May 22: Steinbeck writes at length of his decision to use the "perplexing" Cain and Abel story as a "framework" for his novel, and then he rereads the book of Genesis in search of a title. May 25: Steinbeck acknowledges having worked until about 3 A.M. the previous night, reading, researching, and writing what he calls "one of the most devilish plans I have ever heard of." He chortles, "And the awful thing is that it would work. That is the really terrible thing." May 30: He writes again about his "method," noting that he and Covici might recognize it, but he doubts if "the general reader" would have any "sense of the under thing." June 11: Steinbeck copies the Cain and Abel story in longhand and decides on his title, adding, "In other words, this story [Cain and Abel] is the basis of all human neurosis." The next day he states that he has found the definitive "key." June 21: A long entry discusses the variant meanings of different translations of Genesis 4—the Cain and Abel story—and Steinbeck comments on how different factions have misunderstood the real, underlying meaning. He asks Covici to get him the original Hebrew word that had been variously translated as "thou shalt," "do thou," and "thou mayest" (in *East of Eden*, this word appears as "**Timshel**"). June 26: Noting that he feels better about his "microcosm" than for any of his previous books, he predicts that some of the next day's writing will be "very funny . . . a really amusing venture in scholarship."

On July 2, he tells Covici to notice echoes from his earlier works in this novel and reflects that all his previous writing was "practice for this, I am sure." July 5: Steinbeck acknowledges receipt from Covici of a copy of *Bartlett's Familiar Quotations*, a reference work that will provide him, along with other references, the Matthew Prior quotation that is quoted by Abra's father as the source of her name. That the index for the edition of *Bartlett's* that Steinbeck used also contains sequential entries for Abra, Abram, and Abraham is quite important to an understanding of the use Steinbeck made in the novel of similar given and surnames. July 9: Steinbeck claims that this book will be unique in its attempt "to use both the old [novel forms] and the new." July 13: In this most significant entry, Steinbeck writes about his use of the "C–A theme" and talks about his reversal of the traditional allegorical echoes. He notes that in the first part, his character "Adam . . . was the Abel" and "Charles was a dark principle." Now, however, Caleb has become his "Cain principle." Outlining his plan, he wonders how he will manage to accomplish it. August 12: Noting the significance of the new characters **Cal Trask** and **Abra**, he calls Abra "a new Adam . . . the strong female principle of good as opposed to Cathy." August 21: Steinbeck doubts that readers will understand what the book is really about because they do not read closely enough, and even if they do, they usually misinterpret what they see. October 10: He reflects on previous reviews of his fiction that seem to "show a fear and hatred of ideas and speculations. It seems to be true that people can only take parables fully clothed with flesh. Any attempt to correlate in terms of thought is frightening. And if that is so, *East of Eden* is going to take a bad beating because it is full of such things." October 16: Steinbeck writes what he calls a "fairy tale." This final entry is a fanciful dialogue between the Writer (Steinbeck) and the editors of **Viking Press**, a dialogue in which the editors claim that the readers will not understand his novel. The Writer replies, "Do you?" A response comes from only one editor (Covici): "Yes, but the reader won't."

It is clear from these examples alone that Steinbeck's intent is to correlate history, myth, fairy tale, and religion into what he feels is a "devilish," microcosmic, not-to-be-understood master plan. Thus, *Journal of a Novel* is a significant key to an understanding of his creative process and the meaning not only of *East of Eden* but also of many of his other novels.

Further Reading: Dillman, Mary A. "Contexts of Development in John Steinbeck's *The Journals of the Grapes of Wrath and Journal of a Novel*." PhD diss., The Ohio State University, 1992; Pratt, John C. *John Steinbeck in Christian Perspective.* Ann Arbor, MI: William B. Eerdmans, 1970.

John Clark Pratt

JOY. A veteran labor organizer in ***In Dubious Battle*** who has been nearly driven out of his mind by past beatings yet joins the strikers; he is killed when the first trainload of strikebreakers arrive. His funeral is marked by a great demonstration that helps unite the strikers.

JOYCE, JAMES (1882–1941). Irish novelist and poet. Known for his experimentation with language and form, Joyce revolutionized the literary culture of the early twentieth century, becoming a central figure within a cadre of authors including **Ezra Pound, T. S. Eliot, Ernest Hemingway,** and Gertrude Stein who challenged formal conventions of writing in an attempt to illustrate the subjective nature of human experience. Though a reader and admirer of Joyce's work, Steinbeck found Joyce's writing to be too complex and abstruse to suit his aesthetic taste. Moreover, thematically, Joyce's preoccupation with individual experience tends to run counter to the pervasive social and ecological perspective that runs throughout Steinbeck's work. However, Steinbeck had read Joyce's *Ulysses* and *Finnegans Wake* sometime during the 1930s, and **Jackson J. Benson** notes that Steinbeck's unnamed novel and another unpublished manuscript, **"Dissonant Symphony,"** produced during this time, may have been influenced by Joyce. The extent to which those works may have been influenced remains, nevertheless, a mystery, given that Steinbeck destroyed both manuscripts.

Further Reading: Benson, Jackson J. *The True Adventures of John Steinbeck, Writer.* New York: Viking, 1984.

Gregory Hill, Jr.

JOYOUS GARDE. During the winter of 1954, John and **Elaine Scott Steinbeck** purchased a house in **Sag Harbor** that was private and situated on a small peninsula with a boat dock leading to a cove. Steinbeck had a small writing room built out on the point of his property, where at times he struggled mightily with his adaptation of Malory's ***Le Morte d'Arthur.*** Appropriately, Steinbeck called his writing refuge "Joyous Garde" which is a reference to Arthurian legend. In one of his early adventures, **Lancelot** conquered the castle Dolorous Garde. He then took the castle for his home and renamed it Joyous Garde. It was soon after this feat that Lancelot returned to Camelot and became a full knight of the round table. It is also worth noting, in context of Steinbeck, that there are three Elaines in Arthurian legend. There is Elaine of Corbenic, whom Lancelot saves from a pot of boiling water, and Elaine of Astolat, who dies of a broken heart because of Lancelot's inability to return her love. Most interestingly however, Lancelot was the son of **King Ban of Benwick**, who was one of **Arthur**'s most vigorous supporters. King Ban's wife was **Queen Elaine**. As a romantic gesture for Elaine on her birthday in 1965, Steinbeck had a swimming pool built between the house and Joyous Garde that included a stepping stone with Lancelot's last words to **Guinevere**, "Ladye, I take reccorde of God, in thee I have myn erthly joye." Considering that Steinbeck spent much time struggling with writing in Joyous Garde, its name is ironic. Most probably the last writing he completed in his life was an unfinished letter to his agent, **Elizabeth Otis**, with the final line observing, "my fingers have avoided the pencil as though it were an old and poisoned tool."

Further Reading: Benson, Jackson J. *The True Adventures of John Steinbeck, Writer.* New York: Viking, 1984.

Brian Niro

JUAN CHICOY. *See* **Chicoy, Juan**.

JUAN THOMAS. The older brother of **Kino** in *The Pearl*, Juan Thomas and his wife **Apolonia** stand by Kino and **Juana** when all in the town seem to turn against them. Juan Thomas gives his brother advice on how to deal with the pearl dealers, whom they suspect of collusion, and he also protects and hides Kino after he has killed the man trying to steal his pearl. His opinion appears to represent the natives' attitudes toward their life and tradition. But it is also Juan who first warns Kino of the consequences of his actions: "You [Kino] have defied not the pearl buyers, but the whole structure, the whole way of life, and I am afraid for you." In the end, despite his providing the means for their escape, Juan Thomas's fears prove justified as Kino and Juana are tracked, and their baby dies from a gunshot to the head.

Stephen K. George

JUANA (*THE PEARL*). The wife of **Kino** in *The Pearl*, Juana is one of **John** Steinbeck's most admirable characters. A dutiful wife, she aids her husband in his pearl diving and lovingly cares for their only child, **Coyotito**. She rejoices with Kino over the discovery of the pearl but also is the first to pronounce it as evil; she braves a beating from her husband when she tries to throw it away. Though dependent upon Kino's strength, Juana proves both strong and independent. She insists that they leave the village after Kino kills a man trying to steal the pearl, and she keeps the family from disintegrating once Kino realizes that they are being followed by trackers. At the end, Juana knowingly refuses to throw away the pearl and allows her husband to do it.

Mimi Gladstein, in "Steinbeck's Juana: A Woman of Worth," writes that Juana, with the exception of **Ma Joad**, "is the most positively depicted woman in Steinbeck's work" and indeed "the most admirable, most indomitable character" in *The Pearl*. Although some critics do find fault with Juana, as when Richard VanDerBeets argues that her view of the pearl as evil is "extreme" and actually contributes to the family's demise, most readers find Juana to be the moral center of the work. As Gladstein notes, Juana's "values never change; she is, from beginning to end, devoted to the preservation of her loved ones, man and child."

Stephen K. George

JUANA (*VIVA ZAPATA!*). In ***Viva Zapata!*** she appears in the screenplay, but not in the actual film. She is a rather subservient woman who appears to love **Emiliano**, though we never see that this love is reciprocated.

JUANITO. Young man in ***To a God Unknown*** who volunteers to work without pay for **Joseph Wayne** as his *vaquero* and foreman. He represents a link to an ancient, nonbiblical cultural heritage that becomes fused with contemporary religion and society. He calls himself a Castilian, but others believe his mother was Native American. He becomes central to the action when he kills Joesph's youngest brother, **Benjamin Wayne**, after catching him in bed with his wife. He reappears late in the novel to convince Joseph to visit the priest, **Father Angelo**. After Joseph refuses his offer to stay on the farm, Juanito returns to his wife and new son, named after Joseph Wayne. Juanito asks Joseph to bless his namesake, thus ensuring the passing on of a heritage (albeit not overtly familial, although young Joseph may be Benjamin's son) that Joseph Wayne himself had received from his father. The fact that Juanito has no last name but could possibly be the son of **Old Juan** is significant to Steinbeck's belief (also shown later in ***The Grapes of Wrath*** and especially in ***East of Eden***) that both given and inherited names show a dependence on the past that can often become prescriptively tragic for the name bearers.

JUDGE. Presides at the indictment of the halfwit who confesses to doing away with **Cathy Ames** and setting the fire that killed **William** and **Mrs. Ames** in *East of Eden*. The judge realizes the confession is based only on a desire to please and dismisses the charges and then scolds **Mike**, the constable, for being so gullible.

JULIUS CAESAR. According to **Robert DeMott**, Caesar's *Commentaries* (on the Gallic and Civil Wars) was one of Steinbeck's favorite works. The novelist makes reference to it in *Cup of Gold*, as does the character **Junius Maltby** in ***The Pastures of Heaven***.

JUNG, CARL (1875–1961). Swiss psychologist and psychiatrist who founded analytic psychology, in some aspects a response to Sigmund Freud's psychoanalysis. Jung proposed and developed the concepts of the extroverted and introverted personality, archetypes, and the collective unconscious, and his work continues to be influential in psychiatry and in the study of religion, literature, and related fields. **Robert DeMott** lists nine books by psychologist Carl Jung that Steinbeck at least reviewed, and **Jackson J. Benson** links **Casy**'s phalanx, or group man, philosophy in ***The Grapes of Wrath*** to Jungian psychology. We know from **Carol Henning Steinbeck**, Steinbeck's first wife, that Steinbeck's friendship with Jungian psychologist and mythologist **Joseph Campbell** in the early 1930s had a discernible effect on the writer's intellectual development. The two men met frequently at **Edward F. Ricketts**' laboratory in Monterey where they discussed ideas and books. Recognizing Steinbeck's familiarity with Jung's work, critics have noted the psychoanalytic influences in the novels ***To a God Unknown*** and ***In Dubious Battle*** and in several stories in ***The Long Valley***.

Jung's ideas about the ego and the unconscious self, particularly what Jung calls the "shadow self," have been particularly useful for psychological readings of ***The Pearl*** and ***Of Mice and Men***. Jung describes what he calls a shadow and an anima, or animus, as psychological projections of ego. The shadow is always of the same gender as the subject and may even be recognized as the subject's evil nature. Jung explains that the shadow self is a projection of the ego's dark characteristics, inferiorities of an emotional, obsessive, or possessive quality. **John H. Timmerman** demonstrates in Jungian terms that the imagery in

The Pearl "carefully parallels the disclosure about human nature" and discusses **Kino**'s character development as a parable of self-discovery that "parallels the Jungian confrontation with the shadow of the unconscious, an ultimate act of reading one's own life." Charlotte Hadella also analyzes the relationships in *The Grapes of Wrath* between **George Milton** and **Lennie Small** and between George and **Curley's wife** in Jungian terms: Lennie appears to be George's "shadow self," and Curley's wife is his "anima," archetypes that invade the unconscious. Looking closely at the opening scene of the novel, Hadella explains, "Steinbeck subliminally defines Lennie as George's shadow after drawing our attention to the river, a symbol of the Jungian collective unconscious." Hadella discusses a number of minor details in the novel that point to George's violently aggressive nature, primitive impulses in George himself that he projects onto Lennie. "Unconsciously, [George] projects undesirable characteristics onto his shadow self, then feels the need to control that self by isolating it in the safe haven of the Edenic dream farm. Meanwhile, George inadvertently directs Lennie toward disaster by staying at the ranch even after the trouble with Curley and by making Lennie fearful of Curley's wife. Though George may realize that Lennie will eventually do something terrible for which he will have to be incarcerated or destroyed, he does not take him away from the ranch because of an unconscious desire to rid himself of his shadow." Hadella goes on to show that just as Lennie can be seen as George's shadow self, Curley's wife has characteristics of the Jungian anima, a contra-sexual figure that is usually not recognized by the subject as part of his or her own psyche, but represents the face of absolute evil.

Further Reading: Benson, Jackson J. *The True Adventures of John Steinbeck, Writer.* New York: Viking, 1984; DeMott, Robert. *Steinbeck's Reading; A Catalogue of Books Owned and Borrowed*. New York: Garland, 1984; Hadella, Charlotte. *Of Mice and Men: A Kinship of Powerlessness.* New York: Twayne, 1995; Timmerman, John H.. "The Shadow and The Pearl: Jungian Patterns in *The Pearl*." In *The Short Novels of John Steinbeck: Critical Essays with a Checklist to Steinbeck Criticism*. Ed. Jackson J. Benson. Durham, NC: Duke University Press, 1990.

Marilyn Chandler McEntyre

K

KATRINA, THE. Freighter on which Steinbeck traveled from Long Beach, California, to his first visit to New York in 1925. On board, he met the artist **Mahlon Blaine**, and in going through the Panama Canal, he gained firsthand knowledge of the setting for ***Cup of Gold***.

KATY. Fourteenth-century French pig featured in Steinbeck's satiric treatment of medieval Catholic church doctrines, including exorcism, conversion, sainthood, virginity, and miracles in **"Saint Katy the Virgin."** By having a monk convert Katy to Christianity so that she eschews her formerly wicked ways, Steinbeck uses satirical scenes that feature her crossing herself with her cloven hoof, visiting and comforting the sick and dying, twirling on one hoof for a prolonged period, and, in death, with her bones preserved as relics, helping to cure women with female trouble and ringworm.

KAUFMAN, GEORGE S. (1889–1961). This famous playwright and Broadway director not only encouraged Steinbeck to transform ***Of Mice and Men*** into a play, but also guided Steinbeck personally in molding the play's final form. Due to Kaufman's input, the part of **Curley's wife** was significantly expanded. On November 23, 1937, *Of Mice and Men* opened on Broadway under the direction of Kaufman, and the play later was awarded the New York Film Critics Drama Desk Award. Even after the work had garnered this recognition, Steinbeck failed to show an interest in seeing the production. Eventually, his absence proved offensive to Kaufman and caused a rift in their friendship.

Tracy Michaels

KAY, SIR. Son of **Sir Ector** and foster brother of **Arthur** in ***The Acts of King Arthur***. He is made seneschal and keeper of the lands by Arthur. He also is made a Knight of the **Round Table** on **King Pellinore**'s recommendation after the war with the five kings. Captured and imprisoned by **Tarquin** and released by **Lancelot**, he decides, together with his father, Sir Ector, and his uncle, **Sir Lyonel**, to ride after Lancelot and join him on his quest. When he catches up with Lancelot, he complains that his position as seneschal, responsible for provisioning the king's court, has diminished his reputation as a fighting knight and made him into something of a laughing stock. Lancelot feels sorry for him and carries on his quest disguised as Sir Kay; for some time, Lancelot is able, by his deeds, to restore some of Kay's lost reputation.

Roy S. Simmonds

KAYNES, SIR. In *The Acts of King Arthur*, one of the four knights who protect **Arthur** from his enemies before he becomes king.

KAZAN, ELIA ["GADG"/ELIAS KAZANJOGLOU] (1909–2003). Known for his creative stage direction, Kazan was born in

Istanbul in 1909 to Greek parents and immigrated to the United States in 1913. After studying drama at Yale, he joined the New York Group Theater as an actor in 1930; he directed his first stage play in 1935, and in the 1940s he gained fame as one of Broadway's finest talents. Kazan later founded the Actor's Studio in New York in 1947 with Cheryl Crawford and Robert Lewis. His most famous student was **Marlon Brando**, whom he directed on Broadway in *Streetcar* and with whom he collaborated in the movie version of that play (1951) as well as in John Steinbeck's ***Viva Zapata!*** (1952) and the Oscar-winning *On the Waterfront* (1954). Steinbeck and Kazan met in 1948 after the former agreed to do a screenplay for **Darryl Zanuck** with Kazan as director. Unfortunately, the research for a movie on the Mexican hero, **Emiliano Zapata**, languished as Steinbeck struggled with his deteriorating marriage to **Gwyndolyn Conger Steinbeck**. During this time, however, Steinbeck and Kazan became friends. **Jackson J. Benson** records that Kazan considered Steinbeck "his brother, no matter what" and that the director was essential in consoling Steinbeck and listening to his troubles and anxieties during this trying period. Their close friendship was, no doubt, the reason that Kazan was later chosen to direct ***East of Eden*** after the success of *Zapata!*. Steinbeck trusted him implicitly. When Kazan drew criticism for being among the first Hollywood insiders to cooperate with the investigation held by the House Un-American Activities Committee during the Red Scare in 1952, Steinbeck staunchly defended his friend. Nonetheless, Kazan's testimony cost him dearly among Hollywood's elite.

Michael J. Meyer and Brian Railsback

KAZIN, ALFRED (1915–1998). Literary critic best known for his viewpoints and critiques of the ongoing literary scene. During a review of a critical book about Steinbeck for the *New York Times Book Review* titled "The Unhappy Man from the Unhappy Valley," Kazin added that very little written by Steinbeck after ***The Grapes of Wrath*** had any value. Steinbeck's reputation as a writer suffered greatly from Kazin's article, which characterized many of Steinbeck's later works as overly sentimental. Kazin's article paved the way for **Arthur Mizener**'s "Does a Moral Vision of the Thirties Deserve a Nobel Prize?"—a condescending commentary that appeared in *The New York Times* shortly before the **Nobel Prize** ceremony and suggested that the Swedes had made a terrible error in judgment in honoring the writer.

Ted Scholz

KEEF, MR. R. In ***East of Eden***, **Horace Quinn**'s opponent in the 1903 election for sheriff of **Monterey** County.

KEEHAN, DON. *See* **Don Keehan**.

KELLY, KISS OF DEATH. A welterweight boxer once managed by **Fauna** in ***Sweet Thursday.***

KEMP, CORPORAL. The assistant to **Axel Dane** at the San Jose recruiting office in ***East of Eden***. They allow **Aron Trask** to enlist in the army, even though they know he is underage.

KENNEDY, JACQUELINE BOUVIER (1929–1994). Wife of the thirty-fifth president of the United States, **John Fitzgerald Kennedy**. Shortly after the president's assassination in November 1963, Jackie Kennedy asked Steinbeck if he would be willing to write the definitive biography of her husband's life. Although Steinbeck was sympathetic to Kennedy's politics, he recognized that such a book was really not his kind of project, but, for a time at least, he seems to have considered the request seriously. Perhaps Steinbeck was intrigued by the late president's association with Camelot and **Arthur**ian legend, given that he had spent several years in England researching his own retelling of the Arthurian legend. He wrote Mrs. Kennedy on February 25, 1964, drawing the parallels between the two heroic men, but on April

20 of the same year, he postponed, or abandoned, the project with these words: "One day I do plan to write about what we spoke of—how this man who was the best of his people, by his life and death gave the best back to them for their own." Shortly thereafter, following Steinbeck's death, Mrs. Kennedy wrote to **Elaine Scott Steinbeck** and expressed her deep appreciation for his compassion, his wisdom, and his far-seeing view of things during her period of grief. Regarding the proposed book, she wrote, "His letters say more than a whole book and I will treasure them all of my life."

Further Reading: Steinbeck, Elaine, and Robert Walsten, eds. *Steinbeck: A Life in Letters*. New York: Penguin, 1989.

Michael J. Meyer

KENNEDY, JOHN FITZGERALD (1917–1963). The thirty-fifth president of the United States, he was admired by John Steinbeck. According to **Jackson J. Benson**, Steinbeck at first distrusted Kennedy, but given the president's concern for the arts and literature, the author grew to like him; in 1963 Steinbeck saw Kennedy several times, and in that year the president selected him for the Medal of Freedom. The president suggested Steinbeck visit the Soviet Union as part of a cultural exchange, which he did. In Poland, having recently returned from the USSR trip but still on the official schedule, Steinbeck and his wife, **Elaine Scott Steinbeck**, were shocked when they heard about Kennedy's assassination. **Jacqueline Kennedy** asked Steinbeck to write her husband's definitive biography, but he was not able to do it.

Further Reading: Benson, Jackson J. *The True Adventures of John Steinbeck, Writer*. New York: Viking, 1984.

KING OF THE LAKE. In *Acts of King Arthur,* knight of **King Arthur** who is made a Knight of the **Round Table** on **King Pellinore**'s recommendation after the war with the five kings.

KING OF NORTH GALYS. In *Acts of King Arthur,* one of the four knights beaten in tournament by **Sir Lancelot** and the four white knights as champions of **Sir Bagdemagus**.

KINO. The protagonist of ***The Pearl*** is a poor native diver who lives with his wife, **Juana**, and infant son, **Coyotito**, in a coastal village on the Gulf of Mexico. His story starts one calm morning when, in the midst of a peaceful awakening, Coyotito is bitten by a scorpion, and evil is injected into the lives of the protagonists. Fearing for his child's life, Kino seeks help from the Spanish doctor, imploring medicine and angered by a curt rejection. Later the same day, Kino finds "the Pearl of the World," and his son's health seems assured. Moreover, the pearl represents all the dreams he has ever had for a better life: an education for his son, a church wedding for the couple, a rifle for himself. Unfortunately, none of these dreams materialize, and those in his village, including the doctor and the priest, seem more intent on manipulating and using Kino than on rejoicing in his find. When Kino tries to sell the pearl, the monopoly of pearl buyers in **La Paz** refuse to give him a fair price for it. Later, greed and envy surface as Kino's canoe is destroyed, his hut is burned, and a man is killed in the struggle to wrest the pearl away from its rightful owner. Kino even suggests he will defy precedent and take the pearl to sell in the capital, a decision that most of the townspeople see as dangerous and defiant, a threat to the stability of the social structure. Ultimately, fearful for their lives, Kino and his family flee for cities to the north. But they are eventually tracked down by men Steinbeck describes as similar to the "dark watchers" in **"Flight,"** and Kino is forced to kill his three pursuers in a heroic attempt to save his family. In the end, Coyotito is killed as well by a stray bullet, and Kino and Juana return to La Paz, "removed from human experience," as Steinbeck writes, and carrying "pillars of black fear about them." With the loss of his beloved son, Kino gains a realization of how his soul has been plagued by the worldly value of the pearl. Thus, when he returns to La Paz, he throws the pearl back in the ocean, where it settles calmly in the water. Some of the questions remaining after reading the novella are, as critic **Warren French** asks, "Kino has killed several agents of his pursuers. Can he expect to go unpunished? Even more important, can he really suppress his ambitions and accept his former humble place?"

Critics' responses to Kino have been as contradictory as their appraisals of the work itself. Charles Metzger, in "Steinbeck's *The Pearl* as a Non-teleological Parable of Hope," sees the novella's catastrophes as brought on by Kino's "refusal to face facts," a blinding teleological hope that prevents him from coming to any "understanding-acceptance" until the very end. Tetsumaro Hayashi, in "*The Pearl* as the Novel of Disengagement," attributes idolatry to the diver: "the pearl becomes Kino's new God" and leads him "to become evil-minded, greedy, fearful, and destructive." However, other scholars take an entirely different view. Edward Waldron, in "*The Pearl* and *The Old Man and the Sea*," sees Kino's struggle as admirable, his vision one of "democratic freedom that can only be bought . . . through education and a struggle against the system." Likewise, **Louis Owens** sees Kino as a man who achieves "greatness through the courage to challenge the unknown," despite his shortsightedness. In the end, Kino remains one of many Steinbeck characters who move from a state of innocence to knowledge and acceptance by going "through pain" and coming "out on the other side."

Further Reading: Karson, Jill, ed. *Readings on "The Pearl."* San Diego: Greenhaven Press, 1999.

Kiyoshi Nakayama and Stephen K. George

KIPLING, (JOSEPH) RUDYARD (1865–1936). English writer and Nobel laureate, who wrote novels, poems, and short stories, mostly set in India and Burma (now known as Myanmar) during the time of British rule. Kipling's literary reputation was established by stories of English life in India that revealed his profound identification with, and appreciation for, the land and people of India. Among his best works are *The Jungle Book* (1894) and *Kim* (1901). Like Steinbeck, he was a prolific writer, and much of his work attained wide popularity. He received the 1907 **Nobel Prize** in Literature, the first English author to be so honored. Although Kipling is regarded as one of the greatest English short-story writers, unlike Steinbeck, his renown also extends to his poetry. His poetry is remarkable for its rhymed verse written in the slang used by the ordinary British soldier, a skill Steinbeck mirrored in his use of the vernacular dialects in ***The Grapes of Wrath*** and ***Of Mice and Men***, among other works.

In discussing Steinbeck's biological view of man, critic **Edmund Wilson** praised Kipling as an author capable of romantically raising animals to the stature of humans while denigrating Steinbeck's ability to do so. Benson also mentions Kipling as an integral part of **Edward F. Ricketts**' reading as a young man. According to **Robert DeMott**, Steinbeck owned copies of *The Light that Failed* (1890), *Puck of Pook's Hill* (1906), *The Story of the Gadsbys* (1890), and *The Works of Rudyard Kipling* (1900).

Further Reading: DeMott, Robert. *Steinbeck's Reading; A Catalogue of Books Owned and Borrowed*. New York: Garland, 1984.

T. Adrian Lewis

KITTREDGE, GEORGE LYMAN (1860–1941). American literary scholar and teacher, one of the foremost authorities of his time on the writings of **Shakespeare**, Chaucer, and Sir Thomas Malory. His major writings, along with many journal articles, established him as the then preeminent U.S. scholar of English literature in the early twentieth century. According to **Robert DeMott**, Steinbeck owned Kittredge's *Shakespeare: An Address* (1916).

KLINE, HERBERT (1909–1999). Kline is known for his political films made in the late 1930s and 1940s, especially *The Heart of Spain* (1937), which recorded the bloodshed of the Spanish Civil War. In 1941, Kline, Alexander Hammid, and Steinbeck combined forces to produce ***The Forgotten Village***, a powerful sixty-eight–minute documentary, narrated by **Burgess Meredith**, which takes place in an unnamed, poverty-stricken Mexican community.

KNIGHT, U.S.S. Destroyer that headquartered a secret Navy operation that Steinbeck was attached to as a correspondent in late summer and early fall of 1943. Planning for the unit was directed by the actor **Douglas Fairbanks, Jr.** Some of the most detailed writings on the outfit by Steinbeck involved the taking of the small Italian island of Ventotene, where the author took up arms with his comrades—at great risk to his life.

Further Reading: Benson, Jackson J. *The True Adventures of John Steinbeck, Writer.* New York: Viking, 1984; Steinbeck, John. *Once There Was a War.* 1958. New York: Penguin, 1994.

KNOWLES, FLOYD. Floyd is a young man whom the Joads and **Jim Casy** meet at the Hooverville in ***The Grapes of Wrath***. He tries to explain to the naive Okies how the owner men manipulate the scores of workers who have streamed into their state. His speeches crush the hope that the Joads have nourished for so long, and he presents the reality that California is just as competitive and harsh as the region they have left. In this place the anticipated sharing of wealth has been destroyed by personal greed, and the brotherhood of unions is ironically seen as dangerous and subversive. Floyd tells the Joads that such binding together often results in blacklisting and an inability to find work, and he intimates that when accused of anything, it is better to act ignorant about the charges. Combativeness only results in harsher punishments. Later Floyd makes friends with **Al Joad** as a result of their mutual interest in cars, and he shows his kindness by willingly supplying information about where dependable employment can be gained. However, when another hiring contractor comes to engage workers, Floyd is unable to follow his own good advice and instead verbally confronts the man over the wages he intends to pay, suggesting that the contractor will recruit more men than needed and then lower his price. When an accompanying deputy attempts to arrest Floyd as a troublemaker, he bolts for freedom and is only saved from imprisonment by the interference of **Tom Joad** and the willingness of Jim Casy to take the blame for the incident.

Michael J. Meyer

KNUDSEN, JUDGE. **Salinas** judge who tries unsuccessfully to get in touch with **Mr. Bacon** in ***East of Eden*** to discuss what may be embezzlement charges.

L

"L'AFFAIRE LETTUCEBERG." *See The Grapes of Wrath.*

LA JOLLA. A town in southern California, just north of San Diego, where **Doc** collects marine specimens in both ***Cannery Row*** and ***Sweet Thursday***. Strangely, it is 500 miles from **Monterey** in *Cannery Row*, but just 400 miles away in *Sweet Thursday*. In the latter novel, Doc finds at La Jolla the twenty-eight baby octopi that inspire him to write a scholarly paper titled "Symptoms in Some Cephalopods Approximating Apoplexy." Doc's interest in studying the responses of these "highly emotional animals" is a reflection of his own emotional confusion. When the octopi in the first group die, Doc insists that he cannot proceed with his paper unless he is able to collect more specimens during the spring tides at La Jolla. The planned return to La Jolla gains increasing importance in Doc's mind until it nearly attains the stature of a pilgrimage to Mecca. His spiritual regeneration seems ensured when, at the end of the novel, Doc departs for La Jolla in the company of **Suzy**.

Bruce Ouderkirk

LA PAZ. Located in Baja California, Mexico, La Paz, meaning "peace" in Spanish, ironically, was founded by Hernan Cortez in May 1535. The city of La Paz was called "The Capital of the Pearls" because of the vast exploitation of pearls over the centuries. Steinbeck and his friend **Edward F. Ricketts** visited it when they conducted a scientific research trip to the Sea of Cortez in March and April of 1940.

LADY DE VAWSE. In *The Acts of King Arthur*, holds a tournament in her castle in which **Marhalt**, in the course of the Triple Quest, fights and wins a golden circlet that he presents to her.

"LADY IN INFRA-RED, A." Early short story composed in 1924 while Steinbeck was still at **Stanford University**, this story featured a history of the pirate **Henry Morgan**. It was later developed and expanded to become Steinbeck's first novel, ***Cup of Gold***. Dealing with adventure, exotic locales, and unrequited love, it reflected the early influence of historical romances as well as a preoccupation with the fantastic, magical, and religious elements of fiction.

Michael J. Meyer

LADY OF THE CASTLE, THE. In *The Acts of King Arthur*, she welcomes **Sir Balin** to her castle, but tells him he must conform to the custom that requires any passing stranger to joust with the knight who guards a nearby island. It is this joust that ends with the deaths of both Balin and his brother **Balan**.

LADY OF THE LAKE, THE. In *The Acts of King Arthur*, keeper of the sword **Excalibur** until she allows **Arthur** to receive it from the hand that rises from the waters of the lake. In return for the gift of the sword, she comes to Arthur's court and claims the heads of **Sir Balin** and the damsel of **Lady Lyle of Avalon**, accusing the first of killing her brother and the second of causing her father's death. Sir Balin himself has a score to settle with the Lady of the Lake, for she had by secret craft caused the death of his mother three years earlier. He cuts off her head and gives it to his squire to take back to his friends and relatives in Northumberland.

LADY OF THE ROCK, THE. In *Acts of King Arthur*, a widow, orphan, and gentlewoman, the greater part of whose land, together with her Red Castle, has been taken by the two brothers **Sir Edward** and **Sir Hugh**. During the Triple Quest, **Ewain**, with the guidance of the **Lady Lyne**, fights the two brothers, kills Edward and spares Hugh, and restores the Lady Rock's lands and castle to her.

LADY OF THE RULE, THE. In *Acts of King Arthur*, mother of **Alyne** by **King Pellinore**.

LAGUNA, JOE. A **Salinas** man who buys whiskey for **Cal Trask** in *East of Eden* after Cal takes his brother **Aron Trask** to meet their mother, **Kate Albey**.

LAMARR, HEDY [HEDWIG KIESLER] (1913–2000). Austrian actress who often played a femme fatal in American films such as *White Cargo* (1942), *Strange Woman* (1946), and *Samson and Delilah* (1949). In the 1942 film version of ***Tortilla Flat***, the glamorous Lamarr was miscast as **Dolores (Sweets) Ramirez**, whom Steinbeck describes as being "not pretty, this lean-faced paisana . . . ordinarily her voice was shrill, her face hard and sharp as a hatchet, her figure lumpy and her intentions selfish." It was not Lamarr's fault that her role was rewritten, and she gives an agreeable performance. Although, with a lingering hint of an Austrian accent, she did not seem very Hispanic, in those days Hollywood considered all foreign accents interchangeable.

LANCELOT, SIR. In *The Acts of King Arthur*, son of **King Ban** and **Queen Elaine** of Benwick, originally called **Galahad** but christened **Lancelot**. He fulfills **Merlin**'s prophecy by becoming the world's most perfect knight, occupying the golden-lettered seat, the Siege Perilous, at the **Round Table**. He loves **Arthur** and **Guinevere** and is loved by both of them. With his nephew, **Sir Lyonel**, the least, the laziest, and most worthless of knights, he is sent by Arthur on a quest to search out and correct injustice, punish evils, and overcome traitors to the King's Peace. After many adventures, during which he sends back a line of defeated knights and miscreants to Camelot, he returns in great honor to Winchester, where Arthur is holding his Whitsun court, and, as is the custom, he recounts his deeds and tales of his victories to the king and queen, knights, and assembled company. Afterward, Guinevere invites him into her bedchamber. They fall into each other's arms and passionately kiss, demonstrating the great love they feel for each other, before he breaks away and runs sobbing from the room.

LANGE, DOROTHEA (1895–1965). In 1936, John Steinbeck wrote a series of articles for the *San Francisco News* that were published together two years later as the pamphlet *Their Blood Is Strong: A Factual Story of the Migratory Agricultural Workers in California*. This collection of anecdotes, statistics, and facts about the abysmal living conditions facing these workers was accompanied by several photographs by Dorothea Lange. Born in Hoboken, New Jersey, Lange first studied photography with Clarence White at Columbia University from 1917 to 1918 and then moved to San Francisco to work as a photo finisher and freelance photographer for several years. In 1935 the Farm Security Administration (FSA), an agency started under **Franklin Delano Roosevelt**'s New Deal, hired Lange, Walker Evans, Carl Mydans, and Russell Lee to photograph every aspect of American rural life in hope of generating public and political support for legislation to improve social conditions. The government also wanted a visual record of the rehabilitation work being accomplished by New Deal programs.

During her time with the FSA and the California Rural Rehabilitation Administration (where she worked with Paul Taylor, whom she later married), Lange often captured the psychological and emotional impact of the Depression through photographs of the body. This fascination with bodies can be traced, in part, to her disabling bout with polio at the age of seven, which left her right leg permanently impaired from the knee down. Lange believed that this disability enabled her to empathize with her subjects, and she often used it as a way to win their trust and confidence. Many of her photographs between 1935 and 1942, for example, are powerfully intimate in their focus on body parts to represent the transformation of men and women into tools for labor. Both Lange and Steinbeck used their art to help inspire political and social change, and scholars have often made connections between their 1930s work. Robert Coles, for example, discusses Lange's first assignment with the FSA in Marysville "where she made pictures of **Tom Collins**, the camp manager who was the model for the manager in John Steinbeck's ***The Grapes of Wrath***." Like Steinbeck's California novels, Lange's photography in the 1930s provided vivid firsthand images of working-class life in America, and her famous "Migrant Mother, Nipomo, California, 1936" and "White Angel Breadline" became synonymous with the Depression. Lange's *An American Exodus: A Record of Human Erosion in the Thirties* (1939) was a call to action, capturing through images of the body the misery experienced by so many.

After World War II, Lange's failing health prevented her from active fieldwork for several years, so she began teaching seminars and participating in conferences. She only returned to freelance photography in 1958 and worked continually until her death in 1965.

Further Reading: Coles, Robert. *Dorothea Lange: Photographs of a Lifetime*. New York: An Aperture Monograph, 1982; Meltzer, Milton. *Dorothea Lange: A Photographer's Life*. New York: Farrar, Straus & Giroux, 1978; Stein, Sally. "Peculiar Grace: Dorothea Lange and the Testimony of the Body." In *Dorothea Lange: A Visual Life*. Ed. Elizabeth Partridge. Washington, DC: Smithsonian Institution Press, 1994. 57–90.

Thomas Fahy

LANSER, COLONEL. In ***The Moon Is Down***, the leader of the invading army that occupies a small coastal European town that looks much like a village in Norway. Middle-aged, hard, and tired-looking, Lanser commands a staff of five "herd men" ill-fitted to the task of warfare. However, unlike the rest of his staff, who have never experienced combat and play at war as if it were a game, Lanser is the only one who has actually experienced the sting of battle. Like his symbolic namesake, Lanser is a pointed instrument of war. A veteran of World War I campaigns in Belgium and France, he is a cold realist who recognizes that war is a mix of "treachery and hatred, the muddling of incompetent generals," and "killing and sickness" that ultimately change nothing. Notwithstanding this sobering recognition, he is also a military professional with a blinding sense of duty that allows him to unquestioningly rationalize all his unsavory tasks merely as a matter of following orders. As a result, he views invasion as nothing more than friendly occupation involving an exchange of coal and fish. When the resistance of the townspeople becomes heavier and more violent, however, he gets trapped in a vicious cycle that foments even more revolt because the instructions he receives from "the Leader" (a thinly disguised reference to Hitler) require him to shoot local leaders, take hostages, shoot more hostages, and shoot more leaders. Ultimately, such actions, though forceful, cannot succeed because they are an extension of a sort of limited, dogmatic thinking similar to the kind expressed by the Communist organizers that Steinbeck examines in ***In Dubious Battle***. Thus, when Lanser orders the execution of **Mayor Orden**, he fails to recognize that the temporary gains offered by killing authority figures may provide tactical victories, but in the long run cannot win wars.

Rodney P. Rice

LAO TZE (4TH CENTURY BC). Lao Tze, the founder of Taoism, profoundly shaped the philosophical nature of John Steinbeck's work. This influence was largely through Steinbeck's conversations with his closest friend, **Edward F. Ricketts**. As **Richard Astro** notes, Ricketts' world view was largely Eastern and allied very closely with Taoist philosophy, particularly in his insistence on seeing the world from a **non-teleological**, or "what is," perspective. Steinbeck, although differing with Ricketts in many philosophical respects, shared many of these same views.

Moreover, several of Lao Tze's essential tenets find powerful expression in Steinbeck's literature. For example, Taoism's insistence on seeing the whole clearly and accepting the fundamental nature of things echoes **Doc Burton** of ***In Dubious Battle***, who wanted "to see the whole picture" without "the blinders of 'good' and 'bad'" limiting his vision. In ***The Pearl***, the reader can observe the Taoist principles of antimaterialism and anti-intellectualism in the destruction that follows **Kino** as he struggles against his natural station in life. Even in Steinbeck's last novel, ***The Winter of Our Discontent***, Taoism's insistence on inner harmony is evident in the negative example of **Ethan Allen Hawley**, whose shame and ambition move him toward corruption and suicide instead of toward striving to become one with the Tao, or the ultimate reality. This wonderfully unique blend of Taoist humanism flavors John Steinbeck's writing from beginning to end.

The critical appreciation of Lao Tze's influence on Steinbeck owes much to the work of Richard Astro, as well as to **Peter Lisca**, whose essays in *San Jose Studies* and the *Steinbeck Quarterly* and whose book, *Nature and Myth*, initiated a wellspring of scholarly interest in the philosophical nature of Steinbeck's writing. Such interest continues today, particularly in the scholarship of Michael Meyer, whose collection of essays on Steinbeck and Eastern thought was published in the first issue of the *Steinbeck Review* (Scarecrow). Clearly, much of Steinbeck's rich complexity as a writer and thinker can only be appreciated by recognizing the essential strain of Taoism found within his work.

Further Reading: Astro, Richard. *John Steinbeck and Edward F. Ricketts: The Shaping of a Novelist*. Minneapolis: University of Minnesota Press, 1973; Lisca, Peter. *Nature and Myth*. New York: Crowell, 1978.

Stephen K. George

LAPIERRE, MR. Bartender at the Abbott House in **Salinas** in ***East of Eden*** who tries to convince **Adam Trask** to avoid **Kate Albey's** brothel and go to Jenny's instead.

LARDNER, RING (1885–1933). As Steinbeck points out in ***America and Americans***, Lardner was one of the American authors who started as a journalist. Lardner began publishing short stories in 1914 and, among his other books, published two admired collections of short stories, *How to Write Short Stories* (1924) and *The Love Nest* (1926). According to **Robert DeMott**, Steinbeck reviewed at least *How to Write Short Stories* and *The Round Up* (1929) and particularly enjoyed the story "The Golden Wedding."

"LAST JOAN, THE." Because Steinbeck often mined historical and literary figures for his "heroic" characters, it is not surprising that one heroic figure that intrigued Steinbeck was Joan of Arc (Jeanne d'Arc). Previously, he had shown an interest in the King Arthur legends based on Sir Thomas Malory's depiction of them in ***Le Morte D'Arthur***; he also found the Spanish writer **Miguel de Cervantes**'s quirky hero Don Quixote of interest and planned to write a novel based on his character as well. His interest in Jeanne d'Arc grew primarily with encouragement from his friend **Burgess Meredith**, who wanted Steinbeck to write a play that would star himself and his wife **Paulette Goddard**. Meredith suggested that, since every era has a heroic figure who has an intuition about how to improve the future, the play should focus on a present-day but "last" Joan, depicting her as an individual who would probably also hear voices (like the original Joan) and who would be intent on warning the nation—America, not France—of a current problem: perhaps the threat posed by the discovery of an atom bomb. Although Steinbeck worked conscientiously on the play from February of 1947, he was distracted by his failing marriage to **Gwendolyn Conger Steinbeck** and eventually abandoned the work in April of the same year, preferring to destroy it himself before it was destroyed by critics.

LAUNCEOR, SIR. In ***The Acts of King Arthur***, son of the King of Ireland. He is jealous of **Sir Balin** for winning the magic sword of the **Lady Lyle of Avalon**, and he pursues Balin to avenge an assumed insult to **King Arthur**. He is killed by Balin in combat and is buried with his lover, the **Lady Colombé**, who, in her sorrow, has killed herself with his sword.

LAWRENCE, (CAPTAIN). Pirate captain in ***Cup of Gold***.

LAWRENCE, D. H. [DAVID HERBERT LAWRENCE] (1885–1930). Famous British author of well-known and sometimes controversial novels such as *Sons and Lovers* (1913), *Women in Love* (1921), and *Lady Chatterley's Lover* (1928). His works, especially the earlier ones, were concerned with the tragedy of humankind's separation from nature. Though close Steinbeck friend **Edward F. Ricketts** owned some of Lawrence's books, what Steinbeck read of Lawrence is unknown. Critics have suggested some echoes of Lawrence's view of sexuality in Steinbeck's earlier work, ***To a God Unknown***, in particular. Steinbeck's remarks about Lawrence are often belittling, though he admitted Lawrence was a good writer.

Further Reading: DeMott, Robert. *Steinbeck's Reading; A Catalogue of Books Owned and Borrowed*. New York: Garland, 1984.

LÁZARO. At the beginning of the film ***Viva Zapata!*** he is a member of the peasant delegation that has come to the Presidential Palace in Mexico City for an audience with Porfirio Diáz, their president of thirty-four years, in order to complain about the land that has been taken away from them. He is next seen as a leader of the Native Americans' gathering. When **Emiliano Zapata** is captured and followed by a procession of two columns of *rurales* and mounted men, Lázaro is instrumental in his release. Lázaro appears several more times. He appears as a toughened guerilla fighter with his head in bandages just when **Señor Espéjo** wishes to introduce representatives of Francisco Madero to Zapata, whom he now calls his friend Don Emiliano. Lázaro then appears again as a member of the delegation that has come to see Emiliano in the government office in Mexico City. He is the one who clearly voices the group's complaint against Zapata's brother, **Eufemio Zapata**, for having taken the land that Emiliano had distributed. Lázaro also appears in an excised segment of the film as an old man who is dragged by two soldiers from a deserted hut in a village that has just been entered by federal cavalry. Lázaro's last appearance in the film takes place at the eastern end of the Plaza where Emiliano Zapata's bullet-ridden body has been dumped. Having ridden with Emiliano and fought with him, he cannot be fooled, and he openly declares that the body of the deceased is definitely not that of Emiliano. It is Lázaro who begins the legend that Emiliano is actually still alive somewhere in the mountains.

Further Reading: Steinbeck, John. *Zapata, The Little Tiger*. London: Heinemann, 1991.

LE FIGARO. A sophisticated Paris weekday daily and weekend morning newspaper, noted for its coverage of the arts and satirical political cartoons. During the summer of 1954, when Steinbeck was in Paris, he arranged to contribute a series of seventeen "pieces," as he labeled them—columns written in English under the running title, "One American in Paris"—to *Le Figaro*'s weekend literary supplement. These were translated into French by Jean-François Rozan. A number of them have appeared, some in slightly varying forms, in English, principally in *Punch* in London and in *Holiday, Readers' Digest* and *Saturday Review* in the United States; but numbers 1, 2, 3, 6, 10, and 17 are not known to have been published anywhere in English. Four did not appear in *Le Figaro* in the order that Steinbeck numbered them (numbers 8 and 9 and numbers 11 and 12 were reversed). In this entry, Steinbeck's original numbering is followed by the French title and an English translation by this contributor, the date that the piece appeared in the newspaper and a description of the contents. (See the entry for ***Un Amèricain à New-York et à Paris*** (Paris, 1956), in which thirteen of the columns were published in French.)

1. "John Steinbeck engage un dialogue avec Paris et les Parisiens" ("John Steinbeck Begins a Dialogue with Paris and the Parisians"), June 12, 1954. Steinbeck announces he intends to write a series of articles presenting Paris to the Parisians as seen through one American's eyes, as St. John de Crevecouer had introduced the early United States to the French in *Letters from an American Farmer* (1782).

2. After a space, immediately following piece number 1 on June 12, 1954, the "Second Piece" begins without a new headline. It is a tribute to his friend, photographer **Robert Capa**, who had accompanied Steinbeck to Russia in 1947 and had taken the photographs used in ***A Russian Journal***. Steinbeck was grief-stricken to learn that his friend had recently been killed by a land mine while photographing in the combat zone in Vietnam. The slightly more than thousand-word meditation under the eternal flame in the Arc de Triomphe does not narrate Capa's adventurous career, but pays tribute to his bravery and self-sacrifice in the face of danger to carry on his work of sharing with others visual reminders of great moments of history.

3. "Response aux Francaise demandent: 'Que penzes-vous du MacCarthyisme'" ("Reply to the French demanding, 'What Do You Think about McCarthyism?'"), June 19, 1954. (Note the French spelling of the senator's name.) This response probably disappointed those opposed to the witch-hunting American senator Joseph McCarthy who expected another denunciation, whereas Steinbeck took the longer view that democracies occasionally need demagogic challenges like these to keep on their toes and evolve progressively.

4. "J'aime cette Ile de la Cite" ("I Love that Island of the City"), June 26, 1954. Steinbeck takes his two young sons to the island in the Seine on which Paris was founded to introduce them to some of the great figures and events in French history.

5. "Mon Paris a moi" ("Paris As I See It"), July 3, 1954. Steinbeck rhapsodizes over the scenes that endear the city to him. He reaches the conclusion that the Paris he sees is real only to him because the city is what each individual perceives it to be. Because he does not speak French, he thinks that he sees the city more clearly than others because his visual impressions are not confused by words.

6. Immediately following number 5, with no separate title on July 3 and also in the later book, Steinbeck launches into an enthusiastic account of the hearty reception he received at a "Kermesse aux Etoiles" ("Carnival of the Stars"), an open-air book signing at which he joined a host of other celebrated writers and enjoyed talking with autograph seekers.

7. "Sur les bords de l'Oise" ("On the Banks of the Oise"), July 10, 1954. In one of his least inspired columns, Steinbeck tells about taking his sons fishing on the River Oise, just outside northwestern Paris. The account turns into a comic stereotyping of American, English, and French fishermen, explaining Steinbeck's preference for the French.

8. "Des etoiles . . . et des hommes" ("Of Stars and Men"), July 24, 1954. Some

English translators have missed the play on words with the title of Steinbeck's novel ***Of Mice and Men***, a great favorite in France, and have come up with such pointless titles as "Trust Your Luck" for this meditation on the dangers of stereotyped thinking having a deleterious influence on expanding children's thought.

9. "Une histoire vrai et qui ne parait pas" ("A True Story that Doesn't Seem Possible"), July 17, 1954. An account of the remarkable accomplishments of Joan of Arc as an object lesson to inspire other people. *Le Figaro* probably chose to publish this out of numerical order so that it would appear as close as possible to the French national day, July 14.

10. "Les puces sympathiques" ("The Cooperative Fleas"), July 31, 1954. One of two short stories among the "pieces." Steinbeck narrates in a kind of Rabelaisian humor that he sometimes attempted (as in "**Saint Katy the Virgin**"), how a restaurateur won his coveted second Michelin star with the aid of a secret ingredient supplied by his cat. This ingredient is not identified in the text but suggested by the title. This may never have appeared in an English-language publication because editors may have found it distasteful.

11. "En quête d'un Olympe" ("In Quest of an Olympus"), August 14, 1954. A droll account of Steinbeck's trying to select a restaurant where he could install a waxwork figure that would give diners the impression that they were watching a famous writer at work. Steinbeck ends up praising the hearty food at the now vanished old market at les Halles.

12. "Assez parle du 'bon vieux temps'" ("Enough Said about 'Good Old Days'"), August 7, 1954 (published before number 11). Steinbeck's response to reporter Maria Crapeau's question during a public interview about why American novelists have recently been dwelling so much on the past. In the most self-searching article in the series, Steinbeck admits that he has been guilty of neglecting the exciting present himself and promises to change his ways, as indeed he did in his last two published novels and in ***Travels with Charley*** *in Search of America*.

13. "Français, cher à mon couer" ("The French, Dear to My Heart"), August 21, 1954. Announcing his forthcoming departure from Paris, Steinbeck speaks of the many Parisians he has come to admire, emphasizing the important conclusion that he learned he had not been writing so much about Paris as about what the city had enabled him to learn about himself.

14. "L'Affaire du 1, avenue de M . . ." ("The Affair at 1 Avenue de M . . ."), August 28, 1954. The best known of the *Le Figaro* columns and the only one to be individually titled by Steinbeck is the second short story, a humorous fantasy about the family's desperate efforts to dispose of a piece of their younger son's bubble gum that takes on a life of its own. A long footnote explaining bubble gum to French readers has been dropped in English-language publications, and the address has been changed to "7, rue de M," possibly to avoid protests from Steinbeck's aristocratic neighbors.

15. "Sauce Anglais" ("English Sauce"). The weakest piece in the series collects largely tasteless jokes about the French's low opinion of English cooking.

16. "Un méconnu; le touriste amèricain" ("An Unknown Person: The American Tourist"), September 11, 1954. Steinbeck pleads that the French not stereotype American visitors, given that not all are the often-publicized wealthy showoffs but rather may be ordinary people who have saved all their lives for their dream trip.

17. "Le vraie revolution" ("The True Revolution"), September 18, 1954. Steinbeck answers charges that he is not revolutionary enough by explaining that he is really most dangerous since he is not a slave to ideology but holds **Walt Whitman**'s view that the true revolution will take place when everyone recognizes the greater importance of each individual person than of any political credo.

Further Reading: Benson, Jackson J. *The True Adventures of John Steinbeck, Writer.* New York: Viking, 1984; Covici, Pascal, Jr. *The Portable*

Steinbeck, Revised and Enlarged Edition. New York: Viking, 1971; French, Warren. *John Steinbeck's Nonfiction Revisited*. New York: Twayne, 1996.

Warren French

"LEADER OF THE PEOPLE, THE" (1936). This fourth part of ***The Red Pony*** story cycle was apparently written during the same period in the early 1930s as the other three, but it did not appear in a magazine until August 1936, in the English story magazine *Argosy*. As **Roy S. Simmonds** discovered later, it had long been assumed that the story had not been published until it appeared in ***The Long Valley*** in 1938. The story completes the account of **Jody Tiflin**'s emotional maturing by showing his development of compassion when he begins to understand his grandfather's disappointment at the closing of the frontier and Americans' loss of the spirit of "Westering," the drive to move ever onward like that drive expressed by the Greek hero in Alfred Tennyson's poetic monologue "Ulysses" (one of Steinbeck's favorite poems). The old man's spirit is broken especially when he overhears his son-in-law complaining to his wife about her father's repeated telling of his experiences while leading the wagon trains across the plains during the settling of the West. Jody, on the other hand, listens to his grandfather's tales with rapt attention and tries to console him by speculating that other leaders (perhaps himself) may face similar challenges in the future.

Mimi Resisel Gladstein

LEE. Chinese cook, housekeeper, and lifelong friend to **Adam**, **Cal**, and **Aron Trask** in **East of Eden**. Throughout the novel, Lee acts as an entirely selfless servant, friend, advisor, parent, and teacher. Moreover, Lee introduces key ideas into the novel and articulates much of Steinbeck's thematic material. Yet Lee is an outsider: his Chinese heritage, Eastern thought, and use of narcotics (he drinks ng-ka-py, which he compares to absinthe, and smokes two pipes of opium a day) place him outside the Western and Judeo-Christian tradition. This is important since it means that he is not subject to the culturally inherited patterns that he later identifies in the Cain–Abel story.

Possibly as a result of the circumstances of his birth, Lee understands that human nature includes both good and bad impulses. As he tells Adam, the same men who ravaged his mother while she was in labor afterwards nurtured and mothered him. This "'dreadful beauty'" Lee describes represents, in its paradox, the contradictory impulses with which the individual struggles, the individual's capacity for both good and bad behavior, and the blessing of free will. These understandings are what Lee eventually strives to teach Cal.

At first, Lee wears traditional Chinese dress, sports a queue, plays the fool, behaves subserviently, and speaks Pidgin English. These are forms of camouflage that allow him to adapt to the cultural expectations of both whites and Chinese. As Lee explains to **Samuel Hamilton**, he doesn't fit in as an American in America or as a Chinese man in China; thus, he creates an appearance that reflects the expectations or preconceived notions of others. Because Samuel is able to "separate [his] observation from [his] preconception [and] see what is," Lee reveals himself as he really is: an erudite, perceptive, and articulate man. Consequently, he and Samuel establish a friendship based upon mutual respect and affection—and the sharing of books and ideas. As the novel progresses, Lee slowly learns to relinquish his protective disguise and to find a sense of belonging.

When **Cathy Trask** shoots Adam and deserts him and their infant sons, the yet-to-be-named Caleb and Aron, Lee abandons his guise of ignorant servant, cares for the stunned and wounded Adam, and mothers the twins. Almost a year later, while shopping in King City, Lee encounters Samuel and astounds him with the news that Adam exists in a trance-like state and that the twins remain unnamed. Shortly thereafter, an outraged Samuel rides to the Trask ranch and knocks Adam down. By this time, Lee has abandoned even more of his camouflage:

he has cut off his queue and no longer speaks in Pidgin. When Adam remarks on the change in Lee, Samuel tells him, "He trusts you now. . . . He's maybe a much better man than either of us could dream of being."

After dinner, during a discussion of the **Bible**, Samuel reads aloud the verses from Genesis that make up the Cain–Abel story. Attempting to understand the dynamics of the story and to explain its importance to humankind, Lee suggests, "People are interested only in themselves. If a story is not about the hearer he will not listen." Lee then explains that "this old and terrible story is important because it is a chart of the soul (the secret, rejected, guilty soul)." Here, Lee's exegesis of the Cain–Abel story identifies the paradigm of love, rejection, jealousy, revenge, and guilt that informs the relationships between fathers, sons, and brothers in the novel.

This scene at the Trask dinner table is repeated eleven years later, when again over coffee the three men discuss the story. This time, Lee speaks of how he and some Chinese scholars studied the story intensively, even consulting a rabbi and learning Hebrew. He explains excitedly that the key to the story is realizing that God provided Cain with choice (free will, embodied in the word "**timshel**," meaning "thou mayest [rule over sin]"). Lee calls timshel "the most important word in the world" because it embodies the gift of choice, and indeed it becomes the most important word from this point on in the novel.

When Cal and Aron are twelve, Adam moves the family to **Salinas**. Lee gets them settled and then leaves for San Francisco to fulfill his long-awaited dream of opening a bookstore. But Lee's metamorphosis is complete. Aware that he is no longer a subordinate servant but a devoted friend and member of the family, Lee misses Adam and the boys so much that six days later he returns for good. Over the next few years, Lee develops a tender relationship with **Abra Bacon**, Aron's girlfriend, whom he regards as a daughter. He counsels her wisely when she confides in him her doubts about Aron. When Abra decides to end things with Aron and finds herself attracted to Cal, Lee encourages his two spiritual children. Because Lee has always known that Cal struggles with the good and bad impulses within him, he fervently attempts to convince Cal that his emotions are human nature, not an aberration resulting from a genetic predisposition to evil. He urges Cal over and over to understand that he can control his impulses for bad, that he has the choice. Lee works hard with Cal for Cal is his project—his (and Steinbeck's) Everyman, who must understand that he has the power to change the patterns, that he is not predestined either by genetics or culture because he has free will. When the news of Aron's death causes Adam to have a second, more debilitating stroke, Cal is overcome with guilt and despair, feeling that his actions have killed his brother and destroyed his father. Lee realizes Cal's crisis and speaks with him earnestly about human flaws and the aspiration for perfection. He accompanies Cal and Abra to Adam's bedside and implores Adam to give his blessing to Cal, to forgive and thus free him. In response to Lee's fervent plea, Adam speaks one word—"Timshel!"—a word that is resonant with the promise of what Lee has sought to teach and that offers Cal the same choice, the same free will, that God offered to Cain.

Margaret Seligman

LEE CHONG'S HEAVENLY FLOWER GROCERY. The Cannery Row grocery store, separated by a vacant lot from the **Bear Flag** and located across the street at an angle from **Western Biological Laboratories** in *Sweet Thursday*. Although the store serves as something of a communal gathering place during the time of Lee Chong's ownership, it is a more impersonal setting with **Joseph and Mary Rivas** behind the counter.

"L'ENVOI." This original final chapter of *Travels with Charlie* was not included in the book. In it Steinbeck gives his impressions of **John F. Kennedy**'s inauguration and the fierce snowstorm that accompanied it. For Steinbeck, the inauguration, despite the poor weather and his wife's cold feet in his lap, was a moving one. Ironically, he notes that the Inaugural Ball was the best dance he ever experienced, even though he was not in attendance but merely watched on television. For the strange beauty of his experience, he concludes, "I do know this—the big and mysterious America is bigger than I thought. And more mysterious."

Further Reading: *America and Americans and Selected Nonfiction*. Ed. Susan Shillinglaw and Jackson J. Benson. New York: Viking, 2002.

LESCAULT, SUZANNE. *See* **Hyacinthe, Sister**.

"LET'S GO AFTER THE NEGLECTED TREASURES BENEATH THE SEAS" (1966). Essentially an elongated letter to the editor expressing a plea for equal effort to explore the mysteries of life on earth as well as those that may exist in space. Editor Ernie Heyn writes that Steinbeck, in this open letter, expresses the conviction that exploration of "inner space" and of the sea itself should be as well organized and financed by our government as is the investigation of outer space. "There is something for everyone in the seas—incredible beauty . . . excitement and danger . . . an open door for the ingenuity and inventiveness . . . a new world . . . food for the hungry . . . wealth for the acquisitive . . . in addition to the pure clean wonder of increasing knowledge."

Further Reading: *Popular Science* 189.3 (September 1966): 84–87.

Herbert Behrens and Michael J. Meyer

"LETTERS TO ALICIA" (1965–1967). A series of accounts of Steinbeck's travels to England, Ireland, Israel, and Vietnam published in *Newsday* between 1965 and 1967 and published in other papers as a syndicated column; these pieces were written to Alicia Patterson, *Newsday* publisher (with Harry F. Guggenheim). Though Alicia died in 1963, Steinbeck wanted to write to her as a point of focus and because he greatly admired her curiosity for all subjects. As **Jackson J. Benson** points out, the letters took on an increasingly personal and angry tone, and Steinbeck's comments on Vietnam generated controversy—he was seen as a hawk, someone who had betrayed his liberal ideals. In fact, Steinbeck's tour of Vietnam on behalf of his friend, **Lyndon Johnson**, connected the author with the soldier in the field (as seen in his World War II writings, ***Bombs Away*** and ***Once There Was a War***). Whereas he felt great pride in the soldiers, he could not help feeling some shame about the war protesters, whom he identified as "sour smelling wastelings" in a January 1967 "letter." Steinbeck, already in battle with literary critics by the 1950s, suffered more damage to his reputation among the liberal literary establishment with the Vietnam "Letters to Alicia."

Further Reading: Benson, Jackson J. *The True Adventures of John Steinbeck, Writer*. New York: Viking, 1984; Steinbeck, John. *America and Americans and Selected Nonfiction*. Ed. Susan Shillinglaw and Jackson J. Benson. New York: Viking, 2002.

LEVANT, HOWARD. A Steinbeck critic whose work centers on the author's structural and organizational aptitude, often contending that Steinbeck's ability to edit his own work or to create a disciplined structure resulted in failure in some of his texts whereas those that succeeded were those that were more carefully crafted and planned.

Further Reading: Levant, Howard. *The Novels of John Steinbeck: A Critical Study*. Columbia: University of Missouri Press, 1974.

LEWIN, FRANK (1925–). Lewin served as a professor at the Yale School of Music, teaching composition for film from 1971 to 1992, and at the Columbia University School of the Arts. A widely diversified composer, Lewin has edited and composed music for feature, documentary, and television films and has written incidental music for plays performed at Princeton. In addition, he has scored the work of William Carlos Williams, William Blake, Edward Arlington Robinson, Ogden Nash, and George Gordon, Lord Byron, creating musical adaptations of their poetry for a solo voice. Among his concert compositions are the opera ***Burning Bright***, based on Steinbeck's play of the same name. In October 1950, Lewin—then a composition student at Yale—saw the play off-Broadway in New Haven's Shubert Theater. Although the play was soon on its way to Broadway, it found little favor there. Lewin, however, was deeply impressed by the story and felt it was ideally suited for an opera. In 1967, he took out an option to turn the play into an opera. During the next ten years, Lewin did research and worked on a libretto. In 1977, he began composing the music, completing the score in January 1989 and premiering the entire composition at Yale University in November 1993. Excerpts from the opera were also presented as "a work in progress" at the 5th International Steinbeck conference in San Jose in 1995. In addition, Lewin has published choral works that feature texts from Yeats's "The Cap and The Bells" and Sir Thomas Nashe's poetry. According to Steinbeck critic Robert Morsberger, "Lewin's *Burning Bright* works better as an opera than it does as either a novel or play. . . . Not only does Lewin's music admirably suit Steinbeck's drama, but his libretto in some ways improves on Steinbeck's play."

Further Reading: See Lewin's monograph *Burning Bright, The Genesis of an Opera*, published by The Lyrica Society, 1985. Also see "Burning Bright: An Opera in Three Acts. Music and Libretto by Frank Lewin. Based on the Play and Novel by John Steinbeck" at http://members.aol.com/franklewin/bb.html; the music from the opera may be heard on the Albany Records Label Troy 469-71 in a 2000 performance by the Opera Festival of New Jersey.

LEWIS, SINCLAIR (1885–1951). American novelist and first American to win the **Nobel Prize** in Literature (1930). Born in Sauk Centre, Minnesota, Lewis wrote satirical novels of middle-class life in small-town America. Among his most famous novels are *Main Street* (1920), *Babbit* (1922), and *Elmer Gantry* (1927). In 1959, Steinbeck wrote to Lewis's biographer, Mark Schorer, that he admired Lewis's work, and Steinbeck mentions *Main Street* favorably in ***America and Americans***. He did count Lewis among those authors who fell apart after receiving the Nobel Prize (**Hemingway** and **Faulkner** included), and he felt that Lewis's acceptance speech was "ill-considered rambling." As described in ***Travels with Charley***, Steinbeck stopped at a German restaurant outside of Minneapolis and inquired about the route to Lewis's birthplace in Sauk Centre, but neither the cook nor the waitress had heard of him. As Steinbeck drove through Sauk Centre, he did so without stopping, recalling reading *Main Street* and the few times he met Lewis.

Further Reading: Steinbeck, Elaine, and Robert Wallsten, eds. *Steinbeck: A Life in Letters*. New York: Penguin, 1989.

LIFEBOAT **(FILM)** (1944). World War II proved an important turning point in John Steinbeck's personal and professional life, and his works during the war years remain a strange grab bag of ideas and purposes. None seems odder than *Lifeboat*, the Alfred Hitchcock war thriller for which Steinbeck wrote the original screen treatment. The project began in 1942 when the Merchant Marine asked Hollywood for a movie dramatizing the importance and the danger of their duties supplying the war effort in Europe. Steinbeck took on the task with the same documentary commitment he had displayed in his best works of the Depression decade, and he soon produced a strong treatment of 40,000 words that he called a "novelette" and which unfortunately was never published. His narrative balances the realism of a wartime North Atlantic battle with an allegorical journey of characters representing all the warring nations adrift in an archetypal lifeboat.

However, Hitchcock, the British master of sophisticated suspense, seemed an unlikely choice to direct the American realist, Steinbeck, for the screen. Their problems of collaboration were compounded by the additional efforts of two very different screenwriters—literary adapter MacKinlay Kantor and Hollywood veteran Jo Swerling. Twentieth-Century Fox provided a diverse cast including Tallulah Bankhead as a brassy newswoman, William Bendix as the injured seaman who centered Steinbeck's treatment, and Walter Slezak as a Nazi arch-villain. Steinbeck's subtle allegory was lost in the filmic overlay of home-front propaganda, Hollywood gloss, and Hitchcockian high intrigue. The studio-shot final version proved as false in production values as its committee-produced script. In fact, Steinbeck was so offended when the movie opened in January 1944 that he requested that his name be removed from the credits; contemporary critics such as James Agee and Mary McCarthy confirmed his judgment. *Lifeboat* remains an interesting failure, important only for its transitional place in the careers of both its author and director.

Further Reading: Federle, Steven J. "*Lifeboat* as Allegory: Steinbeck and the Demon of War." *Steinbeck Quarterly* 12 (Winter/Spring 1967): 14–20; Millichap, Joseph R. *Steinbeck and Film*. New York: Ungar, 1983; Morsberger, Robert E. "Adrift in Steinbeck's *Lifeboat*." *Literature/Film Quarterly* 4 (Fall 1976): 325–338.

Joseph Millichap

"LIFEBOAT" (SCRIPT-NOVELETTE). Begun in 1943 as a short story, or novelette, while Steinbeck was working on ***The Moon Is Down***, Steinbeck's "Lifeboat" was later revised at the request of Kenneth MacGowen of Twentieth-Century Fox and became the basic idea for a movie script to be directed by Alfred Hitchcock. The plot dealt with the victims of a U-Boat sinking in the Atlantic, and in depicting the interaction between various strong, allegorical characters, Steinbeck tried to create a microcosm of the real world, a task he later accomplished in ***The Wayward Bus***. Steinbeck envisioned interviewing real-life survivors of such attacks in order to add realism to the work, but Hitchcock was more interested in a simplistic depiction of racial and gender stereotypes. Although Steinbeck finished his adaptation in February 1943 and delivered it to Fox, he seems to have paid little attention to the film's production and was angered when he found that several major changes had been made to the script that he had submitted, including the depiction of a "stock-comedy" Negro and slurs against organized labor. Almost as frustrating were the inaccuracies allowed in the depiction of action on a small boat, details Steinbeck was not only familiar with but also an authority on. After a screening Steinbeck was so upset that he requested that Fox remove his name from the credits, fearing to be associated with what he considered egregious errors and insensitive portrayals of characters. He wanted the blame for the obvious prejudices to fall on Hitchcock, whose penchant for slicker character types all but obliterated the allegorical figures Steinbeck had intended. Fox never approved his request.

Michael J. Meyer

". . . LIKE CAPTURED FIREFLIES" (1959). A 10-inch by 14-inch broadside published by J. Wilson McKenney in 1959 that excerpts an article on teachers originally written by Steinbeck for the *California Teachers' Association Journal* in November 1955. A virtually unknown piece, only twelve copies were hand-set and printed by McKenney, who was the journal's printer as well as the magazine's editor. The publication is so rare that no Steinbeck collection, public or private, is known to have a copy.

LIM, SHORTY. During a fan-tan game at Shorty Lim's place in ***East of Eden***, **Cal Trask** is arrested.

LIPPO, LOUIS. Rancher who introduces **Adam Trask** to **Samuel Hamilton** in ***East of Eden***.

LISCA, PETER (1925–2001). Peter Lisca's groundbreaking 1958 book, *The Wide World* *of John Steinbeck*, was the first major examination of the writer's literary career, spanning from his first novel, ***Cup of Gold***, to what was then his last, ***The Short Reign of Pippin IV***. Lisca was a leader in Steinbeck scholarship—a critic who, despite the author's shifting reputation, could treat his work even-handedly, respond logically to the attacks of his worst enemies, and even revise his own assessment of Steinbeck's later fiction. *The Wide World of John Steinbeck* remains a useful volume of criticism, especially the 1981 edition with its "Afterword" covering the author's last works. Its professed goal is to remedy the critical fixation on Steinbeck's political or social messages (there were those who wanted him to continually rewrite ***The Grapes of Wrath***) by examining, in chronological order, the "craftsmanship" and "content" of his fiction. For an honest appraisal of John Steinbeck's strengths and weaknesses as a writer, Peter Lisca's work remains the starting point for serious Steinbeck scholarship.

Further Reading: Lisca, Peter. *The Wide World of John Steinbeck*. New York: Riverrun Press, 1981.

Stephen K. George

LITTLEFIELD, ANNIE. *See* **Women's Committee at the Weedpatch Camp, The**.

LODEGRANCE, KING OF CAMYLARDE. In ***The Acts of King Arthur***, father of **Guinevere**. When he is attacked by **King Royns** of North Wales, **Arthur** goes to his assistance. Lodegrance gives his daughter's hand in marriage to Arthur, and, as a dowry, gives Arthur the **Round Table** and a hundred knights.

LOESSER, FRANK (1910–1969). Famous songwriter and composer, he is best known for his 1942 song, "Praise the Lord and Pass the Ammunition," his 1949 Academy Award-winning song, "Baby It's Cold Outside," and big Broadway shows *Guys and Dolls* (1950) and *How to Succeed in Business without Really Trying* (1961). Steinbeck met Frank and his wife, Lynn, in 1939 when Steinbeck was beginning to see **Gwyndolyn Conger Steinbeck**, who would become his second wife (Gwyn was a friend of Lynn). In 1944, Frank conceived with John the idea of a musical, ***The Wizard of Maine***, about a snake-oil salesman with a heart of gold, but Steinbeck never completed the work. Loesser remained a lifelong friend, frequently visiting Steinbeck to cheer him in the last year of the author's life.

Further Reading: Benson, Jackson J. *The True Adventures of John Steinbeck, Writer*. New York: Viking, 1984; Loesser, Susan. *A Most Remarkable Fella: Frank Loesser and the Guys and Dolls in His Life*. New York: Dutton, 1993.

LOFT, CAPTAIN. In ***The Moon Is Down***, a young officer who is one of the five members of **Colonel Lanser**'s staff, each of whom displays various "herd men" characteristics that dehumanize and handicap their abilities to act as military professionals. However, unlike his counterpart, **Captain Bentick**, who is older and a dilettante who lacks military aspirations, Loft, as his name suggests, is all ambition, a mechanical man who relies on rigid discipline rather than human sympathy to maintain his mental outlook. Possessing a near encyclopedic knowledge of military customs and courtesies, Loft is also a budding careerist whose driving goals in life are to make brigadier general by the age of forty-five and to be admired by tall, masculine women.

LOG FROM THE SEA OF CORTEZ, THE (1941) The nonfiction narrative of ***Sea of Cortez***, republished in 1951 with **Edward F. Ricketts**' name removed. As an introduction, Steinbeck penned a long memoir of his friend (who had died in 1948) titled "**About Ed Ricketts**."

LOGAN, JOE. A fisherman with an ill daughter. Joe, in briefly meeting **Ethan Allen Hawley** in ***The Winter of Our Discontent***, seems a figure who also is one of life's victims.

L'OLLONAIS. Actual pirate captain and character in ***Cup of Gold***. The real pirate and Steinbeck's character are both renowned among their fellow pirates as exceptionally cruel men.

LONDON. A tough, intelligent migrant in ***In Dubious Battle*** who becomes the leader of the strikers when **Dakin** is jailed. **Mac** wins his confidence by delivering his daughter's baby by lantern light, and the two work together to keep the strike going.

LONDON, JACK (1876–1916). Born in San Francisco, London is best remembered for his larger-than-life adventures and novels *The Call of the Wild* (1903), *The Sea Wolf* (1904), and *White Fang* (1906) and the contemplative *Martin Eden* (1909). As **Jackson J. Benson** notes, Steinbeck enjoyed reading London at an early age. Though in different ways, London and Steinbeck both were influenced by **Darwin**, and both writers tend to place characters in natural settings with an emphasis on the human being's real (rather than preconceived) position in nature as a species subject to natural laws.

LONG VALLEY, THE (1938). Steinbeck's second and arguably best collection of short stories, published in 1938, with the following stories (actual composition dates in brackets): **"The Gift"** [June 1933] *North American Review* 236 (November 1933): 421–38; **"The Great Mountains"** [July 1933] *North American Review* 236 (December 1933): 492–500; **"The Murder"** [Late Summer or Fall 1933] *North American Review* 237 (April 1934): 305–12; **"The Chrysanthemums"** [Fall 1933–February 1934] *Harper's Magazine* 175 (October 1937): 513–19; **"The Promise"** [Winter 1934] *Harper's Magazine* 175 (May 1937): 243–52; **"The Leader of the People"** [Winter 1934] *Argosy* 20 (August 1936): 99–106; **"The Raid"** [May–June 1934] *North American Review* 238 (October 1934): 299–305; **"The Harness"** [May–June 1934] *Atlantic Monthly* 161 (June 1938): 741–49; **"Flight"** [May–June 1934] *The Long Valley* (1938); **"The White Quail"** [May–June 1934] *North American Review* 239 (March 1935): 204–11; **"Johnny Bear"** [late June 1934] (as "The Ears of Johnny Bear") *Esquire* 8 (September 1937): 35, 195–200; **"The Vigilante"** [July–August 1934] (as "The Lonesome Vigilante") *Esquire* 6 (October 1936): 35, 186A–186B; **"The Snake"** [July–August 1934] *Monterey Beacon* (22 June 1935): 10–11, 14–15; **"Breakfast"** [July–August 1934] *Pacific Weekly* 5 (9 November 1936): 300; **"Saint Katy the Virgin"** [1925–26], limited edition of 199 copies (New York: Covici-Friede, 1936).

As a collection of short stories written largely over the course of two years, *The Long Valley* lacks a continuity of characters. Whereas Steinbeck's earlier volume of short stories, ***The Pastures of Heaven***, presents individual short episodes that link together in a narrative, thematic, and geographical whole, one finds little such unity here. The exceptions are the four narratives of ***The Red Pony***. Rather than a unity of characters, however, there appears to be a clear unity of theme in the collection, emanating to a certain degree from the conditions under which Steinbeck wrote the stories. Biographical and historical factors bear upon this collection as powerfully as on any of Steinbeck's work. In 1933 Steinbeck was the author of two published books—***Cup of Gold*** and ***The Pastures of Heaven***—and a soon-to-be released third, ***To a God Unknown***, none of which had or would sell well. His writing career seemed at a standstill, particularly when family matters further compromised the time he could devote to writing. In March 1933, his mother suffered a debilitating stroke, and because he had no evident employment, John was called upon to nurse his mother, beginning with her discharge from the hospital in June, when Steinbeck moved into the family home on Central Avenue in **Salinas**. There he wrote, at the dining room table to be near his mother, most of the stories of *The Long Valley*.

His choice of the short story genre was not incidental. This was a golden age for the American short story, and for Steinbeck it represented a means to acquire recognition. Then, too, he had felt most confident in writing the linked short stories of *The Pastures of Heaven*, works that arose out of the geography and characters he knew firsthand. Once more he turned to such firsthand experience, although far more disparate, in the region of the Long Valley area stretching generally between the San Gabriel and the Gabilan Mountain ranges. Unlike the stories in *The Pastures of Heaven*, set in a relatively small area, these stories are far more varied and individually more complex. For example, "The Murder" may well have been conceived as early as 1931, while Steinbeck was writing *The Pastures of Heaven*, given that it shares setting as well as character and thematic patterns with those stories, but it is far more complex and macabre than any of them. Late in the summer of 1933, Steinbeck felt better prepared to tackle the story's individual demands.

During the year that Steinbeck devoted to these stories, he did devote some time to what he considered a bit of diversion from the real task at hand. In the late summer and early fall of 1933, in just a few casual weeks, Steinbeck penned the draft of a short whimsical novel that would be published in 1935 as ***Tortilla Flat***. Interestingly, this became his first commercial success and encouraged him to return to novels.

The general theme of the *Long Valley* stories appears in the first two composed—"The Gift" and "The Great Mountains," the first of the *Red Pony* stories. Steinbeck stated that theme forthrightly in his later essay, "My Short Novels": "*The Red Pony* was written a long time ago, when there was desolation in my family. The first death occurred. And the family, which every child believes to be immortal, was shattered. Perhaps this is the first adulthood of any man or woman. The first tortured question 'Why?' and then acceptance, and then the child becomes a man. *The Red Pony* was an attempt, an experiment if you wish, to set down this loss and acceptance and growth."

The pattern of "loss and acceptance and growth" was both his personal experience during those trying days and the emerging theme of the short stories. By working through this theme, Steinbeck shows in the stories how one might confront the loss and engage the challenges that lead to growth. In the stories themselves, however, that growth does not always come. Tragedy replaces it. In "Flight" **Pepé Torres** is reduced to an animalistic survival before his death. **Elisa Allen** in "The Chrysanthemums" spots her "bright direction" but at the end cries softly like an old woman facing her lost dream.

Frequently, the loss experienced is that of self-opportunity or personal freedom. **Peter Randall** exemplifies this perfectly in "The Harness," when he is unable to shake off his physical and symbolic harness. His is a psychological enslavement. So, too, many of the characters, like those in "The Raid," find themselves suppressed by a larger social power that Steinbeck describes in *Tortilla Flat* as "civilization." This power bloc has little patience with dreamers, and often Steinbeck's characters are the detritus, the fallout of society. His characters are often improper, chafing at the harness of a civilized order that seems to care for them not at all. They are the voiceless people, the very ones Steinbeck features on the stage of his short fiction.

The value of *The Long Valley* stories, for Steinbeck and the reader, cannot be overestimated. If, as Steinbeck often said, he acquired "sureness of touch" while writing *The Pastures of Heaven*, then the work on these stories fully validated his artistry to himself. Most of the stories were quickly accepted by high-quality publications. Moreover, he stretched and sharpened his artistic skills as never before. After the dismal artistic (and commercial) failures of his previous novels, he had learned precision and direction in craft. Finally, these stories are wonderfully varied. Steinbeck learned here how to look inside the character and let the character do the work. The volume represents a truly stunning variety of characters from this slice of America—from a little boy and an old man struggling with the "desolation of loss" in "The Red Pony," to the fascinating psychological portraits of Elisa Allen and **Mary Teller** and the woman of "The Snake," to renderings of racial conflict as in "Flight" or political conflict as in "The Raid."

John H. Timmerman

LONGINUS THE ROMAN. In *The Acts of King Arthur*, the centurion who wounds the crucified Christ with a spear. The spear lies on the bed alongside the body of **Joseph of Arimathea** in **King Pelham**'s castle and is used by **Sir Balin** to protect himself from and to wound the king.

LOPEZ. Native American worker at **Adam Trask**'s ranch in ***East of Eden***.

LOPEZ, ROSA AND MARIA. *See* **Hueneker, Allen**.

LORAINE LE SAUVAGE. In ***The Acts of King Arthur***, a cowardly knight who wounds **Sir Myles of the Lands** by spearing him in the back while he and his fiancée are on their way to Camelot to wed.

LORENTZ, PARE (1905–1995). Lorentz was a Hollywood film critic who drew the attention of **Franklin Delano Roosevelt** by publishing works on censorship and, in the first year of Roosevelt's presidency, *The Roosevelt Year: 1933*. By depicting the accomplishments of the New Deal in words and pictures, Lorentz emphasized the importance of media in selling the policies of the new administration, and soon he was appointed as film consultant to the Resettlement Administration for a film that was initially designed to depict the environmental conservation promoted by the Tennessee Valley Authority (TVA). However, Lorentz had settled on making a film about the Dust Bowl in the Southwestern United States, a project that he had unsuccessfully tried to pitch to Hollywood a year earlier. Eventually titled *The Plow That Broke the Plains*, the film was written and directed by Lorentz and was an instant artistic success. For Lorentz, the purpose of the film was to depict America as the land of plenty that the country was before the Depression and to suggest the plenty that the United States might again produce if use of the land was brought back into balance. It was also symbolic of Lorentz's sincere belief that America would move forward. The images that Lorentz employed in his films—the lone cowboy, waving fields of grass, the merging of the tributaries into the great Mississippi River, the simplicity of small-town New England life—all spoke to a simpler, golden past. In short, Lorentz's work expressed a belief that in turning away from the negative aspects of the present and looking back to the more successful past, Americans would be able to reclaim the best aspects of that past and bring themselves out of the malaise into which they were floundering.

Lorentz's next project was *The River*, a film that looked at the interrelationships between the land and the people who populated the land adjacent to America's great tributaries and that emphasized the success of the TVA. The film won best documentary at the Venice International Film Festival in 1938, and its script was nominated for the **Pulitzer Prize** in Poetry the same year, reflecting how the filmmaker combined poetic dialogue with powerful visuals and moving music to create a new medium, one complex enough to accomplish the somewhat contradictory task of simultaneously praising and chastening the country that he so loved.

Steinbeck and Lorentz met in February of 1938, with some indication there would be a collaboration between the two. This eventually occurred when the two joined forces in the filming of **Paul de Kruif**'s book, *The Fight for Life* (1938), a semi-documentary whose social message revolved around how to end the poverty and ignorance that caused a high percentage of infant mortality at the Chicago Maternity Center, where the film was made. More important than this joint venture, however, in terms of the connection between Steinbeck and Lorentz, is the fact that Lorentz's experimentation with style, movement, and structure in his films has been cited by critics as a major influence in the composition of Steinbeck's ***The Grapes of Wrath***. Though Steinbeck denied a direct influence, Lorentz's passion for supporting the underdog and his negative reaction to progress as evidenced in *Ecce Homo!* (a film that depicted unemployment from the viewpoint of men displaced by machines) surely found a sympathetic ear in Steinbeck. Whether this influence can be asserted or not, the two artists shared several traits that appealed to their respective audiences although they worked in different media. For example, both employ a lyrical quality of narration, use realistic sound effects, have a sense of epic motion and rhythm, and emphasize realistic human dialogue while developing a musical counterpoint to spoken narration.

Michael J. Meyer

LORRAINE. In *The Wayward Bus*, a friend of **Camille Oaks**. Lorraine is a fellow prostitute who currently lives with a man in advertising whom she infected with gonorrhea. His infection caused him to become mentally unstable, lose his job, and take dangerously large doses of sleeping pills. Camille tells **Norma** a story about how Lorraine incited a fight with her one-time fiancé, **Eddie**, in order to manipulate him through guilt into buying her a mink coat. Lorraine is like Camille—a woman completely devoid of romantic illusions about life or love—and so is both the ideal friend for Camille and the opposite of the romantic Norma, who would like to take Lorraine's place as Camille's new roommate.

Bradd Burningham

LOT, KING OF LOTHIAN AND ORKNEY. In *The Acts of King Arthur*, husband of **Margawse**, the eldest daughter of **Igraine**, and one of the eleven lords of the North defeated by **Arthur** at Bedgrayne. He is delayed by **Merlin**'s trickery until it is too late to lend his army's support to **Nero** in his battle against Arthur. In consequence, he rides against Arthur on his own after Nero has been defeated and in the ensuing fighting is killed by **King Pellinore**.

LOUIE. In *The Wayward Bus*, the driver of the Greyhound bus that brings **Camille Oaks** from San Ysidro to **Rebel Corners**. Louie is large and overweight, but "a dresser" who prides himself on his ability to manipulate women's emotions. Movies and magazines provide Louie with his definitions of style, and he aspires to the images of Bob Hope and Bing Crosby. Louie grows the fingernail on the little finger of his left hand in hopes of setting a trend, which apparently succeeds with coworkers who admire him. With other men, Louie refers to women as "pigs," and he tries to make a play for Camille Oaks, using every technique he has mastered from earlier pickups, but an old, cantankerous woman continually foils his attempts to talk with Camille, threatening to report him to the bus company. Camille has dealt with many Louies before, however, and sees through his attempts to seduce her.

Christopher S. Busch

LOVEJOY, NATALYA (TAL). *See* **Lovejoy, Ritchie**.

LOVEJOY, RITCHIE (1908–1956). Younger than Steinbeck, Lovejoy was an aspiring writer, cartoonist, illustrator, and journalist whom Steinbeck met through Lovejoy's mentor, the writer **Jack Calvin**, who lived in **Carmel**. As friends of Steinbeck and his first wife **Carol Henning Steinbeck**, Lovejoy and his wife Natalya (Tal, 1908–68) were part of the discussion group that gathered at **Ed Ricketts**' lab and were in constant social interaction with Steinbeck while he and Carol lived in **Pacific Grove**. At one time the two wives even planned a business venture together; they planned to develop a home manufacturing firm that would create three-dimensional portraits and department-store dummies in plastic. Steinbeck tried to foster Lovejoy's talent, perhaps alienating Calvin, his initial mentor, at the same time. Steinbeck's most publicized effort at furthering Lovejoy's artistic career was his announcement that he was giving Lovejoy the $1000 stipend awarded as part of the **Pulitzer Prize** he had received for ***The Grapes of Wrath*** so that Lovejoy could take time off from his day job in order to finish a novel that he had in progress. Unfortunately, despite the financial support, Lovejoy was unable to complete the project, and the friendship began to deteriorate in 1944. Perhaps Lovejoy was jealous of Steinbeck's growing success, or perhaps he was angry that because the gift had been so publicized, his failure was even more noticed. The relationship faltered anew when Lovejoy decided to accept an offer from *Life* magazine for a journalistic portrait of **Cannery Row** that Steinbeck himself had refused. Steinbeck considered Lovejoy's action as a double cross and a betrayal—a blatant placing of the need for money above an ethical concern for the denizens of the Row.

Further Reading: Steinbeck, John. *Steinbeck: A Life in Letters*. Ed. Elaine Steinbeck and Robert Wallsten. New York: Penguin, 1989.

Michael J. Meyer

LUCAS THE BUTLER, SIR. In ***The Acts of King Arthur***, one of the rulers of **King Arthur**'s servants.

LUCE, CLARE BOOTHE (1903–1987). Wife of Henry Robinson Luce, world-renowned as the publisher, as well as the founder, of ***Time*** magazine and the business periodical *Fortune*. Clare Luce was an actress, playwright, and journalist before turning her talents to the political scene, where she became a member of Congress in the 1940s and also served as the United States ambassador to Italy and Brazil under President Dwight D. Eisenhower. Luce's association with Steinbeck began when she was chosen to play **Curley's wife** in the stage version of ***Of Mice and Men***, directed by **George S. Kaufman**. The play opened at the Music Box Theater on Broadway in November of 1937. At Kaufman's suggestion, Luce's role was specifically expanded for the play version, and Steinbeck himself carefully wrote out suggestions on how it should be played, suggesting that if one could break down her defenses, she was "really a nice person, an honest person, and you would end up loving her."

Further Reading: Steinbeck, John. "Letter to Clare Luce (1938)." In *Steinbeck: A Life in Letters*. Ed. Elaine Steinbeck and Robert Wallsten. New York: Viking, 1975. 154–155.

Michael J. Meyer

LUDDEN, ALLEN (1917–1981). Known to American television audiences as the host of the television game shows "College Bowl" and "Password," Ludden was a friend of Steinbeck's third wife, **Elaine Scott Steinbeck**, and had gone to drama school with her at the University of Texas. Ludden and his first wife, Margaret, were invited to John and Elaine's wedding and were social friends. Although they were not close, Ludden admired Steinbeck and thought of him as a man of deep spiritual resources. Ludden was a convert to Roman Catholicism and found Steinbeck to be knowledgeable about the faith. They had met on many occasions in New York, and in March 1962 Ludden turned to Steinbeck for support when Margaret died from cancer. Distraught and unable to sleep, Ludden flew to the Italian island of Capri to see and be comforted by the Steinbecks, who welcomed few visitors while there. Steinbeck had suffered in recent months the deaths of several friends besides Ludden's wife, including his publisher, **Harold Guinzburg**, and his beloved friend **Dag Hammarskjöld**. Steinbeck gave Ludden the comfort and listening ear he needed, talking with him all night and into the next day. Finally able to unload his burden with Steinbeck's care, Ludden was able to return to the States rested and refreshed.

Paul M. Blobaum

LYLE OF AVALON, LADY. In ***The Acts of King Arthur***, she sends a damsel to **Arthur**'s court with a sword that can only be drawn from its scabbard by a brave and honorable knight with an unstained character. **Sir Balin** is the last knight to attempt to withdraw the sword and the only one who is successful.

LYNCH, ANNIE. In ***The Winter of Our Discontent***, a waitress in a fast-order grill whom **Ethan Allen Hawley** flatters by using her full name, demonstrating Ethan's sensitivity as opposed to the lack of sensitivity in his fellow townspeople.

LYNCHING VICTIM, THE. Steinbeck based his fictional character's ordeal in **"The Vigilante"** on an actual lynching that occurred in San Jose on November 26, 1933. By transforming the two white lynching victims, Harold Thurmond and John Maurice Holmes, into one nameless black man, Steinbeck injects the issue of racism into the story and thereby intensifies the man's status as victim and helps engender sympathy for him. The victim's crimes are never revealed, possibly because they would detract from Steinbeck's apparent primary goal: examining and illuminating the mentality of an individual member of a lynching mob.

Abby H. P. Werlock

LYNE, THE LADY. In *The Acts of King Arthur,* **Ewain**'s companion on the Triple Quest. She teaches him the arts of knighthood and combat and gives him a magic lightweight suit of armor and a magic sword.

LYONEL, SIR. In *The Acts of King Arthur,* younger brother of **Sir Ector.** Lyonel is chosen to accompany **Lancelot** on his quest so that he might learn all knightly things from him. While Lancelot is sleeping under an apple tree, Lyonel is captured by **Sir Tarquin** and incarcerated in his castle with many other prisoners. All the prisoners are eventually rescued by Lancelot. Together with his brother Sir Ector and his nephew **Sir Kay,** Sir Lyonel decides to ride after Lancelot and rejoin him on his quest.

LYONORS. In *The Acts of King Arthur,* daughter of Earl Sanam. She is loved by **Arthur** and conceives a son, named **Borre,** with him.

LYONSE, SIR. In *The Acts of King Arthur,* Lord of Payarne. He is a knight of the French kings **Ban** and **Bors**.

M

MABEL. One of the prostitutes at the **Bear Flag Restaurant** in ***Sweet Thursday*** who, with **Agnes** and **Becky**, serve as a sort of collective character. Mabel is depicted as being ignorant and at times immature. When **Fauna** is teaching the women about place settings, Mabel screams for her turn to go first. However, she does learn her finishing-school lessons well, naming the pieces of tableware without error and condemning the use of double negatives. Fauna tells Mabel that she may earn a star on the Bear Flag marriage chart soon, but unlike **Suzy**, Mabel informs the madam that she enjoys working at the brothel and has no interest in leaving. Mabel is described as a "natural-born" prostitute; she is in at least the third generation of her family to practice this profession. Although Steinbeck, perhaps recalling his central theme of ***East of Eden***, insists that her involvement in this profession is not fate, he clearly indicates that she is naturally predisposed to it. Although she might choose another line of work, there is little room for free will to operate if her entire nature draws her to prostitution.

Bruce Ouderkirk

MAC (SHORT FOR McLEOD, FIRST NAME NEVER GIVEN). In ***In Dubious Battle***, the experienced and resourceful, but dogmatic party leader who becomes the principal field organizer of the Torgas Valley strike. Much criticism of the novel has focused on his debates with **Doc Burton** about belonging to the party. He instructs **Jim Nolan** until Jim overconfidently declares himself stronger than Mac. However, Mac survives by using Jim's body after he is killed, just as Mac previously used **Joy**'s, to strengthen the group spirit.

MACAULAY, THOMAS BABINGTON (1800–1859). British poet, historian, and politician. Steinbeck probably read at least the first and fourth volumes (of five) of Macaulay's *History of England from the Accession of James II*. **Carol Henning Steinbeck**'s father owned the volumes, and **Robert DeMott** suggests that Steinbeck was interested in the military tactics and weaponry described. **Jim Nolan** of ***In Dubious Battle*** claims in chapter 1 that he read a lot of Macaulay's work.

Further Reading: DeMott, Robert. *Steinbeck's Reading; A Catalogue of Books Owned and Borrowed*. New York: Garland, 1984.

MACHEN, ARTHUR (1863–1947). Welsh novelist; **Robert DeMott** notes Steinbeck read Machen's work in the early 1920s, most likely *The Hill of Dreams* (1923), *The House of Souls* (1923), and *Ornaments in Jade* (1924; Steinbeck owned a signed copy of this one). Critic Joseph Warren Beach suggests that ***To a God Unknown*** indicates some Machen influences.

Further Reading: Beach, Joseph Warren. *American Fiction, 1920–1940*. New York: Scribner, 1972.

MACK. The philosopher king of *Cannery Row* and *Sweet Thursday*. He is the leader of a group of "bums" who live rent-free in a converted shed called the **Palace Flophouse and Grill**. Mack has rejected the getting and spending of middle-class American life. He rules over the Palace, settles disputes, creates fund-raising schemes, and enforces honor among thieves. When they are pressed for cash, Mack and his colleagues will occasionally take work at one of the canneries. Mack's decision to "do something nice" for **Doc** provides the overall dramatic action in *Cannery Row*, and he has a central role in the plot of *Sweet Thursday* as well. Although Mack tells Doc in *Cannery Row* that he himself once had an unsuccessful marriage, he is one of the initiators of the scheme in *Sweet Thursday* to find Doc a wife. Working with **Fauna**, he helps to plan the masquerade party at which **Suzy** is presented to Doc as his future bride. Mack falls into deep despair when the plan for Doc's engagement seems to have failed, but thanks to **Hazel**'s judicious use of an indoor ball bat (to break Doc's arm and win Suzy back to him through sympathy), Doc and Suzy are brought together in the end. Mack also develops the plan to shift the ownership of the Palace Flophouse to Doc by way of a raffle. Thinking that **Joseph** and **Mary Rivas** is the unknowing owner of the Flophouse, Mack cleverly enlists him in the entire raffle process, even to the selling of tickets, so that he cannot later declare the transfer invalid. After the raffle is over, Mack learns that he and the boys actually owned the Flophouse themselves, but he still prefers that Doc be their landlord so that they are unable to sell the place for alcohol. While Mack's schemes never quite succeed as he intends, little serious harm ever comes from them.

At the opening of *Sweet Thursday*, Steinbeck casts Mack in the unlikely role of a literary critic who instructs his class of flophouse scholars in novelistic techniques. Like Huck at the opening of *The Adventures of Huckleberry Finn*, Mack comments on the book in which he first appeared as a character, and he then explains how he believes a novel should be written. His basic requirements are that chapter titles be supplied; that dialogue be the primary method of character development; that there be some descriptive detail; and that lyrical passages, called **hooptedoodle**, be clearly marked and set apart from the narration of the central events.

Steinbeck does supply chapter titles for *Sweet Thursday*—the first time in a novel since ***Tortilla Flat***, where they were similarly used for humorous purposes. He also complies with Mack's requirements regarding the preponderance of dialogue and the disciplined use of descriptive detail. However, the hooptedoodle is not always labeled as such or kept distinct from the central narration. Thus, Steinbeck ultimately shows his disregard for critical advice, even when it is offered by a character of his own creation. Mack's inflated literary diction is one device that Steinbeck uses to distance the events of the novel from the real world, to maintain the fairyland mood of this mock romance.

Some critics have expressed disappointment with the changes in Mack's character from *Cannery Row* to *Sweet Thursday*. However, critics such as **Joseph Fontenrose** who complain that Mack and the boys are now "very respectable bums who promote matrimony" are surely missing Steinbeck's satiric intent in the novel. Mack certainly does not profess a belief in marriage as a valued social institution; he simply believes that Doc needs a woman to fight with in order to keep his mind occupied. Critics such as **Louis Owens** who lament that Mack and the boys are no longer the "tragicomic outcasts" of *Cannery Row* are requiring that Steinbeck write a different novel with their preferred tone. A tragicomic Mack would be grossly out of place in the comic world of *Sweet Thursday*. There was more psychological complexity to the Mack of *Cannery Row*, who admitted that his clowning was a reaction to the sense of personal failure that had haunted him throughout his life. In *Sweet Thursday*, there are few glimpses offered below the surface of his personality, and in this openly stagy world he often assumes the role of a vaudeville comedian, with Doc as his straight man.

What may be more difficult to forgive Steinbeck for is the fact that Mack simply becomes annoying at times. Mack's "little flowers" of wisdom—about the tendency of wealthy women to become hypochondriacs who could be cured by spending some time at a scrub board—are at best inane, and at worst offensive. Likewise, his word play is sometimes so cute as to become cloying, as when he declaims, "Mother, make my bed soon, for I'm sick to the death and I fain would lie down." Although Steinbeck clearly intends for Mack to be a comic character and even a clown, there are times throughout the novel, unfortunately, when his humor falls flat.

Further Reading: Fontenrose, Joseph. *John Steinbeck: An Introduction and Interpretation*. New York: Barnes and Noble, 1963; Owens, Louis. *John Steinbeck's Re-Vision of America*. Athens: University of Georgia Press, 1985; Steinbeck, John. Cannery Row. New York: Viking, 1945.

Charles Etheridge, Jr. and Bruce Ouderkirk

MACMINIMIN, MR. A customer at the Golden Poppy Restaurant in ***Sweet Thursday***.

"MADISON AVENUE AND THE ELECTION." This article records Steinbeck's reaction at the announcement that the Republican and Democratic parties were using New York advertising agencies to design their presidential campaigns for 1956. Steinbeck goes on to speculate about the virtues and the dangers of such a decision, suggesting that the "one difficulty in all of this [is that after] the captive audience has been conditioned to buy Squeakies, the bodybuilding bran dust, then suddenly the message changes and they are told to vote for Elmer Flangdangle for Senator."

Further Reading: *Saturday Review* 39:13 (March 31, 1956): 11.

Herbert Behrens and Michael J. Meyer

MADOR DE LA PORTE, SIR. In ***The Acts of King Arthur***, one of the four knights beaten in tournament by **Sir Lancelot** and the four white knights, the champions of **Sir Bagdemagus**.

MAE, THE TRUCK STOP WAITRESS ON ROUTE 66. Introduced by Steinbeck as a character in intercalary chapter 15 of ***The Grapes of Wrath***, her name is unimportant, but her attitude is pervasive as the migrants stop along the road. Although she is initially reticent about sharing, she is ultimately depicted as generous to a fault, offering large slices of pie to the truckers and giving essential food, such as bread, to the migrants at a reduced price. Along with Al the cook, Mae helps supply the desperate Okies with essentials and provides treats for their children. She buoys their hopes in a time of trial by offering two pieces of five-cent candy for a penny. In return, Al and Mae's actions are rewarded with hefty tips left by the truck drivers.

Michael J. Meyer

MAHLER, HAL V. Owner/operator of a pool hall in Santa Cruz where **Joe Valery** goes to search for **Ethel**, in ***East of Eden***. Hal tells Joe that Ethel was found dead, probably as a result of being pushed off a sardine boat by a bunch of drug-crazed sailors.

"MAIL I'VE SEEN, THE" (1956). In this essay, which appeared in *Saturday Review* (4 Aug.), Steinbeck notes that "A writer's mail is very interesting, but gradually over the years the letters fall into categories." Among these categories are fan letters, critical letters, denunciations, requests for autographs and pictures, thoughtful and intelligent letters, letters requesting money, letters pointing out errors, and invitations to collaborate. Steinbeck laments in particular the number of teachers who encourage their students to write him asking for commentary on his work, because he cannot possibly answer so many requests.

"MAKING OF A NEW YORKER" (1953). Nostalgic article by Steinbeck (first published in the *New York Times Magazine* on February 1, 1953) that concerns his evolving relationship with the city—from being terrified and beaten by the place in 1925 to finally being able to call New York home, which it was for the rest of his life.

Further Reading: Steinbeck, John. "Making of a New Yorker." In *America and Americans and Selected Nonfiction*. Ed. Susan Shillinglaw and Jackson J. Benson. New York: Viking, 2002.

MALKOVICH, JOHN (1953–). Stage and screen actor who often portrays sinister or grotesque characters. His films include *Places in the Heart* (1984), *The Killing Fields* (1984), *Dangerous Liaisons* (1988), *Mary Reilly* (1996), and *Being John Malkovich* (1999). In the 1992 film ***Of Mice and Men***, his portrayal of **Lennie Small** as bald—with a mouthful of rotting teeth and a high, singsong voice—was off-putting to some viewers, though it did not destroy sympathy for the character. Critical response was lukewarm, with Vincent Canby calling Malkovich's Lennie an intelligent, consistent performance, but one that seemed contrived and self-conscious.

MALLOY, MRS. In ***Burning Bright***, she is **Mordeen**'s friend, and the fact that Malloy has a baby and a 19-year-old son, Tom, in college torments **Joe Saul** in the opening scene of the play-novelette. Saul wishes desperately to have children with his second wife, Mordeen, and Mrs. Malloy's apparent fertility makes Saul angry and jealous.

MALLOY, MRS. In ***Sweet Thursday,*** she is a former resident of **Cannery Row** who is now working at a greasy spoon in **Salinas**, waiting for her husband **Sam** to get out of jail. She and Sam formerly lived in an abandoned boiler in the vacant lot between the **Bear Flag Restaurant** and **Lee Chong's Heavenly Flower Grocery**. A dedicated homemaker, she provoked domestic discord by pressing her husband to buy curtains for their solid iron, windowless abode. Although Mrs. Malloy is satirized in ***Cannery Row*** for this impulse of bourgeois domesticity, **Doc** decides in *Sweet Thursday* that **Suzy** is a "brave thing" when he discovers that she actually has glued curtains to the inside of this same boiler.

Charles Etheridge, Jr. and Bruce Ouderkirk

MALLOY, SAM. A former resident of **Cannery Row** who is now a trusty in the county jail. A practical man, he converted an abandoned boiler into a shelter by stripping out the remaining tubes and building a small brick fireplace. However, he could not understand his wife's desire to install curtains in the windowless cylinder. In ***Sweet Thursday***, **Agnes** tells the story of this couple to **Mabel** in order to foreshadow **Suzy**'s later adoption of the boiler as her new home.

Charles Etheridge, Jr. and Bruce Ouderkirk

MALORY, SIR THOMAS. *See* ***Morte d' Arthur, Le.***

MALTBY, JUNIUS. In ***The Pastures of Heaven***, a former clerk in San Francisco who moves to Las Pasturas for health reasons and discovers the positive qualities of a less rigid lifestyle. Laziness becomes a virtue for Junius as he marries a local widow and produces a child of his own, but problems arise when his wife and two stepsons die of a fever, leaving him as a single parent to raise his son, **Robbie**. He lives a life of seclusion with his German servant and companion **Jakob Stutz**, and he teaches his child by the Socratic Method through the discussion of philosophy and great literature, rather than by traditional school approaches. When Robbie is forced to go to school and conform to the rules of the valley community, Junius senses that he has done the boy a disservice by isolating him from others and teaching him the values of freedom and relaxation, rather than the importance of work. Ridden with guilt, Junius moves the family out of Las Pasturas and back to San Francisco, to resume what he considers a more "normal" lifestyle that will be more acceptable to a majority of his neighbors.

MALTBY, ROBBIE. In ***The Pastures of Heaven*** he is **Junius**'s son, a lover of idleness and play like his father. Dressed in ragged clothes and lacking formal manners, he is forced to attend Las Pasturas School, where he becomes the favorite, the class leader, the one to imitate. A learner by doing rather than by rote memory, he does not value the education provided by the school (e.g., reading, arithmetic, spelling). Rather, he has been educated at home through exposure to adult conversations about philosophy and great books. Robbie realizes his reputation as a poor boy when the ladies of Las Pasturas, led by **Mrs. Munroe**, offer him new clothes, supposedly out of their generosity. Unfortunately, their good intentions destroy his independent self-image and cause him harm rather than good.

MANESSEN, SIR. In ***The Acts of King Arthur,*** **Sir Accolon of Gaul**'s cousin and a knight of **King Arthur**'s court. Saved from death by **Morgan le Fay** because of her love for Sir Accolon.

MANSVELDT, EDWARD (d. 1667). Actual pirate captain of Dutch heritage and character who dreams of establishing a nation of buccaneers in ***Cup of Gold***. He enlists **Henry Morgan** as vice admiral in his siege of St. Catherine's Isle. When the conquest is successful, he leaves Henry in command and goes off to recruit citizen pirates for his new nation. He never returns, and it is rumored that he was killed in Cuba by the Spanish. His absence leaves Henry as the preeminent pirate in the Caribbean.

Kevin Hearle

MANUEL. Admitted son of **Old Juan** in ***To a God Unknown***. He is rather a scruffy Pan figure who plays not the pipes, but a guitar.

MARGAWSE. In ***The Acts of King Arthur,*** **the** eldest daughter of **Igraine**. Margawse is married to **King Lot** and is the mother of **Sir Gawain** and **Sir Gaheris**. **Arthur** makes love to her without realizing she is his half-sister, and **Mordred** is born of this incestuous union.

MARHALT, SIR. Son of the King of Ireland in ***The Acts of King Arthur.*** Marhalt meets **Ewain** and **Gawain** after their respective ordered and voluntary banishments from **Arthur**'s court, and he joins them on the Triple Quest.

MARK, KING OF CORNWALL. In ***The Acts of King Arthur,*** after **Sir Launceor** has been killed by **Sir Balin of Northumberland** and **The Lady Colombé** has killed herself in her grief, he buries the two lovers together in a tomb in front of a church altar.

MARN, DR. The local doctor in **"The Harness,"** who sees to **Emma Randall** when she dies and prescribes morphine for **Peter Randall** to sedate him after the funeral.

MARTEL, CHARLES. In ***The Short Reign of Pippin IV,*** Charles is uncle and confidant to **Pippin Héristal**. He is a successful antique dealer, but not overly scrupulous about the authenticity of his wares. He gives Pippin somewhat cynical political advice upon the unhappy event of Pippin's impending coronation, including the suggestion that as king he must have a mistress as well as an advertising agency. He recognizes how the newly established nobility will exploit their ancient rights, including forms of theft. His knowledge of British monarchy and American capitalism makes him a valuable resource for Pippin, who doesn't share his cynicism. Charles sees American corporations as the only viable model for a modern king. He warns Pippin that he will have to appear on television and therefore must cultivate acting skills. Charles is soon distressed, however, to find that his relationship to Pippin has endowed him with unsought notoriety and made him a target for lobbyists and celebrity-seekers.

Marilyn Chandler McEntyre

MARTHA HEASLEY COX CENTER FOR STEINBECK STUDIES, THE. The center, which opened as the Steinbeck Research Center in 1974 at San Jose State University's Wahlquist Library, holds over 40,000 items of Steinbeck materials. The collection includes signed first editions, original manuscripts, and handwritten letters; nearly 3000 scholarly articles and over 6000 newspaper articles; hundreds of foreign language editions; an extensive collection of hard-to-find Steinbeck movies and photographs; and curios and ephemera, such as the Steinbeck family **bible**. The center is now housed in the Dr. Martin Luther King, Jr. Library on the SJSU campus. The center maintains a Web site (www.steinbeck.sjsu.edu) that offers an extensive searchable bibliography of nearly 7000 scholarly articles and provides information about upcoming events, awards and fellowships, including the Steinbeck Fellows Program.

Paul Douglass

MARTIN, WILLIAM J. Husband of **Mollie Hamilton** in *East of Eden*.

MARTIN, OLD. Street-sweeper in Salinas who grubs a cigarette from **Cal Trask** in *East of Eden* and bemoans such progress as the mechanical street-sweeper, which could put him out of a job.

MARULLO, ALFIO. In ***The Winter of Our Discontent***, Marullo is the owner of the store where **Ethan Allen Hawley** clerks. Marullo is an illegal immigrant whose sharp business practices and habit of calling Ethan "kid" lead the latter to dismiss him as a "wop" (Marullo insists that his name is ancient and Roman). In the end, not knowing that Ethan has turned him in to the INS and caused his deportation, but remembering Ethan's earlier refusal to be bribed by the salesman **Biggers**, Marullo leaves the store to Ethan in admiration for what he considers to be Ethan's sterling adherence to ethics and morals. Marullo is also Steinbeck's comment on how recent immigrants have displaced Americans with heritage, and how greed in the business world has replaced the God-centered morality of an earlier day.

MASTER OF THE *BRISTOL GIRL*. Captain of the ship on which **Henry Morgan** first sails to the Caribbean, in ***Cup of Gold***. He is a Puritan, and each Sunday he delivers a sermon full of threats of hellfire to the assembled crew. The master knows that Henry has not been informed he will be sold into indentured servitude when they arrive in the West Indies, and he instructs **Tim** not to tell Henry.

Kevin Hearle

MATHILDE. Young Danish girl who works for **Olive Hamilton (Steinbeck)** in *East of Eden*.

MAUPASSANT, GUY DE (1850–1893). French novelist, journalist, and short story writer. Considered a master of the short story and known for his pessimistic view of humanity, Maupassant wrote in a terse, yet evocative style, creating stories that poignantly describe the sordid details of existence in a form that is praised for its conciseness. Usually associated with Naturalism, Maupassant is difficult to pin down because he was such a versatile writer. Steinbeck read Maupassant's short stories in the 1920s, admiring them for their "deft characterization, suggestive plot, and immediacy of detail," as **Robert DeMott** notes. He particularly liked Maupassant's "The Piece of String," and in a letter to his friend, the novelist **George Albee**, Steinbeck advised Albee to use Maupassant's story as a model for his own writing.

Despite the fact that Steinbeck claimed he never read the story, it has been suggested that the concluding scene in ***Grapes of Wrath*** was influenced by Maupassant's "Idylle" (1884), which contains a description of a wet nurse breast-feeding a hungry man. Steinbeck owned a copy of Maupassant's *The Complete Short Stories* (1903), but "Idylle" is not among the stories in that collection. In addition, Steinbeck wrote to **Pascal Covici** in 1939 that he had never read that story.

Further Reading: DeMott, Robert. *John Steinbeck's Reading; A Catalogue of Books Owned and Borrowed.* New York: Garland, 1984.

T. Adrian Lewis and Janet L. Flood

MAY. Blonde woman in **"The Murder"** whom **Jim Moore** is on his way to see on the night of the murder. She is one of the prostitutes at the Three Star in **Monterey** with whom he has amused himself, both before and after his marriage to **Jelka Moore**. On this night, because he is late leaving for town, he idly worries that someone else may already have claimed her attentions.

MAYOR PRO TEM. The successor to **Mayor Cristy** of **Pacific Grove** in ***Sweet Thursday***. On the second Sweet Thursday of the spring, the mayor pro tem writes a proclamation for the evening paper about the arrival of the long-awaited butterflies.

McBRIDE & COMPANY, ROBERT M. New York publishing company. In 1926, while Steinbeck was eking out a living in New York, a McBride editor named Guy Holt read a number of short stories by Steinbeck and asked him to write six or so more for a collection. Most of the resulting, hastily written stories were not representative of his best work. They were unified by their New York settings, however, so Steinbeck took his old pirate story **"A Lady in Infra-Red,"** which would eventually be the genesis of *Cup of Gold* and tacked on an introduction that claimed he had picked the story up on the streets of the city. Unfortunately for Steinbeck, by the time he returned to McBride a few weeks after his first meeting there, Holt had left the company. Steinbeck was so incensed to learn that Holt's replacement had no interest in his short stories that he had to be forcibly escorted out of the building.

Shortly after this fiasco, a defeated Steinbeck returned to California on a freighter. In 1929, McBride notified Steinbeck's old **Stanford University** friend and unofficial agent, **Ted Miller**, that they would publish *Cup of Gold* that fall. They would pay Steinbeck as much as $400 in royalties up front on the initial shipment to bookstores, and they hoped to use the lure of a cover by Steinbeck's old shipboard and New York friend, the illustrator **Mahlon Blaine**, to get the novel picked up by a book club. When the book was published, Steinbeck was not pleased. He felt that the lurid cover made it look like a swashbuckling tale for adolescents, and he was disappointed with McBride's feeble attempts to market the book. Not only did they not send him a copy of the book, they failed to send out copies to reviewers. However, because part of his *Cup of Gold* contract gave McBride an option on his next two books, Steinbeck sent them a manuscript entitled "To an Unknown God," which would later become ***To a God Unknown***. McBride quickly rejected that manuscript, and Steinbeck's affiliation with the publisher was at an end. *Cup of Gold* sold 1533 copies two months after the beginning of the Great Depression (during which the firm would go bankrupt).

Further Reading: Benson, Jackson J. *The True Adventures of John Steinbeck, Writer.* New York: Viking, 1984.

Kevin Hearle

McELROY. In ***The Wayward Bus***, owner of a Black Angus bull worth $1800. In an ominous foreshadowing, **Walter Breed** sees the dead bull wash past him as he checks the bridge near his general store.

McGREGGOR. Father of **Elizabeth** in ***To a God Unknown***. He is a harness maker and saddler who is known as a philosopher, even though he has renounced his former devotion to Karl Marx. He refuses to visit the **Waynes** at their farm, thereby symbolizing the willful (as opposed to the accidental) dismemberment of family and historical continuity.

McINTOSH & OTIS, INC. Established in 1928, a reputable and successful literary agency that represented John Steinbeck during his lifetime; the firm was the only agency he worked with as a writer. (*See* **McIntosh, Mavis**, and **Otis, Elizabeth**).

McINTOSH, MAVIS (1906–1986). Literary agent and founding member of **McIntosh & Otis, Inc.** In the mid-twenties, McIntosh met **Elizabeth Otis** while working for a literary agency that the pair ultimately discovered to be highly suspect in its practices. Although still a student, McIntosh left the agency along with Otis. Both were upset with the integrity of the office, and they opened their own literary agency soon after. By 1928 the team had become incorporated, and by the early 1930s McIntosh & Otis was a reputable and successful agency.

Although **John Breck** (Elizabeth Smith) first brought Steinbeck and his friend **George Albee** to the attention of McIntosh & Otis, it was **Carl Wilhelmson** who actually recommended Steinbeck specifically to Mavis McIntosh in early 1931. Increasingly disaffected with **Ted Miller** and impressed with the ability of McIntosh & Otis to find publication for Breck, Steinbeck had Miller send the agency a number of manuscripts, including "**Murder at Full Moon**" and "To an Unknown God" (which later became ***To a God Unknown***). Although initially unable to find a publisher for these early manuscripts, McIntosh and Otis were both tremendously supportive of Steinbeck and offered him encouragement at a pivotal time in the infancy of his career. Steinbeck stuck with his newfound literary agents for the rest of his career, nearly forty years.

Although Steinbeck's relationship with McIntosh was eventually overshadowed by the very close friendship he enjoyed with Otis, much of his early correspondence with the agency was addressed directly to McIntosh. This arrangement lasted through publication of ***The Pastures of Heaven, To a God Unknown***, the first two parts of ***The Red Pony***, **"The Murder,"** and up to ***Tortilla Flat***. By approximately the middle of 1935, Steinbeck's correspondence with McIntosh & Otis Inc. shifted to Otis as the primary recipient of his communication.

Brian Niro

McNALLY, TERRENCE (1939–). While a student at the Actors Studio, McNally was hired by **Elaine** and John **Steinbeck** to serve as a tutor for Steinbeck's sons, **John IV (Catbird)** and **Thom**, from 1961 to 1962. He was the main disciplinarian and guardian for the boys during stays at Sag Harbor and then traveled with Elaine and John on an extensive tour through Europe, with stops in England, Wales, Scotland, France, and Italy. McNally often took the brunt of Thom's and John's rebellious teenage natures as he tried to calm their contentious relationship with their father and stepmother. Later, McNally became a famous writer himself, composing such controversial plays as *Love! Valor! Compassion!*, *Corpus Christi*, and *Master Class*. One of his earliest attempts at theater was writing the book for a musical adaptation of Steinbeck's ***East of Eden*** (entitled ***Here's Where I Belong***), a venture that collapsed after one day on Broadway in 1968.

McWILLIAMS, CAREY (1905–1986). Nonfiction writer and author of *Factories in the Field* (1938), McWilliams was known for prose that documented the real problems of migrant workers in California. Like Steinbeck, McWilliams predicted that with more than 50,000 workers destitute and starving, there would be some sort of revolution or armed uprising in protest of the atrocious conditions they were forced to endure. *Factories in the Field* reaffirmed that many of the conditions and events recorded in ***The Grapes of Wrath*** were real, rather than fiction, and Steinbeck enthusiastically endorsed McWilliams's book as a "complete study of Californian agriculture past and present."

Further Reading: Cannon, Lou. "Profile: Carey McWilliams," *California Journal*. November 1999.

Michael J. Meyer

"MEDAL FOR BENNY, A" (1945). Using a plot line proposed by **Jack Wagner**, the brother of his friend **Max**, Steinbeck collaborated on a movie script with this title in 1943. The movie was released to little acclaim in 1945, but it later won Oscar nominations for best story and for J. Carrol Naish as Benny's father. Described by Steinbeck as a kind of vicious comedy, the film is about a bad kid from a California fishing village who is awarded the Congressional Medal of Honor posthumously for wiping out 100 Japanese soldiers before taking a sniper's bullet himself. Though Benny is never seen in the movie, his character is fascinating. It helps viewers explore the nature of heroes and heroism in America and shows how fame, recognition, and honor can change people's opinions and lead them to give hypocritical accolades based on hearsay, rather than fact.

Michael J. Meyer

MEEK, TOM. Salinas constable in ***East of Eden*** who kids **Cal Trask** about his relationship with **Abra Bacon** now that his brother **Aron Trask** has enlisted in the army. Meek also questions Cal about the money Cal and **Will Hamilton** made selling beans, and he thinks Cal is joking when he says he burned it.

MELIOT OF LOGURS, SIR. In ***The Acts of King Arthur***, the brother of Sir Bryan of the Isles, both of whom are encountered by **King Pellinore** during the Quest of the Lady. Meliot is the cousin of **Nyneve**.

MELVILLE, HERMAN (1819–1891). American novelist, short story writer, and poet, best known for his masterpiece *Moby-Dick* (1851). Having gained a great deal of success early in his career with his high-seas adventure tales, Melville experienced a steady decline in popularity throughout his later years, marked most prominently by the popular and critical rejection of *Moby-Dick*. By the time of his death in 1891 his work had been largely forgotten, and it took several years before Melville was recognized as one of the foremost American writers of all time.

Steinbeck was introduced to Melville's work sometime between 1949 and 1950 while working on ***East of Eden***. Known for its use of allegory and symbolism, Melville's work became a literary model—Steinbeck's main character **Adam Trask** becomes obsessed with **Cathy Ames**, just as Captain Ahab is with the whale. Ultimately, both Steinbeck's and Melville's protagonists are threatened with destruction by letting evil overcome them, rather than resisting it.

At the time of Steinbeck's reading, Melville's works were in the midst of a literary revival; *Moby-Dick* especially began to attract a great deal of critical attention. As **Robert DeMott** notes, Steinbeck appreciated Melville's "reflexive and symbolic technique" and adapted it for his use most visibly in *East of Eden*, where in a manner reminiscent of *Moby-Dick*, Steinbeck attempted to "create a counterpoint . . . between dark allegory and 'natural history'" that provided a "non-teleological answer to the theological question about the existence of evil." Along with his love for *Moby-Dick*, Steinbeck also had a small interest in Melville's *Journal of a Visit to Europe and the Levant*. He discovered, by way of a perspicacious dinner guest he met during his tour through the Holy Land in 1966, that Melville's *Journal* actually mentions Steinbeck's great-grandfather, "Deacon Dickson," a missionary to Israel.

Aside from expressing his affinity for Melville's work, on several occasions Steinbeck marked the lack of critical attention paid to *Moby-Dick* in the past as indicative of the poor judgment exercised by critics past and present. In a 1963 letter to **Pascal Covici**, his editor at **Viking Press**, he references *Moby-Dick* in order to lambaste literary critics **Alfred Kazin** and **Arthur Mizener**. He later refers to the novel again, stating, "you can almost hear Kazin's and Mizener's guffaws of rage if a book should come out called Moby-Dick. They would do just what the critics did when it was published" (Fensch, *Steinbeck and Covici* 230).

Later, in ***America and Americans,*** Steinbeck continues his assault on literary critics. Although the actual facts of these allusions to Melville's work are somewhat tenuous (Kazin actually edited the Riverside Edition of *Moby-Dick*), they do speak for Steinbeck's disdain for the critics of his time and earlier, as much as they speak for his deep respect for Melville and his work.

Further Reading: DeMott, Robert. "'Working at the Impossible': *Moby-Dick's* Presence in *East of Eden*." In *Steinbeck and the Environment*. Ed. Susan F. Beegel, Susan Shillinglaw, and Wesley N. Tiffney, Jr. Tuscaloosa: The University of Alabama Press, 1997. 211–28.

Gregory Hill, Jr.

MEMBER OF THE DELEGATION. In ***Viva Zapata!***, he is also recognized as "a man who stands behind **Emiliano**" when **Eufemio Zapata** and Emiliano confront each other in the central hall of the semiruined hacienda that Eufemio has appropriated. Eufemio has also apparently taken this delegate's wife, and he looks directly at the man as he boasts of his own amorous deeds and the taming not only of the people's lands but their wives, as well. This delegate is also looking at the Indian woman behind Eufemio, and evidently recognizes her as his wife. Steinbeck describes the scene as one in which "murder is in the air." Steinbeck soon labels the Member of the Delegation as the "Husband" who kills Eufemio and is killed in turn.

MERCHANTS. In ***Cup of Gold***, the merchants are "a different breed of men, . . . keenly decisive when there was a farm to be wrested by law from its owner, or when the price of food was raised for outland colonists." Like the Genoese slave dealers, they are part of the backdrop of general inhumanity against which the specific psychological portrait of **Henry Morgan** is drawn.

MEREDITH, BURGESS [GEORGE BURGESS] (1908–1997). Film and stage actor and occasional director who played **George Milton** in the 1939 film ***Of Mice and Men*** and narrated ***The Forgotten Village*** (1941). A feisty, diminutive, somewhat eccentric performer, Meredith was only briefly a star but had a long career as a supporting character actor. Among his notable pictures are *Winterset* (1936), *The Story of G. I. Joe* ([as Ernie Pyle] 1945), *The Magnificent Doll* ([as James Madison] 1946), *The Man on the Eiffel Tower* (1949), which he also directed, and *Rocky* (1977). Meredith and Steinbeck became close friends. They would often discuss the novelist's work in progress, but they quarreled in 1958 during a Caribbean vacation and the friendship ended.

Further Reading: Benson, Jackson J. *Looking for Steinbeck's Ghost*. Norman: University of Oklahoma Press, 1988; ——. *The True Adventures of John Steinbeck, Writer*. New York: Viking, 1984.

MERLIN. In ***The Acts of King Arthur***, the magician who casts a spell on **Igraine**, causing her to sleep with **Uther Pendragon** in the belief that he is her husband. In return for his help, Uther must give the child of this union (**Arthur**) into Merlin's care. Merlin advises and assists Arthur in all his endeavors. He warns him against marrying **Guinevere**, for she will be unfaithful to him with his dearest and most trusted friend. Merlin becomes besotted with the damsel **Nyneve**, who leads him on, trading her favors for the secrets of his magic arts. Eventually, by a spell that cannot be broken, she imprisons him for all time in a room under a great rock cliff in Cornwall.

MERLIN. In ***Cup of Gold***, he is reputed to be a seer and bard. **Henry Morgan** seeks his advice before leaving home at the age of fifteen to seek fame and fortune in the Indies. He tells Henry that he is "a little boy" who wants "the moon to drink from as a golden cup." Similarly, fifteen years later he tells Henry's father, **Old Robert**, that Henry "is still a little boy and wants the moon." This image of the golden cup loosely ties this story to the Grail legend.

MESSENGER OF DON ESPINOZA, THE. The man who comes through the ranks of pillaging pirates carrying a white flag to offer a ransom for **La Santa Roja** in ***Cup of Gold***. When **Henry Morgan** demands 20,000 pieces of eight, the messenger's reaction is that Henry doesn't want to ransom her. Henry assures him that what he wants is the gold, and the messenger returns in three days with the ransom. At the ransoming, the messenger explains to Henry that his master is willing to pay the ransom because La Santa Roja, his wife, is the sole heir to ten silver mines.

Kevin Hearle

MEYTHER. Pirate captain under **Henry Morgan**'s command in the campaign against Panama in ***Cup of Gold***.

MIKE. A constable investigating the deaths of **William** and **Mrs. Ames** and the disappearance of **Cathy Ames** in ***East of Eden***. During the hearing, he is brought to task for believing the confession of a half-wit.

MIKE. The protagonist of **"The Vigilante"** (published in ***The Long Valley***) whom Steinbeck uses to examine the effects of mob violence on the individual. Mike has been a willing, even eager, participant in the storming of the jail, the grabbing of the black prisoner, and the lynching of his corpse. In the aftermath, feeling unaccountably lonely and solitary, he enters a bar and discusses the entire night's events with **Welch** the bartender, another loner, who plies him with questions. Through Mike's wife's suspicious reaction to his late return home, Steinbeck implies the sexual dimension of the violence in which Mike has participated.

Abby H. P. Werlock

MIKE'S WIFE. Minor character in **"The Vigilante"** (published in ***The Long Valley***) who becomes suspicious about her husband's whereabouts during the night and accuses him of infidelity. Her accusation functions to make him and the reader aware of the sexual element in the lynching mob mentality.

Abby H. P. Werlock

MILES, SIR. A good knight, slain by **King Pellinore** in ***The Acts of King Arthur***.

MILESTONE, LEWIS (1895–1980). Film director most notable for *All Quiet on the Western Front* (1930), for which he won the Academy Award, and for ***Of Mice and Men*** (1939), which was nominated for best picture, best musical score (by **Aaron Copland**), and best sound recording. Milestone also directed the 1949 film of ***The Red Pony*** with less success. Among his more memorable pictures are *The Front Page* (1931), *Rain* (1932), *The General Died at Dawn* (1936), *A Walk in the Sun* (1946), and *Mutiny on the Bounty* (1962). For *Of Mice and Men*, Milestone visited Steinbeck in Los Gatos to have the author look over the screenplay. Steinbeck made minor revisions in short order, albeit reluctantly. He tried to help Milestone scout out ranch locations for filming, but would not stop the car for fear he would be shot with rock salt by local ranchers who hated him for his pro-migrant labor books and articles. Milestone did the rest of the scouting without Steinbeck.

Further Reading: Benson, Jackson J. *The True Adventures of John Steinbeck, Writer.* New York: Viking, 1984.

MILLER, AMASA "TED." Steinbeck's friend from the English Club at Stanford University and one of his constant companions during his first residence in New York. He arranged Steinbeck's passage back to California and, although unpaid and underappreciated, began serving as his first literary agent in 1928. Although a lawyer by trade, Miller arranged for ***Cup of Gold*** to be typed, and for eight months he personally delivered the manuscript to book editors and plied them with meals. He succeeded in arranging for *Cup of Gold* to be published by **Robert M.**

McBride & Company, but his subsequent efforts on Steinbeck's behalf were met with rejection letter after rejection letter. In 1931, at Steinbeck's suggestion, he turned over his collection of manuscripts and his records of their rejection history to the professional literary agents, **McIntosh & Otis**.

Further Reading: Benson, Jackson J. *The True Adventures of John Steinbeck, Writer.* New York: Viking Press, 1984; Steinbeck, John. *Steinbeck: A Life in Letters.* Ed. Elaine Steinbeck and Robert Wallsten. New York: Penguin, 1989.

Kevin Hearle

MILTON, GEORGE. In *Of Mice and Men*, a character with small but quick, restless eyes and sharp features. He travels with **Lennie Small**, a mentally deficient companion, and protects him from harm. To prevent Lennie from getting into any trouble, he either talks for him or asks him to keep silent. George has promised Lennie's aunt that he will take care of her nephew. George and Lennie dream about having a little house with a couple of acres, a cow, and some pigs, where they would "live off the fatta the lan.'" In the meantime, George frequently gets frustrated with Lennie because the responsibility to look after Lennie burdens him and prevents their dream from coming true. George expresses his wish to be free of Lennie, but he realizes that he needs Lennie for company, just as much as Lennie needs him.

When Lennie accidentally kills **Curley's wife**, George is forced to shoot Lennie to keep him from being subjected to the cruel wrath of **Curley**. The moment George points the gun at Lennie, he seems to be motivated by the feeling that he is leading the social cripple Lennie to his dream world. George's words as he raises the gun enable Lennie to die happy with their dreams in mind: "We'll have a cow. . . . An' we'll have maybe a pig an' chickens . . . an' down the flat we'll have a . . . little piece alfafa. . . . An' you get to tend the rabbits." All this creates a positive mood for the final moments of Lennie's life. For Steinbeck, as he wrote years later in a letter to **Annie Laurie Williams**, this act constitutes a rare heroism: "George is able to rise to greatness—to kill his friend to save him. George is a hero and only heroes are worth writing about."

MILTON, JOHN. *See* ***Paradise Lost***.

"MIRACLE ISLAND OF PARIS." One of a series of articles Steinbeck wrote about Paris while residing there in the mid-1950s. Awed by the city's magnificence, Steinbeck suggests that it would be impossible to write anything new or original about Paris, and that he feels at home when he resides there. Steinbeck writes: "(I) find myself drawn to the Ile de la Cite, that stone ship on the Seine whose cargo has gone to the whole world. . . . How (this island) reassures me that the world is not about to disappear and that men and ideas are eternal."

Further Reading: *Holiday.* February, 1956, 42–43.

Herbert Behrens and Michael J. Meyer

"MIRACLE OF TEPAYAC, THE" (1948). Short story by Steinbeck first published in *Collier's* for, appropriately, Christmas Day, 1948. The story is based on the miracle at Tepeyac, in Mexico, which the Catholic Church says occurred in December of 1531 and involved a Chichimec man named Juan Diego (who was canonized on July 31, 2002). As the story is retold by Steinbeck, Juan Diego is an Indian who grieves the recent loss of his wife. While wandering he encounters the Virgin Mary on a hill at Tepayac, and she tells him to go to the bishop so that a temple might be built for her on the hilltop. The bishop does not believe Juan until Mary provides a sign in the form of fresh roses—impossible to find in that part of the country at that time of year. Juan Diego brings the beautiful roses to the bishop, who then believes. A chapel is built on the hilltop, and Juan happily tends to it for the rest of his days. The story is strikingly spare and unadorned in Steinbeck's telling—stylistically, it fits the humble nature of Juan Diego. This tale is another example of Steinbeck's interest in translating old tales for modern reading, as evidenced in ***The Pearl*** and the unfinished ***The Acts of King Arthur***.

Further Reading: Steinbeck, John. "The Miracle of Tepayac." In *Uncollected Stories of John Steinbeck*. Ed. Kiyoshi Nakayama. Tokyo: Nan'un-do, 1986.

MIRRIELEES, EDITH RONALD (1878–1962). Steinbeck's beloved short story teacher at **Stanford University**. She published in such magazines as the *Atlantic Monthly* and produced two short story anthologies and a creative writing text. He was her most accomplished student, though he never earned more than a B grade in her class. She suggested that Steinbeck's work deserved publication, but was unsure of the appropriate medium for his writings. As **Jackson J. Benson** points out, her inluence—her belief that short stories should be written in terse, unornamented prose with a sense of truth—is seen in Steinbeck's more successful efforts in the 1930s. In 1962, Steinbeck wrote the foreword for a paperback edition of her text, *Story Writing*.

Tracy Michaels

MIZENER, ARTHUR (1907–1988). Well-known American professor and critic who wrote numerous essays and reviews. Among his books was the first biography of **F. Scott Fitzgerald**—*The Far Side of Paradise* (1951). In response to Steinbeck's receipt of the **Nobel Prize** in 1962, Mizener wrote a damning summation of the author's career for *The New York Times*. Mizener considered Steinbeck's works to be time-bound in the 1930s, rife with a fascination for primitive characters, and hopelessly sentimental. In sum, Mizener asserted that serious readers no longer bothered with Steinbeck. Steinbeck himself found Mizener's attacks to be baffling and ill-mannered. Mizener's essay fueled the debate as to whether Steinbeck deserved the Nobel Prize.

Further Reading: Mizener, Arthur. "Does a Moral Vision of the Thirties Deserve a Nobel Prize?" *New York Times*. December 9, 1962, 4.

MODDYFORD, CHARLES (SIR). Governor of Jamaica in ***Cup of Gold***. He and his wife take in **Elizabeth Morgan** after the death of her father, **Sir Edward Morgan**. He greets **Henry Morgan** upon his return from Panama, informs him of the royal summons, and accompanies him to England to meet with King Charles II.

MODDYFORD, LADY. In ***Cup of Gold***, she is the wife of **Sir Charles Moddyford**, governor of Jamaica. She helps to arrange the marriage of **Henry Morgan** and **Elizabeth**, who is Henry's cousin and the daughter of **Sir Edmund Morgan**.

"MODEL T NAMED 'IT,' A" (1953). Short nostalgic piece published in 1953 that was culled from an anecdote recounted in ***East of Eden***, in which **Olive Steinbeck**, the author's mother, had been sprayed by an explosion of oatmeal that her prankster son had put into the radiator of the family car. It was one of several nostalgic stories written by Steinbeck shortly after the completion of his epic novel, perhaps reflecting his need to center himself in memories of the past.

Further Reading: Steinbeck, John. "A Model T Named 'It.'" In *America and Americans and Selected Nonfiction*. Ed. Susan Shillinglaw and Jackson J. Benson. New York: Viking, 2002.

Michael J. Meyer

MONTEREY. A seaside town in central California, Monterey has a rich history and was capital of California under Spanish, Mexican, and U. S. flags from 1777 to 1849. Some twenty miles from his inland birthplace of **Salinas** and adjacent to **Pacific Grove**, where the Steinbecks had a summer cottage, Monterey was the setting for a variety of John Steinbeck's fiction and nonfiction, as well as for significant events in the writer's life. As a young man living in Pacific Grove or attending the 1923 summer session at the **Hopkins Marine Station** in Monterey, Steinbeck spent a great deal of time in and around Monterey during his formative years as a writer.

Edward F. Ricketts operated his **Pacific Biological Laboratory** on **Cannery Row** in Monterey, and this was the scene of much of Steinbeck's reading and thinking during the 1930s. By the time Steinbeck left the Monterey Peninsula, after the fame resulting from publication of ***The Grapes of Wrath*** in 1939 made life there impossible, the author felt nostalgic for the place. When he joined Ricketts on their collecting trip to the Sea of Cortez in 1940, they left Monterey Bay on the ***Western Flyer***. During World War II, Steinbeck considered Monterey, rather than Salinas, as his home, and in particular he hoped that when his war travels were over he could work back in Pacific Grove. **Jackson J. Benson** notes that by 1944 Steinbeck's longing for the simpler life on the Row inspired the author to write ***Cannery Row***. Nearly a decade later a similar nostalgia and a longing for his deceased friend Ricketts would inspire Steinbeck to write a sequel—***Sweet Thursday***.

In 1944, while living in the historic Soto House in Monterey, Steinbeck found that as a writer he could not get an office to rent in the town. He knew that Monterey's business community was not pleased with his publications that featured their community. His second wife, **Gwendolyn Conger Steinbeck**, did not feel welcome down on the Row (his first wife, **Carol Henning Steinbeck**, had been part of the original group), and in 1945 the Steinbecks returned to New York City. After Ricketts had died and Gwyn had divorced him, Steinbeck returned to the cottage in Pacific Grove, where he spent the fall and winter of 1948 and the spring of 1949 in deep depression. After he married his third wife, **Elaine Scott Steinbeck**, and completed ***East of Eden***, he left Monterey behind forever as a home.

Throughout the 1950s and until his death in 1968, Steinbeck made trips to the Monterey area to visit family members, including his sister, **Mary (Steinbeck) Dekker**. When he traveled to the Monterey Peninsula in 1960 as part of his journey for ***Travels with Charley***, he found his old haunts changed because he himself had become a "ghost." He agreed with Thomas Wolfe that one can't go home again, and generally his account of returning to Monterey is rather depressing. He describes it as a place where "they fish for tourists now." As Benson recounts, Steinbeck was terribly embarrassed to see that a local theatre bore his name. Still, as a setting for many of his works—including his first popular novel, ***Tortilla Flat***—and the scene of much of his education as a writer, Monterey is one of the most important locations in Steinbeck's life and writing.

Further Reading: Benson, Jackson J. *The True Adventures of John Steinbeck, Writer*. New York, Viking: 1984; Ricketts, Edward F. *Renaissance Man of Cannery Row: The Life and Letters of Edward F. Ricketts*. Ed. Katherine A. Rodger. Tuscaloosa: University of Alabama Press, 2002; Steinbeck, John. *Travels with Charley In Search of America*. 1962. New York: Penguin, 1980.

MOON IS DOWN, THE **(BOOK)** (1942). Steinbeck's one true war novel and the second of his "play-novelette" forms, published in 1942. As a result of his volunteer work with several government intelligence and information agencies during 1940 and 1941, Steinbeck had decided by September of 1941 to write a work of fiction about the psychological effects an invaded country sustains as a result of enemy occupation. He set the earliest draft of his story in America and submitted it for approval to the U. S. Foreign Information Service, one of the agencies he was associated with. His superiors at the FIS rejected the work, fearing that the mere suggestion of a foreign occupation of U. S. territory might be demoralizing. Steinbeck changed the setting to an unnamed country highly reminiscent of Norway, which had been overrun by the

Nazis in a surprise attack on April 9, 1940. Steinbeck completed the work on December 7, 1941, and borrowed its title, suggestive of spiritual darkness, from the beginning of Act Two of *Macbeth*. **Viking Press** published it on March 6, 1942. A dramatic version ran on Broadway from April 7 to June 6, 1942, and the Twentieth Century-Fox movie premiered on March 14, 1943.

One quiet Sunday morning an unnamed coastal town is unexpectedly invaded by sea and air, and without a declaration of war. The town has been a peaceful democracy for so long that its militia consists of only twelve young men. At the time of the invasion, all are away in nearby hills participating in a shooting competition staged by the local quisling, the popular storekeeper, **George Corell**. When they see the enemy's planes and parachuting invaders, they hurry back to town but are too late to offer more than token resistance. Overwhelmed by superior forces, six are killed, three are wounded, and three escape. Minutes later, the invaders' brass band plays "beautiful and sentimental" music to a bewildered populace in the town square, while the enemy commander, **Colonel Lanser**, formally requests an audience with the mayor, an elderly gentleman named **Orden**. The mayor's wife and their servants, **Joseph** and **Annie**, prepare his house and dress him appropriately for the meeting, while he and his lifelong friend **Doctor Winter**, the town's physician-philosopher, discuss their enemy—an impatient people who "push the rolling world along with their shoulders."

During their conversation, Colonel Lanser treats Mayor Orden with distinguished consideration. Their meeting is disturbed only when the mayor learns that his longtime acquaintance, George Corell, is a fifth columnist. Colonel Lanser pleads for cooperation, comparing his country's invasion to a "business venture." The invaders simply need coal and fish, and they will inconvenience the townspeople as little as possible. They will be harsh only if the locals do not cooperate, and Colonel Lanser asks the Mayor to order the townspeople to obey. Mayor Orden expresses doubt that he could control his independent-minded citizens in such a way, even if he wished to.

During the Mayor's conversation with Colonel Lanser, Annie, the temperamental maid, throws boiling water on one of Lanser's soldiers who is guarding the back porch. This early spontaneous act of rebellion presages organized resistance. Colonel Lanser commandeers the upstairs of Mayor Orden's palace for himself and his staff: the engineer **Major Hunter**, "a gaunt little man of figures"; the Anglophile **Captain Bentick**, who loves "dogs and pink children and Christmas"; the militaristic **Captain Loft**, who "clicked his heels perfectly"; and the idealistic young lieutenants, **Prackle** and **Tonder**, who maintain unquestioning belief in the genius of their Leader. In his new quarters, Colonel Lanser receives the traitor, Mr. Corell, who arrives to claim a role in the new civil administration as a reward for his treason. Colonel Lanser advises Corell to leave the country for his own safety. The Colonel understands that the citizens of the town, only momentarily defeated, will soon strike back. During the course of that conversation, Captain Loft rushes in to report that Captain Bentick has been killed by a local miner, **Alex Morden**, who objected to being ordered to work.

Colonel Lanser, eager to present an illusion of legitimacy for his authority, asks Mayor Orden to sentence Morden to death. The mayor refuses, maintaining that in doing so he would be breaking the law, just as Lanser's troops did when they killed the six local soldiers in the course of invading a peaceable country. Alex Morden is executed after a hasty trial, and the sullen townspeople quickly turn to sabotage. Over the next few months, the coal miners work more slowly, machinery breaks mysteriously, and "accidents" disrupt rail deliveries. Colonel Lanser's troops shoot local hostages in reprisal, but such responses only increase the townspeople's hatred. Eventually, the invaders find themselves cut off from all human warmth and kindness. The isolated conquerors, in effect, become the conquered; in Lieutenant Tonder's words, "The flies conquer the flypaper." Craving companionship and attention, Tonder visits Alex Morden's widow, **Molly**. Molly promises to make love to him for the price of two sausages. When he returns later, Molly kills him with a pair of scissors. The revelation of Tonder's death coincides with fresh reports of breaks in the rail lines and with the arrival of English bombers that drop small packages of dynamite for the townspeople to use in carrying out new acts of sabotage.

As Colonel Lanser and his officers plan their response to the most recent outbreaks of resistance activity, Corell, who was recently wounded in a partisan attempt to kill him, arrives with a letter granting him "certain authority." Corell demands that Mayor Orden and Doctor Winter be held as hostages against further sabotage. Despite doubt that such a move would forestall partisan activity, Lanser orders the arrests of the two men. The mayor refuses to order the townspeople to cease resistance, observing that he would not be obeyed in any event. The sound of new explosions seals his fate. As Mayor Orden is led to his execution, he quotes Socrates to his old friend, Doctor Winter: "Crito, I owe a cock to Asclepius. . . . Will you remember to pay the debt?" Winter responds, "The debt shall be paid."

Critical reviews of *The Moon Is Down* appearing in major U. S. newspapers and literary magazines for several months following its publication constituted the most heated literary debate in the United States during the Second World War. The novel appeared during the bleakest period of the war for the United States—the months between the devastating Japanese attack on Pearl Harbor and the first significant American victory over Japanese forces in the Battle of Midway. During those six months, Americans were confronted by depressing daily accounts of unchecked Japanese victories throughout Southeast Asia and across great stretches of the Pacific Ocean. Understandably, reviewers focused on the question of how effective the novel would be as propaganda.

Although *The Moon Is Down* clearly damns the Nazis, Steinbeck deliberately eschewed the demonizing stereotypes characteristic of World War II propaganda by depicting the invaders as occasionally thoughtful and intelligent. The most trenchant critics, consequently, attacked Steinbeck as naïve, suggesting that such a "soft and dreamy" work could actually demoralize the major audiences he wished to encourage—readers in occupied countries experiencing Nazi brutality directly. These critics included those who also objected to what they perceived as Steinbeck's dangerously optimistic view that an Allied victory was inevitable because the free peoples of democracies are stronger that the "herd people" of totalitarian regimes.

Postwar research has revealed that in fact the novel was effective as propaganda in several Nazi-occupied countries, enjoying particular popularity in France, the Netherlands, Denmark, and Norway. Resistance organizations in those countries published numerous illegal editions of translations of the novel and distributed them, often at great risk, through underground networks. Steinbeck's idea that the exaggerated stereotypes of the usual run of propaganda would not be effective among those who were experiencing the rigors directly proved accurate. Although *The Moon Is Down* was conceived and written mainly as propaganda, it survived remarkably well during and after the crisis that produced it. Since 1945, it has been translated into twenty-two languages and has appeared in roughly one hundred editions in twenty-eight countries.

Further Reading: Benson, Jackson J. *The True Adventures of John Steinbeck, Writer*. New York: Viking, 1984. Coers, Donald. *John Steinbeck as Propagandist: "The Moon Is Down" Goes to War*. Tuscaloosa: The University of Alabama Press, 1991. Hayashi, Ted. *Steinbeck's World War II Fiction, "The Moon Is Down": Three Explications*. Essay Series, No. 1. Muncie, IN: Steinbeck Research Institute, Ball State University, 1986. Simmonds, Roy S. *John Steinbeck: The War Years, 1939–1945*. Lewisburg: Bucknell University Press, 1996.

Donald Coers

MOON IS DOWN, THE* (FILM)** (1943). In some ways, the 20th Century Fox film is the most successful version of *The Moon Is Down*. **Nunnally Johnson**, who had done the screenplay for ***The Grapes of Wrath, wrote the screenplay and produced the film. When he asked Steinbeck for suggestions about adapting the novel and play to the screen, Steinbeck advised, "Tamper with it." Even so, Johnson remained faithful to Steinbeck's plot and used much of his dialogue verbatim. Johnson's main innovation was to open up the action and dramatize scenes that are offstage in the play and novel. Although Steinbeck never specifies the locale of the work, the film never leaves us in doubt. It opens with a map of Norway, while we hear Hitler's voice shouting in rage, "Norway, Norway, Norway." The movie then shows the initial Nazi invasion, storm troopers slaughtering a handful of Norwegian soldiers, numerous details of Nazi brutality, and a crescendo of Norwegian fury. Accordingly, *Time*'s reviewer called the Nazis much harsher in the film and the story more effective than in the novel, using "the sharp language of action rather than introspective comment" to "describe the villagers' growing hatred and resistance, the Nazis' growing fear."

When the novel and play first appeared, some critics, most notably **James Thurber**, attacked Steinbeck for being allegedly "soft" on Nazism by showing some of the invaders as lonely, frightened, and homesick, even though there is no doubt that they are the enemy, carrying out the cruel orders of a mad tyrant. Consequently, when the film was released Bosley Crowther was gratified to find that Nunnally Johnson had "carefully corrected the most censurable features of the work" by making **Colonel Lanser**, the Nazi commander played by **Sir Cedric Hardwicke**, "cold and ruthless, . . . a cold, contemptuous intellectual." Likewise, *Newsweek*'s reviewer noted the "cold, impersonal intelligence" that Hardwicke gave Lanser and stated that he much preferred the casting of Hardwicke and Henry Travers (as **Mayor Orden**) in the film to that of Otto Kruger and Ralph Morgan in the stage version of the work. At the same time, Hermine Rich Isaacs wrote in *Theatre Arts* that Johnson's adaptation was "faithful to the author's almost revolutionary concept of the Nazis as credible human beings, invested with intelligence as well as sheer brute strength and subject to the fallibility of mortals. They have a three-dimensional quality that stands out in bold relief against the usual run of Nazi villain, Hollywood style. . . . In Lanser's sense of the futility of the Nazi brutalities is the most convincing promise of their eventual nemesis."

The Moon Is Down was filmed on a low budget with no major Hollywood stars. The biggest expense was $300,000 paid to Steinbeck for the film rights, indicative of the way his stock had gone up since he received $75,000 for *The Grapes of Wrath*. To save on production costs, Fox simply re-dressed the sets for the Welsh mining village of **John Ford**'s *How Green Was My Valley* (1941) and used them for Norway. Irving Pichel's direction received critical acclaim, and even the lack of star performers was considered an asset in contributing to the film's realism. Bosley Crowther found it the "most persuasive philosophical indictment of the 'new order' that the film is ever likely to contain." After he saw the film, Steinbeck congratulated Johnson, acknowledging, "There is no question that pictures are a better medium for this story than the stage ever was. It was impossible to bring the whole countryside and the feeling of it onto the stage, with the result that the audience saw only one side of the picture."

Further Reading: Morsberger, Robert. "Steinbeck on Screen." In *A Study Guide to Steinbeck: A Handbook to His Major Works*. Ed. Tetsumaro Hayashi. Metuchen, NJ: The Scarecrow Press, 1974; Simmonds, Roy S. "The Metamorphosis of *The Moon Is Down*: March 1942–March 1943." In *After 'The Grapes of Wrath': Essays on John Steinbeck in Honor of Tetsumaro Hayashi*. Ed. Donald V. Coers, Paul D. Ruffin, and Robert J. DeMott. Athens, OH: Ohio University Press, 1995.

Robert E. Morsberger

***MOON IS DOWN, THE* (PLAY)** (1942). The second and arguably the least dramatically arresting of Steinbeck's three published excursions into the play-novelette genre. It was presented on Broadway on April 7, 1942, only a month after the publication of the novel of the same name. The British novelist and critic Frank Swinnerton has suggested that *The Moon Is Down* can be viewed as the World War II companion piece to Maurice Maeterlinck's World War I play *Le Bourgmestre de Stillemonde* (1918). The bracketing of the two works is valid, for they have something more in common than the basic theme of a small town invaded by brutal enemy troops. In each play, a lieutenant of the occupying force is murdered and the town's leading citizen taken hostage, finally to be executed by firing squad. Both are also static plays, in that the whole of each respective drama is enacted within the confines of typically bourgeois rooms, with all the motivating action occurring offstage. But whereas the Belgian playwright presents his thesis in terms of psychological tension, Steinbeck relies for the most part on philosophical debate. Indeed, Steinbeck was forced to admit that *The Moon Is Down* was "not a dramatically interesting play," and that his dialogue did not seem to succeed in crossing the footlights and engaging audiences as a good play should.

In keeping with Steinbeck's definition of a play-novelette, the play closely follows the dialogue of the novel. There was criticism by some contemporary book reviewers, however, regarding (among other matters) what was seen as the unduly sympathetic portrait of **Colonel Lanser**, the commander of the occupying force. Steinbeck did endeavor in the play version to harden the character of the colonel, the better to conform to the current conceptions of the cold ruthlessness with which a Nazi officer would be expected to behave, but the author's efforts in this respect were of little avail. When the play opened on Broadway after an unhappy tryout in Baltimore and some further judicious revision of the dialogue, the New York critics were generally unimpressed. They blamed (in addition to the "pedestrian prose," as one reviewer referred to it) the slow-paced production, the heavy-handed direction, and perhaps most of all, the uninspired casting and weak acting. Among the few positive reactions to the play, the *Theatre Arts* critic maintained that Steinbeck had "succeeded in expressing in pure theatric terms an eloquent plea for democracy, a stirring call-to-arms to all free fighting spirits." The play was withdrawn by the producer on June 6, after only fifty-five performances. It acquired the reputation of being one of the major disappointments of a disappointing theatrical season—a season in which the New York Drama Critics' Circle decided that no play merited their annual award.

With a different cast, the play had more success on a subsequent nationwide tour with a road company. It was also extremely well-received when, with a first class British cast and director, it was staged in London in June of 1943. This time there was no coy attempt to disguise the nationalities of the conquered and the conquerors, as there was in the original Broadway production. But the play had its greatest success in Scandinavia during the war. When first presented in Stockholm in March of 1943, it was such a smash hit that it had to be transferred to a larger theater. With reports filtering through from neighboring Norway of increasing resistance to the Nazi oppressors in that country, critics in neutral Sweden praised Steinbeck for his prophetic vision and declared that the play was even more true-to-life than at the time Steinbeck conceived it.

As a play, and despite its Broadway debacle, *The Moon Is Down* admirably served its propaganda purpose during those wartime days and during the immediate postwar period in liberated Europe. Even though it would still have a burning relevance to the people of any enslaved nation today, and although as a novel the work continues to be published and read by succeeding generations, the play has lapsed into obscurity. Unlike ***Of Mice and Men***, the play-novelette that preceded it, *The Moon Is Down* is not a classic work of the theater. As Robert E.

Morsberger has observed, it is difficult to envisage any circumstance in which it might become the subject of a major revival.

Further Reading: Ditsky, John. "Steinbeck's European Play-Novella: *The Moon Is Down*." *Steinbeck Quarterly* 20 (Winter–Spring 1987): 9–18; French, Warren. "*The Moon Is Down*: John Steinbeck's 'Times'," *Steinbeck Quarterly* 11 (Summer–Fall 1978): 77–86; *The Best Plays of 1941–42 and the Yearbook of the Drama in America*. Ed. Burns Mantle. New York: Dodd, Mead & Company, 1942; Morsberger, Robert E. "Steinbeck and the Stage." In *The Short Novels of John Steinbeck: Critical Essays with a Checklist to Steinbeck Criticism*. Ed. Jackson J. Benson. Durham, NC: Duke University Press, 1990; Steinbeck, John. *The Moon Is Down: A Play in Two Parts*. New York: Viking, 1942.

Roy S. Simmonds

MOORE, JELKA SEPIC. The "Jugo-Slav" wife of **Jim Moore** in **"The Murder."** After committing adultery with her cousin, whom Jim shoots and kills, Jelka meekly submits to Jim's whipping. Steinbeck's depiction of her raises questions of implicit racism and sexism on Jim's part. Numerous critics also find it disturbing that Jim treats Jelka as an animal or a pet. Her Slavic background can be viewed as a pun on the word "slave," and her "foreignness" becomes a metaphor for the enigmatic mystery of the women who remain so incomprehensible to so many men in the stories of ***The Long Valley***.

Abby H. P. Werlock

MOORE, JIM. In **"The Murder,"** a rancher who, when his marriage to a woman he considers unfathomable and "foreign" fails to meet his expectations, returns to the bars and the girls of his bachelorhood at the Three Star in **Monterey**. When a neighbor reveals evidence of cattle thieves on Jim's property, he takes his rifle along, expecting to shoot the thieves. Instead, he shoots the man who has stolen his wife's affections. The old-fashioned male standards by which Jim decides to kill his wife's lover, as well as those by which the coroner and deputy sheriff avoid pressing criminal charges, raise a number of disturbing questions about Jim's attitude toward his wife, whom he beats almost senseless with a bullwhip, and about his self-satisfied view of his place in the universe.

Abby H. P. Werlock

MORALES, MRS. In ***Tortilla Flat***, **Danny**'s next-door neighbor and, briefly, his lover. Mrs. Morales raises chickens, and when **Pilon** moves into Danny's house he immediately contrives a way to lure her chickens into the tall weeds of Danny's backyard. Although she is rumored to be fifty years old, Danny strikes up a romance with her when she accidentally poisons her chickens and uses the proceeds from selling their remains to buy wine. When Danny hears the news of the fire at his second house, he is in Mrs. Morales's bed and is more interested in the task at hand. Mrs. Morales is a good example of the somewhat complicated interplay of romantic and commercial interests involving Danny and the paisanos.

MORDEEN. **Joe Saul**'s wife in Steinbeck's third and last play-novelette, ***Burning Bright***. She is described as beautiful, with blue eyes and blonde hair in tight curls, and she is much younger than her husband. At the time of the play, she has been married to Saul for three years. Mordeen is something of a paradox, for although she suggests a past as a prostitute (or at least a woman with a prostitute's knowledge), she loves Saul as if he were a "god." She will do anything for him, so to give him the child he desperately wants she secretly conceives a child with **Victor**. Mordeen hopes that Saul will believe he is a father at last, although she is sure he is impotent. When Victor bridles at his hapless role as a stud, Mordeen tries to explain to the young man the love she feels for Saul—a love that is selfless and beyond mere animal desire. Although Mordeen would represent a higher love, she becomes like a "mother cat" when Victor threatens to reveal the true paternity of the **Child**.

In the third act of the play version, while Mordeen is beginning her labor, Victor exclaims that he can keep the secret no longer, and she rather calmly tells him that she will have to kill him. In the novella, she is about to stab Victor with a knife when **Friend Ed** helps her by dealing Victor a "crunching blow" and pitching him over the side of a ship (he arranges for Victor to be shanghaied in the play version). When Saul finds out that he is impotent and storms off in a rage, Mordeen acts as if she were dead without him. Later, however, with mediation from Friend Ed, Saul accepts her gift of the Child and she can live again. The characterization of Mordeen, which oscillates between a wife of selfless love and an ex-prostitute capable of murder, contributes to *Burning Bright's* theme of the human paradox (a species that aspires to become god, yet remains animal). However, her characterization also reflects the play-novelette's poor, even ridiculous, execution.

MORDEN, ALEXANDER. In *The Moon Is Down*, a common citizen and one-time alderman who never broke the law before the war. In a fit of anger after the invasion, however, he kills **Captain Bentick** with a pickax after being ordered to perform forced labor. His violent act and subsequent execution at the hands of the enemy galvanize local resistance against the occupation.

MORDEN, MOLLY. In *The Moon Is Down*, a school teacher who is also the youthful, pretty wife of **Alexander Morden**, a man who is executed for killing one of the invading officers, **Captain Bentick**. After her husband is killed, she becomes despondent until she is wooed by the young enemy **Lieutenant Tonder**, a sentimental officer who writes love poems addressed to her. At first she is somewhat attracted to the man. Later, sensing that freedom exacts a higher price than personal satisfaction, she kills Tonder with a pair of scissors, partly out of fear that her knowledge of resistance activities may be compromised by her relationship.

MORDRED. In *The Acts of King Arthur*, the son of **Arthur**, born of Arthur's incestuous union with his half-sister **Margawse**. **Merlin** prophesies that Mordred will destroy Arthur's knights and his kingdom, and Arthur himself. When he is four weeks old, he escapes death at Arthur's hands as the sole survivor of all the babies born on May Day and cast adrift by Arthur in a little ship, an attempt by Arthur to conceal his incestuous sin and guilt. Mordred is one of the four knights beaten in tournament by **Sir Lancelot** and the four white knights, as champions for **Sir Bagdemagus**.

"MORE ABOUT ARISTOCRACY: WHY NOT A WORLD PEERAGE?" (1955). Published in the December 10, 1955, edition of *Saturday Review*, this essay by Steinbeck proposes that men will rise to greatness if they have a motive to do so. Like the Congressional Medal of Honor, a world peerage would provide such a goal for mankind. This honor would be bestowed by the United Nations General Assembly on those who have made unique contributions to civilization, making them citizens of the world. He hopes that as individuals strive for this honor, they will work to avoid dividing the world by practicing meanness and self-interest.

Further Reading: *Saturday Review* 38:50 (December 10, 1955): 11.

MORGAN, EDWARD (SIR). Lieutenant Governor of Jamaica, older brother of **Robert Morgan**, father of **Elizabeth Morgan**, and uncle of **Henry Morgan**, in *Cup of Gold*.

MORGAN, ELIZABETH. Daughter of **Sir Edward Morgan** and cousin to **Henry Morgan**, in *Cup of Gold*. After the death of her father, she follows the advice of **Lady Moddyford** and disingenuously turns to Henry for protection, manipulating him into an unwitting proposal of marriage. On his deathbed, Henry is surprised to discover that Elizabeth seems to feel real affection for him.

MORGAN, GWENLIANA. Paternal grandmother of **Henry Morgan**, in *Cup of Gold*.

Among the townsfolk, her reputation as a seer and necromancer is strong, but her family mostly humors her.

MORGAN, HENRY. He is the protagonist of ***Cup of Gold***, the only one of Steinbeck's works that may be labeled as historical—although it is only loosely so. The epigraph on the title page states that *Cup of Gold* is "A Life of Sir Henry Morgan, buccaneer, with Occasional Reference to History"—a fittingly lengthy title in the seventeenth-century fashion. In this work, Steinbeck draws a psychological portrait of a person whose very limitations lead to fame, or notoriety, through acts of piracy. His father predicts such an outcome as he tries to prepare his wife for the fifteen-year-old boy's departure from home. Henry goes to sea to pursue his desire for a thing he could not name: "This son of ours will be a great man, because—well—because he is not very intelligent. He can see only one desire at a time. . . . He will murder every dream with the implacable arrows of his will."

This description captures much in little, for Henry will not be burdened, as his father has been, with a sense of alternatives—of what might have been. Unlike his father, he will not be "smothered" by the valley, for he "finds it in his power to vault the mountains and stride around the world." But neither will Henry find satisfaction, contentment, peace, or love. He will be consumed by the endless pursuit of his own desires—symbolized by the beautiful woman, **La Santa Roja**—which cease to be desirable after they are attained.

MORGAN LE FAY. In ***The Acts of King Arthur***, she is Queen of the Land of Gore, half-sister of **King Arthur**, wife of **King Uryens**, and mother of **Sir Ewain**. She becomes proficient in the art of necromancy and plots against Arthur, fashioning a counterfeit **Excalibur** and scabbard, drugging Arthur, and imprisoning him in the castle of **Sir Damas**. She steals the true Excalibur, which she gives to her lover, **Sir Accolon of Gaul**. In a fight between Arthur and Accolon, the respective champions of Sir Damas and his younger brother **Sir Outlake**, Arthur unknowingly fights with the counterfeit Excalibur and is terribly wounded without the scabbard's protection. But as the result of a spell cast by **Nyneve** against Accolon, be manages to recover his sword and mortally wound his adversary.

Unaware of Arthur's survival and Accolon's death, Morgan plans to kill her husband and make Accolon king. Eventually, however, her son Ewain prevents her from killing Uryens, but she still manages to steal the scabbard of Excalibur and throw it into a little lake. She rescues **Sir Manessen**, Sir Accolon's cousin, from death and then retires to her lands in the country of Gore to protect herself from Arthur. Morgan tries to kill the king again by sending him a beautiful cloak that has been poisoned, but she is foiled by Nyneve's intervention. She is the leader of the **Four Queens** who capture **Lancelot** and throw him into a dungeon at Maiden's Castle until such time as he submits to the power of one of them. Lancelot escapes from the dungeon and the castle with the assistance of **Sir Bagdemagus**'s daughter.

MORGAN, MOLLY. In ***The Pastures of Heaven***, the sensitive school teacher in Las Pasturas. An understanding woman, Molly tries to pacify the mutant **Tuleracito** by valuing his art, and she attempts to understand the different learning styles of **Robbie Maltby** and the different lifestyle his father has chosen for him. Possibly modeled after Steinbeck's mother, **Olive**, Molly recognizes that what is done to each of these students is abusive, primarily because her own individual history includes an emotionally unstable family. She had a ne'er-do-well father who tried to make up for his absenteeism with little gifts and fantasy stories and a mother who was overly dependent on her children for love and protection. Molly's own impoverished upbringing has led to a teaching career and a rich fantasy that her father is not dead, but merely having fantastic adventures that she will be able to share vicariously when he returns. When **Bert Munroe** describes a drunken migrant who works on his ranch, Molly observes many similarities between the hobo's character and that of her father. Ultimately unwilling to face the possibility that the tramp might be her real father and that her dream world is grounded on fragile assumptions, she leaves her job and Las Pasturas and returns to the safety of the city, where she can keep her fantasies about her father alive.

MORGAN, "MOTHER." Mother of **Henry Morgan**, in ***Cup of Gold***. Her range of concerns is limited to the Christian religion, the cost of things at market, and little else. Totally given to the mundane practicalities of running a household, it is difficult for her to accept the fact that Henry wants to leave home.

MORGAN, ROBERT. Father of the protagonist, **Henry Morgan**, in ***Cup of Gold***. He is a farmer and the younger son of a family of minor nobility in Wales. He is wise about human nature, but incapable of great action. He knows Henry wants to leave before Henry tells him, and he asks only that Henry confer with **Merlin** before setting out. His nickname is "Old Robert."

Kevin Hearle

MORPHY, JOEY. In ***The Winter of Our Discontent***, Joey is a regular customer of **Ethan Allen Hawley**'s for lunchtime sandwiches. A teller at **Baker**'s bank, he is something of a joker and insider who gives Ethan the impression that he knows much more than he lets on. He plants the idea of robbing the bank in Ethan's mind and even suggests ways to make the holdup successful. Mocking the "Great God Currency," Joey still has an instinctual expectation of Ethan's abortive robbery. It is also Joey who suggests to Ethan that the store owner, **Marullo**, is an illegal immigrant.

MORRISON, AGNES. Wife of **Clarence Morrison** and patron of **Dessie Hamilton**'s dressmaking shop in **Salinas**, in ***East of Eden***.

MORRISON, CLARENCE. Husband of **Agnes Morrison** and owner/operator of a **Salinas** dry goods store, in ***East of Eden***.

MORTE D'ARTHUR, LE (CA. 1470). A collection of Arthurian legends written in the fifteenth century by Sir Thomas Malory (1405–1471), *Le Morte* is drawn from a variety of sources both English and French. It is considered an early prose masterpiece for both its style and its use of dialogue, a work that is noteworthy in its attempts to collect and organize the various Arthurian legends that had arisen in different places and times. Steinbeck was given a copy of Malory's work when he was young, and it became "the initial stimulus for [his] becoming a reader" (**Benson**, 20). As a result of the gift, Steinbeck wrote that "magic happened. . . . I loved the old spelling of the words. . . . Perhaps a passionate love for the English language opened to me from this one book." The Middle English of Malory became a "secret language" for both John and his much-loved younger sister, **Mary Steinbeck Dekker**.

Le Morte d'Arthur and its themes became a major influence on much of Steinbeck's fiction. Biographer **Jay Parini** writes, "The structure of these heroic stories would explicitly undergird many of his best novels, such as ***Tortilla Flat*** and ***Cannery Row***, while aspects of the Camelot myth implicitly influenced almost everything he ever produced." Writing about *Tortilla Flat*, for example, Steinbeck noted "The book had a very definite theme . . . The form is that of the Malory version, the coming of **Arthur** and the mystic quality of owning a house, the forming of the round table, the adventures of the knights and finally, the mystic adventures of **Danny**." In ***Sweet Thursday***, Steinbeck makes the book's debt to Malory clear by, among other things, adding descriptive chapter headings reminiscent of the style of *Le Morte d'Arthur*. The Arthurian motifs—ennobling friendship; people living and working together for a common cause; noble women; worthy leaders; and betrayal are all themes that recur, both comically and seriously, throughout Steinbeck's work.

Late in his career, Steinbeck wanted to "set [the tales] down in plain present-day speech for my own young sons, and for other sons not so young," while at the same time "keep[ing] the wonder and the magic" of Malory's work. Consequently, he rented a cottage in England, traveled extensively, and met and corresponded with a number of experts on Malory and on Arthurian legend. Ultimately dissatisfied with his efforts, Steinbeck abandoned the project after having completed a great deal of work, and it was never published during his lifetime. *The Acts of King Arthur and His Noble Knights*, with the subtitle *From the Winchester Manuscripts of Thomas Malory and Other Sources,* was published in 1976, eight years after Steinbeck's death.

Further Reading: Parini, Jay. *John Steinbeck: A Biography.* New York: Holt, 1995; Steinbeck, John. *The Acts of King Arthur and His Noble Knights*. New York: Ballantine, 1976.

Charles Etheridge, Jr.

MUNROE, BERT. In ***The Pastures of Heaven***, the head of the family that buys the Battle House and restores it to its original state as a premier property in Las Pasturas. He is a symbol of middle-class morality and its tendency toward materialism and progressive thought. Often his good intentions backfire, causing pain and anguish for his neighbors. Either he or one of his family members is involved in each of the ten episodes Steinbeck records in *The Pastures of Heaven*.

MUNROE, JIMMIE. In ***The Pastures of Heaven***, he is the Munroes' older son, symbolic of the progress embraced by a new generation and of the sexual appetite of youth. His interest in the beautiful **Alice Wicks** eventually causes her father's downfall due to rumors of their romantic interest in each other. Steinbeck describes Jimmie as sullen and secretive, but possessing a great interest in machines and in his potential to become an inventor.

MUNROE, MAE. In ***The Pastures of Heaven***, the Munroes' daughter. Much like her mother, she is physically attractive, though intellectually submissive and weak. Fashionable in clothing and possessions, she seems too stereotypically feminine, having little interest in areas that require aggressive behavior. Mae is sought after by **Pat Humbert**, and her beauty inspires him to redecorate his house in an attempt to leave the past behind. She eventually makes a match with **Bill Whiteside**, the son of the town's leading citizen. After her marriage, she decides to leave Las Pasturas for the adventures of a bigger city.

MUNROE, MANNY. In ***The Pastures of Heaven***, he is the youngest of the Munroe family. Manny is of subnormal intelligence because of an adenoidal condition that has stunted his brain growth. Because this condition is unknown to his parents and because he is compatible and seldom violent, he is not subjected to the exile and imprisonment imposed on the other Las Pasturas residents (**Tuleracito** and **Hilda Van de Venter**) who suffer from mental defects of a similarly serious nature.

MUNROE, MRS. In ***The Pastures of Heaven***, she is **Bert Munroe**'s wife, a typical homebody whose supposed concern for those less fortunate than herself is easily mistaken for prying and interfering where she doesn't belong. She is portrayed as a conformist, one who very seldom seeks out change or modification of her surroundings.

"MURDER, THE" (1934). First published in the *North American Review* in 1934, "The Murder" depicts the oft-told tale of a love triangle and its tragic consequences. Its immediate effect on the critics is reflected in the 1934 O. Henry Prize that Steinbeck was awarded for the best short story published that year. Apparently the story is based on the wife of a friend, and its setting, the Cañon del Castillo in **Monterey** County, is actually located in a canyon off the road to Corral del Tierra, where the sandstone cliffs resemble a medieval fortress. Significantly, this is also the setting for Steinbeck's ***The Pastures of Heaven***, another story of individuals trapped in a primitive environment. The artistic merits of "The Murder" are manifold, with some of Steinbeck's most vivid writing achieving a mood that holds the reader spellbound. In a letter to **George Albee** he revealed that he was striving not for characterization, but for "a dream-like feeling."

Steinbeck's allusive use of the medieval setting has provoked various critical interpretations. As with many of stories in ***The Long Valley***, a key lies in the positioning of the stories within the collection. "The Murder" follows **"Johnny Bear"** and examines more explicitly the themes of race, sex, and gender differences in a defiled paradise. The story is followed by **"Saint Katy the Virgin,"** with its medieval setting and its continued use of animal imagery to score ironic points against human foibles.

Although critics continue to puzzle over ways to interpret **Jim Moore**'s callous treatment of his wife **Jelka** and the brutal murder of her lover—actions apparently far more reprehensible in our day than they seemed when Steinbeck wrote the story—the author provides in the character of Jim an important clue as to how readers should interpret the story.

The story opens after the murder with a view of Jim and Jelka, who have moved to a new house outside the Cañon del Castillo. Significantly, however, Jim has refused to burn the house because it signifies a "great and important piece of his life," for which people regard him with "awe" and with "admiration." Early in the story, Steinbeck establishes Jim's pride, vanity, and condescending treatment of others—particularly women and foreigners. He has inherited his parents' ranch, and he celebrates his male adulthood by ridding himself of pigs, buying "a fine Guernsey bull," and spending Saturday nights in Monterey, where he gets drunk and socializes with the "noisy girls" of the Three Star. Within a year he marries a foreign girl whose background and large family make him ashamed. It quickly becomes clear that he considers Jelka to be a "Slav girl" that he treats as if she were a domestic inferior. Jim sees her in animal terms, as many critics have noted: she is a doe, a horse, a puppy that he pets and strokes. In terms of how she discharges the household responsibilities, Jim finds her to be the perfect wife, but he complains that she is not a good companion, one with whom he can share his thoughts.

Steinbeck, however, has given each spouse clear gender differences that suggest a subtle examination of the unfathomable gap between men like Jim, who live according to a one-dimensional male code, and women such as Jelka, whose mysterious femininity proves too complex for her husband to fathom. Jim interacts with women only on the most superficial levels, as demonstrated in his preference for the "shrill" chatter, small talk, and "vulgarity" of the Three Star "girls." With them he mocks his wife, who becomes the butt of a joke. Each time Jim visits the Three Star, when the girls ask where his wife is, Jim replies that (like an animal) she is "home in the barn." These superficial women speak his language.

The story contains evidence that Jim's vain and self-absorbed existence might make him almost unbearably dull, with his talk of stallions and farm chores. Not surprisingly, Jelka looks at him as a foreigner who means to be pleasant, despite the fact that she finds him incomprehensible. Just as **Henry Allen** of **"The Chrysanthemums"** and **Harry Teller** of **"The White Quail"** fail to understand their wives, Jim displays absolutely no understanding of his. Like the eyes of the woman in **"The Snake,"** Jelka's "dusty black eyes" are unfathomable.

Jim observes the moon on his way to town, and Steinbeck's imagery suggests Jelka's mystery and femininity, shimmering and glowing. In a fine Steinbeckian touch, Jim rides a gelding rather than a stallion, perhaps suggesting the cuckolding that he will experience later in the evening. At this point, however, rather than thinking of his dark wife Jelka, Jim thinks of "blond May" at the Three Star, and he hopes that she will not have given herself to another patron before he arrives. His male arrogance and insensitivity to those different from himself having been well established, Jim's role is predictable as the story builds to its awful ending.

His neighbor **George** reports finding the remains of a calf with Jim's brand (Jim owns the calf just as surely as he owns his wife), and Jim readies his shotgun, listening for rustlers. Shortly thereafter he thinks of Jelka's unnamed cousin as a pig ironically, as it turns out, for he then finds his wife and her cousin in bed together. In a clear case of first-degree murder, he retreats, ponders the situation, returns to the bedroom with a shotgun, and blows out the cousin's brains. He rides into town to fetch the proper authorities, but when he returns, Jim somewhat arrogantly tells the sheriff and coroner that he feels too exhausted to go with them into the house. After ascertaining that he did not kill his wife and admonishing him to deal gently with her, the sheriff and the coroner depart. Their collusion with Jim is complete: not only did the cousin cuckold him, thus breaking one of the world's most ancient male codes, but their attitude clearly implies that he is a foreigner and therefore not worthy of equality before the law.

After the sheriff and the coroner depart, Jim finds Jelka in the barn. The animal allusions established earlier continue to resound as he whips her until she can no longer stand, branding her forever as if she were one of his calves. In the very last line of the story, he strokes her like a pet. Jelka's last act in the story is to serve him bacon and eggs that she herself declines, because her mouth is so sore from the beating.

The story has been criticized as antifeminist and racially biased, with a clear sexual double standard, but modern studies of spousal abuse should leave us unsurprised that Jelka apparently does all she can to appease this man who has blown out her lover's brains and then beaten her. She remains with him, as we know from their appearance together at the beginning of this violent tale. Although it appears as the penultimate story in *The Long Valley*, "The Murder" was among the first to be written (along with "The Chrysanthemums"), and thus it is open to the same sorts of questions in terms of Steinbeck's personal situation. If, in the aftermath of his wife **Carol Henning Steinbeck**'s relationship with **Joseph Campbell**, Steinbeck contemplated through his fiction the various possible outcomes to marital infidelity, this one is certainly the most violent. The story is of interest because of its medieval allusions and the decision to allow the guilty wife to live; in both "The White Quail" and **"The Harness,"** the wives either literally or figuratively die.

Further Reading: Davis, Robert Murray. "Steinbeck's 'The Murder.'" *Studies in Short Fiction* 14 (1977): 63–68; Ditsky, John. "Steinbeck's 'Slav Girl' and the Role of the Narrator in 'The Murder.'" *Steinbeck Quarterly* 22: 3-4 (Summer-Fall 1989) 68-76; "Point of View in John Steinbeck's 'The Murder,'" *Steinbeck Quarterly* 22.3–4 (Summer–Fall 1989): 77–83; Hughes, Robert S., Jr. *John Steinbeck: A Study of the Short Fiction*. Boston: Twayne, 1989; Mandia, Patricia M. "Sexism and Racism, or Irony? Steinbeck's 'The Murder.'" In *Steinbeck's Short Stories in* The Long Valley*: Essays in Criticism*. Ed. Tetsumaro Hayashi. Muncie, IN: Steinbeck Research Institute, Ball State University, 1991. 62–69; Steinbeck, John."The Murder." In *The Long Valley*. New York: Viking, 1939.

Abby H. P. Werlock

"MURDER AT FULL MOON." Steinbeck wrote this unpublished potboiler in November or December of 1930, completing the manuscript in just nine days. In a letter, Steinbeck noted that the work was written in a burlesque tone. It does suggest a Poesque influence, though less seriously than in the story, **"The Days of Long Marsh."** Steinbeck wrote the manuscript using the pseudonym Peter Pym, borrowed from Edgar Allan Poe's *The Narrative of Arthur Gordon Pym*. Mac, the murderer, kills dogs and people out in the marshes near Cone City (a setting similar to Long Marsh and the setting of **"Johnny Bear"**). Mac has a split personality, the evil half being triggered by the full moon. When Mac is caught, a psychiatrist on the scene, "Hair Doktor Schmelling," diagnoses the strange effects of the moon upon Mac's personality.

This tale may be the first of Steinbeck's that bears some influence from discussions with **Edward F. Ricketts**, whom Steinbeck had met a month or two before he wrote out the manuscript. Both were interested in the impact of environment, including the moon, upon the human psyche, Along with Mac, the characters of "Murder at Full Moon" suffer moods that mirror the melancholy dankness of Gomez Marsh. This story, though clearly playful, is yet another example of Steinbeck's fascination with the impact of setting upon human emotion. Or, in a more Poesque sense, this work is a study of the way in which setting (particularly a natural one, in Steinbeck's work) parallels the interiors of the human mind. "Murder at Full Moon" is part of the collection of Steinbeck manuscripts in the Harry Ransom Humanities Research Center at the University of Texas, Austin.

Further Reading: Railsback, Brian. *Parallel Expeditions: Charles Darwin and the Art of John Steinbeck*. Moscow, ID: University of Idaho Press, 1995.

MURPHY, DR. H.C. Salinas doctor who treats **Adam Trask** in ***East of Eden***, after Adam suffers his first, and then his second stroke.

MURPHY, FATHER. In ***Sweet Thursday***, a young priest in Los Angeles who once tried to draw **Joseph** and **Mary Rivas** into the church. He taught Rivas the theory, if not the practice, of honest labor. Through his influence in city government, Father Murphy was able to secure Rivas a position in which he was responsible for watering and cultivating plants in the Plaza, but the incorrigible Rivas simply used the job as an opportunity to grow marijuana for sale. The failure of a priest to reform the man from his criminal propensities suggests that Rivas is morally irredeemable.

Bruce Ouderkirk

MUSTROVICS. In ***Pastures of Heaven***, the second owners of the "cursed" Battle farm. Described as thin people with yellow skins, they disappear mysteriously after two years of trying to reclaim the soil from misuse by its previous owner, **John Battle**.

"MY SHORT NOVELS" (1953) First published in *Wings* (Oct. 1953); reprinted in *The English Journal* 43 (1954). This preface to a collection of six short novels gives Steinbeck an opportunity to comment on his reasons for writing each. The piece includes such Steinbeck titles as ***The Red Pony, Tortilla Flat, Of Mice and Men, The Moon Is Down, Cannery Row***, and ***The Pearl***. Regarding any type of composition, Steinbeck remarks that "when a book is finished, it is a kind of death, a matter of pain and sorrow to the writer. Then he starts a new book, and . . . a whole new life starts."

Further Reading: Steinbeck, John. "My Short Novels" in *America and Americans and Selected Nonfiction*. Ed. Susan Shillinglaw and Jackson J. Benson. New York: Viking, 2002; also available in Benson, Jackson J. *The Short Novels of John Steinbeck*. Durham: Duke University Press, 1990.

Eric Skipper

MYLES OF THE LANDS, SIR. In ***The Acts of King Arthur***, the fiancé of **Alyne**. While Myles and Alyne are on their way to Camelot to be wed, he is wounded by **Loraine le Sauvage**.

N

NACIO DE LA TORRE Y MIER, DON. In *Viva Zapata!*, Don Nacio advises **Emiliano Zapata** to make peace with the forces in control of the country, since the president is watching him. A scene with Don Nacio that appears in the published screenplay but is completely excised from the film shows which side Don Nacio is on politically (in favor of the peasants). At a dinner party with two anti-peasant *hacendados*, **Don García** and **General Fuentes**, Don Nacio becomes drunk and admits that the reason he arranged the party was to call the *hacendados* together and ask them "to stop this tragedy," referring to Emiliano's request for help "in restoring the village lands before the country burns up with fighting." Don Nacio is ashamed because he knows Emiliano is right, but he doesn't have the courage to help him with money, food, and weapons. Yet Don Nacio admits that he did not send for the army, and when General Fuentes pulls out a pistol and aims it at Emiliano's back, it is Don Nacio who grabs his wrist and prevents Emiliano's murder.

Marcia D. Yarmus

"NAIL, THE." Along with **"East Third Street," "The Days of Long Marsh,"** and **"A Lady in Infra-Red,"** this story is an example of the short fiction written by Steinbeck in his early **Stanford University** years (1924–26). The idea for "The Nail" was taken from the fourth chapter of the book of Judges, which relates the tale of Jael and Sisera. According to **Jackson J. Benson**, this tale inverts the **biblical** message by suggesting that the lives of the pagan Canaanites were far richer and more beautiful than those of the fanatical Jews.

Michael J. Meyer

NAKAYAMA, KIYOSHI (1935–). An important Steinbeck scholar in **Japan** and leading figure in the John Steinbeck Society of Japan, Nakayama was born and raised in Osaka and became a specialist in English and twentieth-century American literature at Kansai University. Nakayama has published twenty-five books, nineteen of which are on or relate to John Steinbeck. Among them is a trilogy of critical studies written in Japanese: *John Steinbeck's Writings: The California Years* (1989), *The Post-California Years* (1999), and *The New York Years* (2002). He compiled *Steinbeck in Japan: A Bibliography* (1992) and translated ***The Grapes of Wrath*** (1997) into Japanese.

"THE NAKED BOOK" (1951). Published in *Vogue* (5 Nov. 1951: 119, 161), this article is a slightly abbreviated version of "Some Random and Randy Thoughts on Books," which appeared in *The Author Looks at Format* (1951). Steinbeck criticizes publishers' methods for selling books, in particular the packaging, which often gives a false impression of the book's contents. He ponders the future of books, "one of the very few authentic magics our species has created," and he wonders whether they can "continue to compete with the quick, cheap, easy forms of entertainment which do not require either reading or thinking."

NANTRES, KING OF GARLOT. In *The Acts of King Arthur,* husband of the **Lady Igraine**'s youngest daughter, **Elaine**.

NANTUCKET. Historic island off southeastern Massachusetts, and in the nineteenth century, the fabled center of the U.S. whaling industry. John, his third wife, **Elaine Scott, John IV**, and **Thom Steinbeck** spent the summer of 1951 on Nantucket Island, where they stayed in an old Victorian beach house near San Katy Light. The house, called "Footlight," was owned by Robert Benchley and was located on a part of the island known as Siasconset. (Steinbeck and his sons also returned to Nantucket in the spring of 1953 for a brief holiday.) For Steinbeck, the time spent on Nantucket during the summer of 1951 was a peaceful but intense period. Often, he would work with great energy through the morning, finishing around one o'clock, and spend the rest of the day in some leisurely activity with the family. It was here that Steinbeck made major strides toward the completion of his "big" novel, which he decided to name ***East of Eden***. Although relatively isolated, the Steinbecks were not completely separated from friends. The **Benchleys (Nat** and Margery) had a summer home close by, and there was a consistent stream of significant visitors. **Elizabeth Otis** and **Pat Covici** appeared over the course of the summer, and these visits seemed to spur Steinbeck on in his creative intensity. By the time of the family's departure from Nantucket, Steinbeck was extremely close to completing the novel, although he would spend a great deal more time rewriting the final version.

Brian Niro

NARAM, SIR. In *The Acts of King Arthur,* one of **King Arthur**'s knights. When **King Royns of North Wales** invades the kingdom, Naram warns Arthur that Royns is one of the best fighting men alive.

NATIONAL STEINBECK CENTER, THE. The 37,000–square foot Center, located in the heart of downtown **Salinas**, opened in 1998. The original structure houses the John Steinbeck Exhibition Hall, where visitors may explore the life of John Steinbeck, his writings, and characters through engaging exhibitry, one-of-a-kind artifacts, and films. There are interactive multi-sensory exhibits for all ages with seven themed theaters showcasing ***Cannery Row, The Grapes of Wrath, East of Eden, Of Mice and Men, The Red Pony*** and much more. In 2003, a 6,500–square foot expansion, now named The Rabobank Agriculture Museum, formerly known as the Valley of the World Agricultural Wing, was opened; this area shares the stories of the Salinas Valley "from field to fork," with hands-on displays, computer stations, and interactive games. The mission of both these arms of the NSC is to inspire people to learn and expand their horizons by demonstrating how the arts and humanities can enhance an individual's understanding of the history, agriculture, and diversity of **Monterey** County. Programs are specifically designed to build bridges between disparate communities by serving as a forum for learning about the literary and artistic treasures, multiculturalism, and social concerns of the Central Coast. For national audiences, the Center's goal is to reveal how John Steinbeck's writings address universal themes and how the people and products of the Salinas Valley touch the world.

NELLIE. In **"The Promise,"** Nellie is the mare **Jody** takes to be bred so that he can have another pony to replace **Gabilan**. When it turns out that the colt is turned wrong for a normal delivery, **Billy Buck** must choose between saving the mare's life or the colt's. Billy kills the mare by smashing in her skull and then performs a caesarian to deliver the colt successfully.

NERO. In *The Acts of King Arthur*, the brother of **King Royns of North Wales**. After his brother's capture by Sir **Balin** and Sir **Balan**, Nero rides into battle against **King Arthur**, but despite his superior forces, he is defeated and his power destroyed when his ally, **King Lot of Lothian and Orkney**, is delayed by **Merlin**'s trickery from reaching the battlefield to support him.

NEW YORK DRAMA CRITICS CIRCLE AWARD. Won by Steinbeck for the play version of ***Of Mice and Men*** in 1938, defeating Thornton Wilder's *Our Town* by a vote of twelve to four. Citing "the bite into the strict quality of its material" and "its refusal to make this study of tragical loneliness and frustration, either cheap or sensational," the critics honored a production that Steinbeck himself never saw (at the time of its run, he was revising and rewriting "L'Affaire Lettuceburg," a draft that would later be abandoned as Steinbeck began work on the novel that would become ***The Grapes of Wrath***. The play version of Steinbeck's novel ***The Moon Is Down*** was also nominated for this award in 1942 but came in second.

Michael J. Meyer

NICHELSON, ALF. In ***East of Eden***, **Salinas** Jack-of-all-trades. Leaving the **Nigger**'s funeral, **Joe Valery** runs into Alf. Over beers at **Mr. Griffin**'s saloon, Alf tells Joe about **Kate Albey/Cathy Trask** and suggests pointedly that Kate may be a poisoner who killed **Faye** to inherit her brothel.

NIGGER, THE. In ***East of Eden***, owner of the Long Green, a brothel that contrasts with **Faye**'s or **Jenny**'s because of its serious, dignified, and almost spiritual atmosphere.

NOBEL PRIZE. Named for Alfred Nobel, the inventor of dynamite, the Nobel Prize was the first prize awarded internationally for achievements in such areas as chemistry, literature, economics, medicine, peace, and physics. Awarded since 1901, the Nobel Prize consists of a cash award and medal, presented by the reigning monarch of Sweden. Steinbeck learned he had been awarded the Nobel Prize for Literature on October 25, 1962, when he turned on the morning news. Although proud, he wrote that he was "afraid of it," and that it would be hard to handle. The American press criticized the selection and denounced the Nobel committee for being out of touch with contemporary American writing. When asked at a press conference if he deserved the prize, Steinbeck responded, "Frankly, no." Still, the criticisms stung Steinbeck and put pressure on him to write a **Nobel Prize acceptance speech** worthy of the award. Negative criticism continued, most devastatingly with **Arthur Mizener**'s *New York Times* article published on the eve of the prize ceremony, December 9, 1962, titled "Does a Moral Vision of the Thirties Deserve a Nobel Prize?" Mizener charged that serious readers had stopped reading Steinbeck after ***The Grapes of Wrath***, and that the Swedes had made an error by honoring Steinbeck. The *New Yorker* was one of the few major American publications that did not treat Steinbeck with disapproval or sarcasm. After surveying other authors who had won the prize, Steinbeck feared winning it would dim his ability to write; sadly, his prophecy proved partly correct, since he would not complete a novel after he won the Nobel.

Paul M. Blobaum

NOBEL PRIZE ACCEPTANCE SPEECH. Following the onslaught of American academic criticism over his award, Steinbeck crafted his acceptance speech so as to be worthy of receiving a **Nobel Prize**. Prize winners customarily commented on current trends and the nature of literature. Steinbeck used his acceptance speech to transcend the critics at home and speak of the responsibilities of those who make literature, and of literature's need to serve the common person, not the scholarly critics. His remarks celebrated the essential humanism of words, the power of the human imagination, and the need for writers to expose human faults and celebrate human greatness. Alluding to the invention of the atomic bomb, Steinbeck wrote, "Man himself has become our greatest hazard and our only hope."

Further Reading: Steinbeck, John. "Nobel Prize Acceptance Speech." In *America and Americans and Selected Nonfiction*. Ed. Susan Shillinglaw and Jackson J. Benson. New York: Viking, 2002.

Paul Blobaum

NOBLE, OSCAR. Deputy sheriff in **Salinas** in ***East of Eden***. Before her suicide, **Kate Albey** sends a message to be given to the sheriff, **Horace Quinn**, in which she exposes **Joe Valery**'s past. When Oscar is taking Joe in for questioning, Joe breaks free and runs. While trying to stop him, Oscar shoots and kills Joe.

Margaret Seligman

NOLAN, JIM. Nolan is the idealistic young leader and central character of *In Dubious Battle*. After losing his job at a department store and being unjustly jailed, he is recruited by **Mac**, a strike organizer; Jim joins the Party to help the strike effort in the Torgas Valley. He rises rapidly and begins to challenge both the strike organizers and, with a fatal result, the associated farmers and their vigilantes. Responding to a fake call to help **Doc Burton**, Nolan's face is blown away by a shotgun blast from the owners' thugs. The novel ends with Mac using Jim's funeral to make good use of his martyrdom, as Jim is idolized in ways he never was during his short and doleful life. Nolan is a void of a man, an empty space, until he discovers some power in his ruthless ability to manipulate the strikers, becoming better at it than Mac, for he lacks even Mac's slight humanity. Like **Pepé Torres** in the short story **"Flight,"** Nolan is destroyed—his literal identity ripped from his face—just as he is on the verge of finding his spiritual identity as a man and, however cold, a place in society.

NON-TELEOLOGICAL THINKING. A method of examining the world that concerns itself primarily not with what should be or could be, but rather with what actually *is*—attempting, at most, to answer the questions *what* or *how* rather than *why*. This idea, developed at length in chapter IV of ***Sea of Cortez*** in the passage sometimes referred to as the "Easter Sunday Sermon," is considered by many to be the key to understanding both Steinbeck's world view and his novelistic methods. The section in *Sea of Cortez* that defines non-teleological thinking is indebted to **Edward F. Ricketts**. **Richard Astro** writes that much of it was "lifted verbatim" from an unpublished work by Ricketts. According to Steinbeck and Ricketts, the problem with conventional teleologies is that they seek to assign blame for the troubles of the world to some party or cause rather than to accept the world as it is. Unemployment during the Depression era is one of the major illustrative examples used in *Cortez*. Many lamented that "the country had to support" the unemployed "because they were shiftless and negligent," and Henry Ford had said that "everybody ought to roll up his sleeves and get to work." The difficulty with the teleological perspective—blaming the unemployment rate on workers' laziness—is that it ignores the fact that "at that time there was work for only about seventy percent of the total employable population." The non-teleological perspective assigns "no blame, at least no social fault . . . to these people; they are what they are 'because' natural conditions are what they are." Although some of the unemployed may be blamed as individuals for their plight, the non-teleological perspective is "more real and less illusionary and even less blaming than more conventional methods of consideration." Several other examples are cited, each giving evidence that the non-teleological perspective is more accurate, more useful, and, in many cases, more compassionate than the teleological one. The doctrine of non-teleological thinking is crucial to an understanding of Steinbeck's work as a whole. Richard Astro, for example, suggests it was "very much on Steinbeck's mind" during the composition of ***In Dubious Battle*** and ***The Grapes of Wrath***.

Further Reading: Astro, Richard. *John Steinbeck and Edward F. Ricketts: The Shaping of a Novelist*. New Berlin: University of Minnesota Press, 1973; Railsback, Brian. *Parallel Expeditions: Charles Darwin and the Art of John Steinbeck*. Moscow: University of Idaho Press, 1995; Ricketts, Edward F. *The Life and Letters of Edward F. Ricketts*. Ed. Katherine A. Rodger. Tuscaloosa: University of Alabama Press, 2002.

Charles Etheridge, Jr.

NORMA. In ***The Wayward Bus***, the latest in a series of waitresses at the garage/lunchroom/bus station belonging to **Juan Chicoy** and his wife, **Alice**. Norma is presented as interchangeable with her predecessors: "gawky and romantic and homely." She is preoccupied with fantasies of life in Hollywood and in particular is obsessed with **Clark Gable**, to whom she writes love letters. On the day of the bus trip, she catches Alice going through her personal effects, which precipitates her quitting and booking passage on the bus with the idea of finally going to Hollywood. Norma is befriended by **Camille Oaks**, a blonde stripper of pinup beauty and proportions, who exudes a powerful sexuality to which virtually all men around her respond. Camille instructs Norma in the use of makeup and provides other suggestions that help to increase Norma's self-confidence, although Camille is cautious and noncommittal about Norma's suggestion that they find an apartment together in Los Angeles. Norma is pleased by the effect her new look and carriage have on at least some of the males on the bus. However, the reality of her new sexual allure—something well understood by Camille—has a downside, too, as Norma finds out when another passenger, **Pimples Carson**, tries to force himself on her. Norma has a practical side, however, and is not without some skills of self-preservation. Although she dispatches Pimples with ease, it is suggested she will survive but not thrive in her new home in Los Angeles. Ultimately, Steinbeck leaves the reader with a sense of the innocence and the impossibility of Norma's dreams when, on the novel's last page, she makes her wish upon a star and indicates that the future, either with Camille or alone, holds no guarantees.

Christopher S. Busch and Bradd Burningham

NORRIS, FRANK. (1870–1902). American novelist known for his naturalistic presentations of life in the United States, Norris's works include *Vandover and the Brute* (1898), *Moran of the Lady Letty* (1898), *A Man's Woman* (1900), and *Blix* (1900). He was also the author of *The Octopus* (1901) and *The Pit* (1903), the first two books in an unfinished trilogy about the wheat-producing industry. **Robert DeMott** says that Norris and Steinbeck "shared thematic and aesthetic affinities." DeMott also quotes critic Leonard Lutwack, who said, "The line of descent from *The Octopus* to ***The Grapes of Wrath*** is as direct as any that can be found in American literature." In the mid-1930s, political fiction was becoming popular again, and Norris's novels from the turn of the century were being read. Steinbeck read *The Octopus* in the early 1930s and admired its dramatization of the clash between ranchers and workers in California's San Joaquin Valley. At this time, Steinbeck was getting the idea for *The Grapes of Wrath* after he became involved with the laborer and migrant worker situation in the **Monterey** area. Norris's most significant work, *McTeague* (1899), is an impressive story of avarice in the lives of everyday people. Many critics believe that Steinbeck, like Norris, was greatly influenced by the French naturalistic writer Emile Zola, who attempted to remain fearlessly realistic (to the point of brutality) in his description and analysis of the soft underside of human motives. In addition, Steinbeck shares with Norris the theme of the individual victimized by an unforgiving and brutal social system. It has been documented that Steinbeck read *McTeague* in the early 1930s, and there is evidence of its influence on ***Of Mice***

and Men. In fact, **F. Scott Fitzgerald** wrote to **Edmund Wilson** about Steinbeck's stealing a scene from *McTeague* and including it in *Of Mice and Men*. In *McTeague*, the character Maria Macpa is forced by the junk dealer Zerkow to tell her dream of the good life and of her escape from grinding poverty. Similarly, in *Of Mice and Men*, **George Milton** tells **Lennie Small** to relate all his expectations. Fitzgerald said that the rhythms of Norris's dialogue are echoed in Steinbeck's, but others have pointed out that Zerkow forces Maria's confession in order to hurt her, while George coaxes Lennie's thoughts to make him feel better. Parini says that Steinbeck often used a source, but then built something entirely different from it.

Further Reading: DeMott, Robert. *Steinbeck's Reading: A Catalogue of Books Owned and Borrowed*. New York: Garland, 1984; Parini, Jay. *John Steinbeck: A Biography*. New York: Holt, 1995.

Brian Niro and Janet L. Flood

NORRIS, MISS. **Cal Trask**'s high school English teacher in ***East of Eden***.

"NOTHING SO MONSTROUS" (1936). One of two special editions of Steinbeck stories issued in 1936. Three hundred seventy copies of this book were printed, containing the **Junius Maltby** episode of ***The Pastures of Heaven*** plus a short epilogue written by Steinbeck for this limited edition. Later **Covici** also created a limited printing of **"Saint Katy the Virgin,"** Steinbeck's animal fable from ***The Long Valley***, and marketed it as well.

Michael J. Meyer

NURSE. The efficient, condescending, and racist woman sent by **Dr. H. C. Murphy** to care for **Adam Trask** in ***East of Eden*** after his second stroke.

"NYMPH AND ISOBEL, THE." An early short story that Steinbeck most likely wrote in 1924, in which a tired shop girl talks to a Greek nymph in a Los Angeles fountain. This piece contrasts the real world with a fantasy/mythological one and, in doing so, prefigures a later Steinbeck who preferred natural settings for his fiction. Real life is shown with all it flaws, including the fictions humans devise to deal with reality.

Michael J. Meyer

NYNEVE. In ***The Acts of King Arthur***, female cousin of Sir Bryan of the Isles and **Sir Meliot of Logurs**. Encountered by **King Pellinore** during the Quest of the Lady and brought to the court of **King Arthur**, where she becomes the object of **Merlin**'s desires. Eventually, Merlin divulges all his secrets, and she then imprisons him for all time in a room under a great rock cliff. She loves Arthur and casts a spell that enables him to recover **Excalibur** during his fight with **Sir Accolon of Gaul**. She saves Arthur from death a second time when she prevents him from donning the poisoned cloak **Morgan Le Fay** has sent him. She saves **Sir Pelleas** from his despair and lives happily with him for the rest of their lives.

O

O. HENRY'S FULL HOUSE. Filmed in 1952 and narrated by Steinbeck (a very rare endeavor for him, as he hated to narrate or give public readings), this anthology film assembles five respected directors and a top-notch cast to bring a handful of stories by the great American author O. Henry to the screen. The cast includes Hollywood notables Charles Laughton, Marilyn Monroe, Richard Widmark, Jeanne Crain, Farley Granger, Anne Baxter, and **Fred Allen.**

OAKS, CAMILLE. In *The Wayward Bus*, a blonde stripper presented as the incarnation of the busty, long-legged calendar girls adorning the walls of the lunchroom belonging to **Juan** and **Alice Chicoy** in **Rebel Corners**, California. Her name is an alias she invents on the spot, inspired by an advertisement she notices for Camel cigarettes combined with the sight of the mature oak trees that are visible for miles and "define" Rebel Corners. Her name is as artificial as the calendar girls pictured on the lunchroom walls—creatures whom the jealousy-prone Alice Chicoy is not in the least bit jealous of, because "she had never seen anyone like them and she didn't think anyone else ever had." However, there is more to Camille than either her name or appearance suggests. Well-dressed and self-composed, yet marred physically by the facial scars left by forceps used during her birth, Camille claims to be a dental nurse but is, in fact, a stripper who performs for stag parties at conventions. Since her youth, she has found herself irresistibly attractive to men. She has become hardened by this situation and, although the narrator claims that she dreams of having a normal family life, is destined to remain a high-class prostitute as long as her appearance holds. Virtually everyone notices Camille's entrance, for she charges a room with sexual energy.

The Wayward Bus is a sexual bus, and the resolutions of many of the conflicts in the novel are sexual in nature. However, Camille is more catalyst than participant in these resolutions. With the possible exception of **Ernest Horton**—with whom she may or may not get together in Los Angeles—Camille's interactions with the other characters serve largely to remind them of their own sexual natures, help them to discover their sexuality, or highlight their hypocrisy or duplicity in this area. For example, Camille converses with **Norma** primarily as a way of avoiding the difficulties associated with rebuffing the male passengers, but she finds Norma's pathetic dreaminess and clutching dependency to be burdensome and unwelcome in a prospective friend. Camille will most certainly return to her own world—without Norma—once the bus reaches **San Juan de la Cruz**.

Christopher S. Busch and Bradd Burningham

"OF FISH AND FISHERMEN" (1954). Published in *Sports Illustrated* (4 Oct. 1954) and earlier that year in *Punch* and *Le Figaro*, this essay compares the Parisian approach to fishing with that of the Americans and

British. Whereas Americans invest excessive time and money in fishing and the British follow a ridiculous code of decorum in which the prize fish is elevated to mythical status, Parisians seem purposely to fish for hours without catching anything. Steinbeck admires the Parisian approach: "From the sanctity of this occupation, a man may emerge refreshed and in control of his own soul. He is not idle. He is fishing."

Further Reading: Steinbeck, John. "On Fishing." In *America and Americans and Selected Nonfiction*. Ed. Susan Shillinglaw and Jackson J. Benson. New York: Viking, 2002.

Eric Skipper

OF MICE AND MEN **(BOOK)** (1937). Published in January 1937, the novella *Of Mice and Men* marks a deliberate change from Steinbeck's previous book, ***In Dubious Battle***, a novel about a contemporary farm strike. In this new project, Steinbeck chose to work within a much narrower framework; consequently, *Of Mice and Men* concentrates on a small number of characters—**George Milton**, **Lennie Small,** and a few others—as Steinbeck tells the story of the migrant ranch laborers through carefully detailed settings. Only a short time before the composition of *Of Mice and Men*, thousands of itinerant single men had roamed the western states, following the harvests. Many of them traveled by rail, arriving in the fields in empty boxcars that were later used to transport the grain. However, in the first two decades of the twentieth century, migrant workers were disappearing because the farmhands who used to do the farm work were being replaced by machines. The loneliness and frustration experienced by these men set the tone of the novel, a story about ranch workers' lives and broken dreams.

The story concerns George Milton and Lennie Small. George is small but quick whereas Lennie is huge but mentally deficient. The first scene of the book shows George and Lennie on their way to a ranch near Soledad, California, where they will work as farmhands. From the conversations between George and Lennie, the reader learns that Lennie is always in trouble because he loves to stroke soft things; however, because he is so strong, he often destroys whatever he touches. The reader also learns why they left the previous ranch–they had to run away because Lennie tried to touch a girl's dress, and the girl screamed. George had to hide Lennie in a ditch to save him from a lynch mob whose members assumed Lennie had assaulted the girl. Before they get to the next ranch, George warns Lennie to stay out of trouble so they can have a new life. George dreams of making enough money to buy a piece of land where he and Lennie can have their own place. Whenever George talks about their dream—"we're gonna have a little house and a couple of acres an' a cow and some pigs"—Lennie breaks in and adds to their dreams that "we're gonna have in the garden and about the rabbits in the cages." All Lennie cares about is that he will tend the rabbits. Clearly, George and Lennie need each other's company as they try to survive the lonely life of migrant workers.

When George and Lennie arrive at the bunkhouse of the ranch to sign up to work, their meeting with the **boss** is not pleasant, and soon after they start working, **Curley**, the boss's son, tries to pick a fight with Lennie. Curley's hostility is based on the fact that he is small in stature, and large men make him feel inferior. To make matters worse, George learns that **Curley's wife** has the reputation of being a woman with a wandering eye when it comes to ranch hands. George feels the danger from this woman and warns Lennie to stay away from her; he is afraid that Lennie may approach Curley's wife as he did the girl at the previous ranch.

At the new ranch, it seems that George and Lennie's dream of finding a place of their own might soon be realized when, unfortunately, Lennie gets in trouble. One day, Curley comes to the bunkhouse to look for his wife because he suspects she is having an affair with **Slim**, a lead ranch hand. Embarrassed by Slim, who ridicules him, Curley is ready to pick a fight. When other ranch hands join Slim to attack Curley, Curley picks Lennie to fight with because Lennie is standing aside and laughing, an act Curley feels is insulting, especially from a big guy. In their fight, Lennie crushes Curley's hand. George and Lennie's fate is not simply determined by their actual encounters on the ranch; their future destiny seems unavoidably related to what is happening to individuals around them, including the fellow ranch hands, Curley, Curley's wife, **Crooks**, Slim, **Candy**, and even the dog. For example, the fight between Curley and Lennie is triggered by the conflict between Slim and Curley; Lennie is not much more than a bystander in the hostile atmosphere.

Another bad omen occurs with the shooting of Candy's old dog. Steinbeck vividly describes this incident. Candy, the old swamper in the bunkhouse, has a dog that is too old to eat or walk properly. **Carlson** encourages Candy to have the dog killed to save the animal from further suffering, because he considers the old dog useless. Steinbeck links the dog's fate to Lennie's imminent death: "After a moment the ancient dog walked lamely in through the open door. He gazed about with mild, half-blind eyes." Another connection of the event to the last scene of the story occurs when Candy expresses his regret that "I ought to of shot that dog myself, George. I shouldn't ought to of let no stranger shoot my dog." This event anticipates George's shooting of Lennie later in the book.

Although different things are happening to the individual characters in this work, almost all the characters share one common problem: a lack of communication and companionship. This problem is to the result of differences in race, gender, mental abilities, and physical skills. In one instance, Steinbeck conveys this theme through the dialogue between Crooks and Lennie, the former a black and the latter a developmentally disabled man. One Saturday night, when all the ranch hands but Crooks, Lennie, and Candy have gone to town, Lennie comes to Crooks's room in the barn, where Crooks philosophizes about companionship, and Lennie talks about his dreams of tending the rabbits. However, even though he is lonely himself, Crooks hesitates about whether Lennie, a white man, should come into his room. Similarly, Candy expresses feelings of loneliness, especially when he is made to feel useless because of a disability, and he wants to join in on George and Lennie's plan to own a ranch. In a third instance, the loneliness of Curley's wife seems to be the result of the almost complete lack of communication between her and the men; as the solitary female character, she often shows up simply to find someone to talk to, although her efforts are rebuffed or viewed with suspicion by the men.

Lennie's fate is sealed when Curley's wife comes to the bunkhouse to seek some companionship with Lennie and finds him stroking his dead puppy that he has just killed, and she learns that Lennie likes soft things. In an attempt to get Lennie's attention, she assumes a pose designed to attract Lennie's attention. She tells Lennie that she does not love Curley, and she even compliments Lennie on his strength and congratulates him for hurting Curley's hand in the fight. Then, seeking some physical pleasure she has no doubt been denied, she encourages Lennie to stroke her hair but panics when Lennie holds on too tightly. In an attempt to quiet her screams, Lennie accidentally breaks her neck and kills her. Frightened, Lennie vanishes into the brush to hide himself. The farmhands find the body of Curley's wife, and an enraged Curley organizes a search party.

Late that afternoon, Lennie comes to the river, knowing he has broken his promise to George that he will not get into any more trouble. Soon George shows up and reassures Lennie of their dream to own their own place and tend the rabbits. While keeping Lennie talking about their dream, George puts a gun to the base of Lennie's skull and fires before the other men arrive.

According to Steinbeck, George is a hero who is "able to rise to greatness—to kill his friend to save him." However, readers should not consider the novel simply as one that advocates for heroism in such a brotherhood. A careful reading should also stress developing an understanding of the deep loneliness experienced by characters as they pursue their dreams.

Of Mice and Men was an immediate success upon its publication, even though Steinbeck said he was not expecting a large sale. The novel was chosen as a Book of the Month Club selection, and 117,000 copies were sold in advance of the official publication date, February 25, 1937. An obvious characteristic of the novel is its conversational style. Steinbeck later explained that he was teaching himself to write for the theater, and late in 1937, he translated the novel into a play. In fact, he considered the novel an experiment in writing a play that could be read, or a novel that could be played. Steinbeck worked together with playwright **George F. Kaufman**, who was going to direct the stage version of *Of Mice and Men*. Steinbeck took advice from Kaufman and made some changes for the play version. In the play, Steinbeck preserved the marvelous tenderness of the book, but he also enlarged the role of Curley's wife, who is presented in the play as a person with strongly articulated feelings about her past history and family relationships. The play *Of Mice and Men* opened at the Music Box Theater in New York on November 23, 1937, with Wallace Ford as George and Broderick Crawford as Lennie. Claire Luce appeared as Curley's wife. A movie based on the play was produced soon thereafter.

The initial reviews regarding *Of Mice and Men* were enthusiastic. Ralph Thompson wrote in the *New York Times* that "the boys have whooped it up for John Steinbeck's new book." Henry Seidel Canby wrote in the *Saturday Review of Literature* that "there has been nothing quite so good of the kind in American writing since Sherwood Anderson's early stories." Nevertheless, there was also resistance expressed in the reception of the novel. The most damaging assessment was from **Edmund Wilson,** who stated that Steinbeck's preoccupation with biology led him "to present life in animal terms," to deal "almost always in his fiction . . . with lower animals or with human beings so rudimentary that they are almost on the animal level." Wilson found a prime example of his point in the character of Lennie. But other critics such as **Jackson J. Benson** and **Peter Lisca** argue that science and nature provided a philosophical framework for Steinbeck's animalistic characterizations. According to this view, Steinbeck's concern with biology gave him a sense of connection with the natural universe. Lisca further notes that "the world of *Of Mice and Men* is a fallen one, inhabited by sons of Cain, forever exiled from Eden, the little farm of which they dream." However, **Louis Owens** points out that there are no Edens in Steinbeck's writing, only illusions of Eden, and that in the fallen world of the **Salinas** Valley, the Promised Land is an illusory and painful fantasy. Lennie's yearning for the rabbits and for all soft, living things symbolizes the yearning all men have for warm, living contact. It is this yearning, as Owens notes, that makes George need Lennie just as much as Lennie needs George, and that sends Curley's wife wandering despairingly about the ranch in search of companionship.

In *Of Mice and Men*, Steinbeck questions the meaning of life itself. The story may be read as Steinbeck's **non-teleological** thinking about life: life is what it *is*, rather than what it *should be*. This is in accord with the original title of the work, "*Something That Happened*." In addition to the theme of loneliness in *Of Mice and Men*, recent critics including Charlotte Hadella believe that the contextual overtones in the novel are twofold: mythical and communal. The description of George and Lennie's dream to own a couple of acres of land is delivered as a religious incantation. George's partnership with Lennie and the notion of living in a place where he can keep Lennie safe from the real world are the results of a promise George made to Lennie's **Aunt Clara**. Their plan reflects the illusion of the American Dream and the mythic innocence of Eden. Nevertheless, most critics consider *Of Mice and Men* one of Steinbeck's most compressed and unified works, and agree that it achieves an artistic richness in exposing the conditions of human beings as individuals and as members of social groups. For decades, critics have focused on Steinbeck's treatment of a recurring theme in *Of Mice and Men*: the inherent loneliness of the itinerant farm laborers and their desperate desire for land of their own. Loneliness and the dream of land are personified in the characters of George and Lennie. Such desires and dreams also parallel the fundamental themes in one of Steinbeck's earlier works, ***To a God Unknown***.

Further Reading: Hadella, Charlotte. "*Of Mice and Men.*" In *A New Study Guide to Steinbeck's Major Works with Critical Explications*. Ed. Tetsumaro Hayashi. Metuchen, NJ: Scarecrow Press, 1993. 149–59; Levant, Howard. *The Novels of John Steinbeck*. Columbia: University of Missouri Press, 1983; Lisca, Peter. *The Wide World of John Steinbeck*. New Brunswick, NJ: Rutgers University Press, 1958; Loftis, Anne. "A Historical Introduction to *Of Mice and Men*." In *The Short Novels of John Steinbeck: Critical Essays with a Checklist to Steinbeck Criticism*. Ed. Jackson J. Benson. Durham, NC: Duke University Press, 1990. 39–47. Owens, Louis. *John Steinbeck's Revision of America*. Athens: University of Georgia Press, 1985. Steinbeck, John. *A Life in Letters*. Ed. Elaine Steinbeck and Robert Wallsten. New York: Viking Press, 1975; ———. *Of Mice and Men*. (1937) New York: Penguin Books, 1993.

Luchen Li

OF MICE AND MEN **(FILM AND TELEVISION VERSIONS)** (1939, 1968, 1981, 1992). On December 22, 1939, producer Hal Roach premiered the first film version, directed brilliantly by **Lewis Milestone**, as a low-budget production that cost less than $300,000 to produce. The screenplay by Eugene Solow retained most of Steinbeck's dialogue but opened up the action using Norbert Brodine's lyric photography of the fields and hills of California and of the actual work of the migrant farmhands, rather than confining events to the bunkhouse and the pond where the story opens and ends. **Spencer Tracy**, James Cagney, and **John Garfield** had all wanted to play **George** but were either too expensive or otherwise committed, but Milestone got memorable performances from **Burgess Meredith** as George, **Lon Chaney, Jr.,** as **Lennie**, and Betty Field as **Curley's wife** (called Mae in this and subsequent films), all then comparatively unknown. **Aaron Copland**'s score (his first for a dramatic film) was groundbreaking, largely because he took three times as long as most studios allowed for composition, and he avoided the symphonic orchestration that was then customary for films in favor of a more subdued realism, providing the sorts of tunes farmhands might whistle, scored for only one or two instruments. The score was nominated for an Oscar (but lost to *Stagecoach*), and Copland later used parts of it for two movements of his suite *Music for Movies.* Critical response was mostly ecstatic: "Hollywood for once displays deep respect for a serious writer," wrote Frank Hoellering in *The Nation.* The reviewer for *The New York Times* admired "the feeling of seeing another third, or thirtieth of the nation, not merely a troupe of playactors living in a world of make-believe." In 1970, Charles Higham and Joel Greenberg praised the film's "background of economic misery coupled with rural lyricism, a combination that brings out some of Milestone's finest qualities: a beautiful feeling for the farm, the land and its workers . . . and an instinctive sympathy for the pathos, loneliness, and tawdry pleasures of the itinerant farm hands." Despite critical raves and an Oscar nomination for best picture, *Of Mice and Men* fared poorly at the box office, edged out by the many blockbuster productions of 1939, the year *Gone with the Wind* won the Oscar for best film. Since then, *Of Mice and Men* has become valued as a classic.

Nearly forgotten is a 1968 version for television, which suggested a homosexual relationship between **George Segal** as George and **Nicol Williamson** as Lennie that is not in Steinbeck's novel or play.

NBC offered a television version in 1981, directed by Reza Badiyi and produced by **Robert Blake**, who also played George opposite **Randy Quaid**'s Lennie. All the cast gave solid performances, but the most profoundly moving characterization was given by Lew Ayres as **Candy**, the one-legged swamper. Except for a scene where the fugitive George and Lennie go to Lennie's **Aunt Clara** (who is dead in the novel and play), E. Nick Alexander's script was based on Eugene Solow's screenplay. The main flaw in this otherwise effective version is the score by George Romanis, which is too often intrusive, sometimes loud enough to obscure the dialogue, and makes painfully obvious use of conventional folk songs to underscore the action and emotions.

In 1992, MGM released a new theatrical version, in which **John Malkovich** and **Gary Sinise** reprised their roles as Lennie and George from the 1980 Steppenwolf Theatre production in Chicago. Sinise had also previously played **Tom Joad** in the Tony-winning Steppenwolf stage version of ***The Grapes of Wrath***. As film director, Sinise provided vivid period detail and location photography so beautiful as to undercut the bleak loneliness of Steinbeck's story. Horton Foote's screenplay mostly followed Steinbeck but flaws the scene with **Crooks**, the only black man on the ranch, by exaggerating his taunting of Lennie and then omitting him from the group that plans to join forces to buy a small farm. It also spoils the ending by cutting all the dialogue after Lennie's "and I get to tend the rabbits," leaving out George's description of a peaceful, painless heaven across the water, and Lennie's rapturous "I can see it" just as he is shot.

The film is capable but less than compelling. As George, Sinise seems too young and handsome and too emotionally low keyed. John Malkovich's Lennie is even more of a problem: he played Lennie as bald, with a mouthful of rotting teeth and a high, singsong voice. Many critics considered Malkovich's characterization as much off-putting as sympathetic, and at times his Lennie almost becomes a terrifying monster. Vincent Canby observed that it is an intelligent, consistent performance but one that seems too contrived. The other performances are fine, especially that of Ray Walston as Candy.

Further Reading: Morsberger, Robert. "Tell Again, George." In *John Steinbeck: The Years of Greatness, 1936–1939*. Ed. Tetsumaro Hayashi. Tuscaloosa: University of Alabama Press, 1993.

OFFICE OF WAR INFORMATION. Perhaps best known as the adolescent manifestation of the Central Intelligence Agency (CIA), the Office of War Information was the product of the 1942 merger of two other fledgling government agencies, the Foreign Information Service and the Office of Strategic Services. Early in 1940, in a letter to President **Franklin Delano Roosevelt**, Steinbeck proposed the creation of a wartime office that might match the propaganda efforts being lobbied abroad. At first, his offers were dismissed as the well-wishing of a patriot who could offer no expert advice on the situation. The urgings of FDR's Civilian Coordinator of Information (COI), William J. Donovan, however, apparently won over Roosevelt and eventually led him to develop an agency, the Office of Strategic Services, to counter the Axis spread of misinformation. It can be argued that Steinbeck's persistent correspondence helped establish this office.

Although initially fairly reluctant to become more involved—he was offered a job with the Coordinator of Information and turned it down—Steinbeck began to feel increasingly obligated to participate personally. In a letter to the president, Steinbeck noted that although he had already turned down one job offer, the conditions in the United States led him to believe that he already had "a job whether I want one or not."

The Foreign Information Service (FIS) was created in 1941, and in October of that year, Steinbeck was requested (read "instructed") to participate. Although there is little official record of Steinbeck's involvement in the transforming agency, it is highly likely that he worked as an unpaid consultant, an arrangement the FIS guarded with some jealousy. In a manner capable only of a government agency, the FIS would not hire him on a permanent basis, nor would it allow him to work elsewhere. Despite this fact, Steinbeck continued to work for the FIS, preparing overseas broadcasts.

Later, Steinbeck worked in the Office of War Information and other government agencies, including the air force, where he gathered information and produced propaganda. It was not until the agency became operational that Steinbeck was ever actually offered a genuine job. The offer, however, was tainted by the possibility that Steinbeck's ultimate employment might be stopped because of his limited contributions to ambulances for Spain; in addition, there was the possibility he might be labeled a Communist. Steinbeck continued to be met with a kind of bureaucratic impasse as his projects were continually delayed or blocked from the outset, leading him to conclude in a 1943 letter to **Webster "Toby" Street** that although private industry might not support his work, "neither does the army nor the gov't." Nevertheless, Steinbeck persevered and was able to produce a fair number of wartime pieces, including ***The Moon Is Down***, ***Bombs Away***, and a series of articles as a correspondent (published together in ***Once There Was a War***).

Brian Niro

O'HARA, JOHN (1905–1970). An American author of novels and short fiction, O'Hara was greatly concerned with the relationship between social history and fiction. Many of his novels and short stories are set in realistic, but fictional, towns in Pennsylvania. His most famous works include *Appointment in Samarra* (1934), *Butterfield 8* (1935; film 1960), *A Rage to Live* (1949), *From the Terrace* (1958; film 1960), and *Ten North Frederick* (1955; film 1958), which won the National Book Award. Steinbeck and O'Hara met in 1936 when O'Hara was asked to do the script for ***In Dubious Battle***. Although O'Hara never completed the project, the pair shared an initially awkward acquaintance that eventually grew into a lasting friendship. In stark contrast to Steinbeck, O'Hara took himself and his work very seriously. O'Hara enjoyed a flair for the dramatic that stretched across his diet, his choice of tailor-made suits, and his hypersensitive response to his critics. Steinbeck enjoyed O'Hara's company but, according to **Jackson J. Benson**, secretly thought O'Hara's work was sloppy. Despite their occasional differences, O'Hara was a close and loyal friend to Steinbeck. At one point, when Steinbeck and his third wife, **Elaine Scott Steinbeck**, observed a very drunk O'Hara on the street, the complexity of the authors' relationship came out as Steinbeck observed that O'Hara had really come to ruin. Many years later, while Steinbeck suffered in a hospital bed after surgery for a detached retina, O'Hara read to him nearly every day. Loyal to the end, O'Hara arrived at Steinbeck's funeral an hour early to pray.

Further Reading: Benson, Jackson J. *The True Adventures of John Steinbeck, Writer*. New York: Viking, 1984; Steinbeck, John. *A Life in Letters*. Ed. Elaine Steinbeck and Robert Wallsten. New York: Viking, 1975.

OLD EASTER. In the short story **"The Great Mountains,"** a thirty-year-old horse, who is past his days of usefulness on the ranch. **Mr. Tiflin** makes an analogy between the horse and **Gitano**, suggesting that it might be better to shoot the old horse and put him out of his misery. **Warren Graham French** sees both Gitano and Old Easter as suggesting renewal, if not resurrection and perpetual life.

OLD JUAN. The first Mexican settler **Joseph Wayne** meets in ***To a God Unknown*** when he arrives in the Nacimiento Valley. Old Juan tells Joseph to remember him when he kills his first deer. Later, Old Juan organizes the New Year's fiesta. He could possibly be the father of **Juanito**, thus a patriarch in his own right, but this fact is intentionally obscured.

OLD MAN FROM GAMBAIS. In ***The Short Reign of Pippin IV***, a peasant and recluse whom **Héristal Pippin** encounters on a solitary motorcycle ride in the woods. Pippin later shares a bottle of wine with him, and in return, the old man answers Pippin's questions about why he does what he does for so little visible remuneration, using simple sentences that articulate a work ethic free from both greed and a political agenda.

OLD MEXICO. In *The Wayward Bus*, the subject of **Juan Chicoy**'s nostalgic longings. Chicoy yearns to return to the Mexico of his youth. He looks for a sign from the Virgin that he may leave his present life and responsibilities behind and head for freedom in Mexico, but he ultimately finds that he cannot abandon the passengers to follow his dream. The **Pritchards** are also bound for Mexico, but as tourists rather than as natives.

Christopher Busch

OLD STAGECOACH ROAD. In *The Wayward Bus*, the road the bus takes as its alternate route in order to avoid the bridges imperiled by the rising **SanYsidro River**. Symbolically very important in the novel, the old road embodies the history of the American West. Once traversed regularly by stagecoaches, wagons, and men on horseback, and once bounded by active, self-sufficient farms, the road is now nearly abandoned, with occasional drab houses scattered here and there. A second symbolic association of the road is connected to Steinbeck's epigram from the medieval morality play, *Everyman*. The modern-day pilgrims on the bus traverse the road much as their cultural ancestors did, yet with markedly less purpose and dignity than their predecessors possessed, for they have neither the intensity of the religious conviction expressed in medieval times nor the purpose of frontier development that marked the nineteenth-century American experience.

Christopher Busch

OLD TENNIS SHOES. A local nickname for Old Tennessee whiskey, a cheap blend sold at **Lee Chong**'s grocery store in *Sweet Thursday* and consumed in large quantities on **Cannery Row**.

OLD WOMAN PASSENGER, THE. In *The Wayward Bus*, a cantankerous passenger on **Louie**'s Greyhound bus. The old woman interrupts Louie's attempts to seduce **Camille Oaks**.

OLDER MAN AND THE SILENT BOY BY THE COLORADO RIVER, THE. Like the **ragged man** before them, these two characters in *The Grapes of Wrath* also offer a premonition of the evils that await the **Joads** in California. Although the two affirm the state's status as "the purtiest country you ever seen," they also relate stories of discrimination against the Okies, the first time the Joads have heard this derogatory label. They also tell how the surplus of crops is wasted by farm owners, and how conglomerates and monopolies rather than individually owned farms have begun to dominate the truck crop industries. Sensing that **Pa Joad** at least does not believe his story, the older man remarks on the futility of trying to eradicate so strong a dream as the Joads have through rumor and hearsay. The Joads will have to experience California firsthand before the reality of its inhumanity will truly sink in.

Michael J. Meyer

"OLIVE WOOD CROSS, THE." An old story written in Steinbeck's early years (mid-1920s), which the author mentions in a letter to his friend, **Kate Beswick**, as having been lost in making the rounds of every publisher in the country.

ONCE THERE WAS A WAR (1958). First published in 1958, this volume reprints sixty-six of the eighty-five war dispatches Steinbeck published in the *New York Herald Tribune* during the period June 21 through December 15, 1943. The dispatches cover his experiences as an accredited war correspondent for the newspaper from June to October 1943 in England, North Africa, and Italy.

Steinbeck did not make the initial decision to publish the book nor did he choose which of the dispatches should be reprinted. Certainly, he complained to his publishers at the exclusion of some of the pieces and asked that they be reinstated, but they were not. Since virtually all the reprinted dispatches carry the datelines corresponding to the actual dates they were originally published in the *New York Herald Tribune* and not the dates on which they were written, they should not be regarded as providing an exact sequential record of Steinbeck's travels overseas. This confusion is further compounded by the fact that, with their appearance one by one in the newspaper, the dispatches frequently failed to keep the true chronological order of the events they described, and, moreover, all the later pieces datelined November 15 onward (which relate to events that had occurred during the first half of September) were actually written after Steinbeck returned to the United States in October 1943.

Unfortunately, Steinbeck did not use the original dispatches, in possible conjunction with any unused on-the-spot notes he made while overseas, as background material for a comprehensive account of his time in the war zone, as he did with ***A Russian Journal***. This later work was developed from the series of articles he had published in the *New York Herald Tribune* following his investigative visit to the Soviet Union with photographer **Robert Capa** from July through mid-September 1947. Not using the original dispatches for *Once There Was a War* was probably related to the fact that when he returned home from the war in the autumn of 1943, he was in bad physical shape and somewhat psychologically scarred by some of his experiences. He declared that he had seen enough of war to last him for the foreseeable future, and he clearly had no stomach to write about it in depth once he had completed his contract with the newspaper. He publicly argued that he was still too close to events to fashion his material into a book-length narrative and needed to let it incubate in his mind for at least a couple of years before putting pen to paper.

Even though Steinbeck had the intention of eventually writing such a book, it was never a project he seriously contemplated after those two designated incubatory years had passed. Apart from anything else, other projects and personal problems soon crowded out any plans he may have had for the book. In his introduction to this volume, he refers to the reprinted dispatches as "period pieces, fairy tales, half-meaningless memories of a time and of attitudes which have gone forever from the world." He goes on to remind his readers that the dispatches were written under circumstances of pressure and tension, and that his reason for eschewing the initial impulse to change or rewrite them in any way was that "their very raggedness is . . . a parcel of their immediacy," making them "as real as the wicked witch and the good fairy, as true and tested and edited as any other myth."

It had never been Steinbeck's intent to report the day-to-day hard news on the progress of the war and, by so doing, trespass on the territory of the professional war correspondents. Instead, he saw his role as that of a mere observer of the ordinary men and women in wartime, who were doing a difficult, dangerous, and sometimes boring job to the best of their abilities. His adherence to this aim can be seen in some of the titles given to the dispatches by the **Viking Press** editors: "Stories of the Blitz," "Lilli Marlene," "War Talk," "Growing Vegetables," "Bob Hope," and "Chewing Gum." Steinbeck writes about the homesickness of American troops in London on the Fourth of July; the indomitable spirit of the people of Dover, who were under continual bombardment from German guns across the Channel; the hardships and perils of the men on unglamorous British minesweepers; the value of good luck charms; and the servicemen's concern about the postwar world. Even semifictitious stories are included, such as those about a ghost cottage and the "elf" in Algiers, and those about Steinbeck's own official driver, the colorful Big Train Mulligan, whose character and exploits briefly captured the imagination and delight of readers back in the United States.

The book is divided into three sections, "England," "Africa," and "Italy," containing thirty-four, six, and twenty-six dispatches respectively. The falloff in the number of dispatches in the second section reflects not only the shorter period of time he spent in Africa, but also his growing disillusionment with the task he had set for himself, his restlessness to return home to his wife, **Gwyndolyn Conger Steinbeck**, and his doubts about the quality of the stories he was finding. The first twelve dispatches reproduced in the book—the six that describe the voyage across the Atlantic on a large troopship and the subsequent six that describe life at a U.S. bomber station in England, from which almost daily missions were flown over Europe—are brilliant pieces of reportage, vividly putting the reader into the shoes of the servicemen themselves. Almost all the England dispatches, in spite of their occasional mundane element, possess the immediacy and telling observation of Steinbeck, the novelist. If there is a certain falloff in the Africa pieces, the volume springs into life in the third section, with the advent of action and, as it were, the real war. This final section is principally taken up with the preparation for and the execution of the Allied invasion of Italy. Not all that is described is based on Steinbeck's firsthand knowledge, however. For instance, he did not experience landing in an LCI (Landing Craft Infantry boat) under fire on a hostile beach, although he was ashore on Red Beach at Salerno for several hours while it was under fierce bombardment by the Germans. As he notes in the introduction, "I never admitted having seen anything myself. In describing a scene, I invariably put it in the mouth of someone else" (xvi). The last thirteen dispatches he wrote (written after he had returned home), of which nine are reprinted in *Once There Was a War*, cover Steinbeck's experiences in September 1943 with a small task group, consisting of a single American destroyer and a flotilla of American, British, and Dutch small naval craft (units of the "Plywood Navy," as he refers to them). The task group had the two-fold purpose of capturing various small German-held offshore islands in the vicinity of the Bay of Naples, and of generally, under cover of darkness, creating confusion and panic among enemy troops on the mainland by giving the impression that other landings in force were about to take place. These later dispatches were frequently heavily censored, and unfortunately do not tell the whole story, further details of which have since been related in **Douglas Fairbanks, Jr.**'s, autobiographical *A Hell of a War.*

Once There Was a War had, on the whole, a good reception when it appeared in 1958. The contemporary critics were predictably divided almost equally between those who accepted the book's format and the fact that its content told the truth, if not the whole truth, and those who regretted that Steinbeck had not taken time to write a more substantial work. In the former group were those critics who thought the pieces not merely excellent journalism but fine literature. In the latter group were those who questioned the whole rationale of reprinting what were seen as thin feature stories that had no relevance to the current times. Subsequent scholarly opinion, while being similarly divided, has nevertheless been generally more appreciative of the book.

Further Reading: Fairbanks, Douglas, Jr. *A Hell of a War.* London: Robson Books, 1995; French, Warren. *Steinbeck's Non-Fiction Revisited.* New York: Twayne Publishers, 1996; Simmonds, Roy S. "John Steinbeck's World War II Dispatches: An Annotated Checklist." *Serif* 11 (Summer 1974): 21-30; ———. *John Steinbeck: The War Years, 1939–1945.* Lewisburg, PA: Bucknell University Press, 1996; Steinbeck, John. *Once There Was a War.* New York: Viking Press, 1958.

Roy S. Simmonds

ONE-EYED MAN AT THE JUNKYARD, THE. This character demonstrates generosity to **Tom** and **Al Joad** in ***The Grapes of Wrath*** by helping them find a bearing replacement for their car. Not only does the one-eyed man sell this part at a reasonable price, unlike the car salesmen, but he also provides tools to remove it and then lets Tom and Al purchase several other necessities they find lying around. Although he despises his boss, the junkyard owner, because of the constant mockery he must endure regarding his physical deformity, the one-eyed man has not been able to break free from his negative influence. In an almost uncalled for upbraiding, Tom criticizes him for his whining and complaining and urges him to seek independence, encouraging him to take some sort of action and to recognize that no change can take place without movement of some type. Critics who have compared the **Joads**' journey to Homer's *The Odyssey* have identified the one-eyed man as a Cyclops figure, repeating Polyphemus's "Woe is me!" attitude but, unlike Poseidon's one-eyed son, also demonstrating hospitality and generosity to the traveling Joads.

Michael J. Meyer

O'NEILL, EUGENE (1888–1953). American playwright and winner of the 1936 **Nobel Prize** for Literature; Steinbeck read O'Neill's plays during the 1920s and was especially taken with *The Hairy Ape* (1922). As an expressionistic writer, O'Neill's writing style stands largely in contrast to Steinbeck's more naturalistic and sentimental style. Steinbeck, however, did incorporate expressionistic elements reminiscent of O'Neill's work into the stage adaptation of his novella ***Burning Bright***. In spite of poor reviews by critics, Steinbeck nevertheless defended his work by drawing upon O'Neill as an authority in using this technique.

Further Reading: DeMott, Robert. *Steinbeck's Reading: A Catalog of Books Owned and Borrowed*. New York: Garland, 1984.

Gregory Hill, Jr.

ONTELAKE OF WENTELAND, SIR. In ***The Acts of King Arthur***, the "forceful knight" who snatches the lady from the court of **King Arthur**. Killed by **King Pellinore** during the Quest of the Lady.

"OPEN SEASON ON GUESTS" (1957). The editor of *Playboy* magazine described Steinbeck's 1957 piece as a withering satire that offers some bloodcurdling tips for the taming of unhousebroken housebreakers. Discussing the perennial conflict between a host and his guests, Steinbeck writes that "etiquette is the body of truce terms between those natural enemies which prevents them from killing each other on sight." In order to win, the host must fight back with a suave deadliness; one solution Steinbeck suggests is holding a cocktail party, then locking every door, removing all the furniture, and preparing a witches' brew. The next step requires turning off the air conditioning, lighting the furnace, and smiling with happy malice as the offending guests slowly die.

Further Reading: *Playboy*, September 1957, 21.

Herbert Behrens and Michael J. Meyer

OPERA ADAPTATIONS. *See* **Floyd, Carlisle; Lewin, Frank**.

ORDEN, MAYOR. In ***The Moon Is Down***, the elderly mayor of a small coastal village in northern Europe that is suddenly overrun by a group of invaders who bear close resemblance to Hitler's army. With his white hair and large mustache, Orden cuts a stately figure and frequently wears a heavy chain of office around his neck, a medallion that symbolizes his role as mayor. A mannered, unassuming man who before the war seems content to go quietly about his civic duties, Orden becomes Steinbeck's figure for enduring central democratic ideals, especially freedom, after the invasion. When an invading officer is killed by an angry citizen, for example, **Colonel Lanser** asks Orden to mete out punishment to the offender. However, Orden refuses and points out that even if he were to comply with Lanser's wishes, it would be impossible to break the independent-minded spirit of his people. Later, outbreaks of sabotage increase throughout the village and Orden is arrested. After refusing to order the townspeople to cease their resistance activities, he is executed and becomes something of a martyr figure, not unlike the preacher **Jim Casy** in *The Grapes of Wrath*. Fittingly, before he dies, Orden voices his own epitaph, using Socrates' prophetic words: "a man who is good for anything ought not to calculate the chance of living or dying; he ought only to consider whether he is doing right or wrong."

Rodney P. Rice

ORDEN, SARAH. In ***The Moon Is Down***, the dutiful wife of **Mayor Orden.** She is preoccupied with appearances and manners, and spends most of her time tending the household and maintaining the mayor's meticulous deportment. After **Alexander Morden** is executed for killing an enemy officer, she provides comfort to Morden's widow, **Molly**.

OTHER SIDE OF EDEN: LIFE WITH JOHN STEINBECK, THE. Posthumous autobiographical account of Steinbeck's youngest son, "Catbird," published by his wife, Nancy, in 2001. As the son of a celebrated literary icon, **John Steinbeck IV** grew up in a privileged world peopled by the literati and the intellectual elite. Sadly, it was also a world of alcoholism, bitter divorce, estrangement, and abuse, on the part of both his mother, **Gwendolyn Conger Steinbeck**, and his father. In his memoir, the late son and namesake of John Steinbeck tries to make sense of an often painful youth. Left unfinished at his untimely death as a result of back surgery in 1991, this testament to his life is reconstructed by his wife of twelve years. Interweaving reminiscences of her life with John Steinbeck IV, Nancy Steinbeck created an account from two perspectives: her husband's memories of his chaotic and adventurous upbringing, and her own thoughts on their journey together to make a new life apart from the long shadow of a famous father and a troubled past.

Although laboring under the burden of being the son of a twentieth-century legend, the younger Steinbeck established himself as a respected journalist in his own right, mainly through his writing on wartime Vietnam, which had a profound impact on his life. *The Other Side of Eden* contains many thoughts on Vietnam, including a memorable scene of his father's visit to the war-torn country while the younger Steinbeck was in the army. There are also vivid recollections of his mother's abusive, alcoholic rages; his lonely years in boarding school; his long battle with drug addiction; his strained relationship with his remote, conflicted father; and the connection of ***East of Eden*** to Steinbeck's real-life family. Nancy Steinbeck adds perspective as an outsider, getting to know this complex family through her husband and, in the end, helping him put his life on solid footing.

Nancy Steinbeck

OTIS, ELIZABETH (1900–1981). Literary agent and founding member of **McIntosh & Otis, Inc**. In the mid-1920s, Otis met **Mavis McIntosh** while they were working for a literary agency that the pair ultimately discovered to be highly suspect in its practices. At this time, Otis was still a student at Vassar. The two ambitious women left the corrupt agency to start their own offices in New York. By 1928, the agency was incorporated, and by the early 1930s, McIntosh and Otis had established a reputable and successful business. Although initially introduced to Mavis McIntosh, Steinbeck soon enjoyed an extremely close friendship with Elizabeth Otis. Somewhere near the middle of 1935, Steinbeck began to correspond increasingly, and then almost exclusively, with Otis in his dealings with the agency. For her part, Otis represented one of the limited number of readers whom Steinbeck considered friends and whose criticism he appreciated as honest, fair, and incisive. Indeed, the correspondence between Steinbeck and Otis remained nearly constant from 1935 until Steinbeck's death. It is thought, in fact, that the last letter Steinbeck composed was meant for Otis. The typical Steinbeck letter to Otis seems to wander from some professional concern, or comment on his most recent project, to matters much more personal. As both confidante and mentor, Otis stood in an extremely privileged circle. In one letter to Otis, Steinbeck confessed, "I wonder why I always fool myself and, through myself, other people. But I don't think I fool you." Elizabeth Otis was one of a select group of friends who were present the day Steinbeck died in 1968.

Brian Niro

"OUR 'RIGGED' MORALITY." This three-page essay appeared in the March 1960 issue of *Coronet* (144–147) and reprinted correspondence between Steinbeck and **Adlai E. Stevenson** regarding the state of America's values.

"OUTER SHORES, THE." **Edward F. Ricketts** had planned to complete this work with Steinbeck; it was to have been the third part of a kind of trilogy—***The Sea of Cortez*** and ***Between Pacific Tides*** are the other parts. The project began to take shape with Ricketts' collecting voyages in 1945–46 in the waters around Vancouver Island and the Queen Charlotte island group, off the coast of British Columbia. The narrative portion of the text was to be written by Steinbeck after a final voyage with Ricketts to this area in the summer of 1948. With endorsements from Steinbeck and the **Viking Press**, Ricketts applied for a Guggenheim award, but the proposal was turned down. Steinbeck looked forward to the expedition with Ricketts and his wife, Alice, as a break from his work on his "big book" (***East of Eden***) and his troubled marriage to **Gwendolyn Conger Steinbeck**. The trip to the Queen Charlottes that was to culminate in "The Outer Shores" never occurred, however, because Ricketts was killed in May 1948 when his car was hit by a train.

Further Reading: Benson, Jackson J. *The True Adventures of John Steinbeck, Writer*. New York: Viking, 1984; Rodger, Katherine A. *Renaissance Man of Cannery Row: The Life and Letters of Edward F. Ricketts*. Tuscaloosa: University of Alabama Press, 2002; Tamm, Eric Enno. *Beyond "The Outer Shores."* New York: Four Walls Eight Windows, 2004.

OUTLAKE, SIR. In ***The Acts of King Arthur***, a kind and just knight, the brother of **Sir Damas,** a knight who has refused to share inherited lands with his brother. **Sir Accolon of Gaul** acts as Sir Outlake's champion against **King Arthur,** who is the champion of Sir Damas. Arthur subsequently divests Sir Damas of his whole manor and gives it to Sir Outlake.

"OVER THERE" (1944). An article based on Steinbeck's experiences as a war correspondent; this essay appeared in the February 1944 issue of *Ladies Home Journal*. It included several of Steinbeck's insights about World War II, based on his personal experiences; it also reprinted some of the author's journalistic correspondence to *Newsday Magazine* on pages 20–21, 137, 139–142, and 144–158. (*See* also ***Once There Was a War.***)

OVERSEER, THE. The indentured manager of **James Flower**'s plantation on Barbados in ***Cup of Gold***. He enjoys punishing slaves, and has erected a gallows in front of their quarters. When his period of indenture ends, he goes violently crazy. To prevent him from burning the fields, **Henry Morgan** shoots and kills him. Henry subsequently assumes the position of overseer.

Kevin Hearle

OWENS, LOUIS D. (1948–2002). Steinbeck critic and novelist. Born in Lompoc, California, where his father was stationed in the army, Owens spent his early years moving regularly between the Mississippi home of his father's Choctaw-Irish-French family and California, with sojourns in Oklahoma, the birthplace of his Cherokee-Irish mother. When he was seven years old, his family settled in the southern end of California's **Salinas** Valley. While attending public schools and working on farms and ranches up and down the Salinas Valley, Owens encountered the writings of John Steinbeck and became fascinated with the author's ability to turn the valley and its people into complex fictions. Owens attended Cuesta Community College for two years before transferring to the University of California–Santa Barbara, where he completed a BA degree in English in 1971 and, after working for the U.S. Forest Service, returned to earn an MA in English in 1974. After additional time working as a firefighter and wilderness ranger for the U.S. Forest Service, Owens received a doctorate in 1981 from the University of California–Davis, with a dissertation on the fiction of John Steinbeck. Following a year as a Fulbright lecturer in American literature at the University of Pisa in Italy, Owens became an assistant professor of English at California State University–Northridge in 1982 and went on to teach at the University of New Mexico and the University of California–Santa Cruz. At the time of his death, he was a professor of English and Native American studies at the University of California–Davis. Although he had previously published on other aspects of American literature, Owens's first Steinbeck publications came in 1977, 1979, and 1980, with articles on ***Once There Was a War, The Wayward Bus, To a God Unknown, The Log from the Sea of Cortez,*** and **"Flight."** Among his twelve published critical monographs, essay collections, and novels are *John Steinbeck's Re-Vision of America* (Georgia 1985), a broad critical analysis of Steinbeck's fiction, and *The Grapes of Wrath: Trouble in the Promised Land* (G.K. Hall 1989). Of his more than 100 published essays, 25 focus on Steinbeck's writing and have appeared in a wide variety of journals, periodicals, and anthologies. He served as editor of *American Literary Scholarship* and received the American Book Award (in 1997, for his novel *Nightland*), the PEN Josephine Miles Award, National Endowment for the Humanities and National Endowment for the Arts fellowships, and the Outstanding Teacher of the Year Award for 1985–86 from the International John Steinbeck Society.

Further Reading: LaLonde, Chris. *Grave Concerns, Trickster Turns: The Novels of Louis Owens.* Norman: University of Oklahoma Press, 2002.

Louis Owens and Brian Railsback

P

PACIFIC BIOLOGICAL LABORATORY. A biological supply house located in **Monterey**, California, and the central location for the important friendship between John Steinbeck and **Edward F. Ricketts**. Albert E. Galigher originally opened the Pacific Biological Laboratory in 1921. After leaving the University of Chicago in that same year, Ricketts moved to California to become Galigher's partner in the burgeoning business. After a dispute between the two men, Galigher moved to Berkeley, leaving Ricketts as sole proprietor. Ricketts soon made Pacific Biological both his place of business and his home. Ricketts collected a wide variety of marine specimens and prepared slides to be shipped to schools for exhibition, experimentation, and dissection. Particularly through the 1930s, Steinbeck spent a great deal of time at the lab, and he at times assisted Ricketts in his labor; thus, the author learned a keen appreciation of ecological matters and the rigors of scientific investigation. **Carol Henning Steinbeck** also came to benefit from the arrangement and worked for a brief period as Ricketts' secretary in 1932. In 1936 the lab burned down, but Ricketts had it rebuilt without much alteration from the original design; to help with the cost of rebuilding, Steinbeck became a silent partner in the business.

The social life at the lab was most famously fictionalized in Steinbeck's humorous novels ***Cannery Row*** and ***Sweet Thursday***. Though the composition of the group changed over the years, the lab was the site of a near-constant social gathering, the size and social dimension of which was created by whoever happened to wander in for the day (which might include local prostitutes, college students from the region, and some great thinkers such as **Joseph Campbell**). These gatherings are remembered fondly by various participants as being part intellectual stimulation and part revelry, with many sessions leading well into the early hours of the morning. For Steinbeck's literary and intellectual development, the makeshift library Ricketts had at the lab was as important as the social gatherings and discussions. Steinbeck continued to visit the lab through the 1940s until Ricketts' tragic death in May 1948.

Further Reading: Benson, Jackson J. *The True Adventures of John Steinbeck, Writer.* New York: Viking, 1984; Lynch, Audry. *Steinbeck Remembered, Interviews with friends and acquaintances of John Steinbeck.* Santa Barbara, CA: Fithian Press, 2000; Rodger, Katherine A. *Renaissance Man of Cannery Row: The Life and Letters of Edward F. Ricketts.* Tuscaloosa: University of Alabama Press, 2002

PACIFIC GROVE. A community adjacent to Monterey, California, where Steinbeck's parents owned a cottage in which John lived for many years. This was his primary residence (with his first wife, **Carol Henning Steinbeck**) until he gained financial success after the publication of ***Tortilla Flat*** in 1935. He returned to the cottage occasionally thereafter, staying for the longest period after his divorce from his second wife, **Gwyndolyn Conger Steinbeck**, in 1948.

In ***Sweet Thursday,*** Pacific Grove is the subject of two chapters of vitriolic satire that diverge from the central plotline. The first of these, "The Great Roque War," traces the absurd origins and insane results of rampant bigotry. After the Pacific Grove community is introduced to the game of roque, a rivalry quickly develops between the two major teams, eventually becoming so extreme that the Blues and Greens murder their opponents. When the donor of the roque court has it bulldozed to end this pointless violence, the community becomes so incensed that it burns him in effigy each year. The second episode, entitled "**Hooptedoodle** (2), or The Pacific Grove Butterfly Festival," focuses on the commercial exploitation of nature and the irrationality of social scapegoating. The Pacific Grove community, noticing that swarms of monarch butterflies generally arrive at a certain time each spring, capitalizes on this event by developing a Great Butterfly Festival to draw tourists. However, when the butterflies fail to arrive at their appointed time after years of clockwork regularity, the community is unwilling to accept this change as a natural phenomenon. Instead, the people seek scapegoats, directing their anger at the mayor, the city council, unidentified sinners, the chief of police, the water commissioner, Roosevelt-Truman socialism, and even a local first-grade teacher. In both episodes, Pacific Grove serves as a foil for **Cannery Row**, with the aggressive and vindictive behavior of "respectable" middle-class citizens set against the cooperative and harmonious ethos of the social outcasts on the Row.

Bruce Ouderkirk

PALACE FLOPHOUSE AND GRILL, THE (PALACE FLOPHOUSE). In *Cannery Row,* the Palace was formerly a shed used to store fish meal and was owned by Horace Abbeville, who deeded the building to **Lee Chong** as payment for a grocery debt. It becomes the domicile and headquarters for **Mack** and the boys when they agree to pay a rent of $5 per week (though this is never paid, they protect the property and surrounding area). The Palace Flophouse serves as the setting for a number of important scenes in ***Sweet Thursday,*** including the masquerade party that creates a rift between **Doc** and **Suzy**. By the postwar period of *Sweet Thursday,* the Flophouse roof leaks so badly that each of the men has constructed a makeshift canopy over his bed. However, this modest shelter elevates the social status of Mack and the boys, much as **Danny**'s house does for the loafers in ***Tortilla Flat***. Thus, when Mack begins to fear that Lee Chong sold this property along with the grocery store to **Joseph and Mary Rivas**, he develops an elaborate—and ultimately unnecessary—scheme to prevent their eviction.

Bruce Ouderkirk

PARADISE LOST (1667). Steinbeck found the title for his fifth novel, ***In Dubious Battle***, in a line taken from Milton's famous epic (Book I, line 104), and critics such as **Jay Parini** have suggested that Steinbeck's characters in *Battle* mirror the fallen angels of *Paradise Lost* and that their commitment to defiance of the owners is similar to Satan's defiance of an "Almighty Father" (Book III, line 386) in its futility. *Paradise Lost* also provided Steinbeck with the concept of "felix culpa," a belief expressed by Adam in Book XII, lines 470–484, that even though evil seems to triumph, in reality it becomes a necessary agent for the attainment of righteousness. In ***The Pastures of Heaven***, the author used this concept to suggest that the evil observed in and associated with the **Munroe** family might be questionable. Though the Munroes ultimately burst the illusions, or fantasies, of other families in the little valley, perhaps their actions are redemptory rather than reprehensible. Yet a third Steinbeck book related to Milton's epic is ***East of Eden***, in which Steinbeck portrays

Adam Trask and his deceitful wife **Cathy** trying to reclaim Eden in southern California, offering a parallel not only to the original Adam and Eve but also to the fallen angels in hell trying to recreate a home to rival Heaven, even though they have been exiled. Steinbeck once commented on *Paradise Lost* that it was a work he had read when he was very young and that he remembered it not as a book he read but as an event that that happened to him—something powerful.

Michael J. Meyer

PARINI, JAY (LEE) (1948–). Educator and writer whose book, *John Steinbeck: A Biography,* was published in 1995. Born April 2, 1948, in Pittston, Pennsylvania, Parini attended Lafayette College and the University of St. Andrews, where he received his PhD in 1975. In addition to being an assistant professor of English at Dartmouth College, he served as editor for the "North Star" poetry series, has been on the teaching staff of the Bread Loaf Writers' Conference, and served on the board of the National Book Critics Circle from 1996 to 1999. A writer of literary essay and biography as well as original poetry and fiction, Parini has published such recent works as *Some Necessary Angels: Essays on Writing and Politics* (1997), *Robert Frost, A Life* (1999), *The Apprentice Lover* (2003), *One Matchless Time: A Life of William Faulkner* (2004) and *The Art of Teaching* (2005).

John Hooper

PARKER, DOROTHY [ROTHSCHILD] (1893–1967). American writer of short stories, verse, and criticism whose work was known for its satirical bent, Parker was the drama critic for *The New Yorker* and *Vanity Fair* and a member of a discussion group called the Algonquin Round Table. **Robert DeMott** notes that Steinbeck read *The Collected Stories of Dorothy Parker* (1942), *The Portable Dorothy Parker* (1944), and *The Ladies of the Corridor* (1954), a play written by Dorothy Parker and Arnaud d'Usseau (Steinbeck praised this play in ***America and Americans***). Steinbeck knew Parker socially in New York during the late 1940s.

T. Adrian Lewis and Jan Flood

PASTURES OF HEAVEN, THE (1932). [For commentary on the book's plot, see the subsequent chapter summaries.] Biographer **Jackson J. Benson** suggests that during the 1920s and 1930s, Steinbeck was intrigued by innovation and that the construction of *The Pastures of Heaven*, his second novel, published in 1932, may have been influenced by new structures for fiction as well as by **Sherwood Anderson's** groundbreaking short story cycle, *Winesburg, Ohio* (1919). Another important source for the central idea of *Pastures* was supplied by Steinbeck's friend and fellow writer **Beth Ingels**, who had been raised in Corral de Tierra, a little valley in the hills west of **Salinas**. Originally, Ingels envisioned a book about the strange people whose fates influenced the emotional development of a young girl and the interaction of people in a small confined valley. However, when she repeated her ideas within the intellectual circle of friends fostered by John and **Carol Henning Steinbeck**, it was inevitable that the more famous author would pick up on a potential storyline and shape it to fit his own ends. As early as 1930, Steinbeck wrote his friend **Ted Miller** about his desire to gather a series of short stories in *Decameron* fashion. Thus, by combining his interest in experimental form, his interest in **Jungian** actions motivated by the unconscious, and the biblical story of fallen Eden and separated generations, Steinbeck generated the essential qualities that make up *The Pastures of Heaven*. According to Benson, another letter to Miller in May 1931 specifies Steinbeck's intention to relate the stories to each other and to draw a parallel to a Miltonian Lucifer. The interrelated stories that make up *Pastures* were originally meant to be combined with Steinbeck's novella **"Dissonant Symphony"** (never completed). *Pastures* eventually emerged as a separate work and gained a life of its own. Steinbeck spent most of 1931 refining the stories, yet the completed manuscript was greeted with little outward enthusiasm by his agents, **McIntosh and Otis**, who feared that too warm a reception might raise their client's hopes unwarrantedly. Surprisingly, *Pastures* was accepted almost immediately by Cape and Smith, leaving its author free to turn his attention to a revision of ***To a God Unknown***.

Pastures, like *God*, can be said to emphasize a mechanistic world in which there is no ultimate cause or design; evidence of Steinbeck's fascination with the rather arbitrary nature of life can also be found in the fact that the story endings in the book often leave the reader unsure of the eventual outcome for the protagonists. Each is an objective tale, something that happened. Benson suggests that *Pastures* provides one of the first indications that Steinbeck was attracted to **non-teleological** philosophy, a concept that grew even more significant during his association and friendship with **Edward F. Ricketts**. In an interview with Benson, Steinbeck's close friend **Dook Sheffield** identified one significant interest of Steinbeck at this time as the observation that "personalities are seldom fixed or stable but are subject to and influenced by the interpretations of the observer almost as if the two were chemicals interacting with each other."

This principle is at work in *Pastures* as the reader observes a tale ostensibly tied together by a single family, the Munroes, a family who supposedly causes many of the problems that occur in Steinbeck's idyllic valley. According to Sheffield, the plan for *Symphony*, perhaps later transferred and adapted to *Pastures*, was to base the composition on the structure used by **Robert Browning** in "The Ring and the Book": to observe a central character never in a direct manner but rather through the eyes of those around him. As Benson notes, "Each of these narrator/observers would not only see the character differently but the character would in effect become a different person in response to each observer." Steinbeck employs this methodology in *Pastures* by using different perspectives in order to provide a fluctuating perception of each of the valley residents. Even the reading audience falls under the spell of the narrator's arbitrarily shifting opinions. As John Timmerman contends, "The Munroes may be only catalysts rather than causers of action, all depending upon reader viewpoint."

Another significant influence for the author at the time of the composition of *The Pastures of Heaven* was **Carl Jung**. While exploring the black and sluggish depths of the unconscious through reading Jung's treatises, Steinbeck seems to have discovered how much individuals were influenced by their unrealized dreams and desires, which he illustrates through each of the portraits he paints of the book's characters. Although the Munroes are frequently seen as the antagonists of the short story cycle, Steinbeck deliberately leaves open the possibility that each of the residents of the *Pastures* is responsible for the loss of his or her own dreams and idealism as the harsh world of reality breaks in on their isolated existences. In Jung's terminology, their shadow world may be far more responsible for their situations than the family they choose to blame.

Although *The Pastures of Heaven* sold poorly in its first printing, it was initially well-received by critics who noted its author's social and psychological character development. However, several critics were uncomfortable with the structure of the book. Later analyses suggest that the message of *Pastures* is best served by approaching it as a whole rather than as nine separate entities and a frame. As Timmerman puts it, *Pastures* was "envisioned together as one piece and is not a random accumulation of the odds and ends of a writer's scrapbook." Critics such as **Warren French** also call attention to the book's prevailing ironic tone and to the paradoxes which abound in each story. Of the major critics, only **Howard Levant** believes that *Pastures* is a significantly flawed piece of art, contending that Steinbeck's overt aims in the novel are badly confused despite his cogent letter outlining his intent for its composition. Following the lead of **Lisca** in *Nature and Myth*, more recent assessments have tended to stress the book's reliance on biblical mythology and its portrait of a type of "fallen" Eden. Timmerman, for example, states that "the Eden of *Pastures* measures what the inhabitants could be but more decisively what they are, mortals discovering the fallenness of human nature, not sons of God." Timmerman goes on to draw three distinct parallels to the biblical Eden myth in the story cycle, pointing out that *Pastures* displays not only disorientation from God that leads to enmity with neighbors, but also an initiation into human knowledge of evil as a personal experience and an exile from the rich beneficence of Eden to a lifetime of toil and troubles.

Similarly, **Louis Owens** recalls the words of Satan in *Paradise Lost* in his analysis, citing the lines "the mind itself is its own place and in itself / Can make a Heav'n of Hell, a Hell of Heav'n." But though giving credit to biblical allusion and acknowledging earlier critics in the process, Owens shifts his personal assessment to private human illusions, stressing their connection to the greater illusion of an American Eden that can somehow be regained. Owens implies that Steinbeck's intent is to draw the reader into a deceptive trap of blaming the Munroes for the decay in *Pastures* rather than acknowledging that every dilemma faced there is attributable to human nature rather than to an individual scapegoat.

Perhaps the closest reading of the interconnectedness of the stories is provided in **Joseph Fontenrose's** *Steinbeck's Unhappy Valley*. In this insightful study, Fontenrose outlines the complexity of this outwardly simple book and explains how Steinbeck manipulates the effect of time and the importance of the locale (houses, gardens, and farms) in order to create generous parallel and antithetical elements that exist between each story and its precursors as well as its followers.

Further Reading: Benson, Jackson J. *The True Adventures of John Steinbeck, Writer.* New York: Viking, 1984; Steinbeck, John. *Steinbeck: A Life in Letters*. Ed. Elaine Steinbeck and Robert Wallsten. New York: Viking Penguin, 1975; Fontenrose, Joseph. *John Steinbeck: An Introduction and Interpretation*. New York: Holt, Rinehart, and Winston, 1963.

Michael J. Meyer

PASTURES OF HEAVEN, THE **(CHAPTER I)**. Steinbeck begins his short story cycle with a cynical look at the Catholic religion and its domination and oppression of local Native American tribes. Despite the contention that these Christian invaders were helping the pagan natives find the "truth," Steinbeck implies that what really occurred was merely slavery and that the exploitation that benefited the Spanish could not be justified on the basis of their religious principles. Their imposition of "civilization" can hardly be said to have benefited the natives. As the novel begins, somewhere around 1776 (thus creating a clear tie to the establishment of America as a new Eden), a troop of Spanish soldiers attempts to recapture a group of twenty Native Americans who have escaped their domination (a number Steinbeck will later parallel with the number of residents in the valley). By chance, one of their number, an unnamed corporal, discovers the verdant valley of the title. Shocked and surprised, the soldier shouts out an exclamation that gives the valley a name that will follow it throughout its future history, Las Pasturas de Cielo. To the corporal, it appears to be a lush new Eden, a paradisal area like that described in the biblical Psalm 23. But in a sarcastic tone, Steinbeck notes that this paradise is ironically one of the few spots that has not already been claimed by the greedy Spaniards and thus is still available to be settled and claimed by the first discoverer. Unfortunately, the corporal is not fated to enjoy such a benefit, and Steinbeck records that instead he contracts a sexually transmitted disease from a Native American woman and eventually dies. The author then shifts the story to 100 years later when Las Pasturas has been settled by twenty families who, like the original discoverer, are determined that its lush surroundings will bring them the peace and prosperity that they seek in life. It is their individual and collective stories that follow, eventually bringing a return to a frame episode that will bring the text full circle as a new group of individuals, this time tourists, see the lush valley for the first time.

***PASTURES OF HEAVEN, THE* (CHAPTER II).** The story paradoxically begins with a description of the property that is now the least desirable in Las Pasturas, the Battle Farm. Its earliest owners created an image of their property that called up associations with tangled trees, brambles, and weeds as well as the run-down haunted atmosphere of its farmhouse. The history of this plot of land is then recounted, beginning with its settlement by Easterner **George Battle** and his early commitment to its blossoming and growth. The elder Battle tills the land even at the expense of his human relationships with his own family, relationships that are shown to deteriorate and fail even as the land offers its increase.

After George Battle's death, perhaps in an effort to deny his heritage of land and increase, Battle's son, John, inheriting his mother's physical and emotional flaws, becomes the exact opposite of his father: an eccentric, even fanatic proponent of God and religion. Overcome by religious fervor and a crazed opposition to Satan and evil, John Battle eventually succeeds in reversing his father's success and ruining the property. Encouraged by his neglect, the once fruitful land recedes into unproductivity. Eventually, after his death from a virulent snake bite (another Edenic reference), John Battle's plot of land in Las Pasturas becomes so run down that it stands vacant for a time. Then in 1921, it is occupied by foreign immigrants, the Mustrovics, who, though both quiet and introverted, work hard to reclaim the land from its state of disrepair. After attaining this difficult goal, however, the Mustrovics mysteriously disappear from the area, demonstrating the Must-rove-itch of many early settlers in the West. Consequently, the deserted farm again reverts to wildness, to what critic John Timmerman identifies as the frenzied conflict of order versus disorder, of community versus personal demons. At this point Steinbeck mentions the local superstition that begins to develop: that the farm is cursed and its owners will continue to be plagued with disasters. However, this rumor does not prevent a third individual, **Bert Munroe**, from buying the property.

The Munroes' purchase, of course, elicits a great deal of curiosity and scrutiny as once again the Battle farm undergoes reclamation. The Munroes, representative of a new progressive era and a developing middle-class citizenry at the turn of the century, exude the qualities of modernity (efficiency, management skills, scientific knowledge) while at the same time suggesting weakness in their stereotypical superficialities and their empty values. This strange combination of attributes creates a family that exerts an ambiguous influence on the community at best. Such ambiguity is reflected in Bert's belief in his own personal curse long before he buys the Battle farm. Despite his determination to challenge fate head-on, his lack of self-confidence has resulted in several failed endeavors in the past, and only in the Edenic Las Pasturas can he envision a new hope, a hope similar to that expressed by the corporal in the first chapter. By reuniting with the land, Bert achieves a temporary peace, and a recurrent Steinbeckian theme is established. Yet Bert Munroe's apparent success in restoring the Battle property meets with little approval from his neighbors, who see his efforts at renewal as antithetical to their long-held beliefs about the property. The chapter ends by suggesting two possibilities for the Munroes' good fortune: the two curses have canceled one another out or the curses have merely gone underground and have begun breeding a passel of new curses. Despite the seeming impossibility of the latter suggestion, the remaining chapters of the novel examine the possibility of just such an occurrence as other property owners and residents of Las Pasturas are affected by the acts of the various members of the Munroe family.

***PASTURES OF HEAVEN, THE* (CHAPTER III).** This chapter introduces other residents of Las Pasturas de Cielo, the Wicks family:

Edward "Shark" Wicks, his wife, **Kathryn**, and their daughter, **Alice Wicks**. The Wicks' farmhouse, described as debris-strewn and unbeautiful, is evidence of Edward Wicks's miserly qualities and his neglect of his family at the expense of fostering his business acumen. Yet Wicks, described as a successful vegetable and fruit farmer, has been nicknamed "Shark" because of his reputation for being a clever and skilled manipulator of money. Ironically, this reputation is undeserved given that Wicks's skill is really nonexistent, a product of his own rich fantasy life that he has cultivated like his orchards and gardens until his neighbors actually begin to accept outward appearance as reality. He is not the wealthy individual many in the Valley take him to be, but his inflated reputation gives evidence of how human ingenuity can create deception.

Besides his financial preeminence, Wicks has only one other possession of note, the exceptional beauty of his daughter, Alice. His family relationships and the appearance of his land pale in comparison with his concern for the richness of his "fantasy" wealth and the richness of his daughter's virginity and purity. Soon Alice becomes a virtual prisoner, with her father confining and sheltering her from the outside world as a miser would hoard his money from the prying eyes of others. But Steinbeck also ironically reveals that Alice's outer beauty is countered by a lack of inner worth, and she is described as "incredibly stupid, dull and backward." Nevertheless, Wicks persists in hovering over her in hopes of preserving her so-called perfection and retaining the envy and respect of his fellow townspeople. After she reaches puberty, his concern for her chastity becomes almost monomaniacal. As his fantasy investments in land multiply, so does his investment in Alice. His contrived gains and losses seem so real to him that he feels he must protect them at all costs, and consequently Alice too must be guarded and kept safe.

The eldest Munroe boy, **Jimmie**, enters the picture at this time as a love interest for Alice and as a threat to Shark Wicks's perception of himself as a rich man. Shark's attempt to repress his daughter's interest in any type of meeting with Jimmie merely incenses and fuels her curiosity about the "forbidden fruit." When Wicks is called out of town for a family funeral, an opportunity for Alice and Jimmie's first meeting presents itself. Alice convinces her mother to let her attend a local dance, and she is immediately drawn to Jimmie, and a sexual attraction develops. Although Jimmie and Alice only kiss at the dance, rumors of their romantic attachment flood the town, and when Wicks returns, he overreacts, even thinking of shooting Jimmie. The Munroes, especially **Bert**, anticipate Wicks's violent reaction and call the sheriff to place him under bond before any violence can occur. The size of the bond that Bert requests is large because of Wicks's reputation, and Shark's fantasy investments are destroyed when he is forced to admit in court that he has no real money to cover the $10,000 request. Wicks's dream world is dashed, his vitality gone.

The destruction of his fantasy proves positive as the chapter ends and Shark learns to rely on a real relationship with his wife, Kathryn, who comes into her own as a compassionate helpmeet. The Wicks' decision to move away from Las Pasturas is a sad one, though there is some joy as the characters face truth for the first time. The first curse attributed to the Munroes is thus seen to bring both good and evil.

PASTURES OF HEAVEN, THE* (CHAPTER IV).** Although seemingly unconnected by any transition to the previous tale, the fourth chapter begins the story of another Las Pasturas resident, **Tuleracito**, a dwarfish outcast child who is discovered in the sage brush as a baby. Slightly deformed and initially unable to speak, Tuleracito, often assessed as a forerunner of such characters as **Lennie Small** in ***Of Mice and Men and Johnny Bear in ***The Long Valley***, seems physically rather than emotionally cursed although he has no initial contact with the Munroes. Yet despite his ugliness and lack of mental ability, he demonstrates a number of talents (including gardening and drawing) that surprise even his detractors in Las Pasturas, who sometimes refer to him as the spawn of the devil. His fierce temper when any of the products of his handiwork is destroyed indicates to the town that he is someone to be feared. When he reaches the age of eleven, the town tries to regulate him by forcing him to attend the public school, where his talent in art is first appreciated by the teacher Miss Martin. But her appreciation is short-lived when she discovers that her pupil becomes enraged when his chalk drawings are erased from the classroom blackboard. He even attacks fellow students and partially destroys the schoolroom in his fury. After the incident, Miss Martin requests a flogging as a punishment, indicating that the teacher's initial good opinion of him is shattered and that now she sees him only as a creature or a type of animal.

When Tuleracito's guardian, **Franklin Gomez**, counters that the boy is merely one "whom God has not quite yet finished," his analysis is dismissed as nonsense, and shortly thereafter Miss Martin quits her job and a new teacher, **Molly Morgan**, replaces her. The model for these two teachers is generally agreed to have been Steinbeck's aunt, Molly Martin, a former resident of the Corral de Tierra and a neighbor of **Beth Ingels**. A totally different type of educator, creative and innovative by nature, Ms. Morgan excites her classroom and helps her students enter fantasy worlds as well as real ones through the reading of books. Her stories of fairies and gnomes create a startling discovery for Tuleracito, who feels for once a connection with a "society," albeit a mythical one. Unwittingly, Ms. Morgan encourages Tuleracito's search for "little people" as a way to further his imagination and experience a sense of belonging. Unfortunately, the isolate is intent on finding real gnomes rather than fantasy figures, and he begins his search in earnest by enlarging any holes where they might be hiding. When the Munroes discover holes dug on their property as the result of Tuleracito's search, they fill in the empty spaces and consequently incur Tuleracito's rage. Not knowing any better, Tuleracito attacks **Bert Munroe** as a punishment for obliterating his work, beating him over the head with a shovel.

It is not surprising that when Tuleracito is captured after the attack, he is treated as a dangerous individual and as a potential killer. Despite the fact that real justice is not being done, Tuleracito is committed to an insane asylum, suggesting the fate of any lower life form who is at variance with society's conventions. His dream world of belonging is also destroyed.

***PASTURES OF HEAVEN, THE* (CHAPTER V)**. Tragedy strikes **Helen Van de Venter**, another resident of Las Pasturas who is introduced at the start of the fifth chapter, often and hard, though Steinbeck records that she "hungered for tragedy and life had lavishly heaped it on her." After losing her husband in a hunting accident, Helen gives birth to a daughter, **Hilda Van de Venter**, who unfortunately turns out to be psychologically unsound, not unlike **Tuleracito**. Yet Hilda's social class is shown to prevent the fate reserved for the dwarf. Although Mrs. Van de Venter's protective hovering only serves to intensify her daughter's unstable condition, it also suggests a parallel for readers to the plight of **Alice Wicks**, given that both parents attempt to control a child who possesses a limited mental capacity. It seems as if Helen revels in the burdens she must bear as her daughter matures. Thus, when Hilda begins to make up dreams and nightmares, her mother becomes even more protective about allowing her freedom in the real world. Imprisoned in her own home, Hilda eventually rebels and runs away, and when she is caught and returned, she concocts even more ridiculous fantasy stories to plague her warden mother. When Hilda approaches adolescence and her mother refuses to seek psychiatric help for her, Hilda's condition begins to worsen. Although her regular doctor assesses the problem, he is unable to convince Helen to deal with it. Like Tuleracito, Hilda is ignored or treated as a beast. It is at this point that Mrs. Van de Venter contemplates the Pastures of Heaven as a retreat, a perfect place to isolate her unstable daughter from society. She creates a paradisal setting in Christmas Canyon, complete with a beautiful house and elegant landscaping and lawn decorations. Although the outside is beautiful, the home is like a mental hospital that keeps Hilda away from society. It is another of Steinbeck's settings that function as metaphor, depicting the personality of a character who is outwardly stable but inwardly warped and troubled.

Again it is a Munroe who invades this privacy with the stated intent of being helpful. In typical moral ambiguity, Steinbeck questions whether the Munroes' helpfulness is not instead motivated by their "prying curiosity." Finding Hilda alone and imprisoned in the home, **Bert Munroe** makes the mistake of talking to her and of re-forming her fantasies about escape, this time with a man, a sexual partner, who will save her from despair. Meanwhile Helen's own isolation and fantasy world is growing, and her own mental stability is becoming questionable. Although she has suddenly found a haven of quiet and solitude, because of the strain and stress of her responsibilities to Hilda, she gradually begins to crack as well. When she discovers Hilda has met a real rather than a fantasy outsider (Munroe) and that she has hallucinations about him as a lover, the stress is unbearable, and once again, a personal paradise is destroyed. Helen discovers that Hilda has again escaped her prison, and after looking upon her husband's trophy game in the living room, Helen speculates on what might be necessary to control Hilda in the future and eventually decides there is no solution but to track her down and shoot her. Though the doctor delivers a verdict of suicide, Steinbeck has led the reader to see past this inaccurate conclusion and to observe the acts of a mentally unstable mother to whom pain is a necessity and a fact of life. Again, allegedly through their carelessness, the Munroes and their curses destroy an "ideal" world, shattering an Eden and creating a living hell in its stead.

***PASTURES OF HEAVEN, THE* (CHAPTER VI).** The sixth chapter of the story cycle focuses on the Maltby family, and readers are introduced to another character who has sought out Las Pasturas as an answer to a dream. It is also the only *Pastures* story that was published separately, appearing in 1936 as an illustrated monograph titled *Nothing So Monstrous*. **Junius Maltby** experiences a midlife crisis when he discovers that city living has resulted in the deterioration of his health and will force him to move to a drier climate. Yet Junius's reaction to this "disaster" is positive for the situation allows him to cut the strings of his dull clerkship and to find a relaxation he had never previously known. He uses the opportunity to renew his health, marry, and develop the positive quality of laziness, able to lose himself in just sitting with a good book. The Maltby farm in Las Pasturas, of course, suffers from neglect as Junius satisfies his personal needs and ignores his land. He is so entranced by his fantasy world that it becomes his bulwark against reality when his wife and two stepsons die from influenza. He is left with only an infant son who learns from his father to value leisure rather than work. Although criticized by the townspeople, the Maltbys are happy and content, and soon they are joined by a German "servant" **Jakob Stutz** (ironically Steinbeck's initials), who offers Maltby a sounding board for his philosophical ideas. The older men's discussion of art and literature prevents them both from facing the traumatic realities that exist around them, and the baby, **Robbie Maltby** (named after author **Robert Louis Stevenson**), matures quickly given that he is treated like a little adult and his father indulges him with gleaming experiences others would consider valueless. Robbie's learning is from life rather than from school books, and Steinbeck describes the boy's conversations with the adults as planting seedlings that sprout, sending out branching limbs and bearing strange fruit despite lack of rigid structure and organization and practical applications. Steinbeck implies that these teachings are worthless only in the eyes of the other townspeople, revealing the crisis that results when middle-class respectability and mediocrity confront rebellious nonconformity and nontraditional lifestyles. The townspeople grow to deplore Junius's actions, feeling that he not only neglects his child, but also ignores his land, thus giving the community of Las Pasturas a bad name. Although his poverty makes him an isolate in the area, Junius is not fazed by the criticism until Robbie is forced by the residents to attend school. Of course, the child's nonconformity and lack of normative values draw attention to him, but surprisingly he does not become isolated. Rather, his behavior is picked up by other children, and to the horror of the townspeople, he becomes imitated rather than rejected. Soon Robbie's teacher notices him as well—because despite his maturity in conversation and his general knowledge, he refuses to master basic concepts such as writing and arithmetic.

Yet despite these failures, Robbie's leadership abilities and his insight into ways of making learning fun excite his teacher, **Molly Morgan**, who determines to visit his home in order to discover what strange elements influence and inspire him. When she arrives, she is struck by the delightfulness of the disarray and lack of organization at the Maltby home, but she is even more surprised to see Junius and Robbie set up a learning experience for Robbie's peers. The experience is constructed as a game or role play in which the students act out the simulated rescue of the President of the United States. Impressed by the way games and role plays enhance the involvement of the learners and foster their retention of the material, Miss Morgan returns to the humdrum of the regular classroom with a mild sense of disapproval of her traditional schooling techniques. Unfortunately, she is unable to institute positive changes in methodology and produce a favorable outcome when the school board comes to visit her classroom. Instead, the board members are impressed with her sense of discipline and order and commend her for her firm hand. Of course, Robbie Maltby is singled out by the visitors as one deserving of notice for his less than rigid adherence to the school rules. Motivated by **Mrs. Munroe**, whose husband is its newest member, the school board suggests that the school help the odd student to fit in by offering him new clothes and by attempting to force him into conformity with the social norms held by the rest of the community. Their offer stuns Robbie into embarrassment; the revelation is so harsh that eventually the Maltbys decide to return to the hectic life of the city and re-embrace its materialistic values and rigid work ethic. Sadly, society's norms have been imposed on an individual, and another dream bubble is burst.

***PASTURES OF HEAVEN, THE* (CHAPTER VII).** In the seventh chapter, Steinbeck provides a picture of a small farm owned by **Rosa** and **Maria Lopez**, a property that produces little in terms of material wealth. In order to supplement their meager income, the sisters decide that they will become vendors of tortillas and enchiladas and will reshape their small dwelling place as a Mexican restaurant. When their plan for business is not as successful as they wish, the sisters eventually decide to foster a happier and more avid clientele by offering sexual favors as part of their dinner packages. Although the act is initially repulsive to their very Catholic upbringing, they believe it is a necessary extra that will encourage more customers to try their wares; not surprisingly, they are correct. Because of their sincere faith, however, after each sin they confess to the Virgin and ask forgiveness, thus justifying the practice of prostitution and absolving themselves from any guilt they may feel. Like **Junius** and **Robbie Maltby**, the Lopez sisters are able to create joy and happiness from what others may consider shameful and incorrect. They reason that the sex act itself is not being sold; it is only being offered as encouragement to those who spend freely for food.

Their happiness is short-lived, though, because rumors spread in the town of Las Pasturas that the sisters are running a house of ill repute. When Maria Lopez heads toward **Monterey** to pick up supplies and picks up **Allen Hueneker**, whom Steinbeck describes as ugly and ape-like, the rumor mill begins to grind in earnest. Observed by the Munroes, the "couple" are fair game for a practical joke at their own expense. As a result of the joking, however, the rumor spreads to the authorities of the town, and by the time Maria returns from Monterey, the sheriff has been to visit the Lopez ranch and has closed down the restaurant. Again middle-class morality destroys the potential happiness of a lower-class citizen and appears insensitive and inhumane. The two sisters are, of course, devastated by the charges of prostitution for they believe they have not sold their flesh but only their mother's fine cooking. In despair, they decide like the Maltbys and the Wicks before them that it will be necessary to leave the Pastures of Heaven for a new place, for an immoral city life of real prostitution that has none of the happiness or purity present in the rural neighborhood in which they now reside. Although the Munroes are unaware of the influence of their actions, they have caused another fantasy world to fall.

PASTURES OF HEAVEN, THE **(CHAPTER VIII)**. This story returns to a previously introduced character, the new teacher of the local school, **Molly Morgan**. Though Miss Morgan has been a factor in both the **Tularecito** and the Maltby stories, the narrative begins with her arrival in the secluded valley for an initial interview for a teaching position with the school board president, **John Whiteside**, who himself is the center of a narrative in Chapter XII. Initially portrayed as a fearful young applicant for a new job, Miss Morgan finds herself confronted with questions about herself that probe her inner being rather than her outward persona. Her reflections about her past are recorded in italics, as through a stream of consciousness. Steinbeck reveals details about the real character of the new schoolmarm. By now, readers are not surprised when they observe that she is another character who needs a rich fantasy life in order to bear the burden of the cruel realities that surround her. By observing her clipped responses and comparing them with the rich texture of her unexpressed thoughts, readers can see Whiteside is only seeing part of Molly Morgan in his interview. Readers, on the other hand, see that Miss Morgan has been born into an emotionally needy family with an absentee father and a mother who is overly demanding of attention and love, especially from her young daughter. It is a different image, weaker and less competent than the reader has seen in other episodes featuring Miss Morgan, and this new perspective helps us see that no individual has only one facet. Molly's terse replies to Whiteside in no way convey the emotions she is feeling as she probes her psyche to answer the interview questions. Whereas her actual conversation is nondescript, the words in italics reveal a scared little girl within the woman, an individual who is both confused and sad. By blocking out past elements of sadness, she can, like her father, recapture the wonderful dreams and fantasies of her childhood. Despite the unlikelihood of his return, Molly firmly believes that eventually her father will come to rescue her from her life of drudgery and criticism. She does receive a warm response from the Whitesides, who see her as a potential bride for their son, **Bill.** Molly's discussions with Bill, however, reveal his far-different personality, and eventually his sense of practicality and his realistic attitude begin to impede on her dream world. As critic John Timmerman suggests in his Jungian reading, Molly may be reluctant to face her shadow, the dark side of her psyche—and Bill's practical side will ultimately force her to confront it. When **Bert Munroe** visits the Whitesides, he mentions his new temporary farmhand, a lonely drunken hobo whose actions and conversation suggest a clear parallel to Molly's lost father. Unwilling to face the possibility that the idealized vision of her father may be false and that he is no more than a vagrant con-man, Molly becomes an isolate, trying to avoid the cold harsh truth that may be awaiting her. Eventually recognizing that she is unable to confront her worst fear, she decides to leave both Las Pasturas and her new job, believing that only through distancing from the truth will she be able to sustain her unwillingness to believe in reality and thus maintain her positive image of her father.

***PASTURES OF HEAVEN, THE* (CHAPTER IX).** Chicken farmer **Raymond Banks** and his idyllic farm are analyzed in this chapter as Steinbeck examines the contrast between Banks's immaculately clean whitewashed house and his own personal, seemingly perverted interest in death and dying. Ironically, Steinbeck portrays Banks's appearance as a mirror to his personality; his positive physical traits are balanced by other, more fearsome personal characteristics, and his cheerful attributes are balanced by contrasting evil actions as well. Banks's actions suggest his duality as well. For example, he functions as the Santa Claus for the children of Las Pasturas, but he also is the first to initiate the children to the rituals of death by demonstrating the humane way to kill his chickens.

Each year, the Banks family is host to a barbeque for the community, and it is at this event that **Bert Munroe** questions Banks about his frequent trips to San Quentin prison in order to observe hangings. In the eyes of the community members, Banks's trips seem to indicate that he revels in the excitement and emotional high he receives from his observances and that he finds fulfillment in sharing the intense emotions often present at the gallows. However, his sensitivity to avoiding needless suffering for animals would appear to be paradoxical with such an obsession with human violence. When Munroe suggests that he accompany Raymond on his next trip, Banks agrees to arrange it, but Munroe's change in temperament is evident as the discussion continues. After it is apparent he will be able to attend, Munroe becomes nauseated and physically upset at the thought of witnessing violent death. At the same time he expresses a "strange, panting congestion of desire." Later, Bert confesses that he has a morbid curiosity about the execution process, inquiring about the reactions of the victims as well as of the observers. Nonetheless, his physical reaction of nervousness and irritability persists until he eventually feels compelled to refuse Banks's invitation to accompany him to the hangings.

Surprisingly, at this point Munroe tells his own personal story of an experience with the cruel death of a chicken during his childhood when his uncle missed a chicken's head and instead seriously injured it with the ax blade. The story reinforces Munroe's own reticence to watch an execution of any type, but more importantly it allows Banks to see a parallel to his own farm and his insistence on a painless death for the animals he raises. This parallel leads Banks to a self-evaluation of his attitude toward death and eventually causes him to invent a specious excuse to avoid attending another hanging at San Quentin. His former pleasure, seen from a different and new perspective, has been turned into a terror, and he has seen a part of himself he had previously kept hidden or unrecognized. A Munroe action has once more turned a pleasure into a pain.

***PASTURES OF HEAVEN, THE* (CHAPTER X).** The story of **Pat Humbert** is the central focus of the tenth chapter. Humbert, an only child, is one who has been influenced by the aches, illnesses, and complaints of his older parents, who show little or no consideration for his youth. Consequently, early on in his existence, they cumber him with excessive responsibility and a sense of guilt. Until their deaths, when he is almost thirty, Pat remains under the influence of their dreary negativism, and their cold authoritarian attitudes continue to shape his actions. In an attempt to reject their continuing repression, even in death, of his freedom, Pat shuts off the sepulchral living room area of the house and tries to forget his unhappy childhood and young adult memories. However, he finds himself constantly feeling guilty and in need of companionship. To cope with his feelings, he often avoids returning to the house of ghosts, preferring instead to sleep in the barn or to interact with his neighbors and thus avoid the past events that plague him. Ironically, while neglecting the house and trying not to live in it, he does not neglect his farm, using his work ethic to avoid a continuing confrontation with the values of his parents. Eventually, his benign neglect of his home results in a fostering of a lovely white rose bush that covers the side of the house and attracts the attention of young **Mae Munroe**. When Pat observes her passing his house, she is at first just another antidote for the poison of loneliness, but later he is genuinely moved when he overhears her admiration of the roses and her query whether the inside of the farmhouse is as beautiful. From then on, Humbert's major task becomes the transformation of the dusty house of the dead into a warm Vermont home, complete with up-to-date decorations. Again, the changing environment of the house serves as a metaphor for Humbert's changing attitude. After serious research, he plans to recreate a lovely living area and to exorcise the dreary and musty past of which the interior of the home reminds him. Once he has begun the work, Pat avoids the community in order to concentrate on his task of change; the work moves quickly as he knocks out a partition and makes the two small rooms—signifying his parents—into one larger one: a symbol of his new self. However, Humbert's fantasy of marrying Mae Munroe and removing his parents' somber influence on his life remains unachieved since he is reluctant to share his preparations either with his intended bride or with his neighbors. As he anticipates Mae's reactions, his own exultation at his success soars until he is suddenly and harshly brought back to reality by the announcement of Mae's engagement to **Bill Whiteside**. Disillusioned and upset, Pat returns to his lonely home only to sleep in the barn, saddened that the ghosts of the past rather than the dreams of the future have won the battle for his soul.

***PASTURES OF HEAVEN, THE* (CHAPTER XI)**. The story of the Whiteside family is the longest episode in *The Pastures of Heaven*, primarily because it covers two generations of settlers and begins a look at the third. **Richard Whiteside** is the forefather of the present-day residents of Las Pasturas, having arrived in the 1850s to find gold and then realizing that the land of Las Pasturas was a greater treasure. Richard's vision is to establish a new cite or state modeled on the Greeks and to populate it with his descendants. He also hopes to establish a personal dynasty and tradition so that future Whitesides will not think of leaving the area and their family heritage. After building a sturdy house of redwood, Richard marries a distant relative named **Alicia Whiteside** and begins plans for a family and for the exposure to classical thinking and philosophy that his new race will need to continue. When the first child is conceived, Richard prays that his family curse of producing an only child will be removed, and he studies classical society and literature carefully, determined to recreate an intellectually and culturally superior tribe. When Alicia delivers the child, her doctor forbids Richard to endanger her health with another conception, and the Whiteside dream of a dynasty begins to falter. Critic John Timmerman notes the impending failure of Richard's ideal society as the child's name is changed from David, the founder of a famous biblical line and the favored king of Yahweh, to John, the lonely and isolated prophet who prepared the way for Christ but was eventually executed without producing an heir. Defying the doctor's order, Alicia conceives again five years later and not only loses the baby, but becomes an invalid in the process. Thus the Whitesides' dream must be postponed for a generation, and **John Whiteside** becomes the center of the family's hopes and dreams. Steeped in the classical education process his father so values, John receives the dictate to make the dream a reality. When he returns from Harvard, his father has already died, but Alicia clings to life in hopes of seeing grandchildren, a concrete symbol of John's success.

Eventually John does propose to Willa, the sister of a friend, and she is forced to undergo a stern inquisition by Alicia before being approved. Unfortunately, by this time, John, bound to the land and the Whiteside home, finds his position in the valley more tenuous than his father did, primarily because he is so willing to compromise rather than to set standards. Yet the Whiteside name remains the most influential in the valley. John and **Willa Whiteside**'s home becomes a place where the politics and social values of the valley are discussed and determined, yet there is no indication that the previous generation's passion for a dynasty and a new race exists.

When Willa and John produce an only child, **Bill Whiteside**, the dormant dream resurfaces in John, and the farm flourishes under his determination to pass on a worthy heritage to his offspring. However, when he attempts to pass on the classical precepts that he has so valued, John finds that Bill is uninterested. Instead the new generation is concerned with practical ideas and material goods rather than with deep thinking and philosophical possibilities. When the Munroes move into the valley, **Bert Munroe** is quick to recognize the power of the Whiteside approval and to attempt to ingratiate himself with it. Therefore he joins the community discussions at the Whiteside home and expresses interest in the classics and the books John Whiteside values. Within a year, the family intimacy grows, and Bill and **Mae Munroe** decide upon marriage, while at the same time determining to move to **Monterey** rather than maintain the homestead in Las Pasturas.

With different values, Bill's vision of the dynasty is centered more in the material goods and progress offered by the city, and consequently, the delayed dream of the family suddenly withers even more and heads toward destruction. Though John persists in believing that Bill will return to his roots and to the family property, he does indeed move away after the marriage, disappointing both his father and his mother. In despair, John begins to think of ways to renew his precious land and make it produce more.

Unfortunately, his plan to burn off the brush surrounding his property with the help of Bert Munroe backfires, and his beloved house is set on fire. Though there is a chance to save the property, John's reaction is to let it burn to the ground, considering that there seems to be no one in the next generation who values it. As the flames surge throughout the dwelling, all dreams of a dynasty and a new race flicker and then die out. Even John's valued meerschaum pipe, a symbol of a lasting generational inheritance, is destroyed. With the loss of the fabled Whiteside residence, itself another indicator of stability and timelessness, an era and an attitude have passed into oblivion. The Whitesides therefore decide to move in temporarily with Bill and Mae in Monterey, and Steinbeck demonstrates that even the strongest dream has fallen victim either to the Munroe curse or to its own unattainability.

PASTURES OF HEAVEN, THE **(CHAPTER XII).** The final chapter shifts the reader from the early twentieth century to the present day of the late 1920s or early 1930s as a tourist bus stops to observe the secluded Edenic valley. In a parallel to the initial chapter, which records the discovery of Las Pasturas by the Spanish corporal, these six new sightseers rediscover the land, and their shocked reactions are similar to those that occurred over a century before. A sort of camaraderie among the passengers motivates a sharing of their perceptions as they pause for a moment and look down into the lush valley. Though Steinbeck earlier has recorded the many pains and problems that are concealed beneath the outward beauty of the area, each passenger brings a different positive perspective to his or her observations. The successful rich man, for example, envisions the valley's potential in terms of urban development and its ability to make money through subdivisions. The newlyweds are at first attracted to the lovely appearance of the land, but then they come to the recognition that ambition and responsibilities will prevent them from attaining a leisurely and entertaining lifestyle. They must pursue success and money first. A young priest also decides to reject Las Pasturas, assuming that it lacks an appropriate challenge for a religious man; because it appears so idyllic, it does not suggest any possibilities for true spiritual wrestling with sin and evil. Therefore, the priest decides that perhaps its appeal is only an escape from the reality of God's testing and that staying there may eliminate a heavenly reward at death. Finally, the aged man revels in the potential in the valley to escape the trials of the outside world and take the time to think, to piece together meaning from a life of trouble and confusion.

As they reboard the bus, the driver's speech summarizes the tourists' reactions to Las Pasturas: it is to them an Edenic valley where one can experience quiet and easy living. It is truly Las Pasturas de Cielo rather than Las Pasturas de Tierra. Readers, of course, having seen the real valley and the real people who live there, quickly recognize how vacuous and shallow the observations of these tourists are. The little valley presents just as many dilemmas and challenges as the world the tourists will return to, although such problems are seldom evident in its outward appearance. Ironically, the tourists, like the residents, find that Eden is impossible to restore or keep. They all decide to search onward for something better, an effort Steinbeck suggests is doomed to failure even in the most positive of environments—for either by the interference of others or because of one's own flaws, idealism falters, and even the Pastures of Heaven cannot be transformed from a valley whose residents are sin-sick, fallen men.

Michael J. Meyer

PAULETTE. **Henry Morgan**'s first mistress in ***Cup of Gold***. She is a mixed-race house servant he bought for **James Flower** in Port Royal. She falls in love with Henry and is jealous of **Elizabeth Morgan**. Her plan to get him drunk and marry him fails; however, before he leaves the plantation, Henry exacts a promise from James Flower not to put her to work in the fields.

Kevin Hearle

PEARL, THE **(BOOK)** (1947). When Steinbeck and his close friend **Edward F. Ricketts** made a scientific expedition in the Gulf of California in 1940, they heard of a folktale that Steinbeck reported in the narrative section of ***Sea of Cortez***. It is a story of a native Mexican boy who found a pearl of great size. He knew its value was so great that he imagined he could get drunk often and have his pick of the girls. But every pearl broker offered him so little that he refused to sell it and hid it under a stone; because of the pearl, he was attacked, waylaid, and tortured. Fed up, he cursed the pearl and threw it into the sea to make himself a free man again. Steinbeck considered the boy "too heroic, too wise" and the legend "far too reasonable to be true," but he thought it "probably true."

Steinbeck nursed the story in his mind for four years before he started writing the novella, *The Pearl*, at his new home, an adobe called the Soto House, in **Monterey**, just after Thanksgiving of 1944; he finished the first draft by early February 1945. The story first appeared in the *Woman's Home Companion* (December 1945) under the title, "The Pearl of the World," and then the novella in book form as *The Pearl* was published by Viking Press in November 1947.

Steinbeck expanded the seed story, thinking of making it into a screenplay. Therefore, his own version had to be believable as well as true—beyond a folktale. He converted the heroic figure of the unnamed native Mexican boy to a young married man, **Kino**, who has a wife, **Juana**, and an infant son, **Coyotito**. The book reviews were generally favorable; though some reviewers sniffed at the utter simplicity of Steinbeck's novella, more noted that Steinbeck was at the top of his game. Orville Prescott of the *New York Times* begins his review of *The Pearl* by observing that Steinbeck's recent works have been "wretched," but concludes that the novella represents the author's best work since ***The Red Pony*** and ***The Grapes of Wrath***. Maxwell Geismar writes in the *Saturday Review of Literature*, "The writing is very good, as are the descriptions of village life and Mexican types, and the Gulf scene itself: the land, the climate, even the various hours of the day."

The Pearl begins with a description of Kino and his family in the early morning, living a simple and peaceful life. The opening scenes are developed effectively with light and sounds as though the reader were seeing the movie. A scorpion appears and stings Coyotito on the shoulder, and the peacefulness suddenly turns into a panic. Juana wants to see the doctor in town; however, the doctor will not see the baby because Kino has no money, but only several valueless seed pearls. After all, the doctor is of a race called "conquistadors," a group that has exploited, beaten, and despised Kino's people. After this anguishing experience, the family sets out to sea, and Kino happens to find a pearl that is as large as a sea gull's egg. Back home, as he gazes at the silver surface of the pearl, he sees what he could get if he becomes rich—fine new clothes, a new harpoon, even a rifle—and he also envisions sending his boy to school and having a church wedding with his common-law wife. But he is unable to sell the pearl for the price he has expected, so he refuses to sell it, knowing that he and his people have always been cheated by the pearl buyers. He declares that he will sell his pearl in the capital, but this means betraying his people's way of life and traditions, which inevitably causes the family's tragedy. First, Kino's house is searched, and then he is attacked and hurt by a man. Kino kills a man when attacked a second time. Meanwhile, his canoe is destroyed and his house is burned down. When Kino and his family flee, three "dark trackers" come after them. Kino manages to kill the trackers, but one of them has already shot Coyotito to death. At last, Kino and Juana return to La Paz and walk straight to the beach, where Kino throws the great but cursed pearl back into the sea.

The surface story of the book is a morality play as well as a parable. As Steinbeck notes in his introductory remarks, "As with all retold tales that are in people's hearts, there are only good and bad things and black and white things and good and evil things and no in-between anywhere." Thus, everything in the story seems to possess a dual quality, the quality of which has been embodied, for instance, in the history of Mexico as a country—that of the descendants of the conquistadors and the native people. When a scorpion moves delicately down the rope to Coyotito at the outset of the novella, Kino hears in his mind "the Song of Evil" on top of "the Song of the Family," whereas Juana "repeated an ancient magic to guard against such evil, and on top of that she muttered a Hail Mary between clenched teeth." Only when it is possessed in the hand of a person of pure heart is the great pearl Kino holds gray and beautiful. In the last scene of the story, in which Kino looks into the surface of the pearl, he finds it is ugly. Once the pearl settles into the water, however, "The lights on its surface were green and lovely." Additionally, Steinbeck incorporates an atmosphere of hazy mirage into this story in order to overlay the dual quality of the landscape and environment—to show how, rather symbolically, the local people "trust things of the spirit and things of the imagination, but they do not trust their eyes." (The locale of the story is La Paz, though he actually came across mirages around Pulmo and in Estero de la Luna on the eastern coast of the Gulf.)

Though it features moments of beauty, *The Pearl* is, in fact, a brutal story in which the ruthless, deadly fights for survival take place in the dark. Steinbeck symbolically portrays how, in the estuary or elsewhere, the strong eat the weak under the law of the jungle (similar to the writer's point in chapter 6 of ***Cannery Row,*** in which all the little animals in the Great Tide Pool are struggling—killing and eating one another to live). In the middle of third chapter of *The Pearl,* the people in the house can hear the swish of a tight-woven school of small fishes and the bouncing splash of the bigger fishes from the estuary as the slaughter goes on. The passage, based on a phenomenon Steinbeck witnessed not in **La Paz**, but near Guaymas on the other side of the Gulf, symbolically falls between the doctor's two visits to Kino's house at night. One can readily suspect his medical treatment for the baby to be dishonest. One may even suspect that he is deeply involved in the whole criminal project of robbing Kino of the great pearl. The estuary, like a tide pool, represents a microcosm, just as a town represents a human habitat. To Steinbeck, a town epitomizes the universe, as does a human community such as those in ***Tortilla Flat*** or **Cannery Row** in **Monterey**, California. The microcosm functions as part of a greater ecosystem. It is a motif Steinbeck persistently uses throughout his entire canon. Another significant landscape description in the story is that of the mountainous area where Kino's family arrives and finds an oasis in its desperate flight from the dark trackers (just as **Pepé Torres** in **"Flight"** was tracked by "dark watchers"). The family will surely die unless it finds the little pools. Again, to Steinbeck, the little pools are, like the Great Tide Pool in *Cannery Row,* not only "places of life" but also "places of killing because of the water."

The Pearl is a symbolic parable with moral lessons and also a realistic, humanistic novella with ecological and sociological insights. In the final impressive scene of the novella, the only thing Kino holds in his hand is a rifle that he has taken from the dark trackers. At the outset of the story Kino and Juana had a brush house, a canoe, and, most of all, their beloved son, Coyotito. They have lost everything. Many readers might question the ending: how will they be able to live when all they possess is a rifle, and nothing to live by and on? And Kino will always be in danger of being shot. Nothing meaningful and productive can be achieved by violence only. Another possible interpretation of the ending, however, depends on how Kino will contribute to his people's needs with his courage and weapon. The native people need someone to protect them, or at least to prevent them from being cheated. To work for the betterment of society seems to be Kino's only recourse. Steinbeck did not make Kino "laugh a great deal" against modern capitalism, social injustice, and human greediness, as the young boy of the seed story did. Can it be that the writer wanted to leave the protagonist something else to do? Kino can be, in Steinbeck's terms in ***In Dubious Battle***, the "head" or the "eyes" of the "groupman" or "phalanx," a great individual who willingly sacrifices himself to the whole. In this sense, *The Pearl* is a humanistic or a realistic novella going beyond the limits of a parable or a morality play. Steinbeck's use of the environment and his holistic worldview interrelate the protagonists' lives and the themes of the novella. In his fiction the environment appropriately functions as a microcosm in which the protagonists live as a family of the world and in which Kino as the hero could gallantly act as what critic Lester Jay Marks calls a "Steinbeck hero."

Further Reading: Gladstein, Mimi Reisel. "Steinbeck's Juana: A Woman of Worth." *Steinbeck Quarterly* 9.1 (Winter 1976): 20–24; McElrath, Joseph R., Jesse S. Crisler, and Susan Shillinglaw, eds. *John Steinbeck, The Contemporary Reviews.* New York: Cambridge, 1996; Morris, Harry. "*The Pearl*: Realism and Allegory." In *Steinbeck: A Collection of Critical Essays, Twentieth Century Views.* Ed. Robert Murray Davis. Englewood Cliffs, NJ: Prentice-Hall, 1972. 149–162; Owens, Louis. *John Steinbeck's Re-Vision of America.* Athens: University of Georgia Press, 1985; Meyer, Michael J. "Precious Bane: Mining the Fool's Gold of The Pearl," and Simmonds, Roy S. "Steinbeck's *The Pearl*: Legend, Film, Novel" In *The Short Novels of John Steinbeck: Critical Essays with a Checklist to Steinbeck Criticism.* Ed. Jackson J. Benson. 161–172 and 173–184; Steinbeck, John. *The Pearl.* New York: Viking, 1947; ———. *The Log from the Sea of Cortez.* New York: Viking, 1951.

Kiyoshi Nakayama

PEARL, THE **(1947 FILM).** John Steinbeck heard the story that became ***The Pearl*** during his expedition to the Gulf of California in 1940, and he briefly recounted it in ***Sea of Cortez***. An expanded version was written in early 1945, appearing in the December issue of *Woman's Home Companion* that year; book publication was postponed until

November 1947 in anticipation of the film's release. The short novel received positive reviews in publications as diverse in viewpoints as ***Time*** and *Commonweal*; over the years *The Pearl* has become a minor classic among Steinbeck's works. Part of its status can be attributed to its widespread use in high school classes; however, the narrative neatly balances the harsh, almost filmic realism of Steinbeck's best works with a powerful allegory about the dangers and disillusionments of success. The primitive setting on the Mexican coast provides a universalized context for a subject that must have held considerable personal importance for the author, who was unable to reprise his earlier success in the postwar years. At the conclusion of the tale, **Kino**, the protagonist, has lost his infant son to the corruption created by this pearl of great price, which he casts back into the sea. He stands matured and hardened, like Steinbeck's **Zapata**, a defeated but stronger hero.

Unfortunately, this powerful characterization of Kino did not receive the successful filmic treatment that made ***Viva Zapata!*** a screen classic. Steinbeck wrote the initial screenplay with his old Hollywood friend, **Jack Wagner**, but Mexican director Emilio Fernandez also took a hand in shaping the story. The Mexican and American co-production falters in a hodgepodge of clichés from both cultures, despite more than adequate performances by the principals, Pedro Armendariz as Kino and Maria Elena Marques as **Juana**. Director Fernandez, perhaps Mexico's best-known filmic auteur, fluctuates in style between arty tableaux and interpolated dancing señoritas and macho brawling dear to the popular audiences of both countries. Critics considered the result a confused production at cross-purposes with itself. Steinbeck was embarrassed by the results at the preview, and the reviews only corroborated his reaction. Its only interest for a contemporary audience is as a curiosity of co-production in this period and for its somewhat oblique connection to John Steinbeck's minor literary classic.

Further Reading: Metzger, Charles. "The Film Version of Steinbeck's *The Pearl*." *Steinbeck Quarterly* 4 (Fall 1976): 88–92; Millichap, Joseph R. *Steinbeck and Film*. New York: Ungar, 1983; Simmonds, Roy S. "Steinbeck's *The Pearl*: Legend, Film, Novel." In *The Short Novels of John Steinbeck*. Ed. Jackson J. Benson. Durham, NC: Duke University Press, 1990; Steinbeck, John. *The Pearl*. New York: Viking, 1948.

Joseph Millichap

PEARL, THE **(2005 FILM)**. Written and directed by Alfredo Zacharias, the 2005 version of *The Pearl* starred Lukas Haas as **Kino** and Richard Harris, appearing in one of his last movie roles, as Doctor Karl Gottleib. Zacharias took significant liberties with Steinbeck's original plot, and Harris's role combined the novel's Spanish **doctor** with a charlatan and medic created by Zacharias, who controls both the people and the pearl-buying business in an anonymous village and impedes the residents from obtaining economic independence. Though still retaining some of the important dialogue of the original story, the director and screenwriter added several subplots not found in the original story line: a different type of corruption in the church and the priest; an emphasis on primitive medicine, including a curandera (perhaps an echo of ***The Forgotten Village***); a geologist who wants to replace the doctor and who agrees to track Kino and obtain the pearl; and finally a suggestion that others in the past have died trying to defy the collusion practiced by the village buyers. The most drastic changes employed, however, involve ending the movie happily: the evil doctor and geologist are punished, the latter stabbed to death; **Coyotito** is not harmed by random gunfire; and the people of the village decide to relocate and leave behind the oppression that has been their heritage for generations.

A low-budget production ($8 million), the movie began filming in 2001 in Baja California, around La Paz (the original location described by Steinbeck) and Mazatlan. Because of controversy over the script (the substantial alterations of Steinbeck's story), the film was never released in theaters and went straight to video with a release scheduled for January 2003 but delayed until November 2005. A review in *Variety* states that the adaptation "has almost none of the original novel's narrative or mythic potency." Other faults cited include the observation that the doctor's role was enhanced to star quality explicitly for Harris and that Haas was hopelessly miscast. The performances of Mexican actress Tere Tarin-Perez (as **Juana**) and of Harris, however, seem much closer to Steinbeck's original intentions in the novel.

Michael J. Meyer

PEARL BUYERS, THE. Along with the doctor and the priest, the pearl buyers in ***The Pearl*** form the third element of oppression for **Kino** and his people. Although the natives suspect them of holding a monopoly on the market price, past efforts to sell their pearls at the capital have failed, so the natives remain under the power of these crafty men. When **Kino** goes to sell his "Pearl of the World," the buyers already know what price will be offered and stage an elaborate show, with the first buyer offering a thousand pesos, the second nothing, and the last five hundred. Still, the pearl buyers are but cogs in the machine; it is their employer in La Paz who will discipline them for failing to purchase Kino's pearl.

Stephen K. George

PEELE, DOC. Physician who attends to the death of **Mary Hawley**'s brother Dennis in ***The Winter of Our Discontent***, he testifies to **Ethan Hawley** about how remarkably persons can change character under stress.

PELHAM, KING. In ***The Acts of King Arthur***, brother of **Sir Garlon**. When his brother is killed before his eyes by **Sir Balin**, a guest at his court, King Pelham endeavors to avenge his brother's death. He is wounded by Balin with the spear of **Longinus the Roman** and his castle is destroyed by an earthquake. A blight of sickness, hunger, and despair spreads over his land.

PELLEAS, SIR, LORD OF THE ISLES. In ***The Acts of King Arthur***, a sad knight and one of the best knights in the world who overturns five hundred knights in a single tournament. He vainly loves the **Lady Ettarde**, and when he finds her sleeping with **Sir Gawain**, his heart is broken and he retires to his bed to die. Lady Ettarde is persuaded by a spell cast by **Nyneve** that she does in fact love Sir Pelleas after all, but the good knight rejects her and lives the rest of his life happily with Nyneve.

PELLINORE, KING. In ***The Acts of King Arthur***, father of **Percival** and Lamorake. He is known as the Knight of the Fountain and challenges every knight who passes by. He kills **Sir Miles** and wounds **Sir Gryfflet**. He overcomes **Arthur** when Arthur seeks revenge and spares Arthur only through **Merlin**'s magical intervention. Subsequently, he becomes a loyal friend to Arthur and fights in the first line of his knights. He kills **King Lot** in battle and is made a Knight of the **Round Table**. He is sent by Arthur on the Quest of the Lady, and by ignoring the calls for aid of his daughter, **Alyne**, he causes her death and earns her curse—that his best friend will fail him in his greatest need and the man he trusts the most will leave him to be killed.

PEPYS, SAMUEL (1633–1703). Famous English diarist. Steinbeck read and admired Pepys's diaries and claimed that Pepys allowed readers to understand not only what happened in the seventeenth century but also what people at the time thought about it. Steinbeck owned the two-volume 1946 edition of *The Diary of Samuel Pepys*, edited by Henry B. Wheatley.

Janet L. Flood and T. Adrian Lewis

PERCIVAL. Son of **King Pellinore**, in ***The Acts of King Arthur***.

PEREZ DE GUZMAN, JUAN (DON). Governor of Panama in ***Cup of Gold***. He tries to bribe **Henry Morgan** to stay away from

Panama and then prepares for the attack by paying for masses in the cathedral and gathering bulls with which to stampede the invading buccaneers. It is a wholly ineffectual defense. During the sacking of the city, he confronts Morgan, but is overcome by cowardice. He drops his sword and drunkenly heads out of the ruined city on foot.

Kevin Hearle

PERYNE DE MONTE BELYARDE, SIR. In ***The Acts of King Arthur***, the second knight to be killed while in the company of **Sir Balin** by a great spear thrown by the invisible knight **Sir Garlon**.

PERYS DE FORESTE SAVAGE, SIR. In ***The Acts of King Arthur***, a cruel knight, a molester of damsels and gentlewomen, killed by **Lancelot**.

PETRARCH [FRANCESCO PETRARCHA] (1304–1374). Italian scholar, poet, and humanist whose poems addressed to Laura, an idealized beloved, contributed to the Renaissance flowering of lyric poetry. Several of Petrarch's sonnets were read at Steinbeck's funeral by his close friend **Henry Fonda**. According to **Jackson J. Benson**, Petrarch, along with Malory, **Shakespeare**, Verdi, and Wagner, led Steinbeck to consider love the noblest of all emotions, a powerful force that could elevate the soul, overcome all obstacles, and even transcend death. Benson also notes that Steinbeck often relied on Petrarch as a way to end a long evening of talk and music with friends. Before his guests left, Steinbeck would read Petrarch's verse in a simple low voice full of emotion. These sonnets were also some of Steinbeck's favorites, and he read them countless times. They may have also served to alleviate the pain he was experiencing as a result of his deteriorating relationship with his wife **Gwyndolyn Conger Steinbeck**. In a 1962 letter to **Elizabeth Otis**, Steinbeck wrote, "Oddly the real depth both of style and thought I have found lately has been in Petrarch."

Further Reading: Benson, Jackson J. *The True Adventures of John Steinbeck, Writer*. New York: Viking, 1984.

T. Adrian Lewis and Michael J. Meyer

PHALANX. *See* **"Argument of Phalanx."**

PHARIANCE, SIR. In ***The Acts of King Arthur***, knight of **Kings Ban** and **Bors**.

PHILLIPS, DR. In "**The Snake**" he is the researcher in the **Monterey** lab who is surprised and repulsed by a strange woman who enters his lab to buy a rattlesnake and watch it eat a rat. The fictional Dr. Phillips is an early avatar of Steinbeck's friend Edward F. Ricketts. Phillips is so absorbed in his research that he has no outside interests and he eschews emotions that are inherently nonscientific, a theme Steinbeck explored in a more humorous vein with another Doc character in ***Sweet Thursday***.

Abby H. P. Werlock

"PIECE OF IT FELL ON MY TAIL, A." Title of a novel Steinbeck began shortly after abandoning ***The Acts of King Arthur and His Noble Knights***. Taking his title from the children's story about Henny Penny and Chicken Little, Steinbeck proposed to retell the tale with an emphasis on the nature of reality and on the intolerance and conflict produced by differences in personal perception. Although Steinbeck talked about the story to various individuals, including his agent **Elizabeth Otis**, and labored over it from May to October 1966, he was never able to progress, finding it difficult to translate the important message into believable prose. It was the last literary project he planned.

Michael J. Meyer

PIERRE LE GRAND. Actual pirate captain and character in ***Cup of Gold*** under whom **Dafydd** served.

PIGTAILS (AMY). A little girl at the **Weedpatch** Camp who puts an end to **Ruthie Joad**'s selfishness in ***The Grapes of***

Wrath by advising the children to refuse to play with her as long as she tries to boss and domineer them. Providing a parallel to how the unions worked together against the domineering owners, Pigtails's act eventually stems Ruthie's pride, stubbornness, and desire to control others and helps demonstrate that working with others is preferable to subduing and trying to change them by force. *See also* **Arvin Sanitary Camp**.

PILON. In *Tortilla Flat,* the best friend of the main character **Danny** and one of the paisanos who share the latter's house. Pilon is the resident philosopher and logician of the group, not only determining the proper ends for the paisanos but also devising practical strategies for attaining those ends. In each of the friends' setbacks he finds a lesson, which generally points out not how to do the right thing, but how to do the wrong thing without getting caught. He is always cooking up one scheme or another, usually aimed at acquiring more wine, and to facilitate these plots, he keeps abreast of all the details of life on Tortilla Flat. Pilon is with Danny from the beginning of the novel. The preface begins near the end of World War I, with the two friends, along with **Big Joe Portagee**, getting drunk and enlisting in the army. While Danny spends the duration of the war in Texas breaking mules, Pilon spends it in Oregon training for the infantry. But when the two are reunited back in Tortilla Flat, things have changed. Danny has returned to an inheritance of two houses from his grandfather, and Pilon sees his first opportunity. He appeals to Danny's generosity, accusing him of abandoning his friends, and the strategy works: Danny invites him to live with him in one of the houses. But soon, Pilon feels indebted to Danny and longs for the distinction of his own home, so he convinces Danny to rent the second house to him, though he never pays the rent. Through further schemes, Pilon acquires several tenants in his own house. Out of guilt over his inability to pay rent, Pilon makes the sacrifice of a day's work cleaning squid. But the two dollars he earns quickly becomes two gallons of wine, which he shares with his friend **Pablo Sanchez** on the way to Danny's house. Pilon convinces Pablo to rent space in his house, reasoning to himself that he can use Pablo's delinquency as an excuse for his own. Acting on the same reasoning, the two lure **Jesus Maria Corcoran** into their house, this time even acquiring a two-dollar deposit, which is promptly exchanged for wine. After drinking the wine, the three of them let Danny's second house burn down through their negligence. The chain of schemes initiated by Pilon ends with the friends moving into Danny's remaining house, where Pilon can find new ways to take advantage of Danny and others.

As a logician, Pilon is a sophist, always rationalizing for his narrow self-interest, but he is also aware of a very definite code of conduct and tries to operate within its parameters. Occasionally, his resourcefulness in finding loopholes in the code runs up against its limits, as it does in his recruitment of the **Pirate** to Danny's household. Pilon discovers that the Pirate, a dimwitted man who lives in a chicken coop with five dogs, has amassed a sizable savings, and he sets out to acquire it. When he fails to learn the whereabouts of the Pirate's "treasure," he invites the Pirate and his dogs to live in Danny's house, pleading concern for the Pirate's welfare but hoping to frighten the Pirate into revealing his secret with tales of the dire consequences of buried treasure. But the Pirate disrupts their play by entrusting the treasure to them, his friends, and Pilon is forced to give up: the Pirate has become one of the paisanos, and betraying a paisano's trust so overtly would be unthinkable for the more subtle and circumspect Pilon.

At one level, Pilon is certainly an embodiment of the capitalist values of selfishness and greed that Steinbeck despised. In the preface, Steinbeck glosses Pilon's name as "something thrown in when a trade is concluded," and this suggests not only the king of "piling on" of schemes that leads to all the friends living under one roof, but also the capitalist drive to extract surplus value or profit. This is one of Pilon's defining characteristics, in counterpoint to Danny's generosity. But careful reading shows that Pilon's wisdom also contains something admirable for Steinbeck.

Pilon is often called a "realist" in the novel, and much of the time this title seems inappropriate, as in chapter 8, where he is labeled an idealist as he searches for treasure on St. Andrew's Eve. But the sense in which Pilon is a realist is clearer in a passage that occurs after he has decided not to tell Pablo about the Pirate's treasure: "Honor and peace to Pilon, for he had discovered how to uncover and to disclose to the world the good that lay in every evil thing. Nor was he blind, as so many saints are, to the evil of good things." Not only is Pilon aware of these facts about the ambivalence of good and evil, but he also displays them in his behavior. Even though his motives are far from pure, he does help the lonely Pirate find a home and a group of friends. At the end of the novel, he even makes another sacrifice for Danny, proposing that all the friends clean squid for a day to throw Danny a huge party. It is fitting then, that this character, who is the source of so much specious argument in *Tortilla Flat*, also serves as the messenger of its most profound wisdom.

Brian Vescio

PIODA, MR. A man in the **Salinas** Post Office in ***East of Eden*** who assists **Adam Trask** to his feet when Adam collapses after learning of **Aron Trask**'s enlistment.

PIPE DREAM. A 1955 **Rodgers and Hammerstein** musical comedy based on *Sweet Thursday*. Steinbeck had written his novel with its eventual adaptation to the stage in mind, but he had no official role in the production. As he attended rehearsals and out-of-town tryouts, however, he became deeply concerned about the entire tone of the show. Accustomed to creating wholesome, family entertainment, Oscar Hammerstein kept revising the libretto to make the material more and more innocuous, even to the point of clouding the fact that **Suzy** is engaged as a working prostitute at the **Bear Flag**; in this revised version, she may simply be rooming there. Steinbeck protested to Hammerstein, warning in a letter that the show was "in grave danger of mediocrity" because "what emerges now is an old fashioned love story." However, Steinbeck's long letters to the producers with detailed, line-by-line suggestions were simply ignored.

The production opened at New York's Shubert Theatre on November 30, 1955. The reviews, though mixed, were less than enthusiastic and often made exactly the criticisms Steinbeck had anticipated. The show did manage to survive the season, running for a total of 246 performances, but by Rodgers and Hammerstein standards, it could be called a failure. *Pipe Dream* had the shortest run of any of their productions and lost the most money. After this experience, which came on the heels of his disappointment with ***Burning Bright***, Steinbeck made no further attempts to write for the stage.

Further Reading: Morsberger, Robert E. "*Pipe Dream*, or Not So Sweet Thursday." *Steinbeck Quarterly* 21 (Summer–Fall 1988): 85–96; Steinbeck, John. *Steinbeck: A Life in Letters*. Ed. Elaine Steinbeck and Robert Wallsten. New York: Viking, 1975.

Bruce Ouderkirk

PIRATE, THE. In ***Tortilla Flat***, a large, shy, childlike man who becomes one of **Danny**'s paisanos through the greed of the others. The Pirate's only friends appear to be five dogs who live with him in a chicken coop outside an abandoned house and who are utterly belligerent toward everyone and everything else. The Pirate is so named, we are told, because of his bushy black beard, but he also possesses a hidden treasure of sorts. Six days a week he goes into town to beg from **Monterey** restaurants scraps of food, which he then divides equally among his dogs. He spends the rest of the day chopping kindling, which he sells for twenty-five cents. He keeps his treasure hidden, never spending a penny of it because he intends to buy a gold candlestick for Saint Francis when his total reaches a thousand quarters. It is this treasure that inspires the paisanos to invite him into their house. **Pilon** deduces the existence of the Pirate's treasure, but even he cannot discern its whereabouts, even after following the Pirate for weeks and trying to wheedle it out of him in conversation. **Jesus Maria Corcoran** suggests that the paisanos invite the Pirate into their house to get the secret out of him, and they allow him and his dogs to live within a corner of one room, the boundary marked with blue chalk. In conversation, the friends talk constantly about the dangers of hoarding secret treasure, until the Pirate finally gives up his secret. But in doing so, he thwarts their plans: rather than entrusting the secret of the treasure's whereabouts to them, he entrusts them with the treasure itself. This act reveals the limits of the paisanos' willingness to cheat and steal from one another, since even they cannot bring themselves to steal something so freely and guilelessly entrusted to them.

The responsibility of guarding the Pirate's treasure becomes an almost sacred pact among them, and when **Big Joe Portagee** attempts to violate this pact in chapter 12, he is severely beaten by the others. When the friends recover the treasure, they find it has reached the requisite thousand quarters, and they help the Pirate buy the candlestick. The day the candlestick is placed in the church, the Pirate attends alone, leaving the dogs with the paisanos, but the dogs break free and burst into church. The Pirate takes them outside until the service is over, but then takes them up to his customary shelter in the woods and repeats the sermon on Saint Francis for them, arranging them in rows like a congregation. When he hears a sound behind him, the Pirate believes his dogs have had a vision of Saint Francis as a reward. In a sense, the dogs have had a vision of beatitude, since the Pirate himself partakes of sainthood, sharing everything he has with the dogs and using his money not to buy wine but to honor a saint. In his childlike simplicity, he is the only completely generous character in *Tortilla Flat*.

Brian Vescio

PLACIDAS, SIR. In ***The Acts of King Arthur***, French Knight who guards and protects the kingdoms of **Kings Ban** and **Bors** while they are in England helping **Arthur**.

PLATO (C. 428–C. 348 BC). Eminent Greek Philosopher and prose writer, founder of philosophical idealism. As noted by **Robert DeMott**, Steinbeck's library contained *The Dialogues of Plato*. **Jim Nolan**, one of the main characters of ***In Dubious Battle***, mentions that he read Plato's *Republic*, and in ***The Moon Is Down***, **Mayor Orden** recites passages from the *Apology*, a depiction of Socrates' defense at his trial, and the *Crito*, a dialogue between Socrates and Crito in which the latter urges Socrates to escape his imprisonment.

T. Adrian Lewis

PLATT, ALEX. Connecticut neighbor of **Charles** and **Adam Trask** in ***East of Eden***. Alex finds the suitcase of men's clothing, a purse, and a locked box containing almost four thousand dollars, possessions belonging to **Mr. Edwards** and **Catherine Amesbury**, left there the evening of Catherine's brutal beating.

"PLAY-NOVELETTE, THE" (1950). Appearing originally as "The Novel Might Benefit . . ." in *Stage* (1938), this prose piece was reprinted in the "Author's Foreword" to the novelette publication of *Burning Bright*. In this essay, Steinbeck states that *Of Mice and Men* was a failure as a play-novelette because of his lack of knowledge about stagecraft. He believes that the experimental form has a future, however, since it offers potential advantages to both lay readers and players. In the end, he asserts that the novel form might "benefit by the discipline, the terseness of the drama, but [on the other hand] the drama itself might achieve increased openness, freedom and versatility."

Further Reading: Steinbeck, John. "The Play-Novelette." *America and Americans and Selected Nonfiction*. Ed. Susan Shillinglaw and Jackson J. Benson. New York: Viking, 2002.

Eric Skipper

"A PLEA FOR TOURISTS" (1955). Article in *Punch* (January 26) in which Steinbeck defends American tourists in Europe, noting that a few "louts" have created the stereotype of the Ugly American.

Scott Simkins

"PLEA TO TEACHERS, A" (1955). Originally appeared in *Saturday Review* (38.18, April 30, 1955) and was reprinted in National Education Association's September 1955 journal under the title, "Dear Teachers, Sweet Teachers, I Beg You Call Them Off!" In the essay, Steinbeck playfully complains that teachers have unleashed a monster by asking their students to write directly to authors. Specifically, he notes that he has received threatening letters from some students ("and I don't want none of them form letters. I want the real stuff") if he doesn't respond to the thousands of letters he receives daily.

Herbert Behrens and Michael J. Meyer

PLUTARCH (C. AD 46–C. 120). Greek essayist and biographer, his great work is *The Parallel Lives,* comprising forty-six surviving biographies arranged in pairs (one Greek life with one comparable Roman) and four single biographies. The English translation by Sir Thomas North had a profound effect upon English literature; it supplied, for example, the material for Shakespeare's *Coriolanus, Julius Caesar, Antony and Cleopatra,* and *Timon of Athens.* **Jackson J. Benson** records that Steinbeck reread Plutarch's *Lives,* along with other classical historical texts such as Toynbee's *A Study of History* (1934) and Rousseau's *Confessions* (1770, 1781), in an attempt to keep up with the reading of his sons in boarding school and to revaluate texts he had not visited in years. Steinbeck's comments about reading, as noted by **Robert DeMott**, indicate that the author returned to Plutarch again and again throughout his life.

PLUTARCO. In ***Viva Zapata!***, upon the dragging death of **Innocénte**, Innocénte's wife makes reference to Plutarco, who must have suffered a similar fate to that of Innocénte while attempting to plant his field as well. Evidently he was killed, but Innocénte stubbornly refused to learn from Plutarco's fatal experience, much to the chagrin of Innocénte's wife.

POETRY. John Steinbeck loved poetry, and the influence of poets and poetry upon his prose is significant in a way that his own meager output as a poet is not. He read widely; besides owning anthologies of English, Scottish, American and Chinese poetry, he at one time either owned himself or borrowed from **Edward F. Ricketts** individual books of poetry by following writers: **Dante Alighieri**, Matthew Arnold, Charles Baudelaire, Stephen Vincent Benet, Wilfrid Blunt, **Robert Browning**, Geoffrey Chaucer, John Donne, **T. S. Eliot**, Federico Garcia Lorca, Wolfgang Goethe, Homer, Gerard Manley Hopkins, Horace, **Robinson Jeffers**, Li Po, Henry Wadsworth Longfellow, Archibald MacLeish, Sir Thomas Malory, Ogden Nash, Novalis, Ovid, **Petrarch**, **Ezra Pound**, Edwin Arlington Robinson, **Carl Sandburg**, Algernon Charles Swinburne, Rabindranath Tagore, Tu Fu, Francois Villon, Virgil, **Walt Whitman**, John Greenleaf Whittier, Xenophon, and William Butler Yeats. He had special praise for Robert Graves and W. H. Auden. Although he disparaged **Alfred Lord Tennyson**'s *Idylls of the King* (1859) as a gutless version of Malory, he called for a portion of Tennyson's "Ulysses" (1842) to be read at his funeral along with selections from the verse of **Robert Louis Stevenson** and **John Millington Synge**.

The poetry of Robinson Jeffers—especially "The Women at Point Sur" and "Apology for Bad Dreams"—was the single most significant influence upon ***To a God Unknown***. Thomas Malory's ***Morte D'Arthur***, the work Steinbeck credited with awakening his love of reading, was an important influence on ***Cup of Gold, Tortilla Flat, The Winter of Our Discontent***, and, of course, Steinbeck's incomplete attempt to translate Malory into prose, the posthumously published ***The Acts of King Arthur and His Noble Knights***.

A consideration of Steinbeck's titles further indicates his debt to poetry. **John Milton**'s *Paradise Lost* was the source of ***In Dubious Battle***'s title. ***Of Mice and Men*** takes its title from "To a Mouse" by the Scottish poet Robert Burns, and the title of ***Burning Bright*** features the third and fourth words of **William Blake**'s "The Tyger." **Shakespeare** provided titles for both ***The Moon Is Down*** and *The Winter of Our Discontent* (*Macbeth* and *Richard III* respectively), and ***The Pearl*** is not so coincidentally also the title of one of the great religious narratives—in alliterative verse—of medieval English. For ***The Grapes of Wrath*** Steinbeck turned to **Julia Ward Howe**'s "Battle Hymn of the Republic," which itself derived the phrase from both Isaiah 63:3 and Revelations 19:15. With ***East of Eden***, Steinbeck—drawing on Genesis 3:24—created a new biblical phrase for his title, much as he had paraphrased the Vedic hymns in creating the title *To a God Unknown*.

Steinbeck apparently came from a family of failed poets. An untitled, lamely galloping trimeter narrative by his father has its moments of charm, but his mother's "An Autograph" is sentimental doggerel that manages to make the worst poems of the Celtic Twilight, Victorian sentimentalists, and the pre-Raphaelites seem blazingly modern in their diction and prosodically sophisticated vocabulary. Fortunately, those are apparently the only surviving poems by Mr. and Mrs. Steinbeck.

Steinbeck began writing poems occasionally in childhood. What few poems we have from Steinbeck's youth survived because he gave them as gifts to his parents and sisters. Those early poems that are known to have survived were almost uniformly intended to be humorous, and some of them actually were—however briefly. The poems poke mild fun at family members or their friends and erratically display his burgeoning understanding of meter. Many of the poems are about preparing and eating food.

Steinbeck was, however, enough of a reader of poetry to be conscious early on that he was not a great poet. While still a student at **Stanford University**, he addressed a letter to the professor of his versification course, William Herbert Carruth, as to his training in the writing of verse. In that letter, he claims—falsely it seems—to have written verse only during three years, and then only under the influence of two loves, one war, and certain months of May. He jokingly claims that the rejection of his first two-line schoolboy poem by the object of his presumably prepubescent affection causes him to be reticent about publishing his poems.

What remains of the poems he wrote during the 1920s suggests some branching out as to subject matter; however, Steinbeck remained flippant when asked about them, and most of the poems are slight satires composed in fairly mechanical verse with diction drawn from the mock epic. These include eleven lines of what Steinbeck jokingly pretends is a sonnet on the morals of chorus girls; a clunky meditation on a carnival elephant written in iambic heptameter couplets arranged awkwardly into two successive quatrains followed by a sestet, another quatrain, and a single closing couplet; and, by 1928, a few slightly nonsensical, four line, iambic tetrameter epigrams composed of two couplets of modest humor. Although Steinbeck's handling of meter became more appropriate to his subject matter and tone as the 1920s wore on, and though his use of an increasingly colloquial diction represented a significant improvement over the bulk of his surviving student work, it is not surprising that Steinbeck was conscious that his verse did not measure up to his prose.

There are, however, at least two surviving pre-1926 poems that display true poetic talent. One poem, which Steinbeck wrote for his poetry course and sent to his parents from Stanford, was his adaptation of a figure from *Revelations*. "The Whore of Babylon" poem consists of five *abab* rhymed iambic pentameter quatrains. The diction leans toward the melodramatic in some lines, but the poem is technically accomplished—his use of the caesura is in particular a great improvement over his teenage verse—and genuinely worth reading. There is a vaguely Yeatsian quality to the poem. The other remarkable poem is harder to date. The prosodic dexterity it displays suggests that it was written during his Stanford years; however, because the poem describes the Steinbeck family but leaves out the husband of his eldest sister (**Esther Steinbeck Rodgers** was ten years older than John), it is tempting to date the poem from before his 1919 departure for Stanford. Whenever it was written, the poem is a mock epic delight. In charmingly rhymed iambic pentameter couplets, it describes the Steinbeck family barbecue and lays waste to the clichés of epic.

During the 1930s, Steinbeck's poetic production seems to have been insignificant. It is possible that he wrote poems during this period and destroyed them in one of his periodic bonfires of juvenilia. A more likely explanation would be that he felt one poet in the family was enough. Perhaps Steinbeck was intimidated by the poetry written by his wife **Carol Henning Steinbeck**, or maybe he felt it best to let her have the uncontested creative outlet of this one literary field to herself. Whatever his reasons, Carol Steinbeck's poems, published under the pseudonym Amnesia Glasscock, were misattributed to him.

The most important shift in Steinbeck's poetry seems to have occurred as his first marriage was failing and the affair that would lead to his second marriage was beginning. In an undated letter to Professor George F. Sensabaugh written sometime in the early 1940s, Steinbeck declines the request to judge a poetry contest at Stanford University on the grounds that he is unqualified. Steinbeck's argument for his inadequacy as a judge of poetry is based on a crucial distinction between verse and poetry. Although he admits to being capable of checking a poem's scansion, rhyme scheme, and argument, he implies that those characteristics are the necessary constituents of verse rather than poetry. During this same period, Steinbeck's poetic technique underwent a related change. In November 1940, Steinbeck wrote to his old friend and then go-between **Max Wagner**, asking him to tell **Gwyndolyn Conger**—who would later be his second wife—that he was writing a "song" for her. It may be that by thinking of his writing for Gwyn as a "song" rather than as a suite of twenty-five love poems, Steinbeck freed himself from his anxiety about poetic technique. Whatever the impetus for the change, the erotic poems to Gwyn show Steinbeck breaking away from meter and trying his hand at free verse. In the "Girl of the Air" sequence of poems, Steinbeck relies primarily on rhetorical forms such as anaphora and elaboration to give his extended "song" to Gwyn its characteristic sound. Unfortunately, although the suite of poems is rhythmically more sophisticated and satisfying than his earliest verse, it isn't nearly as prosodically accomplished, as euphonious, or as narratively satisfying as his barbecue mock epic or his Whore of Babylon poem. As **Robert DeMott** notes, it contains some of the worst lines that ever attempted to pass for poetry in English. It also is repetitive in a way that begins to seem like a bad parody of Eliot's *Four Quartets*, and its rhythmic slackness at times is reminiscent of the worst of Walt Whitman. Given their private nature—he was still married to Carol when he wrote the poems—it is hardly surprising that he never sought to publish any of them.

After his disappointing marriage to Gwyn concluded, Steinbeck wrote little in the way of poetry and conveniently seemed to have forgotten much of what he had written before in the genre. In a July 10, 1949, letter to his third wife, **Elaine Scott Steinbeck**, he claims to have written only one poem in his life. He then quotes in its entirety a variation on one of his four-line epigrams from the 1920s.

Ultimately, it is interesting to speculate as to what sort of poet Steinbeck might have gone on to be had he considered his poetry as a professional rather than a strictly personal matter. Had he focused on writing rhymed and metered verse, he almost certainly could have given Ogden Nash some competition, and he might even have become an important minor writer of serious verse. His adaptation of Whitman's rhetorical form to a shorter line seems to have provided him with a free-verse technique that, with practice, might eventually have developed into a mature and rhythmically sensitive poetic style, but it makes more sense to be grateful for the influence of poetry upon his prose masterpieces than it does to mourn the death of a minor poet. With the exception of his poem on the Whore of Babylon and his family barbecue mock epic, Steinbeck was right not to try to publish his poems.

Further Reading: DeMott, Robert. "After *The Grapes of Wrath*: A Speculative Essay on John Steinbeck's Suite of Love Poems for Gwyn, 'The Girl of the Air.'" *John Steinbeck: The Years of Greatness, 1936–39*. Ed. Tetsumaro Hayashi. Tuscaloosa: University of Alabama Press, 1993. 20–45; Steinbeck, John. "Then My Arm Glassed Up." *Sports Illustrated*. December 20, 1965, 94–102; "Grover Sherwood Papers," "John Steinbeck Collection," and "Wells Fargo John Steinbeck Collection," Department of Special Collections, Green Library, Stanford University.

Kevin Hearle

POLITICAL BELIEFS. John Steinbeck's political beliefs were those of a Progressive, who believed government exists to help the individual become self-reliant. No perfectionist, Steinbeck saw life as an ongoing conflict between competing economic and political ideologies, between individuals driven by ambition and greed and those with less power and few opportunities under **political tyranny**. He believed government for its own health should give people an opportunity to compete fairly. He thought that the political system most likely to succeed was one in which individuals were allowed to develop fully their own talents. But he also acknowledged that an individual had a moral responsibility to uphold the social fabric. Although a great American patriot, Steinbeck thought in terms of the human species and so felt that human rights everywhere ought to be protected. He based his political creed of individual opportunity and social obligation on psycho-scientific ideas.

Human biological origins, he thought, instinctively pull us backward toward herding and forming schools—as fish do—for protection; thus, the individual becomes insignificant. These unconscious urges he identified with collective or totalitarian movements. But humanity also evolved a desire for individual expression and dignity much as the character **Pepé Torres** displays in Steinbeck's story **"Flight."** Steinbeck thought democracy, which used the group to protect the individual, attempted to balance those two drives. Darwinian competition and adjustment also compose part of Steinbeck's political picture. Nations with the most flexibility will best survive changing conditions, conditions often the result of man's inherent desire to explore and improve. Nations that become complacent and rest on their success, as he feared America in the 1950s had, would lose out to those with greater drives and willingness to sacrifice. He thought this true of individuals and groups as exemplified by the fictitious Joads who grow more determined from their difficulties. For three decades, Steinbeck evaluated world affairs and advised presidents on the basis of these views of human nature.

Further Reading: Britch, Carrol, and Cliff Lewis, eds. *Rediscovering Steinbeck—Revisionist Views of his Art, Politics, and Intellect*. Lewiston, NY: Mellen Press, 1989; Steinbeck, John. *America and Americans*. New York: Viking, 1966.

Clifford Lewis

POLITICAL TYRANNY. Steinbeck's earliest writings were about unconscious drives that brought individuals into conflict with their environment. With the rise of totalitarian movements in California in the Depression, he began to write about drives that led individuals to take upon themselves a group identity. ***In Dubious Battle***, written in 1932 and 1933 before the New Deal altered the political scene, described two totalitarian groups that squashed individual rights because they believed the means justified the end. A wealthy group of landowners controlled public institutions—banks, media, and government—and denied poor individuals their rights. The communist left sought to use these abused poor to acquire the power held by the wealthy. The novel denounced both the fascist and communist organizations for destroying individual rights. Seeing no political support for the well-being of the individual, Steinbeck rejected both camps and called himself a nihilist. When totalitarian regimes emerged as world powers in Japan, Germany, and the Soviet Union, Steinbeck warned of their threat to democracies.

In the Junius Maltby episode (chapter 6) of *Pastures of Heaven*, Steinbeck predicted a Japanese-American war. In 1940, while in Mexico, he informed President **Roosevelt** of German strength there and met with the president to discuss a propaganda or spy agency to replace the FBI's foreign efforts. Steinbeck supported the Allied war efforts. His ***The Moon Is Down*** asserted that occupied democracies would prevail over their totalitarian foes because the urge for liberty was too strong to be smothered. ***Bombs Away***, which he wrote at Roosevelt's request to recruit bombing crews, explained the individual differences necessary for the success of the team.

With the Cold War emerging, Steinbeck traveled to the USSR in 1947 to try to ease tensions between the two super powers by humanizing its citizens. His report in ***A Russian Journal*** presented the idea that communist ideology, with all of its rituals and icons, was the political veneer for religious perfectionism. He disavowed the Marxist requirement that art, an expression of individual uniqueness, serve as a vehicle to support the state. And he predicted that the Soviets would not succeed in denying citizens' democratic aspirations. Nearly two decades later—in a 1965 memo—Steinbeck informed the Johnson administration that from discussions with leaders of Hungary and other satellite countries, he had concluded that these countries intended to carry out policies independent of the Soviets. He expected them to revolt against Moscow, but felt that the Soviet Army would not be used. He reported also that Castro's regime had failed in Cuba but not to expect the elite to return to power. His faith that freedom was too embedded in mankind to be suppressed even by powerful dictators led him to offer valuable advice; he was less successful, however, in understanding political forces in South Vietnam.

To Steinbeck, the North Vietnamese Communists' war in South Vietnam required the United States to continue a postwar policy of opposing totalitarian expansion. He saw the Viet Cong as a group who disregarded human rights and who felt any means justified its end. Through newspaper articles (the **"Letters to Alicia"**), conversations with President Johnson, and letters to White House aides and the Secretary of Defense, Steinbeck defended the war. Once he learned more about the South Vietnamese Government's corruption and its indifference to its people, he realized we were not supporting a fledging democracy. He had not become the reactionary his critics believed; however, he was wrong to think the government in the South was republican. The political debate over our moral responsibility to protect weak nations or victims of evil ideology continues but Steinbeck's stance against tyrants and demagogues is clearly evident in the body of his work.

Further Reading: Britch, Carrol, and Cliff Lewis, eds. *Rediscovering Steinbeck—Revisionist Views of his Art, Politics, and Intellect*. Lewiston, NY: Edwin Mellen Press, 1989.

Clifford Lewis

POM-POM, JOHNNY. In ***Tortilla Flat***, one of the latest arrivals among **Danny**'s motley crew of paisanos. He joins the group late in the novel when he brings news of Danny, who has gone on his prolonged "amok," as Steinbeck calls it. Johnny Pom-pom brings news of Danny's escape from jail, aided by the drunken jailer **Tito Ralph**. When **Torrelli** arrives to evict the paisanos, Johnny proves his friendship by helping to confiscate and destroy the bill of sale for the house, and he also works alongside the others to earn money for Danny's final party. There is nothing very distinctive about Johnny, but his late arrival signals the way that all of Tortilla Flat will come to rally around Danny at the end of the novel.

PORTAGEE, BIG JOE. In *Tortilla Flat*, an animalistic character who enlists in the army with **Danny** and **Pilon** and later becomes one of the paisanos who share Danny's house. In the preface, Big Joe stumbles upon Danny and Pilon drinking in the woods and follows them to the army recruitment office. Even though he begins to sober up and to change his mind, it is too late, and Joe is assigned to the infantry. The most notable fact about Joe is that he has spent a good portion of his life in jail. In fact, Steinbeck tells us that Joe believes a man should spend half his life in jail, just as he spends half his day sleeping. Because the army's regulations are much more onerous than those in civilian life, punishing people for what they don't do as well as for what they do, Joe spends considerably more than half his time in the army in jail. After the war is over, Joe still has six months to serve in jail, and Steinbeck tells us that if the armistice hadn't been signed, Joe probably would have been shot. When Joe returns to **Monterey**, he gets no welcome from friends or the community, so he spends most of a drunken binge with prostitutes, followed by another stint in jail. After he gets out, he meets Pilon on his way to the forest to search for buried treasure, a custom in Tortilla Flat on St. Andrew's Eve. Pilon finds what he believes is buried treasure and marks the spot, but though Big Joe wants to dig immediately, Pilon forces him to stay for an all-night vigil to keep evil spirits and other treasure-seekers away. They return to Danny's house in the morning, planning to dig up the treasure later, and when Joe arrives, Danny knows he has come to stay. Joe's initiation into the group illustrates the foundations of deceit and self-interest on which the paisanos' shaky friendships are built.

When Joe moves into Danny's house, the paisanos have already been entrusted with the **Pirate**'s treasure, and although they have all pledged not to steal it, Joe succumbs to the temptation. He is punished with a shockingly severe beating in the novel's most brutal scene. Later, a woman named **Tia Ignacia** invites Big Joe into her house on a rainy night and tries to seduce him with subtle insinuations and wine. Joe is oblivious to the insinuations and is interested only in the wine, until she kicks him out of the house and he has to hold her tightly to stop her from beating him. These events, along with his descent into "the pit" on his return from the war, portray Big Joe as all appetite, with none of the sensitivities that the other paisanos, for all their selfishness and irresponsibility, possess. Discipline is clearly what has been lacking from Joe's life, and whereas he once found that discipline in the comfort of jail, in the course of the novel he comes to find it in the friendship of the paisanos.

Bryan Vescio

PORTUGUES, BARTOLOMEO. Actual pirate captain and character in ***Cup of Gold***.

"POSITANO" (1953). First appearing in *Harper's Bazaar* (May 1953), this essay was also reprinted with the same title in Salerno, Italy, in *Entre Provinciale Per Il Turismo* (1954). This travel article on the Italian seatown of Positano is a combination of personal experience, deft description, nutshell history, and fanciful anecdotes.

Further Reading: Steinbeck, John. "Positano" in *America and Americans and Selected Nonfiction*. Ed. Susan Shillinglaw and Jackson J. Benson. New York: Viking, 2002.

Eric Skipper

POUND, EZRA (1885–1972). Prominent American twentieth-century poet and critic, a major influence on modernist literature as a whole. Pound's theories about literature have influenced poets and writers alike, most notably **T. S. Eliot**, William Carlos Williams, and **Ernest Hemingway**. During World War II, Pound lived in Italy and broadcast Fascist propaganda over the radio in Rome. He was later tried for treason in the United States and was deemed unable to stand trial for his mental instability. He was then committed to a sanitarium (1946–58), from which countless literary and artistic figures tried to obtain his release. While sitting on a subcommittee of the People to People Program in 1956, Steinbeck had the occasion to disagree with a proposal to release Pound, citing the fact that this proposal might jeopardize the more important aims of the committee, one in particular being the admission of Hungarian refugees into the United States. Steinbeck, as **Jackson J. Benson** clarifies, "was not against freeing Pound; he simply thought it would outrage public opinion if they proposed it." **William Faulkner** won the day, however, and a joint subcommittee statement from Faulkner, Donald Hall, and Steinbeck recommended Pound's release. During the Vietnam War, left-wing critics, because of their politics rather than their aesthetics, compared Steinbeck's support of American soldiers fighting in the war to Ezra Pound's treasonous broadcasts during World War II.

Further Reading: Benson, Jackson J. *The True Adventures of John Steinbeck, Writer.* New York: Viking, 1984.

T. Adrian Lewis

PRACKLE, LIEUTENANT. In ***The Moon Is Down***, the first of a pair of young, idealistic officers who are the junior portion of **Colonel Lanser**'s five-man staff. Prackle is used to symbolize sentimental, inexperienced youth. Prackle carries a lock of hair in the back of his watch, makes pencil sketches of his friends, and dreams of seducing the sister of one of his comrades.

PRESIDENTIAL MEDAL OF FREEDOM. Along with the Congressional Gold Medal, this is the highest civilian award from the U.S. government. President **John Fitzgerald Kennedy** selected Steinbeck for the award, which was given to the author by President **Lyndon Baines Johnson** in 1964 after Kennedy's assassination.

PRIEST, THE. Along with the doctor and pearl buyers, the priest in ***The Pearl*** is also an instrument of oppression. His greed is evident as he gasps at the sight of the pearl and then implores the couple to remember God's goodness to them. It is only after the pearl is discovered that he is willing to marry **Kino** and **Juana**. It is also the priest who conspires in the oppression of Kino's people by urging them to remain in their station and not attempt to find a better market for their pearls.

Stephen K. George

"PRIMER OF THE 30s, A" (1960). A long article written for *Esquire* and published in June 1960. Steinbeck describes the 1930s as almost designed, beginning with a great economic collapse and ending with a great war. His disdain for President Herbert Hoover's ineptitude and his love for **Franklin Delano Roosevelt** is still palpable after thirty years. Steinbeck's personal memories seem a bit romantic, suggesting he was poorer than he was at the end of the 1920s (well-prepared for poverty), even though he describes in modest yet accurate detail how the money came rolling in after the publication of ***Tortilla Flat***. Steinbeck bookends the article with the folly of the stock traders in 1929 and the chilling prospects of contemporary traders still playing a kind of roulette in New York City.

Further Reading: Steinbeck, John. "A Primer of the 30s." In *America and Americans and Selected Nonfiction.* Ed. Susan Shillinglaw and Jackson J. Benson. New York: Viking Penguin, 2002.

PRITCHARD, BERNICE. In ***The Wayward Bus***, wife of **Elliott Pritchard** and mother of

Mildred Pritchard. The Pritchard family, bound for a Mexican vacation, are three of the travelers aboard "Sweetheart" (the bus) on the day of its eventful journey. She is described as "feminine and dainty" and smelling of the lavender toilet water she uses and a natural acidic odor of her own. Bernice is known in her social group for "goodness and sagacity." Yet this reputation is based not on virtues Steinbeck finds admirable, but rather on the result of her never venturing an opinion on any topic beyond perfume or cooking. Bernice's world is almost entirely one of surfaces and superficial relationships, although she rules her own family through guilt and manipulation and metes out her most severe punishment by forcing her husband Elliott and her daughter Mildred to endure the guilt engendered by her lapse into migraine headaches. Always the picture of perfect order and propriety, Bernice arouses anger through her smug and placidly manipulative manner. She is incapable of sexual pleasure, and she has slowly "strangled" her husband's natural sexual drive. Sex is the means by which her husband and daughter finally rebel against her ongoing manipulation, when Elliott sexually assaults her in a cave after the bus breaks down, and Mildred initiates a sexual liaison with **Juan Chicoy**, the bus driver. However, at least in the case of Elliott, it is suggested that his act will supply her with whatever reserves of guilt she will ever need to bend him to her wishes in the future. She leads a vapid, emotionally controlled, and sterile life, a strong counterpoint to the intellectually and sexually charged nature of the life her daughter Mildred experiences.

Christopher Busch and Bradd Burningham

PRITCHARD, ELLIOTT. In *The Wayward Bus*, the father of **Mildred Pritchard** and husband of **Bernice Pritchard**, Elliott is the epitome of the American businessman whom Steinbeck despises. Dressed in a gray suit ornamented with a lodge pin and a gold watch and key chain, Pritchard is the typical "company man." Steinbeck had little sympathy for the segment of American society that Mr. Pritchard seems to represent; in a novel in which none of the characters generates a great deal of sympathy, Mr. Pritchard is portrayed even more negatively than most of the others. He has dedicated his life to conforming to the expectations of his company and his fellow businessmen. He despises and fears anything foreign, politically radical, or different from the narrow conventionality his middle-class situation demands. He was a man who "had given up his freedom and then had forgotten what it was like." He is portrayed as both immoral and weak. For instance, he would steal **Ernest Horton**'s idea for a new product if he thought the theft would be cost-efficient, and the true nature of his proposal to the voluptuous **Camille Oaks** that she "work" for him is something she sees through in an instant. Though he has not yet entered the foreign territory of Mexico, his vacation trip's destination, Pritchard already finds himself in new and discomforting social, as well as geographic, territory. Accustomed to the "respectability" of the middle-class business world, he is embarrassed and a little frightened when **Alice Chicoy** brazenly refuses to serve breakfast in the Pritchards' room. Though hardly a sympathetic character, Pritchard arouses the reader's pity in his subjugation, particularly sexual, by his wife Bernice. This pity approaches revulsion when he forces himself on his wife in the cave near the novel's end in a desperate (though ultimately futile) attempt to express, if only for his own sake, a virile manliness. Pritchard will return from this trip firmly under his wife's control, a figure of diminished American manhood.

PRITCHARD, MILDRED. In *The Wayward Bus*, the twenty-one-year-old daughter of **Elliott** and **Bernice Pritchard**, Mildred Pritchard is an athletic, intelligent, and attractive young woman who is just beginning to experience the moral and emotional complexities of the adult world. She is on a vacation from college and, unlike her parents, has a sincere desire to see Mexico and experience adventure in other forms. Although Mildred is presented as strong willed, she is also still in an uncertain, formative stage of her life—intellectually, emotionally, and sexually. Her convictions are "strong" but "variable." Yet Mildred is also young and inexperienced, a condition emphasized by her extreme nearsightedness (a symbol of her limited knowledge of the world) and her ambivalence toward her parents. Mildred both loves her parents and finds their social views and personal idiosyncrasies revolting. During the bus trip three important events occur to Mildred. She recognizes her mother's convenient headaches for the manipulative device that they are and understands the cruel dimensions of her father's nature as a businessman. The second event is her sexual liaison with **Juan Chicoy**, which she initiates and consummates despite knowing there is no future with him beyond the moment. This experience provides Mildred with an insight into her own sexual desires—as distinct and separate from those of her partner—and adds to a self-knowledge that has gradually grown throughout the novel. Finally, Mildred begins to consider the situation of her gender, finding herself wondering about women's need to affect poses whenever men are present. She recognizes further the aged's fear of "smaller and smaller things." Mildred figures as a life symbol in the novel, in contrast to **Van Brunt**, the personification of death.

Christopher S. Busch and Bradd Burningham

"PROMISE, THE" (1937). The third story in ***The Red Pony*** cycle, it first appeared in *Harper's* (August 1937) and in *O. Henry Prize Stories of 1938*. Because of guilt feelings about the death of the red pony, **Jody Tiflin**'s father promises him a colt if he will take care of the mare **Nellie** during the long gestation period. Also filled with guilt feelings, **Billy Buck** has to kill the mare to deliver the colt when problems arise during the birthing. Buck makes the promise that he can deliver Jody a healthy colt, and he must pay a terrible price to make it so. "The Promise" is another of Steinbeck's tales that is a pointed reminder that human beings have a very limited control over larger, natural forces—one makes a promise against nature at one's peril.

PRYOR, CHARLEY, AND SON TOM. The two who discover the body of **Danny Taylor** near the end of ***The Winter of Our Discontent***.

PULASKI, MIKE. A former Army buddy of **Ethan Allen Hawley** in ***The Winter of Our Discontent***, Mike gives Ethan a formula for putting things out of one's mind when they become troublesome.

PULITZER PRIZE. Won by Steinbeck in 1940 for his 1939 novel, ***The Grapes of Wrath***. Later Steinbeck wrote friend **Joseph Henry Jackson** that he was pleased and flattered that he was chosen for the fiction award in a year when **Carl Sandburg** and **William Saroyan** were honored for poetry and drama respectively. Calling these two "good company," Steinbeck was delighted with the honor but gave away the monetary award to his friend **Ritchie Lovejoy** so that Lovejoy could take time off from his regular job and finish a novel.

Further Reading: Steinbeck, John. *A Life in Letters*. Ed. Elaine Steinbeck and Robert Wallsten. New York: Viking, 1975.

Michael J. Meyer

PUNK KID, THE. In ***The Wayward Bus***, the window washer for the Greyhound Bus Company. He had observed **George** the swamper find a passenger's wallet containing two fifty-dollar bills, which prevented George from keeping the money for himself. The kid discusses the encounter with a second swamper who appears only briefly in the novel.

PURTY (PRETTY) BOY FLOYD (1904–1934). *See* **Floyd, Purty Boy**.

PUSHKIN, ALEKSANDER (1799–1837). Russian author commonly regarded as the father of modern Russian literature. Steinbeck noted in a letter that he went through Pushkin's work "in a maniacal period" during the summer of 1924. In ***America and Americans***, Steinbeck's deep respect for Pushkin is made clear. He praises Pushkin's ability to represent his particular cultural paradigm through language, stating "I do know that if I had only read Russian history I could not have had the access to Russian thinking I have had from reading . . . Pushkin."

Further Reading: Steinbeck, John. *America and Americans*. New York: Viking, 1966.

Gregory Hill, Jr.

PYLE, ERNIE (1900–1945). **Pulitzer Prize**–winning journalist and arguably the most famous American war correspondent of World War II, Ernest Taylor Pyle wrote on-the-ground stories about American GIs that endeared him to the war-weary nation. Tragically, he died in April 1945 from sniper fire on the island of Ie Shima, off Okinawa, not long before the end of the war. Steinbeck, who knew and admired Pyle, approached his own work as a war correspondent as Pyle did: from the soldier's level rather than the large and perhaps more antiseptic view of generals and politicians.

Further Reading: Benson, Jackson J. *The True Adventures of John Steinbeck, Writer*. New York: Viking, 1984; Steinbeck, John. *Once There Was a War*. New York: Viking, 1958.

PYNNEL, SIR. In *The Acts of King Arthur*, unhorsed by **Gryfflet** at Bedgrayne.

Q

QUAID, RANDY (1953–). Hulking actor who gave an effective performance as **Lennie Small** in the 1981 television version of *Of Mice and Men.*

QUINN, ANTHONY (1915–2001). American actor of Irish/Mexican descent who played **Emiliano**'s brother **Eufemio** in the 1952 production of *Viva Zapata!*, directed by **Elia Kazan** with a screenplay by John Steinbeck. Quinn won the Academy Award for best supporting actor for this role.

QUINN, HORACE. Deputy Sheriff in King City who investigates the shooting of **Adam Trask** and the disappearance of his wife, **Cathy Trask**, in *East of Eden*. Later, at **Will Hamilton**'s suggestion, Horace runs for sheriff of **Monterey** County and serves from 1903 to 1919. After **Kate Albey**'s suicide, he burns obscene pictures of prominent **Salinas** residents, which she had used for blackmail purposes. He visits Adam to tell him of her death and urges him to tell his son, **Aron Trask**, that she had willed all her money to him.

QUIXOTE, DON. *See* **Cervantes, Miguel de; Don Keehan.**

R

RAGGED MAN. In ***The Grapes of Wrath***, met by the **Joads** in chapter 16 as they stop at a roadside camp. The ragged man is one of the first who destroys the fantasy of California as Eden when he tells the Joads he has been there and is on his way back, preferring to starve at home with friends than be ignored and abused by strangers.

"RAID, THE" (1934). Set in a nameless California town, and opening with two men striding down its streets, this Steinbeck short story (first published in the *North American Review* in 1934) presents yet another aspect of the lives of workers of the 1930s, one that would echo through ***In Dubious Battle*** and form the core of ***The Grapes of Wrath***. "The Raid" appears in ***The Long Valley***, just after **"Breakfast,"** and focuses on two men known only as Dick, an experienced Communist Party member and strike organizer, and **Root**, his young apprentice. Numerous critics have identified their similarity to **Jim Nolan** and **Mac** in *In Dubious Battle*. According to **Jackson J. Benson**, "The Raid" was written after the Imperial Valley strike, an unusually violent one that resulted in party leaders being beaten, kidnapped, and killed. Despite the violence near the end of the story, "The Raid" is more memorable for the dialogue between Dick and Root and the way it reveals Party policy, the motivations behind the two men's commitment, and the subtle exploration of courage as Root worries about whether he will stand his ground or run if violence occurs. Steinbeck also injects a palpable tension into the story when the two men prepare for their meeting in an old, deserted store as the minutes tick by. The only worker to appear—a nameless man wearing a painter's cap—warns them that someone has betrayed them and that a raiding party is on its way. Dick begins by speaking harshly to Root, telling him that if he performs poorly, Dick will report him to Party officials. His attitude toward Root moves from one of impatience with Root's inexperience and arrogance about his own position to one of sympathetic support and advice for Root as they learn they will indeed be attacked.

Despite his nervousness over being in charge of his first meeting with workers, Root is clearly a committed and talented young man. During the course of his dialogue with Dick, he talks about his own father, a railroad brakeman, who had evicted him from the house after learning that Root had become a Communist. Root is upset about his father's failure to understand his belief in and support of the Party's goals. His father fears for his job, Root explains, and simply refuses to see the truth that burns so clearly for Root. Dick, ever alert for the cause, replies that Root should save the good lines for his speech. Root's bravery in facing up to the raiding party seems convincing, because his fear is so palpable. He is utterly terrified throughout the first three sections of the story as they wait for the black-hearted men who, when they finally arrive, carry sticks and clubs in their hands. After someone hits Root on the side of his head with a two-by-four, the bleeding young man loses all fear and rises to his feet with passionate eloquence, asking the men to understand that he and the other Party members want to improve conditions for all workers, including those who hit him.

The full impact of the religious analogy that has been building during the raid occurs when Root, his face and head swathed in bandages, awakens next to Dick in a hospital jail cell. Dick, who has suffered a broken arm and several broken ribs, praises Root for his bravery and confesses that he had doubted whether the young man could survive the terrible blows he had sustained. When Root tries to explain the compassionate way he feels about the men who hit him, he recalls the words of Christ at the crucifixion ("Forgive them because they don't know what they're doing"), but Dick sternly reminds him that "religion is the opium of the people" and that Root should stay away from it. Ironically, despite the Communist rejection of Christianity, both Dick and Root have behaved very much like Christians: refusing to condemn their attackers, they stand up courageously against anti-Communist bias and violence, even though they each face a six-month jail sentence. Root's views are precursors to those of **Jim Casy** and **Tom Joad** in *The Grapes of Wrath*.

Further Reading: Benson, Jackson J. *The True Adventures of John Steinbeck, Writer*. New York: Viking, 1984; Hughes, Richard S. *John Steinbeck: A Study of the Short Fiction*. Boston: Twayne, 1989. Lisca, Peter. "'The Raid' and *In Dubious Battle." A Study Guide to Steinbeck's* The Long Valley. Ed. Tetsumaro Hayashi and Reloy Garcia. Ann Arbor, MI: Pierian, 1976.

Abby H. P. Werlock

RALPH. House pimp at **Kate Albey**'s brothel in ***East of Eden***. After **Samuel Hamilton**'s funeral, **Adam Trask** visits Kate for the first time since she shot and left him years before. When he rebuffs her advances, she screams, bringing Ralph, who punches Adam and knocks him to the floor but refuses to kick him, despite Kate's order to do so.

RALPH, TITO. In ***Tortilla Flat***, the last of the paisanos to join **Danny** in his inherited house. Tito is a jailer who, as **Johnny Pom-pom** tells us, has one major weakness: when he drinks wine, he forgets he is a jailer and leaves his post, often escaping along with his prisoners. This is just what happens at the beginning of the novel, when Danny lands in jail after his return from the army. Tito shares two gallons of wine with his prisoner, and when they are finished, they go out together for more wine. Danny escapes into the forest, and Tito returns to the jail to report the escape. Later, when Danny trades all his possessions for wine and goes on one final binge, he lands in jail again, and again he escapes with the help of his drunken jailer. This time Tito is fired and, after smashing a window in frustration, is jailed himself. But since he still has the keys to his cell, he escapes and returns with Danny to join the other paisanos, remaining with them until the end. The ineffectual jailer is a sign of the refreshing lack of discipline in the life of *Tortilla Flat*, but he also represents the dialectic of freedom and responsibility that increasingly determines Danny's fate as the novel concludes.

Bryan Vescio

RAMIREZ, DOLORES ENGRACIA ("SWEETS"). In ***Tortilla Flat***, a paisana housekeeper who temporarily "sucks" **Danny** in, with the help of a vacuum cleaner. Although she isn't especially pretty and has a sour disposition, she has earned the nickname Sweets because of certain seductive qualities of voice and movement. When Sweets hears of Danny's inheritance, she seduces him, and he buys her a vacuum cleaner as a present. Although there is no electricity in Tortilla Flat, the present makes Sweets the talk of the town, and she pushes the machine around for visitors, while producing a hum with her own voice, a hum that echoes her seductive growl. In the meantime, Danny is suffering from the less attractive aspects of Sweets's personality, and his friends come to the rescue. They convince Danny to take the vacuum cleaner back and trade it for wine, on the grounds that her having the vacuum cleaner will only cause Sweets to demand more from him, including the wiring to make it work. This has the intended effect of ending the relationship, which suits Danny just fine. The affair between Danny and Sweets in another example of the way the false value of property transforms natural, sexual relationships into alienating commercial transactions.

Bryan Vescio

RANDALL, EMMA. In **"The Harness"** she is the wife of **Peter** and daughter of a respected Mason. Through severe discipline, she manages to shape her husband into one of the most successful and respected men in **Monterey** County. In return for his exemplary behavior fifty-one weeks of the year, she turns a blind eye to his annual week of debauchery in San Francisco. The effect of his behavior is not without consequences, however: each year when Peter returns from San Francisco, Emma becomes a bedridden invalid for several weeks. At age forty-five, already looking far older than her years, she becomes more seriously ill than usual and dies. If Peter's behavior eventually wears her down, her effect on Peter remains profound, even in death.

Abby H. P. Werlock

RANDALL, PETER. Repressed protagonist and husband of **Emma** in **"The Harness,"** who acts as his conscience. Although the common reaction to him is to see him as the henpecked husband, he may additionally be viewed as schizophrenic—a respected man of the community for most of the year, and a sensual lover of drink, women, and beauty for the one remaining week. Emma's death does not eliminate the conscious sense of morality that normally overrides his sensual self. He continues his split-identity behavior even after she is gone, behaving responsibly most of the year and then indulging in his annual, if brief, San Francisco binge.

Abby H. P. Werlock

RANDOLPH, WILLIAM. In ***Sweet Thursday***, the engineer, fireman, and president of the Hediondo Cannery who adapted the front end of a locomotive for use as a boiler. Years later, when the boiler required frequent maintenance, he consigned it to the vacant lot between the **Bear Flag** and **Lee Chong's grocery**, where it became the home of first the **Malloys** and then **Suzy**.

"RANDOM THOUGHTS ON RANDOM DOGS" (1955) Originally published in the *Saturday Review* (October 8, 1955), Steinbeck observes in this essay how the role of dogs in society has changed over the years. Once they were functional, but now "many dogs are used as decorations" and "by far the greatest number are a sop for loneliness." He reflects on a dog he once owned, T-Dog, a seer who wandered off into the world and became a missionary. He describes whimsically his ideal dog, a white English bull terrier, and wonders if he still exists.

Further Reading: Steinbeck, John. "Random Thoughts on Random Dogs." In *America and Americans and Selected Nonfiction*. Ed. Susan Shillinglaw and Jackson J. Benson. New York: Viking, 2002.

Eric Skipper

RANTINI. Swiss-Italian who rents **Adam Trask**'s ranch when the Trasks move to **Salinas** in ***East of Eden***. Later, he contracts out his bean crops to **Will Hamilton** and **Cal Trask.**

"RATIONALE" (1957). Published in *Steinbeck and His Critics*, this essay responds to a university's request for a rationale on why Steinbeck wrote his books: "My basic rationale might be that I like to write. I feel good when I am doing it—better than when I am not." He explains that a writer performs his craft out of hopes for love and acceptance, as a technique for communication, and as a stimulus. But most of all he does it because he enjoys it."

Further Reading: Steinbeck, John. "Rationale." In *America and Americans and Selected Nonfiction*. Ed. Susan Shillinglaw and Jackson J. Benson. New York: Viking, 2002.

Eric Skipper

RATTLESNAKE CLUB. A group of **Salinas** men who, in conducting a memorial meeting for dead members, procure the services of the entire staff of the **Bear Flag** restaurant for a reduced group rate. In ***Sweet Thursday***, their behavior becomes tiresome for the prostitutes, with their songs of Sigma Chi, stories about their children, and practical jokes with a rubber lizard. While **Suzy** wishes there were more dead members, **Fauna** is glad to count among her clientele such solid citizens, who have their fun without damaging her house. This incident is another example of the joy Steinbeck took in ridiculing the middle class—in this case, men of influence in his former hometown of Salinas.

Bruce Ouderkirk

RATZ, MRS. Married to **Timothy Ratz**, Mrs. Ratz is the landlady of the dismal house where the narrator boards in **"Johnny Bear."**

RATZ, TIMOTHY. Husband of **Mrs. Ratz**, the narrator's landlady in **"Johnny Bear."** Timothy, a minor character, functions a bit like a Greek chorus without the voice: he never speaks but is always present in the Buffalo Bar, playing solitaire and cheating at it if necessary, since he treats himself to a shot of whiskey whenever he wins.

RAWLEY, JIM. *See* **Central Committee at Weedpatch Camp.**

RAYNOLD, SIR. In ***The Acts of King Arthur***, he challenges **Sir Lancelot**, who is wearing the armor and bearing the device of **Sir Kay**. Raynold is beaten by Kay and is sent to the court to submit to **Guinevere** as one of Sir Kay's prizes.

"REALITY AND ILLUSION" (1954). Published in *Punch* (227:5958, November 17, 1954, 616–17) and written while John and his wife **Elaine Scott Steinbeck** were living in France, this piece concerns the author's knowledge of the "real" Paris. Steinbeck acknowledges that he has walked the city and sat in local cafés, but he also knows these actions fail to capture the city's essence according to its residents. In his own mind, however, Steinbeck is sure he knows the city well, and he decides to defend his definition rather than to accept local criticism.

Michael J. Meyer

REBEL CORNERS. In ***The Wayward Bus***, site of bus stop/café/garage operated by **Juan** and **Alice Chicoy**. Named in 1862, as a result of the **Blanken** family's decision to secede with 160 acres and their blacksmith shop in order to join the Confederacy during the Civil War. Rebel Corners is lost by foreclosure to the First National Bank of **San Ysidro** following the war. Steinbeck describes it as an "island," from which the bus departs to **San Juan de la Cruz**.

RED. In ***The Wayward Bus***, a bus driver for the Red Arrow line, a jokester whose company **Alice Chicoy** enjoys. She fantasizes about him as she drinks following **Juan Chicoy's** departure for **San Juan de la Cruz**.

RED PONY, THE **(BOOK)** (1933–1936). The stories appeared as individual pieces in 1933–1936, in a 1937 limited edition (first three stories), as part of ***The Long Valley***, in 1945 as an illustrated book, and in 1949 as a movie script. What has come to be known as the novelette *The Red Pony* grew organically from a short story Steinbeck began writing early in 1933. He first called it the "pony story," seeing it as an experiment in telling a story "as though it came out of the boy's mind although there is no going into the boy's mind." The project eventually grew into four stories. The first two were published in the *North American Review* in November and December of 1933. The next two were written shortly thereafter, and one was published in *Harper's* magazine. Few story cycles were ever written under more difficult circumstances, so it is not surprising that the theme of dealing with death permeates the novelette. In early 1933, Steinbeck had moved back to his boyhood home to care for his mother, felled by a massive stroke that left her paralyzed. As John, the son, dealt with the impending loss of his mother, Steinbeck, the author, created a young boy named **Jody** who also goes through the initiating experiences of death. In two cases it is the death of horses, his pony **Gabilan** and the horse **Nellie**; concurrently, Jody touches the lives of two old men in their twilight years—the mysterious stranger **Gitano** and Jody's **grandfather**, who had once been a "leader of the people." Writing about his work many years later, Steinbeck explained that *The Red Pony* was an attempt to respond to the child's question, why, when first experiencing death. It charts the process to adulthood, which moves from loss to acceptance to growth and understanding.

The first story, **"The Gift,"** begins in the early fall of Jody Tiflin's tenth year. Steinbeck signals that this will be a realistic depiction of farm life in the first scene, which includes a detailed and graphic description of **Billy Buck**, the farmhand, clearing his nostrils, currying the horses, and responding to the ringing triangle that announces breakfast. After breakfast, Jody's father and Billy Buck leave, and Jody, after some time spent walking about the farm, is inspected and sent off to school. When he returns, his mother reprimands him for not filling the woodbox properly, and he goes out to do his chores. When the men return, with the smell of brandy on their breaths, Jody senses that something is up, but he does not have any hint of what. The next morning Jody finds, to his great delight, that his father has bought him a pony. He names the pony Gabilan, after the western mountain range and promises to look out for the horse and break him right. Having the responsibility for Gabilan brings Jody a number of new feelings. He rises early to see his pet, creates worrisome fantasies about losing him, and learns a great deal about horses from Billy Buck, who is a consummate instructor. Unfortunately, disaster strikes one day before Gabilan has grown sufficiently to be ridden. Although Jody has been careful to keep Gabilan from getting wet, and has fears about what might happen to the pony in the rain, one day toward Thanksgiving Jody hesitantly leaves Gabilan in the corral when he goes to school. Billy Buck assures Jody that it will not rain and promises to put the horse in if it does. But, for once, the usually infallible farmhand is wrong about the weather and is not available to put the horse in the barn when it does rain. Jody returns to find a wet and miserable horse, soon suffering from a cold that suddenly turns lethal. The narration follows the gruesome details of the pony's illness as Billy Buck and Jody try to save it. Jody sleeps in the barn to be near Gabilan, but awakens to find the barn door open and the pony gone. Following the tracks, he finds the red pony in its death throes as buzzards circle around it. He plunges toward Gabilan to protect him but is not in time to prevent a buzzard from plucking out one of the pony's eyes. In frustration and anger, Jody kills the bird, beating its head to a pulp. **Carl Tiflin**'s patient explanation to his son that it was not the buzzard that killed the pony arouses Billy Buck's anger. The story ends with his furious statement to his boss: "Jesus Christ! Man, can't you see how he'd feel about it?"

R. S. Hughes reads this first story as beginning Jody's initiation into adulthood by teaching him three lessons: "human beings are fallible; nature is uncaring and indifferent; and nature's immutable law for all earthly creatures is death." On another level, according to Thom Tammaro, the story is about "a child's acquisition of responsibility, industry, and independence, and his coming to understand the matrices of society by achieving and feeling a sense of accomplishment through succeeding in tasks assigned." Tammaro uses Erik Erikson's theory about the eight stages of life as a theoretical basis for his reading of Jody's development in this story.

The next story, **"The Great Mountains,"** takes place in the summer. One might assume this is the summer after Gabilan's death, but there are no clear time markers in the story. Jody is listless, taking out his boredom by playing cruel tricks on his dog, Doubletree Mutt, and killing birds. He broods about the dark mountains to the west of the farm, questioning his father, his mother, and Billy Buck, but getting little information, which "made the mountains dear to him, and terrible." **Roy Simmonds** notes that the "romantic mysticism" of the mountains in this story is sometimes seen as a contrast to the realistic nature of the other stories in the cycle. One day, a lean old man comes down the road from **Salinas**, explaining that he is Gitano and that he has come back to the place of his birth, where he plans to stay until he dies. The old man is a paisano, the term used in Steinbeck's time to identify people who were descended from the Spanish or Mexican early settlers of California. Carl Tiflin behaves callously toward Gitano because he cannot afford to feed and maintain the old man. On the other hand, the old man, as mysterious as the mountains, intrigues Jody. Following him to the bunkhouse one night, Jody sees him unwrap a rapier with an intricately carved, golden-basket hilt. Gitano tells Jody that he got the rapier from his father, but he does not know its origin. The next morning, Gitano and **Old Easter**, one of the decrepit ranch horses, are gone, leaving Jody with a sense of longing.

Several key themes resonate in this story. One is the issue of the treatment of those who are too old to work. Within that theme, Gitano and Old Easter are linked. Both have served well in their day, but both are too old to work any longer. In a heated exchange between Carl Tiflin and Billy Buck, Billy defends Gitano and all old paisanos. There is also the underlying issue of Gitano's right to be on the land of his fathers, the rapier serving as a possible link to a past when it was his people who owned the land where the Tiflins' ranch now stands. Several critics have written about the significance of Gitano as an Arthurian figure, who, like King **Arthur**, disappears toward the west, noting that in Steinbeck's personal mythology, there exists a mystical and romantic westward questing of mankind.

In **"The Promise,"** Steinbeck turns from a brooding tale of impending death to a tale of conception, gestation, birth, and violent death. The season is spring, perhaps a year following the summer arrival and departure of Gitano. Jody is in school, and the narrator presents an amusing description of his boyish antics. He marches home at the head of a silent but deadly phantom army, which disappears when Jody's attention is turned toward a horny-toad that he promptly catches and deposits in his lunch pail. Turning from head of the army to stealthy hunter, Jody captures such game as lizards, a snake, grasshoppers, and a newt. Steinbeck is particularly effective in evoking the imaginations and antics of children. His rendition of Jody's Walter Mitty-like fantasies about riding Black Demon to help the sheriff, about winning roping contests, and about helping the president catch a bandit in Washington add to the full characterization of the boy's personality. The promise of the title is multidimensional. First, there is the promise of new life as **Nellie** is bred and Jody awaits the birth of her colt. Next, there are the promises Jody must make to his father about working over the summer to pay for the stud fee and about caring for **Nellie** and raising the colt. Finally, there is the promise Billy Buck makes to Jody that he will get him a good colt. In that promise rests the memory of the death of the other pony. The narration follows Jody through the summer and fall and into the following winter, as he cares for **Nellie** and anticipates the birth of the colt. Impatience and anxiety are the dominant moods, with foreshadowing of possible problems. In a grisly birthing scene, Billy Buck finds that the only way to save the colt is to kill **Nellie**, which he does by smashing her skull. He tears the colt out of the stomach with a knife, sawing and ripping at the tough belly. Finally, Billy Buck takes the colt and walks slowly over and lays it in the straw at Jody's feet, saying, "There's your colt, the way I promised." The story is among Steinbeck's most effective pieces of short fiction, an assessment reinforced by the fact that it was included in the *O. Henry Memorial Award: Prize Stories of 1938*.

"The Leader of the People" returns the cycle of stories to the twilight years of old men. It is March, and Jody is planning a mouse hunt. Billy Buck is finishing raking away the last of a haystack, which has provided a home and some security for the mice throughout the winter. The symbol of the mouse hunt is important later in the story, when **Grandfather** questions the quality of the new generation of people and compares the unequal mouse hunt to the troops "hunting Indians and shooting children and burning teepees." **Mrs. Tiflin**'s father has come for a visit, a visit dreaded by Mr. Tiflin, who has little patience with Grandfather's insistence on repeating the same old stories about Indians and crossing the plains, about "westering," as he calls it. Jody's mother tries to elicit her husband's understanding by explaining, "That was the big thing in my father's life. He led a wagon train clear across the plains to the coast, and when it was finished, his life was done." Jody, who loves the stories, is excited about his grandfather's visit. Tension builds during a dinner scene where Carl Tiflin is barely civil while Grandfather recounts his stories and Billy Buck, whom Grandfather acknowledges as one of the few men in the new generation who hasn't gone soft, is respectful. Jody, however, is interested. The strained relationship between Mr. and Mrs. Tiflin comes to a head the next morning at breakfast when Grandfather overhears Carl Tiflin complaining about how no one wants to hear the stories again and again. In the final scene of the novel, Grandfather acknowledges the fact that "westering has died out of the people. . . . It's all done. . . . It is finished." It is a scene of acceptance by the old man, but it also provides an opportunity for Jody to illustrate his developing maturity and compassion. This he does by choosing to be with his grandfather rather than hunt mice. Jody tries to comfort the old man by offering to make him some lemonade. Mimi R. Gladstein explains that Mrs. Tiflin, who thinks Jody is just finding an excuse to have some lemonade, "begins to understand the significance of his (Jody's) actions," which is evident by her stopping suddenly and saying softly, "Here I'll reach the squeezer down to you."

Individually and as a whole, *The Red Pony* stories are jewels of narrative craft. John H. Timmerman notes the "richness of narrative texture and theme" and the "belying simplicity of tone and point of view." Howard Levant calls it a "completely successful instance of the organic relationship between structure and materials." Louis Owens, on the other hand, disagrees with most of the critics who see the novella as a *bildungsroman* and who chart the development in Jody's maturity through them. He claims that in the last story, "Jody has demonstrated no greater sensitivity to the value of life than he had in the first story."

Further Reading: French, Warren. *John Steinbeck*. Boston: Twayne Publishers, 1989; Gladstein, Mimi R. "'The Leader of the People': A Boy Becomes a Mensch." In *Steinbeck's* The Red Pony: *Essays in Criticism*. Ed. Tetsumaro Hayashi and Thomas J. Moore. Steinbeck Monograph Series, No. 13, 1988; Hughes, R. S. *John Steinbeck: A Study of the Short Fiction*. Boston: Twayne Publishers, 1989; Levant, Howard. "John Steinbeck's *The Red Pony:* A Study in Narrative Technique." In *The Short Novels of John Steinbeck*. Ed. Jackson J. Benson. Durham, NC: Duke University Press, 1990; Owens, Louis. *John Steinbeck's Re-Vision of America*. Athens: University of Georgia Press, 1985; Tammaro, Thomas M. "Erik Erikson Meets John Steinbeck: Psycho-social Development in 'The Gift.'" In *Steinbeck's* The

Red Pony: *Essays in Criticism*. Ed. Tetsumaro Hayashi and Thomas J. Moore. Steinbeck Monograph Series, No, 13, 1988; Timmerman, John H. *The Dramatic Landscape of John Steinbeck's Short Stories*, Norman: University of Oklahoma Press, 1990.

Mimi Reisel Gladstein

RED PONY, THE **(FILM AND TELEVISION VERSIONS)** (1949, 1973). John Steinbeck's classic short story sequence, ***The Red Pony***, began early in his writing career, with the first two sections appearing shortly after they were written in November and December 1933; the third section, although evidently written at the same time as the first two, was not published until May 1937. The fourth and final section, written some years after the first three, appeared abroad in August 1936, and all four were brought together in ***The Long Valley***, which was published in September 1938. A separate illustrated edition under the title *The Red Pony* also appeared in 1945. **Lewis Milestone**, the director of the film ***Of Mice and Men*** (1939), discussed a screen version with Steinbeck as early as 1940, and a partial screenplay was written in 1941; wartime complications kept both men from working on the project until 1947 when they entered into a business partnership. Although aided by a capable cast and production team, Milestone and Steinbeck did not achieve the artistic success of their earlier adaptation, even with Steinbeck writing his own screenplay. *The Red Pony* was released to an indifferent critical and popular reaction in 1949.

Steinbeck's story sequence presented considerable possibilities for film, as it carefully balances naturalistic realism and archetypal symbolism in showing a young boy initiated into the complexities of both nature and culture. The original narrative is elliptical and symbolic in its presentation, however, and when Steinbeck connected and clarified these elements in a straightforward plot line, a great deal of complexity was lost. In particular, a conventional happy ending confirms the Hollywood direction of the movie, also seen in the casting. Robert Mitchum played **Billy Buck**, and Peter Miles, as Steinbeck's autobiographical protagonist, proves inadequate to his part; the rest of the veteran cast is adequate if uninspired. Perhaps the most memorable feature of the entire project remains Aaron Copland's fine score, which, like his music for *Of Mice and Men*, became a concert favorite.

An even less-interesting television-movie adaptation was first broadcast on March 18, 1973, under the direction of Robert Totten. Although it featured more distinguished casting, notably the aging **Henry Fonda** and Maureen O'Hara as young Clint Howard's parents, the scripting is simplified even more by leaving Billy Buck out entirely, and this production lacks the lyric touch of Milestone or Copland. Newer productions have been announced, but none has appeared.

Further Reading: French, Warren. "*The Red Pony* as Story Cycle and Film." In *The Short Novels of John Steinbeck*. Ed. Jackson J. Benson. Durham, NC: Duke University Press, 1990; Millichap, Joseph R. *Steinbeck and Film*. New York: Ungar, 1983; Steinbeck, John. *The Red Pony*. New York: Viking, 1945.

Joseph Millichap

RED SAINT, THE (LA SANTA ROJA). In ***Cup of Gold***, her real name is **Ysobel Espinoza**, but she is known as the Red Saint and is reputed to be the most desirable woman in the world, comparable to Helen of Troy. When **Henry Morgan** finally finds her, he discovers that she is not the woman he has dreamed of, and for whom he has sacked Panama. He returns her to her husband in exchange for a ransom.

"REFLECTIONS ON A LUNAR ECLIPSE" (1963). Appearing in *The New York Herald Tribune*'s Book Week on October 6, 1963, this article was a memoir about the composition of ***The Moon Is Down***, composed after Steinbeck received a mimeographed copy of *Maanen er Skjult*, a Danish translation of the novel. The author relates his personal efforts to stem the tide of war, including his membership in the Writers' War Board and in The Office of War Information.

Fascinated by the resistance movements in occupied Europe, Steinbeck describes his initial intent to set the novel in America, hoping to make it a blueprint that set forth what might be expected if America were invaded and what its citizens might need to do should that happen. After submitting an initial draft to his superiors in the government, Steinbeck was stunned when the War Office labeled the work counterproductive, suggesting that it implied that America might somehow be defeated by the Axis powers. Although he disagreed with that assessment, Steinbeck obeyed the order to abandon his work. Later, however, encouraged by friends overseas, he decided to resurrect it, setting it in an anonymous country rather than in America.

According to Steinbeck, this change involved combining the national characteristics of the people of Denmark, Norway, and France and led to the eventual publication under the title *The Moon Is Down*. Unfortunately, the early criticism returned, but this time it centered on Steinbeck's portrayal of the invading army as "too human," capable of pain and folly and errors just like those they sought to subdue. In defense of a novel that wartime critics labeled as "unrealistic optimism" and "dangerous romanticism," Steinbeck closes his reminiscence by recounting the work's positive influence on nations under severe pressure to submit to Nazi orders and reminds readers twenty years later of the courageous actions that such "propaganda" inspired.

Further Reading: Steinbeck, John. "Reflections on a Lunar Eclipse." *New York Sunday Herald Tribune*, 6 October 1963, *Book Week*: 3.

Michael J. Meyer

"REPENT." In *The Wayward Bus*, word painted in now-faded black lettering on a cliff above the ditch where the bus mires. The passengers seek shelter from the rain in a cave directly below this admonition. The characters seem to live without regard to God or faith. On a bus whose bumper once read *"el Gran Poder de Jesus"* but is now called simply "Sweetheart," the riders find solace not in repentance or in a return to God, but in sex and pies.

"REPORT ON AMERICA" (1955). Humorous, wondering article published in *Punch* (June 22) ranging from wartime anecdotes illustrating British understatement to a discussion of a squirrel that vandalized President Dwight Eisenhower's putting green on the White House lawn. Steinbeck implies that Americans and their news services are preoccupied with trivial matters.

Scott Simkins

"REUNION AT THE QUIET HOTEL" (1958). Short story that originally appeared in a London newspaper, the *Evening Standard*, on January 25, 1958. In it, the narrator, a war correspondent, reminisces about his return to London with his wife six years after World War II. The setting is a small but well-known hotel where the narrator had been quartered during the war. Although his wife considers it a moth-eaten dump and wishes they would have stayed at a more upscale hotel, the narrator (presumably modeled on Steinbeck himself) sees the hotel differently, describing the decor as stately and grand. The narrator has nostalgic memories about his previous stay, memories he hopes to share with the familiar faces who still remain on the hotel's staff. After enduring complaints from his wife about the room, the weather, and the food, the narrator decides to placate her by taking her out to Soho for some Armenian food. The story ends abruptly when the couple, upon returning from their meal, discover that the hotel is no longer there. Instead they find a hole filled with rubble, leaving the reader to conclude that the hotel was probably the victim of the Luftwaffe's blitzkrieg years before. The reunion described on the previous pages may have been just the narrator's imagination, yet he remains puzzled and is worried about what has happened to their luggage and passports. Concerned that these events are too strange to be believable and not wanting to be ridiculed, the narrator fails to tell the story to the police and, when he reports the loss of the passports, simply tells the embassy they have been stolen.

Further Reading: Steinbeck, John. "Reunion at the Quiet Hotel." In *Uncollected Stories of John Steinbeck*. Ed. Nakayama, Kiyoshi. Tokyo: Nan'un-do, 1986.

Michael J. Meyer

RHYS (SQUIRE). Writer of the letter informing **Sir Edward Morgan** of **Robert Morgan**'s odd behavior after the death of his wife in ***Cup of Gold***. Also, probably a relative of the poet from the House of Rhys, whose political influence saw him preferred to **Merlin**.

RICHARD III. Tragedy/history play by **William Shakespeare** that follows the rise and fall of the Yorkist dynasty during The War of The Roses. Of particular interest in the play is Shakespeare's depiction of Richard's questionable ascent to the throne, through machinations and the ruthless murders of those who stand in his way. His Machiavellian villainy causes the death of many characters, including the deaths of his own brother and nephews. The title of Steinbeck's final novel, ***The Winter of Our Discontent***, was taken from the title character's opening soliloquy: "Now is the winter of our discontent/Made glorious summer by this sun of York." Similar to the Yorkists' discontent at the Lancastrian rule, *Winter*'s protagonist, **Ethan Allen Hawley**, is shown to be dissatisfied with his status in the New England village of New Baytown. Like Richard, this discontent leads to a willingness to sacrifice his moral code and even human life in order to increase his own status and assure his financial success. Critics have also noted the parallels between the crafty manipulations of the Yorkist Richard and "Tricky Dick," since Richard Nixon was the Republican candidate for president of the United States as the novel was being completed. Nixon's battle for the presidency with **John F. Kennedy** is no doubt reflected in the novel's examination of the battle between evil and good to attain political power. Moreover, the political intrigue and corruption depicted in *Winter* are shown to be unworthy of the proud American Revolutionary heritage as well as unrepresentative of America's moral and religious beliefs, essential elements in the founding of the country.

Michael J. Meyer

RICKETTS, EDWARD F. (1897–1948). Edward Flanders Robb Ricketts, arguably John Steinbeck's closest friend from 1930 to 1948, had an unparalleled influence on the author. Ricketts was a scientist/biologist by trade, who wanted to be a writer, and Steinbeck was a writer by trade, who, for a time, wanted to be a scientist/biologist—theirs was a natural friendship and exchange of ideas that allowed Steinbeck to produce much of his best work. Steinbeck's various **Doc** characters are fictional avatars of Ricketts. Katherine A. Rodger's biographical essay is a highly readable and useful portrait of his life, while Steinbeck's somewhat fictionalized account in **"About Ed Ricketts"** makes clear the author's high regard for his friend. A fine assessment of Ricketts' work and writing may be found in Eric Enno Tamm's *Beyond The Outer Shores*, and the classic assessment of the literary relationship between Steinbeck and Ricketts is **Richard Astro**'s *John Steinbeck and Edward F. Ricketts: The Shaping of a Novelist*.

Ricketts was born in Chicago on May 14, 1897, to Abbott Ricketts and Alice Beverly Flanders Ricketts. He was the older brother of sister Frances, born in 1899, and of brother Thayer, born in 1902. As early as six years old, Ricketts became interested in zoology. In public school, he proved to be an excellent student who got along well with his teachers and peers; he enjoyed the poetry of Keats, **Robinson Jeffers**, and **Whitman**. In the 1915–16 academic year, he attended Illinois State Normal University but left to travel the country and work such odd jobs as bookkeeper or surveyor's assistant. Drafted in 1917, he worked as a clerk for the medical corps at Camp Grant in Illinois and accepted but did not necessarily enjoy his brief military stint. After the armistice, he was discharged in March 1919. That year, he began his studies at the University of Chicago, and although he earned good grades, he interrupted his academic career for a long walk through the country. He traveled on foot from Indiana all the way to Florida (Steinbeck describes a similar trek made by his fictional Doc character in ***Cannery Row***). Back at the University of Chicago in 1921, Ricketts was influenced by the work of **W. C. Allee**, who inductively studied cooperation and patterns among organisms and would later publish his major work, *Animal Aggregations*, in 1931. Ricketts never completed his degree at the University of Chicago (neither did Steinbeck at **Stanford University**). In 1922, Ricketts married Anna Barbara Maker ("Nan") and they had a son, Edward F. Ricketts, Jr., born on August 23, 1923, the first of three children. Ricketts followed his business partner, Albert E. Galigher, to **Pacific Grove**, where they established **Pacific Biological Laboratories**. The business concerned collecting and preparing specimens—primarily marine—for schools and universities. Although the partnership with Galigher ended in 1924, Ricketts continued the lab business for the rest of his life. He conducted experiments and published some of his writings throughout the 1920s, and his work earned a great deal of respect in the **Monterey** area.

In 1930, Steinbeck met Ricketts in either a dentist's office or the home of a mutual friend, **Jack Calvin** (accounts differ). **Carol Henning Steinbeck** worked for a time as an assistant at Ricketts' lab, and soon the Steinbecks spent a great deal of time there. Conversations at the lab, with many others included (**Joseph Campbell** among them), might have ranged from discussions about anthropology, ecology, mythology, philosophy, or physics that could evolve into the wild parties that Steinbeck fictionalized in *Cannery Row* and ***Sweet Thursday***. Along with creating the opportunity for conversation, Ricketts also provided a makeshift library in the lab, from which Steinbeck borrowed materials. Over time, Steinbeck and Ricketts worked out their ideas about **non-teleological thinking** ("'is' thinking"), most famously articulated in ***The Log from the Sea of Cortez***. In *The Log*, Steinbeck lifted the definition of "'is' thinking" from Ricketts' writing: "Non-teleological thinking concerns itself primarily not with what should be, or could be, or might be, but rather with what actually 'is'—attempting at most to answer the already sufficiently difficult questions *what* or *how*, instead of *why*." Their understanding essentially attempted to apprehend the widest picture possible, consider it inductively without preconceptions, and subsequently discern truth (the what or the how). This view included all species and, in Steinbeck's fiction, considered the human being as well. Ricketts and Steinbeck were holistic thinkers, seeing human beings as part of a much larger picture. The philosophical viewpoint Steinbeck worked out with Ricketts, primarily in the 1930s, informs most of Steinbeck's important work, including ***In Dubious Battle***, ***The Grapes of Wrath***, and ***The Moon Is Down***, and continues to the last book Steinbeck published in his lifetime, ***America and Americans***.

In 1932, Nan Ricketts separated from Ed, and, despite attempts at reconciliation, she began but never completed divorce proceedings in 1946. Throughout the early 1930s Ricketts embarked on expeditions along the Pacific coast and in Alaska and Mexico. In 1936, Ricketts moved into the **Cannery Row** lab on Ocean Avenue, only to see it burn down because of an electrical fire. He lost valuable papers, research information, and his library. In 1939, in spite of considerable delay by the Stanford University Press and the fire at the lab, Ricketts published ***Between Pacific Tides***, a book concerning marine life on the northern Pacific Coast, which received good reviews. Despite help from Steinbeck, he could not find a publisher for his philosophical essays. Much of the holistic, ecological, and even mystic thought contained in these essays found its way into *Sea of Cortez*.

Because Steinbeck was exhausted from the effort of writing and publishing *The Grapes of Wrath*, in late 1939 and early 1940 he studied under Ricketts' guidance to prepare for three collecting expeditions that would lead to a triumvirate of works concerning marine life in San Francisco Bay, the **Sea of Cortez**, and the Pacific Northwest. The only book completed from the plan was *Sea of Cortez*. Having contracted the ***Western Flyer*** and its crew for the expedition, Ricketts and Steinbeck left for a six-week tour in the Gulf of California on March 11, 1940. Although Steinbeck's wife, Carol, went along as cook, the Steinbecks' marital difficulties are evident as she is not referred to by name in *Sea of Cortez*. The work was a true collaboration, with Steinbeck assembling the narrative portion from Ricketts' journal of the trip and his earlier philosophical essays, and from Captain **Tony Berry**'s bare log. Ricketts assembled the accompanying annotated phyletic catalogue of marine specimens, including photographs. As Rodger states in her biographical essay about Ricketts, the two authors did not realize "that more than fifty years later their study of the Gulf of California would still be considered one of the most comprehensive accounts of the region."

The collaboration experienced on *Sea of Cortez* did not occur for Steinbeck's next project, the filming of ***The Forgotten Village*** (1941). The point of contention was essentially between Steinbeck's view that modern medicine needed to be brought to the villages of Mexico, and Ricketts' belief that the local indigenous culture and belief system should not be disturbed or replaced. Ricketts went so far as to write an anti-script to Steinbeck's project: "Thesis and Materials for a Script on Mexico: Which Shall Be Motivated Oppositely to John's 'Forgotten Village.'" As Rodger points out, the rift did not last. During the time Steinbeck and Ricketts were finishing up *Sea of Cortez* back in Monterey, Ed began a relationship with **Toni Jackson**, the woman who would be his common-law wife until 1947. The social life at the lab continued, and Ricketts and Jackson struck up a friendship with author Henry Miller. Sales of *Sea of Cortez* were disappointing; the book was released in the first week of December 1941, amid the uproar over the U.S. entry into World War II.

Ricketts made contributions to the war effort as a lab technician at the Presidio in Monterey. Ricketts had planned a substantial contribution in the form of ecological and topographical information on the Palau Islands, of strategic importance in the Pacific campaign, but the military showed little enthusiasm. With Pacific Biological Laboratories faltering financially, he took a job as a chemist for the California Packing Corporation and recorded the sardine populations for the *Monterey Peninsula Herald*. Given his background as a biologist and ecologist, Ricketts carefully observed the results of overfishing and the drastic depopulation of sardines in the 1940s.

The most famous of the Doc characters Steinbeck created based on versions of the real Ricketts, the Doc of *Cannery Row* and *Sweet Thursday*, was introduced to the country with the 1945 publication of *Row*. Although Ricketts was approached by fans not quite able to separate the real man from the fictionalized version of Doc, including one man who broke into the lab wanting to ask Doc some questions, Ricketts took it with his usual patience and ability to accept unexpected circumstances—a reflection of his philosophical practice of integrating the small things of life into the larger picture.

In 1947 and 1948, Ricketts worked on what was meant to be his next collaboration with Steinbeck, **"The Outer Shores,"** which would result from an expedition to Vancouver Island and the Queen Charlottes. During this time, however, both men were working under personal duress. Steinbeck's second marriage, to **Gwyndolyn Conger Steinbeck**, was falling apart. Toni Jackson's daughter, Kay, was dying from a brain tumor, and therefore Toni was away at the hospital a great deal of the time. With Kay's death, a grieving Toni left Ricketts in 1947, married a marine biologist, and left with him for Palestine in 1948. Ricketts was denied financial support for "The Outer

Shores" project when, despite an endorsement from Steinbeck, a proposal for a Guggenheim Fellowship was turned down. By the end of 1947, however, Ricketts met Alice Campbell, a twenty-five-year-old student at the University of California–Berkeley, and married her in January 1948 (although the marriage was not legal, as Ricketts was technically still married to Nan). Ricketts was looking forward to the expedition to the Queen Charlottes in May 1948 with Steinbeck (who was living in New York throughout most of the 1940s and out of touch). Ricketts, however, was driving across the railroad tracks near Cannery Row when his car was struck by the Del Monte Express on May 8, 1948. Although mortally wounded, Ricketts had the presence of mind to urge people not to blame the train's motorman. Steinbeck tried desperately to reach his friend from New York, but Ricketts died on May 11, 1948, just before Steinbeck was able to make contact.

The immense impact of Ricketts on Steinbeck is implicitly made by the thematic explorations in Steinbeck's fiction and nonfiction that were inspired by Ricketts. The informal education Steinbeck received through conversations at the lab and use of Ricketts' library paralleled the novelist's earlier education at such places as the **Hopkins Marine Station**. Ricketts' influence and collaboration came at the critical period of the author's development in the 1930s. Steinbeck was most explicit about Ricketts' importance to him, and, in the 1951 preface to *The Log from the Sea of Cortez*, "About Ed Ricketts," Steinbeck makes this clear: "Very many conclusions Ed and I worked out together through endless discussion and reading and observation and experiment. We worked together, and so closely I do not know in some cases who started which line of speculation since the end thought was the product of both minds." Speaking of Ricketts' death ten years later, Steinbeck is quoted in Thomas Fensch's *Conversations*: "He was my partner for eighteen years—he was part of my brain . . . when he was killed, I was destroyed." Edward F. Ricketts was among Steinbeck's best friends and certainly his most important collaborator. Independent of Steinbeck, Ricketts was a man of importance, as Rodger concludes: "While his influence on Steinbeck alone makes Ricketts a significant figure in literary history, his own writings—his letters in particular—merit attention that is long overdue."

Further Reading: Astro, Richard. *John Steinbeck and Edward F. Ricketts: The Shaping of a Novelist*. New Berlin: University Minnesota Press, 1973; Benson, Jackson J. *The True Adventures of John Steinbeck, Writer*. New York: Viking, 1984; Fensch, Thomas, ed. *Conversations with John Steinbeck*. Jackson: University Press of Mississippi, 1988; Railsback, Brian. *Parallel Expeditions: Charles Darwin and the Art of John Steinbeck*. Moscow: University of Idaho Press, 1995; Rodger, Katherine A. *Renaissance Man of Cannery Row, The Life and Letters of Edward F. Ricketts*. Tuscaloosa: University of Alabama Press, 2002; Steinbeck, John. "About Ed Ricketts." In *The Log From the Sea of Cortez* (1951). New York: Penguin, 1978; Tamm, Eric Enno. *Beyond The Outer Shores*. New York: Four Walls and Eight Windows, 2004.

Brian Railsback

RITTER, WILLIAM EMERSON (1856–1944). Ritter combined philosophical discourse with biology when he served as the head of the zoology department at the University of California–Berkeley. C. V. Taylor was one of his students, and it was through Taylor at **Stanford University** that Steinbeck was exposed to Ritter's doctrine of the "organismal unity of life," wherein all parts of a whole are interdependent and cooperative with each other to ensure the well-being and smooth functioning of the whole. Much of Steinbeck's work, in particular such books as ***In Dubious Battle*** and ***The Moon Is Down***, reflect this philosophy in that his characters are not treated as isolated individuals but rather as parts of the whole, namely, human and general ecology.

Further Reading: Ritter, William Emerson. *The Unity of the Organism or The Organismal*

Conception of Life. 2 vols. Boston: Gorham Press, 1919.

Tracy Michaels

RIVAS, CACAHUETE. In *Sweet Thursday,* the nephew of **Joseph and Mary Rivas,** who plays trumpet with the Espaldas Mojadas band. He is described as a lean, handsome, and somewhat sullen young man. When he is not practicing or performing, he is generally seen idling about his uncle's store, reading *Downbeat*. His uncle sends him to the beach to practice, hoping that the waves and the sea lions will drown him out. There, Cacahuete creates minor mischief, confusing the crew of a tugboat by imitating the passing signal of a ship on his trumpet and startling people in the neighborhood by blowing into a sewer pipe and making their toilets resound with "Stormy Weather." Cacahuete performs with the Espaldas Mojadas at the masquerade party, opening the event with "Whistle While You Work" and playing "The Wedding March" from *Lohengrin* just before **Suzy** is unveiled to **Doc** in the costume of Snow White. The presence of Cacahuete and the Espaldas Mojadas surely is owing to the novel's original conception as a musical comedy for the stage.

Bruce Ouderkirk

RIVAS, JOSEPH AND MARY (THE PATRON, J AND M). In *Sweet Thursday,* Joseph and Mary is a young Mexican American who has bought **Lee Chong's Heavenly Flower Grocery** on **Cannery Row**. His religious name is ironic because he is a man congenitally predisposed to a life of crime. He functions primarily as a foil and rival to **Doc** in the novel. Cynical and self-seeking, Joseph and Mary is ultimately less successful in achieving his ends than are characters like **Fauna,** who willingly become duped now and then to carry out benevolent impulses. As the presumed owner of the **Palace Flophouse**, Joseph figures in the plot when **Mack** and the boys try to trick him into helping them transfer the ownership of the property to Doc. The attention that Steinbeck devotes to Rivas's background in the early chapters of *Sweet Thursday* seems disproportionate to the relatively limited role he later assumes. Although Mack explains to Doc what he knows about the other significant members of Cannery Row in the opening chapter, the entire second chapter is devoted to Joseph and Mary alone.

All of Joseph and Mary's natural impulses lead to illegality. As a child, he stole without qualms, led a gang, hustled sailors at pool, and sold a variety of weapons. By the age of twelve, he entered reform school. Following puberty, he took a respite from illegal activities to concentrate on women, and he then served in the army, where he earned a dishonorable discharge. A priest assisted him in securing a job as caretaker of plants in the Los Angeles Plaza, but he was fired for growing marijuana. Seeking an illicit occupation that kept him safe from prosecution, he eventually aspired to become the hiring agent and exploiter of illegal alien workers from Mexico. This plan backfired, however, when his Mexican work crew formed a band that his nephew joined. Since then, he has had to satisfy himself with booking them to perform at dances. Such is the lengthy initial description of Joseph and Mary's criminal past.

Beginning with his entry into the novel, Joseph and Mary s main function is to serve as a foil and rival to Doc, his antithesis. Since all of his impulses lead him toward dishonesty, he finds the scientist baffling and marvels over Doc's assertion that chess is a game at which it is impossible to cheat. However, Rivas is not really needed as a foil in *Sweet Thursday,* at least for those readers familiar with ***Cannery Row,*** where Doc's honesty was well established. It may be that Steinbeck initially intended to have Rivas play a larger, continuous role as Doc's rival for **Suzy**'s affections. It is not until after the masquerade party, when Suzy begins to live independently, that Rivas suddenly decides to try his luck with her. This change of heart seems unmotivated, but it is crucial to Steinbeck's plot. Once Doc finds himself with his hands around Rivas's neck, ready to kill this rival to keep him away from Suzy, Doc is forced to admit that it is futile for him to try any longer to resist her attraction. Rivas, hardly the criminal thug he is depicted as at the outset, offers to help Doc pick her a bouquet.

Bruce Ouderkirk

RIVERS, CONNIE. Recently married to the eldest Joad daughter, **Rose of Sharon**, in *The Grapes of Wrath*, Connie seemingly joins the migrant family for lack of anything better to do. When the group arrives in California, Connie and his wife plan to build a little white house and settle down. His own dream is to study nights through a cheap correspondence school, hoping to become an electrician and thus become successful. But after the first negative glimpses of California life, Connie is disillusioned and disgruntled. Soon after they reach the Hooverville, Connie deserts his wife to fend for himself, resenting the fact that he could have stayed home and tractored off other Okies for a steady salary like that received by **Joe Davis's boy** and **Willie Feeley**. Through Connie, Steinbeck is able to present a contrary, cynical view from within the family, a view sympathetic to the banks. Never a real part of the **Joads** or of the twelve followers of **Jim Casy**'s new religion, Connie remains an outsider, a Judas betrayer of commitment and brotherhood. (*See also* **Rivers, Rose of Sharon Joad**; **Rosasharn's baby**.)

Michael J. Meyer

RIVERS, ROSE OF SHARON JOAD ("ROSASHARN"). Recently married to **Connie Rivers**, the oldest **Joad** daughter in *The Grapes of Wrath*. During the family's trek, she develops into an ever more sensitive and less selfish individual. Early scenes depict Rosasharn as largely dependent on her weak husband, whiny and childlike when he seems nonsupportive. Initially, she is shown to selfishly pursue her own desires regardless of others' needs. For example, she engages in a sexual encounter with her husband beneath the blankets while **Granma** is seriously ill in the truck, and she complains when she has no milk, although the family cannot afford even the most meager supplies. Although some critics censured Steinbeck for what they considered to be an abrupt shift in character traits, Rosasharn is constantly exposed to **Ma**'s generosity and ever-expanding appreciation of the brotherhood of all mankind. Thus, the ending vignette in the barn, after **Rosasharn's baby** is stillborn, where the grieving mother offers her breast to a starving old man is definitely not as abrupt as some critics have argued.

Although readers may remember Rosasharn's complaining and her superstitious fears—including her encounter with **Mrs. Sandry**, her pleas for milk and special consideration for food, her concerns about how the unexpected deaths of the dog and of **Granpa** will impact her health and her baby's—toward the end of the novel, these qualities have begun to be tempered. Rosasharn insists that she will participate with the family as they pick cotton despite her advanced pregnancy. Also, after a momentary lapse into self-concern in upbraiding **Tom** for risking a return to the family after the murder of the vigilante and **Casy**'s death, Rosasharn realizes that her initial reaction of Tom as uncaring is inaccurate. Rather than accuse her brother of an act that might endanger her and her baby, she keeps watch over him during his sleep and promises to warn him of any impending danger.

Several critics have called attention to Rose of Sharon's biblical heritage, citing the name as it appears in *Song of Solomon* 2:1 and its association with "breasts like clusters of grapes" (*Song of Solomon* 7:7). **Louis Owens** has drawn attention to Solomon 8:7, where the biblical writer states "many waters cannot quench love: neither can floods drown it." The flooding river of the book's end, while more reminiscent of the Red Sea that drowned the Egyptians than of a pleasant stream of renewal, is ultimately unable to destroy or denigrate Rose of Sharon's symbolic gesture of suckling a dying man that closes the novel. The grapes of wrath are seemingly conquered by "the milk of human kindness." On the other hand, the ending has also been labeled as melodramatic and even banal and manipulative in its bathos. Leslie Fiedler suggests that "the milk of a half starved Okie girl is not likely to be rich enough to sustain life and that the old man she suckles is beyond the point of saving." He further asserts that the novel thus ends not on a note of pseudo-Emersonian cosmic optimism but rather on a note of tragic despair. Readers themselves will have to judge whether the characterization is sturdy enough to withstand the heavy symbolism associated with it, and whether Steinbeck was cynical rather than hopeful in his portrait—whether, in fact, the closing suggests not hope but despair, with death and destruction superseding the Joads' attempt at salvation.

Michael J. Meyer

Further Reading: Fiedler, Leslie. "Looking Back after 50 Years." *San Jose Studies* 16.1 (1990): 54–64; Owens, Louis. *The Grapes of Wrath: Trouble in the Promised Land*. Boston: Twayne, 1989.

ROARK. The bad man responsible for setting **Katy,** the "bad pig," on the road to hell in "**Saint Katy the Virgin.**" Roark displays a dim view of religion and delights in mocking it, finding particular pleasure in Katy's wicked behavior. When he tricks the monks into taking Katy with them, he thinks he has hoodwinked them—until, seeing Katy converted to Christianity, he renounces his evil ways, telling her inspirational story over and over to all who will listen.

ROBBIE, THE PROPRIETOR'S SON. After he crosses the Great Divide in Idaho in ***Travels with Charley,*** Steinbeck rents a cabin for the night. The proprietor's ambitious and worldly twenty-year-old son tells Steinbeck that he would like to be a hairdresser, much to the dismay of his father. Steinbeck manages to persuade the father that a hairdresser is most influential: because women place their hair in the hairdresser's hands, he gains authority beyond the reach of most men.

ROBINSON, JOEL. Foreman at **William Ames**'s tannery in Massachusetts in ***East of Eden***. He discovers the robbery at the tannery, thereby changing the way the fire at the Ames's house is viewed. Subsequent investigation reveals **Cathy Ames**'s necklace and a bloodstained hair ribbon, further fueling the speculation about what had happened.

ROCINANTE. The name Steinbeck gives to the three-quarter-ton, custom-built pickup truck he uses to travel around the United States in ***Travels with Charley***. Because many of his friends thought that the trip was "quixotic," Steinbeck called his journey-to-be "Operation Windmills" and named his truck "Rocinante," after the horse of the hero of Spanish novelist and dramatist **Miguel de Cervantes'** most famous work, *Don Quixote de la Mancha* (1605). In Spanish, a *rocin* is a kind of work or draft horse.

RODGERS, (OLIVE) ESTHER STEINBECK (1892–1986). Steinbeck's oldest sister, named after their mother but always referred to by her middle name. Motivated by her mother's emphasis on the importance of education for both sexes, Esther graduated from Mills College in Oakland, California, earning a degree in home economics in 1914. She later taught that subject at Watsonville High School and then served the county as a home economist for the farm advisory office. In 1924, she married Carroll James Rodgers and moved from **Salinas** to Watsonville. After her mother's death in 1934, she took in her invalid father, **John Ernst Steinbeck**, and cared for him until his death a year later. Her second home at 825 Asilomar Avenue in **Pacific Grove** was rumored to have been used by Steinbeck and **Gwyndolyn Conger Steinbeck**, his future wife, for romantic trysts while Esther was not in residence. Steinbeck also wrote large portions of

The Log from the Sea of Cortez at this address. Innately more conservative than her brother, Esther routinely argued with John over social issues, but they remained close as siblings. Her major contribution to Steinbeck studies was her role as a reliable resource for Steinbeck's biographer, **Jackson J. Benson**, providing firsthand accounts of her brother's childhood and adolescence. She also donated many Steinbeck artifacts and memorabilia that now are part of the collection at the Steinbeck family home, located at 132 Central Avenue in Salinas.

Michael J. Meyer

RODGERS, RICHARD (1909–1979) **AND OSCAR HAMMERSTEIN II** (1895–1960). This pair formed one of the most successful and creative teams in American musical theater history. Rodgers wrote the music, and Hammerstein wrote the lyrics. *Oklahoma!,* Rodgers and Hammerstein's first musical collaboration, was based on a play called *Green Grow the Lilacs* by Lynn Riggs; it opened in 1943 with **Elaine Scott Steinbeck** (later to become Steinbeck's third wife) as stage manager. As a musical, *Oklahoma!* was very different from most musicals written up to that time because the songs were integrally involved with a plot or story line. It was a combination of old-fashioned musical comedy and more serious operetta in the manner of the British team of Gilbert and Sullivan.

In the early 1950s, Rodgers and Hammerstein briefly considered an adaptation of Steinbeck's *In The Forests of The Night,* later retitled ***Burning Bright,*** but by 1954, they had settled on a musical version of Steinbeck's ***Sweet Thursday*** entitled ***Pipe Dream.*** Though hopes were originally high for the adaptation's success, it seemed difficult for the artistic pair to create a more realistic, tougher plot rather than their usual soft romantic ones. When the adaptation started to sour, Steinbeck tried to salvage the show by passing on several suggestions for revision to both the librettist and the composer. **Jackson J. Benson** records that despite Steinbeck's attempts to restore his original intent evidenced in the novel, much of the show was "conventional pap." He also quotes a letter from Steinbeck to **Elia Kazan** in which the author declares that, although Rodgers and Hammerstein were attracted to his writing, they were "temperamentally incapable of doing it." The show previewed in New Haven and Boston but never made it to Broadway. It was one of the few failures of the writing team, who went on to compose *Flower Drum Song* (1958) and *The Sound of Music* (1959) before Hammerstein's death from cancer.

Further Reading: Benson, Jackson J. *The True Adventures of John Steinbeck, Writer.* New York: Viking, 1984.

Michael J. Meyer

RODRIGUEZ. Captain of the army defending Panama in ***Cup of Gold***. He leads a beautiful cavalry charge directly into a marsh.

RODRIGUEZ, MRS. Friend to **Mama Torres**, whom **Pepé** visits on his trip to **Monterey** in "**Flight**." Although she never appears in the story, her kitchen is the scene of Pepé's quarrel with and murder of the unidentified man who called him insulting names.

ROLETTI, MR. A ninety-three-year-old man who develops senile satyriasis and has to be restrained from chasing high school girls. Early in ***Sweet Thursday,*** this unusual behavior is cited as one portent of the great changes coming to **Monterey**, to **Cannery Row**, and to **Doc**.

ROLF, MR. Young Episcopal clergyman in **Salinas** who counsels and encourages **Aron Trask** in ***East of Eden*** when Aron decides to enter the ministry. Under Mr. Rolf's tutelage, Aron's quest for purity—which includes becoming celibate—is furthered. When Mr. Rolf tells Aron of the sinful woman who has begun to attend church, he does not know that she is **Kate Albey,** who attends not for salvation but to see her son, Aron.

Margaret Seligman

ROMAS. The old driver in ***To a God Unknown*** who delivers **Joseph**'s house-building materials.

ROMAS, WILLIE. In *To a God Unknown*, he is a lumber-wagon driver and friend to **Juanito**. He has bad dreams and becomes a carousing companion of **Benjamin Wayne**. He later commits suicide.

ROMERO, MAE. The pretty half-Mexican girl with whom the narrator in **"Johnny Bear"** has several dates in the village of Loma. Johnny Bear follows the pair one night and later regales the clients of the Buffalo Bar (while humiliating the narrator) by mimicking the voices of Mae and the narrator. More seriously, Mae's slightly accented voice foreshadows the accented voices of **Amy Hawkins** and her Chinese lover, who engage in a mixed-race affair that, unlike the dalliance between Mae and the narrator, ends in tragedy. The contrast between the presentations of Mae and Amy amplifies the story's implied meanings.

Abby H. P. Werlock

ROOSEVELT, ANNA ELEANOR (1884–1962). Wife of President **Franklin Delano Roosevelt**, in April 1940 she publicly corroborated Steinbeck's descriptions of migrant camps in ***The Grapes of Wrath*** from observations she made herself. Her support helped blunt the invective directed at Steinbeck after the novel's publication in 1939.

Scott Simkins

ROOSEVELT, FRANKLIN DELANO (1882–1945). Longest-serving American president, Roosevelt held office from March 1933 to April 1945, when he died shortly after winning his fourth term and seeing the end of World War II. FDR presided during the decade of America's worst economic depression and during the war against the Axis powers. An innovative reformer, he restored faith in economic democracy by passing legislation that raised wages, provided jobs, developed water power, improved the environment, and assisted the elderly. He passed on to his successor the plan to house and educate returning veterans, and so fueled the postwar boom. As a wartime president, he set impossible production goals that manufacturers met, funded atomic research, and left the nation with an international political vision. The efforts of the Roosevelt administration to better lives at home and to fight tyranny abroad persuaded John Steinbeck to turn his talent to political ends. After observing the federal government's aid to California migrants, Steinbeck, in his novel ***The Grapes of Wrath***, contrasted the suffering the **Joads** experienced when on their own with the improvements that came when Washington provided help. Roosevelt recognized that Steinbeck had written a national epic about life without a New Deal and encouraged his friendship. Steinbeck's first contacts were brief telegraph messages sent in the spring of 1939, asking Roosevelt to continue funding federal camps, to extend the LaFollette Civil Liberties Committee, and to continue funding **Pare Lorentz**'s U.S. Film Service, which made, among other documentaries, *The Plow That Broke the Plains*. The first of a series of Steinbeck letters to FDR offered the Sea of Cortez trip as an opportunity to collect naval information about Mexican coastal activities. FDR took the matter up with naval intelligence, which chose not to pursue it. Another Steinbeck letter (1940), which led to a meeting with FDR, suggested spreading counterfeit money throughout occupied countries in order to destroy the German economy; however, the secretary of the treasury opposed the plan. An important letter Steinbeck sent from Mexico to FDR (1940) warned Roosevelt of German agents' successes there, and said America would lose Mexico's allegiance unless a counterintelligence organization replaced the FBI's foreign efforts. FDR discussed the organization with Steinbeck, offered him a job in it, which Steinbeck rejected, and one year later created a counterintelligence agency for which Steinbeck did some work. But a letter Steinbeck sent to the agency's head, William Donovan, on December 15, 1941, did not persuade FDR to allow Japanese-Americans their freedom during the war in exchange for their spying on disloyal groups. Steinbeck's play ***A Medal for Benny*** might be a protest against California's abusive treatment of these loyal citizens.

Steinbeck's public support of the war effort is well known. ***The Moon Is Down,*** a novel written for Donovan's intelligence agency, described the democratic instincts that spelled defeat for the Germans in Norway. ***Bombs Away,*** a book Roosevelt personally asked Steinbeck to write, recruited volunteers into the army air force. In the film script for ***Lifeboat*** (1943), Steinbeck condemned war profiteering and spending money for war but not for civilian needs. It was Steinbeck's contribution to FDR's 1944 campaign, however, that developed respect for Steinbeck within the inner circles of the Democratic Party. First Steinbeck fulfilled a request to write a "Letter" in FDR's name that explained why the president felt it a military duty to run for another term. In slightly altered form, the "Letter" announced Roosevelt's candidacy in newspapers on July 11, 1944. In July of that year, as FDR requested, Steinbeck composed a two-hundred-fifty-word "Gettysburg Address" intended to be FDR's valediction. Had Roosevelt left the powerful and visionary policy address unchanged, the speech would be famous. But speechwriters and FDR mangled the prose, and also dropped the most significant of the postwar goals Steinbeck wanted, civil rights legislation.

After the deaths of his political heroes, Roosevelt and his chief aide, Harry Hopkins, in 1945, Steinbeck performed one more writing duty for them: a eulogy for the New Deal on the occasion of a memorial service for Hopkins in May 1946, in Washington, DC. Of the three pages Steinbeck composed, actor **Burgess Meredith** read but half a page. Following the rhythm of Lincoln's Gettysburg Address, Steinbeck listed the achievements of the New Deal. Then he concluded with what he thought would be FDR's revolutionary contribution, an "idea" that "flows in the veins and shines in the eyes of the people and it will be there just as enduring in their children": "human welfare is the first and final task of government. It has no other." This idea is a New Deal principle that guided Steinbeck's political writing.

Further Reading: Benson, Jackson J. *The True Adventures of John Steinbeck, Writer.* New York: Viking, 1984; Goodwin, Doris Kearns. *No Ordinary Time.* New York: Simon & Schuster, 1994; Lewis, Cliff. "Art for Politics: John Steinbeck and FDR." In *After* The Grapes of Wrath. Ed. Donald Coers, Paul Ruffin, and Robert DeMott. Athens: Ohio University Press, 1995, 23–29; Rosenman, Samuel I. *The Public Speeches and Addresses of Franklin Roosevelt.* Vol. III. New York: Da Capa, 1969. (*See also* the Steinbeck-Roosevelt Collection, Roosevelt Library, Hyde Park, NY.)

Clifford Lewis

ROOT. Novice in the Communist Party, who in "**The Raid**" is educated by Dick, an older and experienced Communist. As Dick and Root wait for the party members to appear for the meeting, Root is nervous and unsure of himself; this will be his first public speaking engagement. He also fears that he lacks the courage to stand up to violence should they be raided, as indeed they are. His bravery is, in fact, commendable, and after he has been seriously wounded, Root explains the source of his bravery in apparently Christian terms, thus earning another admonition from Dick. Finally, though, Dick is impressed by the courage with which Root has acquitted himself.

Abby H. P. Werlock

ROSASHARN. *See* **Rivers, Rosasharn Joad.**

ROSASHARN'S BABY. The child of **Rosasharn Joad Rivers** and **Connie Rivers** in ***The Grapes of Wrath*** is stillborn in a boxcar while torrential rains flood California. The death is caused by its mother's malnutrition during pregnancy, but the child's fate has been foreshadowed throughout the novel, making the death less of a shock. For example, the prediction of **Mrs. Sandry** at the Weedpatch Camp (**Arvin Sanitary Camp**) and Rosasharn's often-expressed fears for the baby's well-being during the journey predict its failure to survive. The shriveled body is taken by **Uncle John**, who, rather than burying it, deposits it in an apple box that he sets adrift on the flood, telling it to "go down and tell 'em. Go down in the streets and rot and tell 'em that way." As Moses in the bull rushes was a symbol of salvation in Genesis, so this baby on the water is a reverse symbol of death and destruction—a member of the generation of the poor and downtrodden, fated to die before it has even lived because of the greed of owners. The baby's death is compared to the wasting away of overripe fruit on the trees or to the surplus harvest that is dumped and allowed to rot in order to decrease supply and increase prices.

Michael J. Meyer

ROSEN, DR. **Salinas** doctor consulted by **Kate Albey** in *East of Eden*.

ROUND TABLE, THE. In *The Acts of King Arthur*, the Round Table is originally given by **Uther Pendragon** to **King Lodegrance** of Camylarde; it seats one hundred fifty knights. Subsequently the table, together with one hundred knights, is given to **King Arthur** by King Lodegrance as a dowry on the occasion of his daughter **Guinevere**'s marriage to Arthur. Arthur asks **Merlin** to search his kingdom to find an additional fifty brave and perfect knights to fill the Round Table, but Merlin is able to find only twenty-eight such knights. Of the remaining seats, two must be held only by the most honorable knights. The last of these seats is the Siege Perilous, to be occupied by the most perfect knight ever to live, and any other knight who dares to take that place will be destroyed. On the formation of the Fellowship of the Round Table, every knight swears to keep the laws; never to use violence without good reason; never to murder or be guilty of treason; to be merciful when mercy is asked; to protect damsels, ladies, gentlewomen, and widows; and never to fight in an unjust cause or for personal gain. Steinbeck loosely employed the concept of the Round Table in other fiction, most notably in ***Tortilla Flat***.

ROY. **Will Hamilton**'s garage mechanic in *East of Eden*. In a scene that serves as comic relief, Roy teaches **Adam Trask** and **Lee** how to drive the new Ford Adam has just bought. His knowledge about cars and his talent with spitting impress **Cal** and **Aron Trask**, who are nevertheless confused by his repeated exclamation, "Just call me Joe," when his name is Roy. Perhaps this latter idiosyncrasy reinforces Steinbeck's idea that a man's name or initials need not be a factor in predetermining his personality.

Margaret Seligman

ROYCE, JOSIAH (1855–1916). American philosopher and teacher, who was the leading American exponent of absolute idealism. Born in Grass Valley, California, Royce studied engineering but turned to philosophy after graduation. While a student in Europe, Royce was influenced by the writings of the absolute idealist Hegel. Royce held that human thought and the external world were unified. He believed in an absolute truth, which, he argued, everyone must agree exists. He held that humans know truth beyond themselves because they are a part of the logos, or world-mind, a concept that would have appealed to a holistic thinker like Steinbeck. He also believed that the natural order of the world must be also a moral order, and that a person's ethical obligation is to the moral order and takes the form of loyalty to the great community of all individuals. As **Robert DeMott** notes, Steinbeck owned a 1948 edition of Royce's *California*, but it is unknown if Steinbeck read other works by the author/philosopher. Critic Charles Shively asserts that the community of the oppressed in ***The Grapes of Wrath*** resembles the "loyal community" described by Royce: "Royce's terminology and ideas concerning the individual and the community, if not the basis for Steinbeck's social philosophy, can at least illustrate that the novelist does indeed have a definite social theory . . . which is consistent with Steinbeck's view of a unified cosmos."

Further Reading: Shively, Charles. "John Steinbeck: From The Tide Pool to the Loyal Community." In *Steinbeck: The Man and His Work*. Ed. Richard Astro and Tetsumaro Hayashi. Corvallis: Oregon State University Press, 1971.

ROYNS, KING OF NORTH WALES. In ***The Acts of King Arthur***, brother of **Nero** and rebel king who is defeated when **King Arthur** comes to the assistance of **King Lodegrance of Camylarde**. King Royns later claims to have defeated the eleven lords of the North and demands that Arthur cut off his beard and send it to him to use as trimming for his coat; otherwise, he will invade Arthur's kingdom. He raises a large army and invades as he has threatened, but is captured by **Sir Balin of Northumberland** and **Sir Balan** and delivered to Camelot.

RUIZ, CORNELIA. In ***Tortilla Flat***, a woman of apparently easy virtue whose endless parade of love affairs provides the main topic of conversation among the paisanos during their bouts of drinking. The most extensive story we hear of Cornelia comes from **Danny**, who describes how one of her lovers stole a baby pig from its mother to give to Cornelia, only to have the sow burst into Cornelia's house, attack her, and recover the piglet. **Pablo Sanchez** takes from this story the lesson that nothing goes as planned, but it also illustrates how organic relationships can be disrupted by human lust and greed.

Bryan Vescio

RUSSIAN JOURNAL, A (1948). Published in 1948, John Steinbeck's and photographer **Robert Capa**'s collaborative, often wryly humorous, travelogue describes the "private life of the Russian people" in the Soviet Union in the years immediately after the World War II. Steinbeck ostensibly credits his dissatisfaction with contemporary journalism as much as a troubled home life and a curiosity about postwar Europe for his desire to report on the USSR. "News has become a matter of punditry," he writes. "A man sitting at a desk in Washington or New York reads the cables and rearranges them to fit his own mental pattern and his by-line." In short, he wanted to report from firsthand observation, much as he had done from California's migrant camps while researching **"The Harvest Gypsies"** or as he had done with the war correspondence he had just completed (later compiled in the book, ***Once There Was a War***). As he did in his other reporting, he wanted to avoid politics and other big issues typical in the mainstream press. Under the aegis of the *New York Herald Tribune*, Steinbeck and Capa embarked on a forty-day trip, from the end of July to the middle of September 1947, traveling to Moscow, Kiev, and Stalingrad, but mostly in the countryside, visiting the residents of Georgia and Ukraine. As Steinbeck writes, they wished "to avoid politics . . . to talk to and to understand Russian farmers, and working people, and market people, to see how they lived, and to try to tell our people about it, so that some kind of common understanding might be reached." Relying on novelistic techniques and using narrative, anecdote, and dialogue, Steinbeck observes the inception of the project, their struggle with war surplus airplanes and red tape, their impatience in Moscow, their interpreters, and their tours through the towns and farms. To counter the mounting fear of and propaganda about faceless Russians in the postwar United States, Steinbeck records his encounters with individual Russians, Ukrainians, and Georgians. For instance, the driver who took them around the Ukrainian farmlands "had been a pilot during the war as well as a tank-driver," Steinbeck observes. "He had one very great gift, he could sleep at any time, and for any length of time." Mamuchka, the farm wife, who prepares a feast in honor of their visit, keeps a large picture of her son on the wall and, as Steinbeck recalls, she only mentioned him once: "Graduated in biochemistry in 1940, mobilized in 1941, killed in 1941."

Steinbeck devotes much space to narrative, describing the lifestyles and living conditions of ordinary Russians. He reports in thick description on the postwar rebuilding, the great sadness for those killed in the war, the Soviet pride in defeating fascism, as well as the dancing, the drinking, the harvesting, the school plays, the wrestling matches, and the factory work. Steinbeck tries to help his American readers discover a "common understanding" with their Russian peers. He reports on the ubiquity of Josef Stalin's image: "Nothing in the Soviet Union goes on outside the vision of the plaster, bronze, painted, or embroidered eye of Stalin." He reports on the massive war damage in Kiev and on the German prisoners of war forced to help in the cleaning up and rebuilding, the conquered invaders whom the Ukrainians will not look at. "They look through these prisoners," Steinbeck writes, "and over them and do not see them."

The 1930s had set the precedent for this kind of collaborative documentary journalism, particularly in the work of James Agee and Walker Evans on *Let Us Now Praise Famous Men* and **Erskine Caldwell** and Margaret Bourke-White on *You Have Seen Their Faces*. Steinbeck himself experienced this sort of collaboration in his migrant camp travels with photographer **Horace Bristol** and his coverage of bomber pilot training with photographer **John Swope** for the book, ***Bombs Away***. Unlike these consistently serious projects, *A Russian Journal* is invested with Steinbeck's and Capa's humor, and the book is much closer in tone to ***Travels with Charley in Search of America***. For example, reporting on their delay in Moscow awaiting permission to travel and to photograph, Steinbeck also records the details of their hotel room, with its crowded bathroom and rickety bathtub. "It was an old bathtub," he writes, "probably prerevolutionary, and its enamel had been worn off on the bottom, leaving a surface like sandpaper. Capa, who is a delicate creature, found that he began to bleed after a bath, and he took to wearing shorts in the tub." Capa himself wrote a chapter for the book, "A Legitimate Complaint," in which he notices that he is traveling with several Steinbecks. The one in the morning is shy, mostly quiet, and unable to assist with simple tasks like ordering breakfast. Then Steinbeck opens up with the morning questions: "He has obviously spent his three hours of hunger figuring out the damn things, which range from the old Greek table habits to the sex life of fishes." Capa deals with Steinbeck's long silences on the road during the day, but by the evening the social, gregarious Steinbeck emerges and stays until about 3 AM, when he is in bed "holding firmly a thick volume of poetry from two thousand years ago. . . . His face is fully relaxed, his mouth is open, and the man with the low quiet voice snores without restraint or inhibitions."

As the humor would indicate, Steinbeck abandons the objective perspective of his work of the 1930s. Steinbeck's perspective in *A Russian Journal* is remarkably subjective and, in that respect, has much in common with the work of Tom Wolfe and the other new journalists of the 1960s and 1970s. Such journalism not only allowed Steinbeck to comment directly on what he saw in a way his fiction could not, but it also allowed him to account for the effect his own presence as a foreign observer and American celebrity had on what and whom he observed. Steinbeck records in a personal voice the reaction of the people to himself and to Capa, and vice versa. In effect, he and Capa become characters in the travelogue. This is especially evident in descriptions of the occasional meetings Steinbeck had with journalists, poets, and literary critics who quizzed him on his opinions of Russian authors, American poets, and American foreign policy.

When *A Russian Journal* appeared in the spring of 1948, reviews were mixed. While some reviewers praised the efforts of Steinbeck and the photos of Capa, others found the book imperceptive and a bit self-indulgent. "I haven't taken the trouble to count the lines, but my guess is that more space is devoted to Steinbeck's intake of liquor and food and teasing Capa than to any aspect of Soviet life," exclaimed Louis Fischer of the *Saturday Review.* At the conclusion of the book, Steinbeck predicted this kind of reaction: "We know that this journal will not be satisfactory either to the ecclesiastical Left, nor the lumpen Right. The first will say it is anti-Russian, and the second that it is pro-Russian. Surely it is superficial, and how could it be otherwise?" What Steinbeck notes in his conclusion is a good summary for much of his work: he cuts across politics and acknowledges that no one man, or two, can contain all that is true—certainly not in a relatively short trip across a vast, censored country.

Further Reading: Benson, Jackson J. *The True Adventures of John Steinbeck, Writer.* New York: Viking, 1984; McElrath, Joseph R., Jr., Jesse S. Crisler, and Susan Shillinglaw, eds. *John Steinbeck, The Contemporary Reviews*. New York: Cambridge University Press, 1996; Railsback, Brian. "Style and Image: John Steinbeck and Photography." In *John Steinbeck: A Centennial Tribute*. Ed. Syed Mashkoor Ali. Jaipur, India: Surabhi Publications, 2004.

Scott Simkins and Brian Railsback

RUTHIE. *See* **Joad, Ruthie**.

S

SAFEWAY MANAGER. In *Sweet Thursday,* a compassionate man who allows **the Seer** to steal an occasional candy bar but who does finally have him arrested when he steals three on one visit. Later, on the second Sweet Thursday of the spring, the manager speaks to the presiding judge to arrange for the seer's release from jail—another sign of the goodwill and happiness pervading Cannery Row in the end.

SAGRAMOR DE DESYRUS, SIR. In *The Acts of King Arthur,* one of the knights of the **Round Table** imprisoned by **Sir Tarquin** and rescued by **Sir Lancelot**.

SAINT JOAN. See *Last Joan, The.*

"SAINT KATY THE VIRGIN" (1936). Short story published in 1936 as a separate edition of only 199 copies by The Golden Eagle Press for **Covici-Friede**; it was later included as one of the stories in *The Long Valley.* The story is an odd one, with a peculiar choice of subject and burlesque treatment reminiscent of the stories of Mark Twain (see **Clemens, Samuel Langhorne**). The action is set in France in the province of "P—" in the year "13—." **Roark**, a "bad man who kept a pig," a medieval character who sees through the fraud and hypocrisy of the Catholic Church, raises a pig whom he names **Katy** and teaches all manner of irreverent, sinful behavior. The worldly Roark, suspicious of Church teachings and labeled bad simply because he laughs at "the wrong times and the wrong people," may be viewed as an alter ego for Steinbeck himself, who might have been laughing as he wrote this story. As **Jackson J. Benson** notes, Steinbeck's fondness for this story may provide a "key to his secret heart." Katy responds well to Roark's training, moving from stealing milk and eating her own brothers and sisters to devouring the neighbors' chickens and ducks and even the occasional child. When Roark breeds Katy, however, and she eats every single one of her own piglets, even Roark can no longer condone her depravity. Just as he readies her for the slaughter, he encounters **Brother Colin** and **Brother Paul**, two monks who ask him to tithe to the church. To their surprise and gratification, the heretofore-recalcitrant Roark offers them his immense pig. When the monks see Katy, each reacts according to his nature: Brother Colin, round and worldly, sees in Katy a nearly endless supply of bacon and sausage, whereas Brother Paul, lean and ascetic, hopes to please Father Benedict by converting Katy to Christianity. Theirs is not an easy task given that Katy bites Brother Colin and terrorizes them both by chasing them up a tree. Gradually, after musing on Katy's devilish nature and on the reasons why lions rather than pigs appear more frequently in biblical parables, Brother Paul prevails, delivering "the Sermon on the Mount in beautiful Latin to the groveling, moaning Katy," whose eyes appear to beam with repentance.

Arriving at the monastery, Brother Colin and Brother Paul cause a great stir among the Brotherhood, all of whom can envision Katy as food and all of whom are horrified when Katy dips her hoof in holy water and crosses herself. **Father Benedict** tells Paul he is a fool for converting her, for the church is more in need of pigs this year than of Christians. Nonetheless, Katy becomes a fixture of goodness in the monastery, performing good works and blessing the travelers who make pilgrimages to the monastery of "M—" in order to benefit from Katy's healing powers and receive her blessings. After her death, she is added to the Calendar of the Elect, and ultimately—after much discussion of the difference between physical virginity and virginity by intent—she is raised to sainthood. Her relics reside permanently in the chapel, and thus long after her death, Saint Katy continues to do good works and perform miracles.

Steinbeck uses Katy the pig as a humorous device for gently pointing out the foibles of the Catholic Church's teachings on exorcism, virginity, martyrdom, and qualifications for sainthood, among others.

Further Reading: Benson, Jackson J. *The True Adventures of John Steinbeck, Writer*. New York: Viking, 1984; Hughes, Robert S., Jr. *John Steinbeck: A Study of the Short Fiction*. Boston: Twayne, 1989; Marovitz, Sanford E. "The Cryptic Raillery of 'Saint Katy the Virgin.'" In *A Study Guide to Steinbeck's 'The Long Valley.'* Ed. Tetsumaro Hayashi and Reloy Garcia. Ann Arbor, MI: Pierian, 1976. 73–80.

Abby H. P. Werlock

SALAZAR. In *Viva Zapata!* it is the family name of **Emiliano** and **Eufemio Zapata**'s mother, a name that Emiliano proudly shouts to **Josefa Espejo** at their meeting in the church. Her full name was actually Cleofas Salazar.

SALINAS (CALIFORNIA). Central California farm town and place of John Steinbeck's birth in 1902; the author's relationship with his hometown during much of his lifetime was uneasy, especially as his work was perceived as leftist and all too critical of middle-class conservatism. Now, however, **The National Steinbeck Center**—one of the finest facilities built for an American author—commands the town's Main Street. The Steinbeck home, a two-story white Victorian house, is now The Steinbeck House (132 Central Avenue), serving lunch and selling his books.

When Steinbeck was growing up in Salinas, the town had a population of approximately 2500 and served local cattle ranches and small farms in the area. John did not distinguish himself in school and was a somewhat introverted student at Salinas High School, where his junior year was interrupted by a serious bout of pneumonia that nearly killed him. Part of his recovery included a stay in the warmer climate of Jolon on the southern end of the Salinas Valley. According to **Jackson J. Benson**, Steinbeck felt as a teenager that he was rejected, an outsider, and "he nourished a hatred for his home town, adding up its faults as he perceived them—its narrow-mindedness, its prejudices, its clannishness, and the hypocrisy of its respectability . . . for many years, the people of Salinas returned his hostility." Steinbeck worked several jobs in and around Salinas as a teen and young man, most notably at the **Spreckels sugar** plant (which still stands). In the early 1920s, Steinbeck lived at home on and off again when he wasn't enrolled at **Stanford University**. In 1933 and 1934, Steinbeck was brought back to Salinas with his wife, **Carol Henning Steinbeck**, to care for his dying mother and weakened father. During this period he composed stories that reflect the area immediately surrounding Salinas, including some of ***The Long Valley*** pieces and ***The Red Pony*** stories. The surrounding labor strife and general destitution of farm workers occupied him as well, leading to such works as ***In Dubious Battle*** and ***The Grapes of Wrath***. By the 1939 publication of *Grapes*, many of the fine citizens of Salinas were outraged at their hometown author (while attempting to show **Lewis Milestone** locations for the film version, Steinbeck was afraid to stop on the ranches for fear he would be attacked), but by that year, Steinbeck had moved closer to the coast at Los Gatos, and he had lived in **Pacific Grove** and spent much time in **Monterey**. With his parents both dead by 1935 (the Salinas house was sold then), his ties to Salinas were diminished.

With his marriage to **Gwyndolyn Conger Steinbeck** and later to **Elaine Scott Steinbeck**, New York had become Steinbeck's permanent residence by the end of the 1940s. Jackson J. Benson notes that when Steinbeck did feel homesick for California, as he sometimes did during his World War II travels, he longed for Monterey, not Salinas. However, Steinbeck had decided by the late 1940s to attempt an important, longer novel that would encompass his immediate and extended family, a novel that therefore would find Salinas at its center: ***East of Eden***. By 1951, Steinbeck was reading the Salinas paper regularly and had enlisted the aid of the editor for help in researching his old home; he also asked his sisters, **Mary Steinbeck Dekker** and **Beth Steinbeck Ainsworth**, detailed questions about the area to regain his sense of place. Yet he wrote the book on **Nantucket** and in New York. When Steinbeck did visit his old stomping grounds in California, he often felt uncomfortable, particularly after the death of **Edward F. Ricketts** in 1948. The 1952 publication of *East of Eden* did not help how the people of Salinas felt about him, either. In 1955, Steinbeck published a rather disparaging article about his hometown, **"Always Something to do in Salinas,"** for *Holiday* magazine. He gently mocks a town slogan he remembered: "Salinas is." Though he observes the progress of the town in agriculture and development, he notes, "Salinas was never a pretty town. It took a dullness from the swamps." He takes a special interest in the odd characters, people with violent tendencies, and the town's numerous misers, and he details the ugly Salinas lettuce strike. "It is a kind of metropolis now," Steinbeck concludes. "But the high, thin, gray fog still hangs overhead and every afternoon the harsh relentless wind blows up the valley from King City. And the town justifies the slogan given it when it was very young . . . Salinas is!"

Further Reading: Benson, Jackson J. *The True Adventures of John Steinbeck, Writer.* New York: Viking, 1984; Steinbeck, John. "Always Something to Do in Salinas" (1955). In *America and Americans and Selected Nonfiction*. Ed. Susan Shillinglaw and Jackson J. Benson. New York: Viking, 2002.

Brian Railsback

SAN JUAN DE LA CRUZ. In ***The Wayward Bus***, the fictional destination of the passengers, located forty-two miles south of San Ysidro and separated from Rebel Corners by the San Ysidro River. The town is named after St. John of the Cross (1524–1591), a Spanish monk known for mystical poetry, including "The Dark Night of the Soul" and "The Living Flame of Love," and his advocacy of asceticism.

SAN YSIDRO. In ***The Wayward Bus***, the California town used to establish the location of Rebel Corners, forty-two miles to the south; location of the Greyhound bus station where **Camille Oaks** first appears, before she then rides the bus driven by **Louie** to Rebel Corners.

SAN YSIDRO RIVER. In ***The Wayward Bus***, the river that threatens the two bridges over which the bus ordinarily passes on its way from Rebel Corners to **San Juan de la Cruz**. Its seasonal patterns of flood and dryness, as well as the plant and animal life that surround it, resemble those of the Salinas River described elsewhere in Steinbeck's fiction. Symbolically, though, it looks back to Genesis for its origins, for the river is both serpent-like in its movements from one side of the valley to the other and clearly linked with Noah's flood in its threat to the "world" of the bus. Further, the swollen river, passing through the saturated countryside, becomes an important aspect of a general motif in the novel, that of modern-day excess, be it sexual, gustatory, or material.

SANCHEZ, PABLO. In *Tortilla Flat,* the second paisano to join **Danny**'s household. Readers first hear of Pablo in chapter 1, when Danny and **Pilon**, having just returned from the war, discuss the fates of their old friends and recount the story of how Pablo found himself in jail for stealing a goose. In chapter 3, Pilon encounters Pablo in a ditch and invites him to share two gallons of wine in the house he is renting from Danny. Though Pablo doesn't seem to mind homelessness, Pilon soon convinces him to rent space in the house, and from this point on, Pablo shares with the other paisanos a life of drinking, swindling, and fighting. When Steinbeck lists the special attributes of all the paisanos, he assigns Pablo artistic ingenuousness. The only evidence of this quality in the novel seems to be Pablo's tendency to use more poetic language than the other paisanos. In chapter 4, he proclaims, "If all the dew were diamonds . . . we would be very rich. We would be drunk all our lives." In chapter 5, he says of **Jesus Maria Corcoran**, "His is a grasshopper brain . . . He sings and plays and jumps. There is no seriousness in him."

Pablo also demonstrates an unusually strong religious sensibility for a paisano. He is the one who buys the candle for St. Francis that eventually burns down Danny's second house, and he alone suspects divine intervention in this event. Pablo claims to have seen a vision like the Angel of Death hovering over Danny just before the climactic party, a vision not shared by his companion Pilon, and he claims to have crossed himself and to have said two Hail Marys, something likewise not witnessed by Pilon. But as this last episode suggests, Steinbeck shows that Pablo, despite some minor distinctions, isn't much different from the other paisanos after all. All Pablo's friends pay lip service to religion, and this may be all Pablo is doing when he describes his vision of Danny.

SANDBURG, CARL (1878–1967). Noted twentieth-century American poet and historian, Sandburg first drew the attention of the public with Whitmanesque free verse with the works that make up his *Chicago Poems*, some of which appeared in *Poetry* magazine in 1914. His book after the Great Depression, *The People, Yes* (1936), was a poetic testament to the will of the people to conquer even the most severe tests of their physical and emotional stamina, and some critics attribute **Ma Joad**'s comments about the power of the people in Steinbeck's ***The Grapes of Wrath*** to Sandburg's influence. In addition to poetry, Sandburg published two collections of American folksongs and is most respected for his six-volume biography of Abraham Lincoln, *Abraham Lincoln: the Prairie Years* (1926), and *Abraham Lincoln: the War Years* (1939). The latter work was awarded the **Pulitzer Prize** for History in 1940, a time when Steinbeck, the award winner in fiction for *The Grapes of Wrath*, expressed his pride at being in such distinguished company as Sandburg and the drama winner, **William Saroyan**. Soon the two authors developed a solid friendship, and they often met and talked or sang when Sandburg visited New York.

According to **Jackson J. Benson**, Sandburg and Steinbeck shared a similar trait: the ability to maintain sophistication and intellectual flair while remaining capable of reaching the common people. Both also had a significant nationalistic bent, singing of America and sustaining a deep feeling for the land and its people, and perhaps it was these similarities that drew them together. In the late 1950s, when Steinbeck was in some trouble over a letter he had written to Adlai Stevenson criticizing the American nation for overindulgence and materialistic excess, Sandburg rose to his defense. When Steinbeck detractor **Alfred Kazin** questioned whether Steinbeck was worthy of the 1962 **Nobel Prize**, Sandburg, who remained fiercely loyal to his friend, responded by boycotting a Kazin reception for foreign literati, making sure that the critics clearly understood that Sandburg considered the attack on his friend unwarranted and rude. It is clear that Steinbeck held Sandburg in high respect and valued his friendship strongly. Steinbeck's personal library contained several of the poet's books, collected from 1940, with a gift from Sandburg himself, through to 1960.

Further Reading: Benson, Jackson J. *The True Adventures of John Steinbeck, Writer.* New York: Viking, 1984; DeMott, Robert. *Steinbeck's Reading: A Catalogue of Books Owned and Borrowed.* New York: Garland, 1984.

Michael J. Meyer

SANDRY, MRS. This woman from the Weedpatch (**Arvin Sanitary**) camp in ***The Grapes of Wrath*** provides an illustration of how the religious beliefs of extremely conservative individuals can have evil consequences on others. Mrs. Sandry takes immediate notice of **Rose of Sharon Rivers**'s pregnancy and tells her to be careful about avoiding sin, especially such things as hug dancing and play acting, both of which seem to be occurring at the camp as ways of entertaining the residents. Mrs. Sandry's bleak portrait of God as a punisher rather than a deliverer reinforces Steinbeck's hatred of rigid fundamentalism and parallels the earlier episode with the six Jehovites who also brought pain and disturbance rather than relief when **Granma Joad** fell ill. Rose of Sharon is cowed by Mrs. Sandry's prediction that she will lose her baby as a result of her sin. Mrs. Sandry is convinced that such a miscarriage could be God's punishment for a life spent on personal pleasure rather than on spiritual concerns. When Mrs. Sandry is later confronted by **Ma**, who threatens to harm her physically unless she stops harassing Rose of Sharon, Ma causes Mrs. Sandry to fall into an epileptic fit, complete with animal-like howling that signifies the inhumanity of her religious faith (or, ironically, suggests demon possession). Even the Weedpatch camp director classifies her as "crazy" and urges Ma not to harm her.

Michael J. Meyer

SANTA ROJA, LA. Spanish for **"The Red Saint."** The woman whose legendary beauty (she is compared to Helen of Troy) sets off **Henry Morgan**'s desire to capture Panama in ***Cup of Gold***. She turns out to be older than Henry had imagined, married, and to Henry's great discomfort, very much a woman of the world. A disappointed Henry still tries to enact the romantic scenario of his dreams, but she laughs at his foolishness and confesses that she is disappointed in him also. Enraged and embarrassed at his failure to capture her, Henry kills the cockney pirate **Jones** on a minor pretext and then kills his favorite lieutenant and only friend, **Cocur de Gris**, in a fit of misguided jealousy. Disillusioned at last, Henry demands and receives a ransom of twenty thousand pieces of gold for her from her husband. She recognizes that their confrontation has aged them both, and she leaves Henry feeling sad for both of them. The historical account of the siege of Panama written by Alexandre Exquemelin, who claimed to have been one of Morgan's men, mentions an unnamed woman of Panama who spurned the romantic advances of Henry Morgan and was eventually ransomed.

Further Reading: Eddy, Darlene. "To Go A-Buccaneering and Take a Spanish Town: Some Seventeenth-Century Aspects of Cup of Gold." *Steinbeck Quarterly* 8 (Winter 1975): 3–12.

Kevin Hearle

SAROYAN, WILLIAM (1908–1981). Prolific author of short stories, novels, plays, memoirs, and other pieces, he was born in Fresno, California, and often tended toward works that reflected his life experiences and Armenian heritage. Steinbeck became acquainted with Saroyan but did not care much for his writing. After reading one of Saroyan's most critically acclaimed works, *The Daring Young Man on the Flying Trapeze* (1934), Steinbeck noted in a 1935 letter, as recorded by DeMott, that "**Willa Cather** writes the best prose in America and William Saroyan the worst." In 1940, when Steinbeck won his **Pulitzer Prize** for ***The Grapes of Wrath***, Saroyan won for drama with *The Time of*

Your Life. When Saroyan turned his award down and Steinbeck was asked about it, he commented diplomatically that he was simply pleased to be in the company of Saroyan and **Sandburg** (who had also won that year for poetry).

Further Reading: DeMott, Robert. *Steinbeck's Reading: A Catalogue of Books Owned and Borrowed*. New York: Garland, 1984.

SAUL, JOE. Protagonist in ***Burning Bright***, Steinbeck's last "play-novelette," Joe Saul is a man nearing 50, feeling his powers wane. He is intent on having a child with his young wife, **Mordeen**, who surmises that her husband is impotent because of an earlier bout with rheumatic fever, though Saul himself does not know. Mordeen uses **Victor**, a young man who senses Saul's weakness, as a kind of stud animal so that she can have the **Child** that Saul so desperately wants. At first delighted to be a father, Saul becomes suspicious and visits **Dr. Zorn**. Learning he is sterile, Saul becomes enraged at Mordeen. Through discussions with **Friend Ed** (another Steinbeck character based on **Edward F. Ricketts**) and through introspection, Saul overcomes his anger and comes to accept the Child and Mordeen's love offering (in the book version, Friend Ed has killed Victor, so this complication is eliminated). Like the other characters in the allegorical *Burning Bright*, Saul is more a walking symbol than a flesh-and-blood character. He is an **everyman** in three acts with different settings—thus a circus performer, farmer, and seaman. Saul is man in transition: a bitter old man consumed by waning passions who becomes intellectually enlightened, seeing past his own desires for the love of the Child. He is the Old Testament Saul, a king threatened by a young David, but he is also the New Testament Saul, a selfish man who becomes enlightened on the road to Damascus and becomes Paul, the greatest of the apostles. Acknowledging that humans have one foot in hell and the other in heaven, Saul exclaims near the end of the book, "With all our horrors and our faults, somewhere in us there is a shining." At the end of the play, Saul literally illuminates the darkened stage with his light.

SAWKINS, (CAPTAIN). Puritan pirate captain under **Henry Morgan**'s command in the campaign against Panama in ***Cup of Gold***.

SCARDIGLI, VIRGINIA (1916–). Virginia Scardigli was one of several friends of John Steinbeck and **Edward F. Ricketts** who met on a regular basis at Ed's lab on Cannery Row. After graduating from the University of California at Berkeley, she moved to Carmel in 1935 and eventually fell in with the group at the lab. This group included (at various times throughout the 1930s and early 1940s) **Ritch** and **Tal Lovejoy, Richard** and Jan **Albee, Toby** and Peggy **Street**, Bruce and Jean Arris, Ellwood and Barbara Graham, and **Toni Jackson**. Most of these people were artists, writers, or students. Their parties consisted of such varied activities and trappings as poetry readings, jazz, costumes, wine, and a very informal variety of philosophical inquiry. After Ricketts' death on May 11, 1948, many of these same friends met for his funeral. As the service began, Steinbeck and Scardigli led the others to the chapel, which rested above the ocean, and then down to the water to gaze at the tide pools. More recently, Scardigli has remained active as an eyewitness at Steinbeck conferences, including the Fourth International Steinbeck Congress held in San Jose and Monterey in March 1997.

Further Reading: Benson, Jackson J. *The True Adventures of John Steinbeck, Writer*. New York: Viking, 1984; Lynch, Audry. *Steinbeck Remembered, Interviews with friends and acquaintances of John Steinbeck*. Santa Barbara, CA: Fithian Press, 2000.

Stephen K. George

SCHNEIDER, LOUIS. In ***East of Eden*** a resident of **Salinas** who buys the underage

Cal Trask a pint of whiskey to give to **Rabbit Holman**.

SCHULBERG, BUDD (WILSON) (1914–). Hollywood screenwriter, American novelist and journalist, and winner of the Academy Award for the screenplay for *On the Waterfront* in 1954. Schulberg was a good friend of Steinbeck late in the author's life. Steinbeck considered Schulberg exemplary in his personal concern for minorities and for those who had few opportunities for success. With Steinbeck's help, Schulberg acquired funding for a writing workshop he had established in Watts, a racially heated neighborhood of Los Angeles. By acquiring grants from the National Endowment for the Humanities, the Rockefeller Foundation, and the state of California, Schulberg was able in the 1960s to convert the workshop into a school for about 250 students, later called Douglass House Watts Writers Workshop. In 1971, he founded a parallel school in New York with a similar name, the Frederick Douglass Creative Arts Center. During the Watts riots in 1968, Schulberg went to the school while "buildings were still smoking" and produced with young writers a book entitled *From the Ashes* (1967); later, while Steinbeck prepared for an operation to repair a ruptured spinal disk, Schulberg visited him in the hospital and presented a signed gift copy of this book to his friend. A later publication, *The Four Seasons of Success* (1972), examined six American novelists—**Sinclair Lewis**, **F. Scott Fitzgerald**, **William Saroyan**, Nathanael West, Thomas Heggen, and Steinbeck—and their relationship to success and failure.

During his long career as a writer, Schulberg also taught writing at Columbia University, New York; Phoenixville Veterans Hospital; and University of the Streets, New York. He also received awards from the American Literary Association, as well as from the New York Critics, the Foreign Correspondents, and the Screen Writers Guild.

Further Reading: Benson, Jackson J. *The True Adventures of John Steinbeck, Writer.* New York: Viking, 1984.

Michael J. Meyer

SCOT, LEWIS. Pirate captain in ***Cup of Gold***.

SCOTT, ELAINE. *See* **Steinbeck, Elaine Scott**.

SCOTT, SIR WALTER (1771–1832). Scottish poet, novelist, and biographer who is often considered the inventor of the historical novel. Scott's works include *Waverley* (1814), *Rob Roy* (1818), *Heart of the Midlothian* (1818), and the historical romance *Ivanhoe* (1819). Along with the works of Alexander Dumas, **Robert Louis Stevenson**, and **John Bunyan**, Scott's works impacted the young Steinbeck and led to his fascination with romance and adventure as well as his preoccupation with the fantastic, magical, and religious elements of fiction. Like Steinbeck, Scott was concerned about recording the mores and attitudes of his society and was known for his depiction of all ranges of society, from beggars and rustics to the middle class to the land-holding nobility. His emphasis on ordinary people and their eccentricities and his style that mixed lyric beauty with clarity of description also seem to have influenced the early work of Steinbeck. Scott's interest in the **Arthur** legend as depicted in poetic romance *The Lady of The Lake* (1810) later led the mature Steinbeck to visit Scott's house in Abottsford in 1965 as he did research for his ***The Acts of King Arthur*** and as he searched for undiscovered manuscripts that might shed more light on Arthurian legend.

Michael J. Meyer

SEA OF CORTEZ: A LEISURELY JOURNAL OF TRAVEL AND RESEARCH (1941). Often referred to simply as *Sea of Cortez*, this nonfiction ecological study, coauthored with **Edward F. Ricketts**, includes a narrative portion and a phyletic catalog of marine animals from the Gulf of California that includes photographs. The book in its entirety was published in 1941 and is the record of a journey undertaken to the Sea of Cortez, better known to American readers as the Gulf of California, from March 11 to April

20 of 1940 aboard the ***Western Flyer*** (the authors contend they went with the less well-known name because it was "better sounding and more exciting"). At the time of the book's publication, Steinbeck resisted any efforts by his editor, **Pascal Covici**, to not list Ricketts as an equal coauthor. In 1951, after Ricketts' death, Steinbeck did bow to pressure and allow Viking to publish the narrative portion of the work (***The Log from the Sea of Cortez***) under his name only. Covici expected that the change in authorship would help sales. Though Steinbeck did write most of the *Log*, using the journals of the trip written by Ricketts and the *Western Flyer*'s Captain **Tony Berry**, parts of the narrative portion are taken word for word from Ricketts' earlier work (including the critical section defining **non-teleological thinking**). Thus, the published authorship of the *Log* is a bit misleading. In the 1951 publication, however, Steinbeck added a substantial introductory essay, "About Ed Ricketts," that lauds his coauthor and friend.

In 1939, Ricketts had published (with **Jack Calvin**) a book titled ***Between Pacific Tides***, a book that was described by **Richard Astro** as "a definitive sourcebook for studying marine life on the Pacific Coast." During this period, Steinbeck was quite involved with the lab work at Pacific Biological Laboratories (he eventually became part owner), and he and Ricketts conceived of a trip that was intended to advance Ed's reputation as a scientist and to establish Steinbeck's bona fides as a scientific writer.

Jackson J. Benson reports that the idea for such a trip had "been in the back of [Steinbeck's] mind at least as far back as the writing of the final draft" of ***The Grapes of Wrath***. Plans for the trip came to fruition in the spring of 1940, when Steinbeck chartered the *Western Flyer* and set sail with a crew that included Ed Ricketts, Tony Berry, **Tex Travis** (the engineer), **Sparky Enea** and **Tiny Colletto** (seamen), and **Carol Henning Steinbeck**, the author's wife (who is, curiously, not mentioned in the narrative). Composition was interrupted by the filming of ***The Forgotten Village*** and the decay of Steinbeck's marriage to Carol and the beginning of his relationship with **Gwyndolyn Conger Steinbeck**, who would become the author's second wife. Steinbeck began writing early in 1941, finishing in the summer of that year; ***Sea of Cortez*** was published in December. The staff of his publisher, **Viking**, were not enthusiastic about the work and were unhappy about his insistence that the book bear both his and Ricketts' names. In a letter dated August 25, 1941, and signed by both men, the compositional method of the work is described:

> Originally a journal of the trip was to have been kept by both of us, but this record was found to be a natural expression of only one of us. This journal was subsequently used by the other chiefly as a reminder of what had actually taken place, but in several cases parts of the original field notes were incorporated into the final narrative, and in one case a large section was lifted verbatum [sic] from other unpublished work. This was then passed back to the other for comment, completion of certain chiefly technical details, and corrections. And then the correction was passed back again.

In short, Steinbeck went to great trouble to assure his publishers that the work was indeed a collaboration.

The work challenges a number of prevailing scientific views, but perhaps the most significant challenge is to the idea of objective reality itself. The introduction states, "The design of a book is the pattern of a reality controlled and shaped by the mind of the writer. This is completely understood about poetry or fiction, but it is too seldom realized about books of fact." Steinbeck and Ricketts anticipate what later generations of social scientists will come to realize: that when a process or a system is observed, the presence of the observer changes the process or affects the system. They go on to note, "We knew that what seemed to us true could be only relatively true anyway. There is no other kind of observation." Their stated purpose in the journey is to "go wide open. Let's see what we see, record what we find, and not fool ourselves with conventional scientific strictures." The book is divided into twenty-eight sections or chapters, each of which can, according to **Joseph Fontenrose**, be broken "into two parts, narrative of events and reflections upon them." The first four chapters deal with preparation for the journey and then getting underway. Each of the crew members (save Carol) is introduced and background is given on each. Preparations for the journey are recounted in loving detail, and readers are told which books were brought, what sort of camera was purchased, and how many specimen barrels were included. Interwoven within the narrative are references to the work of other scientists, and comic incidents are abundant (the evil outboard motor, the Hansen Sea-Cow, is vilified, and the whiskey brought along for the trip disappears before the ship gets underway). Observations about humanity and the nature of scientific thinking are included as well; chapter 2 contains a rumination about the relationship between humanity and the boats it builds: "There is an 'idea' boat that is an emotion, and because the emotion is so strong it is probably that no other tool is made with so much honesty as a boat." This relationship is described in terms that are virtually Jungian; the boat is an archetype, and the relationship between person and boat is nearly a part of the collective unconscious: boats have been "designed through millenniums of trial and error by the human consciousness." The narrative mixes these various elements—detailed observation, scientific reference, comic incident, and philosophizing about human nature—with great relish, resulting in a tone that Fontenrose calls "lively, vivid, and entertaining." Furthermore, the method used to narrate the voyage is in keeping with the collecting method used to gather marine samples: there is an attempt to see a larger truth, to record details and behaviors and moods and attitudes, to perceive as much as possible and let whatever patterns or truths exist become slowly apparent, or, in the words of **John H. Timmerman**, "one must observe the specimen in its living reality, in its relation to other things, and in our relation to it. Ideally, the observer should . . . enter the environment."

Chapters 5 and 6 deal largely with the sea voyage to Mexico and the establishment of a shipboard routine. Once the action of the narration is in Mexico, the narrative alternates between descriptions of various ports and what has been written about them, accounts of collection stations (including the species collected and, when of interest, the countryside surrounding the collecting area), and reports of people encountered during the journey (human behavior in bars is subject to the same kind of observation and analysis that is given to sea urchins).

The narration recounts the twenty-one collecting stations; the visits to some stations, such as Cape San Lucas, are recounted in great detail, whereas others are quickly summarized. Throughout the narrative, Steinbeck's love of and respect for the Mexican people is evident; they "were outgoing in a wholesome way, truly interested in their visitors, and always courteous. They confirmed Steinbeck's doctrine . . . that money and possessions poison human relations if they are lifted about human values."

Most Steinbeck scholars point to chapter 14, often called "The Easter Sunday Sermon," as critical to an understanding of Steinbeck's thinking. This section outlines the doctrine of **non-teleological**, or "is," **thinking** and formally states a position on the psychology of groups. Another oft-quoted passage occurs during the stopover in La Paz, when the narrative recounts the tale of an "Indian boy" who "by accident found a pearl of great size" and how the possession of this rare and valuable object so very nearly ruins the young man's life that he "threw it as far as he could into the channel." This tale became the basis for Steinbeck's ***The Pearl***.

The final product of *Sea of Cortez* is a remarkable book, virtually *sui generis* in American literature. The first section, the narrative, is called "pure poetry" by Astro, and the second part, the "phyletic catalogue," as Fontenrose calls it, which includes color plates, black and white photos, and drawings, catalogues approximately 550 species, and ten percent of those species had never before been depicted. The book is a contribution both to American letters and to scientific knowledge. Yet despite its contribution to scientific knowledge, Steinbeckian mischief and humor are apparent. At one point, the group's collecting had discovered what they thought was a new species, and they had planned to name it "Proctophilus winchellii," after Walter Winchell, a sensationalistic and gossiping radio broadcaster. The authors write that the fish so honored "lives in the anus of a cucumber, flipping in and out, possibly feeding on the feces of the host but more likely merely hiding in the anus from possible enemies." Steinbeck defends the choice of name by maintaining it was an attempt to carry "on the ancient and disreputable tradition of biologists."

The book was published December 5, 1941, and the hope was that it would appeal to Christmas shoppers, but sales were disappointing, perhaps because of the holiday spirit–sombering effects of that month's attack on Pearl Harbor. Initial reviews were positive. The reviewer for the *Library Journal* said it is "filled with colorful Steinbeckian philosophy and spicy anecdotes." The reviewer for *Books* pronounced it "a fine-flavored sketch of travel and biological field work," and the *Scientific Book Club Review* was even more generous with its praise: "The first half of the book is highly recommended as good reading for anybody; the second half as a valuable reference work for the marine biologist."

The critical establishment has held the book in high regard; most of the analyses quote from the "Easter Sunday Sermon" and argue that to understand *Sea of Cortez* is to understand Steinbeck's thinking. **Peter Lisca** writes that it is "above all a very entertaining book, full of gusto for all forms of life, and reverence for the known and unknowable universe" and notes that it is indispensable for "knowledge of the intellectual backgrounds of Steinbeck's fiction." Richard Astro, who has written admirably in many places about the relationship between Steinbeck and Ricketts, writes about understanding the truly collaborative nature of the composition process of *Sea of Cortez* and calls the work "an extremely valuable creation in its own right." Brian Railsback notes that the book is ideal as a sourcebook of Steinbeck's thinking in terms of holism, biology, physics, and important connections to **Charles Darwin**'s work. Louis Owens argues that Steinbeck operates "*a priori*," bringing "to his work the pattern of thought according to which reality will be shaped," and concludes that *Sea of Cortez* is Steinbeck's most effective nonfiction book because of the high quality of "the pattern" Steinbeck brought to the work's composition and his fidelity to that pattern. Warren French suggests that the book is an attempt for Steinbeck to establish a new direction for his work and writes about the book both as autobiographical writing and as metaphysical speculation, but cautions that the work "may provide a small reward for the reader's investment in it." French also calls the decision to include **"About Ed Ricketts"** as the preface to *The Log from the Sea of Cortez* an "unfortunate one" and argues instead it should have been "an epilogue to a new edition of ***Cannery Row***."

Sea of Cortez remains the most important of Steinbeck's nonfiction work for readers interested in the philosophical and scientific concepts that drove much of the author's fiction.

Further Reading: Astro, Richard. *"Sea of Cortez."* In *A Study Guide to Steinbeck: A Handbook to His Major Works*. Ed. Tetsumaro Hayashi. Metuchen, NJ: Scarecrow Press, 1974. 168–186; Benson, Jackson J. *The True Adventures of John Steinbeck, Writer.* New York: Viking, 1984; Bracher, Frederick. "Steinbeck and the Biological View of Man." In *Steinbeck and His Critics: A Record of Twenty-Five Years*. Ed. E.W. Tedlock and C.V. Wicker. Albuquerque: University of New Mexico Press, 1957. 183–196; (Fontenrose, Joseph. *"Sea of Cortez."* In *Steinbeck: A Collection of Critical Essays*. Ed. Robert Murray Davis. Englewood Cliffs, NJ: Prentice-Hall, 1972. 122–134; French,

Warren. *John Steinbeck*, 2nd ed. Boston: Twayne Publishers, 1975; ———. *John Steinbeck's Nonfiction Revisited*. New York: Twayne, 1996; Lisca, Peter. *John Steinbeck: Nature and Myth*. New York: Thomas Y. Crowell, 1978; Owens, Louis. "Patterns of Reality and Barrels of Works: From *Western Flyer to Rocinante* in Steinbeck's Nonfiction." In *The Steinbeck Question: New Essays in Criticism*. Ed. Donald R. Noble. Troy, NY: Whitson Publishing, 1993. 171–182; Railsback, Brian. *Parallel Expeditions: Charles Darwin and the Art of John Steinbeck*. Moscow: University of Idaho Press, 1995; Timmerman, John H. *John Steinbeck's Fiction: The Aesthetics of the Road Taken*. Norman: University of Oklahoma Press, 1986.

Charles Etheridge, Jr.

"SECRET WEAPON WE WERE AFRAID TO USE, THE" (1952). Written in 1952 as part of an agreement with *Collier's* to produce three articles for publication in the magazine, "Secret Weapon" was the only one of the three that eventually appeared in print in *Collier's*. Autobiographical in nature, it dramatized Steinbeck's proposal to **Franklin Delano Roosevelt** during World War II that counterfeit American currency be dropped in Europe in order to disrupt the Nazi economy and cause its downfall. The other pieces Steinbeck produced as part of the *Collier's* agreement, **"The Making of a New Yorker"** and **"Positano,"** eventually appeared in the *New York Times Magazine* and *Harper's Bazaar*.

Michael J. Meyer

SEER, THE. In ***Sweet Thursday***, a big, bearded stranger with the eyes of a baby who lives on the beach under the sheltering boughs of a stand of pine trees. Many critics have pointed out that the seer resembles the old man in ***To a God Unknown*** who makes daily sacrifices to the setting sun. He also has some kinship with the old man from Gambais in ***The Short Reign of Pippin IV*** who pulls things out of the moat that other people push in. These grotesque figures are portrayed as being out of touch with reality, yet as perhaps having greater access to the truth than those who lead a more mundane existence. The description of the Seer's eyes—"the lively, innocent eyes of a healthy baby," eyes with "the merry light of a wise baby"—suggests that his natural vision has been uncorrupted by contact with society. The seer assumes a central thematic role in *Sweet Thursday*. To **Doc**, the seer represents a simpler, self-sufficient mode of existence that he feels he has left behind. As Doc reclines in the seer's bed of pine needles, a sense of peacefulness returns to him. In words that echo his comments about **Mack** and the boys in ***Cannery Row***, Doc expresses his admiration for the way the seer has escaped the driving ambition for material acquisition that he feels is symptomatic of the times. However, as the two of them discuss Doc's unease, which is obvious to the perceptive eyes of the seer, it is not a life of self-sufficiency or natural simplicity that the seer recommends for Doc. Instead, he advises that Doc may not be able to move forward in his search for the meaning of his personal existence without love. Along with his overt messages, the seer offers Doc other lessons through example. When he perceives beauty, for instance, the seer makes no attempt to rationally analyze it or even to determine whether what he sees is real or illusory, but simply accepts his vision and responds to the beauty. Similarly, Doc later has to suspend his rational examination of whether **Suzy** will be a suitable mate and simply accept and act upon the beauty that he perceives in her. The seer's example also provides Doc with a naturalistic lesson about the insistence of human drives. Although the seer tells Doc that appetites are good—"the more appetites a man has, the richer he is"—the seer tries to suppress his own appetite for candy bars so that he won't have to steal. This attempt to suppress a strong basic drive, even for a rationally determined good, is shown to be futile, for eventually he is unable to enforce the unnatural austerity on himself. Likewise, Doc's attempt to disregard the voice of his marrow, which urges him to seek love as a salve for his loneliness, is destined to fail. Finally, the seer represents the lonely, isolated existence that could be in store for Doc if he fails to find love. The Seer, far from leading an idyllic life in his nature bower, finds himself watching the sunset each night simply because it is the one activity in his solitary life that makes him "seem needed."

Toward the conclusion of the novel, the seer also serves to advance the plot to its final outcome. When **Hazel** is considering breaking Doc's arm to bring his friend together with Suzy, the seer's advice commits him to this course. Speaking in terms that echo **Lee** in ***East of Eden*** and **Friend Ed** in ***Burning Bright***, the seer says, "If you love him you must do anything to help him—anything. Even kill him to save him incurable pain. This is the highest and most terrible duty of friendship." Hazel follows the seer's advice, and the union he hoped for is achieved.

Bruce Ouderkirk

SEGAL, GEORGE (1934–). Film actor who played **George Milton** in a 1968 television version of ***Of Mice and Men*** opposite Nicol Williamson as **Lennie Small**. Among Segal's more notable films are *Who's Afraid of Virginia Woolf?* (1966), *The Quiller Memorandum* (1966), and *A Touch of Class* (1973).

SHAKESPEARE, WILLIAM (1564–1616). Elizabethan playwright and poet who is arguably the most famous author in English letters. According to **Robert DeMott**, John Steinbeck had a complete twelve-volume 1887 edition of Shakespeare's works in his personal library (though only volumes 3 through 9 have survived). Throughout his lifetime, Steinbeck also owned other editions of Shakespeare's works and individual plays. Steinbeck appreciated the bard's works throughout his lifetime, an appreciation that grew over the years. The title of ***The Moon Is Down*** comes from a line in *Macbeth* (Act II, scene 1), and Steinbeck's last novel, ***The Winter of Our Discontent***, is derived from *Richard III* (Act 1, scene 1). DeMott surveys Steinbeck's letters, quoting comments made from 1943 to 1960, and writes, "In his letters JS often drew on Shakespeare for statements on character, symbolism, theme, inspiration, and personal and historical parallels."

Further Reading: DeMott, Robert. *Steinbeck's Reading: A Catalogue of Books Owned and Borrowed*. New York: Garland, 1984; Hayashi, Tetsumaro. "Steinbeck's *Winter* as Shakespearean Fiction." *Steinbeck Quarterly* 12 (1979): 107–115.

SHAW, GEORGE BERNARD (1856–1950). Controversial Dublin-born playwright, critic, economist, reformer, and novelist. Shaw was a prolific playwright, writing over fifty plays during his long lifetime, works that included *Major Barbara* (1907), *Pygmalion* (1912), and *Heartbreak House* (1917). Although Steinbeck enjoyed Shaw's work in his teens, even attempting to write a sequel to *Caesar and Cleopatra* (1913) when he was seventeen, he believed Shaw's literary persona obscured the vacuous nature of much of his writing. For example, **Jay Parini** reports that while in isolation at Lake Tahoe in 1936, Steinbeck wrote to friend **Bob Cathcart** about Shaw, commenting that the British author appealed to the young mind because "his wit is so dazzling that we never stop to consider that he had never said anything very important." **Jackson J. Benson** writes that it was, however, Shaw's shameless self-promotion and self-aggrandizing nature that led Steinbeck to quip, "he is the greatest press agent . . . pretending to be a genius, and pretending with such force that he convinces himself first and then other people." Steinbeck felt that future generations would see Shaw as a "charlatan." Although he admitted that Shaw was "an artist," he added, "he is never able to be all artist and no charlatan." Steinbeck saw Shaw as a "self-advertiser," the "greatest press agent" of the day, and felt that after Shaw died, people would forget about him. However, Steinbeck appears to retract this sentiment in a letter to **Carlton (Dook) Sheffield** on November 28, 1962, written while he was working on his **Nobel Prize acceptance speech**. Although Steinbeck expressed the fear of the Nobel Prize being an "epitaph" as it was for many writers, he made an exception for George Bernard Shaw. Nevertheless, his rejection of Shaw's so-called publicity-seeking remained adamant. In fact, Steinbeck worked conscientiously to formulate his own vision of the relationship between the artist and his work, believing that, as Jackson J. Benson claims, the artist's personal life "stays in the background," letting "his work speak for itself." Though much of Steinbeck's work was, in a sense, just as controversial as Shaw's, Steinbeck always attempted to remove himself, and his personal life for that matter, from those controversies. Steinbeck's library contained four works by Shaw: *Man and Superman* (1903), *Caesar and Cleopatra* (1913), *Pygmalion* (1912), and *Saint Joan* (1924).

Further Reading: Benson, Jackson J. *The True Adventures of John Steinbeck, Writer.* New York: Viking, 1984; DeMott, Robert. *Steinbeck's Reading: A Catalogue of Books Owned and Borrowed.* New York: Garland, 1984; Steinbeck, John. *Steinbeck: A Life in Letters.* Ed. Elaine Steinbeck and Robert Wallsten. New York: Viking, 1976.

Janet L. Flood and T. Adrian Lewis

SHEBLEY, LLOYD. Naturalist and friend of Steinbeck during the late 1920s and 1930s. As an employee of the Department of Fish and Game, Shebley ran a local fish hatchery near Lake Tahoe where Steinbeck would often visit and sometimes work. Though not nearly to the extent that **Edward F. Ricketts** did, Shebley provided Steinbeck with several scientific concepts incorporated in his fiction, primarily influencing his discourse on the behavioral patterns of his characters. While Steinbeck was working at the fish hatchery in Tahoe City in 1928, Shebley was out when guests, two sisters, came looking for him, so the author entertained the visitors; one of the sisters was **Carol Henning Steinbeck**, who would later become Steinbeck's first wife.

Further Reading: Benson, Jackson J. *The True Adventures of John Steinbeck, Writer.* New York: Viking, 1984.

Ted Scholz

SHEFFIELD, CARLTON "DOOK" (1901–1989). One-time roommates and longtime friends, Sheffield and Steinbeck first met during registration at **Stanford University** in January 1923. While at Stanford University, they each had dreams about being writers and would often confide in one another on different matters of life, ethics, and philosophy. In an early letter, Steinbeck describes their relationship as one that "supplement[ed] and strengthen[ed] the other" through the years, and he notes that although they were "opposites," they were also "equals." Though they remained faithful correspondents with one another throughout their lives, their relationship at times became strained as they were each forced to come to terms with Steinbeck's increasing popularity. Sheffield's book on their friendship, *Steinbeck: The Good Companion*, was published in 1983 by American Lives Endowment and offers keen insights into their long friendship.

Further Reading: Benson, Jackson J. *The True Adventures of John Steinbeck, Writer.* New York: Viking, 1984; Sheffield, Carlton. *Steinbeck: The Good Companion.* Berkeley, CA: Creative Arts Books, 1983; Steinbeck, John. *Steinbeck: A Life in Letters.* Ed. Elaine Steinbeck and Robert Wallsten. New York: Viking, 1976.

Ted Scholz

SHERIFF (*EAST OF EDEN*; CONNECTICUT). Unnamed Connecticut sheriff who goes to the Trask farm in *East of Eden* to question **Cathy Ames** and is duped by her feigned amnesia.

SHERIFF (*EAST OF EDEN*; KING CITY). Unnamed King City sheriff who investigates the shooting of **Adam Trask** and the disappearance of **Cathy Trask** in *East of Eden*. On the basis of the information given to him by **Faye**, he concludes that her new girl, **Kate Albey**, is the missing Mrs. Trask. He goes to talk to Kate and makes her promise to maintain her new identity, to stay away from King City, and to dye her hair black so that no one will recognize her, all of which she does.

Margaret Seligman

SHERIFF ("THE VIGILANTE"). In **"The Vigilante,"** the sheriff is a clearly hypocritical figure bent solely on furthering and maintaining his official and political power. He offers practically no resistance to the lynching mob, merely exhorting them to capture the correct prisoner, even identifying the jail cell so that the mob can storm it. A minor character, he is the negative stereotype of American law enforcers.

Abby H. P. Werlock

SHIRER, WILLIAM (1904–1993). In the 1920s and 1930s, stationed in Europe and in India as a foreign correspondent for the *Chicago Tribune* and the Universal News Service. In addition, he served from 1937 to 1941 as radio broadcaster for the Columbia Broadcasting System (CBS), relaying to America news of the European crises leading to World War II. His impassioned statements alerting America to the Nazi danger earned him several journalistic awards. Steinbeck first met Shirer through his publisher **Lewis Gannett** in 1944. Soon Steinbeck sought advice about his new position as a war correspondent because he was impressed with Shirer's recollection of European political events in *Berlin Diary: The Journal of a Foreign Correspondent, 1934–1941* (1941), which gained an international audience for its simple documentation of survival amid horror. In the 1950s Shirer began his research for *The Rise and Fall of the Third Reich*, his massive study of the Nazi movement that won a National Book Award in 1961. Other notable books include *The Collapse of the Third Republic: An Inquiry into the Fall of France in 1940* (1969), *Gandhi: A Memoir* (1979), and his autobiographical *Twentieth-Century Journey* (1976, 1984, 1990), published in a three-volume set.

SHOLOKOV, MIKHAIL (1905–1984). Russian writer at odds with the Stalinist writing establishment whom Steinbeck considered one of the best living Russian authors. The two authors met in Helsinki in 1957, and Sholokov expressed his admiration for Steinbeck's work. According to **Robert DeMott**, Steinbeck likely read *And Quiet Flows the Don* (1934) and *The Don Flows Home to the Sea* (1940).

"SHORT, SHORT STORY OF MANKIND, A FABLE" (1966). First published in *Adam* in August 1966, this short piece is a comical take on man's instinct for survival. Steinbeck depicts two cavemen discussing members of another tribe who have adopted so-called "normal" ways of living and have made 'technological" advances. Soon, the tribe develops a series of inventors and freethinkers who influence the other people around them, primarily because individuals realize that a group's failure to go along with change usually results in extinction. As Steinbeck's fable continues, the tribes merge into a state, a league, and then a nation. The latter development works well until the clever inventors discover long-range missiles and the atom bomb. The question the author poses is how mankind will deal with this challenge; Steinbeck, of course, hopes that the human race will be smarter than the cavemen and will knuckle down and do what is necessary for survival.

SHORT REIGN OF PIPPIN IV, THE (1957). Although *Pippin*, Steinbeck's fifteenth novel (1957) and certainly one of his lesser works, received mixed reviews—some loving Steinbeck's high-spirited and uncharacteristic foray into political satire, others seeing in its lightness of tone and content another failure to measure up to the talent that produced ***The Grapes of Wrath***—writing it gave the author particular pleasure. The idea of a spoof on the restoration of the French monarchy occurred to him during his stay in Paris in 1954. He sketched the piece out as a story at that time, but didn't return to it until 1956, when he produced a book-length manuscript within a month. "I could not resist writing it," he wrote to **Toby**

Street, adding, "I do have fun with my profession."

The book, which Steinbeck called a "fabrication," satirizes French politics and the Americanization of modern French culture. The title character, **Pippin Héristal**, is a mild-mannered astronomer in midlife who lives comfortably with his wife, daughter, and telescope in a leased apartment at Number One Avenue de Marigny, a venerable house originally built as the headquarters of the Knights of St. John (not coincidentally, this was Steinbeck's Paris address). Supported by the income from a small estate in the Loire that produces wine "tasting like the odor of spring wildflowers," Pippin pursues his pleasures—plays, concerts, ballets, learned societies, and, chiefly, amateur astronomy—largely undisturbed. Except for sometimes-complicated financial negotiations with his practical and frugal wife, **Marie Héristal**, and the shifting cultural and political passions of his twenty-year-old daughter, **Clotilde Héristal** intense, violent, star-struck, pretty, and overweight—his life is satisfactorily routine. One February 14, that routine life is disrupted by an unseasonable meteor shower that convinces the excited Pippin that he needs a new camera. Marie is convinced he does not, inquiring pointedly, "Can one eat meteors, M'sieur?" Pippin visits his uncle, **Charles Martel**, to complain of his domestic predicament, and Martel suggests a diplomatic plan whereby the camera can be paid for in small increments that Marie will not notice. Marie, in the meantime, consults her friend and confidante **Sister Hyacinthe**, a former dancer in the Follies Bergère and now a nun. Sister Hyacinthe advises a little reverse psychology, assuring the ambivalent wife that should she insist Pippin buy the camera, he will very likely be reluctant to spend the money himself. The ensuing negotiations lead to a hilarious confusion of hidden agendas, interrupted conveniently by Clotilde's appearance to announce that she's leaving for a screen test for a part in an American film. Once the principals' characters are established, the writer turns to a broadly comic characterization of the French government where "anarchy has been refined to the point of reaction" and instability is the norm. Two days before the aforementioned meteor shower, all parties have been summoned to the Elysée Palace to deliberate a course of action following the failure of M. Rumorgue's Proto-Communist government. The parties represented include "The Conservative Radicals; The Radical Conservatives; The Royalists; The Right Centrists; The Left Centrists; The Christian Atheists; The Christian Christians; The Christian Communists" and other equally oxymoronic denominations. After much debate, the National Assembly decides to restore the monarchy. Before they settle upon the Bourbon pretender, however, various subgroups of Royalists, including vestigial Merovingians, Orleanists, and Caesarians who claimed descent from Julius Caesar, appear to be contenders. After much debate, they agree upon Pippin Arnulf Héristal, descendant of Charlemagne.

Preoccupied with his efforts to photograph the meteor shower, Pippin is one of the few who, on the following day, is unaware that the French Republic has been voted out of existence and that he has been elected King of France by acclamation, his line having been traced from Charlemagne through one Pippin III, who died in 768. When a coronation committee surprises him with the announcement, he dismisses it as "a joke not in good taste." After a number of failed attempts to argue his way out of the appointment, he sends the committee away, hoping the preposterous appointment will dissolve as a dream in the interim. A "royal salute" of antiaircraft batteries awakens him. He flees to his uncle's antique establishment; Charles musingly decides that since the French want anything but a stable government, Pippin has been thrust into the role of "what the Americans call a 'patsy.'" He has no way out; he's "sunk." He must accept the crown or be guillotined.

Pippin's first official act, finding that the monarchy's total balance in the bank is 120,000 francs, is to request one subsidy from America "for the purpose of making France strong against Communism" and an equal subsidy from the Communist nations "in the interests of world peace." The coronation itself proves to be a major undertaking, requiring, as it does, that costumes be exhumed or made, requisite courtly servants be appointed, and industries be given time to make millions of ceramic souvenirs. Pippin mourns the loss of privacy and leisure to pursue astronomy. He wants to wear his own clothes—most especially a favorite old corduroy jacket—and drive himself around on his motorbike. Madame Héristal, however, takes on her new status with "realism and vigor." She makes lists of things to be done. Clotilde, in the meantime, has fallen in love with **Tod Johnson**, a fellow member of the Tab Hunter fan club and scion of a wealthy chicken-ranching family in Petaluma. Once it is established that his father is an authentic king (Egg King, as American ads have it), the match passes muster as appropriate to Clotilde's new status. Tod's explanations of American business and corporate profit strategies aim sharp satirical barbs at capitalism and the postwar culture of the 1950s. When Tod tries to advise the king to run France on an American corporate model, the assumptions behind both monarchy and capitalism are reduced to absurdities.

Though Pippin makes periodic attempts to escape and drowns his sorrows in occasional drinking sprees with Uncle Charlie, a summer of relative peace and benevolence ensues, but the monarchy runs into trouble when the people begin to be suspicious of so much peace and prosperity. McCarthy-style witch-hunts place the king in a cross fire of confused purposes. When Pippin begins to articulate democratic–socialist sympathies with the laboring people, he finds himself increasingly lonely and disillusioned about the government, particularly with respect to its similarities to American capitalism. He takes solitary rides in the woods on his motorcycle and on one of these rides, he visits an old man who helps clarify his emerging political philosophy. He also seeks wisdom from Sister Hyacinthe, who encourages him to follow his own lights. Uncle Charlie warns him that if he exceeds his role as figurehead and presumes to make suggestions to the senate, he'll become a martyr to his cause. Pippin, however, decides to follow his conscience.

Pippin's moment of greatness comes when he addresses a convention of party leaders and makes a plea for more equitable distribution of resources, wages keyed to profits, low taxes collected from all, health insurance, pensions, and restoration of badly used land. He ends with a plea for "Liberty, Equality, Fraternity and Opportunity." Having delivered himself of this shocking speech, he leaves the various parties and the press to their devices, quietly slips out into the woods and back into his corduroy jacket and crash helmet, and rides his motorcycle to his old home where, he believes, he will be left to happy obscurity and amateur astronomy while the factions carry on their riotous debates.

Although the satire is very broad, the characters thin, and the plot often ridiculous, *Pippin* is a book with heart and surpasses simple allegory or parody. In various dialogues and speeches, Steinbeck provides a sense of his political philosophy and raises questions about poverty and privilege that deserve reflection. A much more serious, often angry, consideration of these issues occurs later in ***America and Americans***.

Marilyn Chandler McEntyre

SIMMONDS, ROY S. (1925–2001). England's leading Steinbeck scholar was a civil servant who made extensive studies of Steinbeck's manuscripts as the basis for a series of articles. He also wrote *Steinbeck's Literary Achievement* (Muncie, IN: Steinbeck Research Institute, 1976) and *John Steinbeck: The War Years, 1939–1945* (Lewisburg, PA: Bucknell University Press, 1996) and several books about the Southern novelist William March. One of his final Steinbeck criticisms appears in Edwin Mellen Press's *A Biographical and Critical Introduction of John Steinbeck*, published in 2000.

SINGLE, JENNY/JENNIE. A sidewalk encounter with **Ethan Allen Hawley** (***The***

Winter of Our Discontent) convinces Ethan that she would be the least likely witness in town.

SINISE, GARY (1955–). Stage and screen actor who played **Tom Joad** in the Steppenwolf Theatre production of ***The Grapes of Wrath*** and both directed and played **George Milton** in the 1992 film of ***Of Mice and Men***. Sinise has also recorded *Of Mice and Men* on audiotape. Sinise says that seeing a stage production of *Of Mice and Men* when he was a teenager reduced him to tears and made him determined to become an actor. Among his subsequent films have been *Forrest Gump* (1994), *Apollo 13* (1995), *Mission to Mars* (2000), and *The Human Stain* (2004).

SLIM. A jerkline skinner and quietly grave authority of the ranch hands in ***Of Mice and Men***. He wears a Stetson, and his long black hair is combed straight back. When his dog gives birth to nine pups, he tells **Carlson** that he "drowned four of 'em right off" because he does not believe that the mother dog can feed that many puppies. Slim is one of the ranch hands whom **George Milton** trusts. At a card game, George tells Slim that they have left the previous ranch so that **Lennie Small** would not be lynched by a mob after he was falsely accused of raping a girl. Slim is quick to notice that it is "funny" that George and Lennie stick together because "hardly none of the guys even travel together." As Slim perceives it, ranch hands normally come and go alone. Slim is also the character who stirs up a fight between Lennie and **Curley**, who suspects that Slim is having an affair with **Curley's wife**.

At the end of the novel, there seems to be a closer bond between George and Slim, who may be the only person on the ranch that understands George's shooting of Lennie. After Slim reaches the site where George has just shot Lennie, Slim tries to comfort George, and they depart together.

SMALL, LENNIE. In ***Of Mice and Men***, **George Milton**'s companion. He is a huge man and mentally deficient. Steinbeck describes Lennie as the opposite of George, who is physically small but mentally sharp: "Behind him [George] walked his opposite, a huge man, shapeless of face, with large, pale eyes, with wide, sloping shoulders; and he walked heavily, dragging his feet a little, the way a bear drags his paws. His arms did not swing at his sides, but hung loosely." Lennie loves soft, furry things, and he keeps a dead mouse in his pocket and strokes it. Lennie's only desire is to live on a ranch with George and tend rabbits. Lennie always forgets what George tells him, but he remembers that George promises him that he can tend some rabbits when they own their place. George knowingly tells Lennie to stay away from **Curley's wife**; although simple, Lennie is attracted to Curley's wife, who, out of loneliness, often comes to the bunkhouse to look for the company of the ranch hands. One day, when all other ranch hands are playing horseshoes, she approaches Lennie and invites him to stroke her hair. Being a giant with enormous strength, Lennie holds her too tightly, panics, and accidentally breaks her neck and kills her when she tries to get away. George, his companion and loyal friend, is forced to kill Lennie in order to save him from the cruel wrath of **Curley**. In explaining what he intended Lennie to convey to readers, Steinbeck wrote in a letter that Lennie "was not to represent insanity at all but [rather] the inarticulate and powerful yearning of all men."

Because Steinbeck uses animal imagery on several occasions to describe Lennie, critics often speak of Lennie as a symbol of humankind's animal nature. When Lennie drinks from the pool in the grove, he "dabble[s] his big paw in the water"; at the end of the novel, Lennie appears out of the brush as silently as a creeping bear moves. Lennie represents the frail nature of primeval innocence and is the id to George's ego or the body to George's brain. George tells **Slim** that his relationship with Lennie "made me seem God damn smart alongside of him" because Lennie seemed to be a natural part of himself. To prove that Lennie was as obedient to him as one's body to his brain, George relates that one time he told Lennie to jump into the Sacramento River from a cliff, and Lennie, who couldn't swim a stroke, jumped in without any hesitation and almost drowned. In the novel, Lennie is repeatedly associated with animals or described as childlike. Moreover, Steinbeck portrays Lennie as an innocent and natural being, harmless to no one unless danger is imposed on him. If there is anything flawed in Lennie, it is the inherent imperfection in humanity that renders the farm with the rabbits—Lennie's dream—forever an impossibility. In this sense, the title, *Of Mice and Men*, a fragment from the poem by **Robert Burns**, gives emphasis to the idea of the futility of human endeavor or the vanity of human wishes.

Further Reading: Steinbeck, John. *Steinbeck: A Life in Letters.* Ed. Elaine Steinbeck and Robert Wallsten. New York: Viking, 1975.

Luchen Li

SMASHER. In **"The Gift,"** Smasher is described as a shepherd dog who had lost an ear fighting a coyote. He chases chickens as he makes the farm rounds with **Jody Tiflin**.

SMITH, ELIZABETH. *See* Breck, John.

SMITH, E. C. A. *See* Breck, John.

SMITTY. In ***Of Mice and Men***, a skinner who fought with **Crooks** earlier at a Christmas party.

SMUTS, J. C. (1870–1950). Jan Christian Smuts was a votarist of **Darwin**'s theory of evolution; he found evolution the key to a wider vision, a holistic way of viewing nature and its interrelations among species. He also recognized evolution as a progressive, creative force, interpreting the struggle for survival as a "form of comradeship, of social cooperation and mutual help." **Edward F. Ricketts** owned Smuts's *Holism and Evolution*, and he and Steinbeck likely discussed it in the spring of 1932. The viewpoint of struggle as a positive, progressive force is evident throughout Steinbeck's writing, particularly in ***The Grapes of Wrath*** and ***The Log From the Sea of Cortez*** and most explicitly in ***America and Americans***. Steinbeck's close attention to Smuts is evident in *The Grapes of Wrath*, for his definition of a tenant farmer closely parallels Smuts's definition of a whole. Smuts writes, "A whole, which is *more* than the sum of its parts, has something internal, some inwardness of structure and function, some specific inner relations, some internality of character or nature, which constitutes that *more*." Steinbeck's description of the farmer notes inner relations (chemistry and elements) and external connections with the land, all with the same rhetorical emphasis on "more": "Carbon is not a man, nor salt nor water nor calcium. For he is all these, but he is much more, much more; and the land is so much more than its analysis. The man who is more than his chemistry, walking on the earth, turning the plow point for a stone . . . that man who is more than his elements knows the land that is more than its analysis."

Further Reading: Astro, Richard. *John Steinbeck and Edward F. Ricketts: The Shaping of a Novelist.* New Berlin: University of Minnesota Press, 1973; Railsback, Brian. *Parallel Expeditions: Charles Darwin and the Art of John Steinbeck*. Moscow: University of Idaho Press, 1995; Smuts, Jan Christian. *Holism and Evolution*. New York: Macmillan, 1926.

"SNAKE, THE" (1938). This fourth story in Steinbeck's collection, ***The Long Valley***, continues to demonstrate the author's interest in the psychology of gender and sex. Originally appearing in a February 1938 edition of *Esquire* under the title "A Snake of One's Own," it has been interpreted from **Freud**ian and **Jung**ian perspectives, of course, as well as from biblical, Edenic ones, and most critics also point to Steinbeck's juxtaposing of the natural world to the scientific method.

"SOME RANDOM AND RANDY THOUGHTS" (1951). Appeared in *The Author Looks at Format* (1951); in this essay,

Steinbeck ponders the disingenuous methods of publishers for selling books, and the survivability of the book form amid the advent of other kinds of entertainment. He makes clear his preference for cheap paperbacks, which can be passed from reader to reader, over expensive, handsome editions, and his belief in the sacredness and immortality of books.

Further Reading: Steinbeck, John. "Some Random and Randy Thoughts on Books." *America and Americans and Selected Nonfiction.* Ed. Susan Shillinglaw and Jackson J. Benson. New York: Viking, 2002.

Eric Skipper

"SOME THOUGHTS ON JUVENILE DELINQUENCY" (1955). A brief article in the *Saturday Review* (May 28, 1955) in which Steinbeck argues that juveniles need to exercise responsibility and loyalty to a unit and tend to look to gangs to fulfill that need.

Scott Simkins

SOMERS, OLD LADY. A **Monterey** resident who figures briefly in one of ***Sweet Thursday***'s many slapstick incidents. When **Cacahuete Rivas** aims his trumpet into a sewer pipe, every toilet in the neighborhood, including hers, erupts with "Stormy Weather." Old lady Somers is taking an enema at the time of this brass explosion, and the rectal result is left to the reader's imagination.

SONNY BOY. The plump Greek owner of a restaurant and bar on the wharf in **Monterey** where **Doc** has his first date with **Suzy** in *Sweet Thursday*. **Fauna**, telephoning as Doc's secretary, has made elaborate arrangements with **Sonny Boy** to ensure that the dinner date is a romantic success. Sonny Boy scrupulously performs his role as Cupid, having a fireside table ready, high-powered martinis mixed, Chablis chilled, and a meal prepared of crab and pompano, which combines the couple's presumed astrological signs of Cancer and Pisces. Fauna and Sonny Boy's efforts are successful to the extent that Doc and Suzy end up spending a pleasant evening together walking on the beach.

Bruce Ouderkirk

SORLUS OF THE FOREST. In *The Acts of King Arthur*, brother of **Brian of the Forest**, both of whom are encountered by **Gawain** on his Quest of the White Stag.

"SOUL AND GUTS OF FRANCE, THE" (1952). Appeared in *Colliers* (August 30, 1952: 26–30); this travel account is an homage to the hardworking, fiercely individualistic province dwellers of France. Steinbeck tells of a visit to the village of Poligny, which defended itself valiantly against German occupation. He relates how the men responded to his defense of the United States and its policies with innate skepticism and how talk always returned to the subject of wine, which was the town's foremost love and occupation. According to Steinbeck, "the future of France will be decided by people such as these."

Further Reading: Steinbeck, John. "The Soul and Guts of France." In *America and Americans and Selected Nonfiction.* Ed. Susan Shillinglaw and Jackson J. Benson. New York: Viking, 2002.

Eric Skipper

SPANISH CORPORAL. In ***Pastures of Heaven***, as the initial discoverer of Las Pasturas, he finds the Edenic valley by accident as he chases a deer to the top of the ridge and exclaims, "Here are the green pastures of heaven which the Lord giveth us." Unfortunately, he contracts a sexually transmitted disease from one of the Native Americans he is escorting back to servitude and dies before he can return to take advantage of the beautiful and fruitful surroundings.

SPECTATOR, THE. One of the books brought along in ***Travels with Charley***. Early in part 2, during a stop in the White Mountains of Vermont, Steinbeck takes great delight in reading from the first volume of Henry Morely's 1883 edition of **Joseph Addison's** (British, 1672–1719) most famous collection of essays. In the selection that Steinbeck reads, Addison writes that readers seem more interested in the biography of the writer than in the writer's work. Steinbeck agrees and, in the style of Addison, offers a prose vignette describing himself and his travel clothing for his readers.

Further Reading: Addison, Joseph, and Henry Steele. *The Spectator.* Ed. Henry Morley. London: Routledge, 1883.

SPENGLER, OSWALD (1880–1936). German philosopher with a background in science, mathematics, history, and art. Spengler developed an explanation of the history of human culture in his significant work *The Decline of the West* (1918). Much of the volume is meant to demonstrate that every individual culture had a unique "soul" and that each facet of this cultural core (art and thought) passed through a cycle of growth and decay that resembled the biological cycle of living organisms. In particular, Spengler controversially argued that European culture had completely matured in its period of technological and political expansion. **Joseph Campbell** lent Steinbeck *The Decline of the West* for a brief period in 1932. Steinbeck soon returned the volume, apparently without finishing it. In fact, for the most part, Steinbeck consistently obscured the substance of his philosophical reading. **Carlton Sheffield**, for example, remembers Steinbeck as having read Spengler years earlier, leaving the question of Spengler's potential influence in some doubt. Eventually, Steinbeck purchased a complete copy of *The Decline of the West*, although exactly when remains uncertain. It seems that Steinbeck was at least slightly alarmed by the potential implications of Spengler's thought and the destructive repercussions that it might have for his art.

Further Reading: DeMott, Robert. *Steinbeck's Reading: A Catalogue of Books Owned and Borrowed.* New York: Garland, 1984.

Brian Niro

SPRECKELS SUGAR. The Spreckels family owned a sugar-beet processing plant south of Salinas, California, as well as sugar-beet ranches and other plants at other locations. Steinbeck worked for the company as a teenager and young man, working at various times as a maintenance man, ranch worker supervisor, and bench chemist. He based his material in ***Of Mice and Men*** on the Spreckels ranch hands or "bindlestiffs" who roamed the country looking for work.

Paul M. Blobaum

SPRINGSTEEN, BRUCE (1949–). American singer-songwriter most famous for the populist, working-class appeal of his depiction of American angst. Springsteen enjoyed his greatest popularity during the early 1970s through to the mid-1980s. During this period, Springsteen's music moved progressively from a folksy blues-driven rock toward a more accessible pop-rock market. In 1995, and after several years of absence from the spotlight, Springsteen released a solo album titled *The Ghost of Tom Joad*. The album is a low-key effort featuring the harmonica and guitar combination that reaches back to the isolated and intimate simplicity of folk music traditions. Springsteen expands the significance of the character **Tom Joad** to represent the entirety of migrant exploitation in America. In the title track of the album, Springsteen's narrator embarks on a migrant voyage where he searches, waits, and eventually sits by the fireside with the ghost of Tom Joad. Although Springsteen nearly failed to acknowledge Steinbeck's role in the creation of the character Tom Joad, he did perform a benefit concert in October 1996 for the Steinbeck Research Center (now **The Martha Heasley Cox Center for Steinbeck Studies**). Afterward, Springsteen was given the John Steinbeck Award. Interestingly, the album liner notes recognize as sources two books, two *Los Angeles Times* newspaper articles, and **John Ford**'s film version of ***The Grapes of Wrath*** (1940), written by **Nunnally Johnson**, and Steinbeck is mentioned only as the inspiration for Johnson.

Brian Niro

STACKPOLE, PETER (1913–1997). Stackpole was a *Time-Life* photographer in 1936 when he was assigned to do portraits of various prominent people on the **Monterey** Peninsula. More by chance than by intent, Stackpole found Steinbeck in **Pacific Grove** shortly after the author had published ***Tortilla Flat***, and his photos are among the first to record Steinbeck's image for posterity. During the initial shoot, Steinbeck was reluctant to stand still for a portrait, so many of the photos depict him quite casually in his home and garden. One of these photos appeared in *Time* when the magazine reviewed Steinbeck's best seller. In 1945 Stackpole returned with *Time* reporter Bob DeRoos to take photos of **Cannery Row**. Although Steinbeck himself managed to evade Stackpole, the photographer was able to meet **Edward F. Ricketts** and record on film such scenes as Ricketts working in the **Pacific Biological Laboratory** and collecting specimens near the **Great Tide Pool**. Other shots depicted areas in Cannery Row that were the staging grounds for scenes in Steinbeck's novel as well as individuals who served as inspirations for **Mack** and the boys. In a 1975 interview, Stackpole said that he tried to interest Steinbeck in collaborating on a book that would feature Stackpole's work in underwater photography but that he failed to convince the author to join him.

Further Reading: Cox, Martha Heasley. "Interview with Peter Stackpole–July 1975." *The Steinbeck Newsletter* 9:1 (Fall 1995): 19–22.

Michael J. Meyer

STANFORD UNIVERSITY. At age seventeen (1919), Steinbeck entered Leland Stanford Junior University (as it was called then) in Palo Alto, California. He did not embrace life in academe and was an average student, fitfully attending the university until the spring of 1925, when he quit for good without a degree. He did pick up scientific philosophies at the Stanford-affiliated **Hopkins Marine Station** and concepts in writing from professors **Edith Mirrielees** and Margery Bailey. He was a member of the Stanford English Club, and he developed important friendships with **Carlton "Dook" Sheffield**, **Carl Wilhelmson**, and **John Breck**. The Wells Fargo Steinbeck Collection at Stanford University, which features notebooks and drafts associated with his earliest works, is described in the 2000 Stanford Library publication, *John Steinbeck: From Salinas to Stockholm* by William McPheron.

STANTON, HENRY. Member of the **Salinas** draft board in ***East of Eden*** who encourages his coworker **Adam Trask** to relax because he does his job too scrupulously and seriously. Henry tries to divert Adam when he becomes concerned about the war lasting so long that he might have to draft his own sons, **Cal** and **Aron Trask**.

Margaret Seligman

"STARVATION UNDER THE ORANGE TREES" (1938). Encouraged by Helen Hosmer of The Simon J. Lubin Society, Steinbeck collected the articles he had written for *The San Francisco News* and added an epilogue with this title to the seven journalistic pieces he had already written. Hosmer wrote the preface to the pamphlet and also came up with a title for the collection, *Their Blood Is Strong*. By acquiring photographs by **Dorothea Lange** for the front and back covers and by using the popularity of Steinbeck, Hosmer all but assured high sales for this political tract, and Steinbeck designated the proceeds from the work to benefit the very neediest of the migrant workers whose stories he had told. (*See also* ***The Harvest Gypsies***.)

Michael J. Meyer

STEFFENS, LINCOLN (1866–1936). Famous American journalist of the early 1900s and part of the muckraking school that included fellow novelist Upton Sinclair. Steffens is most well known for his exposé of political corruption in *The Shame of The Cities* (1904). As an editor and author he held positions at *McClure's*, *The American*, and *Everybody's Magazine* in the early 1900s and established himself as one of the foremost social critics of America and as a strong voice for reform. His 1931 *Autobiography* also reiterates his commitment to radical causes. Along with his wife, Ella Winter, Steffens was an influential supporter of labor-organizing and strike efforts in the Carmel area and was a member of such leftist organizations as the John Reed club and the Young Communist League. Steinbeck's association with Steffens and Winter may account for his early on being depicted as a radical and for the leftist viewpoints seemingly espoused in his work being deplored by conservative groups. From 1933 up to Steffens's death in 1936, Steinbeck often visited Steffens and Winter at their home in Carmel. Here Steffens urged the young writer as well as college students to observe firsthand the labor strife in the surrounding area. Through Steffens, Steinbeck met strike organizers. The call to observe and the contacts made through Steffens helped the young writer prepare some of his greatest works, including ***In Dubious Battle*** and ***The Grapes of Wrath***. Though Steinbeck and Steffens shared similar concerns, Steinbeck did not agree with Steffens's more traditionally leftist views or his enthusiasm for the communist experiment in the Soviet Union.

Further Reading: Benson, Jackson J. *The True Adventures of John Steinbeck, Writer.* New York: Viking, 1984.

STEINBECK ARCHIVES. *See* **Appendix**.

STEINBECK, CAROL HENNING (?–1983). Carol Henning, the daughter of middle-class parents from San Jose, California, was John Steinbeck's first wife and, with the exception of **Edward F. Ricketts**, arguably the most powerful influence on his early writing. John and Carol met in June of 1928. Carol, a tall, athletic woman with long brown hair who was described as more handsome than pretty, came up from San Francisco with her sister Idell and stopped to take a tour of the hatchery at Tahoe City. Their young tour guide, John Steinbeck, was immediately drawn to her wit and good looks; for her part, Carol was fascinated by this hulk of a man who wryly described himself as "a midwife to lady trout," and the two traded barbs during the entire tour. Before they left, John had set up a double date for that night with his roommate, **Lloyd Shebley**, which after a rocky start culminated with John and Carol dancing to soft jazz under a star-filled sky. After a period of eighteen months of bohemian courtship—rendezvousing at the **Pacific Grove** cottage, drinking wine on the beach, arguing the merits of a particular author—John and Carol were married on January 14, 1930, in a ten-minute ceremony at the courthouse in Glendale, California. In many ways Carol was the perfect fit for John. Though John could be shy, introverted, and brooding, Carol was the opposite: outgoing, forthright, upbeat, energetic. Although a very independent woman, Carol was also completely devoted to Steinbeck as both a husband and writer. **Jackson J. Benson** notes that **Mary Talbot**, the woman in ***Cannery Row*** who continually lifts the spirits of her despondent husband and sees them both as "magic people," is largely based on Carol.

The early years of their marriage, in which they shifted from broken-down homes in southern California to the cottage in Pacific Grove, were, ironically, the happiest of their time together. Often penniless, they were able to live rent-free at the cottage and received a meager monthly allowance from Steinbeck's parents. This money, combined with what Carol earned from a succession of temporary jobs, enabled John to continue to write and provided sufficient funds for the elaborate parties and celebrations the couple and their circle of friends loved. Carol was also a talented writer and published some of her light verse in several issues of the *Monterey Beacon* under the pseudonym, Amnesia Glasscock, a play on the name of Carl Burgess Glasscock, California's poet laureate.

It was during the early and mid-1930s that Carol's influence on Steinbeck as a writer was felt. In a purely practical sense, Carol's devotion to her husband made the work of this most productive time of his life possible. In addition to supporting both of them financially, Carol also spent hour upon hour typing, editing, and proofreading Steinbeck's manuscripts, which were difficult to read (he had very small handwriting) and weak in spelling and punctuation. Emotionally she helped John fend off the depression and anxiety that attended the daunting task of writing two thousand words a day, his self-proclaimed goal; she lifted him with her faith in his ability and refused to allow him to wallow in self-pity. As part of the dedication to ***The Grapes of Wrath*** affirms ("To CAROL who willed it"), it was her sheer strength of character that enabled John to face and overcome the challenges of a beginning writer bursting with ideas but unsure of his own talent.

Just as important, however, was Carol's influence on John's social conscience. Steinbeck was always a compassionate man who was most concerned with the "little guy," the misfits and downtrodden of society. But according to several critics, it was Carol who helped develop and focus John's social conscience, particularly concerning the injustices of Depression-era America. In addition to being more politically active and introducing her husband to various socialist groups, Carol began working in November of 1933 for the Emergency Relief Organization (E.R.O.), which attempted to alleviate the worst effects of the Great Depression. Carol mainly served the destitute families of immigrant Mexican workers and would relate the details of starving children and slave wages to Steinbeck each night, making him keenly aware of the poverty and injustice in his own backyard. Thus, Carol played a major role in encouraging the artistic compassion and consciousness that would later find voice in the literary masterpieces ***In Dubious Battle, Of Mice and Men***, and *The Grapes of Wrath*.

Finally, Carol influenced John's writing by helping curb his natural tendencies for weakness in plot and sentimentality. As a writer, Steinbeck's talent lay in powerfully describing characters and situations within a vividly detailed environment, not in tying all these situations or scenes together in a cause-and-effect sequence that gave unity to the story as a whole. Carol recognized this tendency in John's work and helped him come up with other devices (such as the Arthurian theme in ***Tortilla Flat***) to unify his work. She also sought to restrain the emotional excesses that at times entered Steinbeck's fiction. Carol was one of the few people in Steinbeck's life who could read something he wrote, look him straight in the eye, and say, "That's just a load of crap." Carol's intelligence and complete honesty with John made him a better writer, as when she read *L'Affaire Lettuceberg*, the seething satire that would prove to be a dry run for *Grapes*, and pronounced, "Burn it." Steinbeck did.

After the immense success of *The Grapes of Wrath* in 1939, which brought money, publicity, and constant traveling, the Steinbecks' marriage quickly began to crumble. Part of the blame rests with Carol, who had had an affair with **Joseph Campbell**, a mutual friend, and was now prone to outbursts and bouts of drinking that were a great embarrassment to John. But much of the blame must rest with Steinbeck, who could be terribly insensitive and emotionally withdrawn and who never seemed to fully appreciate the tremendous sacrifices Carol made on behalf of their relationship and his career. After a period of attempted reconciliation and then separation (during which Steinbeck's affair with the young singer, Gwyn Conger, surfaced), Carol obtained a divorce on March 18, 1943. Eleven days later, John married **Gwyndolyn Conger Steinbeck** in New Orleans.

Carol Henning Steinbeck, while eventually softening toward her former husband, did feel some measure of resentment toward John for the rest of her life. During their separation she wrote him cheerful letters and survived emotionally by entering mechanics' training school at Fort Ord at the beginning of World War II, eventually graduating at the top of her class. But the divorce itself and its aftermath were full of bitterness and pain; she had devoted so much of her life to John and his career and seemed to receive so little in return. To the end of his life, John thought of Carol as a "good person" and felt guilty for the failure of their marriage and his part in it.

Many years later, on the eve of Steinbeck's **Nobel Prize acceptance speech**, John received a telegram from Carol that read, in effect, "Congratulations—I always knew that it would come to you someday." One wonders if, without Carol's determination and support, that great American epic, *The Grapes of Wrath*, which bears the name she herself suggested, would have been written at all.

Further Reading: Benson, Jackson J. *The True Adventures of John Steinbeck, Writer.* New York: Viking, 1984; Parini, Jay. *John Steinbeck, A Biography.* New York: Holt, 1995.

Stephen K. George

STEINBECK, ELAINE SCOTT (1914–2003). Of all of John Steinbeck's personal relationships—and he was a man with many that were deep and abiding—his third marriage, to Elaine Scott, was his most rewarding. Although never a direct influence upon his writing craft as **Carol Henning Steinbeck** had been, Elaine gave Steinbeck the emotional confidence and security he needed after his second divorce (from **Gwyndolyn Conger Steinbeck**) to complete some of his most provocative works, including ***East of Eden*** and ***The Winter of Our Discontent***. The last twenty years of Steinbeck's life were satisfying, artistically and personally, largely because of Elaine.

Elaine Anderson Scott grew up in Fort Worth, Texas, the daughter of a prominent oilman. She studied drama production at the University of Texas, where she met and fell in love with the aspiring actor, Zachary Taylor. Upon his graduation, the couple, with their young daughter Waverly, moved to New York to start careers in theater. After a short time both were hired by the Westport Community Playhouse and eventually made it to Broadway, where Zachary was offered several leading roles and Elaine rose to the station of stage manager, a position unheard of for a woman at that time. Elaine eventually went on to manage several Broadway productions, including **Rodgers and Hammerstein**'s *Oklahoma!* After a few years, Zachary Scott was offered a contract with Warner Brothers, and the family relocated to Hollywood. But the show business lifestyle proved detrimental to their marriage, and by 1949 they had drifted apart.

John Steinbeck first met Elaine in the spring of that year through a mutual friend, the actress Ann Sothern, whom John had invited to come up to **Monterey** for a few days. Reluctantly, Steinbeck agreed that Ann could bring a friend to act as a chaperone; this friend was Elaine Scott. Over that Memorial Day weekend, John gave them the complete Steinbeck tour, including **Edward F. Ricketts**' lab, his **Pacific Grove** cottage, and all the good restaurants. Almost immediately, he and Elaine felt a strong attraction for each other.

In many ways Elaine Scott was the woman Steinbeck had waited for his entire life. Attractive, feminine, strong, and witty, Elaine was a genuinely loving person and, after Steinbeck's tormenting second marriage, the perfect companion for John, who later wrote, "Both of my wives were somehow in competition with me so that I was ashamed of being noticed. I am not a bit ashamed now. Elaine is on my side, not against me. The result is that I am more relaxed than I have ever been."

By the end of the summer, John and Elaine had fallen deeply in love, with John (who was shy in conversation) bombarding her with letters delivered secretly by friends. On November 1, 1949, Elaine called and told him she was breaking up with her husband, who was convinced that Steinbeck would flee with the news. John didn't. Her divorce hearing came a month later, and by the next week, John and Elaine had rented two apartments in the same building in New York in order to be close to each other. They enjoyed a very happy first Christmas together with his sons and her daughter.

Although hesitant to give their approval, Elaine's family members met John in the spring of 1950 and were quickly won over. John's sister, **Mary Steinbeck Dekker**, who had never liked Gwyn, also approved of Elaine. The couple was married on December 28, 1950, at the home of Steinbeck's publisher, **Harold Guinzburg**. It was a very traditional and peaceful ceremony, in contrast to Steinbeck's second wedding, with about fifty close friends and family attending. The couple later honeymooned in Bermuda and then returned to find their apartment crowded wall to wall with people in a welcome home party reminiscent of ***Cannery Row.***

The Steinbecks quickly settled into their life together, though it was often stressful with worries over the children, money, and Gwyn. But Elaine created a loving environment in the four-story brownstone they bought on Seventy-second Street, and took care of all the day-to-day details so that Steinbeck could concentrate on the project he had been anticipating and yet dreading for years, the semiautobiographical *East of Eden.* Although their marriage had its moments of friction, often as a result of Steinbeck's possessiveness and insecurities, Elaine provided the confidence and stability that Steinbeck had so lacked with Gwyn and that enabled his artistry to flourish.

However, unlike Carol, Elaine had very little direct influence on his writing—not by her choice, but because of John. The very first time he sat down to read her one of his manuscripts, she had tried, during a break in the reading, to give him her take on what he had written. John stopped her and said, "I don't want a critic, I just need an audience." This Elaine provided for the rest of his life. And just as his former wives found their way into Steinbeck's literature—Carol as *Cannery Row*'s **Mary Talbot** and Gwyn as the unenviable **Cathy Ames** in *East of Eden*—so does Elaine provide the model for the warm and amused **Mary Hawley** in Steinbeck's last novel, *The Winter of Our Discontent.*

Throughout their marriage, John and Elaine Steinbeck were nearly inseparable. Spending almost as much time overseas as at home, they traveled to Europe in 1952, with Steinbeck writing a series of articles for *Collier's* and Elaine contributing as a photographer. They also celebrated New Years nine years in a row by vacationing in the West Indies. But their favorite time together was the year they spent at Discove Cottage in Somerset, England, while Steinbeck researched his beloved project ***The Acts of King Arthur*** (published posthumously in 1976). They also had wonderful celebrations together, with none more magnificent than Elaine's birthday. On one such occasion, Steinbeck arose before dawn and, using a small cannon designed for starting yacht races, fired off a forty-one–gun salute that brought the local Coast Guard down on him.

The depth of their relationship is revealed in a detailed questionnaire Steinbeck filled out in 1964 for his friend and new doctor, Denton Cox. In the four-and-a-half-page letter he attached at the end, Steinbeck wrote, "And now the last thing you should know. I love Elaine more than myself. Her well-being and comfort and happiness are more important than my own. And I would go to any length to withhold from her any pain or sorrow that is not needful for her own enrichment." Four years later, John Steinbeck died in their New York apartment at 5:30 PM on December 20, with Elaine lying at his side.

Following his death, Elaine Scott Steinbeck continually furthered the literary reputation of her husband, particularly in her editing (with **Robert Wallsten**) of the first major collection of Steinbeck's correspondence, *Steinbeck: A Life in Letters* (published in 1975), and in her cooperation with biographers **Jackson J. Benson** and **Jay Parini**. Elaine Steinbeck died in 2003.

This strong yet deeply devoted woman, whom John affectionately referred to as the "Fayre Eleyne," both enabled the writing of Steinbeck's later fiction and encouraged the flowering of Steinbeck literary criticism to come. Steinbeck scholarship owes much to Elaine Scott Steinbeck.

Further Reading: Benson, Jackson J. *The True Adventures of John Steinbeck, Writer.* New York: Viking, 1984; Parini, Jay. *John Steinbeck, A Biography.* New York: Holt, 1995.

Stephen K. George

STEINBECK, ELIZABETH (1894–1992). *See* **Ainsworth, Elizabeth Steinbeck**.

STEINBECK, (OLIVE) ESTHER (1892–1986). *See* **Rodgers, Esther Steinbeck**.

STEINBECK, GWYNDOLYN (GWYN) CONGER (1916?–1975). Unlike his first wife, **Carol Henning Steinbeck**, Steinbeck's second wife, Gwyndolyn (Gwyn) Conger, had little positive influence on John as a writer. However, their brief marriage, from 1943 to 1948, while proving to be the most painful relationship of Steinbeck's life, did influence the writing of what he later described as his greatest literary achievement, the epic novel ***East of Eden***. Even more important, she bore her husband his only children, sons **John Steinbeck IV** and **Thom Steinbeck**.

Steinbeck met Gwyn in June of 1939 during the publicity blitz concerning ***The Grapes of Wrath*** and while experiencing marriage difficulties with Carol. Gwyn was a very pretty twenty-year-old, about five feet six inches, with dark blonde hair and a nice figure. Since the age of fourteen she had been singing professionally, both with bands and on the radio, and now she was in Hollywood working as a vocalist for CBS, doing bit parts in movies, and making the nightclub circuit. While holed up in his small Hollywood apartment, John Steinbeck was visited by **Max Wagner**, who was so concerned over Steinbeck's physical and emotional state that he asked Gwyn to go over and cheer him up without telling her who this old friend was. Steinbeck met Gwyn at the door and introduced himself as "Mr. Brooks;" their first date was over a bowl of chicken soup in Steinbeck's small, dimly lit kitchen.

Despite the eighteen years Steinbeck had in seniority, it was Gwyn who was the adult in their early relationship. Somewhat tentatively, like a school-aged boy, Steinbeck would go to the clubs where Gwyn was performing and watch from the sideline, talking occasionally with her between shows. On their first dates Steinbeck forgot to bring money, forcing Gwyn to pay while he mumbled excuses. On their fourth date, he asked her how she felt toward him; she replied that she liked him a great deal.

After almost two years of secret rendezvous, capped by a cabin stay outside **Monterey** while Carol was in Hawaii recuperating from the flu, Steinbeck confessed his love affair with Gwyn. After a famous confrontation, in which Steinbeck placed the two women together and told them to decide for themselves who would get him, John and Carol Steinbeck were reunited; according to John, Carol took the outside and Gwyn had his heart. But this reconciliation lasted just a week. Near the end of April 1941, the couple had separated permanently, and in March 1943 Carol was granted a divorce on the grounds of mental cruelty.

Eleven days later, on March 29, John and Gwyn were married in New Orleans at the home of the writer Lyle Saxon. But the ceremony itself foreshadowed the unsteady nature of their relationship, with Gwyn in tears from losing her ring and the minister tipsy from all the liquor he had consumed while waiting. It ended with two policemen bursting into the room and demanding that Steinbeck go with them; a young lady was waiting outside, claiming that he was the father of her child. After a moment of stunned silence, the room broke into laughter at the practical joke. Steinbeck later wrote of it, "People cried and laughed and shouted and got drunk. Oh! It was a fine wedding."

This joy, however, was short-lived, for Steinbeck had very few happy times with Gwyn, who though lively and pretty could also be petty and cruel. From the start of their marriage, as John prepared to leave for Europe as a war correspondent for the *New York Herald Tribune*, Gwyn tried to control him by accusing him of choosing the war over his new bride and then claiming (falsely) that she was pregnant. Later, while he was overseas, Gwyn would punish him by not answering his constant flow of letters or by writing him about all the advances from men she was receiving and how lonely she was. Tortured emotionally, Steinbeck fell into bouts of deep anger and depression, even questioning if he was man enough to hold on to his young wife.

After John's return from the war, there was some reconciliation, particularly with the birth of their first son, Thom, on August 2, 1944. (Steinbeck even won a bet of twenty dollars from Gwyn for finishing his novel ***Cannery Row*** before she gave birth.) Gwyn went on to work as a music consultant for the film version of ***The Pearl*** and also wrote a play with **Nat Benchley**, "The Circus of Doctor Lao," which had a short run in Chicago with their friend, **Burgess Meredith**, in the lead role. But at the same time, Gwyn felt that her creativity and career were being smothered by the fame of her husband and the increasing demands on her as a wife and mother, and this feeling intensified after the birth of their second son, John IV, on June 12, 1946, after which Gwyn spent two months in recovery. The atmosphere in their marriage, unlike the open and volatile confrontations between John and Carol, was one of simmering tension and retaliation. After Steinbeck returned from **Edward F. Ricketts'** funeral in May 1948, Gwyn unloaded her bombshell: she wanted a divorce. The awful timing of the announcement, coupled with her revelations about infidelity and not having loved him for years, nearly broke Steinbeck, who eventually moved into the cottage at **Pacific Grove** while Gwyn and the boys remained in New York. Their divorce became final in October of that year.

The failure of Steinbeck's second marriage seems to be the fault of both John and Gwyn. In a parallel to **Adam** and **Cathy Trask** of *East of Eden*, neither of them saw each other clearly: John wanted the feminine homemaker whose first concern would be his own well-being, whereas Gwyn wanted a career and to control John. The age difference and John's celebrity didn't help either. But what turned many people against Gwyn is the cruelty with which she continued to treat John and the bitterness that remained with her until she died. Never remarrying, she used her custody of the boys and John's payment of alimony to afflict John the rest of his life, eventually filing a frivolous suit for an increase in financial support just four years before his death. As for John, he reserved his greatest personal hatred for his second wife.

This extreme emotion led to the single greatest contribution of Gwyn Conger Steinbeck to her husband's writing. As critics such as **Jay Parini** have observed, Steinbeck's most evil creation, *East of Eden*'s sadistic whorehouse proprietor, **Kate Albey (Cathy Ames)**, is patterned after Gwyn. Moreover, the novel's dominant theme of *timshel*, or "thou mayest," is directly tied to Steinbeck's own personal fear that Gwyn's negative influence over Thom and John might be too great for his sons to overcome. Thus, one of Steinbeck's most powerful and positive themes, his belief in the potential for human greatness of heart and spirit, ironically owes its expression in *East of Eden* to his most painful relationship, his marriage to Gwyn Conger.

Note: From 1941 on, Gwyn preferred the spelling of her first name to be "Gwyndolyn" rather than "Gwendolyn," as she was known when she and Steinbeck first met; for the sake of consistency, this book uses the former spelling.

Further Reading: Benson, Jackson J. *The True Adventures of John Steinbeck, Writer.* New York: Viking, 1984; Parini, Jay. *John Steinbeck, A Biography.* New York: Holt, 1995.

Stephen K. George

STEINBECK, JOHN, IV (CATBIRD) (1945–1991). The son of John Steinbeck and **Gwyndolyn Conger Steinbeck** was born on June 12, 1945, in New York City, and, although he was the younger of Steinbeck's two sons, he was his namesake. His father nicknamed him "Catbird" because of his penchant for crouching on the floorboards under the glove compartment of their car, which Steinbeck referred to as "the catbird seat." Gwyn suffered a severe case of postpartum depression after the birth, partly due to traumatic events that preceded it.

Burdened by the reality of domestic responsibilities, Steinbeck was not eager to have a second child. This dynamic caused even further strain on the marriage, which had begun to unravel with the birth of their first son, **Thom Steinbeck**. After his parents divorced in 1949, John IV continued to live with his mother and brother in their four-story brownstone on East Seventy-eighth Street in Manhattan. Steinbeck lived only six blocks away, so his sons ran back and forth often between the two houses.

John was first introduced to mood-altering chemicals at the age of four when he raided his mother's supply of codeine. He was eventually hospitalized for an addiction that was never discovered. This began a lifelong struggle with alcoholism and drug addiction. John attended private day schools until 1955 when he was sent to Eaglebrook, a boarding school in Deerfield, Massachusetts. In 1961, Steinbeck took both boys on an extended trip throughout Europe, tutored by the young playwright, **Terrence McNally**. Upon returning, John entered Hebron Academy in Maine in 1962.

In 1965, John was drafted into the Vietnam War, and he became a journalist for Armed Forces Radio and TV as a war correspondent for the Department of Defense. As John IV states in his memoir, *The Other Side of Eden: Life with John Steinbeck*, "As a reporter for the Army in Vietnam, I had gone out looking for a good human interest story, and I found instead more marijuana than Cheech and Chong's best dream." Upon his return to the United States prior to his discharge, he was asked by the *Washingtonian* to write an article, which he titled, "The Importance of Being Stoned in Vietnam." He was called to testify in front of a Senate subcommittee on drug abuse. Despite General William Westmoreland's statement that Private John Steinbeck's comments on the use of marijuana in Vietnam were baseless, John received an honorary discharge. During that time, John was arrested for "maintaining a common nuisance," upon the discovery of twenty pounds of marijuana in his apartment, which was confiscated along with the manuscript for the *Washingtonian* article. Charges were dropped, but the incident was of great embarrassment to the family. Steinbeck's last words to his son were "They should have thrown you in jail."

John's Vietnam memoir, *In Touch*, was published by Knopf in 1969. He writes about his experiences with the Vietnamese, the GIs, and his romantic interlude with that culture. He describes the tense and surrealistic atmosphere of demonstrations in the streets, knifings in bars, and bombs exploding everywhere. His testimony in front of the Senate is included as an appendix. John had gone to Vietnam as a hawk, but he returned to Washington as a dove. He writes about his drug bust, the trial, and acquittal. In the final chapter, he tells the reader about a drive across the United States as he talks with friends about issues that were urgent to his generation freedom, responsibility, education, the direction of their lives, meditation, and drugs. A reviewer commented, "He tells how it is to be 'the son of the novelist' and in what ways this has helped and hindered him so far. He has written a book whose direct, quiet spoken, non-dogmatic quality conveys with particular force what it is like to be twenty-one at this time, in this country, questioning, experiencing, enjoying, trying to get in touch."

In 1968, John returned to Vietnam as a journalist. Along with Sean Flynn, son of actor Errol Flynn, he started *Dispatch News Service*. Fluent in street Vietnamese, they quickly became independent of the flow of information dispensed by the United States Press Office. Hence, they were the first to disclose the truth about the My Lai massacre and the Con Son tiger cages. Sean disappeared in Cambodia on a photo shoot. In 1969, John took the vows of a Buddhist monk while living on Phoenix Island in the middle of the Mekong delta, under the tutelage of the politically powerful Coconut Monk, a silent tree-dwelling Buddhist yogi. This tiny, stooped mendicant adopted John as a spiritual son and invited him to live in the peace zone he had created in the midst of the raging war. Howitzer shells were hammered into bells by the 400 monks who lived on the island.

In 1971, John won an Emmy for the work he did on the CBS documentary "The World of Charlie Company" with Walter Cronkite. He traveled back and forth between Asia and the United States several more times before settling in Boulder, Colorado, where he began to study Tibetan Buddhism at the Naropa Institute. He met his future wife, Nancy Harper, there in 1975. They were married on March 11, 1982, and her two children took John's last name. In 1983, the family traveled around the world for a year, living in Kathmandu in order to further their Tibetan Buddhist studies.

In 1984, John was diagnosed with hemochromatosis, a genetic disease that causes iron retention in the organs. This life-threatening illness, combined with his excessive drinking and drug use, created a healing crisis for John that resulted in his successful quest for sobriety. In 1987, the family moved to La Jolla, California. John pursued his journalistic career, writing articles about their travels with the Dalai Lama, Tibetan Buddhism, and the genetic aspects of alcoholism and drug addiction. In 1989, John IV began writing his autobiography, *The Other Side of Eden*, which was completed by Nancy Steinbeck and published posthumously in 2001. The memoir contains many thoughts on Vietnam, including a memorable scene of his father's visit to the war-torn country while the younger Steinbeck was in the army. There are also vivid recollections of his mother's abusive, alcoholic rages, his lonely years in boarding school, his long battle with drug addiction, his strained relationship with his remote, conflicted father, and the connection of ***East of Eden*** to Steinbeck's real-life family. In 1990, John was diagnosed with a ruptured disc. He underwent corrective surgery on February 7, 1991, but did not survive the operation, leaving behind his wife, Nancy, and their two children, Megan and Michael Steinbeck.

Further Reading: Benson, Jackson J. *The True Adventures of John Steinbeck, Writer.* New York: Viking, 1984; Steinbeck, John IV. *In Touch.* New York: Knopf, 1969; Steinbeck, John IV, and Nancy Steinbeck. *The Other Side of Eden: Life with John Steinbeck.* New York: Prometheus Books, 2001.

Nancy Steinbeck

STEINBECK, JOHN ERNST (1862–1935). Unlike Steinbeck's mother, John Ernst Steinbeck influenced his son more by his absence than by his presence and more by his failures than by his successes. A tall, dignified, unassuming man, John Ernst made possible Steinbeck's early career by his unflagging financial support and his desire that his son pursue his passion for writing. Yet in his passivity and fears of failure, the father encouraged a lack of confidence that would remain with his son for much, if not all, of his life. John Ernst's father was John Adolph Grossteinbeck, a pious German from Düsseldorf who once led a quixotic venture to the Holy Land in the early 1850s that ended with the stabbing death of his brother and the rape of his sister-in-law. While there, John Adolph fell in love with a fellow missionary's daughter, Almira Dickson, and the couple eventually immigrated to Massachusetts, where John Adolph labored as a woodcarver in a shed behind his father-in-law's house. After an episode in which Grossteinbeck (who now called himself Steinbeck) was drafted into and then deserted the Confederate Army, the family moved to California around 1870 and settled on a ten-acre farm near Hollister, about thirty miles from **Salinas**. There, John Ernst, who was one of six boys, milked cows, worked in the orchard, and helped at his father's mill.

Although John Ernst enjoyed the land and gardening (a pleasure that he passed on to his son), he entered business and management as a profession. He was managing a mill in King City when he met **Olive Hamilton**, a pretty teacher and aspiring socialite, and after a secret engagement, the couple married and moved to **Salinas**, where John Ernst managed the Sperry Flour Mill. In 1910, five years after the birth of the last of their four children, John Ernst lost his job at Sperry Mill. After failing with his own business, a feed store that opened just as automobiles and tractors were replacing horses, John Ernst suffered from depression and a mounting sense of despair, often sitting alone for hours at a time in his darkened bedroom. Despite the help of friends, which eventually led to his appointment as county treasurer, a position of some social weight in Salinas, John Ernst never fully recovered from his professional failures. A sensitive and withdrawn man all his life, these fears were passed on to his young son, John, who likewise felt financially and emotionally insecure despite his many successes.

When the future author Steinbeck grew old enough to attend college, John Ernst hoped that he would study engineering, law, or some other promising profession. However, unlike Olive, who never really accepted John's chosen vocation as a writer, John Ernst admired his son's determination to pursue his dreams; he helped Steinbeck find jobs when he was away from **Stanford University** and later provided a stipend of fifty dollars a month while John and his young wife **Carol Henning Steinbeck** struggled with his writing career. Despite lacking a basic faith in himself, John Ernst had an abiding belief in his son, so much so that he would often carry John's new books around with him to display to neighbors and friends.

After his wife's stroke in March of 1933, John Ernst began to unravel; Olive had always been the pillar of the family, and he could not imagine a life without her. As Steinbeck's father's behavior became more erratic—he would sometimes wander into the study as John was writing, glare at his son, and then stumble off—Steinbeck retreated deeper into his work. **Jay Parini** reports that according to Steinbeck, the horrible part was the "slow torture wherein a good and strong man tears off little shreds of himself and throws them away" (Parini 140). A little more than a year after Olive's death, John Ernst died in May 1935.

John Ernst Steinbeck has been cited as the model for many of the emotionally restrained westerners of Steinbeck's fiction, including the distant **Carl Tiflin** in ***The Red Pony***; the lonely and dominated husband, **Harry Teller**, in **"The White Quail"**; and the well-dressed county supervisor, **Mr. Bacon**, in ***East of Eden***. In his father, John Steinbeck found not only an explanation for the fears within himself, but also the resolve to lead his own life differently. After his father's death, Steinbeck wrote in a letter, "Poor silent man all his life. I feel very badly . . . for he told me only a few months ago that he had never done anything he wanted to do. Worst of all he hadn't done the work he wanted to do." John Steinbeck, who pursued his artistic passion all his life, clearly avoided this same mistake.

Further Reading: Benson, Jackson J. *The True Adventures of John Steinbeck, Writer.* New York: Viking, 1984; Parini, Jay. *John Steinbeck, A Biography.* New York: Holt, 1995; Steinbeck, John. *A Life In Letters.* Ed. Elaine Steinbeck and Robert Wallsten. New York: Viking, 1975.

Stephen K. George

STEINBECK, JOHN ERNST (IN *EAST OF EDEN*). Husband of **Olive Hamilton (Steinbeck)** and father of **John** and **Mary Steinbeck**—a fictionalized version of Steinbeck's real father. After building a flour mill in King City, he becomes engaged to Olive in secret. When they marry, they move from Paso Robles to King City and finally to **Salinas**.

Margaret Seligman

STEINBECK, MARY (1905–1965). *See* **Dekker, Mary Steinbeck**.

STEINBECK, MARY (IN *EAST OF EDEN*). Daughter of **Olive Hamilton (Steinbeck)** and **John Ernst Steinbeck** and sister of **John Steinbeck**—fictionalized version of Steinbeck's real sister. In addition to her close relationship with her brother John, Mary had a special fondness for her uncle, **Tom Hamilton**. However, when the tomboyish Mary asks Tom how to become a boy, she becomes disillusioned with him when he admits to her that he likes girls. During World War I, Mary joins John in insulting the German **Mr. Fenchel**.

Margaret Seligman

STEINBECK, OLIVE HAMILTON (1866–1934). John Steinbeck's relationship with his mother, Olive Hamilton Steinbeck, was complex and enduring. Many critics, including **Jay Parini and Jackson J. Benson**, attribute Steinbeck's love of language, clear sense of right and wrong, and outrage at social injustice to his mother's curious mix of artistic and religious values. Yet, regrettably, Olive Steinbeck's vast energy and high expectations also encouraged in her talented son an insecurity that never left him. To the end of his life, John Steinbeck believed that he had not accomplished enough and felt a keen sense of failure, some of which can be traced to Olive's demanding influence.

Olive Hamilton was born in San Jose, the youngest of five girls in a family of nine children. Her father, Samuel Hamilton, hailed from Northern Ireland, came to America at the age of seventeen, and married Elizabeth Fagen in 1849 in New York City. A year later, they moved to California and eventually settled on a dry, rocky, 1600-acre ranch sixty miles south of **Salinas**. Although the land was poor, Samuel made an adequate living working as a blacksmith and inventor while Elizabeth tended both the farm and children.

But farm life was never for Olive, who aspired to greater things. At seventeen, she passed the county's school board examinations and began teaching in a one-room school south of **Monterey**. At the age of twenty-four, she married **John Ernst Steinbeck**, the founder and manager of a flour mill in King City. Eventually John Ernst took a position with the Sperry Flour Mill in **Salinas**, and with the acquisition of a large Victorian house on Central Avenue, the Steinbecks set themselves firmly in the upper echelon of Salinas society.

In time the Steinbecks had four children, Esther (1892), Beth (1894), John (1902), and Mary (1905). Olive, though a devoted mother, was also involved in any number of charitable and society organizations. Peers described her as a woman who would take charge and end up doing much of the labor herself; as a result, John was often taken care of by his older sisters or a friend's mother. Olive did profoundly influence John's exposure to the literary and imaginative world. Books were an everyday part of the Steinbeck household, which was a place of song, poetry, recitation, and storytelling. The family also subscribed to the leading magazines of the time, including *Collier's*, *The Saturday Evening Post*, and *National Geographic*. Olive's love of learning and her creative energy are clearly a part of John Steinbeck's artistic makeup.

However, Olive also influenced her only son negatively in her constant insistence that his best efforts were never good enough. Such extreme expectations did not sit well with Steinbeck, who rebelled at the pressure and fled a home life in which Olive was the dominant figure. Ironically, John returned some years later to nurse his almost helpless mother, who was now suffering from high blood pressure and clogged arteries. When Olive experienced a severe stroke in March of 1933, the month that Steinbeck says she always dreaded ("Mother never drew a carefree breath in March"), John stayed at her side in the Salinas Valley Hospital. Upon her release in June, John and **Carol Henning Steinbeck** moved to the Steinbeck home to care for both Olive and John Ernst, who was also rapidly deteriorating.

This time of caring for Olive was very painful for John, who felt so depressed and filled with anger and guilt that he wondered if he would ever be able to write again. Nonetheless, during these dark days Steinbeck wrote some of his most memorable fiction, including stories that would later be found in ***The Red Pony, The Long Valley***, and his first commercial success, ***Tortilla Flat***. It was as if the passing of his mother's powerful influence had finally allowed the writer to explore his own creativity to its fullest. Olive Hamilton

Steinbeck died on February 19, 1934, with John sitting at her side.

The first in a line of strong women who had an impact on both Steinbeck's writing and his life, Olive finds her way into many of his most memorable characters, from the young unmarried school teacher, **Molly Morgan**, in ***The Pastures of Heaven*** to the indomitable **Ma Joad** in ***The Grapes of Wrath***. Other figures include **Joseph Wayne**'s sacrificial spouse, **Elizabeth McGreggor Wayne**, in ***To a God Unknown***; **Mary Teller** in **"The White Quail,"** the domineering wife of milquetoast **Harry Teller**; and, of course, the biographical **Olive Hamilton** of ***East of Eden***, whose "theology was a curious mixture of Irish fairies and . . . Old Testament Jehovah" and whose commitment to selling war bonds resulted in an airplane ride that seems strangely out of place in the novel. Certainly, the novel's deathbed scene with **Cal** and **Adam Trask** is a direct corollary to Steinbeck's own nursing of Olive after her stroke. And perhaps as Adam released his son from his sense of guilt, John Steinbeck's loving portrait of Olive in *East of Eden* reflects some reconciliation with Steinbeck's own mother, a woman who, as Parini surmises, likely never saw "her son for who he really was." (*See also* **Ainsworth, Elizabeth Steinbeck**; **Dekker, Mary Steinbeck**; and **Rodgers, Esther Steinbeck**.)

Further Reading: Benson, Jackson J. *The True Adventures of John Steinbeck, Writer.* New York: Viking, 1984; Parini, Jay. *John Steinbeck: A Biography.* New York: Holt, 1995; Steinbeck, John. *Steinbeck: A Life in Letters.* Ed. Elaine Steinbeck and Robert Wallsten. New York: Viking, 1975.

Stephen K. George

STEINBECK, THOM (1944–). The firstborn son of Steinbeck and his second wife, **Gwyndolyn Conger Steinbeck**. Growing up in a rather volatile environment that involved being shuttled back and forth between his warring parents after their acrimonious divorce, Thom and his brother **John Steinbeck IV** (nicknamed "Catbird") were of great concern to their father, who dedicated ***East of Eden***, his self-proclaimed master work, to his sons. Because the novel includes two sons of opposite temperaments, the siblings often were exposed to speculation over which of the Trask sons, **Charles** or **Adam Trask** (or in the second generation **Cal** and **Aron Trask**) was intended to stand for which Steinbeck son. As they grew up, Thom and Catbird often traveled with their father and his third wife, **Elaine Scott Steinbeck**, and had a tutor, **Terrence McNally**, who helped them keep up with their studies. Thom has contributed important views about his father, and he has become a successful author in his own right. In 2002, along with critic **Louis Owens**, he participated in C-SPAN's *American Writers II* series, in a two-hour television special that discussed the work of his famous father. He also appeared on the *Oprah Winfrey Show* in 2003 when Oprah selected *East of Eden* as the first classic to be discussed by her book club. In 2002, Ballantine published Thom's critically acclaimed collection of short stories, many set in "Steinbeck Country" in California, *Down to a Soundless Sea*. According to a recent interview (http://www.fwomp.com/Int_steinbeck.htm), he is planning a new book on his father, tentatively entitled *Notes from an Ungrateful Child*. Also in progress is a novel-length work entitled *Caverns Measureless to Man* about an Irish immigrant coming to California. Presently (2006) residing California, Thom Steinbeck serves on the boards of directors of the Stella Adler Theater in Los Angeles, California, and the National Steinbeck Center in Salinas, California. He frequently speaks about his father at the yearly Salinas Steinbeck festivals and at scholarly gatherings.

Further Reading: Benson, Jackson J. *The True Adventures of John Steinbeck, Writer.* New York: Viking, 1984; Steinbeck, John IV, and Nancy Steinbeck, *The Other Side of Eden: Life with John Steinbeck.* Amherst, NY: Prometheus

Books, 2001; Steinbeck, Thom. *Down to a Soundless Sea*. New York: Ballantine, 2002.

Michael J. Meyer

STEINBECK SOCIETIES. Several organizations have been developed to encourage the study of John Steinbeck. The first was The Steinbeck Bibliographical Society, begun in February 1966. Under the leadership of Tetsumaro Hayashi and Preston Beyer, this society became The Steinbeck Society of America a year later. Under Hayashi's guidance, the society began publishing the *Steinbeck Newsletter* in 1968, which in turn became *The Steinbeck Quarterly* (appearing four times a year until 1978 and then published biannually from 1978 to 1993). The society sponsored a monograph series from 1971 to 1991. Hayashi found assistance from several Steinbeck scholars, including **Peter Lisca**, **Warren French**, **Robert DeMott**, **Roy Simmonds**, Reloy Garcia, **Richard Astro**, and Yasuo Hashiguchi. Hayashi also published three Steinbeck bibliographies for Scarecrow Press and three study guides to Steinbeck. When Hayashi retired from Ball State University in 1993 and moved to Japan to teach, the society became inactive.

A formal organization devoted to Steinbeck also developed in Japan in 1977 in commemoration of the First International Steinbeck Congress held in Fukuoka in 1976. The John Steinbeck Society of Japan has continued ever since. This organization aims to conduct research and promote friendship among its members. It holds an annual conference in Japan and publishes an annual journal, *Steinbeck Studies* (formerly *The John Steinbeck Society of Japan Newsletter*). The society also hosted international conferences in Hawaii (1999) and Kyoto (2005) and helps sponsor conferences in the United States as well.

After 1993, the work of *The Steinbeck Quarterly* moved to the **Marsha Heasley Cox Center for Steinbeck Studies** at San Jose State University. Under Susan Shillinglaw, the Center's director, the *Quarterly* merged with the Center's newsletter. In 2001, the *Steinbeck Newsletter* expanded its format to become *Steinbeck Studies*.

In 2003, a new group of Steinbeck scholars headed by Barbara Heavilin and Stephen K. George (who had both studied under Hayashi) worked to invigorate the Steinbeck Society in the United States. They created the New John Steinbeck Society of America and introduced *The Steinbeck Review*, a formal adjudicated journal. In 2006, plans were underway to merge the *Steinbeck Newsletter* and *The Steinbeck Review* into one publication (*The Steinbeck Review*).

STERNE, LAURENCE (1713–1768). English novelist and clergyman. Steinbeck read Sterne's *The Life and Opinions of Tristram Shandy* (1760), and in a 1935 letter to **Robert O. Ballou**, his publisher, Steinbeck said he had been reading Macaulay's account of the siege of Limerick in *History of England* (1849) and Sterne's account of it in *Tristram Shandy* at the same time. He added, "What contempt was felt for the Irish before they went into ward politics." Later, in 1945, Steinbeck wrote to **Pascal Covici**, his publisher and editor at **Viking Press**, about his progress on ***The Wayward Bus***, which he indicated was "growing to the most ambitious thing I have ever attempted." He told Covici that it would be as funny as *Tom Jones*, *Tristram Shandy*, and *Don Quixote*. Steinbeck again expressed appreciation for Sterne's humor when he wrote in the introduction to *The World of Li'l Abner* (1965) that Al Capp was the best satirist since Laurence Sterne.

Further Reading: DeMott, Robert. *Steinbeck's Reading: A Catalogue of Books Owned and Borrowed*. New York: Garland, 1984.

Janet L. Flood

STEVENSON, ADLAI EWING (1900–1965). U.S. politician and statesman who eventually attained worldwide recognition for his steady-handed practice of diplomacy on an international level. Elected governor of Illinois for one term in 1948, Stevenson was the surprise candidate of the

Democratic Party in 1952 and 1956 but was defeated in both elections by charismatic war hero Dwight D. Eisenhower. After his defeat in 1956, Stevenson returned to Chicago to practice law and continued to live in Illinois until he was appointed U.S. ambassador to the United Nations in 1961, a position he held until his death in 1965.

First drawn to Stevenson as an articulate intellectual he believed was both honest and trustworthy, Steinbeck was soon convinced to write the foreword for a thin volume edited by Richard Harrity entitled *Speeches of Adlai Stevenson*; in this volume, released in 1952 as a campaign device, John Steinbeck wrote of Stevenson's speeches with admiration: "I can't ever remember reading a political speech with pleasure, sometimes with admiration, yes, but never with pleasure." Steinbeck's respect for Stevenson's eloquence in expressing his political thoughts was a key factor in the initiation of one of Steinbeck's most treasured friendships and caused him to become a "Stevenson Democrat" for the rest of his life.

Although most critics and Steinbeck aficionados are under the misconception that Steinbeck was an active member of Stevenson's speech-writing teams, the two never met personally until 1958, long after the elections. According to Tetsumaro Hayashi, Steinbeck confessed "he did not write speeches directly for the candidate," though he often drafted ideas for the candidate's consideration—ideas that were combined with those of other supporters of Stevenson in the artistic community, including Archibald MacLeish and **Bernard DeVoto**; these concepts were sometimes converted to Stevenson's own speech pattern by his team of advisors. When it became clear that Stevenson's 1956 campaign was failing, Steinbeck wanted to help in any way possible; "I wish to God they would let me write one violent fighting speech and then get it delivered," he wrote to a friend.

In the years following the actual meeting of two at a Chicago dinner party in 1958, they exchanged frequent correspondence and enjoyed personal contact on a regular basis. According to Hayashi, Steinbeck felt the relationship to be "comfortable, congenial, private and respectful." For his part, Stevenson found Steinbeck to be a friend who sought no personal political reward and who could be counted on not to divulge information meant to remain private. Since Stevenson's moral political vision was so appealing to Steinbeck, he even advocated the candidate's third run for the presidency, opposing **Lyndon Baines Johnson** and **John F. Kennedy**, both of whom he later would later serve as advisor and confidante. Hayashi notes that, for Steinbeck, "Adlai Stevenson was an endearing friend, a moral crusader, and an ideal torch bearer for America and Americans."

Prior to the crucial 1960 election, Steinbeck, who felt Eisenhower was "lazy, tired, ignorant and incredibly vain," was even more worried about his would-be successor. Particularly, he and Stevenson discussed **Richard Nixon**, agreeing that Eisenhower's vice-president was a "dangerous" man. (Both **Jackson J. Benson** and Hayashi note that Steinbeck wrote political lampoons and slogans satirizing Nixon for the 1960 campaign.)

Another indication of Steinbeck's hostility toward Nixon was displayed in his final novel, *The Winter of Our Discontent*, as indicated by his choice of Richard III as an analogue to *Winter*'s major character, Ethan Allen Hawley. Most critics feel the image of Richard Lancaster was deliberately intended to suggest Nixon, as another villainous Richard, who would stop at nothing until he had attained his goal: the highest office of the land.

However, Steinbeck was not content with blaming an individual or a party. Instead he saw the increasing popularity of Nixon (and the rejection of Stevenson) as an indication of the growing moral malaise in the country and as an indication of its increasing reliance on money and possessions as indicators of success. Honesty, truth, and integrity seemed to have taken back seats in governmental affairs; in a November 5, 1959, letter to Stevenson, Steinbeck lamented, "Having too many things, they [Americans] spend their hours and money on the couch, searching for a soul. We can stand anything God and Nature throw at us save plenty."

Unfortunately, controversy erupted when the letter was published in March of the following year in *Coronet* with an introduction by Stevenson. Steinbeck's harsh view of America and Americans did not sit well with the press or with readers; and, as a result, he was roundly rebuked by critics and supporters alike. There is speculation that the press release of the letter may have been a ploy to sway the results of the campaign for the presidential primary later that spring, but despite this negative publicity, Steinbeck continued to support Stevenson.

After JFK's victory, Stevenson's appointment as Ambassador to the UN in 1961 along with Steinbeck's move to Long Island allowed the friends to see each other more regularly; the two also met abroad several times a year, usually in Paris or London

News of Stevenson's death in July 1965 hit Steinbeck hard. In a July 16, 1965, letter to Jack Valenti and his wife, he wrote, "My first reaction to his death was one of rage that Americans had been too stupid to avail themselves of his complete ability." After the rage came sadness, not only for the loss of a good friend, but also for the loss of what Steinbeck considered "the representation . . . of American politics brought to its highest level."

Steinbeck did not plan to attend any of the memorial service but when he thought of how Stevenson would have reacted at *his* death, he made plans to attend the funeral in Bloomington, Illinois, with President Johnson. This was done at the president's request—because, Benson writes, "with Steinbeck, Johnson would feel more comfortable attending the funeral of a man whom he had not treated well."

In a letter to long-time friend **Carlton "Dook" Sheffield** on August 5, 1965, Steinbeck explained his emotional tie to the man he came to call "Guv". "He was a lovely man. You would have liked him. The fine, sharp, informed and humorous quality of his mind was unique in public men whom I have met." Steinbeck had a dream for America and the world, a dream he felt Stevenson shared; it is no wonder he urged him to champion his cause for America and the world. Nor is it surprising that, with Adlai Stevenson's death, part of Steinbeck's dream for "democracy, freedom, and world peace" died as well.

Further Reading: Benson, Jackson J. *The True Adventures of John Steinbeck, Writer.* New York: Penguin, 1990; Hayashi, Tetsumaro. "John Steinbeck and Adlai Stevenson: Their Moral and Political Vision." *Steinbeck Quarterly* 24.34 (1991): 94–107; Steinbeck, John. Foreword. *Speeches of Adlai Stevenson*. Ed. Richard Harrity. New York: Random House, 1952; Steinbeck, John. *Steinbeck: A Life in Letters*. Ed. Elaine Steinbeck and Robert Wallsten. New York: Penguin, 1989. Stevenson, Adlai. *A Call to Greatness*. New York: Harper, 1954; ———. *Friends and Enemies: What I Learned in Russia.* London: Rupert Hart-Davis, 1959; ———. *Putting First Things First*. New York: Random House, 1960.

Michael J. Meyer

STEVENSON, ROBERT LOUIS (1850–1894). Scottish novelist, poet, essayist, playwright, and travel writer, primarily known for his novels *Treasure Island* (1883), *The Strange Case of Dr. Jekyll and Mr. Hyde* (1886), and *Kidnapped* (1886). Steinbeck read and enjoyed Stevenson's work as a young boy, and he continued to reread his works throughout his life. He particularly appreciated how Stevenson allowed the reader to affectively and imaginatively participate in his novels, making the text reflect, as DeMott explains, "the reader's subjective state, which then 'keys into' the story and makes him part of it." Stevenson's poetry was no less important to Steinbeck. His favorite book of verse by Stevenson, *A Child's Garden of Verses* (1885), was eventually set to music by Steinbeck's second wife **Gwyndolyn Conger Steinbeck**. Stevenson had lived in **Monterey** in the early 1880s, which Steinbeck noted in ***Cannery Row***: "Monterey . . . remembers with pleasure and some glory that Robert Louis Stevenson lived there." In Monterey, Stevenson met Edith Wagner as a young girl, and this chance meeting provided Steinbeck with the material for his article **"How Edith**

McGillicuddy Met Robert Louis Stevenson," which appeared in *Harper's Magazine* in 1941. In the mid 1940s, **Pascal Covici** asked Steinbeck to edit a collection of Stevenson's work, going so far as to send him a very rare edition of Stevenson's work as an incentive. Steinbeck agreed to write the introduction, but gave the chore of text selection to Gwyn. The volume never came to fruition. A decade later, Steinbeck wanted to turn Stevenson's *The Wrong Box* (1889) into a film, believing the book would make a great comedy. From Steinbeck's childhood reading of Stevenson's adventure tales to a selection of Stevenson's verse being read at his funeral, Steinbeck carried his love for the writer's work to the end of his life. At his death, Steinbeck's library contained six works by Stevenson.

Further Reading: DeMott, Robert. *Steinbeck's Reading: A Catalogue of Books Owned and Borrowed.* New York: Garland, 1984.

T. Adrian Lewis

STOWE, HARRIET BEECHER (1811–1896). American writer and novelist most famous for her abolitionist work *Uncle Tom's Cabin* (1852). The book itself is a forceful remonstration against social injustice and slavery, demonstrating Stowe's understanding of the artist as a social reformer. Perhaps because of her political agenda, Stowe was criticized for the highly sentimental content of her writing and for her creation of overly idealized characters. Regardless, the novel's tremendous popularity helped polarize public sentiment and played a significant role in crystallizing the American Civil War.

Steinbeck did own and had read *Uncle Tom's Cabin* before writing ***The Grapes of Wrath***, although how long before is uncertain. Steinbeck's *The Grapes of Wrath* has been compared to Stowe's *Uncle Tom's Cabin* for the stinging indictment contained in each novel's social criticism. Steinbeck's creation of dispossessed migrants who are ultimately exploited by an economic system reminiscent of the slave era for its ruthlessness if not for its institutional bigotry parallels Stowe's major themes. Although *The Grapes of Wrath* did not polarize the nation in the same manner as *Uncle Tom's Cabin*, the novel nevertheless created a considerable amount of discontent among those who empathized with the migrant laborers and, alternatively, those who were wary of the communist influence they perceived in Steinbeck's "subversive" criticism.

Brian Niro

STREET, WEBSTER "TOBY" (1899–1984). In 1927, this early friend of John Steinbeck supplied that author with the unfinished script of his play ***The Green Lady,*** which Steinbeck eventually reworked into his second novel ***To a God Unknown***. **Robert DeMott**, in his 1995 introduction to the Penguin edition of that novel, observes that Street's play concerned a man named Andy Wane whose wife and children are "torn apart by [his] pathological preoccupation with the trees on his land." Steinbeck rewrote the character and expanded on the pantheism of Street's Andy Wane to create his own tragically myth-driven **Joseph Wayne**. One of several friends with whom Steinbeck maintained a lifelong correspondence, Street met Steinbeck while both attended **Stanford University** in the early 1920s and the latter years of the previous decade. Along with **Carlton "Dook" Sheffield**, another of Steinbeck's lifelong friends and correspondents, they had joined the English Club, through which they discussed literature and shared their own writing. Street also helped to set Steinbeck up with the job as winter caretaker at a Lake Tahoe resort where, in 1928, the author completed the manuscript of his first novel, ***Cup of Gold***.

Further Reading: Benson, Jackson J. *The True Adventures of John Steinbeck, Writer.* New York: Viking, 1984.

STUTZ, JAKOB. In ***Pastures of Heaven,*** an older German man who comes to work for **Junius Maltby**. He holds philosophical discussions with Junius and his son and acts in the role-plays that help Robbie learn. He follows a laid-back lifestyle of ease and relaxation, but he has a high degree of self-attained knowledge that he shares with both the Maltbys.

SULLIVAN. Pirate captain under **Henry Morgan**'s command in the campaign against Panama in ***Cup of Gold***.

"SUMMER BEFORE, THE" (1955). Part of a series of intermingled stories based on Steinbeck's experience as a youngster growing up in **Salinas**. According to **Jackson J. Benson**, only two or three were put on paper, and only "Summer" was ever published, appearing in the British magazine *Punch* in May 1955. The story is now only extant in Kiyoshi Nakayama's edition of *Uncollected Stories of John Steinbeck*, published in 1986 by Nan' un-do, Tokyo. It also is in the collection of the Harry Ransom Humanities Research Center at The University of Texas at Austin, the repository for the papers of **Pascal Covici**, Steinbeck's close friend and editor.

The story relates the adventures of a six-year-old Steinbeck and his sister, Mary, and a group of their Salinas friends the summer before John is to enter first grade or Baby School, yet another step toward maturity. Written in retrospect, "Summer" is sprinkled with typical Steinbeckian descriptions of the shifting setting and attempts to recapture a childlike view of the world. This viewpoint combines an innate curiosity about the natural world (including hair worms and mosquito larvae) with a serious description of the competition between boys and girls even at a young age. John's sister Mary is depicted as a "tough little monkey" who rises to meet any boy's challenge and usually is successful in defusing their teasing about a girl's inferiority.

Using stream-of-consciousness techniques, Steinbeck's plotline wanders freely, suggesting the inability of youngsters to concentrate on a single object for a long time. The story skips between episodes that recall humorous childhood naïveté to the real difficulties Steinbeck experienced in controlling and saddling his red pony, Jill.

Several sections of "Summer" focus on Willie Morton, a new resident of Salinas who tries to fit in with the local children. Willie is described as controlled by his mother, who is so concerned for his welfare that she refuses to let him join the other children and go swimming in the Salinas River.

As fall approaches, the children plan one more trip to the swimming hole, this time deciding to roast franks rather than pack traditional lunches of jelly sandwiches and hard-boiled eggs. As Steinbeck and his friends assert a newly formed maturity, Willie becomes more determined to join this second trip despite his mother's objections. Defying her control, Willie accompanies his newfound friends to the swimming hole but isolates himself by refusing to strip and swim naked. As Steinbeck describes the frolic and joy that he and his friends experience, readers see the children experimenting with adulthood, reveling in nudity and in trying out smoking. Both activities suggest a growing rebellion against societal norms and rules.

Unfortunately, the story ends with the drowning death of Willie, whose body is discovered beneath the water, caught on the branch of an old cottonwood tree. By refusing to strip, he has been ignored by the others, so no one has noticed him entering the water. But Steinbeck reserves his biggest surprise for the ending, for as Willie's body is recovered by a local farmer, it is discovered that Willie is a girl, thus returning the story to the gender inequities young children often find so divisive.

Thus, "Summer" ends with an event that requires a real rite of passage: an encounter with death. Like **Doc**'s discovery of the body in the tide pool in ***Sweet Thursday***, the children are faced with an uneasy and confusing look at reality as Steinbeck combines fictionalized events with a nonfiction memoir.

Michael J. Meyer

SUMMERS, ELLA. *See* **Women's Committee at the Weedpatch Camp**.

SUSY. In *Of Mice and Men,* owner of a house of prostitution that has five girls. Whit tells **George Milton** of the place and says that the boys normally spend Saturday nights at Susy's house.

SUZY. The love interest for **Doc** in *Sweet Thursday,* she is a twenty-one-year-old woman who arrives in **Monterey** by bus and begins to work at the **Bear Flag**. Her background is so typical of the prostitutes there that the madam is able to guess it at their first meeting. At sixteen, Suzy left an unhappy home and ran off with a man who treated her well, but he abandoned her when she became pregnant, and she ended up losing the baby. Her previous work experience consisted of being a waitress, a clerk in a dime store, and a small-time hustler. Her hard life has damaged her self-esteem and made her angry, but her good nature shines through when she lets down her defenses. Doc eventually comes to love her for her vulnerability as well as her strength of will.

On her arrival in Monterey, after being warned not to work the streets, Suzy proceeds directly to the Bear Flag to seek employment as a prostitute. She tells **Fauna**, the madam, that the only difference in being a waitress is that "you get took to a movie instead of three bucks." From the beginning, Fauna believes that Suzy would make a better wife than a hooker because "she's got a streak of lady in her." Although Suzy shows herself to be ignorant and bad-tempered in her brief encounters with Doc, Fauna manages to arrange a successful date for the couple. Emboldened, Fauna plans to use an upcoming masquerade party to announce their engagement and convinces Suzy to dress as Snow White. However, when Fauna presents the transformed Suzy and says, "Doc, come get your girl!" his face tells of his distaste, and Suzy runs away, determined to reform herself. Although she believes that there is no longer any prospect of a union with Doc, she wants to be sure that the next time she falls in love with a man, she'll "be good enough for him, inside and outside." She takes a job at a local restaurant, transforms an abandoned boiler into her home, and gains a feeling of self-respect for the first time in her life. She turns Doc away when he calls on her to apologize, but once she sees that he truly loves and needs her, she assures him, "You got yourself a girl!"

For a leading character in a novel by a major author, Suzy has seemed to many critics to be too one-dimensional. **Louis Owens**, for instance, has labeled her simply as "the whore with a heart of gold." This description doesn't quite seem accurate, however, for Steinbeck takes pains to depict Suzy as a young woman with a bad temper who is only temporarily working as a failed, miscast prostitute. On her initial appearance in the novel, Suzy looks enough like a potential hustler that the local constable warns her against working the streets. However, from the time she meets Fauna to apply for work, she is depicted as being out of place in this profession. Those convinced that Suzy will leave the business soon include not only Fauna and the other women in the house, but also **Joseph and Mary Rivas**, who considers himself a shrewd judge of hustlers. The Patron even considers her physically unfit for the work. Her discomfort in this profession is revealed most directly in her hostility toward Doc when he refers to prostitution as a "sad substitute for love." Just as Suzy is not a prostitute by calling, so is it questionable that she has a heart of gold. Her fiery temper is evident from her initial description, when she walks down the street limping "slightly on her right foot," a "scuff on the right toe," as if she has recently kicked something. She argues with Doc at every opportunity, and the other women at the Bear Flag complain that she argues with the customers as well. At one point, she herself admits, "I don't know how to be nice." The irascibility she demonstrates toward **Joe Elegant** and Doc is apparently caused by an inferiority complex. As with many of the youth depicted in ***East of Eden***, Steinbeck suggests that her low self-esteem is the product of parental rejection, for the sole memory she shares about her parents is of their failure to accept a gift she offered them. Only after she leaves prostitution behind do her old wounds begin to heal. By the end of the novel, her heart has not undergone an alchemical conversion to gold, but its brassy shrillness has finally been muted.

If Steinbeck avoids this particular stereotype, that is not to say that he invests Suzy's character with complexity or appeal. Brian Railsback notes that Suzy "embodies all the elements of Steinbeck's best people," making her "an ideal match for Doc." However, Doc himself recognizes that she is ignorant, hot-tempered, and opinionated, qualities that are neither characteristic of Steinbeck's best people nor compatible with Doc's personality. When Doc finally comes to respect her for her gritty type of courage, which he labels as gallantry of the soul, he seems self-deluded. This recalls a similar overstatement he makes earlier when, confronted by her tactlessness and pugnacity, he says of her, "That's probably the only completely honest human I have ever met." Though Suzy is certainly depicted as having some redeeming qualities, such as her candor and zest, her incompatibility with Doc is more than superficial.

Further Reading: Owens, Louis. *John Steinbeck's Re-Vision of America.* Athens: University of Georgia Press, 1985; Railsback, Brian. *Parallel Expeditions: Charles Darwin and the Art of John Steinbeck.* Moscow: University of Idaho Press, 1995.

Bruce Ouderkirk

SWEET THURSDAY (1954). Steinbeck's sequel to ***Cannery Row***, this work had its origin in Steinbeck's abortive attempts to adapt *Cannery Row* to the stage. He twice attempted an adaptation, first in the summer of 1950 as a dramatic play and again in the fall of 1952 as a musical comedy, but both times, he gave up in frustration. After the second attempt failed, he decided to write a new play, initially titled "Bear Flag," using the same setting and some of the same characters as in *Cannery Row.* Encouraged by producer Ernest Martin to develop a musical that focused on a love story involving **Doc**, Steinbeck set to work on the play at the beginning of 1953. However, after nearly two months of dictating the script, he decided that instead of writing directly for the theater, he would develop his new material into a novel that could then be adapted for the stage by himself or someone else. Eventually, *Sweet Thursday* was indeed adapted into the **Rodgers and Hammerstein** musical ***Pipe Dream***, and the novel was clearly shaped by this conceptual plan. As **Jackson J. Benson** has noted, Steinbeck tailored his novel "to the idea of its eventual conversion to a musical comedy, which may be one of the most peculiar frameworks of development ever used for an American novel." Steinbeck's use of the genre's traditional boy-meets-girl love story as his central plot in *Sweet Thursday* has accounted for much of the negative criticism directed at the novel.

Upon its publication on June 10, 1954, *Sweet Thursday* surged to the top of the best-sellers list and finished as the seventh–best-selling book of the year. Although the reading public embraced the novel, its critical reception was mixed. Characteristically, ***Time* magazine**, which never published a favorable review of Steinbeck's work, flatly labeled the novel "a turkey." Other extremely negative assessments appeared in such prestigious publications as the *New Yorker*, *Harper's*, *America*, and *Commonweal*. Gilbert Highet, writing for *Harper's*, called the novel "a corny farce," and Brendan Gill of the *New Yorker* concluded, "Steinbeck's talent is diminishing with each book." The caustic tone found in many of these notices suggests, however, that the reviewers had such a thorough distaste for Steinbeck's subjects and themes as to preclude a fair aesthetic assessment. On the other extreme, a few major publications featured rave reviews, including the *Atlantic Monthly*, whose critic praised the novel's dialogue, and the *New York Times*, whose reviewer insisted that the book showed "Steinbeck at his best." Despite these divided opinions, the disparaging voices were more numerous and more shrilly insistent. Even the largely favorable assessments often carried a qualifying caveat—that the book could be enjoyable if accepted on its own terms, but it was not quite the novel expected of a major author. Harvey Curtis Webster, writing for the *Saturday Review*, reflected this mixed reaction to *Sweet Thursday* most directly when he termed it one of Steinbeck's "good-and-bad books," placing it on the middle level of the oeuvre.

Literary scholars have, on the whole, expressed even less enthusiasm for the novel. The first generation of Steinbeck scholars tended to devalue all of his postwar work, arguing that his artistry diminished as he lost touch with his native Californian locales or as he assumed a less scientific and more moralistic point of view. Thus, **Peter Lisca**, **Warren French**, and **Joseph Fontenrose**—the three most influential Steinbeck scholars of the 1960s—all regarded *Sweet Thursday* as an inferior novel, and they did not change their stance in the studies they published subsequently. Lisca insisted that the novel betrayed Steinbeck's "relaxation of attention" as an artist, French called it "an insensitive book by a disgruntled man" (*John Steinbeck*, 1st ed.), and Fontenrose faulted the novel for both its "tasteless slapstick" and its "sententious statements." More recently, critics of such stature as Jackson J. Benson and **Louis Owens** have added their voices to the chorus of disparagement. Jackson J. Benson has said that Steinbeck "indulged himself rather shamelessly in fantasy, whimsy, nostalgia, and sentimentality," and Owens has described the novel as a self-parody, a conscious "sell-out." With so many scholars dismissing *Sweet Thursday* out of hand, it is not surprising that the novel has received little serious attention.

Those scholars who have taken the novel seriously have evinced a willingness to look beyond its musical-comedy plotline. **Richard Astro**, for instance, insists that Steinbeck takes an ironic stance toward the romantic resolution so that the novel actually demonstrates his increasing pessimism in the ability of the visionary, embodied by **Doc**, to survive in contemporary society. Other scholars have gone even further in approaching the novel from fresh perspectives. Charles Metzger has studied it as an example of the pastoral tradition; Lawrence William Jones, as a modern parable; **Howard Levant**, as a semi-allegory; and **John H. Timmerman**, as a farce with parallels to the Western. Brian Railsback observes that the novel underscores Steinbeck's interest in the inductive method, truth, and a desire to at last complete his "Doc" character. The most inventive approach to the novel has been advanced by **Robert DeMott**, who reads the book as a postmodern portrait in which the creative artist has been transmuted into the scientist Doc. DeMott builds on Jones's theories to argue that Steinbeck's later writing "moved farther away from naturalism and closer toward fabulation, parable, . . . and magical realism."

It is certainly tempting to read *Sweet Thursday* as more than a realistic narrative because the central plotline is so conventional. Discharged from the military, Doc returns to Cannery Row two years after the war has ended to find both the Row and himself deeply changed. Although he was once satisfied by his "appreciative contemplation" of the world, he now feels lonely and discontent. He comes to believe that writing a scientific paper will restore his equanimity, whereas the more mundane view of the community is that he just "needs a dame." As he develops a block that prevents him from writing his paper, the community focuses its attention on matching Doc with **Suzy**, a twenty-one-year-old woman who has recently arrived in town and gone to work at the local brothel. Despite the obvious incompatibility of the couple, they both feel drawn to one another, and the community conspires to entangle them in a matrimonial snare. Suzy eventually leaves the brothel, and once she is convinced that Doc truly needs her, the two acknowledge their love and drive away together into the sunset.

If this trite love story were all that *Sweet Thursday* had to offer, critics would be correct in finding the novel unworthy of serious attention. However, it differs from a conventional romance or musical comedy in a number of important respects. First of all, with the romantic plotline providing a sense of direction for the novel, Steinbeck frequently diverges from it into subplots that allow him to develop themes commonly found in his serious work. Early in the novel, for instance, Steinbeck introduces a self-professed **seer** whom Doc meets on the beach and engages in discussion about a lifestyle of natural contentment versus an endless struggle for material acquisition. In a passage reminiscent of *Cannery Row,* Doc tells this friend of nature, "It's one of the symptoms of our time to find danger in men like you who don't worry and rush about.... It's a crime to be happy without equipment." Similarly, the introduction of colorful **Old Jingleballicks** allows for the development of some of Steinbeck's other recurrent themes. In discussing the tax laws, which allow him to deduct donations to organizations but not to individuals, Old Jay restates the credo of ***East of Eden***: "The only creative thing we have is the individual." His discussions with Doc also raise ecological ideas that echo ***Sea of Cortez*** and theories about human population that anticipate those expressed in ***America and Americans***. Furthermore, Steinbeck interpolates into the novel some short narratives like "The Great Roque War" to continue the inversion of social values evident in *Cannery Row,* where the people most respected by society are the most rapacious. At various times, Steinbeck also engages in satire about the marriage institution, literary criticism, McCarthyism, and the spread of neurosis ("new roses"). Given the wide scope of the novel's thematic concerns, some critics have agreed with Warren French's contention that *Sweet Thursday* becomes "a patchwork quilt of reworked materials" (*John Steinbeck,* 2nd ed.). Yet the presence of these themes certainly frees the novel from the predictable patterns of the typical romance and enhances its conceptual depth.

In addition to inserting his wide-ranging social commentary, Steinbeck satirizes some of the conventions of the romance itself so that *Sweet Thursday* essentially becomes a mock-romance. To begin, he parodies the very concept of "star-crossed" lovers by having Doc and Suzy declared compatible on the basis of spurious astrological findings, Doc having lied about his birthday. The two lovers are the antithesis of the stock romance figures, the heroic male being transformed into a small businessman-scientist with a PhD, the virtuous female turned into a former runaway and occasional hooker. Furthermore, the two are brought together not by divine destiny but by the elaborate machinations of a whorehouse madam working in collusion with a drunken bum, their efforts supported by a half-wit who thinks himself destined to become president of the United States. Whereas the typical hero and heroine of romance have some differences in temperament or background, Steinbeck portrays Doc and Suzy as being thoroughly incompatible. Indeed, he considered this to be such an essential element of the novel that he pleaded with Oscar Hammerstein not to eliminate it from the stage adaptation: "The only thing this story has, besides some curious characters, is the almost tragic situation that a man of high mind and background and culture takes to his breast an ignorant, ill-tempered little hooker.... He has to take her, knowing that a great part of it is going to be misery, and she has to take him knowing she will have to live the loneliness of not even knowing what he is talking about ... yet each of them knows that the worse hell is the penalty of separation."

Although the situation that Steinbeck describes seems just as sentimental, it is a more pathetic resolution than the happily-ever-after ending of the typical romance. This impression is all the stronger given that not a single happy couple, married or otherwise, appears in the entire novel. Beyond his explicit parody of romance conventions, Steinbeck invests the entire action with a sense of unreality, as though from the beginning one were watching actors on a stage. **Roy Simmonds** has noted that "the whole tone of the book is, as it were, two removes from reality, its setting and its characters filtered first through the process of the author's creativity into the fictional ambience of *Cannery Row,* then that fictional ambience itself filtered and transformed into the veritable fairyland that is *Sweet Thursday.*" One might add that when Steinbeck moves all of his actors to a Snow White costume party, the play within a play, he places them at yet a third remove from reality. It is in this surreal atmosphere—the floor seeming "to rise and fall like the deck of a stately ship," the whole building seeming to "swell and subside like rising bread"—that the climax of the mock-romance is attained. The two star-mismatched lovers gaze at each other through the pervading "fog of unreality," fall in love, and then go their separate ways, estranged. Through this climactic scene, Steinbeck reveals the artificiality of the romance genre.

Steinbeck's intentional violations of the mimetic tradition clearly lend the novel, as DeMott has suggested, to be viewed as metafiction. In fact, the prologue begins with one of the characters, **Mack**, explaining how he would have written *Cannery Row* differently than Steinbeck did, an opening that invites readers to consider the novel about to unfold as purely a work of fiction. In the opening chapter, "What Happened in Between," Mack is the source of most of the narrative events, and the events definitely have the ring of fictional tales—a Marine collecting pickled ears, prostitutes singing mournful hymns over the death of their madam, a mentally challenged man studying astrophysics, a storekeeper buying a schooner to sail away to the South Seas, Mack himself pursuing a girl's watch with a Geiger counter halfway across the country. This sense of unreality is carried on throughout the novel, keeping a reader aware of the unfolding work as a piece of fiction. There are literary chapter titles and punning paraphrases of such authors as Coleridge and Pope. There are improbable events, such as "The Great Roque War," a tale of a deadly feud developing over croquet, which the narrator openly admits "didn't necessarily happen." There is anti-mimetic dialogue, as when Mack, a man of no apparent education, suddenly speaks in Latin or makes erudite literary allusions. There is a portrait of a novelist writing a novel that has no connection to the fictional world in which he lives as a character. There is one character disavowing the existence of another, when Doc, like an editor participating in the story, tells Jingleballicks, "You're just not possible! You're a ridiculous idea." There are surreal details, as when, on the second Sweet Thursday, "a squadron of baby angels maneuvered at twelve hundred feet." There are false prophecies and delusional seers. From the beginning of the novel to the end, Steinbeck keeps his readers aware that they are in a fictive world where fantasy and reality are hardly distinguishable.

By developing a secondary world where basic certainties are so elusive, Steinbeck ultimately addresses the more enduring questions posed by the confusion of the times. How can one know what is real and what isn't? The novel's seer does not even attempt to distinguish between visions and reality; he accepts the images he sees without judgment and enjoys their beauty whether they are illusory or not. Apart from external reality, how can one know oneself with any degree of certainty? When Doc looks within, he hears multiple voices, each insisting on its own version of truth. How can one communicate one's vision to others? **Joe Elegant**, the novel's novelist, wants to convey "the reality below reality" as he sees it, but he creates such a dense swamp of symbols as to make his vision incomprehensible to anyone, possibly even himself. Again, how can one make accurate judgments of others? Perhaps there is no reliable basis to determine whether Suzy is, as she is called at various times, an illiterate tramp, a brave thing, Snow White the bride, a grandstanding bitch, a two-bit hustler, a nice kid, or all of these or none. Perhaps, after all, it is impossible to predict whether or not she would be a good wife. The novel does not provide definitive answers to any of the questions it raises—in the end, Doc has to make a major decision without knowing at all whether his choice is advisable—but in raising such epistemological questions, Steinbeck elevates the novel above the genre of its surface story.

Sweet Thursday is obviously not among Steinbeck's greatest novels. It becomes excessively sentimental, especially when Doc decides that he can't live without Suzy; it becomes too cute, as when Mack spouts nonsense like "God works in his tum-te-dum way his tum-tums to perform"; it becomes sententious, especially when Doc and Old Jingleballicks engage in debate; it even becomes ludicrous, as when the prostitutes fight over who gets to be first to lay out the fancy silverware and correct each other's grammar, "Double negative! Double negative!" Yet it is a more artistically complex novel than has usually been recognized. Steinbeck loved to read **Shakespeare** and surely knew that in many of his comedies the master parodied certain conventions of the theater at the same time that he employed them. So, too, Steinbeck created a romantic comedy for the stage that satirizes many of the conventions of the genre he adopted. Although time has tarnished the relevance of many of the topical concerns discussed in the novel, the epistemological questions that Steinbeck raised in *Sweet Thursday* will remain important to readers in any age.

Further Reading: Astro, Richard. *John Steinbeck and Edward F. Ricketts: The Shaping of a Novelist*, Minneapolis: University of Minnesota Press, 1973; Benson, Jackson, J. *The True Adventures of John Steinbeck, Writer.* New York: Viking, 1984; DeMott, Robert J. "*Sweet Thursday* Revisited: An Excursion in Suggestiveness." In *After "The Grapes of Wrath": Essays on John Steinbeck in Honor of Tetsumaro Hayashi.* Ed. Donald V. Coers, Paul C. Ruffin, and Robert J. DeMott. Athens Ohio University Press, 1995; Fontenrose, Joseph. *John Steinbeck: An Introduction and Interpretation.* New York: Barnes and Noble, 1963; French, Warren. *John Steinbeck.* New York: Twayne, 1961; French, Warren. *John Steinbeck*, 2nd ed. Boston: Twayne, 1975; Lisca, Peter. *The Wide World of John Steinbeck.* New Brunswick, NJ: Rutgers University Press, 1958; McElrath, Joseph R., Jr., Jesse S. Crisler, and Susan Shillinglaw, eds. *John Steinbeck: The Contemporary Reviews.* New York: Cambridge University Press, 1996; Morsberger, Robert E. "*Pipe Dream*, or Not So Sweet Thursday." *Steinbeck Quarterly* 21 (Summer–Fall 1988): 85–96; Owens, Louis. *John Steinbeck's Re-Vision of America.* Athens: University of Georgia Press, 1985; Railsback, Brian. *Parallel Expeditions: Charles Darwin and the Art of John Steinbeck.* Moscow: University of Idaho Press, 1995; Steinbeck, John. *Steinbeck: A Life in Letters.* Ed. Elaine Steinbeck and Robert Wallsten. New York: Viking, 1975.

Bruce Ouderkirk

SWEETHEART. In ***The Wayward Bus***, the commonly recognized name of the "wayward" bus. "Sweetheart" is an ancient, aluminum-paint colored passenger bus that makes the run from **Rebel Corners** to San Juan de la Cruz. Although the new name is saccharine, secular, and slightly hokey, the former inscription on the bumpers is still legible: *"el gran Poder de Jesus"* (the great power of Jesus). Sweetheart is described as "an old, old bus, and it had seen many trips and many difficulties," as evidenced by the many dents and scratches and "home paint job" on its exterior and the inoperable windows, worn floorboards, and worn driver's seat. Yet as a symbol of technology in the novel, Sweetheart facilitates Steinbeck's contrast between Juan's capability as a mechanic and the passengers' helplessness before the mechanized modern world, which becomes clear when the bus mires. Steinbeck creates a symbolic "world" in the bus itself, much as Melville does through the Pequod in *Moby Dick*; in **Jackson J. Benson**'s words, Steinbeck's metaphor reveals a "world in microcosm adrift in the universe." Peopled by self-indulgent, physically or morally repugnant passengers who are seemingly incapable of noble action, the motorized (i.e., modern) bus mires on the old road over which stagecoaches used to pass and thus symbolically represents the shrinking, diminution, and corruption of modern American culture as compared with the storied frontier past.

Further Reading: Benson, Jackson J. *The True Adventures of John Steinbeck, Writer.* New York: Viking, 1984.

SWIFT, JONATHAN (1667–1745). Irish writer widely regarded as the most important prose satirist in the English language. Little is said about Swift's impact upon Steinbeck's writing, but **Robert DeMott** suggests that Steinbeck was most likely rereading Swift sometime during the early 1940s, as evinced by a short holograph accompanying a letter to his publisher **Pascal Covici** and his use of "A Modest Proposal" (1729) in ***Sea of Cortez***. In his short note to Covici, he lauds the timelessness of Swift's stories, stating that "the poetical satires in Gulliver have long been forgotten but the stories go on." Regarding his own use of "A Modest Proposal," Steinbeck stated simply that it was an "addenda to Swift's suggestion about a use for Irish babies and drawn out by the myth that the Seri Indians of Tiburon are cannibals."

Further Reading: DeMott, Robert. *Steinbeck's Reading: A Catalogue of Books Owned and Borrowed.* New York: Garland, 1984; Fensch, Thomas. *Steinbeck and Covici.* Middlebury, VT: Paul S. Eriksson, 1979.

Gregory Hill, Jr.

SWOPE, JOHN (1908–1978). An accomplished pilot and photographer who took photos for ***Bombs Away*** (Steinbeck wrote the text). Swope was an early advocate for air power in war, and in 1940 he worked as a flight instructor for pilots as the government readied for the inevitable involvement in World War II. Although Swope was excited about the project, Steinbeck felt he was doing a job for President **Franklin Delano Roosevelt** (who in person asked Steinbeck to do the work). They spent some thirty days in the air for over twenty thousand miles in different types of aircraft, and, as **Jackson J. Benson** points out, Steinbeck found the time tiresome, and the author was not thrilled by Swope's propensity to get shots of Steinbeck in the shower or waking up. Swope and Steinbeck donated their royalties from *Bombs Away* to the U.S. Army Air Forces Aid Society Trust Fund.

Further Reading: Benson, Jackson J. *The True Adventures of John Steinbeck, Writer.* New York: Viking, 1984; Railsback, Brian. "Style and Image: John Steinbeck and Photography." In *John Steinbeck, A Centennial Tribute.* Ed. Syed Mashkoor Ali. Jaipur, India: Surabhi, 2004.

Brian Railsback

SYNGE, JOHN MILLINGTON (1871–1909). Steinbeck enjoyed the work of this Irish playwright and poet; though Steinbeck owned a 1936 edition of *The Complete Works of John M. Synge*, **Robert DeMott** notes that Steinbeck likely read Synge earlier than that. **Henry Fonda** read Synge's "**Petrarch's** Sonnets to Laura" at Steinbeck's funeral.

Further Reading: DeMott, Robert. *Steinbeck's Reading: A Catalogue of Books Owned and Borrowed.* New York: Garland, 1984.

T

TAGUS RANCH. A 4,000-acre peach ranch in Tulare County, south of Fresno, that employed migrant workers and Dust Bowl refugees. It was the site of a workers' strike in August 1933, which served as a model for the strike depicted at the Hooper Ranch, an important setting in ***The Grapes of Wrath***. The wage at Tagus (15 cents an hour) was barely enough to buy food in the company store in 1933 and was the same paid by the Growers Association in *The Grapes of Wrath*. The workers at the ranch were organized by labor unions and struck for 30 cents an hour. Although the company settled for 25 cents an hour after state mediation, company officials were so angered by having to give in that the company later ripped out the peach trees and planted cotton. The Tagus Ranch strike also prompted a cotton workers' strike, after which most of the major events of *The Grapes of Wrath* are modeled.

Paul Blobaum

TALBOT, MARY. In Chapter 24 of ***Cannery Row,*** Mary Talbot is a beautiful, eccentric young woman who defies the realities of poverty with gaiety and a propensity to throw parties on the cheap. She is a tonic for her husband Tom, who is often despondent about their financial troubles and their dwindling prospects. When he asks her to face the fact that they are going down, she continues to be Tom's cheerleader. **Jackson J. Benson** notes that Steinbeck may have modeled Mary on **Carol Henning Steinbeck** and the Steinbecks' friend, Natalya (Tal) Lovejoy, who both were adept at putting together parties on a shoestring during tough times. Just as Mary worked to cheer Tom, Carol strove to pull John up.

Further Reading: Benson, Jackson J. *The True Adventures of John Steinbeck, Writer.* New York: Viking, 1984.

TARQUIN, SIR. In ***The Acts of King Arthur,*** brother of **King Carados**, who was killed by **Sir Lancelot**. In honor of his hatred of Lancelot, Tarquin fights, captures, and imprisons any knight of **King Arthur**'s fellowship he finds. He is finally granted his wish to meet Lancelot and is killed by him.

TAULAS. In ***The Acts of King Arthur,*** the brother of **Taulurd,** a giant who lives in Cornwall and who once bested **Sir Marhalt** in a fight.

TAULURD. In ***The Acts of King Arthur,*** the giant killed by **Sir Marhalt** during the Triple Quest.

TAYLOR, DANNY. In ***The Winter of Our Discontent***, Danny is the town drunk of New Baytown. He is also like a "brother" to **Ethan Allen Hawley,** who routinely advances Danny sums of money for drinks. After being expelled from Annapolis, Danny maintains his reputation by holding on to a family property known as Taylor

Meadow, a level field that Ethan knows is the only suitable site for a needed new airport. By offering Danny money, which had been inherited by **Mary Hawley**, for alcohol treatment, Ethan plans to acquire his friend's land, realizing that Danny will eventually waste the money drinking himself to death. Although he understands the duplicitous nature of his "brother," Danny nonetheless wills the land to Ethan after his death. Ethan's awareness that Danny knows what he is up to is a major factor in the latter's final despair over his betrayal.

John Ditsky

TAYLOR, JESS. A neighbor of the **Tiflin** family in ***The Red Pony***, Taylor appears briefly in two stories. It is he who brings news of seeing **Gitano**, riding on **Old Easter** and headed for the Santa Lucia Mountains. In **"The Promise," Jody** takes **Nellie** to be bred by Taylor's stallion, Sundog, for a $5.00 stud fee.

TAYLOR, OLD MAN. In ***East of Eden***, an eccentric **Salinas** man who buys old houses and then moves and crowds them onto a vacant lot he owns. **Dessie Hamilton** speaks of an encounter with him one afternoon in order to amuse **Agnes Morrison**, who is visiting her dressmaking shop.

TAYLOR, WILLIAM, 4TH. In *Sweet Thursday*, a first-grader in **Pacific Grove**. He sparks a scandal when he comes home from school with his crayons wrapped in the dust jacket of the Kinsey report, a controversial analysis of human sexual behavior by Alfred Kinsey that had appeared in 1948 and was based on data collected and interviews held at the Kinsey Institute at Indiana University.

TEGNA. Pirate captain under **Henry Morgan**'s command in the campaign against Panama in ***Cup of Gold***.

TELLER, HARRY. Like **Peter Randall**, Harry is a repressed and lonely husband. His actions in **"The White Quail"** are constantly in conflict with those of his wife, **Mary**, a woman who definitely knows her own mind. His loneliness echoes that of others in ***The Long Valley*** stories (**Dr. Phillips** of **"The Snake,"** for instance, or **Jim Moore** in **"The Murder"** and **Mike** in **"The Vigilante"**). Harry's infatuation with Mary gradually turns to resentment of Mary's love for her garden and her identification with the white quail, and anger at his own failure to find a more prominent place in her affections. In retaliation, Harry shoots the solitary white bird that is such a clear symbol for his wife, but it is his own sense of loneliness and isolation that ends the short story.

Abby H. P. Werlock

TELLER, MARY. In **"The White Quail"** Mary marries **Harry** because he can afford to provide her with the garden of her dreams. This garden is far from "natural," as Mary artificially imposes order and structure on the "wild"erness. Within this personal Eden she creates, Mary sees the solitary white quail that frequents the garden as emblematic of her true self. Although Mary's independence has been read positively as self-sufficiency, more frequently, it is seen negatively as reflecting her self-absorption and ruthless egotism. Mary especially fears a local cat as a potential destroyer of the quail and urges her husband to scare it away or shoot it. Instead Harry shoots the white quail and removes its corpse from the garden, in the process metaphorically killing his wife and leaving readers and critics alike divided over which spouse most deserves sympathy: the neglected husband or the obsessive, selfish wife.

Abby H. P. Werlock

TENNER, WILLIAM (BILL). In ***Of Mice and Men***, a former pea cultivator operator at the ranch who quit the job three months before **George Milton** and **Lennie Small** arrive. He is the one whose letter to the editor of a magazine earns respect from his fellow ranch hands. In the letter, he tells the editor that he had been reading the magazine for six years and particularly likes the stories by Peter Rand, whom he calls a "whing-ding." **Whit**, another ranch hand, who had worked with Tenner before he left the ranch, calls him "a hell of a nice fella."

Luchen Li

TENNYSON, ALFRED LORD (1809–1892). Prominent Victorian poet, who was named the poet laureate of England in 1850. His poems "Ulysses," "Locksley Hall," "Charge of the Light Brigade," and the lengthy elegy *In Memoriam A. H. H* are among his most well-known works. Steinbeck refers to Tennyson in the first version of ***To a God Unknown***, and he also was intrigued by Tennyson's epic poem, *The Idylls of the King* (1889), which he considered a "pale echo" of the Arthurian cycle. Steinbeck believed Tennyson's *Idylls* took the "toughness out" of Sir Thomas Malory's ***Le Morte D'Arthur*** (1470, pub. 1485) in order to suit "his soft Victorian audience." Despite this criticism of Tennyson's work, **Henry Fonda** read from "Ulysses" at Steinbeck's funeral. According to **Robert DeMott**, Steinbeck's library contained a copy of *The Idylls of the King*.

T. Adrian Lewis

THACKERAY, WILLIAM MAKEPEACE (1811–1863). English satirical novelist, who wrote *Vanity Fair*. Steinbeck is described as admiring writers who, like Thackeray, had thought deeply about what they had written. In 1936, fired from the *New York American* and disappointed by not having any stories published, Steinbeck returned to California. He found work as a caretaker on the Lake Tahoe estate of Mrs. Alice Bingham. He spent the next two years in almost complete solitude, doing heavy physical labor, reading, and, most importantly, writing. During this time, Steinbeck read extensively from the novels of Thackeray, Dickens, and **Scott**. He realized that he needed solitude to create, and throughout his life, Steinbeck would often retreat when he felt his writing was suffering.

Janet L. Flood

THEIR BLOOD IS STRONG. *See* ***The Harvest Gypsies***.

THELMA. Prostitute at **Kate Albey**'s brothel in ***East of Eden***.

"THEN MY ARM GLASSED UP" (1965). In this epistolary piece, published in *Sports Illustrated* (December 20, 1965), Steinbeck reflects on his experiences as an observer and participant in sports, while maintaining that he is largely ill-equipped to talk about sports because his interests are "scattered" and "unorthodox." He pokes fun at sport fishers and hunters and calls into question the true courage of bullfighters. His observations are often metaphorical: "It seems to me that any sport is a kind of practice, perhaps unconscious, for the life-and-death struggle for survival."

Further Reading: Steinbeck, John. "Then My Arm Glassed Up." In *America and Americans and Selected Nonfiction*. Ed. Susan Shillinglaw and Jackson J. Benson. New York: Viking, 2002.

THERESE. Prostitute at **Kate Albey**'s brothel in ***East of Eden***.

THINKING MAN'S DOG, THE. Written by Ted Patrick in 1964, this book is a humorous indictment of individuals who think that they own their dogs, rather than the other way around. Knowing Steinbeck was a dog enthusiast, Patrick invited him to write the introduction to the book. When the book was published, Patrick included Steinbeck's letter explaining why he had to decline the offer.

THOMAS, MR. Through the intercession of the **Wallaces**, Mr. Thomas, a farm owner in ***The Grapes of Wrath***, offers work to **Tom Joad** shortly after his arrival at the Weedpatch camp (**Arvin Sanitary Camp**). Although Thomas ultimately capitulates to the pressures of the Farmers Association and the Bank of the West in their insistence that he lower wages, he is sympathetic to the plight of the migrants and thoughtfully warns the three workers of the impending fight being planned at the Saturday night dance at the camp. He also relates how the growers' association manipulates public opinion against the migrants by fostering fears about "red" agitators. Like **Mae** and Al at the truck stop, Mr. Thomas is evidence that not all humans are motivated by greed and selfishness, and that some people have empathy for others.

Michael J. Meyer

THOREAU, HENRY DAVID (1817–1862). Steinbeck's indebtedness to the American transcendentalists has been noted frequently. His specific debt to Thoreau is not hard to discern; the key ideas in *Walden* that have fueled generations of writers and environmentalists since its publication in 1854 surface clearly in Steinbeck's major works. These ideas include seeing nature as teacher and text, model and parable—that which connects us intimately and directly with the divine; observing nature, society, and self to gain wisdom; embracing simplicity and economy over material excess; maintaining a skeptical distance from institutions and their claims; questioning the norms that define "civilized" behavior; and resisting technological and imperialistic expansionism. Like Thoreau, Steinbeck looks upon the natural world as a source of knowledge, a text to replace or expand upon scripture, which teaches those who have eyes to see and ears to hear.

For Steinbeck, as for Thoreau, the wise man was defined above all else by his discerning relationship to the natural world, allowing it to inform his understanding of human relations and enterprises. In several of Steinbeck's novels, readers encounter variations on this type of wise man—a character whose unusual self-knowledge and sharp intuitions come from close association with the natural world. Two of the most notable of these are **Casy** in ***The Grapes of Wrath*** and **Doc** in ***Cannery Row***. Both are solitaries, men who take frequent "flights into the wilderness" but who live among people who rely upon them for guidance. Both are more educated than those around them, but each, like Thoreau, has rejected the institutional forms and frameworks that endowed him with professional credentials and, instead, lives as a maverick, moving easily among circles of people where he does not belong, functioning as a kind of prophet. Indeed it might be said that in such characters Steinbeck is working out a definition of the prophet as one who sees into the heart of nature and speaks forth the lessons it teaches, often producing lyrical moments, philosophical insights, or prophetic soliloquies. In such passages, the writer, in effect, issues a warning and a call to turn away from those forms of civilized life that remove us from nature.

And like Thoreau, Steinbeck writes as one who is himself a visionary, trying to find a language for the ultimate interconnectedness of all creation as a means for understanding what humans must do. Stei beck's most explicit articulation of this vision is given in ***Sea of Cortez***, where he describes **non-teleological thinking** as a way of understanding the natural as well as the social world, independent of the causal relations and presumed purposes that individuals so readily posit to satisfy their need for comprehensible meaning. To think in such a way entails a rejection of the myopic anthropocentrism that distorts our understanding of the functioning of whole systems; instead, the large patterns of evolution are valued, and natural and human communities are seen as organic wholes that transcend the life and purposes of any individual within them. More generally, in almost all the novels, the natural world is featured as a place of Edenic retreat and as an image of hope and renewal, as well as a place where seekers find wisdom—by wandering the broad valleys, farming the land, visiting the tide pools, camping in the wilderness, or gazing at the stars.

Marilyn Chandler McEntyre

THUCYDIDES (456?–404? BC). Classical Greek historian and author. In 424 BC, he was elected one of the ten *strategoi* of the year and, because of his connections, was given command of the fleet in the Thraceward region, based at Thasos. He failed to prevent the capture of the important city of Amphipolis by the Spartan general Brasidas, who launched a sudden attack in the middle of winter. Because of this blunder, Thucydides was recalled, tried, and sentenced to exile. This, he says later, gave him greater opportunity for undistracted study for his *History* and for travel and wider contacts, especially on the Peloponnesian side—Sparta and its allies. His *History*, which is divided into eight books, probably not by Thucydides' design, stops in the middle of the events of the autumn of 411 BC, more than six and a half years before the end of the war. Thucydides was writing what few others have attempted—a strictly contemporary history of events that he lived through and that succeeded each other throughout almost his whole adult life. He endeavored to do more than merely record events, some of which he took an active part in and in which he was a direct or indirect spectator; instead, he attempted to write the final history for later generations, and, as far as a writer can and as no other has, he succeeded. During his last years, he was observing, inquiring, writing his notes, adding to or modifying what he had already written; at no time before the end, during the twenty-seven years of the war, did he know what that end would be, nor, therefore, what the length and the final shape of his own *History* would be. It is evident that he did not long survive the war, but, in what he lived to complete, he wrote a definitive history.

In a 1962 letter to **Elizabeth Otis**, Steinbeck noted that in his evaluation of older texts that he had read in the past, some of the things he admired had fallen off and others had become far greater. He included the *History* of Thucydides in the latter group, books whose stock seemed to improve with rereading and evaluation.

Further Reading: DeMott, Robert. *Steinbeck's Reading: A Catalogue of Books Owned and Borrowed.* New York: Garland, 1984.

Michael J. Meyer

THURBER, JAMES (1894–1961). American artist, cartoonist, humorist, and critic whose 1942 vitriolic review of Steinbeck's ***The Moon Is Down*** in *The New Republic* created some controversy in its own right (**Viking** editor **Marshall Best** came to the book's defense, only to bring out another attack from Thurber). Thurber accused Steinbeck of being too optimistic and idealistic about the war and, in particular, he decried what he felt was Steinbeck's sympathetic handling of the Nazis.

Further Reading: McElrath, Joseph, Jr., Jesse S. Crisler, and Susan Shillinglaw, eds. *John Steinbeck: The Contemporary Reviews.* Cambridge: Cambridge University Press, 1996.

TIFLIN, CARL. **Jody**'s father in ***The Red Pony*** is a strict disciplinarian, who is not sensitive to other people's feelings. He is described as a man who "hated weakness and sickness, and he held a violent contempt for helplessness." In some instances, he even behaves cruelly, although the narrator sometimes provides rationalizations for his behavior. Still, he does the best he can, buying a pony and saddle for his son when he has the opportunity. After **Gabilan** dies, he arranges for the mare, **Nellie**, to be bred so that Jody can have another pony, at the same time requiring that Jody earn the right and behave responsibly. In **"The Great Mountains,"** Tiflin notices parallels between **Old Easter** and **Gitano**, saying "old things ought to be put out of their misery." He tells Gitano, "If ham and eggs grew on a side-hill, I'd turn you out to pasture . . . but I can't afford to pasture you in my kitchen." The last time he is seen in the novelette, he experiences shame for his cruel treatment of **Grandfather**. He apologizes, and Jody understands the price that the apology extracts from his proud father; "It was a terrible thing to him to retract a word, but to retract it in shame was infinitely worse."

Mimi Reisel Gladstein

TIFLIN, JODY. In ***The Red Pony***, the boy protagonist whose experiences with the violent death of horses and the waning years of old men form the plots of the four related but distinct stories that make up the novelette. During the course of the seasonal cycle the stories record, Jody grows from a petulant, aggressive, but appealingly imaginative youngster into an ambitious but considerate person, greatly chastened by grim encounters with human and natural shortcomings—the death of his red pony in **"The Gift,"** the disappearance and seemingly certain suicide of old **Gitano** in **"The Great Mountains,"** the necessity of killing the favorite mare, **Nellie**, to save her colt in **"The Promise,"** and the death of an old man's dream and the spirit of "westering" with the closing of the frontier as recounted in **"The Leader of the People."**

In "The Gift," Jody is ten years old and all boy, smashing muskmelons with his heel, feeling pride in the distinction his pony gives him among his classmates, and learning from **Billy Buck** how to care for his new pony. Steinbeck presents Jody as imaginative, sometimes destructive, but also compassionate, especially toward older men. He does the best he can with the care of his pony, **Gabilan**. His treatment of the mare, **Nellie**, in "The Promise" has been compared to that of an expectant father. His final gesture in the novelette is an attempt to make his grandfather feel better. The focus on Jody provides a thread of unity through the distinct stories, which are told as though the reader is in Jody's mind and shares his perceptions.

Mimi Reisel Gladstein

TILSON, DR. King City doctor in ***East of Eden*** who treats and upbraids **Cathy Trask** when she attempts to induce an abortion with a knitting needle. Later, when **Dessie Hamilton** becomes critically ill, **Tom Hamilton** rides to **Red Duncan**'s house to telephone Dr. Tilson.

TIFLIN, MRS. In *The Red Pony,* **Jody**'s mother is a farm housewife who tries to teach him responsibility and ameliorate the sometimes callous behavior of her husband toward her son and her father. She plays a minimal role in the stories, appearing briefly in each of the stories. In **"The Gift,"** she prepares meals and reminds Jody to do his chores. When **Gitano** arrives in **"The Great Mountains,"** she does not know how to deal with him and so calls her husband. In **"The Promise,"** she is depicted as full of concern for household matters and as rather impatient with her son's immaturity. As the story progresses, she gives Jody some responsibility by showing him how to prepare warm mash for **Nellie**, but her insensitivity returns when it is time for the mare to give birth, and she does not recognize the importance of the foal to her son, preferring instead to emphasize rules and order. Her role in **"The Leader of the People"** is larger than in the other stories. She is angered by her husband's behavior toward her father and tries to get him to be more understanding. Whereas **Carl Tiflin**, her husband, is usually the one in control of all aspects of life on the ranch, the narrator explains "when occasionally her temper arose, he could not combat it." She is critical of Jody, calling him "Big-Britches." When Jody asks for lemons to make lemonade for his grandfather, she mimics him because she thinks it an excuse to have a treat. The final words in the novel are hers, though, words that demonstrate her appreciation for her son's show of compassion to his grandfather.

Margaret Seligman

TIM. Bosun from Cork, Ireland, and former pirate who, in ***Cup of Gold***, befriends **Henry Morgan** in an inn. Tim immediately takes advantage of Henry's naïveté by getting Henry to pay for his meal and promises to get Henry aboard the ***Bristol Girl*** as a cabin boy for the voyage to the West Indies. What Tim fails to mention is that on arrival, Henry will be sold into five years of indentured servitude.

Kevin Hearle

***TIME* MAGAZINE**. Throughout his career, Steinbeck's relationship with *Time* fluctuated from receiving unflattering to, at times, openly hostile reviews of his fictional output.

For approximately thirty years, *Time* criticized and mocked Steinbeck's "proletarian" themes, rarely missing an opportunity to add hue to the portrait painted of Steinbeck as a "red" writer. Nevertheless, the magazine tacitly acknowledged Steinbeck's significance as a major American writer and never failed to print every major event of his life. For his part, Steinbeck seemed largely uninterested in the quality of his reviews. However, Steinbeck often wrote to *Time* to protest condescending reviews made by the magazine regarding writers Steinbeck either knew or admired. This, in turn, became a source of ridicule for the people at *Time.* In a rather pathetic reversal of position, *Time* abandoned its antagonistic stance toward Steinbeck only when composing and printing his obituary.

Brian Niro

"TIME THE WOLVES ATE THE VICE-PRINCIPAL, THE" (1947). This gruesome short story was written as one of the interpolated chapters in ***Cannery Row***, but Steinbeck had dropped it before the manuscript was completed. It first appeared obscurely in the first issue of the short-lived *'47: Magazine of the Year* (March 1947) and was reprinted much later in the *Steinbeck Newsletter* (Fall 1995). As the overworked and overtired Mr. Hartley, vice principal in the high school of Steinbeck's home town, **Salinas**, California, is walking home in the middle of the night, he is killed and eaten by a pack of wolves that has invaded the city. The woman on whose porch he has taken futile refuge does not even wake up. In *John Steinbeck: The War Years 1939–1945* (1996), **Roy Simmonds** discusses the deletion of the chapter from *Cannery Row* as well as **Warren French**'s comments about Steinbeck's attack on Americans' complacency when people are dying on their doorsteps.

Further Reading: Steinbeck, John. "The Day the Wolves Ate the Vice-Principal." In *Uncollected Stories of John Steinbeck*. Ed. Kiyoshi Nakayama. Tokyo: Nan'undo, 1986.

TIMMERMAN, JOHN H. (1945–). Steinbeck scholar and author of two books: *John Steinbeck's Fiction: The Aesthetics of the Road Taken* (1986) and *The Dramatic Landscape of Steinbeck's Short Stories* (1990). Both of these works were written in the 1980s, a period during which critics were re-examining critical dogma concerning Steinbeck's work and were beginning to evaluate it on its own terms. *John Steinbeck's Fiction* is the first major critical study written after **Jackson J. Benson**'s definitive biography was made available, and the analysis relies on extensive biographical reference. His second book, *The Dramatic Landscape of Steinbeck's Short Stories*, explores Steinbeck's literary apprenticeship in the 1920s and 1930s. The relationship between Steinbeck and creative writing professor **Edith Mirrielees** is examined. The book deals with nearly all of Steinbeck's short stories. Each section offers an interpretation of the story at hand, but also examines the composition of the story, alterations made during the composing process, and biographical information relating to the work's composition.

Charles Etheridge, Jr.

TIMSHEL* [TIMSHOL; TIMSHOL-BO].** Steinbeck's spelling of the Hebrew verb, *timshol-bo*, a command stated in the future tense that literally means "you will rule" (*timshol*) "in him" (*bo*), and which has been variously translated as "thou shalt rule over him," (King James **Bible**); "do thou rule over him" (American Standard Bible); and "thou mayest rule over it" (the Holy Scriptures). Steinbeck learned about and studied this word during the time he was writing ***East of Eden. Fascinated by the possibilities of meaning in the word, and with his thematic intentions well in mind, Steinbeck used the variant spelling, *timshel*, and the meaning "thou mayest [rule over sin]."

Timshol-bo appears in Genesis 4:7, the section of the Cain and Abel story in which God attempts to console and direct Cain after rejecting Cain's offering. In *East of Eden*, this story is read prior to the naming of the **Trask** twins, and the lines in question read, "If thou doest well, shalt thou not be accepted? And if thou doest not well, sin lieth at the door. And unto thee shall be his desire, and thou shalt rule over him." Later, and after much study (possibly a parallel to Steinbeck's own), an exegesis of this biblical passage is offered by **Lee**, the Chinese servant, who explains excitedly, "Don't you see? . . . American Standard translation orders men to triumph over sin. . . ." The King James translation makes a promise in 'Thou shalt,' meaning that men will surely triumph over sin. But the Hebrew word, the word *timshel*—'Thou mayest'—that gives a choice. . . . For if 'thou mayest'—it is also true that 'Thou mayest not.'"

After this point in the novel, Steinbeck uses *timshel* to establish a dichotomy between psychological, genetic, or generational predestination and free, individual development and action, ideas that are central to the story. In this way, *timshel* functions to inform characters and to direct their actions and development, to provide an impetus for plot events, and to articulate and enhance symbolism and the book's thematic design.

As Steinbeck suspected, scholars have continually challenged his interpretation of *timshel*. **Peter Lisca**, who forgives Steinbeck's use of *timshel*, believes nevertheless that the structure and thematic content of the book are flawed. Taking a different approach, **Joseph Fontenrose** scrutinized Steinbeck's translation of *timshel* and identified the errors in the Hebrew spelling and grammatical usage. Fontenrose argued that these errors weakened the thematic coherence and narrative unity of *East of Eden*, and his linguistic analysis of *timshel* has remained widely accepted. **Warren French** believes that the book is essentially a failure, although, like Lisca, he is willing to excuse Steinbeck's use of *timshel*. Finally, **Robert DeMott** points out that although "Steinbeck has been accused of appropriating and translating timshol improperly . . . [he was adhering] to the artist's freedom . . . to distort facts for artful purposes."

In other critical views, John L. Gribben, Lester J. Marks, and Barbara McDaniel examine the ways in which the structure of the novel is connected to the themes of good vs. evil, rejection and alienation, and free will; in their analyses, *timshel*, "thou mayest," becomes the mechanism by which these themes are resolved. Gribben, Marks, and **John Ditsky** assert that, as Ditsky puts it, "the epiphany of Timshel! puts an end to strict determinism," thus articulating Steinbeck's **non-teleological** view of the human condition.

Further Reading: DeMott, Robert. *Steinbeck's Typewriter: Essays on His Art*. Troy, NY: Whitston Publishing Co., 1996; Ditsky, John. *Essays on* East of Eden. Muncie, IN: John Steinbeck Society of America/Ball State University, 1977; Fensch, Thomas. *Steinbeck and Covici: The Story of a Friendship*. Middlebury, VT: Paul Eriksson, 1979; Fontenrose, Joseph. *John Steinbeck: An Introduction and Interpretation*. New York: Barnes and Noble, 1963; French, Warren. *John Steinbeck*. Rev. ed. Boston: Twayne Publishers, 1975; Gribben, John L. "Steinbeck's *East of Eden* and Milton's *Paradise Lost:* A Discussion of Timshel." *Steinbeck Quarterly* 5 (Spring 1972): 35–43; Lisca, Peter. *The Wide World of John Steinbeck*. New Brunswick, NJ: Rutgers University Press, 1958. Marks, Lester Jay. "*East of Eden:* 'Thou Mayest.'" *Steinbeck Quarterly* 4 (Winter 1971): 3–18; McDaniel, Barbara. "Alienation in *East of Eden*: The 'Chart of the Human Soul.'" *Steinbeck Quarterly* 14 (Winter–Spring 1981): 32–39. Steinbeck, John. *Journal of a Novel: The* East of Eden *Letters*. New York: Viking, 1969.

Margaret Seligman

TINKER. Initially appearing as a romantic figure in **"The Chrysanthemums,"** a wandering man enviably free of property or a wife, the tinker later reveals himself as a manipulative, dirty man who is ultimately without a soul. Shamelessly toying with the admirable and complex **Elisa Allen**, he plays on her emotions in return for money and falsely promises to deliver her flowers to another woman. He clearly demonstrates his utter disregard for her when he dumps the chrysanthemums (a metaphor for the thirty-five-year-old woman) onto the road.

Abby H. P. Werlock

TO A GOD UNKNOWN. This 1933 novel is important for two reasons: first, the circumstances of composition and publication provide insights into the early development of a struggling writer, and second, many of the themes, character types, attitudes, and locations that Steinbeck was to use in his later, more significant works are prefigured here. The novel is the first example, albeit a rough one, of the technique—syncretic allegory—that Steinbeck was to perfect in ***The Grapes of Wrath*** and ***East of Eden***. In a note accompanying the manuscript, he called it "a novel about the world" with "new seeing," adding, "It is probable that no one will know it for two hundred years. It will be confused, analyzed, analogized, criticized, and none of our fine critics will know what is happening."

Steinbeck got the idea for this novel from a play, ***The Green Lady***, written by his friend **Webster "Toby" Street** for a **Stanford University** creative writing class. In Street's play, the main character, Andy Wane, tries to save his Mendocino County, California farm while at the same time keep his daughter from leaving home. Intrigued by this subject, Steinbeck started a novel in the fall and winter of 1927–28 with the same title, naming Street as coauthor. Within a year, he had changed the location to the Nacimiento River Valley and the name of the major character to **Joseph Wayne**. After completing more than 100 draft pages, he put the project aside in favor of writing short stories. In December of 1928, however, he resumed work on the novel, now titled *To the* [later *an*] *Unknown God* and creating different conflicts. In the spring of 1930, he sent the completed manuscript to his first publisher, **Robert M. McBride & Co.**, which turned it down, as did numerous other houses. In August 1931, Steinbeck withdrew the manuscript from circulation and, at about the same time, had the idea for ***The Pastures of Heaven***, which was published in 1932. No doubt influenced by mythologist **Joseph Campbell**, who had become a friend and neighbor, Steinbeck produced a major rewrite of *To a God Unknown* by February 1933. Accepted by his former editor, **Robert Ballou** (who had joined the Putnam publishing company), the novel was published that year but received negative reviews and minimal sales, and was remaindered early in 1934. The *Nation* called it "pitifully thin and shadowy," and the *New York Times* saw it as "little more than a curious hodge-podge of vague moods and irrelevant meanings"; the *Saturday Review of Literature* acknowledged Steinbeck's talent but hoped that "he [could] find a more stable and definite principle upon which to build his next novel." Soon afterward, however, editor **Pat Covici** of the **Viking Press** obtained the rights to *To a God Unknown* and *The Pastures of Heaven* and reissued both books in the fall of 1935.

The plot of *To a God Unknown* appears at first rather forced, simplistic, and linear. In 1903, having left his Vermont family after receiving his father's reluctant blessing, Joseph Wayne homesteads 160 acres in the Nacimiento River Valley. Shortly after, he hires a local named **Juanito** as his farm foreman. Wayne's brothers, **Burton, Benjamin**, and **Thomas** also leave Vermont, their father having died, and acquire adjoining homesteads in the fertile valley. Because of ample rain, the crops and animals flourish, and Joseph marries **Elizabeth**, an intellectual school teacher from **Monterey**. Shortly thereafter, tragedy occurs when Juanito discovers Benjamin Wayne, an alcoholic and womanizer, in bed with his wife. After killing Benjamin as a punishment for his adultery, Juanito vanishes. A more positive note for the family is sounded when Elizabeth becomes pregnant and, with Joseph assisting at the birth, has a son, whom Wayne names **John**. At the same time, the deepening drought affects everyone, and brother Burton's religious fanaticism causes an increasing rift among the remaining brothers. Especially incensed by what he thinks is Joseph's continuing naturalistic idolatry of a giant oak tree (which Wayne believes contains the spirit of his father), Burton girdles the tree's roots, killing it, and then leaves the farm. Shortly afterward, Joseph and Elizabeth visit an ancient grotto (the other main symbol in the novel), where Elizabeth falls from the rock and dies. Distraught, Joseph and Thomas (who is seen doubting everyone and everything around him with increasing frequency) look for ways to save the farm and the animals.

Despite their efforts, the drought continues and Thomas is forced to drive the 416 remaining cattle to the ocean, taking Joseph's infant son with him. Joseph does not join him, feeling compelled to remain on his land because he has been "appointed" to do so. Upon arriving at the coast, Thomas writes that over 300 of the cows did not survive the trip, but that the remainder are well.

Juanito mysteriously reappears and convinces Joseph to talk with the local priest, who agrees to pray only for Joseph's soul, not for rain. In a confusing mixture of religious imagery, the priest does pray for rain after Joseph leaves, but, by then, Joseph has chosen a pagan ritual, having found a newborn calf and sacrificed it at the rock. Joseph then climbs to the top and slits his own wrists, sacrificing himself for his now deserted land. The rains come immediately, and, although the priest believes that his prayers have caused the drought to end, the villagers celebrate with a fiesta that includes primitive rituals. By the end of the novel, only nature itself remains unspoiled. All the attempts to understand and control nature and to assert godlike power for human beings have proven futile.

To a God Unknown shows Steinbeck's early interest in writing about the structure and interdependence of family, the relationship of human to nature, and the tragic results of believing blindly in specific and exclusive historical, natural, or religious cause-and-effect relationships. In short, it is the first time Steinbeck employs **non-teleological** thinking in a novel. Reviewers, as noted above, disliked this novel, and even the most serious Steinbeck critics have had difficulty resolving and explaining Steinbeck's method of syncretic allegory, his use of multiple allegorical referents in a distinctly unconventional way. In *To a God Unknown*, Steinbeck's use of this technique is abundant, especially when compared with his later novels. Refusing to accept *any* existing theories, especially religious, of cause and effect (teleology), Steinbeck instead tries to combine and echo all of them to show the limitations of human ability to understand and explain the world, especially in religious terms.

Thus his Joseph (whose name echoes that of the biblical Joseph with his many brothers) also shows characteristics of God, Moses, and Christ but is unable to inspire or lead his people anywhere, and there will be no resurrection after his self-sacrifice. The giant oak tree that contains Wayne's father's spirit comes from Joshua 24:26, where Joshua, who had completed the exodus started by Moses, preserved the laws of God in "a great stone . . . under an oak." What Steinbeck has done in this novel is to invert and combine many biblical legends and referents; his characters have been called rather than led by a patriarchal God/Christ/Moses/Joshua/Aaron figure to a land where, after their arrival, they suffer the same adversities (deaths, droughts, dying animals, adultery, lack of water) as did their migrating biblical predecessors, who were en route to their "promised" land. Although Wayne, for instance, is unable to get water from *his* stone as Moses did (Numbers 20:15), at the end of the novel he dies like Aaron at the top of a mountain (Numbers 20:23–4). Aaron, however, was denied any entrance to the Promised Land by God, so he sent his son on with his brother, Moses. In an inverted echo, Wayne sends his son on with his own unreligious brother, after voluntarily refusing to participate in a slimmed-down exodus to the verdant California coastal area. For Steinbeck, no promised land exists (nor, by inference, did it ever exist), even though his well-intentioned characters try to create one in terms of their various teleological beliefs: Roman Catholic (represented by the priest, **Father Angelo**), Protestant (Burton Wayne), Darwinian-animalistic (Thomas Wayne), hedonistic (Benjamin Wayne), or primitivistic (the locals). *To a God Unknown* demonstrates that neither faith nor the intellect can provide solutions to life's problems, and shows that to follow any one belief exclusively produces conditions that range from ignorance to tragedy. For Steinbeck, the only promised land is understanding itself. This theme and this allegorical technique pervade all of Steinbeck's subsequent works.

Further Reading: Benson, Jackson J. *The True Adventures of John Steinbeck, Writer.* New York: Viking, 1984; DeMott, Robert. "Steinbeck's *To a God Unknown.*" In *A Study Guide to Steinbeck.* Ed. Tetsumaro Hayashi. Metuchen, NJ: Scarecrow, 1974; Lisca, Peter. "*Cup of Gold* and *To a God Unknown:* Two Early Works of John Steinbeck." *Kwartalnik-Neofilologiczny* 22, 00311 (Warszawa, Poland, 1975): 173–83; Owens, Louis. "John Steinbeck's 'Mystical Outcrying': *To a God Unknown* and *The Log from the Sea of Cortez.*" *San Jose Studies* 5.2 (1979); 20–32; Prindle, Dennis. "The Pretexts of Romance: Steinbeck's Allegorical Naturalism from *Cup of Gold to Tortilla Flat.*" In *The Steinbeck Question: New Essays in Criticism.* Ed. Donald Noble. Troy, NY: Whitson, 1993.

John Clark Pratt

TOBINUS STREAT OF MONTROY, SIR. Steinbeck's Arthurian pseudonym for **Webster "Toby" Street**, his longtime friend and attorney of **Monterey**, California. Sir Tobinus distinguishes himself in the service of **King Arthur** during the battle with **Nero**, the brother of **King Royns of North Wales**.

TOLSTOY, LEO (1828–1910). Eminent Russian novelist, moral philosopher, and religious mystic. His novels *War and Peace* (1866) and *Anna Karenina* (1877) are among his most famous works. *War and Peace*, a vast novel that depicts characters from all social backgrounds during the Napoleonic period, is considered one of the greatest novels of world literature, and certainly Steinbeck thought so, at one time claiming that it was his favorite novel, perhaps because it often offered moral advice that could be applied to the lives of common people. Tolstoy believed that individuals do not make history; they are mere agents of historical forces that are beyond their control or comprehension. Thus, the character of Napoleon in *War and Peace* became a prime example of Tolstoy's view of history. Tolstoy's philosophy undoubtedly appealed to Steinbeck, who later claimed that "it would be difficult to get an army to fight if every member of it had . . . read *War and Peace*." While visiting Stockholm in 1957, Steinbeck met the Russian writer Mikhail Sholokhov, and they discussed the relationship between Tolstoy and Turgenev. Sholokhov believed that it was a good thing for writers to get together and discuss their work, speculating that perhaps the richness in both writers' compositions grew from their interchange of thoughts and the ensuing discussions. Steinbeck disagreed, citing the fact that it was frequently difficult for the two writers to get along. He went on to tell Sholokhov that "most American writers were kind of lone wolves who believed that two good men could not write one good book." This stance of Steinbeck's was in sync with his comments elsewhere that no great work was ever done in collaboration, and that the free, exploring mind of the individual is the most valuable thing in the world. According to Robert DeMott, Steinbeck's library contained a copy of *War and Peace*.

Further Reading: DeMott, Robert. *Steinbeck's Reading: A Catalogue of Books Owned and Borrowed.* New York: Garland, 1984.

T. Adrian Lewis and Michael J. Meyer

TOMAS, JUAN. Kino's brother in ***The Pearl***. Juan is married to **Apolonia** and has four children; with more experience, he serves as an advisor to Kino. Juan is the one man Kino can trust, and he advises Kino to be cautious of the danger the great pearl brings and that safety and family are more important than the possibility of great profit. After Kino has killed a man to keep the pearl, Juan hides him away in his home with Apolonia and the children despite the danger. To help Kino escape, Juan tells the people of the village that his brother may have fled to the sea and drowned. Juan is the example of a true family man, one who puts blood before money—a lesson Kino learns the hard way.

TONDER, LIEUTENANT. In ***The Moon Is Down***, the second of a pair of young, idealistic officers who form the junior portion of **Colonel Lanser**'s staff. Like his counterpart, **Lieutenant Prackle**, Tonder is a green, "undergraduate" lieutenant, who symbolizes sentimental, inexperienced youth. A budding poet, whose aspirations have been shunted by the war, he is a dark romantic at heart; he occasionally pens blank verse to imaginary dark women, and, like Henry Fleming in **Crane**'s *The Red Badge of Courage* (1895), longs for glorious death on the battlefield. Eventually, his romanticism is blunted when he realizes the futility of the occupation, an operation he likens to flies conquering flypaper. Later, he is killed by **Molly Morden**, the widow of an executed villager, after a failed attempt to woo her.

Rodney P. Rice

TONY. In ***Sweet Thursday***, a piano player who, at **Fauna**'s request, is supposed to play at **Sonny Boy**'s restaurant on the night of **Doc**'s date with **Suzy**. Although Tony is ill and unable to play, he represents one more element in Fauna's elaborate plans for the evening.

TORRE, SIR. In ***The Acts of King Arthur***, natural son of **King Pellinore**. Presented at the court of **King Arthur** by the cowherd **Aryes**, whom he had always regarded until then as his father. As the first knight to be made after the formation of the Fellowship of the **Round Table**, he is sent by Arthur on the Quest of the White Brachet, which he fulfills so well that Arthur gives him an earldom of lands and a place of honor in the court. He is made a Knight of the Round Table after the war with the **five kings**, in preference to **Sir Bagdemagus**.

TORRELLI. In ***Tortilla Flat***, the local wine merchant, whose business thrives in spite of prohibition. Wine is the most precious commodity in *Tortilla Flat*, so Torrelli is among its most important citizens, especially to **Danny** and his friends. Between being swindled out of wine and cuckolded repeatedly, Torrelli suffers much at the hands of the paisanos, and, late in the novel, he believes he will get his revenge when Danny, on a prolonged binge, signs his house over to Torrelli for more wine. Torrelli, who is portrayed as the devil in Steinbeck's chapter heading, presents the bill of sale to Danny's friends and attempts to evict them, but they steal the paper and burn it. Steinbeck describes this episode as the triumphant salvation of the community of paisanos, and it certainly represents a victory for the values of friendship and communal life over those of commerce and property.

Bryan Vescio

TORREON. In ***The Wayward Bus***, mentioned as the boyhood home of **Juan Chicoy**, where he used to lie in bed and listen for gunfire during the Mexican Revolution.

TORRES, EMILIO. **Pepé**'s twelve-year-old brother and **Mama Torres**'s youngest son in **"Flight."** Because of the questions he poses to his savvy older sister, **Rosy**, the reader learns that Pepé is doomed: he has become a man, is embarking on a journey, and will die before he can return.

Abby H. P. Werlock

TORRES, MAMA. Widowed mother of **Pepé**, **Rosy**, and **Emilio** in **"Flight,"** Mama has the wisdom and endurance to survive even though her husband and eldest son do not. She has run the farm for ten years, and, despite his laziness, she loves her nineteen-year-old son Pepé, who is approaching manhood and whom she hopes will share some of the responsibilities she has borne since her husband's death. The complex meaning of manhood, however, is entwined not just with strength and agility, but also with violence and death. When Mama learns that Pepé has killed a man, she knows instantly that their days together have ended; she can only warn him of the dangers he will face from his pursuers, give him advice that may keep him safe a little longer, and then bid him farewell before she emits the traditional lament for the death of a loved one. Mama's strength and powers do not extend into the male realm of violence and death.

Abby H. P. Werlock

TORRES, PEPÉ. All the ingredients of his tragedy are present in the initial descriptions of the nineteen-year-old protagonist of **"Flight."** The fact that Pepé inherits all his father's accoutrements, whether material, cultural, or gendered, suggests he will share his fate and thus contribute to the deterministic nature of his story. Even as Pepé assumes some responsibility for his mother and his siblings, he cannot help using his skill with a knife to kill the **Monterey** man who insults him; so, from the beginning, the concept of manly adulthood is inextricably bound up with the concept of violence and death. Seen as the protagonist of either a *bildungsroman* or a morality tale, Pepé cannot escape his destiny, for his journey leads him straight to his death. At the end, as with a **Hemingway** hero, the best that Pepé can do is to face death with courage and dignity.

Abby H. P. Werlock

TORRES, ROSY. **Emilio**'s and **Pepé**'s prescient fourteen-year-old sister in **"Flight."** She seems to understand the male world, and thus, when her younger brother, Emilio, asks her when Pepé became a man, she knowingly answers that it happened the previous night in **Monterey** (referring to Pepé's murder of a man who insulted him). She knows, further, that this "manly" act of Pepé's will lead to his own death; she tells her younger brother, Emilio, that Pepé has embarked on a journey, and that he will never return.

Abby H. P. Werlock

***TORTILLA FLAT* (BOOK)** (1935). In 1932, Steinbeck's friend **Edward F. Ricketts** introduced him to a high school teacher from **Monterey** named **Susan Gregory**, who entertained Steinbeck with tales of the paisanos, residents of a shantytown in the hills above Monterey known as Tortilla Flat. These stories were the genesis for what Steinbeck worked out as his 1935 novel, *Tortilla Flat*.

The summer of 1933, when he began work on the novel, was a particularly bleak time for Steinbeck, both professionally and personally. His novel ***The Pastures of Heaven*** was selling poorly, and the lack of income was making the task of revising ***To a God Unknown*** (published in September 1933) increasingly difficult. In March, his mother suffered a massive stroke from which she would never recover, and his father's health was seriously deteriorating by the end of the summer. Curiously, though, despite his own financial troubles and the added burdens of caring for his ailing parents, Steinbeck was able to make this dark period one of the most productive in his career. In addition to completing the revisions on his third novel, he produced such enduring works as **"The Chrysanthemums"** and ***The Red Pony.*** He also began working feverishly on *Tortilla Flat*, completing three fourths of it in a little over a month and the entire novel by mid-March 1934, just after his mother's death in February. The novel was published by **Covici-Friede** in late May 1935, five days after the death of Steinbeck's father.

Steinbeck himself provided the reason behind this incongruous productivity, and in particular the whimsical tone of *Tortilla Flat*, when he wrote of the latter that it "is a direct rebellion against all the sorrow of our house." After his father's collapse, he had written to his publisher **Robert Ballou**, "Our house is crumbling very rapidly and when it is gone there will be nothing left." Significantly, the novel that Steinbeck wrote as his house was crumbling around him takes as its central theme what he called "the mystic quality of owning a house."

The main action of the novel begins when **Danny**, the central character who becomes by the end the binding force of the entire community of Tortilla Flat, inherits two houses from his grandfather. After a brief stint in jail, Danny comes upon his wily friend, **Pilon**, who extracts from Danny an invitation to share one of the houses. Pilon then convinces Danny to let him rent the other house, but the rent is never paid, since Pilon uses any money that comes into his hands to purchase wine from an Italian bootlegger named **Mr. Torrelli**. Furthermore, Pilon convinces another paisano, **Pablo Sanchez**, to rent space within his rented house, fully expecting a similar delinquency on the part of his tenant. Through various adventures, Danny's houses acquire several more tenants, including **Jesus Maria Corcoran**, a "humanitarian" of questionable motivation, the **Pirate**, the dull-witted owner of five beloved dogs and a sizable savings, and **Big Joe Portagee**, a huge, animalistic man who has spent half of his life in jail.

Life among the paisanos consists largely of drinking wine and devising various schemes for getting more wine, the cause of most of the group's adventures. Drinking bouts, which begin gently with song and conversation, frequently end in physical bouts of a more violent nature. But while hard feelings among the paisanos are quickly forgotten, these fights serve to remind the reader that each of the characters is driven primarily by self-interest, no matter how much they justify their actions by appeals to camaraderie. Pilon, in particular, is a master of rationalizing self-serving acts by appealing to higher principles. He pretends to extract a lesson from each of the novel's frequent mishaps, but, in each case, the "lesson" avoids the obvious moral message of the event in favor of a justification for pragmatic self-interest.

The most notable law among the paisanos is total disrespect for private property of any kind. Danny's house, of course, is the central example of private property converted into community property. Characters are always conspiring to steal some or all of each other's wine, that most precious commodity in Tortilla Flat, and money and other goods are considered fair game as well, since they can be exchanged for wine. In chapter VII, for example, the Pirate becomes one of the paisanos as a result of the others' attempts to appropriate the "treasure" he has saved through years of selling kindling to local restaurants. Women occasionally enter the lives of Danny and his friends, but only as property, to be treated the way they treat all other property. **Cornelia Ruiz**, a woman who appears to be community property in the Flat, is the chief topic of drunken conversation at Danny's house. In chapter IX, when Danny acquires the charms of **Dolores ("Sweets") Ramirez** in exchange for a vacuum cleaner, his friends promptly attempt to unburden him of her. The paisanos also swindle Mr. Torrelli out of his wife's affections nearly as often as they swindle him out of his wine.

But the most critical episodes in the novel center on the fates of Danny's inherited houses. In chapter V, while Danny is away romancing a neighbor named **Mrs. Morales**, Pilon, Pablo, and Jesus Maria dispose of some of Danny's money and the wine they acquired for it. As they sleep off their overindulgence, a single candle left burning touches off a fire that destroys the house. Surprisingly, rather than inspiring Danny's wrath at their irresponsibility, his friends' actions only enhance the camaraderie among them by uniting them under a single roof. In chapter XV, this renewed unity is threatened when a restless Danny goes on a prolonged binge, trading most of the remaining house's furnishings and finally signing over the house itself to Mr. Torrelli for wine. But when Torrelli, portrayed as the devil, presents the bill of sale to Danny's friends, they seize it and burn it, protecting the community of paisanos once more.

As the novel winds down, Danny becomes strangely apathetic, a sign of his impending death. His friends make the ultimate sacrifice by performing a full day's work cutting squid in order to throw a party to cheer Danny up, a party that brings together all of Tortilla Flat, but at the end of his party, Danny plunges to his death in the gulch south of the Flat. The friends mourn him, fittingly, with wine and song, but when a stray match sets Danny's remaining house on fire, this time they purposely let it burn. The novel ends with the paisanos going their separate ways, having lost both the agent and the symbol of their unity.

When Steinbeck's literary agent read the completed manuscript, she complained that it was trivial and lacked a clear theme. Steinbeck responded in a letter describing the theme as a function of the novel's structure, which was taken from Malory's version of the Arthurian cycle. In fact, the Arthurian parallels are made explicit in the novel's preface, where Steinbeck writes, "For Danny's house was not unlike the **Round Table**, and Danny's friends were not unlike the knights of it." Danny's house and its inhabitants may well seem trivial in comparison with Camelot and the Knights of the Round Table, but Steinbeck's fascination with the legend of Camelot was always a fascination with the ideal of community itself, depicting the ways in which individuals with diverse and even conflicting interests can be reconciled—if only temporarily—in a higher purpose. The paisanos are certainly a community in this sense, and although many readers have taken the parallels to Camelot as gentle mockery of Danny and his friends, *Tortilla Flat* can also be read as a kind of mock epic in reverse, demonstrating that it doesn't take kings and noblemen to make a community.

Although the importance of details about Arthurian analogs in *Tortilla Flat* has become a matter of dispute among critics, Arthur Kinney's guide to those details in "The Arthurian Cycle in *Tortilla Flat*" remains probably the most important work of criticism on the novel to date. This interest in community is most famously embodied in Steinbeck's phalanx theory, which he first articulated in a letter to **George Albee** shortly before he began writing *Tortilla Flat*. Steinbeck alludes to this idea in his preface as well when he writes, "No, when you speak of Danny's house you are understood to mean a unit of which the parts are men, from which came sweetness and joy, philanthropy and, in the end, a mystic sorrow."

Not only does Danny's house function as a single organic unit, but the larger communities of Tortilla Flat and Monterey do, too. These communities often become characters in the novel, as in chapter V, where Steinbeck provides a long description of how "[a]ll Monterey began to make gradual instinctive preparations against the night." This phenomenon is clearest at the end of the novel, when all Tortilla Flat comes together in celebration of Danny's life and in mourning over his death. *Tortilla Flat* marks a turning point in Steinbeck's career in a number of senses, one of which is that it contains early signs of the social criticism that would increasingly occupy Steinbeck in his later work, beginning with his next novel, ***In Dubious Battle***. Early reviewers were charmed by *Tortilla Flat*'s colorful characters and good humor, and while it can still be read profitably at this level, its subtle social commentaries are more apparent in light of subsequent Steinbeck works. One of the novel's consistent targets is the military mentality, which creates a false, alienating community that contrasts with the organic community of the Flat. This is evident in Big Joe Portagee's difficulties adjusting to military life, but it is even more prominent in chapter X, where the friends encounter a sixteen-year-old **corporal** with a baby. The corporal's wife has been stolen by a captain, but rather than seeking revenge as the paisanos recommend, the boy vows to make his son a general so he, too, can enjoy the spoils of an officer. This shows that the boy has internalized the hierarchical values of the military at the expense of the values of Tortilla Flat, where distinctions of rank do not exist.

But, more importantly, the entire novel is an assault on America's worship of private property, whose effects were especially obvious to Steinbeck in 1933, at the height of the Depression. Money and property divide the paisanos from the beginning of the novel when Danny inherits his two houses. As long as Danny is a landlord and Pilon and the others are his tenants, they are divided, emotionally as well as physically. It is only when the rented house burns down and the pretense of rent is abandoned that the true bond develops among the friends. Little wonder that Danny is not at all bothered by the destruction of his property—on the contrary, he is relieved to be spared the responsibilities of ownership. When Mr. Torrelli legitimately acquires Danny's house and tries to evict his friends, their destruction of the bill of sale is portrayed as a heroic act that preserves their community.

As in Steinbeck's later works, the highest value is community, and what is most antithetical to this value is the drive to acquire wealth and property. Critic **Louis Owens** finds the encroaching values of capitalism to be the difference between the paisanos and their precursor Knights of the Round Table, and he also finds them to be the source of Steinbeck's ironic tone toward the former. Part of the justification for classifying the novel as a mock epic lies in Steinbeck's attempts to alternate between the simple speech patterns of the paisanos and a more elevated language—that of the King James Bible—which appears when the characters' "chivalry" is invoked. Some critics have complained, however, that Steinbeck's treatment of poverty in the novel, which reemerges in later works like ***Cannery Row*** and ***Sweet Thursday***, is too gentle, even romanticized, compared to the more sober, critical eye he casts on this subject in his protest novels. But the gentle irony of much of the novel and the genuine tragedy of its conclusion also make it an authentic tragicomedy, and there is evidence in the text that this is the vision Steinbeck intended.

Pilon, who is portrayed rather sardonically as the novel's voice of wisdom, seems to embody the true wisdom of Steinbeck's novel when he decides not to confide in his friend Pablo about his discovery of the Pirate's treasure: "Honor and peace to Pilon, for he had discovered how to uncover and to disclose to the world the good that lay in every evil thing. Nor was he blind, as so many saints are, to the evil of good things." The characters, for all their individual imperfections, for all their irresponsibility and petty selfishness, are able to unite and to perform some genuinely good deeds. But as Owens indicates, life in Tortilla Flat is always imperfect, a mixed blessing, just as paisanos, who claim pure Spanish blood, are really a mixture of Spanish, Indian, Mexican, and assorted Caucasian bloods. Even the name "Tortilla Flat" evokes this sense of impurity and imperfection, since, as readers are told, it is applied to a geographical feature that is not a flat at all. At the end of the novel, Steinbeck reminds his readers that even the ultimate good, a human community, is ultimately fallible, imperfect, and fragile. The best mode through which to convey this message is the one Steinbeck chose, the mixed mode of tragicomedy.

The most important sense in which this novel marked a turning point in Steinbeck's career, however, is that it marked his first real critical and commercial success. *Tortilla Flat* received warm reviews in both the *New York Times* and the *New York Herald Tribune*, as well as in the *Los Angeles Times*, and it put Steinbeck on several best-seller lists for the first time. Paramount bought the film rights to the novel for $4,000, four times what Steinbeck's writing had earned him to that point, and a film version, starring **Spencer Tracy** and **John Garfield**, was released in 1942. A much less successful Broadway version of *Tortilla Flat* opened in January 1938, but closed after only four performances. Still, Steinbeck's earnings from this book gave him enough financial security that he could begin to ponder the "big book" that would become his true ambition. But more importantly to Steinbeck, this novel gave him the serious recognition as a writer he had sought from the beginning of his career, and which he has enjoyed ever since.

Further Reading: Kinney, Arthur F. "The Arthurian Cycle in *Tortilla Flat*." *Modern Fiction Studies* 11 (Spring 1965): 11–20; Lisca, Peter. Tortilla Flat, *The Wide World of John Steinbeck*. New Brunswick, NJ: Rutgers University Press, 1958; Owens, Louis. "*Tortilla Flat:* Camelot *East of Eden*." *John Steinbeck's Re-Vision of America*. Athens: University of Georgia Press, 1985; Prindle, Dennis. "The Pretexts of Romance: Steinbeck's Allegorical Naturalism from *Cup of Gold* to *Tortilla Flat*." In *The Steinbeck Question: New Essays in Criticism*. Ed. Donald Noble. Troy, NY: Whitston, 1993. 23–36; Steinbeck, Elaine, and Robert Wallsten, eds. *Steinbeck: A Life in Letters*. New York: Viking, 1975; Tavernier-Courbin, Jacqueline. "Social Satire in John Steinbeck's *Tortilla Flat* and *Cannery Row*." *Thalia* 17.1–2 (1997): 51-60.

Bryan Vescio

***TORTILLA FLAT* (FILM)** (1942). *Tortilla Flat*, the novel published in 1935, is Steinbeck's bittersweet comedy about the paisanos of **Monterey**, California, and was the author's first financial success. In 1938, Jack Kirkland, who had dramatized the enormously successful *Tobacco Road*, adapted *Tortilla Flat* for the stage, but it was a dismal failure. Steinbeck predicted that a movie would fare no better, but in 1942, MGM came out with a reasonably successful film version, directed by **Victor Fleming**. The screenplay by John Lee Mahin and Benjamin Glazer takes considerable liberties with Steinbeck's episodic narrative, focusing on the one chapter in which **Danny** is seduced by the hatchet-faced but voluptuous **Dolores ("Sweets") Ramirez**. In the novel, both he and Sweets are cheerfully promiscuous, but **Pilon, Pablo**, and Danny's other friends prevent him from marrying her. In contrast, the film makes Sweets (**Hedy Lamarr**, anything but hatchet-faced) virginal, angry at Danny's crude embraces. But Danny is sufficiently clean-cut that he will do the honorable thing, and his friends' plot to keep him from marrying Sweets is ultimately unsuccessful. In the novel, Danny dies, but in the film, he is merely hurt in an accident, in response to which the cheerfully amoral Pilon becomes so pious that numerous critics objected to an inserted sentimental religiosity. As for the film version's Danny, he gets a job (unthinkable for Steinbeck's character) and marries Sweets as the film ends.

A major problem with the film is the players' accents. The quintessentially Irish **Spencer Tracy**, perhaps cast as Pilon because he had won an Academy Award as Manuel, the Portuguese fisherman in Victor Fleming's *Captains Courageous*, at times attempts a minimal Mexican accent but does not sustain it and often lapses into his normal voice. As Danny, **John Garfield** does not even bother with an accent except to follow the script in speaking without contractions; otherwise he uses his New York tough-guy voice. As Sweets, the Austrian Hedy Lamarr is not very successful in sounding Spanish, and Akim Tamiroff sounds more Russian (which he was) than Hispanic. The other players try to sound Mexican with uneven success. For example, Frank Morgan, as the **Pirate**, does not attempt an accent, yet he won an Academy Award nomination as best supporting actor.

Despite distortions and some miscasting, the film does salvage much of Steinbeck's humor as well as the flavor of *Tortilla Flat* (the screenplay calls the paisanos "a warm-hearted people of laughter and kindness"), and it was a modest critical and popular hit. Philip T. Hartung in *Commonweal* called it "an intelligent, charming film"; ***Time*** found it "human and appealing"; *Newsweek* admired its atmosphere and character and thought the screenplay had more continuity than the novel, while retaining "a reasonable facsimile of the Steinbeck flavor"; and Bosley Crowther in the *New York Times* praised its "solid humor and compassion," calling it "a winning motion picture and a deterrent to respectable enterprise." But Crowther and Manny Farber in *New Republic* faulted it for sentimentality and complained of the exaggerated religiosity of Pilon's newfound piety, which is not in the book. The film is now available on videotape.

Robert E. Morsberger

TORTUGA. Caribbean island and center of buccaneering in ***Cup of Gold***.

TRACY, SPENCER (1900–1967). Actor who won an Academy Award as best actor for *Captains Courageous* (1937) and *Boys' Town* (1938) and played **Pilon** in ***Tortilla Flat*** (1942). Although Tracy's background was Irish, he played Hispanics three times, with a marginally successful and not entirely sustained accent—in *Captains Courageous*, *Tortilla Flat*, and *The Old Man and the Sea* (1958). Tracy was a Hollywood crony of Steinbeck and wanted to play **George** in the film version of ***Of Mice and Men*** (1939), but his salary requirements were too expensive and other commitments hampered his involvement.

TRASK, ADAM. Oldest son of **Cyrus Trask** and his first wife in ***East of Eden***, who is known only as **Mrs. Trask**. Husband of **Cathy Trask**, and father of **Cal** and **Aron Trask**. Adam is scrupulously honest and kind and also somewhat of a dreamer (even in certain respects a visionary). He believes that an individual is powerless to change and lacks free will; as he tells Cal, "My father made a mold and forced me into it. . . . I was a bad casting but I couldn't be remelted. Nobody can be remelted." Ultimately, his plans to live in a paradise of his own making cannot be realized because of his lack of insight and self-awareness, his sense of powerlessness and resignation, his good but fundamentally static nature, and his naïveté.

Adam is born six weeks before Cyrus is wounded and discharged from a Connecticut regiment in the Union army. Shortly after Cyrus's return, Mrs. Trask commits suicide. Although Cyrus marries **Alice Trask** within a month, the need for mothering and mother love is strong in Adam, as it is later in his son, Aron Trask.

Approximately eighteen months later, Alice gives birth to **Charles Trask**. While Charles later protects Adam and "felt for his brother the affection one has for helpless things," Adam is "glad of Charles . . . but love, affection, empathy were beyond conception." Charles is competitive and assertive, but Adam is passive and "covered his life with a veil of vagueness" that remains in place throughout his life.

As the boys mature, their relationship is patterned on the love, rejection, jealousy, revenge, and guilt that are the motivational mechanisms of the Cain and Abel story that informs the relationships between fathers, sons, and brothers in the novel. The tyrannical Cyrus arbitrarily prefers Adam to Charles—as Adam later prefers his son Aron to his twin brother Cal. Ironically, the favorites, Adam and Aron, are indifferent to their fathers, while Charles and Cal are, by contrast, desperate for their fathers' love. Such preferential treatment heightens the tension between the brothers, a tension that began when, on Cyrus's birthday, Charles gives him a knife, a gift he has earned the money to buy. However, Cyrus prefers Adam's gift of a mongrel puppy. Two years before, Charles had beaten Adam severely when Adam inadvertently had won a game of peewee and now, jealous, hurt, and angry because of the rejected gift, Charles beats Adam even more viciously, intending to kill him with a hatchet. Three days later, as Adam lies recovering, his father arranges to have him mustered into the cavalry, a career that Adam doesn't want and for which Charles is better suited.

Adam serves in the military in the West for five years, shooting to miss when he is in battle and being much affected by the undeclared war on the Native Americans. However, although he intends to return to the farm in Connecticut, he reenlists, to Charles's disappointment. After another five years, Adam is discharged and for two years wanders as a hobo until he travels east to Florida, this time with the objective of going home. Unfortunately, his intent to return home is thwarted when he is picked up for vagrancy and serves a six month sentence; released, he is picked up again and serves a second term, although he escapes three days before his release. He travels to Georgia, steals clothes from a store, and wires Charles for money for his ticket home. Adam's unequivocal honesty is demonstrated clearly when later he sends money plus 100 percent interest to the storekeeper he robbed and explains to Charles that he escaped with only three days yet to serve because he "didn't feel right about cheating."

Adam arrives home to the news of his father's death and to an unexpected inheritance of over $100,000 to be split between the brothers. While Charles realizes that their father may have come by the money dishonestly, Adam refuses to believe that his father was either a liar or a thief. He admits to Charles that he never loved Cyrus—and now realizes that it was Charles's great love for their father that was the impulse behind the beating and attempted murder fourteen years before.

Adam lives and farms with Charles for a year and then, after an argument, leaves. He returns, and two years later, feeling very restless, leaves again and travels to Rio de

Janeiro and Buenos Aires. When he returns one last time, the brothers continue to farm, although they find that living together is difficult.

When the severely beaten **Cathy Ames** crawls onto the Trask front porch in chapter 11, Adam is immediately taken by her and nurses her attentively. It is as if his yearning for the mother he never had elicits mothering behavior in him. Soon, Adam falls in love with Cathy, despite his brother's admonishments. Charles understands that Cathy is not what she seems, but Adam is incapable of this insight. Not surprisingly, on their wedding night, Cathy drugs the smitten, trusting Adam and climbs into bed with Charles.

Thereafter, Adam and a reluctant, pregnant Cathy move to California, where Adam buys the Bordoni ranch with the money his father left him. He meets and hires **Samuel Hamilton** to dowse for water on his land, and the two begin a lifelong friendship. Adam's joy and love for Cathy completely blind him, and, as his son Aron will do later to his girlfriend **Abra Bacon**, Adam creates an idealized image of Cathy, seeing her as the Eve with whom he will share the Eden he wants to create. Even when she tries to induce an abortion and then tells him that she will leave as soon as she can, he dismisses it as foolishness. His naïveté nearly proves fatal when, a week after she gives birth to their sons, Cathy shoots Adam and leaves him for dead, Adam is overcome with shock and recedes into a trance-like state, not even naming his sons. **Lee**, the Trask servant, cares for the dazed Adam and the boys for over a year until a furious Samuel, told that the boys are yet unnamed, rides to the Trask ranch and punches Adam in order to bring him to his senses. After dinner and a brief discussion of the Cain and Abel story, the boys are named: Caleb and Aron.

About eleven years later, because he and his wife **Liza Hamilton** are leaving their ranch, Samuel rides to Adam's to say goodbye. During a conversation with Samuel and Adam, Lee explains how he and other Chinese scholars had studied the Cain and Abel story and discovered the meaning of the Hebrew word ***timshel*** (thou mayest [choose]). Before he leaves, Samuel decides to tell Adam the truth about Cathy, now **Kate Albey**, thereby giving Adam the choice about how to proceed.

Indeed, sometime later, after Adam attends Samuel's funeral in **Salinas** and then, becomes fortified with liquor, he visits Cathy/Kate for the first time since the shooting. She attempts to manipulate, seduce, and control him but fails—and Adam returns to his ranch feeling free. Seeing Cathy/Kate brings Adam back to life and allows him to pay attention to and develop a relationship with his sons. Ironically, the scrupulously honest Adam keeps the truth about their mother to himself, which contributes to his dilemma when his brother Charles dies and leaves over $100,000 to be divided between Adam and Cathy. Adam is reluctant to give Cathy her share, believing that she will use it for ill, but his honest nature directs him to tell her of the inheritance. While Adam is discussing what to do with Lee, Cal, listening at the door, discovers that his mother is alive.

Adam goes to see Cathy/Kate to tell her about the bequest. She thinks he is trying to trick her and attempts to regain her control by humiliating him. However, despite her attempts, any lingering vestiges of Adam's illusions about Cathy are erased when he understands that she thrives on evil. He tells her, "You don't believe men could have goodness and beauty in them. You see only one side. . . . I seem to know that there's a part of you missing. I think you are only part of a human." By the time Adam leaves, his freedom from her is complete.

Because he wants his sons to attend a better school, Adam buys **Dessie Hamilton**'s house and moves the family to Salinas. He also develops an interest in refrigeration and seeks **Will Hamilton**'s advice about his plan to buy an ice plant and ship lettuce cross-country in refrigerated rail cars. Will cautions Adam about the risks, but Adam, ignoring his advice, proceeds with his enterprise, fails, and ends up close to bankrupt.

Adam's relationships with his sons are emphasized in the context of this failure. Aron, the child Adam prefers, expresses hatred toward his father, while Cal wants to make it up to him. After Cal is arrested during a raid on a fan-tan game, Adam is warm and understanding toward his son. This attention and sense of kinship between them, which enhances Cal's passionate desire to gain his father's approval and love, are his motivation to make money to compensate his father for his loss. Meanwhile, Adam, blind to Cal's devotion, overtly favors and takes pride in Aron, who feels indifference and disdain for his father. Ironically, and ultimately tragically, although Adam tells Cal, "I'm as bad a father as my father was," he does not see that the dynamics of his relationships with his sons and their relationship with each other closely replicates his relationship with his father and brother.

Adam is elected to the draft board in Salinas, a position and responsibility he regards soberly and seriously. Aron goes to college a year early (a source of much paternal pride), and Cal succeeds in his business venture and earns $15,000, which he excitedly plans to give Adam at Thanksgiving dinner. Predictably, and in keeping with Adam's lack of insight and the Cain and Abel pattern, Adam blatantly rejects Cal's gift, telling him first, "You'll have to give it back." When Cal tries to tell him why he earned the money, Adam drives the shaft of rejection deeper by telling Cal "I won't want it ever. I would have been so happy if you could have given me (well, what your brother has) pride in the thing he's doing, gladness in his progress. . . . If you want to give me a present—give me a good life. That would be something I could value." Adam has clearly forgotten what he had experienced with and realized about his brother and father years earlier. His honesty and idealistic nature are his blinders, for, from his perspective, taking the money would be making a profit on the war, on the suffering and perhaps death of others. As Lee explains to Cal, Adam "couldn't help it. . . . That's his nature. It was the only way he knew. He didn't have any choice. But you have."

Nevertheless, later that night, Cal lashes out against his favored brother by taking him to meet their mother. Aron, unable to deal with her depravity and imperfection, runs away and enlists, an event that causes Adam's first stroke. While recuperating, Adam learns of Cathy/Kate's suicide and her willing all her money to Aron. His reaction suggests that he still loves her and is perplexed about how to handle the legacy she has given to Aron, just as he was about Charles's legacy to her and Cal's potential gift to him. Soon a telegram with the news of Aron's death arrives, and Adam suffers a second stroke. As Adam lies in bed, partially paralyzed and not entirely capable of speech, Cal, overcome with guilt, begs his father's forgiveness, but Adam seems indifferent to his pleas. Only when Lee demands that he give Cal his blessing (a parallel to the biblical Jacob and Esau story, also about twins) does Adam respond, offering a blessing that will release him from guilt and free him from the pain of rejection. He struggles to raise his hand and speaks the word "timshel," thus granting to Cal a legacy of free will and choice, just as God offered to Cain. The novel closes without resolving the tensions between father and son, as Adam's "eyes closed and he slept," a slumber that is either literal or metaphorical.

Margaret Seligman

TRASK, ALICE. Second wife of **Cyrus Trask**, mother of **Charles Trask**, and stepmother of **Adam Trask** in ***East of Eden***. Alice was seventeen years old when she married the newly widowed Cyrus. Two weeks later, she was pregnant. Alice was an excellent cook and housekeeper who never complained, quarreled, or showed any emotion. However, one day Adam sees Alice smiling, and it awakens within him a yearning for a mother. He begins to leave her "pretty little things," which, ironically, she believes have been left by Charles. Alice dies of consumption sometime within the five years of Adam's first enlistment, leaving Charles alone on the farm.

Alice's preference for Charles and her misconception about Charles's true nature reflect important elements of the Cain and Abel story as well as the emotional power of parental rejection. Adam's preference for his son **Aron Trask** and Cyrus's preference for his son, Adam, provide further examples of this idea.

Margaret Seligman

TRASK, ARON [AARON]. Son of **Adam** and **Cathy Trask** and twin brother of **Cal Trask** in *East of Eden*. Because he does not want his friends to think he is fancy, he changes the spelling of his name "Aaron" to "Aron," But some critics have suggested that the name shortening also reflects an attempt to avoid being labeled or associated with a biblical namesake. Aron is blond, blue-eyed, and delicate, although "a dogged, steady, and completely fearless fighter, particularly when he was crying." He is also intelligent and does well in school but has limited versatility, dimension, or imagination. He lives in a dream world of his own creation, often appearing self-centered and indifferent toward his brother and father. Although his father dotes on him, he does not respond to his affection and attentions. However, Aron craves a mother, and he is easily duped by the story of his mother's death that **Lee** and his father concoct to protect him and his brother from the knowledge that their mother is alive and running a notorious brothel.

Aron's desperate desire for mother love is satisfied by his relationship with **Abra Bacon**, which begins when she is ten and he is eleven. When Abra tells Aron that she has overheard her parents say that his mother is alive, his passiveness and need to keep his world ordered make him incapable of believing this information or anything that would destroy his concept of how things and people are. These qualities become fatal flaws when he is grown, because they make him fragile, thus easily broken.

As a teenager, Aron develops a strong connection with **Mr. Rolf**, the Episcopal minister. Aron is confirmed in the Episcopal Church, plans to become a minister, and decides to be celibate, thus remaining pure. When he assists Mr. Rolf at the church, his mother attends to look at him, although Aron is unaware who she is. When his father's plan to ship lettuce to the East in refrigerated railcars fails, Aron reacts selfishly, telling Abra that he hates his father for ruining his life. Aron's indifference to his father and complete self-absorption are even more evident when Adam buys a gold watch and plans a festive meal to celebrate Aron's achievement on his examinations, but Aron chooses instead to have dinner with Mr. Rolf and doesn't even bother to tell his father that he passed the exams.

Aron graduates from high school a year early and attends **Stanford University** but quickly becomes disillusioned. He seems to want to run away and hide, whether beneath the branches of the willow tree where he and Abra played house as children or on a farm far away from everything and everyone. He starts to idealize Abra and begins to dream of living with her "in purity and peace" on a ranch. He decides he will not return to college after going home at Thanksgiving.

However, during Thanksgiving dinner, when Cal's gift of money to replace what had been lost in the lettuce venture is flatly rejected by his father, Cal lashes out in revenge and anger at Aron. Desiring to hurt Aron as much as he can, Cal takes him to meet their mother at her brothel. On their way out of the brothel, Aron knocks Cal down and runs away to San Jose, where he lies about his age and enlists in the army. His concept of the world is shattered, and he can do nothing but follow his nature and run away and hide. Aron is killed in battle a short time later.

As in the relationship between Adam and his brother **Charles Trask**, the Cain and Abel story provides the pattern for the relationship between Aron and Cal. Aron, "the golden boy," is preferred by everyone and most significantly by their father, Adam. Cal feels inadequate and jealous but also loves his brother dearly. The crucial scene at Thanksgiving dinner is equivalent to the time when **Cyrus Trask** preferred Adam's gift of a pup to Charles's gift of a knife, and also to the time when Cain and Abel made their offerings to God. In this situation, Adam rejects Cal's gift of money in favor of Aron's gift of "pride in the thing he's doing, gladness in his progress." The rest of the Cain and Abel story then plays out: Stunned and hurt by his father's rejection, Cal "destroys" his brother by taking him to meet their mother. Aron responds by running to hide in the anonymity of the army, an act of self-effacement or a form of suicide. Thus, Aron, like Abel, is "killed" by his brother.

Of further interest is that Aron and Cal are fraternal twins, born from separate placentas. This fact suggests that they may have had different fathers, since their mother drugged her husband, Adam, on their wedding night in order to sleep with his brother, Charles. Aron resembles his mother physically, which is why Cal thinks Adam prefers Aron to him, and, like his mother, Aron's outward appearance also belies his true inner disposition. Like Adam, Aron lives behind a veil in a story of his own creation, and, as his father does with Cathy, Aron idealizes Abra. Moreover, his indifference to Adam, who dotes on him, reflects the relationship Adam had with his father, Cyrus. Finally, like Charles, Aron can be spurred to violence. When Aron knocks Cal down and stands over him after being taken to meet their mother, his act is reminiscent of Charles standing over Adam as he lies prostrate after Charles's relentless, purposeful beating. In this way, Steinbeck seems to suggest that genetic inheritance does not determine the character traits that are handed down from generation to generation.

Aron's ambiguous parentage and character hybridization serve to highlight the meaning and implication of ***timshel***, that character and behavior are the choices of the individual, not predetermined by genetics. However, Aron's aspiration toward purity and his inability to accept human weakness or failing make him entirely one dimensional and, ultimately, a casualty to his own selfish nature.

Margaret Seligman

TRASK, CAL [CALEB]. Son of **Cathy** and **Adam Trask** and twin brother of **Aron Trask** in *East of Eden*. Cal becomes the central focus of parts 3 and 4 of *East of Eden*, for, as Steinbeck writes in a letter to **Pascal Covici**, "Cal is my baby. He is the **Everyman**, the battleground between good and evil, the most human of all." Indeed, Cal represents the tension between good and bad impulses, and his task is to understand and gain control over them.

Since Cal and Aron are born in separate sacks, and since their mother seduced their uncle, **Charles Trask**, on her wedding night after drugging her husband, Adam, the text suggests that Cal and his brother may have different fathers. Although Cal does appear to resemble Charles more than he does Adam, he is also distinct from Charles, who never questions his nature, while Cal consistently struggles with his. As in the case with Aron, this ambiguous paternity merely underscores an important thrust of the novel: that one's parentage is immaterial because liability to sin—or the capability to be pure—is not inherited. This idea is related to the Cain and Abel symbolism that informs a great deal of the book. It also suggests that the obvious Cain and Abel symbolism employed by Steinbeck is far from absolute, since all characters whose names start with *C* do not act like Cain, and all those whose names start with *A* do not act like Abel.

Eventually the jealousy suggested in the Cain and Abel story and exemplified in Cal's behavior and struggles are explained by **Lee**'s exegesis of the sixteen verses of Genesis: "The greatest terror a child can have is that he is not loved . . . and with rejection comes anger, and with anger some kind of crime in revenge for the rejection, and with the crime guilt." This pattern of love, rejection, and retaliation describes the relationships of the Trask brothers, fathers, and sons in the novel, but Cal, the Everyman, seems alone in his self-awareness and painful struggle.

Cal and his brother, Aron, are reintroduced into the story when they are eleven. They have been shooting at rabbits with bows and arrows, and, when one is killed, Cal is eager to give Aron credit for it with their father, even though he himself may have shot it. Cal believes that their father prefers the fair-haired Aron to him, and his feelings make him both love and hate his brother (perhaps representative of the two sides of his nature).

Unlike Aron, Cal is clever and insightful and knows how to hurt or "get" others, although he derives no pleasure from it. When the boys get home from their hunt, they find that **Abra Bacon** and her parents have taken shelter at the Trask ranch during a rainstorm. Cal likes Abra, but she prefers the seemingly helpless, golden Aron. Feeling hurt, Cal retaliates against both of them by humiliating Abra and lying to her about the gift Aron gives her. At this point, Cal does not think about his actions or motivations; he is caught in the pattern of love, rejection, and retaliation that comprise the Cain and Abel story, which Lee calls "the symbol story of the human soul."

However, soon thereafter, Cal begins to gain self-awareness. He listens at the door when Adam and Lee discuss what to do about Charles Trask's bequest to Cathy and discovers that what he suspected is true: his mother is indeed alive. Full of distress and remorse and self-reproach for eavesdropping, Cal prays, "Let me be like Aron. Don't make me mean. . . . If you will let everybody like me, why I'll give you anything in the world, and if I haven't got it, why I'll go for to get it." Cal wants to strike a bargain with God, as if to give God a gift will be to earn God's favor. The parallel with the Cain and Abel story is self-evident, although what also emerges from this brief episode of eavesdropping is dramatic irony for the reader and a bifurcation of the driving forces in Cal's life. Cal must resolve the tension between good and bad within himself by resolving his feelings about and relationship with his mother, the "bad," before he can gain his father's love and approval, the "good."

So that Cal and Aron can attend a better school, Adam moves the family to **Salinas** when the boys are fifteen. While to adults Cal possesses a "precocious maturity," in school he has no friends, isn't particularly liked, and induces fear rather than trust. By contrast, "Aron drew love from every side," and his relationship with Abra excludes Cal. Thus, Cal becomes a brooding, restless loner who walks the Salinas streets at night. One night, from a very drunk **Rabbit Holman**, Cal learns the truth about his mother and accompanies Rabbit to her brothel.

In a conversation with Lee the next morning, Cal expresses resignation, saying, "I've got her in me," for he believes he has a kind of inherited depravity. Lee, who recognizes Cal's struggles with himself and has made Cal his project, knows that Cal's behavior has nothing to do with genetic necessity but is up to him. He tells Cal vehemently, "Whatever you do, it will be you who do it—not your mother." In so doing, Lee is offering Cal the awareness of choice, of free will, embodied by the meaning of ***timshel***.

Cal begins to follow his mother, and after eight weeks confronts her and tells her that he is her son. After talking to her in her lean-to sanctuary, Lee's words begin to have meaning, for Cal tells her, "I'm my own. I don't have to be you. . . . It just came to me whole. If I'm mean, it's my own mean." Cal recognizes that his actions are not predestined but are up to him. By coming to terms with himself in relation to his mother, he can begin to resolve the tensions and struggles within himself.

Part of what allows Cal to reach this point is a change in his relationship with his father. After Cal is arrested in a raid on a fan-tan game and picked up at the jail by Adam, he expects a severe scolding. Instead, Adam is so warm and understanding that "Cal wanted to throw his arms about his father, to hug him and to be hugged by him." The warmth engendered by his honest conversation with his father allows Cal to express the intense love he feels. "The poison of loneliness and the gnawing envy of the unlonely had gone out of him," and Cal basks in Adam's love, for it brings him happiness. Nevertheless, the desire to give him a gift reprises his earlier invocation to God, echoes the Cain and

Abel story, provides dramatic irony, and foreshadows an impending tragedy.

Cal recognizes his opportunity to serve his father soon after the conversation. Adam has lost a great deal of money in his ill-fated venture to ship lettuce to the East in refrigerated railcars, and, unlike Aron, who is angry and hates his father for the failure, Cal wants to make it up to him. He goes to see **Will Hamilton** to find out how to make a lot of money quickly. Will is impressed by Cal's initiative and his frank admission that he is indeed attempting to buy his father's love. Feeling a kinship with Cal, Will makes him his partner in a business venture.

By the subsequent fall, Cal has earned $15,000, which, despite Lee's misgivings, Cal intends to give to his father on Thanksgiving. When the day arrives, Cal is full of excitement: "He had carved this day out for himself and he wanted it." But when it becomes clear that "it would turn out to be Aron's day," Cal retreats to his room feeling shame, disappointment, and jealousy. He thinks he understands why Adam prefers Aron, because of Aron's resemblance to their mother, and the feelings this produces incite the conflict between the two sides of him, the one that feels love and the one that feels hate and anger. "Why not be just what you are and do just what you do?" he thinks, acknowledging that "by whipping himself, he protected himself against whipping by someone else."

Cal then takes Aron to **Joe Garrisiere**'s liquor store to buy champagne, which will be Aron's gift, although Cal pays for it. This incident clearly reflects the one six years earlier, when Cal was anxious to give Aron credit for shooting the rabbit, an episode that prefaced rejection, hurt, and revenge then, as it does in this situation as well.

Later, at the table, when Cal gives Adam the carefully wrapped gift of money, Adam is pleased at first, but, when he sees what the packet contains, he tells Cal, "You'll have to give it back. . . . I won't want it ever. I would have been so happy if you could have given me (well, what your brother has). . . . If you want to give me a present—give me a good life. That would be something I could value." Adam's unmitigated rejection of the gift—and of Cal himself—reverberates with God's rejection of Cain's gift and sends Cal into a tailspin. Despite Lee's insistence that he can control the impulses the rejection has generated, Cal's hurt is so monumental that he is functioning on pure emotion. He waits for Aron and, intent on destroying him as both punishment and revenge, takes him to meet their mother, knowing it will shatter Aron's illusions about her as well as his beliefs about their father and Lee. Indeed, after knocking Cal down, Aron runs from his mother's brothel to San Jose, where he enlists in the army—a prefiguring of his suicidal despair.

As before, Cal gets no pleasure from what he has done. He anesthetizes himself with alcohol to dull the guilt and remorse, and stays drunk for two days before returning home. When a worried Adam asks him where Aron is, Cal responds in a Cain-like manner: "How do I know? . . . Am I supposed to look after him?" He then retreats to his room and burns the now meaningless gift, bill by bill. When Lee tries to tell him that he's just an adolescent, full of good and bad impulses like all human beings, Cal is impervious to Lee's words. Soon thereafter, Adam suffers a stroke when Aron writes of his enlistment, and Cal's sense of worthlessness and guilt increase.

However, during this time, and, because she has come to an awareness of the good and bad impulses within herself, Abra outgrows her relationship with the celibate, pure Aron and becomes interested in Cal. Expecting her to be shocked and repelled, Cal tells her about his mother, the incident with Aron, and Adam's consequent stroke. After explaining that she has known about his mother for a long time and doesn't really love Aron, Abra declares, "I think I love you, Cal." When he counters that he is "not good," she tells him, "Because you're not good." Abra's love for Cal brings him happiness, and, when they cut school at the end of May to pick azaleas in the Alisal, the sweetness of their affection and the lushness of the scene suggest a return to Eden, if only for a transitory moment.

Cal returns home to find that his brother has been killed and that Adam has suffered another, more debilitating stroke. He enters his father's bedroom and confesses to him all he has done, hoping for pardon. But Adam's eyes remain "calm, aware but not interested," as if he continues to reject the offerings of his son. With the arrival of the **nurse**, Cal leaves and, at Lee's urging, goes to see Abra. His despair, guilt, and sense of futility thrust him back to the way he had been thinking before, that he is fated to be bad because he has his mother's blood. Abra's rhetorical responses remind him that the individual, not genetics, is responsible for the choices made.

When they return to the Trask house, Lee is aware that this is the moment of crisis for Cal and tells him that, in contrast to what Adam had told Cal earlier, "every man in every generation is refired," to explain that no one is a replication of his or her parents, and that everyone is made anew. Lee is afraid that Cal will give up and give in to the impulses against which he has been struggling, and he knows that what Cal needs is Adam's love and approval. As they stand at Adam's bedside, Lee demands that Adam bless Cal who, like Cain, is "marked with guilt." Adam struggles to raise his hand and speaks one word: "*Timshel*!" With that word, he offers Cal the forgiveness, free will, and ability to choose that God granted to Cain. The suggestion is that Cal, like his namesake Caleb, will get to the Promised Land, even if he cannot recapture his Edenic birthright.

Margaret Seligman

TRASK, CATHY/CATHERINE. **Cathy Ames**'s married name in ***East of Eden***. Although she is addressed as such, she uses the name only once, when she signs the will through which she bequeaths all her money to her son, **Aron Trask**.

Margaret Seligman

TRASK, CHARLES. Son of **Cyrus** and **Alice Trask** and half-brother of **Adam Trask** in ***East of Eden***. Charles loves Adam, even protecting him from their father's harshness. However, Charles is also fiercely competitive, and, when Adam wins at a game of peewee, Charles hits him in the face, ribs, and head with the bat. After this incident, to Charles's dismay, Cyrus overtly favors Adam, pushing Adam into an army career while understanding that to put Charles "in an army would be to let loose things which in Charles must be chained down, not let loose."

The very qualities to which Cyrus alludes emerge in Charles later that evening, when Charles and Adam are walking. Charles accuses Adam of "trying to take [Cyrus] away" and then confronts Adam, shouting about how Cyrus was disinterested in his birthday gift of a rather expensive knife that Charles had earned the money to buy, preferring Adam's gift of a mongrel puppy he had found. In a rage, Charles begins punching Adam, leaving him partly conscious on the dark road. By the time Charles returns with a hatchet to finish Adam off, Adam has hidden in a ditch, and, despite lighting a series of matches in an attempt to find Adam, Charles is unsuccessful. He throws the hatchet away and walks into town. When he hears that his father is looking for him with a loaded shotgun, he hides out for two weeks before returning to the farm where, in the meantime, Cyrus has had Adam mustered into the cavalry.

During the five years that Adam is in the army, Charles continues to farm. In a letter that he writes to Adam, he alludes to the rejected gift and the beating, saying there is some unfinished business between them. When Adam is discharged, Charles makes elaborate preparations for his return, even living in the shed to keep the house clean. He is deeply disappointed when he learns from Cyrus that Adam has reenlisted and will not return home. Thereafter, Charles goes into self-imposed isolation, becoming more miserly and stingy, although earning the respect of his neighbors for being a good farmer.

Four years after he is again discharged, Adam returns to the farm. Charles informs him that Cyrus has died and has left them a great deal of money. Although Charles suspects that Cyrus might have embezzled the money, he is unable to efface his father's memory because he loves him.

Charles and Adam live and farm together intermittently for five years. This pattern is disrupted when **Cathy Ames** crawls onto their front porch, after being severely beaten by **Mr. Edwards**. Adam, completely smitten by her, nurses her intensively, but Charles sees through her feigned amnesia and perceives that within her "there's something—I almost recognize." Charles tries to warn Adam about Cathy, but, ignoring his brother's admonitions, Adam marries her. On their wedding night, Cathy drugs Adam and climbs into bed with Charles, who "threw back the blanket to receive her."

The relationship between Charles and Adam establishes the paradigm for those aspects of the Cain and Abel story that inform the novel. Charles, as Cain did with God, craves paternal love and approval, and when Adam's gift is favored, Charles lashes out in hurt and rejection, almost killing his brother. Further, Charles bears a "Cain mark," caused by a wound on his forehead that has left a long scar. As he writes to Adam, "It looks . . . like somebody marked me like a cow. . . . It just seems like I was marked." Charles shares this physical trait with Cathy, whose scar results from Mr. Edwards's beating. Both characters bear this "mark of Cain" to establish a kinship between them, which is undoubtedly what Charles recognizes within her.

Charles allows Cathy into his bed on her wedding night because he is, as Cathy calls him, "a devil," and also because he may see it as another way to win in his competition with Adam. When her twins, **Aron** and **Cal Trask**, are born, each with its own placenta, the suggestion is that either one or both of the twins are Charles's. To build on this idea, strong parallels exist between Charles and Cal. Both Charles and Cal are protective of their weaker brothers, both are restless loners who walk out alone at night, both offer gifts to their fathers from money they earned themselves, and both respond to their fathers' rejection of the gift by attempting to destroy their brothers. But while Charles seems lacking in self-awareness and controlled and driven by the negative impulses his father recognizes within him, Cal realizes that he has a choice. Eventually, Cal finds love and acceptance with **Abra Bacon**; Charles lives out his days in grudging isolation, relying on whores at the local inn for impersonal sex and companionship. When Charles dies, he wills a sum of over $100,000 to be divided equally between Adam and Cathy.

Margaret Seligman

TRASK, CYRUS. Father of **Adam** and **Charles Trask** and husband of **Mrs. Trask** and then **Alice Trask** in ***East of Eden***. Cyrus joins a Connecticut regiment in 1862 and, as a result of a wound suffered during his first engagement, loses the lower part of his right leg. He is proud of the prosthetic leg he carves for himself, and stamps loudly around the house as if to accent the tyrannical way he runs his household.

Cyrus returns home six weeks after his son Adam is born and gives his wife, Mrs. Trask, a case of gonorrhea. In paranoiac guilt, she perceives this as punishment for lewd dreams and commits suicide. Within a month, Cyrus marries seventeen-year-old Alice, who becomes pregnant with Charles two weeks later.

Cyrus raises the boys in strict military style and puts unreasonable demands on them, particularly on Adam, whom he arbitrarily prefers to Charles. Charles loves and idolizes his father so passionately that when Cyrus prefers Adam's birthday gift, Charles's intense feelings of jealousy and rejection drive him to beat and try to kill his brother.

Cyrus fabricates the extent of his military experience during the Civil War by reading, studying, and becoming an authority on campaigns and battles in which, after a period of time, he actually believes he had been involved. He writes intelligent and convincing letters and articles about the war, some of which reach the War Department. When the GAR (the Grand Army of the Republic, a Civil War veterans' group) is established with Cyrus's assistance, he becomes its secretary, a lifelong paid position. Further, he becomes a senator and moves to Washington, D.C., where he lives for years before dying of pneumonia. Cyrus leaves his sons over $100,000, to be split between them. It is possible that he came by this money dishonestly.

Cyrus's relationship with his sons is paralleled by Adam's relationship with his sons, **Cal** and **Aron Trask**. Cyrus prefers Adam, favors his birthday gift, and pushes him into the cavalry, a career Adam doesn't desire. Similarly, Adam prefers Aron and the gift he perceives Aron gives him, "a good life," to Cal's gift of $15,000, money Cal made in a business venture with **Will Hamilton**. Adam wants Aron to continue college, although Aron wants to be a minister. Ironically, in both cases, the father prefers the child who is indifferent to him. Moreover, in both cases, the arbitrary preference of one child and the rejection of a heartfelt gift from the other leads to violence and destruction as the rejected child strikes out against the accepted favorite. In this paradigm of the Cain and Abel story, Cyrus and Adam become the godlike fathers who, unlike God, alter the actions and fate of their children.

Margaret Seligman

TRASK, MR. In ***The Wayward Bus***, former road-master of the county through which the bus passes. Trask (now deceased) arouses the wrath of **Van Brunt** for having built the allegedly inadequate bridges now threatened by the flooding river. Van Brunt envies Trask both for his having died "a rich man" and for his sons' attendance at the University of California, where they are, allegedly, "living on the taxpayers' money."

TRASK, MRS. Unnamed first wife of **Cyrus Trask** and mother of **Adam Trask** in ***East of Eden***. She is a pale woman, whose religious beliefs and behavior suggest derangement. When Cyrus goes to war, she believes her god will allow her to communicate with her husband after death. When Cyrus returns and infects her with gonorrhea, her "god of communication became a god of vengeance," and she attributes her infection to the arousing dreams of infidelity she had had in Cyrus's absence. After working for two weeks on a suicide letter filled with confessions of acts she could not possibly have committed, she dresses in a white lawn shroud that she made in secret. She then drowns herself in a pond no deeper than a mud puddle and worries that the mud will sully the shroud.

Margaret Seligman

TRAVELS WITH CHARLEY (1962). Published late in Steinbeck's career, this remains one of Steinbeck's more popular books. Initial sales of 250,000 were far greater than those for Steinbeck's American masterpiece, ***The Grapes of Wrath***. Steinbeck's "dog book," as it is often referred to, was among the top ten best-selling nonfiction books for 1962, remaining on the *New York Times*'s best seller list for fifty-seven weeks. The book received praise from nearly all sectors of the American book-reading public, including academia, where Steinbeck's reputation had been knocked about during the preceding decade. In his 1962 review of *Travels with Charley* for the *New York Times*, Princeton historian Eric Goldman wrote that *Travels with Charley* "is pure delight, a pungent potpourri of places and people interspersed with bittersweet essays."

Serialization in *Holiday* magazine and its designation as a Book-of-the-Month Club main selection catapulted *Travels with Charley* into still greater popular acclaim. In addition, when Steinbeck was awarded the **Nobel Prize** in 1962, sales of the book far exceeded the expectations of his publisher, **The Viking Press**. However, its true popularity rests in its ever-popular, universal theme: the solo journey and adventures of an individual in search of self. A brief look at the background for Steinbeck's motivation to travel across the United States reveals not only a writer in search of his own country, but also a writer in search of his own soul.

As early as October 1954, writing to his agent, **Elizabeth Otis**, from Italy after six months of traveling in Europe, Steinbeck hints at the urge for a trip that he would eventually make six years later. Steinbeck tired, exhausted, and longing for home, wrote, "There is one thing I want to do. When I get home I want to sort of clear my mind and then do some work I have laid out but about the late spring I want to drive through the middle west and the south and listen to what the country is about now. I have been cut off for a very long time, and I think it would be a valuable thing for me to do. New York is very far from the nation in some respects. And it isn't politics so much as the whole pattern. I have lost track of it I think."

Although Steinbeck never got around to the trip in 1955, the idea for such a trip never left him. Nearly six years later, on May 25, 1960, as Steinbeck finished the final draft of his novel ***The Winter of Our Discontent***, he wrote to his friends **Frank Loesser**, the American composer, and his wife that "in the fall—right after Labor Day—I'm going to learn about my own country. I've lost the flavor and taste and sound of it. It's been years since I've seen it. . . . I am going alone, out toward the West. . . . I have to go alone, and I shall go unknown, I just want to look and listen. What I get I'll need badly—a re-knowledge of my own country, of its speeches, its views, its attitudes, its changes. It's long overdue. . . . It will be a kind of rebirth."

Given Steinbeck's lingering desire to make such a trip, it is not surprising to read the following passage from the opening pages of *Travels with Charley*. Not only does the passage echo sentiments expressed years earlier in letters to friends, it also lays out for the reader the intentions of his narrative that follows. "Thus I discovered that I did not know my own country. I, an American writer, writing about America, was working from memory, and memory is at best a faulty, warpy reservoir. I had not heard the speech of America. . . . I had not felt the country for twenty-five years. . . . So it was that I determined to look again, to rediscover this monster land."

However great Steinbeck's desire to rediscover his own country, an even greater and more fundamental desire resonated deep within this Nobel-laureate-to-be: the desire to renew a spirit gone lax, to challenge life itself, to spit in the eye of approaching old age, and to confound a recent stroke, which had resulted in hospitalization and vigorous recuperation efforts. In addition to a "feeling of gray desolation" that followed Steinbeck that September morning in 1960, as he shifted his truck into gear and rolled out of his Sag Harbor driveway, were the haunting specters of failing health, personal doubts about his own artistic powers, and apprehension over critics who, throughout the 1950s, had hounded Steinbeck for producing nothing of significance for nearly two decades.

Realizing the need to examine his own life and, more so, to test his artistic abilities, the fifty-eight-year-old Steinbeck chose to travel the back roads of America as, in his own words, an "antidote for the poison of the professional sick man." A great deal was at risk for Steinbeck as he departed New York in search of America. Steinbeck saw the journey ahead as a way to rejuvenate the spirit—a panacea for both his spiritual and creative crises. And given Steinbeck's physical, psychological, and spiritual condition before undertaking the "Charley" project, one can understand why Steinbeck's biographer, **Jackson J. Benson**, called the writing of *Travels with Charley* "an act of courage."

In his best work, Steinbeck wrote about the issues and struggles of working-class people, especially people of the agricultural working class. There has always been a strong working-class presence in Steinbeck's novels and stories. His works are peopled with blue-collar workers—farmhands, migrants, and the disenfranchised and marginalized Americans, looking for their places in the sunshine of the American Dream. Steinbeck's sensibility was one shaped by sympathy for the struggles of ordinary people, set against extraordinary events, who bond to overcome overwhelming odds that would otherwise defeat individuals. These were not just imagined people and events, but rather ones witnessed by Steinbeck during his early years living and working in the agricultural fields and orchards of California's lush **Salinas** Valley.

Steinbeck's love for the land and the strong presence of a sense of place in his work—coupled with his love for the common worker—are reflected in Steinbeck's attraction to, and appreciation of, the openness of the American landscape, especially the farmlands and plains of the upper Midwest. Steinbeck's appreciation of the land and its people is evident throughout *Travels with Charley*.

Travels with Charley is divided into four parts, each with smaller, chapter-like sections. Part One, the shortest of the four sections (fourteen pages), is an apologia for the trip and the book that follows. On the opening page of *Travels with Charley*, the author's stated reasons for his journey echo those of the narrator of another great travel novel of the nineteenth century, **Herman Melville**'s *Moby-Dick* (1851). Steinbeck writes, "When the virus of restlessness begins to take possession of a wayward man, and the road away from Here seems broad and straight and sweet, the victim must first find in himself a good and sufficient reason for going." Likewise, in the opening paragraph of *Moby-Dick*, Ishmael says, "Whenever I feel myself growing grim about the mouth; whenever it is a damp, drizzly November in my soul; whenever I find myself involuntarily pausing before coffin warehouses . . . then, I account it high time to get to seas as soon as I can."

Part Two begins Steinbeck's 10,000-mile, thirty-four-state, nearly three-month odyssey at his Sag Harbor home in New York shortly after Labor Day 1960, in the wake of **hurricane Donna**. Steinbeck travels north through New York, Connecticut, Massachusetts, Vermont, and New Hampshire, and then into Maine. Along the way, readers experience an archetypal New England autumn through Steinbeck's eyes and lyrical prose vignettes.

Leaving New England, Steinbeck plans to cross into Canada and return to the United States via Windsor, Ontario, and then into Detroit, but his plans are thwarted when he learns from Canadian customs officials that without proof of rabies certification, Charley would not be allowed to reenter the United States. Consequently, Steinbeck follows U.S. 90 through New York, Pennsylvania, Ohio, and Michigan, and then to Chicago, Illinois, where he is joined by his wife, **Elaine Scott Steinbeck**, who had flown out from New York to meet him. Together, they spend a few days enjoying each other's company and the comforts of the Ambassador East Hotel.

Part Three finds Steinbeck and Charley heading west into Wisconsin and through to the dizzying traffic of Minneapolis–St. Paul. Following U.S. 10, Steinbeck traverses Minnesota and crosses the Red River into Fargo, North Dakota, "the crease" in the road maps, where his romance with Fargo is not shattered by the reality. Steinbeck continues his trek across the empty landscapes of the upper plains of North Dakota and Montana, dips briefly into Wyoming and Yellowstone Park, and then returns to Montana and across the Great Divide into Idaho. West of the Idaho mountains, where he stops for the night, Steinbeck is forced to leave early the next morning and "drive hell for leather" to Spokane, Washington, because of a bladder infection that Charley develops. After Charley is treated by a less than sympathetic veterinarian, Steinbeck heads to Seattle. Although Steinbeck is disturbed by a city he no longer recognizes, Charley gets a well-deserved respite from travel and recovers from his illness.

Somewhere along the Pacific coast of Oregon, Steinbeck's camper/truck, **Rocinante** (named after the horse in **Miguel de Cervantes'** *Don Quixote de la Mancha*), blows a tire on a very rainy Sunday afternoon. Frustrated, Steinbeck finds his way to a service station and, with the help of the resourceful owner, is back on the road again, his faith restored in the kindness of strangers.

Setting his compass for California, Steinbeck heads south through the giant redwood country of southern Oregon, where he camps for two days in the shadows of giant redwoods, obviously inspired by the natural beauty of the landscape. The recuperative pause in the journey seems only fitting, a respite in advance of the disappointing and emotionally disturbing homecoming he is about to experience when he returns to his childhood and youthful haunts in **Monterey. Roy S. Simmonds** is correct in calling his return to Monterey "the true emotional climax of *Travels with Charley,* as well as being the book's true narrative climax."

Although pleased to be home to share memories with old friends, Steinbeck soon understands what Thomas Wolfe meant when he called his most famous novel *You Can't Go Home Again*. Arguing politics with his Republican sisters and sharing memories with old friends at **Johnny Garcia**'s bar brings Steinbeck to the realization that return is impossible because they, the living, not the dead, are "the ghosts." The town that was once filled with friendly faces is now filled with "nothing but strangers." His last moments in Monterey are spent with Charley atop Fremont's Peak, waxing philosophical about the nature of memory and change in one of the more lyrical passages of the book.

Rocinante carries its passengers across the Mojave Desert and Arizona and on into New Mexico. Just past Gallup and on the Continental Divide, Steinbeck decides to camp for the night. Here, it appears Steinbeck is tiring of his journey.

Part Four begins with Steinbeck's ruminations on Texas and things Texan. In Amarillo, a cracked windshield forces Steinbeck to stay for three days while Rocinante is repaired. Again, Charley is showing signs of his illness. Summoning help, Steinbeck is pleased to stay another four days at the veterinarian's recommendation, as Charley's prostatitis needs medical attention, and Charley needs rest. Steinbeck's wife flies out to meet him, and they spend Thanksgiving together at the ranch of a friend.

When Charley is well, Steinbeck claims him from the veterinarian and departs for New Orleans, where he experiences the most disturbing moment of his trip: the infamous **"cheerleaders,"** who scream their torrents of hateful, vulgar, racist epithets at two small black children who were enrolled at a previously all-white school. Sickened by the display of open hostility and racism, Steinbeck heads toward home, closing out the last leg of his journey—from Jackson, Mississippi, to Sag Harbor, New York—and the end of his travels with Charley in fewer than six pages.

Travels with Charley is written in the great American tradition of the "road" or travel books—de Tocqueville's *Democracy in America*, Jack Kerouac's *On the Road*, **Erskine Caldwell**'s *Around about America*, Richard Reeve's *American Journey,* and William Least Heat Moon's *Blue Highways*, to name a few. Wonderful passages resonate throughout the text of Steinbeck's book. It is at times sweet and funny, filled with Steinbeck's witty and ironic sense of humor. But it is also a dark, brooding book, with Steinbeck writing not so laughingly about the underside of American life—racism, technological dependency, ecological ignorance—that he witnesses during his journey. Rereading *Travels with Charley* nearly forty years after its publication, one hears Steinbeck's prophetic voice echoing throughout this popular book.

Further Reading: Astro, Richard. "Travels with Steinbeck: The Laws of Thought and the Laws of Things." In *Steinbeck's Travel Literature: Essays in Criticism*. Ed. Tetsumaro Hayashi. Muncie, IN: Steinbeck Monograph Series #10, 1980. 1–11; Ditsky, John. "Steinbeck's *Travels with Charley*: The Quest that Failed." In *Steinbeck's Travel Literature: Essays in Criticism*. Ed. Tetsumaro Hayashi. Muncie, IN: Steinbeck Monograph Series #10, 1980. 56–61; French, Warren. "*Travels with Charley* in Search of America." In *John Steinbeck's Nonfiction Revisited*. New York: Twayne, 1996. 100–107; Heavilin, Barbara. "*Travels with Charley.*" In *A New Study Guide to Steinbeck's Major Works with Critical Explications*. Ed. Tetsumaro Hayashi. Metuchen, NJ: Scarecrow, 1993. 211–239; Simmonds, Roy. "*Travels with Charley.*" In *A Study Guide to Steinbeck* (Part II). Ed. Tetsumaro Hayashi. Metuchen, NJ: Scarecrow, 1979. 165–190; Tammaro, Thom. "Lost in America:

Steinbeck's *Travels with Charley* and William Least Heat Moon's *Blue Highways*." In *Rediscovering Steinbeck: Revisionist Views of His Art, Politics, and Intellect*. Ed. Cliff Lewis and Carroll Britch. Lewiston, NY: Edwin Mellen, 1989. 260–277; ———. "Travels with Steinbeck." *North Dakota Horizons* 22.3 (Summer 1992): 20–27.

Thom Tammaro

TRAVIS, TEX. The engineer aboard the ***Western Flyer***. A native of the Panhandle of Texas, Tex traveled to the coast by "an accident, possibly alcoholic," according to Steinbeck, where he discovered he could combine his "love of Diesel engines" with work onboard boats. Like **Sparky Enea** and **Tiny Coletto**, Tex becomes a competent collector of marine life during the expeditionary journey that Steinbeck and his friend, **Edward F. Ricketts**, conducted in 1940 and described in ***The Sea of Cortez***. Steinbeck and the engineer bunked together during the journey. Early in the journey, Tex claims his engineering duties are too taxing and tries to escape the galley duties that are part of each crew member's responsibility; consequently, the crew exercises maritime justice and begins to store dirty dishes in Tex's bunk. Tex finally agrees to take his turn in the galley, but, the reader is told, he "never did get the catsup out of his blankets." Despite their differences, a genuine friendship developed between Steinbeck and Travis.

Charles Etheridge, Jr.

"TRIAL OF ARTHUR MILLER, THE" (1967). In this piece, which appeared in the June 1967 issue of *Esquire*, Steinbeck observes that playwright Arthur Miller, on trial for contempt of Congress, has one of two unsavory options: inform on friends and acquaintances considered traitors to the nation or keep quiet and be branded a felon. He urges Congress to examine its methods, for, in its attempt to save the nation from attack, it could "undermine the deep personal morality which is the nation's final defense. Congress is truly on trial with Arthur Miller."

Further Reading: Steinbeck, John. "The Trial of Arthur Miller" in *America and Americans and Selected Nonfiction*. Ed. Susan Shillinglaw and Jackson J. Benson. New York: Viking, 2002.

Eric Skipper

TRIXIE. Prostitute at **Faye**'s then **Kate Albey**'s brothel in ***East of Eden***.

TROY, LEGEND OF. The legend of Troy is another backdrop for ***Cup of Gold***. **Merlin** reminds **Henry Morgan** that he is "of the Trojan race." Later, Henry compares the **Red Saint**—reputed to be the most desirable woman in the world—to Helen of Troy, and the sack of Panama itself to the fall of "Troy town."

TRUCK DRIVER, THE. One of the first characters introduced in ***The Grapes of Wrath***, the driver is cleverly tricked by **Tom Joad** into offering him a ride after his release from Macalester Prison. By suggesting the driver is a common man like himself, Tom convinces him to break the rule that forbids hitchhikers. Although initially appearing generous and thoughtful, the trucker is also self-centered, concerned about his personal welfare. Ultimately, Tom discovers that the trucker's interest in his passenger is related to curiosity or nosiness, rather than true concern for Joad as an individual.

Michael J. Meyer

TULERACITO. In ***The Pastures of Heaven***, nicknamed Little Frog, the deformed, dwarf-like baby is found by **Franklin Gomez** in the brush on the side of the road. His artistic talent is discovered when he is forced to go to school, but his violent reaction to the destruction of any of his handiwork makes him feared by society. Eventually, while searching for his own society of gnomes and little people in an attempt to belong to a group, Tuleracito digs holes on the **Munroes'** property and is institutionalized after he violently attacks **Bert Munroe** when Munroe fills in the holes he discovers on his own property.

Michael J. Meyer

TURGENEV, IVAN (1818–1883). Prominent Russian novelist, primarily known for his realistic novel *Father and Sons* (1862) and for *A Sportsman's Sketches* (1852), a collection of tales that realistically depicts the lives of Russian serfs. Turgenev's realism never became naturalistic or overly sentimental; in his fiction, his object was always to depict truth, which at times thwarts his characters' idealism. In 1924, Steinbeck read all of Turgenev's works, during what he called a "maniacal period" of reading. He greatly admired Turgenev's fiction, and he thought that the writer provided the perfect perspective on Russian thought. **Robert DeMott** notes that Steinbeck's library contained copies of *Fathers and Sons* and *A Sportsman's Sketches*.

Further Reading: DeMott, Robert. *Steinbeck's Reading: A Catalogue of Books Owned and Borrowed.* New York: Garland, 1984.

T. Adrian Lewis

TURTLE, THE. The initial animal depicted in the first intercalary chapter of ***The Grapes of Wrath*** is a land turtle that serves as Steinbeck's symbol for determination and perseverance. Like the Okies, it carries its house on its back and, thanks to its hardy constitution, is able to survive natural catastrophes, such as drought and lack of food. In chapter 3, the turtle is shown as a target for a truck driver to hit, suggesting the hardships it must endure, but at the same time it is a carrier of life, bearing the head of a wild oat stem between its legs and eventually succeeding in planting the seed packet when it is spun off the road by the surly driver. A similar or perhaps the same turtle is picked up by **Tom Joad** in chapter 4, and he wraps it in his jacket as a present for his younger brother and sister. Tom's attempt to restrict the turtle's movement is shown to be futile when he later releases it in chapter 6. Although bothered by the Joad cat, which momentarily harasses it, the turtle uses his hard shell to repel the predatory attack, repelling the feline and resuming its journey by heading back in the original direction of its movement. The turtle is later associated with the tenacious gila monster in the California desert that never lets go, even when its head is severed from its body; it is also paralleled with the prolific jack rabbits, which never reach extinction despite frequent attempts by predators to destroy them.

Michael J. Meyer

TWAIN, MARK. *See* **Clemens, Samuel Langhorne**.

TWYM. Father of **Elizabeth**, the young Welsh girl whom the adolescent **Henry Morgan** imagined to be his girlfriend in ***Cup of Gold***.

U

UN AMÉRICAIN À NEW YORK ET À PARIS (1956). This collection of French translations of thirteen of seventeen columns that Steinbeck contributed to the daily newspaper ***Le Figaro*** during his residence in Paris in the summer of 1954 is the only book to include writings by Steinbeck in translation (translated from the American by Jean-François Rozan; Paris: René Julliard). It is also his rarest commercial publication and contains translations of four articles originally published in English—"La Naissance d'un New-Yorkais" ("Autobiography: Making of a New Yorker," *New York Times Magazine*. February 1, 1953, Part II, 26–27, 66–67); "*Quand le printemps se leve*" ("Bricklaying Piece," *Punch*. July 27, 1955, 92); "Les stigmates de la candidature" ("How to Recognize a Candidate," *Punch*. August 10, 1955, 146–48); "Les marches de la noblesse" ("How about Aristocracy: Why Not a World Peerage?" *Saturday Review*. December 10, 1955, 11)—along with a piece not known to have been published anywhere else, "Protestation et Suggestion," a satire of Americans claiming descent from William the Conqueror and following the American cult of momism.

UNCOLLECTED STORIES OF JOHN STEINBECK, THE (1986). Published in Tokyo in 1986 under the editorship of Japanese Steinbeck scholar **Kiyoshi Nakayama**, this small paperback includes **"The Summer Before," "The Time the Wolves Ate the Vice Principal," "Reunion at the Quiet Hotel," "How Edith McGillicuddy Met R. L. Stevenson," "His Father," "The Gifts of Iban: A Short Story,"** and **"The Miracle of Tepayac."** Including stories previously published separately in a variety of periodicals, such as *Collier's*, *Harper's*, *Smokers' Companion*, and *Punch*, the volume is extensively notated in Japanese and was intended to introduce Japanese scholars to previously unobtainable Steinbeck texts. Nakayama notes that three other short stories—**"The Affair at 7, Rue de M——"** (1955), **"How Mr. Hogan Robbed a Bank"** (1956), and **"The History of Mankind"** (1955)—were excluded because of copyright issues.

UNDERHILL, EVELYN (1850–1941). British author of *Mysticism* (1911), *The Mystic Way* (1913), *Man and the Supernatural* (1927), and *The Mystery of Sacrifice* (1938). Under the guidance of Baron Friedrich von Huegel, a writer on theology and mysticism, she embarked on a life of reading, writing, meditation, and prayers.

Underhill (Mrs. Hubert Stuart Moore) taught that the life of contemplative prayer is not just for monks and nuns, but can be the life of any Christian who is willing to undertake it. She also taught that modern psychological theory, far from being a threat to contemplation, can fruitfully be used to enhance it. In her later years, she spent a great deal of time as a lecturer and retreat director.

Michael J. Meyer

"UNSECRET WEAPON" (1953). A two-part story by John Steinbeck published in the February 14 and 21, 1953, issues of *Picture Post.* With its plot to undermine the economic stability of the Soviet Union, this humorous fantasy grew out of Steinbeck's earlier proposal to President **Franklin Delano Roosevelt** to flood the Axis powers with counterfeit currency. Setting this idea in the USSR, the narrator describes the effects of the mysterious wealth, dropped from bombers like leaflets, on the Soviet citizenry and the desperate attempts of Soviet officials to collect the counterfeit rubles and steady their economy.

Scott Simkins

URYENS, KING OF GORE. In *The Acts of King Arthur,* husband of **Morgan le Fay**. One of the **eleven rebel lords of the North**, who were defeated by **King Arthur** at Bedgrayne. He later becomes a friend of Arthur and on **King Pellinore**'s recommendation is made a Knight of the **Round Table** after the war with the **five kings**.

USED CAR SALESMEN. In *The Grapes of Wrath,* these unnamed individuals appear in intercalary chapter 7 as unscrupulous men who treat the Okies with little respect as they try to play on their desperate need for transportation to the West. Using high-pressure tactics and playing on their customers' inexperience and guilt, these crooked businessmen push defective merchandise and offer minimal cash for the Okies' treasured possessions, bartering "junk cars" for "junk lives." Like the bankers, these salesmen are opportunists, ready to make their fortunes from the misfortunes of others.

Michael J. Meyer

USHER. In *Viva Zapata!,* he is dressed "in formal attire" and admits the delegation of peasants into the "Audience Room" of President Díaz's palace, and then leaves.

UTHER PENDRAGON. In *The Acts of King Arthur,* King of England and father of King **Arthur** by **Lady Igraine**, widow of the Duke of Cornwall, who later becomes his wife. As agreed, he gives the newborn baby to **Merlin**. He dies two years later, having blessed Arthur as his true successor.

V

VALERY, JOE. Bouncer who works at **Kate Albey**'s brothel in ***East of Eden***. Kate becomes increasingly and perhaps foolishly dependent on Joe to help her get rid of and then locate **Ethel**, who is attempting to blackmail her by claiming that she has evidence that Kate killed **Faye**. To ensure Joe's loyalty, Kate tells him that she knows he is really **Joe Venuta**, and that he escaped from a San Quentin road gang. Later, when Joe discovers Ethel is dead, he plans to extort money from Kate by withholding the information about Ethel. However, this plan backfires, and prior to her suicide, Kate sends a message to be relayed to the sheriff, **Horace Quinn**, informing him that Joe Valery is, in fact, the wanted Joe Venuta. The next morning, Joe discovers Kate's body, then rifles through her desk and steals incriminating papers, money, her will, and compromising pictures of prominent local citizens, which it is assumed he will use for blackmail purposes. This plan is thwarted as well when, in response to Kate's note, **Oscar Noble** appears to take Joe to the police station for questioning. Joe breaks free, and Oscar shoots and kills him as he tries to escape.

Margaret Seligman

VAN BRUNT. In ***Wayward Bus***, a cantankerous, longtime resident of the county through which the **San Ysidro River** runs and a late addition to the group of passengers taking the eventful journey described in the novel. Van Brunt is presented as frail and elderly, and by the time of the bus trip, he is near death. A series of strokes has altered his personality, making him emotionally volatile, and he finds himself prone to bouts of crying and frightening sexual urges toward women and girls. He is the quarrelsome voice of doom throughout the journey, disagreeing with every decision, then disagreeing again when it is reversed. Van Brunt's sour personality, however, is perhaps excusable in a way that the negative qualities of many of the other characters on the bus are not. Near the end of the trip, he suffers a final stroke that will probably prove fatal or result in what he fears most, an end similar to that of his father, who had "lain like a gray, helpless worm in a bed for eleven months." In fact, anticipating this fate, Van Brunt had previously bought cyanide but was unable to bring himself to commit suicide. When he ultimately falls victim to the dreaded stroke as the bus lies stranded, Juan Chicoy assigns Elliott Pritchard the task of keeping Van Brunt's mouth open to maintain his breathing.

Van Brunt is an image of odious, frightening aging—anathema to the Hollywood culture that embraces youth at all costs. His age and experience seem to have gained little respect or have served little purpose in this world. He and his generation are left to contemplate death alone, bereft of any supportive understanding of aging and dying from contemporary culture. However, his dying presence in the back of the bus at the end of the novel casts at least a partially optimistic light on the fate of the other passengers, who will carry on no matter how great the odds are against their ultimate success.

Christopher S. Busch and Bradd Burningham

VAN DE VENTER, HELEN. In ***The Pastures of Heaven***, the owner of the beautiful ranch in Christmas Canyon. Mrs. Van de Venter has surrounded herself with tragedy, having first lost her husband in a hunting accident and then having given birth to a daughter, **Hilda**, who is psychologically disturbed. Helen seems to thrive on pain and the twists of fate that have devastated her life. Although she tries to isolate her daughter by moving to an idyllic location/prison in Las Pasturas, she soon discovers that it is impossible to conceal her child's defects from the town or to isolate her in Edenic surroundings. When Hilda is accidentally discovered by **Bert Munroe** in his attempt to be a friendly neighbor, the young girl develops a recurrent desire to escape from her prison and find a capable man. Hilda escapes a second time, and Helen recognizes that her daughter's desires will be impossible to control; she concludes that the only answer is Hilda's death. Steinbeck then suggests that Helen deliberately tracks down her daughter and shoots her. Fortunately, because of Hilda's fragile condition, the murder is considered a suicide. Although Helen is ultimately not held accountable for the crime, she loses her fantasy of a stable life and is once more relegated to a world of sadness and guilt amid her paradoxically idyllic surroundings.

Michael J. Meyer

VAN DE VENTER, HILDA. *See* **Van de Venter, Helen**.

VAN DINE, S. S. (1888–1939). Popular mystery writer during the 1920s and 1930s. Steinbeck read his work in the early 1930s, although he was not usually a fan of mystery novels, and he owned two of Van Dine's works, *The Canary Murder Case* (1927) and *The Bishop Murder Case* (1929). **Robert DeMott** notes that Van Dine's mysteries might have in part influenced Steinbeck as he wrote the unpublished potboiler, **"Murder at Full Moon."**

Further Reading: DeMott, Robert. *Steinbeck's Reading: A Catalogue of Books Owned and Borrowed*. New York: Garland, 1984.

VAN FLEET, JO (1914–1996). Already a prominent, award-winning character actor on Broadway, Van Fleet startled moviegoers in her 1955 film debut, playing **James Dean**'s madam-mother in **Elia Kazan**'s adaptation of John Steinbeck's novel ***East of Eden*** (1952), a performance that won her a best supporting actress Oscar.

"VANDERBILT CLINIC, THE." Written by Steinbeck, "The Vanderbilt Clinic" was published in 1947 by the Columbia-Presbyterian Medical Center in New York. This thirteen-page edition, third in a series of reports for the friends and supporters of the hospital, included photographs by Victor Keppler. In it, Steinbeck describes how this book will be issued by the Columbia-Presbyterian Medical Center to "its friends and supporters, to show them the generalized life of the hospital and its Vanderbilt Clinic." Steinbeck's introduction tells the story of "M," who has been a patient at the clinic since she was seventeen months old, and the special treatment and care she has been given by the entire staff. Also discussed are clinic statistics and the importance of the clinic to the community. Steinbeck concludes that "my reason for wanting to write this little piece is very simple. In the files of the Columbia-Presbyterian Medical Center there are four cards and on them are the names of my wife, my two young sons, and myself."

John Hooper

VAUGHAN, LORD AND LADY. Dinner guests of **Henry** and **Elizabeth Morgan** in ***Cup of Gold***.

VAUTIN, SERGEANT. ***In The Short Reign of Pippin IV***, a young guard assigned to the royal palace, who wants to be in Paris where rioting is going on in reaction to **Pippin** Héristal's radical democratic-socialist speech. Pippin relieves Vautin of duty and grants him two weeks' furlough on the spot so he can check out the action in Paris. By doing so, Pippin also relieves himself of one of a succession of invasions of his own privacy and freedom as King Samothrace.

VEDIC HYMN, THE. Source for the title of Steinbeck's ***To a God Unknown***, this work was probably introduced to Steinbeck by mythology expert **Joseph Campbell**. Veda is Sanskrit for "knowledge" and is the name for the most ancient sacred literature of Hinduism, or for the individual books belonging to that literature. This body of ancient literature consists primarily of four collections of hymns, detached poetical portions, and ceremonial formulas. The collections are called the *Rig-Veda,* the *Sama-Veda,* the *Yajur-Veda,* and the *Atharva-Veda.* They are known also as the Samhitas (roughly "collection").

The four Vedas were composed in Vedic, an early form of Sanskrit. The oldest portions are believed by scholars to have originated largely with the Aryan invaders of India sometime between 1300 and 1000 BC; however, the Vedas in their present form are believed to date only from the close of the third century BC.

The first three Samhitas are primarily ritual handbooks that were used in the Vedic period by three classes of priests who officiated at ceremonial sacrifices; thus, they are appropriate texts for the ritualistic and sacrificial life of **Joseph Wayne** in Steinbeck's novel. The *Rig-Veda* contains more than 1000 hymns (Sanskrit *rig*), composed in various poetic meters and arranged in ten books. It was used by the *hotri,* or reciters, who invoked the gods by reading its hymns aloud. The *Sama-Veda* contains verse portions taken mainly from the *Rig-Veda.* It was used by the *udgatri,* or chanters, who sang its hymns, or melodies (Sanskrit *sama*). The *Yajur-Veda,* which now consists of two recensions, both of them partly in prose and partly in verse and both including roughly the same material (although differently arranged), contains sacrificial formulas (Sanskrit *yaja*, "sacrifices"). It was used by the *adhvaryu,* priests who recited appropriate formulas from the *Yajur-Veda* while actually performing the sacrificial actions. **Robert DeMott** points out that Arthur Keith's two-volume work, *The Religion and Philosophy of the Veda and the Upanishads* (1925), was a useful source for Steinbeck.

Further Reading: DeMott, Robert. *Steinbeck's Reading: A Catalogue of Books Owned and Borrowed*. New York: Garland, 1984.

Michael J. Meyer

VENUTA, JOE. Real name of **Kate Albey**'s bouncer, **Joe Valery**, in ***East of Eden***.

VICAR, THE. He is brought by **Elizabeth Morgan** to **Henry Morgan**'s deathbed in ***Cup of Gold***. He tries to have Henry repent his sins so that Henry may be absolved, but Henry dies unrepentant.

VICTOR. In Steinbeck's third and last play-novelette, ***Burning Bright***, Victor is a young man who is used as a kind of stud animal by **Mordeen** so that she can have the **Child** that her impotent husband, **Joe Saul**, so desperately wants. Victor works for Saul as the play takes the characters through three acts with different settings ("The Circus," "The Farm," and "The Sea"). As Saul is much older than Mordeen, Victor senses an opportunity, and he makes advances toward Saul's wife. She is not interested in him but finally makes use of him. Though craven at the beginning of the play, Victor becomes a more sympathetic character as he develops deeper feelings for Mordeen and the Child (his child) that she carries. When Victor threatens to reveal to Saul the true paternity of the Child, Mordeen decides to kill him with a knife. However, **Friend Ed** crushes Victor's skull and gets rid of the body (in the stage version, Friend Ed arranges to have Victor shanghaied). The character of Victor is problematic; he is a dynamic character who begins to have deeper, more mature feelings about Mordeen and their Child. Ironically, these feelings spell his doom in a play-novelette in which love, literally, conquers all.

VIETNAM WAR. *See* **Johnson, Lyndon Baines; Letters to Alicia.**

"VIGILANTE, THE" (1936). Included in ***The Long Valley*** (1938) and first published as "The Lonesome Vigilante" in *Esquire Magazine* in October 1936, this disturbing story opens in an undetermined locale as people begin to leave the aftermath of an initially undisclosed but emotionally searing event. Singled out from this group is **Mike**, the protagonist, who feels disappointed and almost overwhelmingly weary. By the third paragraph, it is revealed that this event had been the lynching of a black man, whose body hangs from a tree in the town park. Even though the man is dead before the mob disperses, a few men try unsuccessfully to burn the body with a lighted twist of newspaper. The rest of the story explores Mike's emotional reaction to his participation in the lynching.

As in another *Long Valley* story, **"Flight,"** in which Steinbeck focuses on **Pepé**'s ability to face death rather than on the crime that forces him to flee his pursuers, in "The Vigilante" Steinbeck provides few details about the prisoner, his crime, or even his lynching. The outline of the story was based on an actual occurrence in San Jose on November 26, 1933, when a mob lynched and burned two men who had kidnapped and brutally murdered the son of a wealthy local family. Steinbeck, however, seems to have purposefully ignored the sensational aspects of the occurrence and, in his story, shows no interest in either the victims' guilt or in their brutal acts. Instead he focuses on Mike's evident need to be part of a group and on the loneliness that gradually envelops him as he distances himself from the mob violence in which he has played such a central role. Indeed, the original version of the story was titled "Case History," and the author uses a simple device to elicit Mike's story.

Mike enters a bar and meets **Welch**, the lone bartender, who evinces a good deal of curiosity and, through questions, extracts information from Mike. Mike is at least partially conscious of his need to remember as much detail as possible, for he knows he has taken part in a "terrible and important affair" and—like a writer—"he would want to remember later so he could tell about it." He thus functions partially as subject and partly as the self-conscious narrator or even as the writer himself. When Mike enters the bar, Welch tells him that he looks like a sleepwalker. Mike is surprised that Welch has described his mood so precisely, just as, at the end of the tale, he will feel astonishment at his wife's similar perceptiveness. Through Mike's responses to the bartender's interested questions, the reader learns that he had participated in the lynching from its inception. It began with drinking in the bar and the decision to storm the jail. The story contains several allusions to unscrupulous lawyers and law enforcers, particularly the sheriff, who remonstrate with the mob to capture the "right" man, even telling them "it's the fourth cell down." Mike is near the front of the mob that successfully rams the door to the jail. Although he explains the way the events of the evening began, Mike does not simply state facts. Much of the information revealed in the exchange between Mike and Welch occurs through Mike's repetition of certain details that suggest his subtly understated feelings of guilt and his attempts at self-justification. Mike's repeated assertions—that this particular black man really was a fiend—demonstrate his need to believe that he has participated in the elimination of a public threat. He seems to need reassurance that he did the right thing, telling Welch that "all the papers" said he was a fiend. Mike's nagging conscience is further suggested when, three times, Mike repeats his belief that the man was killed by the first blow that knocked him down in the jail—almost imperceptibly distancing himself from the actual lynching. And three times before meeting Welch, Mike had repeated that it "don't do no good" to burn the victim, as if the killing and the hanging had been enough. The burning attempts seem to preoccupy him even in the bar when, for the fourth time, he repeats that he sees no point in setting the man on fire.

As the excitement wears off, Mike feels chest pain, loneliness, silence, and weariness. Now, as the town is quiet, Mike says he feels "just like nothing happened." Although the specific comparison does not occur until the end of the story, Steinbeck's language and imagery throughout the story suggest a coming apart similar to the loneliness after sex. When Welch asks him how he feels "afterwards," Mike tells him he feels "tired, but kind of satisfied, too." And as the two men part company and Mike enters his house, his wife takes one look at him and says, "You been with a woman." When she realizes that he has been part of the lynching, he looks in the mirror and, with the same kind of astonishment he felt with Welch, remarks, "By God, she was right. . . . That's exactly how I do feel."

The odd connection between sex and violence, specifically racial violence, has long been noted in prose and poetry; **William Faulkner**'s story, "Dry September," for instance, or Robert Hayden's poem, "Night, Death, Mississippi." Steinbeck seems to have no sympathy for either Mike or his wife, who is notably cold, trying to warm herself by an open stove; indeed, their attitudes are comparable to those of the sheriff and his wife in "Pantaloon in Black," William Faulkner's much more explicit story of racial violence. "The Vigilante," placed as it is between **"The Raid"** and **"Johnny Bear,"** demonstrates Steinbeck's interest in the dominant theme of loneliness that runs throughout *The Long Valley* stories, particularly in the pairings of lonely and isolated men. The story also prepares readers for the much more explicit examination of the forbidden mixing of race and sex that occurs in "Johnny Bear."

Further Reading: Delgado, James. "The Facts behind John Steinbeck's 'The Lonesome Vigilante.'" *Steinbeck Quarterly* 16: 3–4 (Summer–Fall 1983): 70–79; Hughes, Robert S., Jr. *John Steinbeck: A Study of the Short Fiction.* Boston: Twayne, 1989; Meyer, Michael J. "'The Vigilante.'" In *The Facts on File Companion to the American Short Story.* Ed. Abby H. P. Werlock. New York: Facts on File, Inc., 2000. 430–31; Owens, Louis. "'The Little Bit of a Story': Steinbeck's 'The Vigilante.'" In *Steinbeck's Short Stories in* The Long Valley*: Essays in Criticism.* Ed. Tetsumaro Hayashi. Muncie, IN: Steinbeck Research Institute, Ball State University, 1991. 49–53.

Abby H. P. Werlock

VIKING PRESS, THE. Principal hardcover publisher of John Steinbeck's books, beginning in 1938 with ***The Long Valley*** and continuing through posthumous publications to ***America and Americans*** *and Selected Nonfiction* in 2002.

One of New York's strongest and most respected publishing firms, The Viking Press became Steinbeck's publisher when it bought his contract from the struggling **Covici-Friede** for $15,000 in August 1938. Although probably best known for its unsuccessful attempts in trying to persuade Steinbeck to "soften" the language and change the ending of *Grapes of Wrath*, Viking remained Steinbeck's publisher until his death and continues to reprint Steinbeck's books in hardcover; Penguin Books USA now reprints his books in paperback editions.

Further Reading: Fensch, Thomas. *Steinbeck and Covici.* Middlebury, VT: Paul S. Eriksson, 1979.

Ted Scholz

VILLA, FRANCISCO "PANCHO." In ***The Wayward Bus***, the Mexican revolutionary leader featured in a story **Juan Chicoy** heard from his father when Chicoy was a boy in **Torreon**, Mexico.

VINAVER, EUGENE (1899–1979). Malory expert, professor of French language and literature at Manchester University from

1933 to 1966, and Steinbeck friend. Vinaver and Steinbeck first met in 1957, when Steinbeck was collecting materials for ***The Acts of King Arthur and His Noble Nights***. According to **Elaine Scott Steinbeck**, the relationship between the two men was "pure magic"; Vinaver encouraged Steinbeck in his Arthurian endeavor and offered assistance. According to **Jay Parini**, Steinbeck often "worked from Vinaver's annotated edition of Malory." The "Introduction" to *The Acts* proclaims that "no better man could have been chosen for the work [of editing Malory] than Professor Vinaver, with his great knowledge, not only of the 'Frensshe' books, but also of the Welsh, Irish, Scottish, Breton, and English sources. He has brought to the work, beyond his scholarly approach, the feeling of wonder and delight so often lacking in a schoolman's methodology." Given Steinbeck's hostility to literary critics and scholars, the praise heaped upon Vinaver is extraordinary. The two men corresponded for much of the next ten years, both when Steinbeck was working on the Malory project and when he was engaged in other endeavors. In late 1965, the two men were invited by the Duke of Northumberland to use the library at Alnwick Castle (in a continuing search for lost or little-known Arthurian materials). Vinaver found, bound as part of another book, a forty-eight-page manuscript examining the Arthurian legend, one that Steinbeck thought to be unknown, although they later discovered the work had been microfilmed and was available in a number of libraries. Word was leaked to the British press, who, according to Parini, "wildly exaggerat[ed] the importance of the manuscript" and claimed that it was "by Malory, when it was no such thing." Vinaver felt "his reputation was being abused" and the incident damaged the friendship between the two men, despite Steinbeck's January 15, 1966, letter, which stated, "I am miserable if I have been the cause of unease or unhappiness to you." The misunderstanding brought Steinbeck's work on the Malory project to an end, although many years later, after *The Acts of King Arthur* was published posthumously, Vinaver praised it on the BBC.

Further Reading: Benson, Jackson J. *The True Adventures of John Steinbeck, Writer*. New York: Viking, 1984; Parini, Jay. *John Steinbeck: A Biography*. New York: Holt, 1995.

Charles Etheridge, Jr.

VIRGIN DE GUADALUPE. In ***Viva Zapata!***, a picture of the patron saint of Mexico "mounted on a stick" is carried by a boy at the exterior of a fenced field in Morelos—near Ayala, Mexico—and, later, an old Indian "plants it in the ground." The Virgin's story and miraculous appearance before Juan Diego's eyes is told by Steinbeck in his 1948 short story, **"The Miracle of Tepayac."**

VIRGIN OF GUADALUPE. In ***The Wayward Bus***, considered by **Juan Chicoy**'s mother to be her own, protective "personal goddess," the Virgin of Guadalupe figures in Chicoy's life as well. Although his religion is not orthodox, Juan "would have been uneasy driving the bus without the Guadalupana to watch over him." She is represented by a small metal statue affixed to the dashboard. The Virgin was omnipresent for Juan in his childhood, in his thoughts and in statues and images at home and in church. She retains a hold on his conscience. During the trip, Juan has an ongoing conversation with the Virgin, hoping she will intervene by disabling the bus so that he, without pangs of conscience, may escape his responsibilities and return to Mexico. Ultimately, Juan mires the bus himself and starts walking to freedom, but he cannot abandon the passengers and returns to continue the journey.

VITELA, JULE. The mixed-blood Cherokee in ***The Grapes of Wrath***, who instinctively senses the presence of troublemakers at the Weedpatch camp (**Arvin Sanitary camp**) dance and effectively shuts down their attempt to start a riot before it can start.

VIVA ZAPATA!* (FILM, SCREENPLAY, AND NARRATIVE)** (1952). Although John Steinbeck had been reading about **Emiliano Zapata** since the early 1930s, the idea for a screenplay on the life of the Mexican revolutionary came to him in the midst of writing the shooting script of ***The Pearl. In a June 1945 letter from Cuernavaca, Mexico, Steinbeck indicated his strong feelings about the Mexican hero and how he was approached by "an outfit that calls itself Pan-American Films with the proposition" that he do a film on Zapata's life. Fully aware there were "still men living and in power who helped to trick and murder Zapata," Steinbeck was adamant that, in order to make the film, he would "require gov't assurance that it could be made straight historically." He believed the film of Zapata's life could be a great one, as long as the true story was not compromised.

Nothing came of the project until three years later, shortly after the death of his friend, **Edward F. Ricketts**. Steinbeck reflected again upon the possibility of doing a film about Zapata. Early in June 1948, Steinbeck briefly went to Mexico to research Zapata's life, because, to him, Emiliano Zapata was "one of the greatest men who ever lived." Since he was a conscientious researcher with a concern for historical accuracy, Steinbeck continued to return to Mexico for short periods, especially between July and November 1948, and later in January 1949. He prided himself on interviewing every eyewitness he could find.

Steinbeck's editor, **Pascal Covici**, put him in touch with a journalist friend, Magdalena Mondragón, who seemed could help with researching Zapata. According to **Richard Astro**, Steinbeck had first learned about Zapata in 1931 or 1932 at the Hollywood home of his friend **Richard Albee**, where he met Reina Dunn, the Mexican American daughter of an American reporter, Harry H. Dunn. In 1933, the latter published a book about Zapata titled *The Crimson Jester: Zapata of Mexico*. After numerous conversations with Ms. Dunn, Steinbeck felt he had learned, as quoted in Astro, more "about the Mexican freedom fighter from her than from her father's reportage." Steinbeck reputedly had also read a "novelized biography" of Zapata by Edgcumb Pinchón, *Zapata the Unconquerable*, published in 1941. Pinchón had previously prepared a 556-page script narrative for a film, possibly to be done by MGM as a companion picture to his own *Viva Villa* (a popular film in 1934) and for which he, too, had done an enormous amount of firsthand research. Steinbeck gleaned very little from Pinchón's work, since the latter hardly mentioned **Eufemio**, Emiliano's brother, and made no reference to Josefa, Zapata's wife, who is an important figure in Steinbeck's script). However, Robert Morsberger does refer to Steinbeck's use of *Zapata the Unconquerable* and the changes he made to some materials from the Pinchón work. **Jackson J. Benson** indicates that by "going to Cuautla to talk to people there," the author would "just about have to cover the state." Steinbeck even had his second wife, **Gwyndolyn Conger Steinbeck**, go to the National Archives and the National University to do further research on Zapata's life. This was a difficult task for her since her knowledge of Spanish, in contrast to his, was very rudimentary. She often merely copied things that she did not understand personally. From the fall of 1948 until the late summer of 1950, Steinbeck was involved not only with the writing of *Viva Zapata!* but with its filming as well.

The Zapata film became a reality when Steinbeck approached his friend, the director **Elia Kazan**, about doing a movie depicting the life of Christopher Columbus. Since such a movie was already being made, the conversation eventually led to Mexico and the Mexican revolutionary leader, Emiliano Zapata. Both soon became convinced that such a project was viable. Although Kazan credits Steinbeck for being a great writer with much knowledge about Zapata, as the film's director, Kazan credits himself with saving the project from death when Steinbeck and producer **Darryl Zanuck** were at odds over the way it should be written. Not satisfied with the work Steinbeck had done earlier on the script, Kazan became an integral part of the writing, as the two worked together in New York in May 1950: "I had worked up a frame of action for the whole script, and I would ask for lines of dialogue from John, which he'd provide one at a time." Steinbeck wanted to shoot the movie in Mexico, and Kazan agreed, so they both went to Cuernavaca to explore that possibility and further refine the script.

Although Kazan admitted that he made cuts as he shot the film, he still felt it was "a faithful rendering of John's script. He stated 'No actor rewrote it . . . all John's important words and thoughts are faithfully in the film.'" An accurate comparison of the two may be obtained by observing the final product of the film in conjunction with Steinbeck's final shooting script, which Morsberger reproduced in his complete published version (*Viva Zapata!: The Original Screenplay by John Steinbeck,* 1975). According to Morsberger, such a comparison reveals that some major cuts in the film were "indicated by square brackets" and that there were even some cuts not indicated by brackets.

While briefly discussing the film *Viva Zapata!*, **Peter Lisca**, in his seminal work, *The Wide World of John Steinbeck,* not only makes reference to Steinbeck's involvement with "both the story and script" from the fall of 1948 until May of 1950 but also to "a special introduction to the shooting script," which Steinbeck wrote "so that the producer, director, and cameraman would understand what it was about." Undoubtedly, this very long introduction is part of what we now know as the original narrative manuscript from which the screenplay *Viva Zapata!* was derived, and which was discovered by Carolyn and James Robertson in the files of the UCLA film archives. Published privately by the Yolla Bolly Press as a limited edition in November 1991, it contained a commentary written by Morsberger. That same year, it was published in England by William Heinemann, Ltd., under the title *Zapata: The Little Tiger.* In 1993, Penguin released the entire publication, entitled simply *Zapata,* which was edited by Morsberger, together with his Yolla Bolly Press commentary and updated versions of his previous essays on the project. As Morsberger observes, this newly discovered manuscript is not a shooting script, but rather a preliminary treatment that discusses Mexican history—particularly the Mexican Revolution. Steinbeck also gives some suggestions about how the events should be dramatized and filmed. The narrative reflects all of Steinbeck's thorough research, "done over a space of nearly twenty years, much of it oral history that is not in any of the published biographies of Zapata or histories of the revolution" (Morsberger, "Introduction"). The introduction to the narrative is divided into five sections, in which Steinbeck provides the following: a history of Mexico, which he compares to early Greek city-states, beginning with its conquest by Cortez; a history of how the land was "not owned by individual men" but "surely was owned in the sense" that the individual "maintained it during his lifetime"; a discussion of how Indian and Spanish bloods mixed and affected the culture, government, and economy of Mexico; an identification of such leaders as Benito Juárez and Porfirio Díaz; a discussion of the political and economic background of Mexico and the "conditions which brought about Emiliano Zapata," and which prompted Steinbeck to write his story; a discussion of the "customs, habits, costumes and appearances" of Emiliano and his people; and an assessment of the ceremonies—religious and otherwise—common to the town fiestas and fairs, including the types of food and drink vendors sell, *corridos* (folksongs of the nation), music and dances, and many other aspects of Mexican life. He also discusses the economy of Mexico and its landowners, whom he calls intermittently *hacendados* (which is the accurate term) and *haciendado* (the inaccurate form), which he is relating to *hacienda,* the Spanish term for ranch.

Steinbeck pays special attention to the distinctive public characters in a typical town or village, such as the public letter writer, the priest, and the *curandera* (a religious purveyor of faith cures) who "does all of the village healing" sometimes to its detriment. Steinbeck had intended to use a *curandera* throughout his "script as a kind of prophetic character," because in Anenecuilco, the town where Emiliano Zapata was born, a *curandera* predicted his birth a year before he came into the world. A *curandera* also forecast Zapata's death and "climbed to the top of the mountain where his position was and warned him not to go to his death." It is also the *curandera* who contributes to the mythologizing of Emiliano when he is killed by noting that the little *manito* (a birthmark of a little hand, for which Emiliano became famous at his birth and which disappeared at his death) was not present on his chest when she viewed his dead body in the plaza.

In the narrative, Steinbeck also talks of the Mexican territory, particularly around Cuernavaca, an area he knew so well that he could even suggest which surrounding villages would be suitable for filming *Viva Zapata!* It is evident from the recorded details that Steinbeck understood the psychology of the Mexican people and the ways of getting things done in Mexico—as well as their differences from American ways. He offers experienced advice about filming in Mexican territory and discusses how the Mexican authorities should be dealt with, stressing the importance of paying great attention to local courtesies. Since he considered shooting the film in Mexico, Kazan found Steinbeck's knowledge very useful.

Steinbeck's respect and love for the Mexican people in general, and particularly for Emiliano Zapata, shine through all his commentaries. He does not idealize the situation; rather, he keeps a clear and open mind with regard to his details. He felt that Zapata "was a man of great courage" who "never felt fear" and "*was* a better fighter than anyone else . . . a clearer thinker than the people of his time"; in short, for Steinbeck, Zapata was "the symbol of the best there is in the Indian," and he urged that the film be made with "that spirit" in mind.

Following the introduction, the narrative consists exclusively of chapters, each labeled "Scene," with some containing prose sections and others containing dialogue as well as explanatory material. Some elements and characters appear both in the narrative and the screenplay, although with different degrees of emphasis. Many incidents are clear in the screenplay, but were clearer, of course, in the original narrative version. The final shooting script condenses much of the history that Steinbeck explicates in the earlier narrative version. The latter opens before Zapata was born and ends with his death (as does the film script). It builds up certain characters and eliminates others, but although it is a fuller narrative, it is decidedly less cinematic. Jules Buck, a writer assigned to Steinbeck to help him complete the screenplay, described this narrative as being as unwieldy as a PhD dissertation. Buck and Steinbeck worked well together, and the result was *Viva Zapata!*.

The narrative version lacks the tautness and drama of the screenplay, but it serves to explain many facts and issues that the latter leaves unclear. In the narrative, Steinbeck builds up the close relationship between Emiliano and his brother, Eufemio, which is downplayed in the screenplay. Similarly, although he pays a great deal of attention to the character of the *curandera* in the narrative, she does not even appear in the screenplay. Instead, her hysteric fear that Zapata will lose his life if he goes to Chinameca is given more dramatic force in the film as the expression of that fear is transferred to Josefa, Zapata's wife. At the end of the film, instead of the *curandera*, it will be many of the men who fought with Zapata as well as other younger men who confirm that the body dumped in the plaza is not that of Emiliano.

The character of **Fernando Aguirre**, ideologue and friend to no one, is pure fiction and has no reference in the original narrative. Many critics see him as a possible combination of **Jim Nolan** and **Mac** from Steinbeck's strike novel ***In Dubious Battle***, putting "his job as a revolutionary ahead of the people he is supposed to serve" and, in the end, causing the untimely demise of Emiliano Zapata (Lisca). **Jesús Colonel Guajardo**, whose actions are the actual cause of Zapata's demise, also receives much less attention in the screenplay than in the narrative portion. Because of some excisions, he mainly appears in the final scene. On the other hand, a legend described as one that might be true—the deflecting and lassoing of a rifle by a young boy and his brother that leads Emiliano to give his horse, **Blanco**, to the young boy in recognition of his brave act—is briefly recited in the narrative version but dramatized poignantly in a short scene in the screenplay. A similar change involves a story concerning a gold watch and a rifle with which Emiliano teaches Madero a moral lesson—this is merely touched upon in the narrative but very dramatically presented in the screenplay and in the subsequent film.

As Morsberger summarizes, "The two versions of *Zapata* do not duplicate but complement each other; together, they give a more colorful and extensive picture of Emiliano Zapata and the Mexican revolution than either does alone" (*Zapata*, "Preface"). Nonetheless, the focus does differ between the two versions. In the narrative version, Zapata appears more folkloric and mythic. In the screenplay, he appears more of a human being with frailties, but one who is modest and without ambition for the power thrust upon him.

The 1952 film itself received good reviews, and Steinbeck was nominated for an Academy Award for screenwriting. **Marlon Brando** played Zapata, Jean Peters was Josefa, and **Anthony Quinn** won an Academy Award for best supporting actor as Eufemio. John Womack, who published the definitive Zapata biography, titled *Zapata and the Mexican Revolution* (1969), makes reference to the film *Viva Zapata!*, which he considered "a distinguished achievement." He noted that "in telescoping the whole revolution into one dramatic episode," on the one hand "the movie distorts certain events and characters, some grossly," but, on the other hand, "it quickly and vividly develops a portrayal of Zapata, the villagers, and the nature of their relations and movement"—a depiction Womack found to be "subtle, powerful, and true." Womack observed that Steinbeck's research in Mexico not only discovered Zapata's wife, Josefa, but also made his "marriage public for the first time." *Viva Zapata!* is the best film produced from a screenplay by John Steinbeck.

Further Reading: Astro, Richard. *John Steinbeck and Edward F. Ricketts: The Shaping of a Novelist*. New Berlin: University of Minnesota Press, 1973; Benson, Jackson J. *The True Adventures of John Steinbeck, Writer*. New York: Viking, 1984; Fensch, Thomas. *Steinbeck and Covici*. Middlebury, VT: Paul S. Eriksson, 1979; Kazan, Elia. *A Life*. New York: Knopf, 1988; Lisca, Peter. *The Wide World of John Steinbeck*. New York: H. Wolff, 1958; Morsberger, Robert E. "A Note on the Script." Viva Zapata! *The Original Screenplay by John Steinbeck*. New York: Viking, 1975; ———. "Introduction." *Zapata*. New York: Penguin, 1993; Steinbeck, John. *A Life in Letters*. Ed. Elaine Steinbeck and Robert Wallsten. 1975. New York: Penguin, 1989; Womack, John. *Zapata and the Mexican Revolution*. New York: Vintage, 1970.

Marcia D. Yarmus

W

WAGNER, EDITH GILFILLAN (1867–1942). Referred to by Steinbeck as his first writing teacher, Edith Wagner was a local schoolteacher who befriended the author when he was a child, told him stories, and listened to the stories he composed in his youth. A competent journalist herself, she served as a reporter for the *Christian Science Monitor* during the Mexican Revolution, 1910–1912. Mrs. Wagner moved to **Salinas**, Steinbeck's home town, in 1912, along with her four sons, two of whom, **Max** and **Jack**, became fast childhood friends with young John Steinbeck. Both sympathetic to his talent and interested in his creativity, Mrs. Wagner made a singular contribution to the Steinbeck canon when she told him her own story of how she met **Robert Louis Stevenson** when she was a shy twelve year old. Being a compulsive borrower of good material, Steinbeck later remembered the tale and wrote **"How Edith McGillicuddy Met Robert Louis Stevenson"**; however, when he learned that Mrs. Wagner had composed her own version, he politely offered to withdraw his from publication. Although he eventually sold "Edith McGillicuddy" to *Harper's* magazine in August 1941, he sent the royalty he was paid for the short story to Mrs. Wagner. In addition, he acknowledged her strong influence on him by dedicating the short stories in ***The Long Valley*** to her, calling Wagner his "dearest and oldest friend." One might also speculate that Wagner's tales of her early life in Mexico inspired Steinbeck's interest in that ethnic group, motivating his depictions of the paisanos of ***Tortilla Flat*** and his desire to retell the stories of native Mexicans in works like ***The Pearl, The Forgotten Village***, and the historical drama of the life of **Emiliano Zapata** (see ***Viva Zapata!***).

Michael J. Meyer

WAGNER, JACK (1897–1965). Along with his brother, **Max**, Jack Wagner was Steinbeck's friend from childhood. The eldest of the sons of **Edith Wagner**, Wagner grew up with a nonconformist background that made him a perfect fit for **Hollywood**, where he created a career for himself as a screenwriter and as a gag man for the Mack Sennett Studio. Later his life intersected with his boyhood friend once again, when he served as coauthor of the film script for ***The Pearl*** in Mexico in 1947. Wagner also conceived the original story line for the film, ***A Medal for Benny***, but he was unsuccessful in placing it with a studio until Steinbeck agreed to come onboard as a co-writer. After spending a few weekends tinkering with the plot of the movie, Steinbeck and Wagner found that Paramount Studios was interested in the project. *A Medal for Benny* went into production in 1944 and was released in 1945. A mixture of comedy, drama, and natural humor, the film was relatively successful, and Steinbeck and Wagner were nominated for an Oscar for best screenplay in 1946; J. Carroll Naish, who played Benny's father, was nominated as best supporting actor (he won the

Golden Globe award for his portrayal, but not the Oscar).

Michael J. Meyer

WAGNER, MAX (1901–1975). Childhood friend of John Steinbeck. Max and his brother, **Jack**, moved to **Salinas** with their mother, **Edith Wagner**, in 1912. Max and Jack remained lifelong friends with Steinbeck even as they pursued careers in **Hollywood**. While his brother worked behind the scenes as a writer, Max became an actor, working primarily as an extra who seldom spoke on screen. Nonetheless, his career was successful because he was a talented gymnast and a dialectician, skills he taught to other Hollywood actors who had star status. Steinbeck's physical description of the young **Jody Tiflin** in ***The Red Pony*** might have been based on Max Wagner's physique, and Max was known to have ridden Jill, Steinbeck's real-life horse, on occasion. In the 1949 film version of *The Red Pony* that was directed by **Lewis Milestone**, the adult Max appeared as the bartender. Perhaps the most significant influence Max Wagner had on John Steinbeck, however, was that he is rumored to have introduced the author to actress **Gwyndolyn Conger Steinbeck**, who became the second Mrs. John Steinbeck in 1943 (*See also* ***Red Pony, The*** **(film)**.)

Michael J. Meyer

WAINWRIGHT, AGGIE. The eldest daughter of the **Wainwrights**, another migrant couple in *The Grapes of Wrath*, Aggie meets **Al Joad** at the Hooper ranch. Since Al is depicted as sexually promiscuous earlier in the novel, it is surprising that he demonstrates a genuine commitment to Aggie. Some critics have suggested that her name, associated as it is with agriculture, when combined with his mechanical skills offers the only hope for the future for the poor Okies, who will have to combine the ways of the past with the expertise of the future in order to survive. Aggie's commitment to Al also relieves **Rose of Sharon** of the heavy burden of being the only Joad responsible for a new generation. By seeing Aggie's potential as another child bearer, Rose of Sharon is able to abandon her selfishness and her guilt for her stillborn child and to follow more closely **Ma**'s growing example of universal brotherhood. (*See also* **Roasasharn's baby; Joads, The**.)

Michael J. Meyer

WAINWRIGHTS, THE. In ***The Grapes of Wrath***, another migrant couple the **Joads** meet at the Hooper ranch, where they have gone to pick peaches and serve as strike breakers. By the time the Joads are ready to move on to pick cotton, the families have become close friends because of the courtship between **Al** and the oldest Wainwright girl, **Aggie**. The families agree to share transportation and gas, and, as with the **Wilsons** before them, a deeper bond of friendship develops. When the Wainwrights express concern that Aggie may become pregnant and that Al will then desert her, the Joads offer reassurance of Al's commitment. This commitment is later sealed by the couple's engagement, and the families go on to share not only food and work but also the traumatic labor of **Rose of Sharon** and ultimately the death of her child. They also work together to shore up the box cars from the approaching flood. (*See also* **Rosasharn's baby**.)

Michael J. Meyer

WALDER. In ***The Winter of Our Discontent***, he is the INS agent who informs **Ethan Allen Hawley** that the deported **Alfio Marullo** has left his store to Ethan. Walder has driven out to tell Ethan so, as Marullo has put it, "the light won't go out" (a line echoed in the novel's ending), leaving Ethan disconsolate.

WALLACES, THE. In *The Grapes of Wrath*, Timothy Wallace and his son, Wilkie, offer to share their work laying pipe for the electric company with **Tom Joad**. In an episode largely seen as having been developed from the short story **"Breakfast"** in ***The Long Valley***, the two Wallaces, along with an unnamed woman and a child, seem to demonstrate the contentment and peace evident when honest work is done for honest wages and honest employers. Tom is initially invited to share the morning meal with the Wallaces and later is introduced to **Mr. Thomas**, the employer, who agrees to put him on the job, despite the pressure of his fellow owners to cut back on wages and the number of laborers. Later, Tom discovers the Wallaces are both members of the **Central Committee of the Weedpatch Camp**, a council that provides fair self-government. They also explain to Tom the fear the owners have about the organization of labor and about the "red" leaning of those who work toward the unity of the oppressed.

Michael J. Meyer

WALLSTEN, ROBERT. Along with Steinbeck's third wife, **Elaine Scott Steinbeck**, Wallsten edited Steinbeck's letters posthumously, eventually publishing the volume titled *Steinbeck: A Life in Letters*. Wallsten was an actor who knew Elaine Scott when she was a stage manager on Broadway. He later turned to writing as a career and met the author at the premiere of Steinbeck's play ***Burning Bright***. Later he and his wife joined the Steinbecks in Wales, and although he was less intrigued by Steinbeck's Arthurian research than was the author, he was part of a group that examined manuscripts in the surrounding castles. His stay with the Steinbecks at Discove Cottage during this time solidified their friendship and made him a logical choice to help produce the volume of letters.

Michael J. Meyer

WATLING, DANIEL (CAPTAIN). Pious pirate captain in ***Cup of Gold***.

WATSON, TOM. Old man in **Salinas** who, in ***East of Eden***, questions **Caleb Trask** about why he walks the streets at night.

WATT, F(RANK) W(ILLIAM) (1927–). Author of *John Steinbeck* (1962), a pioneering critical summary of John Steinbeck's career. Watt, a scholar, critic, editor, and now professor emeritus at the University of Toronto, examines Steinbeck through paradigms of biology and mythology and describes him as working primarily through the development of particular themes like that of America as Eden. Watt outlines Steinbeck's biography in the first chapter, and while there are some discrepancies—most notably the apocryphal story of Steinbeck traveling west with migrant families—he emphasizes Steinbeck's outlook as a California regionalist working with ordinary speech and with allegory. Watt also explores Steinbeck's use of a **non-teleological** point of view and his concept of the group-man. In chapters 2, 3, and 4, Watt divides Steinbeck's career into phases, providing ample plot synopses and some historical context, starting with Steinbeck's apprentice years from the late 1920s to the mid 1930s and discussing works from ***Cup of Gold*** through ***Tortilla Flat***. Watt credits Steinbeck's "non-teleological discipline" in the latter half of the 1930s, the height of Steinbeck's career, for the success of ***In Dubious Battle***, ***Of Mice and Men***, and ***The Grapes of Wrath***. The fourth chapter includes Steinbeck's postwar work, concluding with ***Travels with Charley in Search of America***. While he agrees with the critical consensus that this was a clear period of artistic decline for Steinbeck, Watt describes it as a more gradual process, and in less damning terms than do many other critics. His fifth chapter contains a review of critical responses to Steinbeck's work up to that time.

Further Reading: Watt, F. W. *John Steinbeck*. New York: Grove Press, 1962.

Scott Simkins

WAYNE, BENJAMIN. Younger brother of **Joseph** in ***To a God Unknown***. An amoral free spirit, womanizer, and alcoholic, he represents the untamable wildness in human beings. He is killed by **Juanito** [little John], the husband of **Alice**, the woman Benjamin has just seduced. It is implied that Benjamin is the father of Alice's son, whom Juanito and Alice name Joseph in honor of their former employer, thus unconsciously carrying on the Wayne family tradition of alternating John and Joseph as generational names. None of the characters seems to understand this relationship or the fact that Benjamin Wayne's son, John (now far away with his uncle), has been effectively replaced by a new son whose name means John in another language.

John Clark Pratt

WAYNE, BURTON. Older brother of **Joseph** in ***To a God Unknown***. He is a Protestant religious zealot who leaves the family homestead because of what he sees as his brother's nature worship. By killing the giant oak tree in which Joseph believes their father's spirit resides, Burton symbolizes the blind conviction that often destroys human continuity in the name of doctrine. What happens to him after that is not known.

WAYNE, ELIZABETH MCGREGGOR. Eighteen-year-old wife of **Joseph** in ***To a God Unknown***. She is an intellectual schoolteacher who loves the literature of the past and leaves her family for Joseph, bears one son, John, then dies from a fall as she attempts to climb up a totem-like rock that symbolizes her husband's belief in the power of Nature. Her death represents the presumed force of accident in human life.

WAYNE, HARRIET. **Burton**'s wife in ***To a God Unknown***.

WAYNE, JENNIE. Wife of **Benjamin** in ***To a God Unknown***. She is a minor character who knows about her husband's philandering but accepts it. After Benjamin's death, she returns to the East.

WAYNE, JOHN. Vermont patriarch of the Wayne family in ***To a God Unknown***. He gives **Joseph** his blessing for his trip west. After John dies, the other sons follow Joseph to the West, and Joseph believes that his father's spirit has joined them, yoked in a large tree that is located on his homestead.

John Clark Pratt

WAYNE, JOSEPH. About thirty-five, the protagonist of ***To a God Unknown***. Although not the oldest son, **Joseph** (whose character has multiple biblical echoes) becomes a patriarch in his own right when he homesteads in 1903 California. He feels "anointed" to care for his land. Even after the death of his wife, **Elizabeth**, and of his youngest brother, **Benjamin**, and even after a drought that decimates his crops and animals, he remains behind when his older brothers leave and sacrifices himself in hopes of producing rain. Single-minded and obsessed, Joseph represents one aspect of the folly of self-deception with his insistence on his responsibilities and place in what he believes is a decipherable universe. Noting the associations with Christ that Steinbeck often applies to Joseph Wayne, **Robert DeMott** invokes the **Jung**ian theory that the conventional Christ symbol "not only fails to include the dark side of things but specifically excludes it in the form of a Luciferian opponent." By believing that Joseph's self-sacrifice does indeed bring the rain and creates "a projected vision of wholeness," DeMott echoes the traditional critical view that shows many of Steinbeck's works ending with a positive affirmation of man's ability to "reconcile the opposition between warring contradictory states, particularly man and nature." **Warren French** comes to the same conclusion in *John Steinbeck's Fiction Revisited* (1994) by stating that "Joseph Wayne does go under, but he saves his land by doing so." **Jackson J. Benson** does not agree, calling the novel "a criticism of closed, man-centered philosophies [and] an attack, generally, on the blindness and self-deception of religion." Brian Railsback, however, in *Parallel Expeditions: Charles Darwin and the Art of John Steinbeck* (1995) most accurately shows Joseph Wayne's final gesture as "useless," demonstrating that "lost in his own preconceptions, Joseph Wayne fails to break through to true understanding." Even though Wayne tries to incorporate all teleologies into his world view, it is what Joseph (who becomes the truly "unknown" God of the title) does *not* understand—the immutable, uncontrollable forces of nature and mankind—that creates his ultimate hubris and causes the tragedy.

Further Reading: Benson, Jackson J. *The True Adventures of John Steinbeck, Writer.* New York: Viking, 1984; DeMott, Robert. "Steinbeck's *To a God Unknown.*" In *A Study Guide to Steinbeck: A Handbook to his Major Works.* Ed. Tetsumaro Hayashi. Metuchen, NJ: Scarecrow Press, 1974; French, Warren. *John Steinbeck's Fiction Revisited.* Boston: Twayne, 1994; Railsback, Brian. *Parallel Expeditions: Charles Darwin and the Art of John Steinbeck.* Moscow: University of Idaho Press, 1995.

John Clark Pratt

WAYNE, MARTHA. Oldest daughter of **Rama** and **Thomas** in ***To a God Unknown***. She correctly predicts rain for the area's first New Year's fiesta, an occurrence that some residents see as the wrath of God.

WAYNE, RAMA. Wife of **Thomas** in ***To a God Unknown***, she dislikes men and expresses a distinct understanding of the difference between good and evil. After **Joseph**'s wife dies, she seduces him in an attempt to make them both "whole" again. She will become the stepmother to Joseph's son, John.

WAYNE, THOMAS. The oldest brother of **Joseph** in ***To a God Unknown***. At times echoing the biblical "doubting" Thomas, he professes no religious beliefs and ends up inheriting the remnants of his brother Joseph's worldly goods. Afraid of any kind of ritual and known as having a "kinship with animals," he represents the natural man, who merely reacts to what happens instead of trying to inflict change.

WAYWARD BUS, THE **(BOOK)** (1947). An allegorical novel, published in 1947 and dedicated to Steinbeck's second wife, **Gwyndolyn Conger Steinbeck**. Originally conceived by Steinbeck as "the Mexican story," and tentatively titled "El Camion Vacilador," *The Wayward Bus* "grew in his mind . . . from a short story, to a short novel, to a very substantial novel" (**Jackson J. Benson**). Steinbeck "wrote the original synopsis in Spanish, thinking that he would publish the short story in Mexico" (Jackson J. Benson). He began the work while living in Cuernavaca, Mexico, restlessly waiting for the film version of ***The Pearl*** to be made. In fact, restlessness and uncertainty, both in terms of his own creative work and in terms of America's postwar future, surrounded the novel's creation. Gwyn was in the midst of a difficult pregnancy and a bout with dysentery, the Steinbecks were supervising the remodeling of two New York City brownstones they had just purchased, and some of Steinbeck's personal items remained in boxes in **Monterey**, California. He wrote for a time in the kitchen of their temporary apartment quarters, then moved to the basement of the brownstone. He experienced a period of despair and the development of marital tensions that would eventually lead to divorce. He wanted to finish the novel quickly, eventually writing 2400 words a day. For the first time, he wrote the draft by speaking into a recorder and, uncharacteristically, finished it ahead of schedule.

Steinbeck had great hopes for the novel, envisioning it as "something like the Don Quixote of Mexico" (Jackson J. Benson). He conceived it to be at first "the most ambitious thing I have ever attempted. . . . It is a cosmic bus. . . . And **Juan Chicoy** . . . is all the god the fathers you ever saw driving a six cylinder broken down, battered world through time and space" (Jackson J. Benson). Steinbeck prefaced the text with a quotation from ***Everyman***, the medieval morality play, concluding with these lines: "That of our lyves and endynge shewes/How transytory we be all daye." He felt the passage would point the way to the novel's meaning, although he was later frustrated by the critics' apparent inability to discern his intent. At one point, Steinbeck decided to shift the novel's setting from Mexico—with the characters riding a tourist bus—to California, probably to allow a parallel with *The Canterbury Tales* pilgrims, coming from all walks of life, to seem more realistic.

Yet, despite his efforts, the novel remained a disappointment. According to Jackson J. Benson, "He needed someone like [first wife] **Carol [Henning Steinbeck]** to tell him, 'this stuff is crap. You had better ditch it or start over.'" According to **Louis Owens**, even Steinbeck recognized its shortcomings, noting in a letter "it was a paste-up job and I should never have let it go out the way it did."

The Wayward Bus was published in February 1947 to mixed reviews. The novel touched off in earnest a debate among critics that would hamper Steinbeck's literary reputation for the rest of his life: does his work after ***The Grapes of Wrath*** measure up to that masterpiece—might it be possible, as Orville Prescott suggested, that Steinbeck "is a one-book author." Other reviewers, including Carlos Baker, wrote supportive and perceptive comments about the book. Probably the reviewer who came closest to Steinbeck's purpose was Harrison Smith, writing in the *Saturday Review* that Steinbeck "is deeply concerned with the second greatest problem of our day, how to preserve the essential simple virtues of human beings from the catastrophe that mechanized civilization is bringing upon all of us." Despite such perceptive comments, Steinbeck was troubled by critics' apparent failure to understand the larger philosophical issues of the book, yet he was pleased by the fact that orders arrived prior to publication for 600,000 copies to the Book of the Month Club and 150,000 copies to the trade. Steinbeck later made the book into a film screenplay with Eugene Solow, which was produced by Charles Brackett.

In terms of plot, the novel is relatively simple. Opening with a historical and physical description of **Rebel Corners**, site of a diner and service station operated by Juan Chicoy and his wife, **Alice**, Steinbeck proceeds to introduce several major characters: Juan, age fifty, Alice, his assistant **Edward "Pimples"/ "Kit" Carson**, and the diner's waitress, **Norma**, all of whom live at the station. Steinbeck describes the bus, **"Sweetheart,"** which will make the journey from Rebel Corners to **San Juan de la Cruz**, and then introduces the passengers who have been stranded at the station overnight as a result of the bus's transmission failure: **Elliott Pritchard**, a businessman, his wife **Bernice**, and their daughter, **Mildred**, who are all at the start of a vacation trip to Mexico; **Ernest Horton,** a traveling salesman hawking novelties; and Van Brunt, an old, local resident traveling to San Juan. As these characters eat breakfast and prepare to board the bus, the narrative shifts to the nearby town of **San Ysidro**, site of the Greyhound bus station, where **Louie**, the driver, and **Edgar**, the ticket clerk, first catch sight of **Camille Oaks**, an exotic dancer who will transfer to "Sweetheart" in Rebel Corners.

As the bus prepares to depart, Norma, long the victim of Alice's tirades, decides that she has had enough and packs to leave. At this point, the novel establishes a pattern that it will sustain to the end: external action, alternating with internal fantasies or musings in each character's mind. Alice Chicoy laments growing older and meditates on her fear of losing Juan to a younger woman. Norma dreams of **Clark Gable** and **Hollywood**; Mildred is attracted to Juan and also imagines an affair with an engineering student she knew; Bernice imagines the stories she will tell when they return from the trip; Pimples fantasizes about holding Camille Oaks in his arms and comforting her; Elliott Pritchard imagines some mild "entertainment" for himself and Ernest Horton with a couple of girls in Hollywood. Here at the novel's midpoint, Steinbeck briefly focuses on the swollen river, described in the iconography of Genesis (serpent and flood). In fact, one of the strongest elements in the novel is its vivid nature description. Steinbeck then quickly turns to Alice, now alone at the diner, first drinking and pampering herself, then reliving her first, emotionally empty sexual encounter. Turning again to the bus, now underway, Steinbeck enters Juan's mind, detailing Juan's memories of his childhood and his fantasy of abandoning his responsibilities and returning to Mexico. Juan recalls rich memories of nature's beauty, the awakening of love, and the solemnity of the Mass as touchstone events of his youth.

Norma dreams of an apartment with Camille, while Pimples brags about his radar correspondence course that will ensure his bright future. After a stop at Breed's General Store and Service Station, Juan asks the passengers to vote on whether to take a detour via the old stage coach road or to turn back, as the bridges seem too imperiled by the raging river to cross. They decide to proceed, and Juan, still wanting to flee to Mexico and freedom, asks the **Virgin of Guadalupe** for some sign affirming his desire. When no sign comes, Juan deliberately mires the bus anyway, and then, ostensibly going for help, walks off down the road.

The bus has been mired beside some caves in a hill bearing a nearly illegible imprecation to **"repent"** at its peak. There is an odor of decay in the air, according to the narrator, presaging the further moral decay of the passengers. Elliot and Bernice Pritchard quarrel, and Mildred leaves, partly in disgust and partly to follow Juan. Moving away from the bus, the narrative follows Mildred to the foreclosed, abandoned **Hawkins farm**. She discovers Juan in the barn and, eventually, they have intercourse. Returning to events at the bus, the narrator recounts discussions between Elliott Pritchard and Ernest Horton regarding the decline of American values, with Pritchard then fantasizing about himself playing the frontiersman and killing a cow to feed the passengers. Shortly thereafter, Pritchard first offers Camille Oaks a job, then forces himself sexually on his wife, who is resting in the cave. Meanwhile, Van Brunt worries about his health, his hereditary propensity toward stroke (which ultimately debilitates him before Juan returns), while Pimples and Norma compare their respective dreams for the future. Pimples fumblingly tries to force himself on Norma, but fails. Juan and Mildred finally return to the bus, and the passengers, working together, finally free it from the ditch and proceed on toward San Juan. The novel ends with Norma's wishing on a star (in the sky this time, rather than on the screen), Camille's refusal to make a solid commitment to Norma regarding their future rooming plans, and Juan's announcement of San Juan's approach, the town marked by "little lights winking with distance, lost and lonely in the night, remote and cold and winking, strung on chains."

Joseph Fontenrose presents a comparatively brief but extremely rich analysis of the novel, focusing on the allegorical function of the bus (the world), the passengers ("journey[ing] toward death"), and the novel's general focus on worldly riches "—money, position, Hollywood glamour, cosmetics." Juan Chicoy appears as "Jesus Christ, who came back to rescue the troubled world" or, seen another way, a "**non-teleological** deity, wedded to the very teleological Alice and carrying a load of teleological passengers." Fontenrose faults the novel for its mismatching of form (allegory) and matter (realistic story), as well as its failure to develop fully the symbolic possibilities of setting or character. **Peter Lisca** views the book as "forming a triptych [with ***Cannery Row*** and ***The Pearl***] which . . . is dedicated to one purpose—an examination of the underlying assumptions of modern civilization." Lisca gives extensive evaluations of the various characters, grouping them as "the damned, those in purgatory, and the saved or elect," and argues that while "none of these characters actually changes during the trip, . . . each . . . undergoes some dark night of the soul in which he achieves a measure of self-knowledge." Lisca argues that on a basic level the book offers a "pitiless examination of . . . [modern] civilization." Yet, ultimately, he suggests that "the allegorical bus . . . does arrive at Saint John of the Cross. The prophet Van Brunt has not really foreseen all. . . . [D]espite the artificial and dishonest Pritchards, the deluded Normas, the cynical Van Brunts, the self-centered Alices and the vulgar Louies, there are also realistic and objective people like Juan Chicoy, without whom the world would founder, who always return to dig it out of the mud." Lisca ultimately judges the book to be a "'well-made' novel from the point of view not only of structure, but of prose style as well."

Warren French presents an alternative grouping of the characters, separating them into the "naturalistic" and the "self-conscious" types (a scheme French suggests Steinbeck uses elsewhere as well). In an apparent battle for the soul of postwar America, these two character types vie for the allegiance of the three young characters, Mildred Pritchard, Norma, and Pimples Carson. Ultimately, because Ernest Horton and Juan Chicoy retain a measure of integrity, French argues, the novel escapes the "naturalistic tragedy" label. It suffers, though, from a tendency to tell rather than to show, particularly with regard to characterization, and contains a structural flaw by drawing the reader's attention away from Chicoy and Horton, the two main characters in French's view. Considering matters of form, narrative point of view, and characterization (among many other concerns), **Howard Levant** suggests that "a severe division between structure and materials is the essential reason for the simple and puzzling impact of *The Wayward Bus*." It is, he argues, "essentially an irresponsible work, an 'open' novel that avoids being either a completed allegory . . . or a thoroughly objective record." Levant argues that this work begins Steinbeck's "irrecoverably steep decline" in reputation among critics, resulting from a "failure [which] is almost entirely artistic." Conversely, Owens argues that "the message that Steinbeck is delivering is simply the most optimistic of all: life will go on; the hills will take in rain and flower and grow, as will certain individuals such as Juan and Mildred," while acknowledging that the book is weakened by the ill-advised allegorical dimension. Readers will also note Steinbeck's descriptions of "excess" in the rain and the raging floodwaters of the river, Norma's fantasies, Alice's fury, Pimples' love of sweets, Elliott Pritchard's sexual violence, and even a fly gorging on spilled wine in the diner—all symptoms of a self-indulgent culture gone soft. Steinbeck juxtaposes this cultural enervation against images of the vanished frontier, seen in the history of the caves, Elliot Pritchard's fantasies, and elsewhere. Overall, the novel is judged to be among Steinbeck's less successful works, perhaps ambitious in conception but flawed in execution.

Further Reading: Busch, Christopher S. "Steinbeck's *The Wayward Bus*: An Affirmation of the Frontier Myth." *Steinbeck Quarterly* 25 (Summer–Fall 1992): 98–108. Ditsky, John. "Work, Blood, and *The Wayward Bus*." In *After* The Grapes of Wrath: *Essays on John Steinbeck in Honor of Tetsumaro Hayashi*." Ed. Donald Coers, Paul D. Ruffin, and Robert J. DeMott. Athens: Ohio University Press, 1994. 136–47; Fontenrose, Joseph. *John Steinbeck: An Introduction and Interpretation*. New York: Barnes and Noble, 1963; French, Warren. *John Steinbeck*. Boston: G. K. Hall, 1975; Levant, Howard. *The Novels of John Steinbeck: A Critical Study*. Columbia: University of Missouri Press, 1974; Lisca, Peter. *The Wide World of John Steinbeck*. New Brunswick, NJ: Rutgers University Press, 1958; McElrath, Joseph R., Jesse S. Crisler, and Susan Shillinglaw, eds. *John Steinbeck, The Contemporary Reviews*. New York: Cambridge, 1996; Owens, Louis. *John Steinbeck's Re-Vision of America*. Athens: University of Georgia Press, 1985; Railsback, Brian. "*The Wayward Bus*: Misogyny or Sexual Selection?" in *After* The Grapes of Wrath: *Essays on John Steinbeck in Honor of Tetsumaro Hayashi*. Ed. Donald Coers, Paul D. Ruffin, and Robert J. DeMott. Athens: Ohio University Press, 1994. 125–35.

Christopher S. Busch

***WAYWARD BUS, THE* (FILM)** (1957). Although planned as a big production for Fox, this black and white 1957 movie was a mediocre work that met with tepid reviews. Posters advertising the *Bus* played off the novelist's name (exclaiming, "The Steinbeck people! The Steinbeck passions! The Steinbeck power!") and sexy leads, with Rick Jason as "Johnny Chicoy" (for **Juan Chicoy**), Joan Collins as **Alice**, and Jayne Mansfield as **Camille Oaks**. According to Jason, both **Anthony Quinn** and **Marlon Brando** considered the part of Chicoy. Victor Vicas, a French documentary filmmaker, waded into his first major **Hollywood** film with *Bus* and created a great deal of tension between himself, the cinematographer (Charles Clarke), the actors, and the crew. Although Steinbeck had worked years before on a screen treatment with Eugene Solow, the screen credit went to Ivan Moffat.

Further Reading: Jason, Rick. *Scrapbooks of My Mind: A Hollywood Autobiography.* New York: Strange New Worlds, 2000.

WEBSTER F. STREET LAY-AWAY PLAN. A martini made with chartreuse instead of vermouth, which is served to **Doc** and **Suzy** by **Sonny Boy** in ***Sweet Thursday.*** The drink's name pays tribute to Steinbeck's long-time friend **Webster "Toby" Street.** When *Sweet Thursday* was adapted into the musical comedy ***Pipe Dream,*** Steinbeck secured his friend's permission to use his name on the stage.

Bruce Ouderkirk

WEEDPATCH. *See* **Arvin Sanitary Camp.**

WELCH. Bartender in **"The Vigilante"** who becomes the sounding board for **Mike** after his participation in the lynching. Although not one of the vigilantes, Welch exhibits much curiosity about the event, even paying Mike extra money for a piece of the denim pants worn by the victim. He is another in the long parade of lonely men in ***The Long Valley.***

Abby H. P. Werlock

WEST, ANTHONY (1914–1987). A reviewer for the *New Yorker,* West wrote a scathing review of ***East of Eden,*** which prompted Steinbeck to muse in a letter to **Carlton "Dook" Sheffield** about the critic's dubious perspective. In this letter, Steinbeck notes the familiar adage that a critic can only offer what a writer should not do—if a critic could offer what to do, then he would be a writer himself. Steinbeck was particularly taken aback by the venom he felt in West's review, leading him to wonder what could possibly have initiated such an animated and resentful response. Steinbeck continued, "I should like to meet him to find out why he hated and feared this book so much." Steinbeck's response demonstrates his ability to both dismiss and fret over the responses made by official representatives of taste.

Further Reading: Steinbeck, John. *Steinbeck: A Life in Letters.* Ed. Elaine Steinbeck and Robert Wallsten. New York: Viking, 1975.

Brian Niro

WEST, ANTHONY (*SWEET THURSDAY*). In ***Sweet Thursday,*** a person to whom **Joe Elegant** begins a letter. The real **Anthony West,** son of Rebecca West and H. G. Wells, was a writer and critic who had published an unfavorable review of ***East of Eden*** in the *New Yorker.* Steinbeck returns fire at West by making him a correspondent of Joe Elegant, the effeminate writer of highbrow, symbol-ridden fiction.

WESTERN BIOLOGICAL. **Doc**'s business, home, and base of operations in ***Cannery Row,*** based on **Edward F. Ricketts'** actual **Pacific Biological Laboratory.** The narrative notes that the lab "sells the lovely animals of the sea, the sponges, tunicates, anemones, the starts and buttlestars, and sun stars, the bivalves, barnacles, the worms and shells, the fabulous and multiform little brothers, the living moving flowers of the sea." In fact, "you can order anything living from Western Biological and sooner or later you will get it." During *Cannery Row*'s first party, the lab is badly damaged by too-enthusiastic revelers, which greatly angers its proprietor, Doc.

WESTERN BIOLOGICAL LABORATORIES. A business operated by **Doc** in ***Sweet Thursday,*** based on **Edward F. Ricketts'** real enterprise, **Pacific Biological Laboratory,** which sells an assortment of animal specimens for use in science classes. Located on **Cannery Row,** it faces the vacant lot that lies between **Lee Chong**'s grocery and the **Bear Flag.** The upper level of Western Biological Laboratory houses Doc's office and living quarters, which are usually in a state of careless disarray. The lower level consists of a storeroom and a laboratory for dissecting, injecting, and embalming specimens. In back, there is a shed on piles over the ocean as well as concrete tanks for storing larger animals. During World War II, Doc had left the facility in charge of **Old Jingleballicks,**

who practically destroyed the place, even selling the expensive museum glass, before abandoning his post. After he returns, Doc restores the building to its former condition, although **Suzy** still calls it a dump. On the day after her dinner date with Doc, she shows her appreciation by giving the place a thorough cleaning.

Bruce Ouderkirk

***WESTERN FLYER*.** The charter fishing boat used by Steinbeck and **Edward F. Ricketts** for their trip to the Sea of Cortez. Described by Steinbeck as "seventy-six feet long with a twenty-five-foot beam; her engine, a hundred and sixty-five horsepower direct reversible Diesel" capable of a speed of "ten knots." Captained by **Tony Berry**, the *Western Flyer* was transformed into a collecting vessel and led Steinbeck to meditate on the "strange identification of man with boat." Her crew included **Tex Travis**, **Sparky Enea**, and **Tiny Colleto**. In addition to John Steinbeck and Ed Ricketts, **Carol Henning Steinbeck** was also present, although she is not mentioned in the narrative of the journey. (*See also* ***Sea of Cortez; The Log from the Sea of Cortez*.**)

Charles Etheridge, Jr.

"WHAT IS THE REAL PARIS?" (1955). Written during Steinbeck's stay in Paris, this article (*Holiday* 18.6, December 1955: 94) discusses different perspectives about the city from the point of view of a real Parisian and from that of a visitor like Steinbeck. Although the length of his visit allows him more insight into the City of Light than a casual tourist might have, Steinbeck acknowledges that critics may feel that he has not seen enough of Paris to write about it, and that he should learn the real Paris. Steinbeck then describes a small bar on the Left Bank and the people and things he has discovered in Paris that are real and unreal simultaneously. Because he is not a true Francophile or fluent in French, Steinbeck observes that he can never know Paris, but that his position as an outsider gives him a perspective that allows him to see a kind of Paris more clearly.

Herbert Behrens and Michael J. Meyer

WHEELER, MR. In ***The Winter of Our Discontent***, he catches **Ethan Allen Hawley** and **Danny Taylor** after they, as youngsters, have underscored what they think is a dirty word in their copy of the *Book of Common Prayer*.

WHITAKER, FRANCIS (1906–1999). A close friend and confidante of John Steinbeck when he was living in **Monterey** during the early 1930s. Whitaker, a sculptor of metal who lived near Steinbeck's Eleventh Street cottage, would often visit during the late afternoons, shortly after Steinbeck finished writing for the day. Whitaker and Steinbeck would spend many evenings together, along with **Edward F. Ricketts** and **Carlton "Dook" Sheffield**, drinking and carrying on discussions. Whitaker was a dedicated socialist, and he would also drag Steinbeck along to meetings at the local socialist club. Whitaker's attempts at converting Steinbeck to socialism, however, remained fruitless at that time—as Steinbeck felt it too idealistic a philosophy to take with any seriousness.

Ted Scholz

WHITE, E(LWYN). B(ROOKS) (1899–1985). American humorist, journalist, and essayist who began the "Talk of the Town" column in the *New Yorker*. Steinbeck owned copies of three of White's books: *Everyday is Saturday* (1934), *Farewell to Model T* (1936), and *One Man's Meat* (1942). In the chapter titled "Americans and the World" of ***America and Americans***, Steinbeck said that essayists like **Nathaniel Benchley** and E. B. White had used the people around them as sources for their work. He added that they did a "new and grand thing." They created an "American literature about Americans."

Further Reading: DeMott, Robert. *Steinbeck's Reading: A Catalogue of Books Owned and Borrowed*. New York: Garland, 1984.

Janet L. Flood

WHITE, T. H. (1906–1964). English novelist and poet, White is primarily known for his works *The Sword in the Stone* (1938) and *The Once and Future King* (1958), both works that developed the Arthurian legend. White's final publication, *The Book of Merlyn* (1977), also was related to the story of **King Arthur**. Steinbeck, also an Arthurian enthusiast (his ***Acts of King Arthur and His Noble Knights***, although unfinished, was edited by his friend **Chase Horton** and published posthumously in 1976), felt that White's work was "marvelously wrought," but that his special talent was putting the story of Arthur in the dialects of the present day, thus updating the legend and moving it into the here and now. That, of course, was also Steinbeck's goal as he conducted research in England in the 1950s and attempted to bring Malory's ***Le Morte d'Arthur*** into a modern and more accessible version that would appeal to both young and old alike.

Michael J. Meyer

"WHITE QUAIL, THE" (1935, 1938). "The White Quail" was originally published in the *North American Review* in March 1935. It was then published as the second story in Steinbeck's collection, ***The Long Valley***, providing thematic continuity with **"The Chrysanthemums,"** the story that precedes it. Likewise set in the Long Valley or **Salinas** Valley, "The White Quail," too, features a married couple, a woman gardener, and an Eden-like setting. **Mary Teller**, like **Elisa Allen**, is talented with flowers, but unlike Elisa, early on in the tale she consciously and overtly compares herself with the garden; indeed, because she knows that "the garden was herself," she can choose only a mate whom the garden would approve. When **Harry Teller**, obviously smitten by Mary's prettiness, agrees to build the house and garden of her dreams, they become engaged and Mary reminds herself to let him kiss her. Soon they marry, Mary having planned the garden exactly as she had always envisioned it. In a burst of gratitude, she offers to let Harry plant some flowers, too, but so thoroughly does Mary identify with the garden that she feels secretly relieved when he declines.

Only a gardener could have written in such detail about Mary's personal metaphor and idyllic retreat. It is obviously Edenic, fashioned to ensure peace and tranquility and to exclude the rough, unpredictable, dark world outside its boundaries. Its rows of fuchsias, "like tropical Christmas trees," ambiguously but repeatedly linked to Christ, form the outer boundary, while within grow cinerarias and live oaks. The garden includes a pool shallow enough so that delicate birds—like Mary—can stand at its edge and drink without fear: "yellow-hammers and wild canaries and red-wing blackbirds, and of course sparrows and linnets, and lots of quail." Mary's devotion to this garden sanctuary comes at a price, though: she has very nearly eschewed marital companionship, and uses her stereotypical "feminine" headaches and locked bedroom doors whenever Harry displeases her. Despite Mary's best efforts, however, intruders penetrate the boundaries of her garden in the shapes of slugs and snails and a gray cat (similar to the serpent, that other intruder in Paradise) that she fears will kill the birds.

When Mary works in the garden, she wears a long dress and sunbonnet that emphasize her femininity. She appears perfectly happy in her outwardly feminine role. As she turns her back on the rough world that appears so very male, she exhibits neither the frustrations nor androgynous appearance of Elisa Allen in "The Chrysanthemums." Critical opinion of Mary runs the gamut from viewing her as a self-absorbed, neurotic, narcissistic, obsessive-compulsive or overly fastidious child-woman, to seeing her as a creative, imaginative, sensitive woman with a strong sense of identity and self-reliance, a woman able to view herself from both without and within. In an intriguing reversal of schoolgirl romanticism, Steinbeck depicts Mary Teller repeatedly writing the words "Mary Teller," only once or twice bothering to write "Mrs. Harry E. Teller." Of course, she unambiguously identifies herself with the white quail in her garden, which appears "like the essence of me, an essence boiled down to utter purity," a secret self that no one can either reach or harm.

Mary's name suggests the biblical Mary, and her chastity—especially as contrasted with Harry's overt, almost clumsy desire for her—suggests a comparison with Louisa Ellis and Joe Daggett in Mary E. Wilkins Freeman's classic story, "A New England Nun." To Mary, Harry is a man who tries to understand her interests, but is incapable of intuition or imagination. Harry is a man who "needed too much light on things that light shriveled." Just as Steinbeck gives Mary some stereotypical qualities, he gives them to Harry as well. Like **Henry Allen** of "The Chrysanthemums," Harry apparently represents the bemused male seeking to understand the mystery of the opposite sex. For example, he cannot fathom Mary's implicit disapproval of his auto loan business during the Depression: to her it sounds "terrible," as if he takes "advantage of people when they [are] down." And although she reassures him that she feels no shame about his profession, she locks her bedroom door that night. Steinbeck realistically depicts Harry's character, especially in the progression of his view of Mary: Harry moves from being so beguiled by Mary's beauty that he barely hears a word she says, to experiencing fear and curiosity about the unfathomable qualities of her mind, to feeling rage and violence when, hysterical and nearly paralyzed with fear, she asks him to poison the gray cat that has crept through her garden. Rather than kill the cat, Harry shoots his air gun and kills the white quail, deliberately carrying her into the rough and chaotic outside world and burying her far away from the garden. On the one hand, the author seems to demonstrate that Mary attempts an impossible task: no one can wall oneself away from the real world. On another level, however, Mary is correct in fearing evil intruding on her Eden: in the end, it is not a grey cat or a serpent, but a man with a gun who symbolically destroys her. The question of the intentional fallacy seems to loom especially large here, particularly for those who turn to biographical information during the period when Steinbeck was writing this story. Again, as with the writing of "The Chrysanthemums," Steinbeck was dealing with his terminally ill mother, and some critics see Mary and Harry as based in part on Steinbeck's mother and father. It was also written after **Carol Henning Steinbeck**'s affair with **Joseph Campbell**. Many critics have noted the shift in focus at the end from Mary to Harry, as if readers should pity the husband who has just metaphorically shot and killed his wife. As the story closes, Harry expresses his own loneliness, but it is unclear whether this is the motive for his action or whether there are other principles involved. The complexity of the characters no doubt accounts for the complexity of interpretations "The White Quail" has elicited. For example, one additional interpretation concerns Steinbeck's equation of the imaginative and artistic process with the need to enclose oneself in a tranquil and beautiful spot, and to try to keep out obtrusions. In this sense, Mary represents Steinbeck himself, with her (and Steinbeck's) disdain for business dealings and ethics, and their difference from outsiders who, like Harry, remain insensitive to nuance and metaphor. Although Steinbeck depicts Mary Teller less sympathetically than he depicts Elisa Allen, he clearly sympathizes with both these women characters. Yet while Elisa merely feels like an old woman at the end of "The Chrysanthemums," Mary drops completely from sight in "The White Quail," as if, like this delicate bird with which she identifies, she herself has been murdered and buried. Like the best of Steinbeck's stories, "The White Quail" raises as many questions as it answers, again demonstrating not only the complexity of marital relationships but also the human need for companionship, and the relation of reality and fallibility to the ideal garden of human perfection.

Further Reading: Busch, Christopher S. "Longing for the Lost Frontier: Steinbeck's Vision of Cultural Decline in 'The White Quail' and 'The Chrysanthemums.'" *Steinbeck Quarterly* 26:3–4 (Summer–Fall, 1993): 81–90; Ditsky, John. "Your Own Mind Coming Out in the Garden: Steinbeck's Elusive Woman." In *John Steinbeck: The Years of Greatness, 1936–1939.* Ed. Tetsumaro Hayashi. Tuscaloosa: University of Alabama Press, 1993. 3–19; Fontenrose, Joseph. *John Steinbeck: An Introduction and an Interpretation.* New York: Holt, Rinehart and Winston, 1963. French, Warren. *John Steinbeck.* 1st. ed. Boston: Twayne, 1961; Hughes, Richard S. *John Steinbeck: A Study of the Short Fiction.* Boston: Twayne, 1989. Meyer, Michael J. "Pure and Corrupt: Agency and Communion in the Edenic Garden of 'The White Quail.'" In *Steinbeck's Short Stories in The Long Valley: Essays in Criticism.* Ed. Tetsumaro Hayashi. Muncie, IN: Steinbeck Research Institute, Ball State University, 1991. 10–17; Owens, Louis. "'The White Quail': Inside the Garden." In *John Steinbeck's Re-Vision of America.* Ed. Louis Owens. Athens: University of Georgia Press, 1985. 113–118; Renner, Stanley. "Sexual Idealism and Violence in 'The White Quail.'" *Steinbeck Quarterly* 17:3–4 (1984): 76–87; Simpson, Arthur L., Jr. "'The White Quail': A Portrait of an Artist." In *A Study Guide to Steinbeck's* The Long Valley. Ed. Tetsumaro Hayashi and Reloy Garcia. Ann Arbor, MI: Pierian, 1976. 11–16.

Abby H. P. Werlock

"WHITE SISTER OF 14TH STREET, THE." A surviving story that was written during Steinbeck's early Stanford University years, "White Sister" is patterned after a Damon Runyan tale, complete with 1920s New York slang and a mismatched romantic interlude between its narrator, Elsie Grough, and a suave Italian named Angelo. Although **Jackson J. Benson** suggests it is not a quality piece of writing, he does indicate that the story reveals Steinbeck's potential and was not a bad effort for a student writer whose primary reason for writing was to get money to eat. **Jay Parini** speculates that the narrator figure was loosely based on Mary Ardath, a Stanford University coed Steinbeck was dating at the time. Following Elsie's pattern in the story, Ardath seems to have revealed her limited cultural awareness to the young Steinbeck, and her insensitivity to him later led to an aborted relationship. "The White Sister" also introduces a repetitive occurrence in the Steinbeck canon, the portrayal of a sensitive young man who is unappreciated by his parents or his girlfriend.

Further Reading: Benson, Jackson J. *The True Adventures of John Steinbeck, Writer.* New York: Viking, 1984; Parini, Jay. *John Steinbeck: A Biography.* New York: Holt, 1995.

Michael J. Meyer

WHITESIDE, ALICIA. In ***The Pastures of Heaven***, as **Richard**'s wife, she is as determined as her husband to produce a dynasty that will carry on a generational heritage. After her difficult first pregnancy, however, the doctor advises the couple not to attempt to have any more children. But Alicia defies the prediction and again becomes pregnant, only to lose the second baby and be confined as an invalid for the rest of her life. Alicia is one of Steinbeck's mystical women who seem to know intuitively. Consequently, she advises her husband to place his faith in the next generation, and she clings to life in order to see her son, **John**, produce the long-awaited dynasty. Only able to survive until John decides to marry **Willa**, she accepts death but still attempts to instill the dynastic dream in the second generation so that the Whiteside heritage will continue.

Michael J. Meyer

WHITESIDE, BILL. In ***The Pastures of Heaven***, the son of **John** and **Willa Whiteside**. He represents the final hope for a dynasty that will carry the rich heritage of patriarch **Richard Whiteside**, one of the first settlers of Las Pasturas. An only child, as was his father before him, Bill does not possess a real interest in land or family; in fact, he ignores and is uninterested in the classical education that his father, John, values. Consequently, John finds his son a disappointment, deploring the fact that Bill prefers a more practical, business orientation to inheriting the family property and presiding over the social affairs of the valley as its leading citizen. John is further hurt when Bill shows no attraction to the local teacher **Molly Morgan**

as a potential wife, and instead announces his intention to move to **Monterey** and marry the middle-class, less-educated **Mae Munroe**. Bill's rejection of the family land is truly the end of the Whiteside hopes for dynasty, and the subsequent destruction of the family's landmark house by fire merely affirms the failure of the clan to maintain the ideals of the past rather than pursue progress and monetary success. With the departure of this third generation of Whitesides, Steinbeck seems to bemoan the fact that the era of farm life is over and the shift of interest to the pastimes of the city has begun.

Michael J. Meyer

WHITESIDE, JOHN. In *The Pastures of Heaven*, the son of **Richard** and **Alicia Whiteside**, he is trained in classical thought and educated at Harvard. When he returns to Las Pasturas, however, he is not as forceful as his father. Although the Whiteside farm remains a focal point for community decision making, Steinbeck describes John's life as "a straight line." He is not as concerned about success, and initially he does not value the land as much as his parents did. It is not until he marries **Willa** and she bears their first child that he begins to have a fierce commitment to the property and to the symbolic Whiteside house and its representation of stability and strong cultural values. However, his son, **Bill**, is uninterested in the classical education John so values and has inherited from his own father. Seeing that Bill rejects his heritage of idealistic and philosophical thought and prefers a more practical, business orientation is a disappointment for John, and he is further hurt when Bill announces his intention to move to **Monterey** and marry **Mae Munroe**. This rejection of the family land leads John to undertake a personal revival of his acreage by burning dead brush, with the help of **Bert Munroe** and his son, **Jimmie**. This decision also causes John's landmark house to be unintentionally set afire, and it is completely destroyed. Ironically, when he observes the structure in flames, John makes no effort to save it, realizing that the next generation has little interest, if any, in the items his generation values, preferring instead to pursue progress and monetary success rather than maintain the ideals of the past.

Michael J. Meyer

WHITESIDE, RICHARD. In *The Pastures of Heaven*, one of the first settlers in Las Pasturas. He came west for gold but realized that the land offered more. Richard hopes the West will remove his family curse of "only" children, and that he will be able to populate the valley with a new dynasty, establishing a race that values classical education and literature. When his wife, **Alicia**, fails to produce more than one child, he invests himself heavily in the education of his son, **John**, as the individual who will create the generational heritage Richard hopes to provide. He immerses his son in his own personal educational ideals and sends him off to Harvard in hopes that he will return to his roots and establish the Whiteside dynasty. Unfortunately, Richard dies before being able to witness either his son's marriage or his attempt to improve the Whiteside property and prestige in Las Pasturas.

Michael J. Meyer

WHITESIDE, WILLA. In *The Pastures of Heaven*, the practical wife of **John Whiteside**, who notes immediately that her child, **Bill**, is unlike his father and grandfather in his interests, and that he is uninterested in the value systems so important to his ancestors. Described early on by Steinbeck as matter of fact and accepting of her son, she is later shown to be critical and upset about her son's decision to leave the family home and move to **Monterey**.

WHITEY (WHIT). A young farm hand on the ranch in *Of Mice and Men*. He calls **Slim**'s attention to a letter in a magazine written by **Bill Tenner**, a former bunkhouse occupant. An overly clean and well-organized person, Whit carefully places the magazine in safekeeping. He also urges **George Milton** to visit **Suzy**'s place, the town brothel.

WHITEY NO. 1. A resident of the **Palace Flophouse** in *Sweet Thursday*. During World War II, he started to work at a war plant in Oakland but broke his leg on the second day. He spent the next three months enjoying himself in the hospital, where he learned how to play rhythm harmonica. His father was a switchman for the Southern Pacific Railroad, and Whitey No. 1 inherited the prestigious railroad hat. On Sweet Thursday, he lets **Mack** wear this status symbol to his conference with the Patron, at which Mack presents the plan to save their home. Once the raffle plan is set in motion, Whitey No. 1 sells tickets in the upscale communities of Pebble Beach, **Carmel**, and the Highlands.

Bruce Ouderkirk

WHITEY NO. 2. One of the idle men living in the **Palace Flophouse** in *Sweet Thursday*. He served in the military during World War II and never forgave the Marine Corps for taking away his most cherished possession, a jar filled with pickled ears. A newcomer to the flophouse, he is apparently the toughest of the men and usually steps forward when the threat of violence is needed. When the raffle tickets are on sale, he throws a rock through the windshield of the first person who refuses to buy one. He offers to beat up **Joe Elegant** when it is discovered that Joe designed the embarrassing costume **Hazel** wears to the masquerade, and near the end of the novel, he stands guard on **Doc**'s porch with a sash weight to discourage anyone but **Suzy** from offering to drive Doc to **La Jolla**. Prior to the masquerade party, it is Whitey No. 2 who teaches **Johnny Carriaga** how to palm cards so that he can pretend to draw Doc's ticket from the lottery bowl. During the party, Whitey No. 2 is seen arm wrestling with **Wide Ida** on the floor.

Whitey No. 2 also figures in a satiric episode about the Red Scare. **Mack** tells Doc that Whitey No. 2 is no longer permitted to caddy at the local country club because he refused to join everyone there in taking a loyalty oath on the eighteenth green. Whitey No. 2 apparently believes he has proven his patriotism by his service in the Marines. He declines to pledge not to destroy the U.S. government because if someday in the future "he gets an idea to burn down the Capitol he don't want no perjury rap to stand in his way." Doc calls Whitey No. 2 a hero for taking this stand based on his ideals.

Having sometimes been labeled, mistakenly, as a Communist sympathizer himself, Steinbeck was deeply disturbed by the Red Scare and the McCarthy hearings. In April 1952, a year before Steinbeck wrote the novel, his good friend **Elia Kazan** had been called to testify before the House Un-American Activities Committee. In a letter written just a week after the publication of *Sweet Thursday*, Steinbeck expressed his concern to his agent that "the effect on young people of the McCarthy hearings is going to be with them all their lives." Later, in 1957, when his friend Arthur Miller refused to testify before Congress, Steinbeck was, according to **Jackson J. Benson**, "the only celebrity to come out publicly in his defense."

Further Reading: Benson, Jackson, J. *The True Adventures of John Steinbeck, Writer.* New York: Viking, 1984; Steinbeck, John. *Steinbeck: A Life in Letters.* Ed. Elaine Steinbeck and Robert Wallsten. New York: Viking, 1975.

Bruce Ouderkirk

WHITMAN, WALT (1819–1892). Considered one of the greatest American poets. His collection of poetry, *Leaves of Grass*, first published in 1855, went through many editions, the last being published in 1892. Influenced by transcendentalism, particularly the philosophy of **Emerson**, Whitman gathered his ideas from many different sources, from the *Divine Comedy* of **Dante** to the works of Greek and Hindu poets. The **Bible** and **Shakespeare** were also very important sources for the ideas Whitman interweaves within his poetry. Whitman's philosophy constantly evolved throughout his life, but in his verse he always sought to reveal man's illimitable freedom, despite being bound up by natural law. Steinbeck first read Whitman in high school, and he particularly enjoyed

"Song of Myself." Throughout his life, Steinbeck always believed Whitman was the greatest American poet, and **Edward F. Ricketts'** admiration for Whitman's poetry also undoubtedly added to Steinbeck's own. Many critics believe that **Tom Joad**'s character in ***The Grapes of Wrath*** draws upon many of the themes Whitman uses in his poetry. Steinbeck's library contained one copy of *Leaves of Grass*.

Further Reading: Benson, Jackson J. *The True Adventures of John Steinbeck, Writer.* New York: Viking, 1984; DeMott, Robert. *Steinbeck's Reading: A Catalogue of Books Owned and Borrowed.* New York: Garland, 1984.

T. Adrian Lewis

WICK, DR. A physician who removes a large kidney stone from **Mrs. Gaston**. Early in ***Sweet Thursday***, this occurrence is ironically cited as one of the portents that major changes are coming to **Monterey** and to **Cannery Row**.

WICKS, ALICE. In ***The Pastures of Heaven***, the Wicks's daughter, Alice, is physically beautiful and universally coveted. Consequently she is closely guarded by her parents, who fear she will be defiled. Considered as a major part of **Edward "Shark" Wicks**'s wealth, Alice is protected from **Jimmie Munroe**, who is suspected of being interested in her. Ironically, Alice is also described as slow and even stupid, and it is clear that her intellect and mental ability do not match her commendable outward features. However, her naïveté is a part of her charm. Later, although her mother lives to regret her decision, Alice is allowed to go to a dance, where she meets and kisses Jimmie Munroe. When her father returns home, rumors of this act infuriate him, and he overreacts by seeking out Jimmie with a shotgun. Although Wicks has no real plans for violence, his actions over his daughter's kiss cause him to lose his fantasy fortune, since he is required to post a safety bond, and it is revealed that he has no extra cash, let alone a considerable fortune.

Michael J. Meyer

WICKS, EDWARD "SHARK." In ***The Pastures of Heaven***, Wicks, nicknamed Shark because of his supposed ability to trade and make money from investments, creates a fantasy world of stock market and financial success that eventually bursts when his other treasure and source of success, his beautiful daughter, **Alice**, is attracted to **Jimmie Munroe**. At all costs, Wicks wants to retain his local reputation for success in both areas, but he eventually loses one when he believes the rumors that his daughter is seeing the Munroe boy, Jimmie, and he decides to punish Jimmie for defiling his treasure. When Wicks seeks revenge on Jimmie, he is arrested and placed under a restrictive bond that causes him to lose his reputed wealth as well. Since his reputation as a wealthy and knowledgeable investor is destroyed, Wicks decides to leave Las Pasturas in disgrace, but Steinbeck records that his losses also create a more positive relationship with his wife, **Katherine**, whom he learns to depend upon and cherish as supporting and encouraging his efforts.

Michael J. Meyer

WICKS, KATHERINE MULLOCK. In ***The Pastures of Heaven***, a strong but common woman who falls into the rut of completing womanly chores after her marriage to **Edward "Shark" Wicks**. After giving birth to a "priceless" daughter, **Alice**, Katherine becomes enamored of the baby's beauty and hovers protectively over her to make sure the child is safe. Later, however, in her husband's absence, Katherine makes the mistake of allowing her daughter to go to a dance and meet **Jimmie Munroe**, an event that will ultimately cause her husband to lose the two elements of his pride: his chaste daughter and his fantasy investments. After these losses, Katherine is able to break free from her former subservient state and serve as a comforter for her despairing husband. Pictured almost as an earth mother, she becomes the source of healing and finds that she possesses knowledge, power, and wisdom that had previously gone ignored and untapped. Eventually, through her inspiration, her husband is able to try again and to renew his belief in himself.

WIFE OF MEMBER OF DELEGATION. In *Viva Zapata!*, she is also known as "woman," called "Chula" by **Eufemio** as she is ordered to follow him. She notes her husband's eyes are upon her and, indeed, within a few moments both he and Eufemio kill each other.

WILDE, DR. Salinas doctor who treats **Faye** and **Kate Albey** in *East of Eden* for what he takes to be botulism caused by home-canned string beans. In actuality, as part of her plot to murder Faye and inherit the brothel, Kate added croton oil, a strong cathartic, to the beans, then swallowed cascara sagrada, a mild laxative, to aggravate her symptoms and to avert suspicion. Kate procures these medicines, plus nux vomica, an emetic containing strychnine, from Dr. Wilde's office, where she goes, ostensibly, to receive further treatment for a kidney ailment. She breaks into the doctor's office and dispensary and copies something from a volume in his bookcase, probably about the substances she has stolen. All of these substances are used by Kate to slowly murder Faye.

Margaret Seligman

WILHELMSON, CARL (1889–1968). Though thirteen years older than Steinbeck, Wilhelmson became a lifelong friend after meeting the author at **Stanford University**, where he enrolled after immigrating from Finland and serving in the Finnish army during World War I. Wilhelmson also associated with the author as a fellow member of the Stanford English Club and later worked with Steinbeck at the **Brigham** estate at Lake Tahoe. Though his writing never attained great popularity, he did manage to publish a novel, *Midsummernight* (1930) and a children's book, *Speed of the Reindeer* (1954).

WILL. The deputy sheriff in **"The Murder"** who, along with the coroner, visits **Jim Moore**'s ranch after Jim has shot and killed the lover of his wife, **Jelka**. Although the coroner reveals the region's lax attitude toward the murder of a wife's lover, Will, through his repeated questions about Jelka's safety, helps underscore the chivalrous attitude toward the erring wife.

Abby H. P. Werlock

WILLIAM. In *Cup of Gold*, a roadmender who has been to London and thinks of the world outside Cardiff as being full of thieves. He runs into **Henry Morgan** as Henry ascends Crag-top to confer with **Merlin**, and he is **Robert Morgan**'s source for information on Merlin and on the outside world.

WILLIAMS, ANNIE LAURIE (1894–1977). As Steinbeck's theater and movie agent, Williams's support was particularly prominent during the theatrical production of *Of Mice and Men*, since she was responsible for getting Steinbeck to adapt his popular short novel into an acceptable script for the stage. Even a novel written in the form of a play cannot be performed as is, and Steinbeck was unfamiliar with the play format. Williams, on the other hand, knew a lot about the theater and was able, with some difficulty, to help Steinbeck recast his story to include appropriate notations for exits, entrances, and set script.

Williams was also a close friend of Steinbeck, as was evident when, in 1943, Williams's husband, Maurice, was reported by the military as missing in action. Steinbeck spent days sorting through what meager information there was available, trying to find out what had happened to him, and he had to argue with the military censors in order to relay the information to her.

Harry Karahalios

WILLIAMS, DR. Massachusetts doctor who examines ten-year-old **Cathy Ames** in *East of Eden*, after her mother discovers her on the floor of the carriage house almost completely naked, with her wrists tied and with two fourteen-year-old boys kneeling beside her. Dr. Williams attends the conference with the boys' families. Despite the boys' protestations of innocence, they are savagely whipped and sent to a correctional facility. Their explanation that Cathy had paid them each a nickel and somehow tied herself up is regarded as ludicrous, despite its veracity. This episode marks the first time Cathy uses sex to manipulate and dupe others.

Margaret Seligman

WILLIAMS, TENNESSEE (1911–1983). American dramatist and author of *A Streetcar Named Desire* (1947) and *The Glass Menagerie* (1944). Steinbeck had ambivalent feelings about Williams's work, at times defending it to critics, as in his letter to Richard Watts, Jr., drama critic for the *New York Post*, where he lauded Williams's *Camino Real* (1953) for its "courage, imagination, and innovation," while vilifying Williams's work in private as indicative of "the neurosis belt of the South" in its preoccupation with "sickness, decay, and abnormality" (**Jackson J. Benson**). Nevertheless, Steinbeck admired his talent and ability, and attended the 1955 opening of Williams's *Cat on a Hot Tin Roof*.

Further Reading: Benson, Jackson J. *The True Adventures of John Steinbeck, Writer.* New York: Viking, 1984; Steinbeck, John. *Steinbeck: A Life in Letters.* Ed. Elaine Steinbeck and Robert Wallsten. (1975). New York: Penguin, 1989.

Gregory Hill, Jr.

WILLIAMSON, NICOL (1936–). British stage and screen actor who played **Lennie Small** opposite **George Segal**'s **George Milton** in a 1968 television version of ***Of Mice and Men*** (1968). He played Hamlet on film and Macbeth on television and had prominent roles in such films as *Robin and Marian* ([as Little John] 1976), *The Seven Percent Solution* ([as Sherlock Holmes] 1976), and *Excalibur* ([as Merlin] 1981).

WILLIE, WEE/FAT, AND STONEWALL JACKSON SMITH. Both are town constables in ***The Winter of Our Discontent***, who exchange news with **Ethan Allen Hawley** during street encounters.

WILSON. In ***East of Eden***, a friend of **Joe Valery**'s in Watsonville, who suggests that Joe talk to **Hal V. Mahler** in Santa Cruz to get information about **Ethel**.

WILSON, EDMUND (1895–1972). Prominent twentieth-century literary critic, Wilson generally was considered a detractor of Steinbeck's artistic merit, primarily because of the author's espousal of naturalism. Steinbeck's celebration of man as a thinking animal drifting in an indifferent universe ran against the humanism that Wilson and other social literary critics of the time advocated. Steinbeck's transgression, according to Wilson, was that he denied the relative importance of man—that he did not see man as the center of the universe but rather as an intelligent animal whose survival depended on the ability to adapt to its surroundings. The undeclared conflict between Steinbeck and Wilson had to do with the question, "What is man?" Wilson understood what Steinbeck was doing in his fiction but could not abide the implications of this philosophy. For Wilson, Steinbeck's biological view of man, his sense of man as part of nature, was a weakness in his conception of character when, in effect, it was really just a difference in philosophy between the two men. Steinbeck's opposition to Wilson, on the other hand, was principled in nature. The essentially elitist position that Wilson and his followers occupied with regard to literature was antithetical to what Steinbeck considered literature to be. Good literature, for Steinbeck, could provoke everyone to self-examination of life and society; it was never intended for the select few, whose sensibilities decided what was good for the people.

Further Reading: Railsback, Brian. *Parallel Expeditions: Charles Darwin and the Art of John Steinbeck.* Moscow: University of Idaho Press, 1995; Wilson, Edmund. *The Boys in the Back Room: Notes on California Novelists.* San Francisco: The Colt Press, 1941; Wilson, Edmund. "John Steinbeck." In *Classics and Commercials: A Literary Chronicle of the Forties.* New York: Farrar, Straus and Giroux, 1950.

Harry Karahalios

WILSON, IVY AND SAIRY. A couple met by the **Joads** on their way to California in ***The Grapes of Wrath***, the Wilsons offer their tent for **Granpa Joad** to rest in when he is overtaken by illness in the middle of the journey. When Granpa succumbs to a stroke, the Wilsons help prepare the body for burial, offer their quilt to wrap the body in, and contribute a page torn from their **Bible** to be used as the last words spoken over a loved one. As a result of this generosity, there is an immediate bonding between the two families, and later **Tom** and **Al Joad** offer to repay their kindnesses by fixing their car. At this point, Sairy expresses her pride in being able to help, identifying this quality as expressing a basic human need and asserting that excessive gratitude is unnecessary. At the end of chapter 13, the two families decide to travel together and work cooperatively to satisfy their basic needs, but they are soon forced to separate because of Sairy's illness. Nonetheless, this connection with the Wilsons is the first example of how the Joads expand their concept of a nuclear family to include an extended family of nonrelated individuals. Before the families part, Sairy is also helpful to the preacher, **Jim Casy**, in formulating the basic concepts of his new creed, rediscovering his supposed lost faith in a higher being, and rekindling his determination to foster a sharing commitment among all humankind.

Michael J. Meyer

WILTS, AL. Deputy sheriff of Soledad in ***Of Mice and Men***. At the end of the novel, **Curley** asks **Whitey (Whit)** to go get Al Wilts while he leads the mob to find **Lennie**.

WINCH, MISS. In *Sweet Thursday*, a **Monterey** resident who usually suffers from a foul disposition before noon but who says good morning to the postman on Sweet Thursday—a bit of proof that it will be a magical day.

WINTER, DOCTOR. In ***The Moon Is Down***, a thoughtful, simple, and benign historian and physician who is a close associate of **Mayor Orden**. A witness to Orden's heroic death at the hands of the invading army, Winter registers Orden's last request, a quotation from Socrates that asks, "Crito, I owe a cock to Asclepius. . . . Will you remember to pay the debt?" Appropriately, Winter responds in the prophetic final lines of the novel, "The debt shall be paid."

Rodney P. Rice

WINTER, ELLA (1898–1980). Along with her husband, **Lincoln Steffens**, the famous muckraker, Winter was an influential supporter of labor organizing and strike efforts in the **Carmel** area. Both husband and wife were also members of leftist organizations such as the John Reed Club and the Young Communist League. Steinbeck's association with them may account for the fact that early on he was depicted as a radical, and that the "red"-leaning viewpoints seemingly advocated in his work were deplored by conservative groups. During the labor disruptions in California, Winter was asked by **Caroline Decker** to provide monetary support for striking workers at the Corcoran Camp. She and Steffens complied, an act that Steinbeck may have used as the basis for a similar offer of support for a radical cause that occurs in ***In Dubious Battle***. Winter and Steinbeck had a brief falling out when she composed a profile of him for the *San Francisco Chronicle* in 1935, a piece Steinbeck felt concentrated too much on his personal life despite the fact they had agreed the journalistic piece would focus on his work. They reconciled, however, and Winter was often part of the group of friends that gathered at **Edward F. Ricketts'** lab for philosophical discussion and serious drinking and partying.

Michael J. Meyer

WINTER OF OUR DISCONTENT, THE (1961). Steinbeck's final finished novel and the last to be published in his lifetime, *The Winter of Our Discontent* is very much a book with an agenda. It is prefaced with a note saying that while its people and places are fictional, readers should search their own hearts and "inspect their own communities," since the book is about "a large part of America today." *The Winter of Our Discontent* is written about New Baytown, a New England town on Long Island—clearly modeled on Sag Harbor, where the Steinbecks had been living and where **Ethan Allen Hawley**, the central character, might be imagined walking the streets as Steinbeck did in real life, knowing the town's folk and events by name and detail.

The town of New Baytown is lovingly described at length at the beginning of the novel's second part, but the lovely old town is quickly also shown as falling into more grasping hands that threaten its traditions in the name of progress and profit. Steinbeck writes here that 1960 was a year in which one could feel the world trembling on the brink of great change—it was the year in which **John Fitzgerald Kennedy** would be elected president, for example, ending the Eisenhower doldrums. Yet things seem poised for further decline in New Baytown. Rather than returning to a promised Camelot existence fostered by a Kennedy presidency, its residents are doomed, victims of their paradoxical pirate/Puritan heritage.

Ethan epitomizes this sense of change, of being on the edge of it. His name suggests how burdened he has been by history—containing as it does the name of a Revolutionary War hero and the once-renowned and historic Hawley family name. The Hawleys have fallen on harder times after Ethan's grandfather was driven out of the maritime business when a likely insurance fire destroyed the *Belle-Adair*, the ship he owned with **Cap'n Baker**, whose profits have made **Banker Baker** a distinguished citizen. In fact, the novel's very structure epitomizes the contrary tugs between traditional values and selfish profiteering in the name of "progress." Ethan's **Great-Aunt Deborah** had always insisted upon the reality of the Easter story of the Crucifixion and Resurrection, and throughout the first part of the novel—which begins on Good Friday and runs to Easter Monday—Ethan is very aware of the liturgical season, which he finds shadowing his own mental state as a meek and suffering Hawley, whose good wife, **Mary**, and children, **Allen** and **Ellen**, seldom cease reminding him that they lack the material possessions their neighbors have.

Many of those neighbors espouse the attitude that eventually corrupts young Allen: "Everybody does it." When Ethan leads Allen to the Hawley library in the attic, Allen finds a volume of early American speeches from which he plagiarizes to write an "I Love America" essay. In Part Two, the essay nearly becomes a public scandal, reminiscent of Charles Van Doren and the rigged quiz shows of the era. While America separates church and state, there is no dissevering religion and politics; *The Winter of Our Discontent* shows how easily people can slide from one set of values to the other without identifying the true nature of the second set.

There is another split in the novel, in this case in point of view. The reader meets Ethan on his way to work at **Alfio Marullo**'s store, where he clerks for low pay. Ethan is seen from without, through third-person narrative, as he confides in animals and canned goods, and then as he encounters customers and townspeople. But Ethan is a thinker—in fact, he can think two lines of thought at once—and soon, first-person introspective narration takes over. But when a more intimate view is needed of the seductress **Margie Young-Hunt**, who is making a play for Ethan and reads his tarot deck fortune as promising future prosperity, the third-person narrative reappears.

On Good Friday night, a restless Ethan prowls the town after leaving a sleeping Mary, encounters his drunken old friend **Danny Taylor**, and—thinking of the past—settles in at his Place, a niche in the old Hawley dock. In the days following, a dinner with Margie and tea with the Hawleys show us a canny, changed Ethan. He will not touch his wife's inheritance from her brother, but he will use the money ostensibly for therapy for Danny, who thereupon signs over to Ethan his family property, a level field that Banker Baker and his cronies covet for a new airport. Predictably, Danny uses the money to drink himself to death, making a Judas of Ethan.

At that point, the religious references largely cease, although Ethan later has a dream in which he, as if a Judas, kisses Danny. Ethan ends the first part of the novel by singing Richard III's famous lines from **Shakespeare**'s play, while Richard II is also quoted and other Shakespearean referents seem to abound (see discussion under Ethan Hawley entry). Steinbeck's novel seems a Shakespearean tragedy, but it stops short of taking Ethan's life, and in other respects Ethan is no Aristotelian tragic hero. Instead, Ethan is a modern tragic hero, stunned by a flash of blinding insight about himself but condemned to go on living.

In addition to Margie's tarot readings, a second element of the occult occurs as Ellen Hawley sleepwalks one night and is found by Ethan caressing a stone talisman from the Hawley case of curios. At the novel's end, it is this talisman that Ethan discovers in his pocket as he prepares for suicide in his Place—having almost robbed a bank, turned in his employer as an illegal alien, sent his friend to a drunken death, and seen his son disgrace himself as a plagiarist. Ethan has Marullo's store, the airport property, and the promise of more. But he thinks he has lost his soul.

The Winter of Our Discontent contains a celebrated passage that sounds somewhat unconvincing coming from the mouth of a preoccupied Ethan. It speaks of 1960 as "a year of change, a year when secret fears come into the open, when discontent stops being dormant and changes gradually to anger"—not just in America, where the coming elections might ensure that "discontent was changing to anger and with the excitement anger brings," but throughout the rest of a restless world. That year, Steinbeck had supported a third candidate for President, **Adlai Stevenson**, but the voters were in more of a mood for dynamic change than he was at first—although Steinbeck eventually became a correspondent of the new first lady. But Steinbeck's assessment of the national and global mood in his novel was on target, and it is hard to read this novel even after so long without reflecting that its seemingly popular trappings only thinly masked enormously more serious concerns.

Those concerns were not necessarily on the minds of Steinbeck's initial reviewers or, for that matter, the many buyers eager to own the latest novel by John Steinbeck—not knowing, of course, that it would also prove to be his last. Thus, as is often the case with the more popular arts, the book sold well enough, irrespective of critical responses. Those responses were mixed, but to some degree their range and tone could have been anticipated. As usual, there were traditional enemies who would not have liked anything the man had written; again, there were those who had lost patience with Steinbeck's stylistic experimentation of the 1940s and 1950s and bewailed his failure to write his early novels all over again. The book's political stance seemed difficult for many to gauge: while Steinbeck clearly means Ethan Allen Hawley to stand for New England values he felt were being jeopardized by the economic freebooting of the postwar years, Hawley's individualism must have struck many as a desertion of Steinbeck's earlier apparent commitment to the notion of a group consciousness, for Hawley's ideas of moral responsibility come down to one person's moral decisions. On the other hand, Hawley clearly views rampant capitalism as sinister in its ability to darken even the noblest conscience. Few reviewers seemed able to come to grips with the novel's conclusion, where a shamed Hawley refuses a noble Roman tragic death—very likely because, Steinbeck might have told them, Hawley does not regard himself as particularly noble, Roman, or tragic in stature.

The politics of the years since the publication of *The Winter of Our Discontent* have provided ample examples of persons in high places who have faced Ethan Allen Hawley's dilemma, and who have vacillated and rationalized in even less heroic terms. Yet it is not all that surprising that the book's earliest reviewers should have largely ignored this aspect of the book's concerns, or considered them secondary, nor that long-standing Steinbeck literary critics should have fit this unusual volume into the patterns of decline they had long since identified in his work—whatever the cause they discerned. Few such critics have taken the book for what it, de facto, is—the writer's final fictional statement about the world he knew. Thus the critical articles on *The Winter of Our Discontent* have been relatively few and far between—although, of course, there is a ready explanation in the patent fact that it was Steinbeck's last—and fewer still have tried to take this volume on its own terms.

Rather, seduced perhaps by the rich overlay of referents in what must be admitted at once is an extremely busy novel, the best writing on *The Winter of Our Discontent* has pursued one or more of its subtexts: the religious, the occult, the civic, and the psychosexual. For instance, there is the matter of the characterization of Ethan's wife, Mary. Is she simply the "little woman" of the 1950s, and is her love play with Ethan merely domestically charming, or is she the sort of arguably passive-aggressive wife that Arthur Miller's Linda Loman in *Death of a Salesman* can be said to be? If so, or not, is Steinbeck's portrayal of her dismissive, or sexist? Or is she simply a kind of wife he had encountered during the process of fictional creation, if seldom in his own contacts?

Few things are certain about *The Winter of Our Discontent*, except that it is far from getting the attention it demands, and very likely merits. There is so much about it that is testamentary—and this is not simply hindsight speaking—that Steinbeck's final novel will have to find newer readers—a newer sort of readers—before it settles into a final critical resting place. Luckily, such finality is unlikely.

Further Reading: Bedford, Richard C. "The Genesis and Consolation of Our Discontent." *Criticism* 14 (1972): 277–94; Gerstenberger, Donna. "Steinbeck's American Wasteland." *Modern Fiction Studies* 1.1 (Winter 1965): 59–65; McCarthy, Kevin M. "Witchcraft and Superstition in *The Winter of Our Discontent*." *New York Folklore Quarterly* 30 (1974): 197–211; Lieber, Todd. "Talismanic Patterns in the Novels of John Steinbeck." *American Literature* 44 (1972): 262–275; MacKendrick, Louis K. "The Popular Art of Discontent: Steinbeck's Masterful Winter." *Steinbeck Quarterly* 12 (1979): 99–107; Meyer, Michael. "Chapter 10: *The Winter of Our Discontent*" in *A New Study Guide to Steinbeck's Major Works with Critical Explication.* Ed. Tetsumaro Hayashi. Lanham, MD: Scarecrow, 1993 240-273; Stone, Donal. "Steinbeck, Jung, and *The Winter of Our Discontent.*" *Steinbeck Quarterly* 11 (1978): 87–96.

John Ditsky

WISTERIA. In ***Sweet Thursday***, a prostitute at **the Bear Flag**, who is unavailable to help service the members of **the Rattlesnake Club** of **Salinas**, since she is spending sixty days in jail for a fight with another prostitute.

"WIZARD, THE." Steinbeck's interest in the theater can be traced back as far as 1932, when he attempted a "practice play" titled "The Wizard." Discussing his interest in wizardry and magic, Steinbeck noted that "my theme old as the shriveling world and as live—magic." The manuscript was written in a student composition book, and Steinbeck's first wife, **Carol,** rescued it from the trash, where Steinbeck had discarded it. The work was never published.

John Hooper

"WIZARD OF MAINE, THE." An unpublished work conceived during the summer of 1944 by Steinbeck and composer and lyricist **Frank Loesser** as a vehicle for their friend Fred Allen. Divided into six sections, it tells the story of a traveling elixir salesman and magician who has set out across the country in hopes of being discovered so that he can perform his tricks professionally on stage. While in Mexico in 1945, working with Jack Wagner on the film version of ***The Pearl***, the two men worked on "The Wizard of Maine," but Steinbeck had his doubts about the project. In mid-summer 1945, Steinbeck completed a 20,000-word treatment of the musical and sent it to his agent, **Annie Laurie Williams**. Steinbeck eventually engaged *Life* magazine entertainment editor George Frazier to write a script for the musical. Frazier quit his job in order to devote time to the work, but received little assistance from Steinbeck and was ultimately unable to produce a script. Eventually, the project and the relationship between Frazier and Steinbeck disintegrated. The unpublished manuscript is now held in the archives of the National Steinbeck Center in **Salinas**, California.

John Hooper

WOMAN. Based on a real woman, the nameless stranger appears unexpectedly in **Dr. Phillips**'s lab to play a major role in **"The Snake."** Although Steinbeck's friends disagree on her appearance and demeanor, Steinbeck unquestionably invented his own version of the temptress, investing her with meanings that were nonexistent in the real woman who walked into **Edward F. Ricketts'** lab. An archetype in both **Jung**ian and **Freud**ian traditions, the dark, mysterious woman exhibits puzzling behavior and a disturbingly sexual interest in the rattlesnake, to which she bears a startling resemblance. She has been seen as a symbol of the unconsciousness, of the Freudian phallus, of androgyny, of base instinct. Additionally, she provides a view of the shallow inadequacy of the life focused on science alone.

Abby H. P. Werlock

"WOMEN AND CHILDREN IN THE U.S.S.R." An article by Steinbeck that was published in the February 1948 issue of *the Ladies Home Journal*. Appearing on pages 44–59, the essay is illustrated with photographs by the famed **Robert Capa**, the last of which was used for the dust jacket illustration for Steinbeck's ***A Russian Journal***. Steinbeck's text and Capa's photographs extend beyond the title's implication to a variety of other USSR topics, and the piece also contains an interesting introduction to the article with a photo of both Steinbeck and Capa on page 3.

Eric Skipper

WOMEN'S COMMITTEE AT THE WEEDPATCH CAMP, THE. This group of women provides an example of how the government camp empowers the migrants with worthwhile tasks. The committee welcomes and educates the new arrivals at the camp, many of whom are unaccustomed to the workings of a democratically run organization or to the modern facilities provided. The committee continually emphasizes the responsibility of each individual toward the group, and reminds those at the camp that the help provided is not charity, but rather requires work and commitment by each resident in order to enjoy fully the privileges offered. (*See also* **Jessie Bullitt; Ella Summers; Annie Littlefield.**)

WONG, MRS. ALFRED. One of the revelers at the masquerade party for **Doc** in ***Sweet Thursday***. Mischievous **Johnny Carriaga** shoots her between the shoulders with a rubber-tipped arrow.

WORKING DAYS: THE JOURNALS OF "THE GRAPES OF WRATH." *See* ***The Grapes of Wrath.***

"WRATH OF JOHN STEINBECK, THE." Written by Steinbeck's **Stanford University** friend, Robert Bennett, this pamphlet was published in 1939 and provided an up-close picture of the author. Although mostly written in a comic tone, "Wrath" does reveal some serious information about Steinbeck, including his views on socialism. Although often criticized for leftist leanings, Steinbeck's skepticism is demonstrated in this essay, particularly through his belief that socialism will not be successful long because it is governed by greed and narrowness of thought. "Wrath" also reveals Steinbeck's espousal of social justice, his indignant criticism of the prejudicial treatment suffered by the lower class, and his willingness to bluntly confront insensitivity to what he considered unwarranted attacks on the poor and helpless. The central incident in the piece involves Steinbeck's rebuttal of a Methodist minister of an Oakland church, who placed an individual's spiritual hunger above her physical needs. Steinbeck's retort could be paraphrased as "feed the body and the soul will take care of itself," illustrating his willingness to stand up and be heard even under difficult circumstances.

WRIGHT, HAROLD BELL (1872–1944). Popular author of eighteen major works published between 1903 and 1942, Wright lived in the Imperial Valley area of Southern California's desert region from 1907 until 1915. Seven of Wright's novels were made into full-length feature films. Steinbeck owned a copy of the very popular romance novel, *The Winning of Barbara Worth* (1911). In ***The Grapes of Wrath***, **Tom Joad** refers to this book as one that made it harder for him to keep Scripture straight, and in ***East of Eden***, the character **Joe Valery** has read it as well, to no great effect.

Further Reading: DeMott, Robert. *Steinbeck's Reading: A Catalogue of Books Owned and Borrowed*. New York: Garland, 1984.

WRIGHT, RICHARD (1908–1960). Prominent African American writer whose work includes the classic novel *Native Son* (1940) and the remarkable autobiography, *Black Boy* (1945). Like Steinbeck, Wright explored but abandoned formal leftist politics and he was considered to be a writer in decline after the publication of his two most successful works. Steinbeck owned *Native Son* and *Uncle Tom's Cabin: Four Novellas* (1938). When they met in Mexico in 1940, while Steinbeck was at work on ***The Forgotten Village***, it seems they would have much in common as writers in top form with recent bestselling novels. However, at first Steinbeck criticized Wright for seeing things within the strictures of race relations, causing tension between the two. Soon Steinbeck relented in his view, the two became friends, and Wright visited Steinbeck and **Herbert Kline** as they worked on the *Village* film project.

Further Reading: DeMott, Robert. *Steinbeck's Reading: A Catalogue of Books Owned and Borrowed*. New York: Garland, 1984; Kline, Herbert. "On John Steinbeck." *Steinbeck Quarterly* 4 (1971): 84.

Y

"YANK IN EUROPE, THE" (1956). In a brief piece that appeared in *Holiday* (19.1, January 1956: 24–25), Steinbeck discussed Americans abroad and the feelings of some individuals that they are scorned and made fun of while traveling on the continent. From his perspective of "belonging" in France, Steinbeck takes issues with the generalities made by tourists, feeling that for the most part they are based on the exceptions rather than the rule. He then defends the American dream of seeing the world, stating, "I believe that tourists are very valuable to the modern world. It is very difficult to hate people you know."

Herbert Behrens and Michael J. Meyer

YOUNG-HUNT, MARGIE. She is the temptress in ***The Winter of Our Discontent***. Widowed and divorced, she is well aware that her chances of establishing a lucrative and secure final relationship are slipping away, and although she has encounters with such men as the traveling salesman **Biggers**, she makes a strong play for **Ethan Allen Hawley**, while also posing as a friend to his wife, **Mary**. Descended from an ancestor exiled to Alaska from Russia for supposed witchcraft, Margie tells fortunes; her reading of the tarot deck assures Mary that Ethan will be rich, while Margie's ability to turn on her sexiness only for males is her major ploy in her quest for security. At a dinner with the Hawleys, she again does a tarot reading and throws out the hanged man card at the end. Although she assures Ethan that the card can mean "salvation," she is troubled by what she sees, including the vision of a snake—Ethan—changing its skin. Her last encounter with Ethan suggests that she understands the changes in Ethan, but expects more distancing to occur between them. "'I don't trust you,'" she says to Ethan. "'You might break the rules. You might turn honest. I tell you I'm scared. . . . I'm betting ten generations of Hawleys are going to kick your ass around the block, and when they leave off, you'll have your own wet rope and salt to rub in the wounds.'" In other word, Ethan's ethical background will eventually resurface, putting any possible relationship with Margie in jeopardy.

YOUNG LIEUTENANT, THE. In ***Cup of Gold***, he suggests to Governor **Don Juan Perez de Guzman** of Panama that when **Henry Morgan**'s pirates attack the city, they should be met by a stampede of wild bulls. The plan backfires disastrously when the pirates fire on the bulls and turn the stampede around onto the Spanish army defending the city.

Z

ZANUCK, DARRYL F. (1902–1979). After a brilliant career at Warner Brothers, where he produced such classics as *Little Caesar* (1931), *Public Enemy* (1931), and *I Am a Fugitive from a Chain Gang* (1932), Zanuck became head of production for 20th Century Fox in 1934, where he produced the film version of ***The Grapes of Wrath*** (1940) and Steinbeck's ***Viva Zapata!*** (1952). Fox also made the films of ***The Moon Is Down*** (1943); ***Lifeboat*** (1944), for which Steinbeck wrote the original screen treatment; and ***O. Henry's Full House*** (1952), in which Steinbeck on camera introduced five stories, but these were not films that Zanuck personally produced. Zanuck did produce most of the distinguished films at the studio, including *Drums along the Mohawk* (1939), *All about Eve* (1950), and such socially conscious pictures as *How Green Was My Valley* (1941), *Gentleman's Agreement* (1947), *The Snake Pit* (1948), and *Pinky* (1949). Zanuck wrote **Ma Joad**'s last speech in the screenplay of *The Grapes of Wrath* to end the film on an upbeat note. "I never have been satisfied with the last scene, when Joad leaves. I have the feeling I'd like to hear from the old man and lady," he told Steinbeck, who replied, "I don't know about that." However, Zanuck respected Steinbeck's novel and worked in secrecy for eight months to produce the film, ignoring threats of a boycott by California agricultural organizations and of a publicity boycott by hostile newspapers. When he saw the film, Steinbeck said, "Zanuck has more than kept his word. He has a hard, straight picture in which the actors are submerged so completely that it looks and feels like a documentary film and certainly it has a hard, truthful ring" (**Jackson J. Benson**). When Steinbeck stalled on drafts of *Viva Zapata!*, Zanuck kept prodding him until he completed a filmable script, for which Steinbeck won an Oscar nomination for best screenplay.

Further Reading: Benson, Jackson J. *The True Adventures of John Steinbeck, Writer.* New York: Viking, 1984; Gussow, Mel. *Don't Say Yes Until I Finish Talking: A Biography of Darryl F. Zanuck.* Garden City, NY: Doubleday, 1971.

ZAPATA, EMILIANO (1879–1919). Leader of the peasant revolt in Mexico from 1910 to 1919, he is fictionalized in Steinbeck's screenplay and screen treatment for ***Viva Zapata!***. Critic and historian John Womack, Jr. observes that although "the movie distorts certain events and characters, some grossly, . . . it quickly and vividly develops a portrayal of Zapata, the villagers, and the nature of their relations and movement."

Further Reading: Womack, John Jr. *Zapata and the Mexican Revolution.* New York: Vintage, 1969.

ZAPATA, EUFEMIO (1873–1917). Older brother of **Emiliano Zapata** who is fictionalized in ***Viva Zapata!***. He is portrayed as a good fighter for land reform but also as a corrupt man, being a womanizer, a drunk, and a man with no compunctions about taking land for himself. The actor **Anthony Quinn** received the Academy Award for Best Supporting Actor for his role as Eufemio.

ZAPATISTA(S). In ***Viva Zapata!***, the generic name given to guerrilla fighter(s) belonging to the Zapata movement.

ZEIGLER (CAPTAIN). Pirate captain under **Henry Morgan**'s command in the campaign against Panama in ***Cup of Gold***. His nickname is "Tavern-keeper of the Sea," because after every victory he would keep his men on board and sell them rum until they ran out of their share of the booty.

ZORN, DR. The doctor in ***Burning Bright*** who is pressed by **Joe Saul** to reveal that Saul is in fact impotent. Enraged by this knowledge, Saul understands that **the Child** his wife, **Mordeen**, carries is not his own.

Appendix

Steinbeck Archives: Universities, Centers, and Libraries

Robert B. Harmon

There are several rich archival collections available to researchers containing Steinbeck's correspondence, manuscripts, personal documents, photographs, home movies, video recordings, memorabilia, and other miscellany.

CALIFORNIA

Within the state of California are several excellent archival collections related to the life and works of John Steinbeck.

Stanford University

Department of Special Collections
Cecil H. Green Library
Stanford, California 94305-6004
(415) 725-1053
Web Site: http://www-sul.stanford.edu/depts/hasrg/ablit/amerlit/steinbeck.html

Housed in the Department of Special Collections, Green Library, the Steinbeck archives at **Stanford University**, where Steinbeck attended classes in the early 1920s, is a collection of materials related to his life and works. Among other things it includes many letters by him to others and letters to him from friends and associates. The Stanford archive also has manuscript and typescript materials to such works as ***Cannery Row*** and many photographs. A *Catalogue of the John Steinbeck Collection at Stanford University* (Stanford, CA: Stanford University Libraries, 1980), compiled by Susan Riggs, lists and describes this archive. An update is "Stanford's Steinbeck Collection—Recent Acquisitions," by Margaret J. Kimball in *The Steinbeck Newsletter*, 6.2 (Summer 1993), 10-11.

San Jose State University

Steinbeck Research Center
Wahlquist Library North 316
San Jose, California 95192-0202
(408) 924-4558
Web site: http://www.steinbeck.sjsu.edu/home/index.jsp

Another important collection is housed in **The Martha Healey Cox Center** at San Jose State University. This center is a repository for all the author's published works as well as unpublished material, including manuscripts, galley proofs, typescripts, movie and television scripts, and correspondence. There is also an extensive collection of secondary materials, files of articles, reviews, commentaries, dissertations, oral histories, photographs, and memorabilia. Robert H. Woodward's "The Steinbeck Research Center at San Jose State University: A Descriptive Catalogue," published in *San Jose Studies* 11.1 (Winter 1985), 1-128, lists and describes this collection in some detail. Two articles that also discuss this collection are "The Steinbeck Collection in the Steinbeck Research Center, San Jose State University," *Steinbeck Quarterly* 11.3-4 (Summer-Fall 1978), 9 & 99, by Martha Heasley Cox and "John Steinbeck Research Center, San Jose State University," in *Dictionary of Literary Biography Yearbook: 1985* (Detroit, MI: Gale Research Company, 1986), 159-161, by John R. Douglas.

The National Steinbeck Center

One Main Street
Salinas, California 93901
(831) 796-3833; (831) 796-3828 fax
Web site: http://www.steinbeck.org/MainFrame.html

Yet another fine California archive was once housed in the Salinas Public Library in Salinas, California, but it has since been moved to the **National Steinbeck Center**, which opened in 1998 in Steinbeck's home town. This collection includes first editions, autographed and inscribed copies of Steinbeck's works, manuscripts, photographs, an extensive collection of oral histories on audiotapes by those who knew Steinbeck, his family, and friends, as well as written, critical works, periodical materials, and memorabilia. The center also houses **Rocinante**, the camper/truck used by Steinbeck in his cross-country journey across America, a trek that resulted in the publication of ***Travels with Charley***, Steinbeck's assessment of his native country after a first-hand observation of its citizens. Also of interest to researchers is the fact that the Center's holdings include holograph copies of ***The Pearl*** and **"The Wizard of Maine."** A catalog of this collection compiled by John Gross and Lee Richard Hayman, *John Steinbeck: A Guide to the Collection of the Salinas Public Library* (Salinas, CA: Salinas Public Library, 1979) lists and describes these materials and also includes photographs. More recent additions to this collection are covered by Mary Jean S. Gamble in her article "Recent Acquisition of the Steinbeck Archives of the Salinas Public Library," in *The Steinbeck Newsletter*, 5.1–2 (Spring 1992), 8–9.

University of California, Berkeley
Bancroft Library
Manuscript Division
Berkeley, California 94720-6000
Web site: http://bancroft.berkeley.edu/collections/

The Manuscripts Division of the Bancroft Library at the University of California, Berkeley, has a significant Steinbeck collection. There are many first and special editions of his works, several manuscripts of his publications in various stages of production, and a collection of photographs of Steinbeck and his family. There are also close to 300 original letters represented in seven manuscript collections. The letters include a large collection written to **Gwyndolyn Conger Steinbeck**, the author's second wife, and letters to **George Sumner Albee, Edward F. Ricketts**, and others. This collection is enumerated by Barbara M. Kennedy in "John Ernst Steinbeck: An Annotated Bibliography of His Personal Correspondence in the Manuscript Collections of the Bancroft Library."

TEXAS

University of Texas at Austin
Harry Ransom Humanities Research Center
Austin, Texas 78713
(512) 471-9119
Web site: http://www.hrc.utexas.edu

The Harry Ransom Humanities Research Center at the University of Texas, Austin, houses Steinbeck manuscript material for ninety separately titled works, the typescript journal of ***The Grapes of Wrath***, over 400 letters (many to his editor **Pascal Covici**), and photographs of Steinbeck's friends and family. Archival items in this collection are enumerated by John R. Payne in "John Steinbeck in the Humanities Research Center, The University of Texas at Austin," *Steinbeck Quarterly* 11.3–4 (Summer-Fall 1978), 100–102. In addition, items listed in the *Bibliographical Catalogue of the Adrian H. Goldstone Collection* (Austin, TX: Humanities Research Center, University of Texas at Austin, 1974), are included in this collection, along with many photographs.

INDIANA

Ball State University
Alexander M. Bracken Library
Special Collections
Muncie, Indiana 47306-1099
(317) 285-5277
Web site: http://www.bsu.edu/library/

Preserved in the Bracken Library at Ball State University in Muncie, Indiana, is a collection of Steinbeck letters and manuscripts, Steinbeck first editions, critical works, and other related materials. A publication to this archive was compiled by Tetsumaro Hayashi and Donald L. Siefker: *The Special Steinbeck Collection of the Ball State University Library: A Bibliographical Handbook* (Muncie, IN: The John Steinbeck Society of America, English Dept., Ball State University, 1972). Nancy K. Turner and Donald L. Siefker provide an update in their article "The John Steinbeck Collection in the Alexander M. Bracken Library, Ball State University, 1980-1990: A Decade in Review," in *The Steinbeck Newsletter*, 5.1–2 (Spring 1992), 9.

MASSACHUSETTS

Houghton Library
Harvard University
Cambridge, Massachusetts 02138
(617) 495-2441
Web site: http://hcl.harvard.edu/libraries/houghton

The small Steinbeck collection at the Houghton Library contains some letters and, most important, four early short stories: "The Nail," "The Days of Long Marsh," East Third Street," and "The Nymph and Isobel." Scholars have in the past debated the authenticity of these stories, but the consensus now is that they are genuine.

NEW JERSEY

Princeton University Library

Rare Books and Special Collections
John Steinbeck: The Collection of Preston Beyer
One Washington Road
Princeton, New Jersey 08544
(609) 258-3184
Web site: http://libweb2.princeton.edu/rbsc2/aids/steinbeck/s-intro.html

The extensive collection of Steinbeck first editions, literary criticism, memorabilia, and artifacts assembled by Steinbeck enthusiast Preston Beyer was donated to the Princeton University Library in 1994 by his daughters. The collection is divided into three sections:

Section I: Books and pamphlets published by Steinbeck.

Section II: Other John Steinbeck material (including biographies, literary criticism, university theses and dissertations, bibliographies, and reference guides).

Section III: Manuscripts and correspondence. Included in the third section are Beyer's correspondence with Steinbeck himself, with his widow **Elaine** and his ex-wife **Gwyndolyn Conger Steinbeck**, and with close friend **Carlton "Dook" Sheffield**. Beyer's letters to Steinbeck scholar **Robert DeMott, John Ditsky, Warren French, Roy Simmonds**, and Tetsumaro Hayashi are also catalogued, as is a signed copy of the author's **Nobel Acceptance Speech** provided by **The Viking Press.** Also housed at Princeton are Beyer's correspondence with libraries, with other collectors, and with early biographer Nelson Valjean and *Life in Letters* editor **Robert Wallsten**.

In his introduction, Beyer explains his early interest in collecting, an activity that began in 1934 after his graduation from Cornell University. Beyer's early association with book dealer **Ben Abramson** (Argus Book Shop) and Marge Cohn (New York House of Books) fostered his interest in Steinbeckiana, especially in acquiring first editions. Initially concentrating on American publications, Beyer later decided to acquire foreign translations of the author's novels and short stories as well as his nonfiction and journalistic output. Later, he added ephemera to his growing collection, deciding that it gave more personality to the collection and enabled researchers to see many sides of Steinbeck. Thus old movie posters, play programs, advertising material, publishers' blurbs, photos, records, and videos are kept side by side with literary criticism and the author's own prodigious literary output. *Further reading*: Princeton University Library. *John Steinbeck: The Collection of Preston Beyer: An Annotated Catalogue*. Princeton: Princeton University Library, 1998.

NEW YORK

Columbia University

Butler Library
Rare Book & Manuscript Library
New York, NY 10027
(212) 854-2231
Web site: http://www.columbia.edu/cu/lweb/indiv/rbml/index.html

The Rare Book and Manuscripts Division of the Butler Library at Columbia University in New York City houses a large Steinbeck collection, most prominently the papers and letters of **Annie Laurie Williams**, one of Steinbeck's literary agents. Bernard R. Crystal describes this collection in "John Steinbeck Letters and Manuscripts in the Columbia University Library, Steinbeck Archive: Part II," in *The Steinbeck Newsletter*, 6.1 (Winter 1993), 1417.

Pierpont Morgan Library

29 East 36th Street
New York, NY 10016
(212) 685-0008
Web site: http://www.morganlibrary.org/

The Pierpont Morgan Library in New York City, once the private domain of the financier-collector Pierpont Morgan and now a public research library, houses the autographed ***Grapes of Wrath*** journal, the working journals for ***The Wayward Bus*** and ***East of Eden***, manuscripts for ***The Short Reign of Pippin IV, Travels with Charley***, and ***The Winter of Our Discontent***, various letters such as those to his British literary agent Graham Watson, and other manuscript materials. This archive is discussed in some detail by Robert Parks in his article "John Steinbeck in the Pierpont Morgan Library," *The Steinbeck Newsletter*, 8.1–2 (Winter/Spring 1995), 19-21.

WASHINGTON, D.C., AND VIRGINIA

There are two smaller archival collections of importance. Housed in the Library of Congress are the typescript manuscripts of ***The Grapes of***

Wrath (1939) and ***The Sea of Cortez*** (1941): The Library of Congress, Manuscript Division, Washington, D.C. 20541; (202) 707-5383; http://www.loc.gov/rr/mss/.

Located in the Special Collections/Manuscripts Department of the Alderman Library at the University of Virginia is the autographed manuscript of ***The Grapes of Wrath*** (1939): Alderman Library, Special Collections/ Manuscripts, University of Virginia, Charlottesville, Virginia 22903-2498; (804) 924-3026, http://www.lib.virginia.edu/alderman/.

Bibliography

PRIMARY WORKS

Fiction

Cup of Gold. New York: Robert McBride, 1929.

The Pastures of Heaven. New York: Brewer, Warren & Putnam, 1932.

To a God Unknown. New York: Robert O. Ballou, 1933.

Tortilla Flat. New York: Covici-Friede, 1935.

In Dubious Battle. New York: Covici-Friede, 1936.

Of Mice and Men. New York: Covici-Friede, 1937.

The Long Valley. New York: Viking Press, 1938.

The Grapes of Wrath. New York: Viking Press, 1939. Also available in revised Penguin Critical Library edition [1996], with text and criticism, eds. Peter Lisca and Kevin Hearle.

The Moon Is Down. New York: Viking Press, 1942.

The Red Pony. Illustrations by Wesley Dennis. New York: Viking Press, 1945.

Cannery Row. New York: Viking Press, 1945.

The Wayward Bus. New York: Viking Press, 1947.

The Pearl. Drawings by Jose Clemente Orozco. New York: Viking Press, 1947.

Burning Bright: A Play in Story Form. New York: Viking Press, 1950.

East of Eden. New York: Viking Press, 1952.

Sweet Thursday. New York: Viking Press, 1954.

The Short Reign of Pippin IV: A Fabrication. New York: Viking Press, 1957.

The Winter of Our Discontent. New York: Viking Press, 1961.

The Acts of King Arthur and His Noble Knights. Ed. Chase Horton. New York: Farrar, Straus & Giroux, 1976. (Includes introduction by Steinbeck, and appendix of 72 letters, written 1956–1965 to Horton and Elizabeth Otis, selected from the 108 letters, cards, and notes housed at Ball State University's Bracken Library.)

Uncollected Stories of John Steinbeck. Ed. Kiyoshi Nakayama. Tokyo: Nan' un-do Company, 1986. (Includes "His Father," "The Summer Before," "How Edith McGillicuddy Met R. L. Stevenson," "Reunion at the Quiet Hotel," "The Miracle of Tepayac," "The Time Wolves Ate the Vice-Principal.")

Film

The Forgotten Village. New York: Viking Press, 1941.

Viva Zapata! Ed. Robert E. Morsberger. New York: Viking Press, 1975.

Zapata. Ed. Robert E. Morsberger. New York: Penguin Books, 1993. (Extended preparatory narrative treatment in dramatic form of the life of Emiliano Zapata, together with filmscript *Viva Zapata!*)

Nonfiction

Their Blood Is Strong. San Francisco: Simon I. Lubin Society, 1938. (Articles first published as "The Harvest Gypsies" in *San Francisco News*, October 5–12, 1936, with new epilogue.)

Sea of Cortez: A Leisurely Journal of Travel and Research. New York: Viking Press, 1941. (Written with Edward F. Ricketts.)

Bombs Away: The Story of a Bomber Team. New York: Viking Press, 1942. (With 60 photographs by John Swope.)

A Russian Journal. New York: Viking Press, 1948. (With photographs and single chapter by Robert Capa.)

The Log from the Sea of Cortez. New York: Viking Press, 1951. (Contains introduction and narrative section from 1941 *Sea of Cortez* and memorial profile, "About Ed Ricketts.") (Introduction by Richard Astro.)

Once There Was a War. New York: Viking Press, 1958. (Collection of World War II dispatches written in 1943 to *New York Herald-Tribune,* plus new introduction.)

Travels with Charley in Search of America. New York: Viking Press, 1962.

America and Americans. New York: Viking Press, 1966. (With photographs.)

America and Americans and Selected Nonfiction. Ed. Susan Shillinglaw and Jackson Benson. New York: Viking, 2002.

Drama

Of Mice and Men: Play in Three Acts. New York: Covici-Friede, 1937.

The Moon Is Down: Play in Two Parts. New York: Viking Press, 1942.

Burning Bright: Play in Three Acts. New York: Dramatists Play Service, 1951.

Correspondence, Journals, Interviews

Journal of a Novel: The "East of Eden" Letters. New York: Viking Press, 1969. (Steinbeck's daily journal—covering January 29 to November 1, 1951—addressed to his editor, Pascal Covici.)

Steinbeck: A Life in Letters. Ed. Elaine Steinbeck and Robert Wallsten. New York: Viking Press, 1975. Also available in paperback, 1989.

Letters to Elizabeth: A Selection of Letters from John Steinbeck to Elizabeth Otis. Ed. Florian J. Shasky and Susan F. Riggs. San Francisco: Book Club of California, 1978. (Publishes 44 letters, written between 1938 and 1965, from the approximately 600 by Steinbeck to Otis at Stanford University; limited edition of 500 copies.)

Fensch, Thomas. *Steinbeck and Covici: The Story of a Friendship.* Middlebury, VT: Paul S. Eriksson, 1979. (Text includes selection of Steinbeck's 350 letters and cards to Pascal Covici, written 1937–1963 and housed at the University of Texas's Harry Ransom Humanities Research Center.)

———, ed. *Conversations with John Steinbeck.* Jackson: University Press of Mississippi, 1988. (Reprints 25 interviews published between 1935 and 1972.)

The Harvest Gypsies: On the Road to "The Grapes of Wrath." Berkeley, CA: Heyday Books, 1988.

Selected Essays of John Steinbeck. Ed. Hidekazu Hirose and Kiyoshi Nakayama. Tokyo: shinozaki shorin Press, 1983. (Includes "Autobiography: Making of a New Yorker," "A Primer on the 30s," "Jalopies I Cursed and Loved," "How to Tell Good Guys from Bad Guys," "My War with the Ospreys," "Conversation at Sag Harbor," "I Go Back to Ireland.")

Working Days: The Journal of "The Grapes of Wrath," 1938–1941. Ed. Robert DeMott. New York: Viking Press, 1989. (Provides diary/journal entries from February 1938 through January 1941, recording Steinbeck's composition of *The Grapes of Wrath* and its post-publication reception)

SECONDARY WORKS

Bibliographies

DeMott, Robert. *John Steinbeck: A Checklist of Books By and About.* Bradenton, FL: Opuscula Press, 1987.

Goldstone, Adrian, and John R. Payne. *John Steinbeck: A Bibliographical Catalogue of the Adrian H. Goldstone Collection.* Austin, TX: Humanities Research Center, 1974.

Harmon, Robert B. *"The Grapes of Wrath": A Fifty Year Bibliographical Survey.* With John F. Early. Introduction by Susan Shillinglaw. San Jose, CA: Steinbeck Research Center, 1990.

———. *John Steinbeck: Annotated Guide to Biographical Sources.* Lanham, MD: Scarecrow Press, 1996.

———. *Steinbeck Bibliographies: An Annotated Guide.* Metuchen, NJ: Scarecrow Press, 1987.

Hayashi, Tetsumaro. *John Steinbeck: A Concise Bibliography (1930–1963).* Metuchen, NJ: Scarecrow Press, 1967.

———. *A New Steinbeck Bibliography, 1927–1971.* Metuchen, NJ: Scarecrow Press, 1973.

———. *A New Steinbeck Bibliography. Supplement I: 1971-1981.* Metuchen, NJ: Scarecrow Press, 1983.

———, ed. *Steinbeck and Hemingway: Dissertation Abstracts and Research Opportunities.* Metuchen, NJ: Scarecrow Press, 1980.

———. *A Student's Guide to Steinbeck's Literature: Primary and Secondary Sources.* Steinbeck Bibliography Series, no.1. Muncie, IN: Steinbeck Research Institute/Ball State University, 1986.

Hayashi, Tetsumaro, and Beverly K. Simpson, comps. *John Steinbeck: Dissertation Abstracts and Research Opportunities.* Metuchen, NJ: Scarecrow Press, 1994.

Meyer, Michael J. *The Hayashi Steinbeck Bibliography 1982–1996.* Lanham, MD: Scarecrow, 1998.

Riggs, Susan F. *A Catalogue of the John Steinbeck Collection at Stanford University.* Stanford, CA: Stanford University Libraries, 1980.

Seifker, Donald L., Tetsumaro Hayashi, and Thomas I. Moore, eds. The Steinbeck Quarterly: *A Cumulative Index of Volumes XI–XX (1978–1987).* Introduction by Robert DeMott. Steinbeck Bibliography Series, no.2. Muncie, IN: Steinbeck Research Institute/Ball State University, 1989.

Biographies, Interviews, and Memoirs

Ariss, Bruce. *Inside Cannery Row: Sketches from the Steinbeck Era.* San Francisco: Lexikos, 1988.

Bennett, Robert. *The Wrath of John Steinbeck or St. John Goes to Church.* Los Angeles: Albertson Press, 1939. Rpt. Norwood, PA: Telegraph Books, 1985. Foreword by Lawrence Clark Powell.

Benson, Jackson J. *The True Adventures of John Steinbeck, Writer.* New York: Viking Press, 1984.

———. *Looking for Steinbeck's Ghost.* Norman: University of Oklahoma Press, 1988.

Enea, Sparky, as told to Audry Lynch. *With Steinbeck in the Sea of Cortez.* Los Osos, CA: Sand River Press, 1991.

Farrell, Keith. *John Steinbeck: The Voice of the Land.* New York: M. Evans and Company, 1986. [Young adult]

Florence, Donnë. *John Steinbeck: America's Author.* Springfield, NJ: Enslow Publishers, 2000. [Juvenile]

Kiernan, Thomas. *The Intricate Music: A Biography of John Steinbeck.* Boston: Little, Brown, 1979.

Lynch, Audrey. *Steinbeck Remembered.* Santa Barbara, CA: Fithian Press, 2000.

Parini, Jay. *John Steinbeck: A Biography.* London: William Heinemann, 1994. New York: Henry Holt, 1995.

Sheffield, Carlton. *Steinbeck: The Good Companion.* Introduction by Richard Blum. Portola Valley, CA: American Lives Endowment, 1983.

Simmonds, Roy S. *John Steinbeck: A Biographical and Critical Introduction.* Lewiston, NY: Edwin Mellen, 2000.

St. Pierre, Brian. *John Steinbeck: The California Years.* San Francisco: Chronicle Books, 1983.

Tessitore, John. *John Steinbeck, A Writer's Life.* New York: Franklin Watts, 2001. [Young adult]

Valjean, Nelson. *John Steinbeck: The Errant Knight.* San Francisco: Chronicle Books, 1975.

Reference Works

George, Stephen K. "John Steinbeck." *The Oxford Encyclopedia of American Literature.* Ed. Jay Parini. Vol. 4. Oxford: Oxford University Press, 2004. 88–98. (A comprehensive overview of Steinbeck's life and literary achievement, including the "early years," "Depression era," "war period," and "mature" and "final years," with a bibliography.)

Mann, Susan Garland. *The Short Story Cycle: A Genre Companion and Reference Guide.* Westport, CT: Greenwood Press, 1989. (Book includes one chapter devoted to *Pastures of Heaven.*)

McElrath, Joseph, Jessie Crissler, and Susan Shillinglaw, eds. *John Steinbeck: The Contemporary Reviews.* Contemporary Reviews Series. New York: Cambridge University Press, 1996.

Li, Luchen, ed. *John Steinbeck: A Documentary Volume.* Vol. 309. Dictionary of Literary Biography. Farmington Hills, MI: Thomson/Gale, 2005.

Critical Studies: Books, Monographs

Ariki, Kyoko. *The Main Thematic Current in John Steinbeck's Works: A Positive View of Man's Survival.* Osaka: Osaka Kyoiku Tosho, 2002.

Barbour, James, and Tom Quirk, eds. *Biographies of Books: The Compositional Histories of Notable American Writings.* Columbia: University of Missouri Press, 1995.

———, eds. *Writing the American Classics.* Chapel Hill: University of North Carolina, 1990.

Belaswamy, Periswamy. *Symbols for the Wordlessness: A Study of the Deep Structure of John Steinbeck's Early Novels.* Chennai, India: Ramath Academic Publishers, 2005.

Benson, Jackson J. *Looking for Steinbeck's Ghost.* Norman: University of Oklahoma Press, 1988.

———. *Steinbeck's "Cannery Row": A Reconsideration.* Steinbeck Essay Series, no.4. Muncie, IN: Steinbeck Research Institute/Ball State University, 1991.

Burrows, Michael. *John Steinbeck and His Films.* St. Austeu, Cornwall, England: Primestyle, 1970.

Chada, Rajni. *Social Realism in the Novels of John Steinbeck.* New Delhi, India: Harman Publishing House, 1990.

Coers, Donald V. *John Steinbeck as Propagandist: "The Moon Is Down" Goes to War.* Tuscaloosa: University of Alabama Press, 1991.

DeMott, Robert. *Steinbeck's Typewriter: A Collection of Essays.* Troy, NY: Whitston, 1996.

Ditsky, John. *Essays on East of Eden.* Steinbeck Monograph Series, no. 7. Muncie, IN: John Steinbeck Society of America/Ball State University, 1977.

———. *John Steinbeck: Life, Work, and Criticism.* Fredericton, New Brunswick: York Press, 1985.

———. *John Steinbeck and the Critics.* Literary Criticism in Perspective Series. Rochester, NY: Camden House, 2000.

Feied, Frederick. *The Tidepool and The Stars: The Ecological Basis of Steinbeck's Depression Novels.* New York: Xlibris, 2001.

Fontenrose, Joseph. *John Steinbeck: An Introduction and Interpretation.* American Authors and Critics Series. New York: Dames and Noble, 1963.

———. *Steinbeck's Unhappy Valley: A Study of "The Pastures of Heaven."* Berkeley, CA: Privately printed, 1981.

French, Warren, ed. *A Companion to "The Grapes of Wrath."* New York: Penguin, 1987. (A reissue of the 1963 original, also in a 1989 paperback edition.)

French, Warren. *Film Guide to "The Grapes of Wrath."* Indiana University Press Film Guide Series. Bloomington: University of Indiana Press, 1973.

———. *John Steinbeck.* Twayne's United States Authors Series, no. 2. New York: Twayne Publishers, 1961.

———. *John Steinbeck.* Twayne's United States Authors Series, no. 2. Rev. ed. Boston: G. K. Hall, 1975.

———. *John Steinbeck's Fiction Revisited.* Twayne's United States Author Series, no. 638. New York: Twayne Publishers, 1994.

———. *John Steinbeck's Non-Fiction Revisited.* New York: Twayne, 1996.

Garcia, Reloy. *Steinbeck and D. H. Lawrence: Fictive Voices and the Ethical Imperative.* Steinbeck Monograph Series, no. 2. Muncie, IN: John Steinbeck Society of America/Ball State University, 1972.

Gladstein, Mimi Reisel. *The Indestructible Woman in the Works of Faulkner, Hemingway, and Steinbeck.* Studies in Modern Literature, no. 45. Ann Arbor, MI: UMI Research Press, 1986.

Gray, James. *John Steinbeck.* Minnesota Pamphlets on American Writers. Minneapolis: University of Minnesota Press, 1971.

Gregory, James N. *American Exodus: The Dust Bowl Migration and Okie Culture in California.* New York: Oxford Press, 1989.

Hadella, Charlotte Cook. *"Of Mice and Men": A Kinship of Powerlessness.* Twayne's Masterwork Studies, no. 147. New York: Twayne Publishers, 1995.

Hayashi, Tetsumaro. *John Steinbeck and the Vietnam War (Part I).* Introduction by Reloy Garcia. Steinbeck Monograph Series, no. 12. Muncie, IN: John Steinbeck Society of America/Ball State University, 1986.

———. *Steinbeck's World War II Fiction, "The Moon Is Down": Three Explications.* Introduction by Reloy Garcia. Steinbeck Essay Series no. 1. Muncie, IN: Steinbeck Research Institute/Ball State University, 1986.

Hughes, R. S. *Beyond "The Red Pony": A Reader's Companion to Steinbeck's Complete Short Stories.* Metuchen, NJ: Scarecrow Press, 1987.

———. *John Steinbeck: A Study of the Short Fiction.* Twayne's Studies in Short Fiction Series, no. 5. Boston: Twayne Publishers, 1989.

Jain, Sunita. *Steinbeck's Concept of Man: A Critical Study of His Novels.* New Delhi, India: New Statesman Publishing, 1979.

Johnson, Claudia Durst. *Understanding "The Grapes of Wrath."* Westport, CT: Greenwood Press, 1999.

———. *Understanding "Of Mice and Men," "The Red Pony," and "The Pearl": The Student Casebook to Issues, Sources, and Historical Documents.* Westport, CT: Greenwood Press, 1997.

Jones, Lawrence William. *John Steinbeck as Fabulist.* Ed. Marston LaFrance. Steinbeck Monograph Series, no. 3. Muncie, IN: John Steinbeck Society of America/Ball State University, 1973.

Levant, Howard. *The Novels of John Steinbeck: A Critical Study.* Introduction by Warren French. Columbia: University of Missouri Press, 1974.

Lisca, Peter. *John Steinbeck: Nature and Myth.* New York: Thomas Y. Crowell, 1978.

———. *The Wide World of John Steinbeck.* New Brunswick, NJ: Rutgers University Press, 1958. Rpt, with new afterword, New York: Gordian Press, 1981.

Marks, Lester. *Thematic Design in the Novels of John Steinbeck.* Studies in American Literature, vol. 11. The Hague: Mouton, 1969.

Martin, Stoddard. *California Writers: Jack London, John Steinbeck, the Tough Guys.* London: Macmillan, 1983.

McCarthy, Paul. *John Steinbeck.* Modern Literature Monographs Series. New York: Frederick Ungar, 1979.

Millichap, Joseph. *Steinbeck and Film.* New York: Frederick Ungar, 1983.

Moore, Harry Thornton. *The Novels of John Steinbeck: A First Critical Study.* Chicago: Normandie House, 1939. Rpt., with contemporary epilogue, Port Washington, NY: Kennikat Press, 1969.

Nakayama, Kiyoshi. *Steinbeck's Writing II: The Post California Years.* Suita, Osaka, Japan: Kansai University Press, 1999.

Owens, Louis. *"The Grapes of Wrath": Trouble in the Promised Land.* Twayne's Masterwork Studies, no. 27. Boston: Twayne Publishers, 1989.

———. *John Steinbeck's Re-Vision of America.* Athens: University of Georgia Press, 1985.

Prabhakar, S. S. *John Steinbeck: A Study.* Hyderabad, India: Academic Publishers, 1976.

Pratt, John Clark. *John Steinbeck: A Critical Essay.* Contemporary Writers in Christian Perspective Series. Grand Rapids, MI: William B. Eerdmans, 1970.

Railsback, Brian E. *Parallel Expeditions: Charles Darwin and the Art of John Steinbeck.* Moscow: University of Idaho Press, 1995.

Satyanarayana, M. R. *John Steinbeck: A Study in the Theme of Compassion.* Hyderabad, India: Osmania Universal Press, 1977.

Shimomura, Noboru. *A Study of John Steinbeck: Mysticism in His Novels.* Tokyo: Hokuseido Press, 1982.

Simmonds, Roy S. *John Steinbeck: The War Years, 1939–1945.* Lewisburg, PA: Bucknell University Press, 1996.

———. *Steinbeck's Literary Achievement.* Steinbeck Monograph Series, no. 6. Muncie, IN: John Steinbeck Society of America/Ball State University, 1976.

Sreenivasan, K. *John Steinbeck: A Study of His Novels.* Trivandrum, India: College Book House, 1980.

Timmerman, John H. *The Dramatic Landscape of Steinbeck's Short Stories.* Norman: University of Oklahoma Press, 1990.

———. *John Steinbeck's Fiction: The Aesthetics of the Road Taken.* Norman: University of Oklahoma Press, 1986.

Watt, F. W. *Steinbeck.* Writers and Critics Series. Edinburgh: Oliver and Boyd, 1962; New York: Grove Press, 1963.

Williams, A. Susan. *John Steinbeck.* East Sussex, England: Wayland Ltd., 1990.

Yano, Shigeharu. *The Current of Steinbeck's World.* Volumes I–IV. Tokyo: Seibido Press, 1978–82.

Collections of Scholarly Essays

Astro, Richard, and Tetsumaro Hayashi, eds. *Steinbeck: The Man and His Work.* Corvallis: Oregon State University Press, 1971.

Beegel, Susan, Susan Shillinglaw, and Wes Tiffney, eds. *Steinbeck and the Environment: Interdisciplinary Approaches.* Tuscaloosa: University of Alabama Press, 1997.

Benson, Jackson J., ed. *The Short Novels of John Steinbeck: Critical Essays with a Checklist to Steinbeck Criticism.* Durham, NC: Duke University Press, 1990.

Bloom, Harold, ed. *John Steinbeck: Modern Critical Views.* New York: Chelsea House, 1987.

———, ed. *John Steinbeck's "The Grapes of Wrath."* Modern Critical Interpretations Series. New York: Chelsea House Publishers, 1988.

Bogardus, Ralph F., and Fred Hobson, eds. *Literature at the Barricades: The American Writer in the 1930s.* Tuscaloosa: University of Alabama Press, 1982.

Britch, Carroll, and Cliff Lewis, eds. *Rediscovering Steinbeck: Revisionist Views of His Art and Politics.* Lewiston, NY: Edwin Mellen Press, 1989.

Coers, Donald V., Paul C. Ruffin, and Robert J. DeMott, eds. *After "The Grapes of Wrath": Essays on John Steinbeck in Honor of Tetsumaro Hayashi.* Athens: Ohio University Press, 1995.

Conner, Ken, and Debra Heimerdinger. *Horace Bristol: An American View.* New York: Chronicle Books, 1996.

Davis, Robert Con, ed. *Twentieth Century Interpretations of "The Grapes of Wrath."* Englewood Cliffs, NJ: Prentice Hall, 1982.

Davis, Robert Murray, ed. *Steinbeck: A Collection of Critical Essays.* Twentieth Century Views Series. Englewood Cliffs, NJ: Prentice Hall, 1972.

Ditsky, John, ed. *Critical Essays on "The Grapes of Wrath."* Critical Essays on Modern Literature Series. Boston: G. K. Hall, 1989.

Donohue, Agnes McNeill, ed. *A Casebook on "The Grapes of Wrath."* New York: Thomas Y. Crowell, 1968.

French, Warren, ed. *A Companion to "The Grapes of Wrath."* New York: Viking Press, 1963. Rpt., Clifton, NJ: Augustus Kelley, 1972. (Includes Steinbeck's *Their Blood Is Strong.*)

George, Stephen, ed. *John Steinbeck: A Centennial Tribute.* Westport, CT: Praeger, 2002.

———, ed. *The Moral Philosophy of John Steinbeck.* Lanham, MD: Scarecrow, 2005.

Hayashi, Tetsumaro, ed. *John Steinbeck: The Years of Greatness, 1936–1939.* Proceedings of the Third International Steinbeck Congress, Honolulu, HI, May 1991. Tuscaloosa: University of Alabama Press, 1993.

———, ed. *A New Study Guide to Steinbeck: Major Works, with Critical Explications*. Metuchen, NJ: Scarecrow Press, 1993.

———, ed. *Steinbeck and the Arthurian Theme.* Steinbeck Monograph Series, no. 5. Muncie, IN: John Steinbeck Society of America/Ball State University, 1975.

———, ed. *Steinbeck's "The Grapes of Wrath": Essays in Criticism.* Introduction by John H. Timmerman. Steinbeck Essay Series, no. 3. Muncie, IN: Steinbeck Research Institute/ Ball State University, 1990.

———, ed. *Steinbeck's Literary Dimension: A Guide to Comparative Studies Series II.* Introduction by Reloy Garcia. Metuchen, NJ: Scarecrow Press, 1991.

———, ed. *Steinbeck's Literary Dimension: A Guide to Comparative Studies.* Metuchen, NJ: Scarecrow Press, 1973.

———, ed. *Steinbeck's Short Stories in "The Long Valley": Essays in Criticism.* Introduction by Warren French. Steinbeck Monograph Series, no. 15. Muncie, IN: John Steinbeck Society of America/Ball State University, 1991.

———, ed. *Steinbeck's Travel Literature: Essays in Criticism*. Steinbeck Monograph Series, no. 10. Muncie, IN: John Steinbeck Society of America/Ball State University, 1980.-

———, ed. *Steinbeck's Women: Essays in Criticism*. Steinbeck Monograph Series, no. 9. Muncie, IN: John Steinbeck Society of America/Ball State University, 1979.

———, ed. *A Study Guide to "The Long Valley."* Introduction by Reloy Garcia. Ann Arbor, MI: Pierian Press, 1976.

———, ed. *A Study Guide to Steinbeck: A Handbook to His Major Works.* Metuchen, NJ: Scarecrow Press, 1974.

———, ed. *A Study Guide to Steinbeck, Part II.* Metuchen, NJ: Scarecrow Press, 1979.

Hayashi, Tetsumaro, Yasuo Hashiguchi, and Richard F. Peterson, eds. *John Steinbeck: East and West.* Proceedings of the First International Steinbeck Congress, Kyushu University, Japan, August 1976. Steinbeck Monograph Series, no. 8. Muncie, IN: John Steinbeck Society of America/Ball State University, 1978.

Hayashi, Tetsumaro, and Thomas J. Moore, eds. *Steinbeck's Posthumous Work: Essays in Criticism.* Steinbeck Monograph Series, no. 14. Muncie, IN: John Steinbeck Society of America/ Ball State University, 1989.

———, eds. *Steinbeck's "The Red Pony": Essays in Criticism*. Steinbeck Monograph Series, no. 13. Muncie, IN: John Steinbeck Society of America/Ball State University, 1988.

Hayashi, Tetsumaro, and Kenneth D. Swan, eds. *Steinbeck's Prophetic Vision of America.* Proceedings of the Bicentennial Steinbeck Seminar. Upland, IN: Taylor University for the John Steinbeck Society of America, 1976.

Heavilin, Barbara A., ed. *The Critical Response to John Steinbeck's "The Grapes of Wrath."* Westport, CT: Greenwood Press, 2000.

———, ed. *John Steinbeck's "The Grapes of Wrath": A Reference Guide.* Greenwood Guides to Fiction. Westport, CT: Greenwood Press, 2002.

———, ed. *John Steinbeck's "Of Mice and Men": A Reference Guide.* Greenwood Guides to Fiction. Westport, CT: Praeger, 2005.

———, ed. *The Steinbeck Yearbook I.* Lewiston, NY: Edwin Mellen, 2000.

———, ed. *The Steinbeck Yearbook II.* Lewiston, NY: Edwin Mellen, 2002.

Heavilin, Barbara A., and Stephen George, eds. *The Steinbeck Yearbook III: Steinbeck's Sense of Place*. Lewiston, NY: Edwin Mellen, 2003

Meyer, Michael J., ed. *Cain Sign; The Betrayal of Brotherhood in the Works of John Steinbeck.* Lewiston, NY: Edwin Mellen, 2000.

Nakayama, Kiyoshi, Scott Pugh, and Shigeharu Yano, eds. *Steinbeck: Asian Perspectives.* Proceedings of the Third International Steinbeck Congress, Honolulu, HI, May 1991. Osaka, Japan: Osaka Kyoiku Tosho, 1992.

Noble, Donald R., ed. *The Steinbeck Question: New Essays in Criticism.* Troy, NY: Whitston Publishing, 1993.

Sharma, R. K., ed. *Indian Responses to Steinbeck: Essays Presented to Warren French.* Foreword by Yasuo Hashiguchi. Jaipur, India: Rachana Prakashan, 1984.

Shillinglaw, Susan, and Kevin Hearle, eds. *Beyond Boundaries: Rereading John Steinbeck*. Tuscaloosa: University of Alabama Press, 2002.

Syed, Mashkoor Ali, ed. *John Steinbeck: A Centennial Tribute.* Jaipur, India: Surabhi. 2004

Tedlock, E. W., and C. V. Wicker, eds. *Steinbeck and His Critics: A Record of Twenty-Five Years.* Albuquerque: University of New Mexico Press, 1957.

Wyatt, David, ed. *New Essays on "The Grapes of Wrath."* The American Novel Series. New York: Cambridge University Press, 1990.

Yano, Shigeru, Tetsumaro Hayashi, Richard F. Peterson, and Yasuo Hashiguchi, eds. *John Steinbeck: From Salinas to the World.* Proceedings of the Second International Steinbeck Congress, Salinas, CA, August 1984; Tokyo: Gaku Shobo Press, 1986.

Journals/Chapters in Books

Cassuto, David. "Turning Wine into Water: Water as Privileged Signifier in *The Grapes of Wrath.*" *Papers on Language and Literature* 29.1 (Winter 1993): 67–95.

Davis, Robert Murray. "The World of John Steinbeck's Joads." *World Literature Today* 64.3 (Summer 1990): 401–04.

Davison, Richard Allan. "Hemingway, Steinbeck and the Art of the Short Story." *Steinbeck Quarterly* XXI.3–4 (Summer/Fall 1988): 73–84.

DeMott, Robert. "Of Ink and Heart's Blood: Adventures in Reading *East of Eden.*" *Connecticut Review* 14 (Spring 1992): 9–21.

Ditsky, John. "California Dreaming: Steinbeck and West." *The Steinbeck Newsletter* 4.2 (Summer 1991): 6–7.

———. "The Depression's 'Graveyard Ghosts': A Shared Motif in *Waiting for Nothing* and *The Grapes of Wrath.*" *The International Fiction Review* 15:1 (Winter 1988): 21–22.

———. "The Devil in Music: Unheard Themes in Steinbeck's Fiction." *Steinbeck Quarterly* XXV.3–4 (Summer/Fall 1992): 80–86.

———. "The Late John Steinbeck: Dissonance in the Post *Grapes* Era." *San Jose Studies* 18.1 (Winter 1992): 20–32.

———. "'Pu-raise Gawd fur Vittory!' Granma as Prophet." *The Steinbeck Newsletter* 6.2 (Summer 1993): 4–5.

Fiedler, Leslie. "Looking Back after 50 Years." *San Jose Studies* 16 (Winter 1990): 54–64. (*The Grapes of Wrath*)

Gladstein, Mimi Reisel. "Deletions from the *Battle*: Gaps in the *Grapes.*" *San Jose Studies* XVIII.1–2 (Winter 1992): 43–51.

Hayashi, Tetsumaro. "John Steinbeck and Adlai Stevenson: Their Moral and Political Vision." *Steinbeck Quarterly* XXIV.3–4 (Summer/Fall 1991): 94–107.

Hearle, Kevin. "The Pastures of Contested Pastoral Discourse." *Steinbeck Quarterly* XXVI.1–2 (Winter/Spring 1993): 38–45.

Heavilin, Barbara. "Ma Joad, Rose of Sharon, and the Stranger Motif: Structural Symmetry in Steinbeck's *The Grapes of Wrath.*" *South Dakota Review* (Summer 1991): 142–52.

Kleis, John Christopher. "*Tortilla Flat* and The Arthurian View." *Cinema Arthuriana*. Ed. Kevin Hartt. Rev. ed. London: McFarland, 2002. 71–79.

Kocela, Chris. "The Redefining of Self in the 'Gradual Flux': An Existentialist Reading of *In Dubious Battle.*" *Steinbeck Newsletter* 10.1 (Spring 1996): 1–6.

Lieber, Todd. "Talismanic Patterns in the Novels of John Steinbeck." *American Literature* 44 (May 1972): 262–275.

Loftis, Anne. "Steinbeck and the Federal Migrant Camps." *San Jose Studies* 16 (Winter 1990): 76–90.

Meyer, Michael J. "Finding a New Jerusalem: The Edenic Myth in John Steinbeck." *Literature and the Bible.* Ed. David Bevan. Amsterdam/Atlanta: Rodopi, 1993. 95–117.

———. "The Search for King Arthur: John Steinbeck's Continuing Preoccupation with the Grail Legend." *Modern Myth.* Ed. David Bevan. Amsterdam/Atlanta: Rodopi, 1993. 7–22.

Morsberger, Robert E. "Play It Again, Lennie and George." *Steinbeck Quarterly* XV.3–4 (Summer/Fall 1982): 123–26.

Mulder, Steven. "The Reader's Story: *East of Eden* as Postmodernist Metafiction." *Steinbeck Quarterly* XXV.3–4 (Summer/Fall 1992): 109–18.

Owens, Louis D. "Camelot, East of Eden: John Steinbeck's *Tortilla Flat.*" *Perspective* 1 (Spring 1984): 1–5. Rpt., in condensed form with the same title, *Arizona Quarterly* 38 (Autumn 1982): 203–16.

———. "Deadly Kids, Stinking Dogs, and Heroes: The Best Laid Plans in Steinbeck's *Of Mice and Men.*" *Steinbeck Studies* (Fall 2002): 1–8.

———. "John Steinbeck's *The Pastures of Heaven*: Illusions of Eden." *Arizona Quarterly* 41.3 (1985): 197–214.

———. "Steinbeck's 'The Murder': Illusions of Chivalry." *Steinbeck Quarterly* XVII.1–2 (Winter/Spring 1984): 10–14.

Quinones, Ricardo. "Chapter 7: The New American Cain: *East of Eden* and Other Works of Post World War II America." In *The Changes of Cain: Violence and the Lost Brother in Cain and Abel Literature.* Princeton: Princeton University Press, 1991.

Railsback, Brian. "Darwin and Steinbeck: The 'Older Method' and *The Sea of Cortez.*"

Steinbeck Quarterly XXIII.1–2 (Winter/Spring 1990): 27–34.

———. "A Frog, a Bear, a Snake and the Human Species: Uncomfortable Reflections in John Steinbeck's Fiction." *Literature and the Grotesque.* Ed. Michael J. Meyer. Amsterdam: Rodopi, 1995. 53–65.

Schmidt, Gary D. "Steinbeck's 'Breakfast': A Reconsideration." *Western American Literature* 26.4 (Winter 1992): 303–311.

Schneer, Deborah. "A Psychoanalytic Reading." *San Jose Studies* 16 (Winter 1990): 107–16.

Timmerman, John H. "The Squatter's Circle in *The Grapes of Wrath.*" *Studies in Short Fiction* 17.2 (Autumn 1989): 203–11.

Visser, Nicholas. "Audience and Closure in *The Grapes of Wrath.*" *Studies in American Fiction* 22 (Spring 1994): 19–36.

Werlock, Abby H. P. "Poor Whites: Joads and Snopeses." *San Jose Studies* 18 (Winter 1992): 61–71.

Winn, Harbour. "The Unity in Steinbeck's *Pastures* Community." *Steinbeck Quarterly* XXII.3–4 (Summer/Fall 1989): 91–103.

Related Sources

Astro, Richard. *John Steinbeck and Edward F. Ricketts: Reshaping of a Novelist.* Minneapolis: University of Minnesota Press, 1973.

Astro, Richard, and Joel W. Hedgepeth, eds. *Steinbeck and the Sea.* Proceedings of a May 1974 Conference at the Marine Science Center, Newport, OR. Corvallis: Oregon State University Sea Grant College Program, 1975.

Christensen, Bonnie. *Woody Guthrie: Poet of the People.* New York: Knopf Books for Young Readers, 2001.

Conner, Ken, and Debra Heimerdinger. *Horace Bristol: An American View.* New York: Chroncile Books, 1996.

Cray, Ed. *Ramblin' Man: The Life and Times of Woody Guthrie.* New York: Norton, 2004.

DeMott, Robert. *Steinbeck's Reading: A Catalogue of Books Owned and Borrowed.* Garland Reference Library of the Humanities, vol. 246. New York: Garland Publishing, 1984.

Fensch, Thomas, ed. *The FBI Files on John Steinbeck.* Woodlands, TX: New Century, 2002.

Gannett, Lewis. *John Steinbeck: Personal and Bibliographical Notes.* New York: Viking Press, 1939.

Hedgepeth, Joel, ed. *The Outer Shore. Part I. Ed Ricketts and John Steinbeck Explore the Pacific Coast.* Eureka, CA: Mad River Press, 1978.

———, ed. *The Outer Shores. Part II. Breaking Through.* Eureka, CA: Mad River Press, 1979. (Includes Ricketts' previously unpublished essays, "The Philosophy of Breaking Through," " A Spiritual Morphology of Poetry," "The Log of the *Western Flyer,*" "Essays on Non-teleological Thinking," "Notes from the Sea of Cortez.")

Heimerdinger, Debra, and Ken Conner. *Horace Bristol: An American View.* New York: Chronicle Books, 1996.

Hemp, Michael Kenneth. *Cannery Row: The History of John Steinbeck's Old Ocean View Avenue.* 2nd ed. Monterey, CA: History Co., 2003.

Hesse, Karen. *Out of the Dust.* New York: Scholastic, 1997.

Larsh, Edward B. *Doc's Lab: Myths and Legends of Cannery Row.* Monterey, CA: PBL Press, 1995.

Lax, Andromeda Romano. *Searching for Steinbeck's Sea of Cortez: A Makeshift Journey along Baja's Desert Coast.* Seattle: Sasquatch Books, 2003.

Mangelsdorf, Tom. *A History of Steinbeck's Cannery Row.* Santa Cruz, CA: Western Tanager Press, 1986.

Maril, Robert Lee. *Waltzing with the Ghost of Tom Joad: Poverty, Myth and Low Wage Labor in Oklahoma.* Norman: University of Oklahoma Press, 2003.

Rodger, Katherine A., ed. *Renaissance Man of Cannery Row: The Life and Letters of Edward F. Ricketts.* Tuscaloosa: University of Alabama Press, 2003.

Schmitz, Anne-Marie. *In Search of Steinbeck.* Los Altos, CA: Hermes Publications, 1978.

Steinbeck, John IV, and Nancy Steinbeck. *The Other Side of Eden: Life with John Steinbeck.* Amherst, MA: Prometheus, 2001.

Tamm, Eric Enno. *Beyond the Outer Shores: The Untold Odyssey of Ed Ricketts, the Pioneering Ecologist Who Inspired John Steinbeck and Joseph Campbell.* New York: Four Walls Eight Windows, 2003.

Weber, Tom. *All the Heroes Are Dead: The Ecology of John Steinbeck's Cannery Row.* San Francisco: Ramparts Press, 1974.

Whitebrook, Peter. *Staging Steinbeck: Dramatising "The Grapes of Wrath."* London: Cassell, 1988.

Index

*Page numbers in **bold** indicate entries in the encyclopedia.*

About the Editors and Contributors

EDITORS

BRIAN RAILSBACK, Co-editor, is Professor of English (Contemporary American Literature and Professional Writing) at Western Carolina University, where he has served as Department Head of English and is presently founding Dean of The Honors College. In 2004 he was named University Scholar at WCU. In both scholarship and fiction writing, he is concerned with environmental issues, a theme that initially attracted him to Steinbeck. He has published essays in several books concerning Steinbeck, including *After "The Grapes of Wrath": Essays on John Steinbeck in Honor of Tetsumaro Hayashi* (Ohio University Press 1995); *Literature and the Grotesque* (Rodopi 1995); *Steinbeck and the Environment* (University of Alabama Press 1997); *Readings on "The Red Pony"* (Greenhaven 2001); *Beyond Boundaries: Rereading John Steinbeck* (University of Alabama Press 2002); and *John Steinbeck: A Centennial Tribute* (U.S. book, Praeger 2002; Indian book, Surabhi 2004). He has presented papers on Steinbeck across the United States as well as in Mexico and Japan. His own study of Steinbeck, *Parallel Expeditions: Charles Darwin and the Art of John Steinbeck,* was published by the University of Idaho Press in 1995. He is presently writing notes (with Robert DeMott) for The Library of America's *John Steinbeck: "Travels With Charley" and Later Novels*, and he is writing the biographical essay on Steinbeck for Blackwell's *A Companion to Twentieth-Century American Fiction*. In addition to his Steinbeck criticism, Railsback has written articles on Kate Chopin and Native American literature and, as a fiction writer, has published short stories and a novel, *The Darkest Clearing* (High Sierra 2004), which the *Charlotte Observer* noted "should satisfy readers looking for a thriller with meat on its bones, especially those passionate about wilderness and intrigued by the dark recesses of the human heart." His short story, "Clean Break," won the 2006 Prose for Papa (Hemingway) competition.

MICHAEL J. MEYER, Co-editor, is Adjunct Professor of English at DePaul and Northeastern Illinois Universities in Chicago. Meyer is a bibliographer for Steinbeck studies, having published *The Hayashi Steinbeck Bibliography (1982–1996)* in 1998 (Scarecrow) as an update to the three previous volumes compiled by Tetsumaro Hayashi. In addition to his bibliographic work, Meyer has served as a member of the editorial board *of The Steinbeck Quarterly* (1990–1993) and as editor of *Cain Sign: The Betrayal of Brotherhood in the Work of John Steinbeck*, (Mellen 2000) a collection that traces the author's use of the Cain and Abel myth throughout his canon. In addition, his essays have appeared in *Steinbeck Quarterly, Steinbeck Review,* and *Steinbeck Newsletter,* and he has contributed chapters to numerous books and monographs, including *The Short Novels of John Steinbeck* (Duke University Press

1990), *A New Study Guide to Steinbeck's Major Works* (Scarecrow 1993), *The Steinbeck Question* (Whitson 1993), *After "The Grapes of Wrath": Essays on John Steinbeck in Honor of Tetsumaro Hayashi* (Ohio University Press 1995), and *Beyond Boundaries: Rereading John Steinbeck* (University of Alabama Press 2002). Since 1994 Meyer has been editor for Rodopi Press's series, Perspectives in Modern Literature, where his seven volumes include *Literature and the Grotesque* (1995) and *Literature and Music* (2002), both of which contain studies of Steinbeck works. Rodopi has also published his essays on Steinbeck in *Literature and the Bible* (1993) and *Modern Myth* (1993). He is presently at work on a book that will review the critical reception of Steinbeck's *Of Mice and Men*. He is currently the vice president of The International John Steinbeck Society.

CONTRIBUTORS

NINA ALLEN is a Master Lecturer in the English department at Suffolk University, Boston, Massachusetts. Her dissertation, entitled "Thomas Hart Benton and John Steinbeck: Populist Realism in the Depression Era, 1929–1941," explores the thematic and aesthetic congruencies in the work of these two men in the 1930s. She also writes on the literature of travel.

JENNIFER BAUMGARTNER earned her MA in English at Western Carolina University and is preparing for doctoral work in English while she is an acquisitions and development editor for WestBow Press.

SUSAN F. BEEGEL holds a PhD in English from Yale University and is editor of *The Hemingway Review,* a publication of the University of Idaho and The Ernest Hemingway Foundation. She has published three books and is the author of more than fifty articles on aspects of American literature and maritime history.

TERRY BEERS is Professor of English at Santa Clara University and Director of the California Legacy Project. He is also the general editor of the California Legacy Series. He recently edited *Gunfight at Mussel Slough: Evolution of a Western Myth* (2004).

HERBERT BEHRENS is a volunteer at the archives of the National Steinbeck Center in Salinas, where he catalogues and indexes the center's holdings in periodicals, photographs, and correspondence related to Steinbeck. Previously, Behrens and his wife, Robbie Behrens, were docents for the Cannery Row Foundation, leading tours at the former Pacific Biological Lab and at the former residence of John, Gwyn, and Thom Steinbeck in Monterey.

JACKSON J. BENSON (see encyclopedia entry on **Benson, Jackson J.**).

PAUL M. BLOBAUM is Assistant Professor of Library Science, Governors State University Library, University Park, Illinois, where he serves as the liaison librarian to the College of Health Professions. His research interests include information organization and distribution regarding health and human services disparities.

BRADD BURNINGHAM is a freelance writer and library consultant in Windsor, Ontario, Canada. His scholarly writing has focused on Steinbeck's *East of Eden and The Winter of Our Discontent*. He is the author of *The Sad Eye* (1991), a book of short fiction.

CHRISTOPHER S. BUSCH is an Associate Professor of English at Hillsdale College, Hillsdale, Michigan, where he teaches courses and seminars in American literature. He has published chapters, articles, and reviews focusing on the literature of the American West, with special attention to intersections of frontier myth, history, and symbol in John Steinbeck's fiction and nonfiction.

MICHAEL CODY is Associate Professor of English at East Tennessee State University. He is the author of *Charles Brockden Brown and the Literary Magazine: Cultural*

Journalism in the Early American Republic (McFarland 2004).

DONALD COERS is Provost at Angelo State University in San Angelo, Texas. He is author of *John Steinbeck as Propagandist: "The Moon Is Down" Goes to War* (1991) and After "The Grapes of Wrath": Essays on John Steinbeck (1995).

ROBERT DEMOTT (see encyclopedia entry for **DeMott, Robert**).

JOHN DITSKY (see encyclopedia entry for **Ditsky, John**).

PAUL DOUGLASS is Professor of English and American Literature at San Jose State University, where he currently serves as the Director of the Martha Heasley Cox Center for Steinbeck Studies and as the editor of *Steinbeck Studies*.

CHARLES ETHERIDGE, JR. teaches English at Texas A&M University–Corpus Christi and is the assistant editor of *The Steinbeck Review*. He has published extensively on twentieth-century American fiction and on composition. He is also the author of the novel *Border Cantos*.

THOMAS FAHY is an Assistant Professor of English and Director of the American Studies Program at Long Island University. He has published several books, including *Freak Shows and the Modern American Imagination: Constructing the Damaged Body from Willa Cather to Truman Capote* (2006), a monograph on Gabriel Garcia Marquez's *Love in the Time of Cholera* (2003), and two novels: *Night Visions* (2004) and *The Unspoken* (forthcoming, 2007). He has also edited numerous collections: *Considering Alan Ball* (2006), *Considering Aaron Sorkin* (2005), *Captive Audience: Prison and Captivity in Contemporary Theater* (2003), and *Peering Behind the Curtain: Disability, Illness and the Extraordinary Body in Contemporary Theater* (2002).

THOMAS FENSCH is the author or editor of twenty-six books. His book, *Steinbeck and Covici: The Story of a Friendship*, the analysis of the relationship between John Steinbeck and his editor and publisher Pascal "Pat" Covici, was published in 1979 and has never been out of print. He is also the editor of *Conversations with John Steinbeck*, a collection of all the public interviews with Steinbeck (1988), *The FBI Files on John Steinbeck* (2002), and the "Introduction" to the latest edition of Steinbeck's *Tortilla Flat* (1997). Awarded a doctorate from Syracuse University, Fensch has also written or edited biographies about Theodor "Dr. Seuss" Geisel and James Thurber.

JANET L. FLOOD earned her MA in writing from DePaul University. She currently teaches there and is the Assistant Director of Graduate Programs in English.

WARREN FRENCH (see encyclopedia entry on **French, Warren**).

STEPHEN K. GEORGE teaches literature, writing, and philosophy at Brigham Young University–Idaho. He is co-editor-in-chief of *The Steinbeck Review* and Executive Director of the New Steinbeck Society of America. His recent publications include *John Steinbeck: A Centennial Tribute* (2002), *The Moral Philosophy of John Steinbeck* (2005), and "John Steinbeck" in *The Oxford Encyclopedia of American Literature*.

MIMI REISEL GLADSTEIN (see encyclopedia entry on **Gladstein, Mimi Reisel**).

ROBERT B. HARMON is an expert on Steinbeck collections and bibliography, and has served as the reference librarian and curator at the Martha Heasley Cox Steinbeck Research Center at San Jose State University. Among his numerous publications are *"The Grapes of Wrath": A Fifty Year Bibliographic Survey* (1990) and *John Steinbeck: An Annotated Guide to Bibliographical Sources* (Scarecrow Press 1996).

YASUO HASHIGUCHI is an expert in bibliography and special collections of John Steinbeck's works, has been a scholar and professor of American Literature in Japan, and served as the First President of the John Steinbeck Society of Japan.

KEVIN HEARLE is a poet, independent scholar, and founding member of the editorial boards of the *Steinbeck Newsletter, Steinbeck Studies*, and the *Steinbeck Review*. He is the author of *Each Thing We Know Is Changed Because We Know It, and Other Poems*, the co-editor of *Beyond Boundaries: Rereading John Steinbeck*, and the revision editor of *"The Grapes of Wrath": Text and Criticism*. His poems have been widely anthologized, and he was the recipient of the Burkhardt Award as Outstanding Steinbeck Scholar of 2005.

BARBARA A. HEAVILIN is Associate Professor of English at Taylor University in Upland, Indiana, and has edited *The Critical Response to John Steinbeck's "The Grapes of Wrath"* (Greenwood 2000) and *John Steinbeck's "The Grapes of Wrath," A Reference Guide* (Greenwood 2002).

GREGORY HILL, JR. is on the English faculty at Robert Morris College, Chicago. His interests lie in modern American experimental fiction and poetry, and in contemporary poetry and poetics.

JOHN HOOPER is the former Registrar of the National Steinbeck Center in Salinas. He is a printer, publisher, and founder of the literary and arts journal, *Grafieka*.

HARRY KARAHALIOS is a graduate student in the PhD program in literature at the University of Notre Dame, Indiana. He studies transnational forms of identity construction and their representation in the novel and in film, as well as questions of national identity in Spain and Greece in areas that have experienced civil war and that are currently experiencing an influx of immigration.

T. ADRIAN LEWIS is an instructor of English and American Studies at DePaul University.

CLIFFORD LEWIS has spent most of his career at the University of Massachusetts at Lowell, where he developed the American Studies program and served as its chair for over twenty years, receiving the Distinguished Teacher Award in Arts and Sciences during his tenure. He has served as a Fulbright Lecturer in Poland and executive officer in the corporation that founded the Lowell National Urban Park. In 1987 he directed "Rediscovering Steinbeck," a conference that featured John Kenneth Galbraith as the keynote speaker. Lewis has published essays on Hemingway, Faulkner, and Steinbeck. He also co-edited, with Carroll Britch, *Rediscovering Steinbeck—Revisionist Views of His Art, Politics and Intellect*.

LUCHEN LI is a Professor of Humanities at Kettering University in Michigan. His writing has appeared in *The Steinbeck Review* and the book *The Moral Philosophy of John Steinbeck*. His *John Steinbeck: A Documentary Volume (Dictionary of Literary Biography*, Vol. 309) was published by Thomson/Gale in 2005, and he is the coauthor of *Critical Companion to John Steinbeck* (Facts on File 2005). Currently he is co-editing a volume of essays from the 6th International Steinbeck Congress held in Kyoto, Japan, in 2005; it is tentatively titled *John Steinbeck's Global Dimensions*.

MARILYN CHANDLER MCENTYRE is Professor of English at Westmont College. She has published extensively on American literature (including her book, *Dwelling in the Text: Houses in American Fiction*), literature and medicine, and theology and the arts. Her two most recent books of poems are *In Quiet Light* (on Vermeer's women) and *Drawn to the Light* (on Rembrandt's biblical paintings).

TRACY MICHAELS was Assistant Professor of English and Literature at Puget Sound Christian College in Everett, Washington, from 1997 to 2004. She lives in Hungary and teaches English as a foreign language to adults with World Gospel Mission. Her other publications include

Research and Writing Skills, a module for the Excel adult continuing education program at Puget Sound Christian College (2003). She has been in *Who's Who Among America's Teachers 2002–2005*.

JOSEPH MILLICHAP is Professor Emeritus of English at Western Kentucky University. He has published widely on many aspects of American literature and film—in particular *John Steinbeck and Film* (1983) and several essays, articles, and reviews on Steinbeck's life and work.

ROBERT E. MORSBERGER is Professor Emeritus at California State Polytechnic University, Pomona. He has published extensively and presented dozens of papers on John Steinbeck and has served on the editorial board of three Steinbeck journals. In addition, he edited Steinbeck's screenplay *Viva Zapata!* for Viking/Penguin and has won the Burkhardt Award for distinguished Steinbeck criticism. He is the author of ten books, including critical analyses entitled *James Thurber* (Twayne 1964) and, in collaboration with Katharine M. Morsberger, *Lew Wallace: Militant Romantic*.

KIYOSHI NAKAYAMA (see encyclopedia entry on **Nakayama, Kiyoshi**).

BRIAN NIRO is a Visiting Assistant Professor at DePaul University, Chicago. He has written previously on Pierre Bourdieu, Michel de Certeau, and Louis Marin. He has also recently authored a book in Palgrave's Transitions series on the concept of *Race* (2003).

GENE NORTON earned his PhD at the University of Kentucky, where his doctoral work concerned William Faulkner. He teaches English and Humanities at Southwestern Community College.

BRUCE OUDERKIRK is Director of Student Support Services at the University of Wisconsin–Eau Claire and has taught English at the University of Nebraska–Lincoln and Iowa State University. He has contributed chapters to *John Steinbeck: A Centennial Tribute* and *The Betrayal of Brotherhood in the Work of John Steinbeck*.

LOUIS OWENS (see encyclopedia entry on **Owens, Louis**).

JOHN CLARK PRATT is a retired Air Force pilot and Professor Emeritus of English at Colorado State University. Among his books are *The Laotian Fragments*, *Vietnam Voices*, and, in the Contemporary Writers in Christian Perspective series, *John Steinbeck*. He has received two Fulbright fellowships: one to the Soviet Union in 1980 and one to Portugal in 1974–75, and has been given the Excellence in Arts Award by the Vietnam Veterans of America (1995).

RODNEY P. RICE is Chair of the Humanities Department and Coordinator for the Interdisciplinary Sciences Degree Program at the South Dakota School of Mines and Technology. He has produced more than fifty publications and presentations on American literature and technical communication. His most recent publication is "Beyond Within: Paths to Moksha in John Steinbeck's *The Pastures of Heaven*" in *The Steinbeck Review*.

KIRSTIN RINGELBERG is Assistant Professor of Art History at Elon University in Elon, North Carolina. She has published essays in *Prospects: An Annual of American Cultural Studies* (2004) and the anthology *Considering Aaron Sorkin: Essays on the Politics, Poetics and Sleight of Hand in the Films and Television Series* (2005).

TED SCHOLZ is a Senior Teaching Fellow at Robert Morris College in Chicago, Illinois.

MARGARET SELIGMAN is a teacher, acoustic musician, and independent scholar. Her articles about *Moby-Dick* and *Billy Budd* have appeared in *Melville Society Extracts*.

SCOTT SIMKINS is an Instructor in the English department of Auburn University,

Auburn, Alabama. Presently serving as the secretary of The New International John Steinbeck Society, he specializes in twentieth-century American literature and maintains the society's Web site.

ROY S. SIMMONDS (see encyclopedia entry on **Simmonds, Roy S.**).

ERIC SKIPPER is Associate Professor of Spanish at Gainesville State College in Georgia. He is a contributor to the *Steinbeck Review,* and author of several articles and short stories. His short story "The Runt" appeared in the textbook, *Literature and Ourselves* (Longman 2001).

NANCY STEINBECK is a graduate of the University of California at Berkeley. She has worked all her life with delinquents, addicts, and the mentally ill. She met John Steinbeck IV in 1975 in Boulder, Colorado, where they studied Tibetan Buddhism for fifteen years. They were married in 1982. Their combined memoir, *The Other Side of Eden: Life with John Steinbeck*, was published in 2001. Upon John's death, Nancy chose to live on a ranch in a remote area of the Ozark Mountains, where she continues to write and speak at conferences, universities, and rural schools about Steinbeck, the craft of memoir writing, and issues concerning the dysfunctional family.

THOM TAMMARO is Professor of Multidisciplinary Studies and teaches in the English department and in the MFA creative writing program at Minnesota State University, Moorhead, where he was named Roland and Beth Dille Distinguished Faculty Lecturer in 2001. He is the author of two collections of poems: *Holding On for Dear Life* and *When the Italians Came to My Home Town.* With Sheila Coghill he is co-editor of *Visiting Frost: Poems Inspired by the Life and Work of Robert Frost; Visiting Walt: Poems Inspired by the Life and Work of Walt Whitman*; and *Visiting Emily: Poems Inspired by the Life and Work of Emily Dickinson,* all published by the University of Iowa Press. With Mark Vinz, he is co-editor of *Imagining Home: Writing from the Midwest* and *Inheriting the Land: Contemporary Voices from the Midwest,* both recipients of Minnesota Book awards and published by the University of Minnesota Press.

JOHN H. TIMMERMAN (see the encyclopedia entry on **Timmerman, John H.**).

BRYAN VESCIO is Assistant Professor of English and Humanistic Studies at The University of Wisconsin–Green Bay. His writing on American authors includes publications on William Faulkner, Nathanael West, and Cormac McCarthy. He also writes on topics in literary theory and film theory.

ABBY H. P. WERLOCK, recently retired from the St. Olaf College English Department and was past President of the Edith Wharton Society. She is the author of articles on Steinbeck, Faulkner, Hemingway, and Wharton. Her books include *Tillie Olsen* (1990), *British Women Writing Fiction* (2000), *Carol Shields's "The Stone Diaries"* (2001), and *The Facts on File Companion to the American Short Story* (2000), which won the American Library Association Outstanding Reference award. Her next book is *The Facts on File Companion to the American Novel* (2006).

MARCIA D. YARMUS is Associate Professor of Spanish Language and Literature at John Jay College of Criminal Justice, The City University of New York (CUNY). Among her Steinbeck publications are articles entitled "The Picaresque Novel and John Steinbeck," "Federico Garcia Lorca's *Yerma* and John Steinbeck's *Burning Bright*: A Comparative Study," "John Steinbeck's *Viva Zapata!* and the Curse of Cain," and "John Steinbeck and the Hispanic Influence." In May 2001, Dr. Yarmus received the Outstanding Teacher Award from the John Jay College of Criminal Justice.

NANCY ZANE is Professor of English at Glenville State College in Glenville, West Virginia, and worked with Robert DeMott at Ohio University, where she earned her MA and PhD.